2021–2022
OREGON BLUE BOOK

Compiled and
published by

Shemia Fagan
Secretary of State

Julie Yamaka, Managing Editor
Phil Wiebe, Copy Editor
Gary Halvorson, Photo and Web Editor

Archives Division
Office of the Secretary of State
Salem, Oregon 97310

Acknowledgements and special thanks to the following people:

Office of the Secretary of State:
 Archives Division, Stephanie Clark, State Archivist
  Fact gathering and verification: Nicholas Adelman, Steve Mabry, Dani Morley,
 Theresa Rea, Layne Sawyer, Todd Shaffer and Ben Zeiner
  Proofreader: Sue White
  Section review: Stephanie Clark, Mary McRobinson and Layne Sawyer
 Business Services Division: Blue Book order processing and fulfillment, Jeff Morgan, Director;
  Michael Hickam and Sarah Roth, Managers; Don Stewart and Debra Wikel
 Elections Division: Candy Mifsud, Lydia Plukchi, and Tami Dettwyler

Department of Administrative Services, Chief Financial Office and Geospatial Enterprise Office, Maps

Employment Department, Research Division: Nick Beleiciks, State Employment Economist,
 Dallas Fridley, Brian Rooney, Damon Runberg, Erik Knoder, Jessica Nelson, Gail Krumenauer,
 Economy Section
 Dave Yamaka, Graphics

Office of the State Court Administrator: Kim Blanding, Judicial Section

Oregon Department of Education: Brian Reeder, Assistant Superintendent, Research, Education Section
Higher Education Coordinating Commission: Endi Hartigan, Education Section

https://sos.oregon.gov/blue-book

Orders:

Office of the Secretary of State
Oregon Blue Book
255 Capitol St. NE, Suite 180
Salem, OR 97310
503-378-5199

TABLE OF CONTENTS

Introduction and Dedication by Shemia Fagan, Secretary of State

Foreword by Kate Brown, Governor

Color illustrations and photographs following page 168

Shemia Fagan
SECRETARY OF STATE

STATE OF OREGON
SECRETARY OF STATE

136 STATE CAPITOL
SALEM, OREGON 97310-0722

January 2021

Fellow Oregonians,

In this introduction to *Oregon's 2021–2022 Oregon Blue Book* — Oregon's biannual publication of our history, economy, government and cultures — I must acknowledge the historic moment we are in as this publication goes to press. On Feb. 28, 2020, the first Oregonian was diagnosed with the novel coronavirus, COVID-19 in Washington County. By March 14, 2020, the first Oregonian died as a result of COVID-19. And, with unprecedented speed, the first Oregonian was inoculated against COVID-19 on DATE with an FDA approved vaccine. As my dedication acknowledges on the next page, 1,708[1] Oregonians have lost their lives to COVID-19. Countless more have lost loved ones, been hospitalized or sick, lost relationships, lost jobs, lost businesses, lost spiritual rituals and ceremonies, lost learning, lost once in a lifetime experiences, and lived under overwhelming stress. As Oregonians, we are together in this historic moment that runs the spectrum from heartbreaking tragedy to extraordinary inspiration.

This historic moment has tested all of us — in some ways shared and in other ways unique to you. We've struggled through new ways of working, teaching, worshiping, parenting, socializing and celebrating life's milestones and losses. We've learned that it is hard to sacrifice to protect people we've never met, from a virus we cannot see, for an unknown duration. We've also been empowered to *do the best we can*, not perfection, but our very best under the unprecedented circumstances — our best work, our best parenting, our best partnership, our best risk reduction, our best self-care, our best housekeeping, our best celebrations and our best friendship. We have hopefully learned to give ourselves and each other grace when we inevitably fall short.

As we enter 2021 — the darkness before the dawn — let us recommit ourselves to *do the best we can* to be safe and bring our loved ones, our neighbors and our fellow Oregonians, through this dark tunnel into the light awaiting us on the other side.

Sincerely,

Shemia Fagan
Secretary of State

---

[1] This is the recorded death total caused by COVID-19 as of the date this *Blue Book* edition goes to press.

Dedication

This year's *Oregon Blue Book* is dedicated to the 1,708 Oregonians who died from COVID-19, their families, all who loved them, liked them and enjoyed their time on this earth. You will be missed but not forgotten.

Please use this page of the *2021–2022 Oregon Blue Book* to write your own dedication to any person or persons whose lives were lost this year.

Kate Brown
Governor

STATE OF OREGON
GOVERNOR
254 STATE CAPITOL
SALEM, OREGON 97301-4047
(503) 378-3111
www.oregon.gov

January 2021

My Fellow Oregonians,

In the pages of this *Blue Book*, you can learn more about what makes Oregon special — its geography, history, symbols and governance. You'll also get a glimpse of the individuals who serve their fellow Oregonians as they work every day to address our state's most important issues through elected office, at state agencies and on boards and commissions.

Especially in the midst of a global viral pandemic, we cannot forget that it is the responsibility of a state's government to serve its people. We must ensure that all students have the tools they need to succeed. We must work toward equity, inclusivity and justice so all people who call Oregon home feel safe, welcome and heard. We must seek to rebuild the state economy so that economic growth and prosperity touch every corner of our great state. We must preserve the beauty and bounty of Oregon for generations to come through careful stewardship of our precious natural resources.

As the state grapples with the COVID-19 pandemic, I strive to protect the health and safety of all Oregonians. And, as our nation grapples with the impacts of systemic racism, I am committed to centering racial justice in a new vision for community safety, in the state budget, and in my administration's agenda.

As we look toward the future — a future where this virus remains a fact of life for months to come — and we focus on building a safer and stronger Oregon, we need to lift up our under-served, rural and tribal communities, as well as our low-income and communities of color. With every great challenge, a new opportunity presents itself. In Oregon, we have the opportunity to come back stronger than before, by lifting up those who have historically been left behind and together, to build a future where everyone can thrive.

Oregon is our home, and this *Blue Book* is a valuable tool for home improvement. So, I urge you to use it for your edification, to inform community projects and as a necessary link between state history, government and the people of Oregon.

Sincerely,

Kate Brown
Governor

NEW IN THIS EDITION . . .

Oregon State Parks Centennial

The featured exhibit in this edition of the *Oregon Blue Book* combines photos and artwork to visually take readers on a tour of the huge variety of state parks in every corner of Oregon.

State parks represent the best of Oregon: from the dramatic vistas of the rugged coastline to the tranquil beauty of mountain lakes, from important historical sites to fascinating natural wonders. State parks have grown into tremendous recreational and cultural assets for Oregonians over the last 100 years.

You can find this exhibit in the color insert located after page 168. An expanded version of this exhibit is available online at https://sos.oregon.gov/blue-book

Interesting and Quirky Oregon State Parks

Keeping with the Oregon State Parks centennial theme, the featured essay that begins on page 312 explores some of the interesting and quirky state parks.

These include the Darlingtonia State Natural Site north of Florence, where the carnivorous cobra lily plant uses its sweet nectar to lure insects into its bright yellow flowers and then eats them.

Another example, Erratic Rock State Park near McMinnville, highlights the power of nature. During the Ice Age, icebergs floated down the Columbia River, flooding the Willamette Valley. One of those floods swept up a 40-ton boulder from the northern Rocky Mountains and deposited it in that spot.

Learn much more about Oregon in this fascinating essay.

Student Essays About Favorite Oregon State Parks

In another reflection of the theme of the Oregon State Parks centennial, we asked Oregon students to write essays describing their favorite state parks. We selected the top essays from the large number of submissions to be displayed in this edition of the *Oregon Blue Book*. All of these essays are illustrated with drawings by the authors.

The essays and drawings help us see the wonder of state parks through the eyes of young students and further reinforce the value of the parks system to all Oregonians.

See the essays, which are shown as submitted, on pages viii, 108, 146, 156, 180, 230 and 324.

Ever-changing Oregon Information

We called, emailed and faxed hundreds of government offices, newspapers, cultural institutions and others in an effort to gather the most up-to-date information for this edition of the *Oregon Blue Book*.

The Oregon History section has been rewritten and illustrated. Several other sections, such as Economy, Government Finance, and Almanac, have been rewritten to reflect changes.

Of course, in addition to this print edition, don't forget the online *Oregon Blue Book*. We continue to add new information as we receive it throughout the year, so you can stay abreast of ongoing changes to Oregon's governmental and cultural institutions. See it at https://sos.oregon.gov/blue-book

STUDENT ESSAY CONTEST WINNER

Wallowa Lake State Park

Halle Krom
John Scanlan's 8th Grade Class
Sunridge Middle School, Pendleton

This drawing by Halle Krom depicts some of the fun things to do in the Wallowa Lake State Park area.

This might seem very cliche, but my favorite Oregon State Parks is Wallowa Lake. I can say with 100% confidence that this is my favorite park, even though I've only been there once.

Wallowa Lake has such amazing views, and just thinking about my experience there brings me great euphoria! The tramway is outstanding and is such a fun little way to the restaurant on top of the mountain. The views up there are even better than the views from down below.

There are quite a few cafes and gift shops if you drive around the area, and each one of them are filled with superior food, and the nicest employees!

There are countless amazing and fun experiences to have at Wallowa Lake, but I'll leave it up to you to check it out for yourself. The fun is endless at Wallowa, and these are just a few of my reasons why I love it so very much.

ALMANAC

Facts, like maps, help us envision a complete picture of Oregon. This section includes an almanac with interesting statistics and general information about Oregon, a list of Oregon Olympic Games medal winners, "Oregon, My Oregon"—our state song and a map of Oregon showing counties and major roads.

For entries with an asterisk (*), see related photo in the color insert pages.

Abbreviation, Oregon: OR (postal)

Alternative Energy

Geothermal (2018)
33 megawatts of capacity
99 megawatts of planned capacity
Three facilities—the largest is 28.5 megawatts
Solar (2018)
295 megawatts of capacity for projects of 1 megawatt or larger
Over 15,000 residential solar projects
685 megawatts of capacity proposed, approved or under review
Wind (2018)
3.383 megawatts of capacity
44 operating facilities (one spans the Oregon/Washington state line)
Sites range from 1.6 to 300 megawatts (13 largest = 69 percent of total capacity)

Altitudes

Highest: Mt. Hood (11,237')
Lowest: Pacific Ocean (sea level)

Amusement Park, Oldest

Oaks Amusement Park, Portland. Opened in May, 1905, is one of the oldest continuously operating amusement parks in the United States.

Animal, State*

The 1969 Legislature named the American Beaver *(Castor canadensis)* the Oregon state animal. Prized for its fur, the beaver was over-trapped by early settlers and eliminated from much of its original range. Through management and protection, the beaver has been reestablished in waterways throughout the state. The beaver has been referred to as "nature's engineer," and its dam-building activities are important to natural water flow and erosion control. Oregon is known as the "Beaver State." The beaver is Oregon State University's mascot.

Apportionment, U.S. House of Representatives
(number of U.S. Representatives from Oregon)
1860–1880....... 1   1940–1970....... 4
1890–1900....... 2   1980–Present.... 5
1910–1930....... 3

Awards (Nobel, Pulitzer)

1934: William P. Murphy, Nobel, Medicine
1934: Medford *Mail Tribune,* Pulitzer, Journalism
1939: Ronald Callvert, *The Oregonian,* Pulitzer, Editorial Writing
1954: Linus Pauling, Nobel, Chemistry
1956: Walter H. Brattain, Nobel, Physics
1957: Wallace Turner and William Lambert, *The Oregonian,* Pulitzer, Local Reporting
1962: Linus Pauling, Nobel, Peace
1990: Nicholas D. Kristof, with wife Sheryl WuDunn, *The New York Times,* Pulitzer, International Reporting
1999: Richard Read, *The Oregonian,* Pulitzer, Explanatory Writing
2001: Carl Weiman, Nobel, Atomic Physics
2001: *The Oregonian,* Pulitzer, Public Service
2001: Tom Hallman, Jr., *The Oregonian,* Pulitzer, Feature Writing
2005: Nigel Jaquiss, *Willamette Week,* Pulitzer, Investigative Reporting
2006: Rick Attig and Doug Bates, *The Oregonian,* Pulitzer, Editorial Writing
2006: Nicholas D. Kristof, *The New York Times,* Pulitzer, Commentary
2007: *The Oregonian,* Pulitzer, Breaking News Reporting
2010: Dale T. Mortensen, Nobel, Economics
2014: *The Oregonian,* Pulitzer, Editorial Writing

Beverage, State

Milk was designated Oregon's state beverage in 1997. The Legislature recognized that milk production and the manufacture of dairy products are major contributors to the economic well-being of Oregon agriculture.

Birds, State*

Songbird: Distinctive for its flute-like song, the Western Meadowlark *(Sturnella neglecta)* was chosen to be the state bird by the Oregon Audubon Society-sponsored schoolchildren's 1927 election. The selection was proclaimed by Governor Patterson in July, 1927, and the 2017 Legislature declared the Western Meadowlark to be the State Songbird. Native to western North America, the bird has brown plumage with buff and black markings. Its underside is bright yellow with a black V-shape on the breast. Outer tail feathers are mainly white and are easily visible when it flies.

Raptor: The Osprey *(Pandion haliaetus)* was designated state raptor by the 2017 Legislature, declaring the large bird with its striking markings to be a fitting symbol of Oregon's rugged independence, strength and resilience, evoking Oregon's lakes, rivers, streams and ocean.

Births: 41,758 (2019)

Borders and Boundaries

Washington on the north; California on the south; Idaho on the east; Pacific Ocean on the west; Nevada on the southeast.

Bridges

Highest: Thomas Creek Bridge, north of Brookings, 345'

Longest: Astoria-Megler Bridge, Astoria, 21,474'

Covered bridges: 51; 33 are located in the Willamette Valley

Buildings, Tallest (Portland)

1. Wells Fargo Tower (1972), 546', 40 floors
2. Park Avenue West (2016), 537', 30 floors
3. U.S. Bancorp Tower (1983), 536', 42 floors

Cities, Total Incorporated: 241

Largest Populations (2020)
1. Portland (664,605)
2. Eugene (173, 620)
3. Salem (168,970)

Counties, Total: 36

Largest Area, Square Miles
1. Harney (10,133)
2. Malheur (9,888)
3. Lake (8,139)

Smallest Area, Square Miles
1. Multnomah (431)
2. Hood River (522)
3. Columbia (657)

Largest Populations (2020)
1. Multnomah (829,560)
2. Washington (620,080)
3. Clackamas (426,515)

Craft Brewing Industry (2019)

311 craft breweries (ranks 10th nationally)
Barrels of craft beer produced per year: 1,012,854 (ranks 9th nationally)

Crustacean, State*

The 2009 Legislature designated the Dungeness Crab *(Metacarcinus magister)* as the official state crustacean. The action followed petitioning by the fourth grade class of Sunset Primary School in West Linn. Common to the Pacific coastline from the Alaskan Aleutian Islands to Santa Cruz, California, Dungeness Crab is considered the most commercially important crab in the Pacific Northwest.

Dance, State

In 1977, the Legislature declared the Square Dance to be Oregon's state dance. The dance is a combination of various steps and figures with four couples grouped in a square. The pioneer origins of the dance and the characteristic dress are deemed to reflect Oregon's heritage. The lively spirit of the dance exemplifies the friendly, free nature and enthusiasm that are part of the Oregon character.

Deaths: 37,236 (2019)

Divorces: 13,304 (2019)

Electoral Votes for U.S. President: 7

Fair, Oregon State: Early History

1858: The State Fair was unofficially started by a group of farmers known as the Oregon Fruit-growers Association.

1861: The first official Oregon State Fair was held along the Clackamas River in the Gladstone/Oregon City area.

1862: The second State Fair took place in Salem, at the same location where it is held today.

Fish, State*

The Chinook Salmon *(Oncorhynchus tshawytscha)*, also known as the spring, king or tyee salmon, is the largest of the Pacific salmons and the most highly prized for the fresh fish trade. Declared the Oregon state fish by the 1961 Legislature, the Chinook Salmon is found from southern California to the Canadian Arctic.

Flag, State*

The state flag, adopted in 1925, is blue with gold lettering and symbols. Blue and gold are the state colors. On the flag's face the legend "STATE OF OREGON" is written above a shield, which is surrounded by 33 stars. Below the shield, which is part of the state seal, is written "1859," the year of Oregon's admission to The Union as the 33rd state. The flag's reverse side depicts a beaver. Oregon has the distinction of being the only state in The Union whose flag has different patterns on each side. The utility flag has a plain border, and the dress or parade flag has gold fringe.

Flower, State*

The Legislature designated the Oregon Grape *(Mahonia aquifolium)* as the state flower by resolution in 1899. A low-growing plant, the Oregon Grape is native to much of the Pacific Coast and is found sparsely east of the Cascades. Its year-round foliage of pinnated, waxy green leaves resembles holly. The plant bears clusters of small yellow flowers in early summer and dark blue berries that ripen in the fall. The fruit can be used in cooking.

Fossil, State*

The Legislature designated the Metasequoia, or Dawn Redwood (Metasequoia glyptostroboides), as the state fossil by resolution in 2005. The Metasequoia flourished in the Miocene Epoch of 25 to 5 million years ago and left its record embedded in rocks across Oregon's landscape. While long extinct in Oregon, paleontologists discovered living 100-foot Metasequoia trees in a remote area of China in the 1940s and brought specimens back to the United States for propagation to ensure Metasequoia trees can be found today.

Fruit, State*

The Legislature designated the pear *(Pyrus communis)* as the state fruit by resolution in 2005. Oregon produces a variety of pears, including Comice, Anjou, Bosc and Bartlett. The pear ranks as the top-selling tree fruit crop in the state and grows particularly well in the Rogue River Valley and in the area between the Columbia River and Mt. Hood.

Gemstone, State*

The 1987 Legislature designated the Oregon Sunstone as the state gemstone. Uncommon in its composition, clarity and colors, it is a large, brightly colored transparent gem in the feldspar family. The Oregon Sunstone attracts collectors and miners and has been identified as a boon to tourism and economic development in southeastern Oregon counties.

Geographic Center

Oregon's geographic center lies in Crook County, 25 miles south-southeast of Prineville.

Gorge, Deepest

Hells Canyon, Wallowa County, Snake River: At up to 7,913' deep, it is the deepest gorge in North America.

Highways, Special Designation

Historic Columbia River Highway: The 74-mile stretch of the Columbia River Highway from Troutdale to The Dalles was built from 1913 to 1922. For many years, it was designated U.S. 30. Beginning in the 1950s, Interstate 84 replaced the historic highway as the main route through the Columbia Gorge. The historic highway became a National Scenic Byway All-American Road in 1999. In 2000, the U.S. Secretary of the Interior designated it a National Historic Landmark, which recognized the highway as a significant national heritage resource. The route became the first highway in the country to be given either of these national designations.

Oregon 99: Originally known as the Pacific Highway, Oregon 99 runs from the Oregon/California border north to Junction City, where it splits into Oregon 99E and Oregon 99W. The Pacific Highway, once designated as U.S. 99, U.S. 99E and U.S. 99W, was the main north–south highway in Oregon from the 1920s until Interstate 5 replaced it in 1964.

U.S. 101: Completed in the 1930s, the Oregon Coast Highway (U.S. 101) runs the length of Oregon's Pacific Coast from Astoria on the Columbia River to the Oregon/California border. The highway was designated an Oregon Scenic Byway in 1991 and a National Scenic Byway All-American Road in 2002.

Veterans Memorial Highways: 479,600 Oregon veterans have served our nation during five major wars—WWI, WWII, Korea, Vietnam, Persian Gulf/Afghanistan/ Iraq. Over 6,000 lost their lives and 15,000 were wounded during those wars. Five border-to-border highways were designated by the Legislature and three governors to honor these veterans:

WWI Veterans Memorial Highway: U.S. 395,
WWII Veterans Historic Highway: U.S. 97,
Korean War Veterans Memorial Highway: Interstate 5,
Vietnam Veterans Memorial Highway: Interstate 84,
Persian Gulf, Afghanistan and Iraq Veterans Memorial Highway: U.S. 101,
POW/MIA Memorial Highway: U.S. 26,
Atomic Veterans Memorial Highway: Interstate 5 from Albany to Salem.

Interstate 5 was also designated a Purple Heart Trail.

The Historic Columbia River Highway has been designated as a National Historical Landmark. (Oregon State Archives scenic photo)

Hops Production (2019)

Acres harvested: 7,306
Yield per acre: 1,783 pounds
Oregon accounted for 12 percent of the United States' hop crop in 2019.

Top varieties grown in Oregon: Nugget, Cascade, Citra, and Willamette, accounting for 50 percent of the state's hop production.

Hydropower (2018)

8,865 megawatts of capacity
88 hydropower facilities—80 in Oregon, 8 crossing state borders
Smallest: 0.04 megawatt
Largest: 2,160 megawatts (John Day Dam, Columbia River)
12 facilities over 100 megawatts
Oregon is the second highest hydropower-producing state in the nation, behind only Washington.

Insect, State*

In 1979, the Legislature designated the Oregon Swallowtail Butterfly *(Papilio oregonius)* as the state insect. A true native of the Northwest, the Oregon Swallowtail is at home in the lower sagebrush canyons of the Columbia River and its tributaries, including the Snake River watershed. This strikingly beautiful butterfly has a wingspan of 2-1/2 to 3 inches and is bright yellow and black with a reddish-orange hindspot.

Judicial Districts: 27

Lakes

Deepest: Crater Lake, 1,943' (deepest in the United States)
Largest:
Upper Klamath Lake, 61,543 surface acres
Malheur Lake, 49,700 surface acres
Note: Sizes may vary depending on seasons and precipitation. At times, Malheur Lake may have a larger surface area than Upper Klamath Lake.

Legal Holidays

New Year's Day (observed)
1/1/21, 12/31/21, 1/2/23
Martin Luther King, Jr.'s Birthday (observed)
1/18/21, 1/17/22, 1/16/23
Presidents' Day
2/15/21, 2/21/22, 2/20/23
Memorial Day
5/31/21, 5/30/22, 5/29/23
Independence Day (observed)
7/5/21, 7/4/22, 7/4/23
Labor Day
9/6/21, 9/5/22, 9/4/23
Veterans Day (observed)
11/11/21, 11/11/22, 11/10/23
Thanksgiving Day
11/25/21, 11/24/22, 11/23/23
Christmas Day (observed)
12/24/21, 12/26/22, 12/25/23
Whenever a holiday falls on a Sunday, the following Monday shall be observed as the holiday. Whenever a holiday falls on a Saturday, the preceding Friday shall be observed as the holiday.

Lighthouses

Cape Arago Lighthouse, Coos Bay: lighted 1934; deactivated 2006 (not accessible to the public)

Cape Blanco Lighthouse, Port Orford: lighted 1870
Cape Meares Lighthouse, Tillamook: lighted 1890; deactivated 1963
Cleft of the Rock Lighthouse, Yachats (privately owned, not open to the public): lighted 1976
Coquille River Lighthouse, Bandon: lighted 1896; deactivated 1939
Heceta Head Lighthouse, Florence: lighted 1893
Port of Brookings Lighthouse, Brookings (privately owned, not open to the public): lighted 1999
Tillamook Rock Lighthouse, Cannon Beach: lighted 1881; deactivated 1957 (privately owned, not open to the public)
Umpqua River Lighthouse, Reedsport: lighted 1894
Yaquina Bay Lighthouse, Newport: lighted 1871–74; reactivated 1996
Yaquina Head Lighthouse, Newport: lighted 1873

The Coquille River Lighthouse in Bandon guided vessels past dangerous shifting sandbars until 1939. (Oregon State Archives scenic photo)

Marriages: 25,212 (2019)

Microbe, State

In 2013, the Oregon Legislature designated *Saccharomyces cerevisiae* as the state microbe. The yeast converts sugar into carbon dioxide and ethanol, an essential process for leavening bread and brewing alcoholic beverages, making Oregon an internationally recognized hub of craft brewing.

Motto, State

"She Flies With Her Own Wings" was adopted by the 1987 Legislature as the Oregon state motto. The phrase originated with Judge Jessie Quinn Thornton and was pictured on the territorial seal in Latin: *Alis Volat Propriis.* The new motto replaced "The Union," which was adopted in 1957.

Mountains, Major

Blue Mountains: This northeastern Oregon mountain chain is part of the Columbia Plateau, which extends into southeastern Washington. Lava flows cover much of the surface, and the upper, wooded slopes have been used for lumbering. Today, recreation and livestock grazing are the principal economic uses. The highest elevation is Rock Creek Butte (9,105'), located on the Elkhorn Ridge a few miles west of Baker City.

Cascade Range: This lofty mountain range extends the entire north–south length of Oregon east of the Willamette Valley. It lies about 100 to 150 miles inland from the coastline and forms an important climatic divide, with the western slopes receiving abundant precipitation but the eastern slopes very little. The western slopes are heavily wooded, with the eastern section mainly covered by grass and scrub plants. Many lakes and several large rivers are in the mountains, the latter harnessed for hydroelectric power. The range is used frequently for outdoor recreation. The highest elevations are Mt. Hood (11,237'), located in Clackamas and Hood River Counties, and Mt. Jefferson (10,495'), located in Jefferson, Linn and Marion Counties.

Coast Range: The Coast Range runs the length of the state along the western coastline, from the Columbia River in the north to the Rogue River in the south. These mountains contain dense softwood forests, which historically made lumbering an important economic activity. Their eastern slopes mark the western edge of the Willamette Valley. The highest elevations are Mt. Bolivar (4,319') in Coos and Curry Counties; and Mary's Peak (4,097') in Benton County.

Klamath Mountains: The Klamath Mountains in southwestern Oregon are sometimes included as part of the Coast Range. These mountains include numerous national forest and wildlife preserves and contain scenic portions of the Klamath River. The highest elevation is Mt. Ashland (7,532') in Jackson County.

Steens Mountain: This is a massive, 30-mile-long mountain in the Alvord Valley, featuring valleys and U-shaped gorges that were cut by glaciers one million years ago. Located in Harney County in southeastern Oregon, it is 9,773' in elevation.

Mushroom, State*

The 1999 Legislature recognized the Pacific Golden Chanterelle *(Cantharellus formosus)* as the state mushroom. This mushroom is a wild, edible fungus of high culinary value that is unique to the Pacific Northwest. More than 500,000 pounds of Pacific Golden Chanterelles are harvested annually, representing a large portion of the commercial mushroom business.

Name of Oregon

The first written record of the name "Oregon" comes from a 1765 proposal for a journey written by Major Robert Rogers, an English army officer. It reads, "The rout . . . is from the Great Lakes towards the Head of the Mississippi, and from thence to the River called by the Indians Ouragon."

His proposal rejected, Rogers reapplied in 1772, using the spelling "Ourigan." The first printed use of the current spelling appeared in Captain Jonathan Carver's 1778 book, *Travels Through the Interior Parts of North America 1766, 1767 and 1768.* He listed the four great rivers of the continent, including "the River Oregon, or the River of the West, that falls into the Pacific Ocean at the Straits of Annian."

While no definitive pronunciation of "Oregon" is given in *Oregon Geographic Names,* the most common pronunciation by long-time Oregonians is "OR-ih-gun."

National Cemeteries

Willamette, Portland (1950); Eagle Point (1973); Roseburg (1973)

National Fish Hatcheries

Eagle Creek, Estacada (1956); Warm Springs (1966)

National Forests

Deschutes (1908); Fremont-Winema (combined 2002: Fremont est. 1908, Winema 1961); Malheur (1908); Mt. Hood (1908); Ochoco (1911); Rogue River-Siskiyou (combined 2004; Rogue River est. 1908, Siskiyou 1907); Siuslaw (1908); Umatilla (1908); Umpqua (1908); Wallowa-Whitman (combined 1954: both est. 1908); Willamette (1933)

National Grassland

Crooked River National Grassland, near Madras (1960)

National Historic Landmarks

Bonneville Dam Historic District, Multnomah County and Skamania County, Washington (1987)

Crater Lake Superintendent's Residence, Klamath County (1987)

Columbia River Highway, Multnomah, Hood River and Wasco Counties (2000)

Deady and Villard Halls, University of Oregon, Lane County (1977)

Fort Astoria Site, Clatsop County (1961)

Fort Rock Cave, Klamath County (1961)

Kam Wah Chung Company Building, Grant County (2005)

Jacksonville Historic District, Jackson County (1966)

Lightship WAL-604 "Columbia," Clatsop County (1989)

Lower Klamath Wildlife Refuge, Klamath County and Siskiyou County, California (1965)

Oregon Caves Chateau, Josephine County (1987)

Pioneer Courthouse, Multnomah County (1977)

Skidmore/Old Town Historic District, Multnomah County (1977—Updated documentation approved 2008)

Sunken Village Archeological Site, Multnomah County (1989)

Timberline Lodge, Clackamas County (1977)

Wallowa Lake Site, Wallowa County (1989)
Watzek Aubrey House, Multnomah County (2011)

National Monuments
Cascade-Siskiyou, near Ashland (2000); John Day Fossil Beds, located in three units near Kimberly, Mitchell and Fossil (1975); Newberry National Volcanic Monument, near Bend (1990); Oregon Caves, near Cave Junction (1909)

National Parks
Crater Lake (1902); Lewis and Clark National Historical Park in Oregon/Washington (1958); Nez Perce National Historical Park in Oregon/Idaho/Montana/Washington (1965)

National Recreation Areas
Hells Canyon National Recreation Area in Oregon/Idaho (1975); Oregon Dunes National Recreation Area (1972)

National Scenic Areas
Columbia River Gorge National Scenic Area (1986); Cascade Head Scenic Research Area (1974)

National Wildlife Refuges
Ankeny, near Jefferson (1965); Bandon Marsh, near Bandon (1983); Baskett Slough, near Dallas (1965); Bear Valley, near Klamath Falls (1978); Cape Meares, near Tillamook (1938); Cold Springs, near Hermiston(1909); Hart Mountain National Antelope Refuge, near Lakeview(1936); Klamath Marsh, near Klamath Falls (1958); Malheur, near Burns (1908); McKay Creek, near Pendleton (1927); Nestucca Bay, near Pacific City (1991); Oregon Islands, off southern Oregon coast (1935); Siletz Bay, near Lincoln City (1991); Three Arch Rocks, off coast near Oceanside (1907); Tualatin River, near Sherwood (1992); Upper Klamath, near Klamath Falls (1928); Wapato Lake, near Gaston (2007); William L. Finley, near Corvallis (1964)

Nut, State*
The hazelnut, or filbert, *(Corylus avellana)* was named the state nut by the 1989 Legislature. Oregon grows 99 percent of the entire U.S. commercial crop. The Oregon hazelnut, unlike wild varieties, grows on single-trunked trees up to 40 feet tall. Adding a unique texture and flavor to recipes and products, hazelnuts are preferred by chefs, bakers, confectioners, food manufacturers and homemakers worldwide.

Outdoor Pageant, State
The 2011 Legislature designated Pendleton's Happy Canyon Indian Pageant and Wild West Show the official outdoor pageant. Presented annually since 1911, local area tribal members worked up the depiction of native village life seen in the present-day script. Acted by a cast of members of local area tribes and local community volunteer actors, the show moves from a depiction of early tribal culture into historic and cultural events such as the coming of Lewis and Clark and the settling of the American West. A live orchestra of Pacific Northwest professional musicians accompanies the show.

Parks, State
256 parks totaling over 109,000 acres; day use attendance of 46 million per year, ranking 4th in the nation; 8 scenic and 4 regional trails; 58 campgrounds

Physical Dimensions
United States rank in total area: 9th
Land area: 95,988 square miles
Water area: 2,391 square miles
Total area: 98,379 square miles
Coastline: 362 miles

Pie, State
Marionberry pie was designated Oregon's official pie by the 2017 Legislature. The Marionberry was an Oregon State University blackberry breeding program's 1950s cross between the "Chehalem" and "Olallieberry." It was named for Marion County where extensive testing found it to have a greater yield and earlier harvest season than the more well-known Boysenberry.

Poet Laureate
In 2020, Governor Kate Brown named Anis Mojgani Oregon's 10th Poet Laureate. Born in New Orleans to Black and Iranian parents, Mojgani earned a BFA in Sequential Art from the Savannah College of Art and Design. He has been awarded artist and writer residencies from the Vermont Studio Center, AIR Serenbe, Bloedel Nature Reserve, Sou'wester, and the Oregon Literary Arts Writers in the Schools. Mojgani came to Oregon in 2004. He has authored five books of poetry, serves on the board of directors of Literary Arts and lives in Portland.

Population
Oregon is ranked 39th in population density with 42 inhabitants per square mile.

1850	12,093	1940	1,089,684
1860	52,465	1950	1,521,341
1870	90,923	1960	1,768,687
1880	174,768	1970	2,091,533
1890	317,704	1980	2,633,156
1900	413,536	1990	2,842,321
1910	672,765	2000	3,421,399
1920	783,389	2010	3,837,300
1930	953,786	2020	4,268,055

Precipitation
Record 24-hour maximum rainfall: 14.3" on November 6, 2006, at Lees Camp in the Tillamook County Coast Range

Average yearly precipitation at Salem: 39.7"

Record 24-hour snowfall: 47" on January 9, 1980, at the Hood River Experimental Station

Record annual snowfall: 903" in 1950 at Crater Lake

Reservoir, Longest: Lake Owyhee, 53 miles

Rivers, Longest

Partially in the State of Oregon:
Columbia River: 1,249 miles; Snake River: 1,040 miles

Entirely in the State of Oregon:
John Day River: 284 miles; Deschutes River: 251 miles

Rock, State*

The thunder egg (geode) was named the Oregon state rock by the 1965 Legislature after rockhounds throughout Oregon voted it as their favorite rock. Thunder eggs range in diameter from less than one inch to over four feet. Nondescript on the outside, they reveal exquisite designs in a wide range of colors when cut and polished. They are found chiefly in Crook, Jefferson, Malheur, Wasco and Wheeler Counties.

Franklin High School in southeast Portland is one of many architecturally significant public schools in Oregon. (Oregon State Archives scenic photo)

Schools, Public

Education Service Districts 19
Schools .... over 1,200
School Districts 197
Student population (2019–2020) 582,661

Seal, State*

On September 17, 1857, the Constitutional Convention adopted a resolution that authorized the U.S. president to appoint a committee of three — Benjamin F. Burch, L. F. Grover and James K. Kelly — to report on a proper seal for the State of Oregon. Harvey Gordon created a draft, to which the committee recommended additions. The state seal consists of a shield, supported by 33 stars and divided by a ribbon with the inscription "The Union." Above the ribbon are the mountains and forests of Oregon, an elk with branching antlers, a covered wagon and ox team, the Pacific Ocean with setting sun, a departing British man-of-war ship signifying the departure of British influence in the region, and an arriving American merchant ship,

signifying the rise of American power. Below the ribbon is a quartering with a sheaf of wheat, plow and pickax, representing Oregon's mining and agricultural resources. The crest is the American Eagle and around the perimeter of the seal is the legend "State of Oregon 1859."

Seashell, State*

In 1848, conchologist John Howard Redfield named the *Fusitriton oregonensis* after the Oregon Territory. Commonly called the Oregon hairy triton, the shell is one of the largest found in the state, reaching lengths up to five inches. The shells are found from Alaska to California and wash up on the Oregon coast at high tide. The Legislature designated it the state shell in 1991.

Shoes, Oldest

Sandals that are 9,300 years old, made of sagebrush and bark, were found at Fort Rock Cave in Central Oregon in 1938 by archaeologist Luther Cressman.

Soil, State

The Legislature designated Jory soil as Oregon's state soil in 2011. Jory soil is distinguished by its brick-red, clayish nature, developed on old volcanic rocks through thousands of years of weathering. It is estimated to exist on more than 300,000 acres of western Oregon hillsides and is named after Jory Hill in Marion County.

Jory soil supports forest vegetation such as Douglas fir and Oregon white oak. Many areas with the soil have been cleared and are now used for agriculture. Jory soil, coupled with Willamette Valley climate, provides an ideal setting for various crops, including wine grapes, wheat, Christmas trees, berries, hazelnuts and grass seed.

Song, State

J. A. Buchanan of Astoria and Henry B. Murtagh of Portland wrote "Oregon, My Oregon," in 1920. With this song, Buchanan and Murtagh won a statewide competition sponsored by the Society of Oregon Composers. The song became the Oregon state song in 1927.

Standard of Time

The standard time zones were established by Congress in 1918. Oregon lies within the Pacific Standard Time zone with the exception of most of Malheur County along the Idaho border, which is on Mountain Standard Time. Daylight Saving Time is in effect from March through November.

Clocks "spring forward" one hour at 2:00 a.m. on the second Sunday of March: 3/14/21, 3/13/22, 3/12/23

Clocks "fall back" one hour at 2:00 a.m. on the first Sunday of November: 11/7/21, 11/6/22, 11/5/23

Tartan, State

Tartan, registration number 36406 was designated Oregon's official tartan by the 2017

Legislature. With colors symbolizing the distinctive features of the state, its blue, gold, green, black, white, taupe, crimson and azure represent the water, mountains, forests, grasslands and volcanic past of our state.

Temperatures, Records and Averages
Highest: 119°F on August 10, 1898, in Pendleton and on July 29, 1898, in Prineville
Lowest: -54°F on February 9, 1933, in Ukiah (50 miles south of Pendleton) and on February 10, 1933, in Seneca (105 miles southwest of Baker City)
Average January/July Temperatures:
Burns .... January 24.8°F/July 66.6°F
Grants Pass .... January 40.9°F/July 71.8°F
Newport ....January 45.0°F/July 57.9°F
Redmond .... January 32.7°F/July 65.9°F
Salem .... January 41.2°F/July 67.6°F

Travel and Tourism (2019)
Total direct spending: $12.8 billion
Overnight visitors: 29.4 million
Travel-generated employment: 117,500

Tree, State*
The Douglas fir *(Pseudotsuga menziesii),* named for David Douglas, a 19th century Scottish botanist, was designated the Oregon state tree in 1939. Great strength, stiffness and moderate weight make it an invaluable timber product said to be stronger than concrete. Averaging up to 200' in height and six feet in diameter, heights of 325' and diameters of 15' can also be found.

Waterfall, Highest
Multnomah Falls, 620'

Wine Industry Production (2018)
Grape production value: $208.7 million.
Number of vineyards: 1,165
Number of wineries: 793
Total planted acreage: 35,972 acres
Leading variety: Pinot Noir—57 percent of all planted acreage and 59 percent of wine grape production

---

Olympic Games Medalists from Oregon (1906–2016)
Note: The 2020 games were rescheduled due the COVID-19 pandemic.

1906
Kerrigan, H.W. (Bert)	High Jump	Bronze

1908
Gilbert, Alfred C.	Pole Vault	Gold
Kelly, Dan	Broad Jump	Silver
Smithson, Forrest	Hurdles	Gold

1912
Hawkins, Martin	Hurdles	Bronze

1920
Balbach, Louis J.	Diving	Bronze
Kuehn, Louis (Hap)	Diving	Gold
Ross, Norman	Swimming	Gold (3)
Sanborn-Payne, Thelma	Diving	Bronze
Sears, Robert	Fencing	Bronze

1924
Newton, Chester	Wrestling	Silver
Reed, Robin	Wrestling	Gold

1928
Hamm, Edward B.	Broad Jump	Gold

1932
Graham, Norris	Rowing	Gold
Hill, Ralph	5000m	Silver
LaBorde, Henri J.	Discus	Silver

1936
Robinson, Mack	200m	Silver

1948
Beck, Lewis W. Jr.	Basketball	Gold
Brown, David P.	Rowing	Gold
Gordien, Fortune	Discus	Bronze

Helser (de Morelos), Brenda	Swimming	Gold
Zimmerman-Edwards, Suzanne	Swimming	Silver

1952
Proctor, Hank	Rowing	Gold
Smith, William T.	Wrestling	Gold

1956
Fifer, James	Rowing	Gold
Gordien, Fortune	Discus	Silver

1960
Davis, Otis	400m	Gold (2)
Dischinger, Terry G.	Basketball	Gold
Imhoff, Darrall	Basketball	Gold
Wood, Carolyn	Swimming	Gold

1964
Carr, Ken	Basketball	Gold
Counts, Mel G.	Basketball	Gold
Dellinger, William S.	Track and Field	Bronze
Freeman, Kevin	Equestrian	Silver
Saubert, Jean M.	Skiing	Silver/Bronze
Schollander, Don	Swimming	Gold (4)

1968
Fosbury, Richard D.	High Jump	Gold
Freeman, Kevin	Equestrian	Silver
Garrigus, Thomas I.	Trapshooting	Silver
Johnson Bailes, Margaret	4x100m Relay	Gold
Sanders, Richard J.	Wrestling	Silver
Schollander, Don	Swimming	Gold/Silver

1972

Freeman, Kevin	Equestrian	Silver
Peyton McDonald, Kim	Swimming	Gold
Sanders, Richard J.	Wrestling	Silver

1976

Peyton McDonald, Kim	Swimming	Gold
Wilkins, Mac M.	Discus	Gold

1984

Burke, Douglas L.	Water Polo	Silver
Herland, Douglas J.	Rowing	Bronze
Huntley (Ruete), Joni	High Jump	Bronze
Johnson, William D.	Skiing	Gold
King (Brown), Judith	400m Hurdles	Silver
Menken-Schaudt, Carol	Basketball	Gold
Schultz, Mark P.	Wrestling	Gold
Wilkins, Mac M.	Discus	Silver

1988

Brown, Cynthia L.	Basketball	Gold
Lang, Brent	Swimming	Gold

1992

Johnson, Dave	Decathlon	Bronze
Jorgenson, Dan	Swimming	Bronze

1994

Street, Picabo	Skiing	Silver

1996

Deal, Lance	Hammer	Silver
MacMillan, Shannon	Soccer	Gold
Milbrett, Tiffany	Soccer	Gold
O'Brien, Dan	Decathlon	Gold
Schneider, Marcus	Rowing	Bronze
Steding, Katy	Basketball	Gold

1998

Street, Picabo	Skiing	Gold

2000

French, Michelle	Soccer	Silver
Kinkade, Mike	Baseball	Gold
Lindland, Matt	Wrestling	Silver
MacMillan, Shannon	Soccer	Silver
Milbrett, Tiffany	Soccer	Silver
Thompson, Chris	Swimming	Bronze

2002

Steele, Dan	Bobsled	Bronze
Klug, Chris	Snow Board	Bronze

2004

Hansen, Joey	Rowing	Gold
Johnson, Kate	Rowing	Silver
Zagunis, Mariel	Fencing	Gold

2008

Cox, Stephanie Lopez	Soccer	Gold
Inman, Josh	Rowing	Bronze
Ward, Rebecca	Fencing	Bronze (2)
Windes, Elsie	Water Polo	Silver
Zagunis, Mariel	Fencing	Gold/Bronze

2012

Eaton, Ashton	Decathlon	Gold
Rupp, Galen	10,000m	Silver
Windes, Elsie	Water Polo	Gold

2016

Crouser, Ryan	Shot Put	Gold
Eaton, Ashton	Decathlon	Gold
Hill, Kim	Volleyball	Bronze
Rupp, Galen	10,000m	Bronze
Zagunis, Mariel	Fencing	Bronze

*Olympic Games medal information courtesy of Jack Elder,
Olympian, Luge 1972*

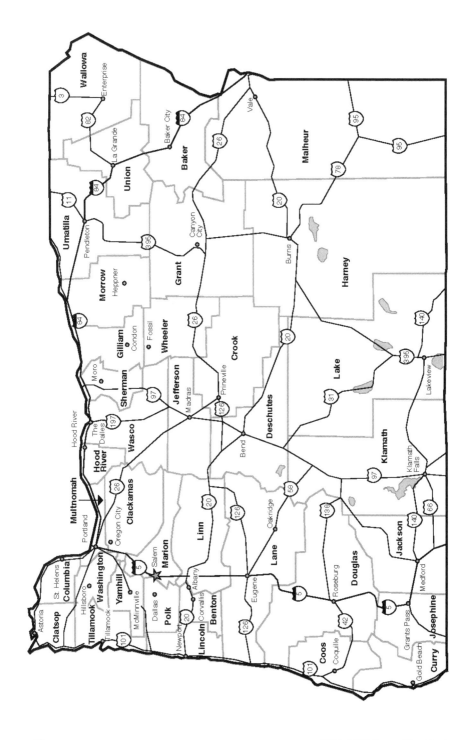

Executive

Oregonians elect five officials for statewide office to manage the executive branch of government: governor, secretary of state, treasurer, attorney general, and bureau of labor and industries commissioner. This section introduces these officials and describes their responsibilities. It also describes the agencies that make up the Executive Branch and the services they provide.

OFFICE OF THE GOVERNOR

Kate Brown, Governor

Address: State Capitol Bldg., 900 Court St. NE, Suite 254, Salem 97301
Phone: 503-378-4582
Web: www.oregon.gov/gov/pages/index.aspx
Kate Brown, Portland; Democrat; appointed 2015; elected 2016; reelected 2018; term expires January 2023.

The governor is elected to a four-year term and is limited to two consecutive terms in office during any 12-year period. The governor must be a U.S. citizen, at least 30 years old and an Oregon resident for three years before taking office.

Bio: After spending most of her childhood in Minnesota, Governor Kate Brown earned a Bachelor of Arts degree in Environmental Conservation with a Certificate in Women's Studies from the University of Colorado at Boulder. She earned her law degree and Certificate in Environmental Law from the Northwestern School of Law at Lewis & Clark College in Portland.

Brown practiced family law in Portland until she was appointed to the Oregon House of Representatives in 1991. She served in both the State House and Senate. In 2004, she became the first woman to serve as Senate majority leader.

In 2008, Brown was elected as Oregon's 24th secretary of state, serving two terms. As secretary of state, she created Business Xpress, an online portal to provide resources for starting, expanding, operating, or relocating businesses in Oregon. Brown also worked to modernize and expand voting access, including launching the country's first automatic voter registration system.

After Governor John Kitzhaber resigned in 2015, Brown was sworn in as Oregon's 38th governor, in accordance with the Oregon Constitution. She was elected governor on November 8, 2016 to finish out Governor Kitzhaber's first term and was reelected in 2018 to a second term.

As governor, Kate Brown has dramatically increased access to the ballot box; made historic investments in addressing climate change, education, transportation, and affordable housing; and expanded the Oregon Health Plan to cover 94 percent of adults and every single child in Oregon.

With her husband Dan, Brown helped raise Dan's son and daughter in SE Portland. When Governor Brown is not busy at the Capitol, you will find her exploring the natural beauty of Oregon with her dog, Jory.

Duties and Responsibilities: The governor is the chief executive of Oregon. The Oregon Constitution charges the governor with faithfully executing the laws, making recommendations to the Legislature and transacting all necessary business of state government.

The governor provides leadership, planning and coordination for the executive branch of state government. She appoints many department and agency heads within the executive branch and members to nearly 300 policymaking, regulatory and advisory boards and commissions. The governor proposes a two-year budget to the Legislature, recommends a legislative program each regular session and may also call special sessions. She reviews all bills passed by the Legislature, may veto measures she believes are not in the public interest and shall fill vacancies by appointment.

The governor chairs the State Land Board, which manages state-owned lands, acts as the superintendent of public instruction, directs state government coordination with local and federal governments and is commander-in-chief of the state's military forces.

The governor appoints judges to fill vacancies in judicial office, has extradition authority and may grant reprieves, commutations and pardons of criminal sentences.

If the office of governor becomes vacant, the office passes, in order, to the secretary of state, state treasurer, president of the Senate and speaker of the House of Representatives. There is no lieutenant governor in Oregon.

Statutory Authority: ORS Chapter 176

Constituent Services

Address: State Library Bldg., 250 Winter St.NE, 3rd Floor, Salem 97301
Mail: State Capitol Bldg., 900 Court St. NE, Suite 254, Salem 97301
Phone: 503-378-4582
Fax: 503-378-6827
Web: https://www.oregon.gov/gov/Pages/request-assistance.aspx
Duties and Responsibilities: The Governor's Constituent Services office assists Oregonians in navigating state services, helping citizens obtain benefits or resolve their problems with government agencies. This team works with individuals and constituency groups to ensure the governor is aware of their concerns, reporting regularly to the governor and policy advisors. The office seeks to treat all inquiries fairly, to examine each situation objectively, and to respond in a clear and helpful way.

Policy Advisors & Governor's Office Staff

The mailing address for all members of the Governor's Office Staff is State Capitol Bldg., 900 Court St. NE, Room 254, Salem, OR 97301. For a full directory, please visit: https://www.oregon.gov/gov/Pages/staff.aspx.

OFFICE OF THE SECRETARY OF STATE

Shemia Fagan, Secretary of State

Address: 136 State Capitol Bldg., Salem 97310-0722
Phone: 503-986-1523
Fax: 503-986-1616
Email: oregon.sos@oregon.gov
Web: http://sos.oregon.gov/Pages/default.aspx
Biography, Clackamas; Democrat; elected 2020; term expires January 2025; Oregon's 28th secretary of state.

The secretary of state is one of three constitutional officers of the executive branch elected statewide. The secretary is elected to a four-year term and is limited to two consecutive terms in office during any 12-year period.

Bio: Born in Portland and raised in Dufur and The Dalles, Secretary Shemia Fagan is a native Oregonian. The politics of Oregon have never been an intellectual exercise for her, they are personal. Fagan knows firsthand the instability facing many Oregon families. During most of her life, her mom struggled with drug addiction and did not have a permanent home. Fagan believes that every person struggling to keep a home or make a home is somebody's somebody. Somebody's son, somebody's aunt, somebody's grandpa or somebody's mom.

Thanks to Oregon schools in Wasco County, Dufur and The Dalles, Secretary Fagan's family had the opportunity to change their lives for the better. She went on to work through college and law school at Willamette University and Lewis & Clark College. Fagan worked as an attorney, advising businesses in employment law, and later representing workers whose civil rights were violated. Secretary Fagan began her political career on the David Douglas School Board in 2011, where she was a proud champion for local public schools. In 2012, Secretary Fagan was elected to the Oregon House from District 51. As a state representative, she delivered millions of dollars for sidewalks in underserved neighborhoods and made sure that vulnerable communities had a voice in our state government. In 2018, Secretary Fagan was elected to the Oregon Senate, where she was the chair of the Senate Housing and Development Committee.

Fagan lives in Clackamas with her two children, Alton and Imogene.

Duties and Responsibilities: The Secretary of State is one of three constitutional offices established at statehood and is the auditor of public accounts, chief elections officer, public records administrator and custodian of the State Seal.

The secretary interprets and applies state election laws, compiles and publishes the *Voters' Pamphlet* and supervises all elections, local and statewide.

She examines and audits accounts of all publicly funded boards, commissions and agencies.

She keeps public records of businesses authorized to transact business in Oregon, nonprofit corporations, and trade and service marks. Other public business records include notices of security interests in movable and personal property, statutory liens and warrants.

As the public records administrator, the secretary houses and provides access to the permanently valuable records of state government through the Archives Division and manages all public records for retention and disposition.

The secretary shares responsibility with the governor and treasurer for supervising and managing state-owned lands and chairs the Oregon Sustainability Board which works to optimize organizations' financial, environmental and social performance. She also regulates Oregon notaries public, and publishes the *Oregon Blue Book*.

Oregon does not have a lieutenant governor. If the office of governor becomes vacant, the office passes to the secretary of state.

Legal Authority: Oregon Constitution, Article VI, Section 2; ORS Chapters 177, 240

Archives Division

Address: 800 Summer St. NE, Salem 97310
Phone: 503-373-0701
Fax: 503-378-4118
Email: Reference.Archives@oregon.gov
Web: https://sos.oregon.gov/archives/Pages/default.aspx
Contact: Stephanie Clark, State Archivist
Statutory Authority: ORS 177.120, Chapter 183, 192.001–192.170, 357.805–357.885
Duties and Responsibilities: The State Archives was created by the Oregon Legislature in 1945 and received its initial funding in 1947. The primary function of the State Archives was to manage public records at all levels of government in Oregon by authorizing their retention and disposition and to identify, preserve and provide access to the permanently valuable public records of the state. Today, the State Archives acts as the state's information manager (Records Management Unit) by managing public records from creation until final disposition, and as the state's information broker (Reference Unit) by identifying, preserving and providing access, through its website and in person, to the permanently valuable public records of the state. In addition, the division is responsible for filing, codifying and publishing Oregon's Administrative Rules; compiling and publishing the *Oregon Blue Book;* filing Official Documents; providing advice and assistance on a variety of public records issues; and managing the State Records Center for non-permanent, paper records storage and the Security Copy Depository for microfilm.

The State Archives is home to the original Oregon Constitution.

State Historical Records Advisory Board

Address: 800 Summer St. NE, Salem 97310
Phone: 503-378-4972
Fax: 503-378-4118
Contact: Mary McRobinson, State Coordinator

Audits Division

Address: Public Service Bldg., 255 Capitol St. NE, Suite 500, Salem 97310
Phone: 503-986-2255; Hotline: 1-800-336-8218
Fax: 503-378-6767
Email: audits.sos@oregon.gov
Web: https://sos.oregon.gov/audits/Pages/default.aspx
Contact: Kip Memmott, Director
Statutory Authority: ORS 177.170–177.180, Chapter 297
Duties and Responsibilities: Created in 1929, the division conducts audits to protect the public interest and improve Oregon government. The division ensures that public funds are properly accounted for, spent in accordance with legal requirements and used to the best advantage. These efforts evoke Oregon's first auditor whose duties were defined in the Territorial Statutes "to lessen the public expenses, use public money to best advantage, promote frugality in public office, and generally, for better management." The division conducts its work according to the professional standards published by the U.S. Government Accountability Office, and all its audits are available to the public on the secretary of state's website.

Corporation Division

Address: Public Service Bldg., 255 Capitol St. NE, Suite 151, Salem 97310
Phone: 503-986-2200
Fax: 503-986-6355
Web: https://sos.oregon.gov/business/Pages/default.aspx
Contact: Ruth Miles, Director
Statutory Authority: ORS Chapters 56, 58, 60, 62, 63, 65, 67, 68, 79, 80, 87, 128, 194, 554, 647, 648
Duties and Responsibilities: The division helps entrepreneurs start a business in Oregon by ensuring state government registration processes are as fast and easy as possible. Specifically, it assists the public in registering business entities and filing public notice of records of debt, commissions notaries public and provides certification of records and notarized documents. The division provides access to public records in the form of copies, certificates, lien searches, computer reports, and on-line database access to allow the public and businesses to know with whom they are doing business.

The Office of Small Business Assistance helps businesses who experience difficulty in their interactions with a state agency and connects businesses with state and non-state resources. The office acts as an ombudsman to help resolve problems between businesses and state agencies.

The origins and functions of the division date back to 1862. Its efforts accomplish the secretary of state's vision to deliver better results to Oregonians through more efficient and effective service delivery, greater transparency and accountability, and by using innovation to connect Oregonians to their government.

Elections Division

Address: Public Service Bldg., 255 Capitol St. NE, Suite 501, Salem 97310-0722
Phone: 503-986-1518
Fax: 503-373-7414
Email: elections.sos@oregon.gov
Web: www.oregonvotes.gov
Contact: Brenda Bayes, Interim Director
Statutory Authority: ORS Chapters 246–260
Duties and Responsibilities: The division ensures the uniform interpretation and application of Oregon's election laws and enforces federal election laws. It monitors and supervises election administration of the country's first vote-by-mail system in all 36 counties and provides the public, elected officials, candidates, media and interested parties advice and assistance in all matters related to elections. Though some of its duties were performed prior to statehood in 1859, the Elections Division was officially created in 1957 when the secretary of state was named the chief elections officer for the state.

The division manages the statewide voter registration database and the electronic system for tracking and reporting campaign finance transactions. The division accepts filings for state offices, receives and verifies initiative and referendum petitions and monitors campaign contributions and expenditure reports. The division publishes and distributes the *Voters' Pamphlet* for all state elections and investigates alleged election law violations.

Internal Support:

Business Services Division
Jeff Morgan, Director

Human Resources Division
Tasha Peterson, Director

Information Systems Division
Chris Molin, Director

OFFICE OF THE STATE TREASURER

Tobias Read, State Treasurer

Address: 159 State Capitol Bldg., 900 Court St. NE, Salem 97301
Phone: 503-378-4329
Email: oregon.treasurer@ost.state.or.us
Web: www.oregon.gov/treasury/Pages/index.aspx
Tobias Read, Beaverton; Democrat; elected 2016; reelected 2020; term expires January 2025.

The state treasurer is elected to a four-year term and is limited to two consecutive terms in office during any 12-year period.
Bio: Tobias Read is Oregon's 29th state treasurer. Born in Montana and raised in Idaho, he moved to Salem, Oregon to attend Willamette University before earning his Master of Business Administration degree at the University of Washington. He brings a wide range of public-sector and private-sector experience to the office. He worked for two U.S. Treasury secretaries, at the Nike Corporation and has most recently served as a state representative in Oregon for a decade.

As a state representative, Tobias was known for focusing on the issues that contribute to a growing economy—a high-quality education, innovation, and funding for our roads and bridges. He strove to fund full-day kindergarten and give all districts the opportunity to offer it. In 2015, he was a chief sponsor of the Oregon Retirement Savings Plan, which in 2017 became the first operating state-sponsored retirement program. Known as OregonSaves, the program enrolls Oregon workers who lack access to a retirement savings option through their employers, allowing hundreds of thousands more Oregonians to retire with dignity after a lifetime of work.

As state treasurer, Tobias' first priority is to focus on managing Oregon's money responsibly and with transparency. He is also working hard to help Oregonians save for college and retirement so that everyone in Oregon has a chance to succeed.

Tobias lives in Beaverton with his wife Heidi and their two children.

Duties and Responsibilities: The state treasurer is a constitutional officer and a statewide elected official. The treasurer serves as the chief financial officer for the state and is responsible for the prudent management of billions of taxpayer dollars.

The treasurer serves as the state's chief investment officer and has the duty of investing the monies of numerous funds such as the Public Employees Retirement Fund, the State Accident Insurance Fund and the Common School Fund.

The treasurer serves on a variety of state financial boards and on the State Land Board, which has a fiduciary duty to manage state trust lands for the benefit of the Common School Fund.

The treasurer's financial responsibilities include managing the investment of state funds, issuing state bonds, serving as the central bank for state agencies and administering the Oregon 529 Savings Network, Oregon Retirement Savings Plan, the Oregon Investment Council and State Debt Policy Advisory Commission.

Statutory Authority: ORS Chapter 178

Executive Division

Address: 159 State Capitol Bldg., 900 Court St. NE, Salem 97301
Phone: 503-378-4329
Contact: Michael Kaplan, Deputy State Treasurer
Duties and Responsibilities: The division coordinates agencywide business services including strategic planning, internal auditing and accounting, human resource functions, project management, procurement and communications.

Debt Management Division

Address: 350 Winter St. NE, Suite 100, Salem 97301-3896
Phone: 503-378-4000
Contact: Jacqueline Knights, Director
Duties and Responsibilities: The division oversees the sale, issuance and ongoing management of all state bonds, serves as a resource for debt-issuing local governments, and serves as the state's liaison to rating agencies and investors with regard to the state's financial condition. The division's work intersects with and is supported by the following three groups.

Municipal Debt Advisory Commission

Statutory Authority: ORS 287.030
Duties and Responsibilities: The commission collects and reports information related to Oregon local government debt and provides policy input to the Legislature on debt matters of local governments.

Private Activity Bond Committee

Duties and Responsibilities: The committee allocates tax-exempt private activity bond allotments provided to the state under federal tax law.

State Debt Policy Advisory Commission

Statutory Authority: ORS 286.550–286.555
Duties and Responsibilities: The commission, chaired by the state treasurer, prepares annual reports regarding outstanding tax-supported and non-tax-supported debt and makes recommendations to the governor and Legislature regarding affordable levels of state indebtedness.

Facilities Authority, Oregon

Address: 1600 Pioneer Tower, 888 SW Fifth Ave., Portland 97204
Phone: 503-802-2102
Contact: Gwendolyn Griffith, Executive Director
Statutory Authority: ORS 289.100
Duties and Responsibilities: The authority was created in 1989 and is empowered to issue low-cost bonds to assist nonprofit organizations with the financing of property and facilities for health, housing, education and culture. The authority reviews proposed projects and makes recommendations to the state treasurer about the issuance of bonds.

Finance Division

Address: 350 Winter St. NE, Suite 100, Salem 97301-3896
Phone: 503-378-4633
Contact: Cora Parker, Director
Duties and Responsibilities: The division provides cash management services to all Oregon state agencies and hundreds of Oregon local government entities, including cities, counties, schools and special districts. The division also helps protect public funds deposited at private banks and credit unions through collateralization requirements governed by ORS chapter 295. As the central bank for state agencies, the division manages millions of financial transactions annually, including cash deposits, electronic fund transfers and check issuance. The division also administers the Local Government Investment Pool, which provides a short-term investment vehicle for local governments.

Short Term Fund Board

Address: 350 Winter St. NE, Suite 100, Salem 97301-3896
Phone: 503-431-7900
Contact: Jeremy Knowles
Statutory Authority: ORS 294.885
Duties and Responsibilities: The board advises the state treasurer and the Oregon Investment Council in the management and investments of the Oregon Short Term Fund and the Local Govern-

ment Investment Pool. The treasurer serves as an ex officio member and appoints three members to the board. The governor appoints the remaining three members.

Investment Division

Address: 16290 SW Upper Boones Ferry Rd., Tigard 97224
Phone: 503-431-7900
Contact: Rex Kim, Chief Investment Officer
Duties and Responsibilities: The division manages the financial and real asset portfolios comprised by the Public Employees Retirement Fund, State Accident Insurance Fund, Oregon Short Term Fund, Common School Fund and other state and agency accounts. On July 31, 2020, the combined market value of these funds totaled approximately $105 billion. The division also manages the investment program for the state's deferred compensation plan and serves as staff for the Oregon Investment Council.

Investment Council, Oregon

Address: 350 Winter St. NE, Suite 100, Salem 97301-3896
Phone: 503-378-4000
Contact: Rex Kim, Chief Investment Officer
Statutory Authority: ORS 293.706
Duties and Responsibilities: The council sets policy for all state investment trust funds, consistent with state law and fiduciary standards. The state treasurer and director of the Public Employees Retirement System are ex officio council members, and the governor appoints four members whose service is subject to Senate confirmation. The council approves guidelines for all state investment activities and delegates day-to-day management authority to the Office of the State Treasurer's Investment Division.

Oregon Savings Network

Address: 350 Winter St. NE, Suite 100, Salem 97301-3896
Phone: 503-373-1903
Contact: Michael Parker, Director
Statutory Authority: ORS 178.200–178.245, 178.300–178.385
Duties and Responsibilities: The Oregon Savings Network enables Oregonians to save for their future, including college and career training, disability-related expenses, and retirement. The network's three programs—the Oregon College Savings Plan, OregonSaves and Oregon ABLE Savings Plan—offer unique, accessible financial tools and investment options that can provide state and federal tax advantages and more flexibility than many other savings vehicles.

BUREAU OF LABOR AND INDUSTRIES

Val Hoyle, Commissioner of the Bureau of Labor and Industries

Address: 800 NE Oregon St., Suite 1045, Portland 97232
Phone: 971-673-0761; Oregon Relay System TTY: 711
Fax: 971-673-0762
Web: www.oregon.gov/boli
Salem: 3865 Wolverine St. NE, Bldg. E-1, Salem 97305; 503-378-3292
Eugene: 1400 Executive Pkwy., Suite 200, Eugene 97401; 541-686-7623
Val Hoyle, Springfield; nonpartisan; elected May 2018; term expires January 2023.
Chief executive of the Bureau of Labor and Industries, the commissioner also chairs the State Apprenticeship and Training Council. The term of the commissioner is four years.
Bio: Oregon's statewide Labor Commissioner Val Hoyle was elected in May 2018. Previously, she was a state representative and House majority leader. Hoyle spent 25 years working in the bicycle industry in domestic and international trade. She lives outside of Springfield, Oregon with her husband and her dog and has two grown children.
Duties and Responsibilities: The Oregon Legislature founded the Bureau of Labor and Industries (BOLI) in 1903, with the mission to protect employment rights, advance employment opportunities and protect access to housing and public accommodations that are free from unlawful discrimination.
The commissioner enforces state laws prohibiting discrimination in employment, housing, public accommodation and vocational, professional and trade schools. The commissioner has the authority to initiate a "commissioner's complaint" on behalf of victims of discrimination.
Through the Wage and Hour Division, the commissioner administers state laws relating to wages, hours of employment, basic working conditions, child labor and prevailing wage rates, and licenses certain labor contractors to protect the workers they employ. The division oversees the Wage Security

Fund that covers workers for unpaid wages in certain business closures and enforces group health insurance termination notification provisions.

The commissioner also directs the state's registered apprenticeship training system that gives workers the opportunity to learn a job skill while earning a living. The program benefits employers by providing a pool of skilled workers to meet business and industry demands.

The agency works to support and train employers so that they can more easily comply with frequently complex state and federal employment law. The Administrative Prosecution Unit prosecutes the agency's contested wage and hour and civil rights complaints. The commissioner issues final orders in all contested cases, except commissioner's complaints.

BOLI employs nearly 100 professionals and is headquartered in Portland. Regional offices are located in Eugene and Salem.

Statutory Authority: ORS Chapter 651

Commissioner's Office and Program Services Division

Contact: Duke Shepard, Deputy Labor Commissioner
Statutory Authority: ORS Chapter 651
Duties and Responsibilities: The office develops legislative initiatives, oversees communications for the agency and manages constituent correspondence and public engagement. The office also oversees legislatively directed reporting and serves as staff for legislative workgroups and the Oregon Council on Civil Rights. Other duties include intergovernmental relations, strategic planning and budget management. The Administrative Prosecution Unit convenes administrative law hearings in contested cases for both wage and hour and civil rights determinations.

Apprenticeship and Training Division

Contact: Lisa Ransom, Administrator
Statutory Authority: ORS Chapter 660
Duties and Responsibilities: The division promotes apprenticeship in a variety of trades by working with business, labor, government and educational organizations to increase training and employment opportunities throughout the state. Apprenticeship is occupational training that includes on-the-job experience with classroom learning. The division registers occupational skills standards and agreements between apprentices and employers and works with local apprenticeship committees to ensure quality training and equal opportunity, especially for women and people of color, in technical craft jobs.

State Apprenticeship and Training Council

Contact: Lisa Ransom, Secretary
Statutory Authority: ORS Chapter 660
Duties and Responsibilities: The council oversees apprenticeship committees, programs and policies and approves apprenticeship committee members. The commissioner of the Bureau of Labor and Industries serves as the chairperson, and the director of the Apprenticeship and Training Division serves as its secretary.

Civil Rights Division

Contact: Cristin Casey, Interim Administrator
Statutory Authority: ORS 25.337–25.424, 171.120–171.125, 345.240, 399.230, 399.235, 408.230, 408.237, 441.178. 476.576, 654.062, Chapter 659A
Duties and Responsibilities: The division defends the rights of all Oregonians to equal opportunity in employment, housing, public accommodations and career schools. It protects employment rights, advances employment opportunities and protects access to housing and public accommodations free from discrimination.

Wage and Hour Division

Contact: Sonia Ramirez, Administrator
Statutory Authority: ORS 279C.800–279C.870, Chapters 652, 653, ORS 654.251, Chapter 658
Duties and Responsibilities: The division enforces laws covering state minimum wage and overtime requirements, working conditions, child labor, farm, forest, construction, janitorial, labor contracting and wage collection. The division enforces the payment of prevailing wage rates required to be paid to construction workers on public works projects. BOLI determines and publishes prevailing wage rates based on an annual construction industry survey.

Prevailing Wage Advisory Committee

Contact: Sonia Ramirez, Administrator
Statutory Authority: ORS 279C.820
Duties and Responsibilities: The committee was legislatively established in 2003 to assist the BOLI commissioner in the administration of the Prevailing Wage Rate Law.

Technical Assistance for Employers Program

Contact: Dylan Morgan, Manager
Duties and Responsibilities: The program offers guidance to Oregon businesses and organizations, so they can understand Oregon employment law and stay in compliance. The program holds employment law seminars throughout the state and

publishes employer handbooks on wage and hour, civil rights, family leave laws and other important topics. The staff fields daily calls from Oregon employers seeking guidance on employment-related matters.

OFFICE OF THE ATTORNEY GENERAL

Ellen F. Rosenblum, Attorney General

Address: 1162 Court St. NE, Salem 97301
Phone: 503-378-4402
Web: www.doj.state.or.us/oregon-department-of-justice/office-of-the-attorney-general/attorney-general-ellen-f-rosenblum/
Contact: Frederick M.Boss, Deputy Attorney General

Ellen F. Rosenblum, Portland; Democrat; appointed June 2012; elected November 2012; reelected 2016; reelected 2020; term expires January 2025.

The term of office for attorney general is four years.

Bio: Attorney General Rosenblum began her legal career as a small firm lawyer in Eugene and later served as a federal prosecutor and state trial and appellate court judge. She is the first woman to serve as Oregon attorney general.

Her priorities as attorney general include consumer protection and civil rights—advocating for and protecting Oregon's children and families, students, seniors, immigrants and refugees, crime victims and survivors. As attorney general, she has established a criminal elder abuse unit and a statewide hate crimes and bias incident response program. She has successfully led statewide task forces on police profiling, hate crimes, public records and consumer privacy. She is committed to supporting law enforcement in investigating and prosecuting complex crimes and to holding corporations accountable when they violate the law.

Attorney General Rosenblum attended the University of Oregon, where she received both her undergraduate degree in sociology and her J.D. (law degree). Rosenblum has served on the Executive Committee of the National Association of Attorneys General, as chair of the Conference of Western Attorneys General, and as co-chair of the Democratic Attorneys General Association. She has also served as secretary of the American Bar Association (ABA) and as chair of the ABA Section of State and Local Government Law.

Duties and Responsibilities: The Legislature created the Office of Attorney General in 1891. The Department of Justice was later established by the Legislature in 1947 and is the equivalent of the state's law firm. The attorney general is the chief law officer of the state and heads the Department of Justice. With a staff of approximately 1,300, the agency, headquartered in Salem, has 10 legal and 13 child support offices throughout the state.

The attorney general appears in and represents the state in all court actions and legal proceedings in which the state of Oregon is a party or has an interest, including proceedings that involve elected and appointed state officials, state agencies, boards and commissions. She appoints assistant attorneys general to act as counsel for state agencies, boards and commissions.

When requested by the governor, any state agency official, or any member of the Legislature, the attorney general gives legal opinions upon any question of law in which the state or any public subdivision may have an interest. Unless expressly authorized by law, the attorney general and her assistant attorneys general may not render opinions or give legal advice to any other persons or agencies.

The attorney general writes ballot titles for measures to be voted upon by the people of Oregon and defends them in the Oregon Supreme Court.

The department advocates for and protects all Oregonians, especially the most vulnerable, such as children and seniors. More than 350 state laws confer numerous responsibilities and authorities to the attorney general. Those responsibilities include supervision of charities, enforcement of antitrust laws, assistance to the state's district attorneys, administration of the state's Crime Victims' Compensation Program, investigations of organized crime and public corruption, and the establishment and enforcement of child support obligations for Oregon families.

Statutory Authority: ORS Chapter 180

Appellate Division

Address: 1162 Court St. NE, Salem 97301
Phone: 503-378-4402
Web: www.doj.state.or.us/oregon-department-of-justice/divisions/appellate-division/
Contact: Benjamin Gutman, Solicitor General
Duties and Responsibilities: The division represents the State of Oregon in all cases in the United States federal courts, Oregon Supreme Court and

Oregon Court of Appeals. Lawyers in the division work on civil and administrative appeals such as tort claims, contract disputes and child welfare cases; defense of criminal convictions in direct criminal appeals; and defense of criminal convictions involving challenges to the validity of convictions or sentences after direct appeals are complete. The division also supports district attorneys throughout the state by providing advice and training on legal issues.

Child Support, Division of

Address: 1215 State St., Salem 97301;
Mail: 1162 Court St. NE, Salem 97301
Phone: 503-947-4388
Web: www.doj.state.or.us/child-support/
Contact: Kate Cooper Richardson,
Administrator
Duties and Responsibilities: The division administers the child support program for the state, providing free child support services to Oregonians. Services include locating absent parents, establishing paternity, assisting with child and medical support orders, modifying and enforcing support orders, and receiving and distributing child and medical support payments. Child support services are provided to all parents. The division maintains local branches around the state and works in partnership with district attorneys' offices to deliver child support services through the Oregon Child Support Program. The program collects and distributes more than $394 million in child support annually, helping to ensure the well-being of Oregon families.

Civil Enforcement Division

Address: 1162 Court St. NE, Salem 97301
Phone: 503-934-4400
Web: www.doj.state.or.us/oregon-department-of-justice/divisions/civil-enforcement/
Contact: Lisa M. Udland, Chief Counsel
Duties and Responsibilities: The division is the Department of Justice's proactive (when the state brings the action) civil litigation arm. Within the division, the Charitable Activities Section enforces laws regarding charitable trusts and solicitations and regulates charitable gaming activities, such as bingo and raffle operations. The Civil Recovery Section is responsible for obtaining judgments and collecting debts owed to state agencies. It also provides legal services to the Division of Child Support. The Financial Fraud/Consumer Protection Section protects Oregon consumers by enforcing the Unlawful Trade Practices Act, commonly known as Oregon's consumer protection law. The section also educates consumers and businesses and enforces antitrust and false claims laws. The division's Medicaid Fraud Unit is part of a federally

subsidized program for deterring fraud committed by Medicaid health care service providers. It also handles cases involving physical or financial abuse/neglect of residents of Medicaid-funded facilities. The Child Advocacy Section helps protect abused, neglected and abandoned children throughout Oregon. Child Advocacy attorneys provide a wide range of legal advice to DHS child welfare workers and often represent DHS in contested juvenile and circuit court hearings and help achieve safe and permanent placement for children.

Crime Victim and Survivor Services Division

Address: 1162 Court St. NE, Salem 97301
Phone: 503-378-5348
Fax: 503-378-5738
Email: cvssd.email@doj.state.or.us
Web: www.doj.state.or.us/crime-victims
Contact: Shannon Sivell, Director
Duties and Responsibilities: The division helps victims cover crime-related costs, protects victims' rights and helps fund local service providers. Through trainings, advisory committees and partnerships, the division helps shape best practices statewide and brings a diverse collection of voices to the issue of victim and survivors' rights. The division connects many different programs with a single goal: to serve victims and survivors effectively and compassionately.

Criminal Justice Division

Address: 1162 Court St. NE, Salem 97301
Phone: 503-378-6347
Fax: 503-373-1936
Web: www.doj.state.or.us/oregon-department-of-justice/divisions/criminal-justice/
Contact: Michael Slauson, Chief Counsel
Duties and Responsibilities: The division provides investigative, analytical, prosecution and training support to Oregon's district attorneys and law enforcement agencies. The division also leads or participates in several important criminal information sharing and analysis programs. The division consists of three sections: District Attorney Assistance, Organized Crime, and the Analytical Criminal Information Services section.

General Counsel Division

Address: 1162 Court St. NE, Salem 97301
Phone: 503-947-4540
Web: www.doj.state.or.us/oregon-department-of-justice/divisions/general-counsel/
Contact: Renee Stineman, Chief Counsel
Duties and Responsibilities: The division acts as the state's in-house counsel and provides a broad range of legal services to state agencies, boards and commissions, including day-to-day legal advice

and representing state agencies in administrative hearings. The division is composed of the following: Business Activities, Business Transactions, Government Services, Health and Human Services, Labor and Employment, Natural Resources, and Tax and Finance.

Trial Division

Address: 158 12th St. NE, Salem 97301;
Mail: 1162 Court St. NE, Salem 97301
Phone: 503-947-4700
Web: www.doj.state.or.us/oregon-department-of-justice/divisions/trial/
Contact: Steve Lippold, Chief Trial Counsel
Duties and Responsibilities: The division defends the state, its agencies, employees and officers in civil lawsuits brought in state and federal courts. The division is divided into three sections.

The Civil Litigation Section handles a wide variety of cases in state and federal courts. These involve disputes over agency orders, tort claims, civil rights, employment and other civil cases involving the state.

The Criminal and Collateral Remedies Section handles cases filed by a convicted person seeking a new trial or a re-sentencing from a trial court. This section seeks to uphold the convictions won by a district attorney when a case reaches the state postconviction and federal habeas corpus stage.

Lawyers in the third section, the Special Litigation Unit, defend state statutes and policies against constitutional challenges in state and federal courts. They also defend the state in complex litigation involving elections law, class action lawsuits and environmental cases.

STATE BUILDINGS

Agriculture Building (1966)*
635 Capitol St. NE, Salem 97301

Barbara Roberts Human Services Bldg. (1992)
550 Summer St. NE, Salem 97301

Capitol Mall Parking Structure (1991)
900 Chemeketa St. NE, Salem 97301

Cecil Edwards Archives Building (1991)
800 Summer St. NE, Salem 97310

Commerce Building (1931)
158 12th St. NE, Salem 97301

Commission for the Blind (1977)
535 SE 12th Ave., Portland 97204

Employment Building (1974)
875 Union St. NE, Salem 97311

Executive Building (1979)
155 Cottage St. NE, Salem 97301

Fish and Wildlife Building (2013)
4034 Fairview Industrial Dr. SE, Salem 97302

550 Building (1992, formerly PUC Building)
550 Capitol St. NE, Salem 97301

Forestry Buildings (1938)
2600 State St., Salem 97310

General Services Building (1954)
1225 Ferry St. SE, Salem 97301

General Services Building Annex (1967)
1257 Ferry St. SE, Salem 97301

Justice Building (1930)
1162 Court St. NE, Salem 97301

Labor and Industries Building (1961)
350 Winter St. NE, Salem 97301

Liquor Control Commission Building (1955)
9201 SE McLoughlin Blvd., Milwaukie 97222

North Capitol Mall Office Building (2003)
725 Summer St. NE, Salem 97301

Public Employees' Retirement System Building (1998)
11410 SW 68th Pkwy., Tigard 97281

Public Service Building (1949)
255 Capitol St. NE, Salem 97310

Real Estate Building (1990)
1177 Center St. NE, Salem 97301

Revenue Building (1981)
955 Center St. NE, Salem 97301

State Capitol Building (1938)
900 Court St. NE, Salem 97301

State Fair Buildings, State Fairgrounds
2330 17th St. NE, Salem 97303

State Hospital Building (1883)
2600 Center St. NE, Salem 97301

State Lands Building (1990)
775 Summer St. NE, Salem 97301

State Library (1939)
250 Winter St. NE, Salem 97301

State Lottery Building (1996)
500 Airport Rd. SE, Salem 97301

State Office Building, Eugene (1961)
165 E 7th Ave., Eugene 97401

State Office Building, Pendleton (1963)
700 SE Emigrant St., Pendleton 97801

State Office Building, Portland (1992)
800 NE Oregon St., Portland 97232

State Police Salem Headquarters (2016)
3565 Trelstad Ave. SE, Salem 97317

State Printing Plant (1980)
550 Airport Rd. SE, Salem 97301

Supreme Court Building (1914)
1163 State St., Salem 97301

Transportation Building (1951)
355 Capitol St. NE, Salem 97301

Veterans' Building (1984)
700 Summer St. NE, Salem 97301

*Year is the date the building was constructed, purchased or occupied by the state.

DISTRICT ATTORNEYS

Oregon's 36 District Attorneys are responsible for safeguarding the rights of all Oregonians, including both victims and defendants in criminal cases. As set forth in the Oregon Constitution, district attorneys represent the public in criminal matters by filing criminal charges where warranted by the law and available evidence. The DA is equally responsible for seeking justice for crime victims while also protecting a defendant's right to due process and a fair trial.

Oregon's district attorneys also enforce child support orders and represent the community in juvenile matters and inquiries into the cause and manner of deaths.

Oregon district attorneys are elected in every county and are required to stand for election every four years, thereby maintaining accountability to the public they serve. Although Oregon's DAs are elected by and accountable to the people in their respective counties, they are considered state officers whose salaries are paid by the state.

Baxter, Greg M.
Baker County DA

Haroldson, John
Benton County DA

Wentworth, John D.
Clackamas County DA

Brown, Ron L.
Clatsop County DA

Auxier, Jeffrey D.
Columbia County DA

Frasier, R. Paul
Coos County DA

Whiting, Wade
Crook County DA

Spansail, Joshua A.
Curry County DA

Hummel, John
Deschutes County DA

Wesenberg, Rick
Douglas County DA

Weatherford, Marion
Gilliam County DA

Carpenter, Jim
Grant County DA

Hughes Ryan P.
Harney County DA

Rasmussen, Carrie
Hood River Co. DA

Heckert, Beth
Jackson County DA

Lariche, Steven F.
Jefferson County DA

Eastman, Joshua J.
Josephine County DA

Costello, Eve A.
Klamath County DA

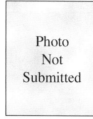

Photo
Not
Submitted

Martin, Ted K.
Lake County DA

Perlow, Patricia W.
Lane County DA

Danforth, Lanee
Lincoln County DA

Marteeny, Doug
Linn County DA

Goldthorpe, David M.
Malheur County DA

Clarkson, Paige E.
Marion County DA

Nelson, Justin
Morrow County DA

Schmidt, Mike
Multnomah Co. DA

Felton, Aaron
Polk County DA

McLeod, Wade
Sherman County DA

Porter, William
Tillamook County DA

Primus, Daniel R.
Umatilla County DA

McDaniel, Kelsie
Union County DA

Frolander, Rebecca
Wallowa County DA

Ellis, Matthew
Wasco County DA

Barton, Kevin
Washington Co. DA

Photo
Not
Submitted

Ladd, Gretchen M.
Wheeler County DA

Berry, Brad
Yamhill County DA

OTHER STATE AGENCIES, BOARDS AND COMMISSIONS

The following section describes agencies, boards, commissions and programs that carry out executive branch duties. Descriptions include basic contact information and a summary of the entity's duties and responsibilities.

Agencies are listed alphabetically by substantive name. For example, the Department of Human Services appears as "Human Services, Department of." Programs under the main agency are listed under that agency's heading. Thus, Child Welfare Programs would appear within the larger entry for Department of Human Services. These subdivisions are also listed alphabetically by substantive name with a few exceptions, such as when a board or commission is connected directly to the main agency office.

The *Blue Book* Index is helpful for locating individual agencies, boards, commissions or programs.

ACCOUNTANCY, OREGON BOARD OF

Address: 200 Hawthorne Ave. SE, Suite D450, Salem 97301-5289
Phone: 503-378-4181
Fax: 503-378-3575
Web: www.oregon.gov/BOA

Contact: Kimberly Fast, Executive Director; Nancy Young-Oliver, CPA, CISA, CFE, Chair
Statutory Authority: ORS Chapter 673
Duties and Responsibilities: Created in 1913 by the Oregon Legislature, the board, with a staff of nine, oversees the licensure of approximately 8,500 Certified Public Accountants (CPAs) and Public Accountants (PAs) and through registration of approximately 1,000 public accounting firms. Applicants for licensure must meet minimum standards in terms of education, work experience and successful completion of the national CPA exam. Thereafter, licensees must demonstrate professional accounting competency at licensure renewal by meeting continuing education standards of 80 hours of education every two years for active licensees.

The CPA profession is fundamentally about trust in the quality of audits, accuracy of financial statements and competency of any other professional service performed by CPAs, including tax services. The board holds licensees accountable for adhering to all professional and ethical standards that apply to their practice. Complaints can be submitted to the board from members of the public, other sources, or may be self-initiated by the board by completing the complaint form which can be found on the board's website. If an investigation finds a violation of board statutes or rules, licensees are held accountable for their conduct through disciplinary action. The public can verify the status and disciplinary history of an Oregon licensee or public accounting firm on the board's website or by calling the board office.

ADMINISTRATIVE SERVICES, DEPARTMENT OF

Address: 155 Cottage St. NE, Salem 97301-3972
Phone: 503-378-3104
Fax: 503-373-7643
Email: oregon.info@oregon.gov
Web: https://www.oregon.gov/DAS/Pages/index.aspx
Contact: Katy Coba, Chief Operating Officer and Director
Statutory Authority: ORS 184.305
Duties and Responsibilities: The Department of Administrative Services (DAS) exists to effectively implement the policy and financial decisions made by the governor and the Oregon Legislature, to manage and coordinate projects involving multiple state agencies and to serve as a catalyst for innovation and improvement across all of state government. DAS serves Oregonians by supporting the state agencies, boards and commissions they rely on each day. DAS employs about 900 people, with offices primarily in the Salem area.

Chief Operating Officer, Office of the

Address: 155 Cottage St. NE, Salem 97301-3965
Phone: 503-378-3104
Fax: 503-373-7643
Email: oregon.info@oregon.gov
Web: https://www.oregon.gov/DAS/Pages/index.aspx
Contact: Katy Coba, Chief Operating Officer and Director
Statutory Authority: ORS 184.315
Duties and Responsibilities: The office provides leadership and policy direction to the department and all other state executive branch agencies. It oversees DAS's public affairs, internal audits, economic analysis, legislative, and information technology (internal to DAS). The office is headed by the Chief Operating Officer, who is appointed by the governor. Staff also provides support to state government's Enterprise Leadership Team, which is comprised of state agency leaders and serves as an advisory board to the governor and the office on long-term strategic policies and statewide initiatives.

Chief Financial Office

Address: 155 Cottage St. NE, U10, Salem 97301-3965
Phone: 503-378-3106
Fax: 503-373-7643
Email: CFO.info@oregon.gov
Web: https://www.oregon.gov/das/Financial/Pages/Index.aspx
Contact: George Naughton, Chief Financial Officer
Statutory Authority: ORS 184.335
Duties and Responsibilities: The office prepares the Governor's Recommended Budget and monitors the development and execution of state agency budgets. The office provides management review services, issues certificates of participation to finance capital construction and infrastructure, helps agencies manage about three million acres of public lands and coordinates the state's bonded debt process. The office manages the financial system infrastructure for state government, which includes accounting, payroll and financial reporting.

Chief Human Resources Office

Address: 155 Cottage St. NE, U30, Salem 97301-3967
Phone: 503-378-3622
Fax: 503-373-7684
Email: chro.hr@oregon.gov
Web: https://www.oregon.gov/das/HR/Pages/Index.aspx
Contact: Madilyn Zike, Chief Human Resources Officer
Statutory Authority: ORS 240.055
Duties and Responsibilities: The office is responsible for statewide human resource systems, policies and initiatives. This encompasses human resource management and consultation and includes establishing and maintaining classification and compensation plans, training and development, administering and maintaining the central state employee database, overseeing personnel recruitment and labor relations and performing Public Employees Retirement System reconciliation for all state agencies. The office also provides direction and services to promote a stable and qualified workforce in state government.

DAS Business Services

Address: 155 Cottage St. NE, U90, Salem 97301-3972
Phone: 503-373-7607
Email: janet.e.savarro@oregon.gov
Web: https://www.oregon.gov/das/Financial/Pages/dbs.aspx
Contact: Janet Savarro, Administrator
Statutory Authority: ORS 184.335
Duties and Responsibilities: This program provides budget, business continuity, performance management and data analysis services for the agency. The program is also responsible for DAS's records management and administrative rules. It coordinates rate development, calculates rates, fees and assessments, performs financial analysis for DAS divisions, develops the statewide price list of

goods and services, and prepares and monitors DAS's biennial budget.

Enterprise Asset Management

Address: 1225 Ferry St. SE, U100, Salem 97301-4281
Phone: 503-428-3362
Fax: 503-373-7210
Email: fac.info@oregon.gov
Web: https://www.oregon.gov/das/Pages/EAM.aspx
Contact: Shannon Ryan, Administrator
Statutory Authority: ORS Chapters 270, 276, 279, 279A, 279B, 279C, 283
Duties and Responsibilities: This program provides services to state government, such as motor pool and surplus property, acquiring and maintaining space for state agencies, property management, real property transaction services (buy, sell and lease), project management, space planning, state building operations and maintenance and landscape maintenance. It also manages parking and commuter programs for state employees in Salem and Portland.

Enterprise Goods and Services

Address: 1225 Ferry St. SE, Salem 97301
Phone: 503-378-4642
Fax: 503-373-1626
Email: brian.e.deforest@oregon.gov
Web: https://www.oregon.gov/das/Pages/EGS.aspx
Contact: Brian E. DeForest, DAS Chief Administrative Officer
Statutory Authority: ORS 184.305, ORS Chapters 278, 279, 282, 283
Duties and Responsibilities: This program provides accounting and payroll, mail distribution and printing, procurement, self-insurance and risk control and financial system management to Executive Branch agencies.

Enterprise Information Services

Address: 155 Cottage St. NE, 4th Floor, Salem 97301
Phone: 503-378-3175
Fax: 503-378-3795
Email: OSCIO.Info@oregon.gov
Web: https://www.oregon.gov/das/OSCIO/Pages/Index.aspx
Contact: Terrence Woods, State Chief Information Officer
Statutory Authority: ORS Chapter 276A
Duties and Responsibilities: Oregon's State Chief Information Officer (State CIO) is an independent official directly responsible to the governor, who operates as the governor's primary advisor for statewide enterprise technology and telecommunication projects and programs, implementation of the Information Technology (IT) Governance framework, and establishment of Oregon's long-term IT strategy using the Enterprise Information Resource Management Strategy. The office is comprised of the following sections: Data Center Services, Cyber Security Services, Project Portfolio Performance, Shared Services, Strategy and Design, and Data Governance and Transparency.

Other Groups:

Economic Analysis, Office of

Address: 155 Cottage St. NE, U20, Salem 97301-3966
Phone: 503-378-3405
Fax: 503-373-7643
Email: OEA.info@oregon.gov
Web: https://www.oregon.gov/DAS/OEA/Pages/index.aspx
Contact: Mark McMullen, State Economist
Duties and Responsibilities: The office prepares state economic and revenue forecasts and long-term population and employment forecasts. It assesses long-term economic and demographic trends, evaluates their implications and conducts special economic and demographic studies. The office also prepares state criminal and juvenile population forecasts and manages the Highway Cost Allocation Study.

Governor's Council of Economic Advisors

Address: 155 Cottage St. NE, U20, Salem 97301-3966
Phone: 503-378-3405
Fax: 503-373-7643
Contact: Joseph Cortright, Chair
Duties and Responsibilities: The council is a group of 12 economists from academia, finance, utilities and industry. It works in conjunction with the Office of Economic Analysis.

Public Lands Advisory Committee

Address: 155 Cottage St. NE, U10, Salem 97301-3965
Phone: 503-378-3106
Fax: 503-373-7643
Email: fac.info@oregon.gov
Web: www.oregon.gov/das/Facilities/Pages/ResPLACProfile.aspx
Contact: John H. Brown, Chair
Statutory Authority: ORS 270.100(1)(d), 270.120
Duties and Responsibilities: The committee's primary role is to advise DAS on all real property acquisitions, exchanges or terminal dispositions valued at $100,000 or more, for which the department must give its consent.

Public Officials Compensation Commission

Address: 155 Cottage St. NE, U30, Salem 97301-3967
Phone: 503-378-2065
Fax: 503-373-7684
Email: Oregon.pocc@oregon.gov
Web: https://www.oregon.gov/das/HR/Pages/pocc.aspx
Statutory Authority: ORS 292.036
Duties and Responsibilities: The commission's primary role is to review and make recommendations to the Legislature on the amount of annual salary to be paid to the governor, secretary of state, treasurer, attorney general, commissioner of the Bureau of Labor and Industries, members of the Legislature, chief justice and judges of the Supreme Court, and judges of the Court of Appeals, Circuit Courts and Tax Courts.

Public Records Advocate

Address: 800 Summer St. NE, Salem 97310
Phone: 503-378-5228
Email: Todd.Albert@oregon.gov
Web: https://www.oregon.gov/pra/Pages/advocate.aspx
Contact: Todd Albert, Acting Public Records Advocate
Statutory Authority: ORS 192.461
Duties and Responsibilities: The Public Records Advocate, appointed by the governor, provides advice, assistance and facilitated dispute resolution services at the request of government bodies or public records requesters, provides training on public records laws and leads the Public Records Advisory Council.

Public Records Advisory Council

Address: 800 Summer Street NE, Salem 97310
Phone: 503-378-5228
Contact: Todd Albert, Acting Public Records Advocate
Statutory Authority: ORS 192.481
Duties and Responsibilities: The council, chaired by the public records advocate, works with the advocate and the State Archives Division to study and make recommendations concerning public records law and the advocate's role, as well as practices, procedures, exemptions and fees related to public records. The council is also responsible for conducting regular surveys of state public bodies to gather information about their public records processes.

ADVOCACY COMMISSIONS OFFICE, OREGON

Address: 421 SW Oak St., Suite 770, Portland 97204
Phone: 503-302-9725
Email: OACO.mail@oregon.gov
Web: www.oregon.gov/OAC/Pages/index.aspx
Contact: Lucy Baker, Administrator
Statutory Authority: ORS 185.005–185.025
Duties and Responsibilities: The office was created in 2005 to support Oregon's Commissions on Asian and Pacific Islander Affairs, Black Affairs, Hispanic Affairs and the Commission for Women. The office supports each commission's work in community based applied policy research; advising the governor, Legislature and departmental leadership on policies affecting communities of color and women; growing leadership from their communities within government; and building success for Asian/Pacific Islander, Black and Hispanic Oregonians and women in Oregon.

Each commission is composed of 11 members, nine of whom are appointed by the governor and confirmed by the Senate to serve four-year terms. The president of the Senate and the speaker of the House each appoint a member to serve a two-year term.

Asian and Pacific Islander Affairs, Commission on

Address: 421 SW Oak St., Suite 770, Portland 97204
Phone: 503-302-9725
Email: OACO.mail@oregon.gov
Web: www.oregon.gov/OCAPIA/Pages/index.aspx
Contact: Hussein Al-Baiaty and Mohamed Alyajouri, Co-Chairs
Statutory Authority: ORS 185.610–185.625
Duties and Responsibilities: The commission was established in 1995 and amended in 1999 to focus on equitable policy advising, advocacy, policy research and leadership development. The goal of the commission is to advise state policy makers on equitable public policy for Asian and Pacific Islander communities and intersectionally among communities of color and women statewide. The commission also works to assure equity focused communication and dissemination of information between state government and Asian and Pacific Islander communities.

Black Affairs, Commission on

Address: 421 SW Oak St., Suite 770, Portland 97204
Phone: 503-302-9725
Web: www.oregon.gov/OCBA/Pages/index.aspx
Email: OACO.mail@oregon.gov

Contact: Jamal T. Fox, Chair
Statutory Authority: ORS 185.410–185.430
Duties and Responsibilities: The commission works for the implementation of economic, social, legal and political equity for Oregon's African American and Black populations. The commission is authorized by law to monitor existing programs and legislation designed to meet the needs of the African American and Black community, identify and research concerns and issues affecting the community in order to recommend actions and programs to the governor and the Legislature, act as a liaison between the community and Oregon's government, encourage African American and Black representation on state boards and commissions and establish special committees as needed.

Hispanic Affairs, Commission on

Address: 421 SW Oak St., Suite 770, Portland 97204
Phone: 503-302-9725
Email: OACO.mail@oregon.gov
Web: www.oregon.gov/Hispanic/Pages/index.aspx
Contact: Irma Linda Castillo, Chair
Statutory Authority: ORS 185.310–185.330
Duties and Responsibilities: The commission was created by the 1983 Legislature to work for economic, social, legal and political equity for Hispanics in Oregon. The commission monitors existing programs and legislation to ensure that the needs of Hispanics are met. The commission researches problems and issues and recommends appropriate action, maintains a liaison between the Hispanic community and government entities and encourages Hispanic representation on state boards and commissions.

In addition, the commission focuses on and responds to the wider statewide context of equity and social well-being, identifies and seeks solutions to disparities in services and programs for the ethnically diverse Hispanic/Latino/Indigenous community, and encourages good public policy development. In networking with numerous Hispanic community, civic, cultural/ethnic and professional organizations, OCHA also promotes civic engagement, economic development and ongoing mentoring for the next generation of leaders.

Women, Commission for

Address: 421 SW Oak St., Suite 770, Portland 97204
Phone: 503-302-9725
Email: OACO.mail@oregon.gov
Web: www.oregon.gov/Women/Pages/index.aspx
Contact: Kasandra Krifka, Chair
Statutory Authority: ORS 185.510–185.560

Duties and Responsibilities: In 1964, Governor Mark Hatfield established the Governor's Commission on the Status of Women to advise him of the needs and concerns of Oregon women. In 1983, the commission gained independent status as the Oregon Commission for Women, with a directive to strive for women's equity through the implementation of beneficial programs and policies. Today, the commission advocates for women in the community, provides information on women's issues to the governor and Legislature, serves as a link for women and their unique equity focused issues to state agencies and the Legislature.

The Agriculture Building in Salem houses the central offices of the Department of Agriculture. (Oregon State Archives scenic photo)

AGRICULTURE, DEPARTMENT OF

Address: 635 Capitol St. NE, Salem 97301-2532
Phone: 503-986-4550
Fax: 503-986-4750
Email: info@oda.state.or.us
Web: www.oregon.gov/ODA/Pages/index.aspx
Contact: Alexis Taylor, Director
Statutory Authority: ORS Chapter 576
Duties and Responsibilities: The Oregon Department of Agriculture (ODA) works to ensure healthy natural resources, environment and economy for Oregonians now and in the future through inspection and certification, regulation, and promotion of agriculture and food.

The agency was formed in 1931 when the Oregon Legislature consolidated 13 separate boards, bureaus and commissions. ODA relies on partnerships with other state and federal agencies, Oregon State University's College of Agricultural Sciences and numerous non-government organizations to help carry out the agency's mission. The 10-member State Board of Agriculture advises ODA on policy issues, develops recommendations on key agricultural issues and provides advocacy of the state's agriculture industry. New responsibilities for the agency include an industrial hemp program and the addition of a cannabis policy coordinator to incorporate the state's cannabis production into existing ODA programs and requirements.

ODA employs about 480 people and is headquartered in Salem with its marketing and laboratory programs located in Portland at the Food Innovation Center. In addition, several inspectors and other staff members' responsibilities are spread geographically to provide services across the state.

Food Safety and Animal Health Programs
Phone:
Animal Health Program (State Veterinarian): 503-986-4680
Food Safety Program: 503-986-4720
Livestock Identification Program (Brands): 503-986-4681
Email: istapleton@oda.state.or.us
Contact: Isaak Stapleton, Director
Duties and Responsibilities: This program area provides inspections for all of Oregon's food distribution systems (except restaurants) to ensure food is safe for consumption. To protect and maintain animal health, it ensures animal feeds meet nutritional and labeling standards. Through registration of brands and brand inspections, it denies a market in stolen livestock.

Internal Service and Consumer Protection Programs
Phone:
Laboratory Services: 503-872-6644
Weights and Measures Program: 503-986-4670
Email: jbarber@oda.state.or.us
Contact: Jason Barber, Director
Duties and Responsibilities: These programs provide consumer protection and fair competition among businesses while facilitating interstate commerce and international trade by ensuring the accuracy and uniformity of Oregon's Commercial Weighing System and the quality of motor fuels sold in Oregon. The program area provides laboratory analysis and technical support to the Oregon Department of Agriculture's enforcement programs and also administers programs dealing with wolf depredation compensation and egg-laying hen cage space.

Market Access and Certification Programs
Phone:
Portland office: 503-872-6600
Salem office: 503-986-4620
Email: jpaulson@oda.state.or.us

Contact: Jess Paulson, Director
Duties and Responsibilities: These programs help Oregon's agricultural producers successfully add value to, sell and ship products to local, national and international markets by promoting and creating demand for products through marketing activities, inspection and certification.

Natural Resources and Pesticide Programs
Phone:
Natural Resources Programs: 503-986-4700
Pesticides Program: 503-986-4635
Email: spage@oda.state.or.us
Contact: Stephanie Page, Director
Duties and Responsibilities: These programs address water quality, quantity and natural resource conservation on agricultural lands. They also address the proper use of pesticides, labeling and sale of fertilizer, as well as field burning in the Willamette Valley. Program goals are accomplished through outreach, regulatory work, monitoring and coordination with other natural resource agencies.

Plant Protection and Conservation Programs
Phone: 503-986-4636
Email: hrogg@oda.state.or.us
Contact: Helmuth Rogg, Director
Duties and Responsibilities: These programs protect Oregon's agricultural industries and natural environment from harmful plant pests, diseases and noxious weeds; enhance the value and marketability of exported nursery stock, Christmas trees, seeds and other agricultural products; register industrial hemp growers and handlers; and further the conservation of threatened and endangered plants.

State Board of Agriculture
Address: 635 Capitol St. NE, Salem 97301-2532
Phone: 503-986-4554
Fax: 503-986-4750
Contact: Karla Valness, Assistant to the Board
Statutory Authority: ORS Chapter 561
Duties and Responsibilities: The 10-member State Board of Agriculture advises ODA on policy, develops recommendations on key agricultural issues and provides advocacy of the state's agriculture industry.

Agricultural Commodity Commissions
Commodity commissions conduct promotional, educational, production and market research projects. The commissions are authorized by ORS chapters 576, 577 and 578 and are funded by assessments on the producers of the commodities.

The director of the Oregon Department of Agriculture appoints the members of all 22 commissions.

Albacore Commission
Address: PO Box 983, Lincoln City 97367-0983
Phone/Fax: 541-994-2647
Web: www.oregonalbacore.org
Contact: Nancy Fitzpatrick, Executive Director

Alfalfa Seed Commission
Address: PO Box 688, Ontario 97914-0688
Phone: 541-881-1335
Email: ddk@fmtc.com
Contact: Edith Kressly, Administrator

Beef Council
Address: 1827 NE 44th Ave., Suite 315, Portland 97213
Phone: 503-274-2333
Web: www.orbeef.org
Contact: Will Wise, Executive Director

Blueberry Commission
Address: PO Box 3366, Salem 97302-0366
Phone: 503-364-2944
Web: www.oregonblueberry.com
Contact: Bryan Ostlund, Administrator

Clover Commission
Web: www.oregonclover.org
Contact Info: See Blueberry Commission

Dairy Products Commission
Address: 10505 SW Barbur Blvd., Portland 97219-6853
Phone: 503-229-5033
Web: https://odncouncil.org
Contact: Pete Kent, Executive Director

Dungeness Crab Commission
Address: PO Box 1160, Coos Bay 97420-0301
Phone: 541-267-5810
Web: www.oregondungeness.org
Contact: Hugh Link, Executive Director

Fine Fescue Commission
Web: www.oregonfinefescue.org
Contact Info: See Blueberry Commission

Hazelnut Commission
Address: 29100 Town Center Loop W., Wilsonville 97070
Phone: 503-582-8420
Web: www.oregonhazelnuts.org
Contact: Polly Owen, Interim Administrator

Hop Commission
Address: PO Box 298, Hubbard 97032
Phone: 503-982-7600
Web: www.oregonhops.org
Contact: Michelle Palacios, Administrator

Mint Commission
Web: www.oregonmint.org
Contact Info: See Blueberry Commission

Potato Commission
Address: 9320 SW Barbur Blvd., Suite 130, Portland 97219-5405
Phone: 503-239-4763
Web: www.oregonspuds.com
Contact: Gary Roth, Executive Director

Processed Vegetable Commission
Address: PO Box 55401, Portland OR. 97238
Phone: 503-702-5707
Web: www.opvc.org
Contact: Jennifer Fletcher, Administrator

Raspberry and Blackberry Commission
Address: 1827 NE 44th Ave., Suite 315, Portland 97213
Phone: 503-274-5458
Web: www.oregon-berries.com
Contact: Julie Hoffman, Associate Director

Ryegrass Growers Seed Commission
Web: www.ryegrass.com
Contact Info: See Blueberry Commission

Salmon Commission
Web: http://oregonsalmon.org
Contact Info: See Albacore Commission

Sheep Commission
Address: 1270 Chemeketa St. NE, Salem 97301
Phone: 503-364-5462
Web: oregonsheepcommission.com
Contact: Richard Kosesan, Administrator

Strawberry Commission
Web: www.oregon-strawberries.org
Contact Info: See Raspberry and Blackberry Commission

Sweet Cherry Commission
Web: www.osweetcherry.org
Contact Info: See Raspberry and Blackberry Commission

Tall Fescue Commission
Web: www.oregontallfescue.org
Contact Info: See Blueberry Commission

Trawl Commission
Address: 16289 Hwy. 101 S, Suite C, Brookings 97415

Phone: 541-469-7830
Web: www.ortrawl.org
Contact: Yelena Nowak, Executive Director

Wheat Commission

Address: 1200 NW Naito Pkwy., Suite 370, Portland 97209-2800
Phone: 503-467-2161
Web: www.owgl.org
Contact: Amanda Hoey, Executive Director

APPRAISER CERTIFICATION AND LICENSURE BOARD

Address: 200 Hawthorne Ave. SE, Suite C-302, Salem 97301
Phone: 503-485-2555
Fax: 503-485-2559
Email: chad.koch@oregon.gov
Web: https://public.orlicensing.oregon.gov/ACLBPortal/Home.aspx
Contact: Chad Koch, Administrator
Statutory Authority: ORS Chapter 674
Duties and Responsibilities: The board was created in 1991 with the responsibility to protect the public and Oregon financial institutions through regulation and supervision of licensed and certified real estate appraisers and appraisal management companies in the state. In addition, the board ensures that real estate appraisals are issued in writing and conducted in compliance with Oregon statutes and administrative rules and the Uniform Standards of Professional Appraisal Practice. The board is a semi-independent agency with six full time staff members and eight board members who are appointed by the governor.

ARCHITECT EXAMINERS, STATE BOARD OF

Address: 205 Liberty St. NE, Suite A, Salem 97301
Phone: 503-763-0662
Email: architectboard@osbae.com
Web: www.osbae.com
Contact: Lisa Howard, Executive Director
Statutory Authority: ORS 671.010–671.220
Duties and Responsibilities: The board was created by the Legislature in 1919 to regulate the practice of architecture. The agency serves Oregonians by assuring that persons practicing architecture in Oregon are properly qualified and registered. The agency determines the standards for architect and architectural firm registration, which consist of a combination of education, examination and experience. The agency enforces the laws governing the practice of architecture in Oregon by investigating alleged violations and disciplining those who violate the law. Headquartered in Salem, the agency consists of seven board members appointed by the governor and five staff.

AVIATION, OREGON DEPARTMENT OF

Address: 3040 25th St. SE, Salem 97302-1125
Phone: 503-378-4880
Fax: 503-373-1688
Email: aviation.mail@aviation.state.or.us
Web: www.oregon.gov/Aviation/Pages/index.aspx
Contact: Betty Stansbury, Director
Statutory Authority: ORS 835.100
Duties and Responsibilities: The department works to provide infrastructure, financial resources and expertise to ensure a safe and efficient air transportation system. It registers airports, pilots and aircraft and is responsible for a Statewide Capital Improvement Program in coordination with the Federal Aviation Administration (FAA) and federally funded public use airports around the state. The department is governed by a seven-member board of directors, appointed by the governor, and employs 14 staff. The Aviation Board was formed in 1921, and it developed the system of airports in Oregon. It performed many of the functions that the FAA does today. The board provides policy oversight for the agency and is the modal committee for the ConnectOregon program.

BLIND, COMMISSION FOR THE

Address: 535 SE 12th Ave., Portland 97214
Phone: 971-673-1588
Fax: 503-234-7468
Email: ocb.mail@state.or.us
Web: www.oregon.gov/blind
Contact: Dacia Johnson, Executive Director
Statutory Authority: ORS 346.110–346.570
Duties and Responsibilities: The mission of the commission is to empower Oregonians who are blind to fully engage in life. Established in 1937, the commission has evolved to be a consumer-driven organization with a citizen governing body, appointed by the governor, representing consumer organizations, education, ophthalmology/optometry businesses and individual citizens who are blind. The commission operates under its enabling statutes and through the Workforce Innovation and Opportunity Act of 2014. The commission has 66 full-time equivalent staff who provide services throughout the state.

The commission's major program objectives include helping Oregonians who are blind get and keep jobs, allowing them to support themselves and their families; training Oregonians in alternative skills related to blindness such as adaptive technology, white cane travel, braille and activities of daily living; helping seniors and individuals with vision loss who are unable to work live with high levels of independence and self-sufficiency so they can remain in their homes and stay active in their communities; and licensing and supporting business owners who operate food service and vending operations in public buildings and facilities throughout the state.

BUSINESS DEVELOPMENT DEPARTMENT, OREGON

Address: 755 Summer St. NE, Suite 200, Salem 97301-1280
Phone: 503-986-0123; TTY: 1-800-735-2900
Fax: 503-581-5115
Web: www.oregon4biz.com
Contact: Sophorn Cheang, Director
Statutory Authority: ORS 285A.070
Duties and Responsibilities: The department, operating as Business Oregon, is the state's economic development agency. Business Oregon has primary offices in Salem and Portland, along with staff located in 12 regions across the state. The mission of the agency is to invest in Oregon businesses, communities and people to promote a globally competitive, diverse and inclusive economy. Business Oregon is focused on five priorities: innovating Oregon's economy, growing small and middle-market companies, cultivating rural economic stability, advancing economic opportunity for underrepresented people, and ensuring an inclusive, transparent and fiscally healthy agency. Core agency functions include rural community development and infrastructure financing; business retention, expansion and recruitment; export promotion and international trade; industry innovation and research and development; entrepreneurship support and small business assistance; and support for arts and cultural organizations.

CHIROPRACTIC EXAMINERS, BOARD OF

Address: 530 Center St. NE, Suite 620, Salem 97301
Phone: 503-378-5816
Fax: 503-362-1260
Email: oregon.obce@oregon.gov
Web: www.oregon.gov/OBCE/Pages/index.aspx
Contact: Cassandra C. McLeod-Skinner, J.D., Executive Director
Statutory Authority: ORS Chapter 684
Duties and Responsibilities: Created in 1915, the board is responsible for administering the Chiropractic Practice Act, as well as establishing the rules and regulations governing chiropractic medicine in Oregon. The seven-member board is comprised of five licensed chiropractors and two public members appointed by the governor for three-year terms.

The board's mission is to serve the public; regulate the practice of chiropractic medicine; and promote quality, competent and ethical health care. The board's programs include application, examination, continuing education, public information and investigation of complaints. If violations are found, the board issues disciplinary actions and/or rehabilitation plans to meet competency standards.

COLUMBIA RIVER GORGE COMMISSION

Address: PO Box 730, White Salmon, WA 98672
Phone: 509-493-3323
Fax: 509-493-2229
Email: info@gorgecommission.com
Web: www.gorgecommission.org
Contact: Krystyna Wolniakowski, Executive Director
Statutory Authority: ORS 196.150
Duties and Responsibilities: The commission was established by a compact between Oregon and Washington in 1987 in response to the 1986 National Scenic Area Act passed by Congress, establishing the 292,500 acre Columbia River Gorge National Scenic Area. The commission works in partnership with the USDA Forest Service, six counties, 13 urban areas and four Columbia River treaty fishing tribes to implement a regional management plan that protects the scenic, natural, cultural and recreational resources of the Columbia River Gorge National Scenic Area and to support the area's economy where it is compatible with resource protections. The commission has 13 members, six appointed by each of the counties, three appointed by the Oregon governor, three appointed by the Washington governor, and one representing the U.S. secretary of agriculture. The agency, governed by the commission, has eight staff specializing in land use planning and resource management.

CONSTRUCTION CONTRACTORS BOARD

Address: 201 High St. SE, Suite 600, PO Box 14140, Salem 97309-5052
Phone: 503-378-4621
Fax: 503-373-2007
Email: ccb.info@state.or.us
Web: www.oregon.gov/CCB
Contact: Chris Huntington, Administrator
Statutory Authority: ORS 701.205
Duties and Responsibilities: The Construction Contractors Board (CCB) serves Oregonians by preventing and resolving construction contracting

problems. The agency licenses contractors, investigates complaints against licensees and penalizes unlawful contractors. The CCB educates the public about how to avoid problems on construction projects and helps mediate disputes between homeowners and licensed contractors.

Formed in 1971 as the Builders Board to license residential contractors, the agency was subsequently renamed and authority expanded to regulate commercial contractors as well. To become licensed, contractors must meet minimum education and experience requirements and pass a test. Licensed contractors are subject to continuing education requirements.

The CCB employs approximately 60 people. Enforcement officers and dispute mediators are deployed across the state. The board is made up of nine members appointed by the governor and confirmed by the Oregon Senate. Members represent different segments of the construction industry, the public and local government.

The Labor and Industries Building in Salem houses the central offices of the Department of Consumer and Business Services. (Oregon State Archives scenic photo)

CONSUMER AND BUSINESS SERVICES, DEPARTMENT OF

Address: 350 Winter St. NE, Salem 97301-3878;
PO Box 14480, Salem 97309-0405
Phone: 503-378-4100
Fax: 503-947-0088
Email: dcbs.info@oregon.gov
Web: dcbs.oregon.gov
Contact: Andrew Stolfi, Director
Statutory Authority: ORS Chapter 705
Duties and Responsibilities: The Department of Consumer and Business Services (DCBS) is Oregon's largest business regulatory and consumer protection agency. The department administers state laws and rules to protect consumers and workers in the areas of workers' compensation, occupational safety and health, financial services, insurance, and building codes. The department was formed in 1993 to serve as an integrated umbrella agency over

most state functions affecting businesses in order to improve efficiency and effectiveness.

DCBS employs about 900 people and is headquartered in Salem. Several of its divisions have offices around the state.

Building Codes Division
Address: 1535 Edgewater St. NW,
PO Box 14470, Salem 97309-0404
Phone: 503-378-4133
Fax: 503-378-2322
Web: oregon.gov/bcd
Contact: Alana Cox, Interim Administrator
Statutory Authority: ORS Chapters 446, 447, 455, 460, 479, 480, 693
Duties and Responsibilities: In 1973, the Legislature established a statewide uniform building code and created this division to administer it. A statewide building code helps ensure a minimum level of safety in all areas of the state and a uniform regulatory environment for businesses, the general public and contractors. The division adopts building codes with the advice of seven statutory boards. The division certifies inspectors, licenses trade professionals and establishes training and education requirements; provides code and rule interpretation and dispute resolution; enforces license, code and permit requirements to prevent unsafe conditions; and conducts inspections where local entities do not.

Building Codes Advisory Boards
Address: PO Box 14470, Salem 97309-0404
Phone: 503-373-7613
Web: www.oregon.gov/BCD/boards/Pages/ index.aspx
Contact: Alana Cox, Policy and Technical Services Manager

Boiler Rules, Board of
Statutory Authority: ORS 480.535, 705.250
Duties and Responsibilities: Created in 1961, the board formulates and adopts rules for the safe construction, installation, inspection, operation, maintenance and repair of boilers and pressure vessels and reviews staff enforcement actions. The governor appoints the board's 11 members to four-year terms, subject to Senate confirmation.

Building Codes Structures Board
Statutory Authority: ORS 455.132, 455.144, 705.250
Duties and Responsibilities: Dating back to 1973, the board helps the DCBS director administer the Structural, Prefabricated Structures, Accessibility to People with Physical Disabilities, and certain energy programs. The governor appoints the board's nine members to four-year terms, subject to Senate confirmation.

Construction Industry Energy Board

Statutory Authority: ORS 455.492, 705.250

Duties and Responsibilities: The board, created in 2009, evaluates proposed state building code standards and proposed administrative rules relating to the energy use and energy efficiency aspects of the electrical, structural, prefabricated structure and low-rise residential specialties. The proposed standards evaluated by the board may include energy conserving technology, construction methods, products and materials. The board has 11 members.

Electrical and Elevator Board

Statutory Authority: ORS 455.138, 455.144, 479.680, 705.250

Duties and Responsibilities: The board, created in 1949, helps the DCBS director administer the electrical and elevator programs. The board oversees the licensing and enforcement of these programs to ensure that the people involved are appropriately licensed and the work meets minimum safety standards. The governor appoints the board's 15 members to four-year terms, subject to Senate confirmation.

Mechanical Board

Statutory Authority: ORS 455.140, 705.250

Duties and Responsibilities: The board, formed in 2004, helps the DCBS director administer the code and associated administrative rules adopted for mechanical devices and equipment. The governor appoints the 10-member board, subject to Senate confirmation.

Plumbing Board, State

Statutory Authority: ORS 693.115, 705.250

Duties and Responsibilities: Created in 1935 under the State Board of Health, the board licenses individuals to engage in the business, trade or calling of a journeyman plumber. The board establishes license, business and supervising plumber registrations, examinations and continuing education fees. The governor appoints the board's seven members, subject to Senate confirmation.

Residential and Manufactured Structures Board

Statutory Authority: ORS 455.135, 705.250

Duties and Responsibilities: The board, created in 2004, helps the DCBS director administer the low-rise residential dwelling program. The governor appoints the board's 11 members, subject to Senate confirmation.

Financial Regulation, Division of

Address: 350 Winter St. NE, Salem 97301-3881; PO Box 14480, Salem 97309-0405

Phone: 503-378-4140

Fax: 503-378-7862

Email: dfr.mail@oregon.gov (financial); cp.ins@oregon.gov (insurance)

Web: dfr.oregon.gov

Contact: T.K. Keen, Administrator

Statutory Authority: ORS Chapters 59, 86A, 97, 446, 465, 646A, 697, 705, 717, 723, 725, 725A, 726, 731–735, 737, 742, 743, 743A, 744, 746, 748, 750, 752

Duties and Responsibilities: Insurance regulation in Oregon began in 1887 when the secretary of state was given ex officio powers as insurance commissioner. The Department of Insurance, which later became the Insurance Division, was created in 1909. Regulation of financial institutions dates to 1907 when banks became subject to the State Banking Board. Securities-related regulation began a few years later in 1913 when the Corporation Department was created to license security brokers and regulate savings and loan associations.

In 2016, the Division of Finance and Corporate Securities and the Insurance Division were merged into the Division of Financial Regulation. The division regulates banks and credit unions, check cashing, debt management services, financial and investment advisors, insurance industry, mortgage industry, money transmitters, pawnshops, payday and title lenders, securities, and drug price transparency. The division investigates consumer complaints, analyzes and monitors financial and insurance institution finances, reviews all insurance policies before they are sold in Oregon, licenses companies and professionals and registers securities and other investments.

Health Insurance Marketplace, Oregon

Address: 350 Winter St. NE, Salem 97301-3883; PO Box 14480, Salem 97309-0405

Phone: 855-268-3767 (Toll-free)

Email: info.marketplace@oregon.gov

Web: healthcare.oregon.gov

Contact: Chiqui Flowers, Administrator

Statutory Authority: ORS Chapter 741

Duties and Responsibilities: The marketplace seeks to improve the lives of Oregonians by providing individuals and small businesses with access to affordable, high-quality health insurance. The marketplace oversees health insurance products sold to Oregonians through HealthCare.gov and provides local support, education and assistance to help Oregonians find the plan that best meets their health and financial needs.

Occupational Safety and Health Division, Oregon

Address: 350 Winter St. NE, Salem 97301-3882;
PO Box 14480, Salem 97309-0405
Phone: 503-378-3272 (Voice/TTY); Toll-free in
Oregon only: 800-922-2689 (Voice/TTY)
Fax: 503-947-7461
Email: web.osha@oregon.gov
Web: osha.oregon.gov
Contact: Michael Wood, Administrator
Statutory Authority: ORS Chapter 654
Duties and Responsibilities: The division, known as Oregon OSHA, was created in 1973 to administer the Oregon Safe Employment Act. Oregon OSHA is responsible for working with employers and employees to reduce and prevent occupational injuries, illnesses and fatalities and for enforcing Oregon occupational safety and health standards. The division inspects workplaces for occupational safety and health hazards, investigates complaints about safety and health issues on the job and investigates fatal accidents to determine if the Oregon Safe Employment Act has been violated. The division also provides technical, educational and consultative services to help employers and employees implement and improve injury and illness prevention plans.

Workers' Compensation Division

Address: 350 Winter St. NE, Salem 97301-3879;
PO Box 14480, Salem 97309-0405
Phone: 503-947-7810
Fax: 503-947-7630
Email: workcomp.questions@oregon.gov
Web: wcd.oregon.gov
Contact: Sally Coen, Acting Administrator
Statutory Authority: ORS Chapters 654, 656, 659A
Duties and Responsibilities: Oregon's workers' compensation system was created in 1913, with major reforms enacted in 1990 and 1995. The division administers and regulates statutes and rules to ensure that employers provide coverage for their workers; provide treatment and benefits to help injured workers return to work as quickly as possible; and resolve disputes as quickly, fairly and with as little litigation as possible. The division facilitates injured workers' early return-to-work through incentive programs funded through the Workers' Benefit Fund; helps resolve medical, vocational, disability and other disputes; and provides consultation, training and technical services to people and businesses within the system.

Injured Workers, Ombudsman for

Address: 350 Winter St. NE, Salem 97301-3878;
PO Box 14480, Salem 97309-0405
Phone: 503-378-3351; Toll-free: 800-927-1271
Email: oiw.questions@oregon.gov
Web: www.oregon.gov/DCBS/OIW/Pages/
index.aspx
Contact: Jennifer Flood, Ombudsman
Statutory Authority: ORS 656.709
Duties and Responsibilities: The Legislature created this office in 1987 to serve as an independent advocate for injured workers and was expanded as part of the major reforms to the workers' compensation system in 1990. The office investigates and attempts to resolve workers' compensation-related complaints, provides information to injured workers to enable them to protect their rights and makes recommendations for improving ombudsman services and the workers' compensation system.

Small Business Ombudsman for Workers' Compensation

Address: 350 Winter St. NE, Salem 97301-3878;
PO Box 14480, Salem 97309-0405
Phone: 971-283-0997
Email: wc.advocate@oregon.gov
Web: www.oregon.gov/DCBS/SBO/Pages/
sbo.aspx
Contact: David Waki, Ombudsman
Statutory Authority: ORS 656.709
Duties and Responsibilities: This office was created as part of the 1990 workers' compensation reforms to educate and advocate small businesses. The ombudsman serves as a workers' compensation resource center, assisting small businesses in the areas of insurance and claims processing. This includes the intervention, investigation and resolution of any workers' compensation-related issue. The office also provides education and information to employers, trade groups, agents and insurers on relevant workers' compensation issues.

Workers' Compensation Management-Labor Advisory Committee

Address: 350 Winter St. NE, Salem 97301-3878;
PO Box 14480, Salem 97309-0405
Phone: 503-947-7867
Fax: 503-378-6444
Email: theresa.a.vanwinkle@oregon.gov
Web: www.oregon.gov/DCBS/mlac/Pages/
mlac.aspx
Contact: Theresa Van Winkle, Administrator
Statutory Authority: ORS 656.790
Duties and Responsibilities: The Legislature created the committee as part of the reform of the workers' compensation system in 1990. It provides

an effective forum for business and labor to meet, and explore and resolve issues involving the workers' compensation system. The committee is charged with reviewing and making recommendations on workers' compensation issues to the DCBS director and the Legislature. Members are appointed by the governor and subject to Senate confirmation. The committee consists of five management and five labor representatives and the DCBS director, who serves as an ex officio member.

Other Groups:

Senior Health Insurance Benefits Assistance

Address: 350 Winter St. NE, Salem 97301;
PO Box 14480, Salem 97309-0405
Phone: 503-947-7979; Toll-free: 1-800-722-4134;
TTY: 1-800-735-2900
Email: shiba.oregon@oregon.gov
Web: healthcare.oregon.gov/shiba/Pages/
index.aspx
Contact: Lisa Emerson
Duties and Responsibilities: Oregon has been providing information to Medicare beneficiaries and their families since the late 1980s. The Senior Health Insurance Benefits Assistance (SHIBA) program officially began in 1992 under a grant from the federal government. Since March 1, 2016, SHIBA has been part of the Oregon Health Insurance Marketplace. SHIBA uses staff and volunteers to help Medicare beneficiaries make health insurance decisions, understand Medicare benefits, choose a supplemental insurance policy and enroll in prescription drug benefits. SHIBA counseling services are free of charge.

Workers' Compensation Board

Address: 2601 25th St. SE, Suite 150, Salem 97302-1280
Phone: 503-378-3308 or 877-311-8061 (Toll-free)
Fax: 503-373-1684
Web: www.oregon.gov/wcb/pages/index.aspx
Contact: Connie Wold, Chair
Statutory Authority: ORS Chapter 656
Duties and Responsibilities: Oregon's workers' compensation system was created in 1913 to resolve workers' compensation disputes. The board was created in 1965 and came under DCBS in 1993. It provides timely and impartial resolution of disputes arising under the workers' compensation law and the Oregon Safe Employment Act. The five-member board is appointed by the governor for four-year terms, subject to Senate confirmation. The board conducts contested case hearings and provides mediation for workers' compensation matters, as well as for Oregon OSHA citations and

orders. The board is the appellate body that reviews administrative law judge workers' compensation orders on appeal, exercises own motion jurisdiction and reviews claim disposition agreements. The board also hears appeals from Oregon Department of Justice regarding applications for compensation under the Crime Victim Assistance Program and resolves disputes between workers and workers' compensation carriers arising from workers' civil actions against third parties.

The central Department of Corrections offices are in the Dome Building in Salem. (Oregon State Archives scenic photo)

CORRECTIONS, DEPARTMENT OF

Address: 2575 Center St. NE, Salem 97301
Phone: 503-945-0927
Web: www.oregon.gov/doc/pages/default.aspx
Contact: Colette S. Peters, Director
Statutory Authority: ORS Chapter 423
Duties and Responsibilities: The department was created by the Legislature in June 1987 and works to promote public safety by holding offenders accountable for their actions and reducing the risk of future criminal behavior. The department has custody of about 14,700 adults sentenced to prison for more than 12 months in 14 state prisons throughout the state. It also oversees community parole and post-prison supervision of about 2,500 individuals in Linn and Douglas Counties. The department is recognized nationally among correctional agencies for providing adults in custody with the cognitive, education and job skills needed to become productive citizens when they transition back to their communities.

Oregon's recidivism rate is about 35 percent when defined as the total percentage of a release cohort that was convicted of any felony at any time within the specified number of months following release from prison or jail. The recidivism rate is 28.5 percent when defined as the total percentage of an admission cohort that was convicted of any felony at any time within the specified number of months after beginning probation.

Administrative Services Division

Address: 2575 Center St. NE, Salem 97301
Phone: 503-945-9859
Contact: Jim Paul, Assistant Director
Duties and Responsibilities: The division supports the daily business of the Department of Corrections. The division encompasses Information Technology, Facility Services and Warehouse Distribution.

Chief Financial Officer, Office of the

Address: 2575 Center St. NE, Salem 97301
Phone: 503-945-9007
Contact: Steve Robbins, Chief Financial Officer
Duties and Responsibilities: The office is responsible for determining the resources necessary to support the existing and growing offender populations. The office develops and executes the department's Long-Range Construction Plan to ensure appropriate institutions are in place to house offenders entering the system. Fiscal Services include contracts, purchasing, accounting and Central Trust.

Communications, Office of

Address: 2575 Center St. NE, Salem 97301
Phone: 503-945-9999
Contact: Rem Nivens, Administrator
Duties and Responsibilities: The office is responsible for furthering the department's mission and goals through close collaboration with external and internal stakeholders, both inside and beyond the realm of public safety. This office ensures the department is a transparent governmental organization that members of the public can access at any time. The office includes internal and external communications, media relations, legislative and government relations and public record/information coordination.

Community Corrections

Address: 3691 State St., Salem 97301
Phone: 503-428-5500
Contact: Jeramiah Stromberg, Assistant Director
Duties and Responsibilities: The Department of Corrections operates Community Corrections in Linn and Douglas Counties, working in partnership with local, county-operated community corrections agencies. Activities include supervision, community-based sanctions and services directed at offenders who have committed felony crimes and have been placed under supervision by the courts (probation), the Board of Parole and Post-Prison Supervision or the local supervisory authority.

Correctional Services Division

Address: 2575 Center St. NE, Salem 97301
Phone: 503-945-9055
Contact: Nathaline Frener, Assistant Director
Duties and Responsibilities: The division is dedicated to applying effective corrections programming, services and support. The division values comprehensive, collaborative partnerships that support the success of individuals during incarceration and through their transition from prison to the community.

The division's wide-ranging responsibilities include intake to prison, sentence computation and offender records, population management, correctional case management and inmate services. In addition, the division provides patient-centered health services covering medical, mental health, dental and pharmaceutical services.

Inspector General, Office of the

Address: 2575 Center St. NE, Salem 97301
Phone: 503-945-9043
Contact: Craig Prins, Inspector General
Duties and Responsibilities: The office provides an oversight function on behalf of the director and deputy director of the Department of Corrections. The office was created in 1990 as recommended by an investigative report to the governor. The inspector general has broad responsibility for oversight of suspected, alleged or actual misconduct within the department, reporting to the director or deputy and to other officials as required by law.

Operations Division

Address: 2575 Center St. NE, Salem 97301
Phone: 503-945-0950
Contact: Mike Gower, Assistant Director
Duties and Responsibilities: Oregon's adult prisons are centrally administered by the assistant director of operations to ensure that Oregon's 14 prisons are safe, civil and productive so that inmates can pursue the goals specified in their corrections plans. The division's responsibilities encompass prison management, inmate transportation, security threat group (gang) management, emergency preparedness and most inmate work crew activities.

Oregon Corrections Enterprises

Address: 3691 State St., Salem 97301
Phone: 503-428-5500
Web: www.oce.oregon.gov
Contact: Ken Jeske, Administrator
Duties and Responsibilities: Oregon Corrections Enterprises (OCE) is semi-independent from the Department of Corrections. By working with the department, state agencies, non-profit agencies and the public, OCE builds partnerships that sustain work opportunities for adults in custody. OCE explores new business opportunities and partnerships while working to reduce recidivism.

State Prisons:

Coffee Creek Correctional Facility
Address: 24499 SW Grahams Ferry Rd., Wilsonville 97070
Phone: 503-570-6400
Contact: Paula Myers, Superintendent
Minimum and medium-security facility accommodating all of Oregon's female inmates and providing intake services to all male inmates, operational since 2001
Capacity: 1,685

Columbia River Correctional Institution
Address: 9111 NE Sunderland Ave., Portland 97211
Phone: 503-280-6646
Contact: Nichole Brown, Superintendent
Minimum-security prison, operational since 1990
Capacity: 553

Deer Ridge Correctional Institution
Address: 3920 East Ashwood Rd., Madras 97741
Phone: 541-325-5999
Contact: Tim Causey, Superintendent
Minimum and medium-security prison, operational since 2007
Capacity: Minimum-security, 774 (not currently in operation); Medium-security, 1,228

Eastern Oregon Correctional Institution
Address: 2500 Westgate, Pendleton 97801
Phone: 541-276-0700
Contact: Sue Washburn, Superintendent
Medium-security prison, operational since 1985
Capacity: 1,659

Mill Creek Correctional Facility
Address: 5465 Turner Rd. SE, Salem 97317
Phone: 503-378-2600
Contact: Brandon Kelly, Superintendent
Minimum-security work camp, operational since 1992
Capacity: 240

Oregon State Correctional Institution
Address: 3405 Deer Park Dr. SE, Salem 97310
Phone: 503-373-0125
Contact: Garrett Laney, Superintendent
Medium-security facility, operational since 1959
Capacity: 890

Oregon State Penitentiary
Address: 2605 State St., Salem 97310
Phone: 503-378-2453
Contact: Brandon Kelly, Superintendent
Multi-security penitentiary, operational since 1866
Capacity: 2,194

Powder River Correctional Facility
Address: 3600 13th St., Baker City 97814
Phone: 541-523-6680
Fax: 541-523-6678
Contact: Tom Mclay, Superintendent
Minimum-security prison, operational since 1989
Capacity: 286

Santiam Correctional Institution
Address: 4005 Aumsville Hwy. SE, Salem 97317
Phone: 503-378-2144
Fax: 503-378-8235
Contact: Kimberly Hendricks, Superintendent
Minimum-security prison, operational since 1992
Capacity: 440

Shutter Creek Correctional Institution
Address: 95200 Shutters Landing Ln., North Bend 97459
Phone: 541-756-6666
Contact: Julie Martin, Acting Superintendent
Minimum-security prison, operational since 1990
Capacity: 302

Snake River Correctional Institution
Address: 777 Stanton Blvd., Ontario 97914
Phone: 541-881-5000
Contact: Brad Cain, Superintendent
Multi-security prison, Oregon's largest correctional institution, operational since 1991
Capacity: 3,062

South Fork Forest Camp
Address: 48300 Wilson River Hwy., Tillamook 97141
Phone: 503-842-2811
Contact: Nichole Brown, Superintendent
Minimum-security work camp, operational since 1951
Capacity: 204

Two Rivers Correctional Institution
Address: 82911 Beach Access Rd., Umatilla 97882
Phone: 541-922-2001
Contact: Tyler Blewett, Superintendent
Medium and minimum-security facility, operational since 2000
Capacity: 1,878

Warner Creek Correctional Facility
Address: 20654 Rabbit Hill Rd., Lakeview 97630
Phone: 541-947-8200
Contact: Steve Brown, Superintendent
Minimum-security facility, operational since 2005
Capacity: 406

CRIMINAL JUSTICE COMMISSION, OREGON

Address: 885 Summer St. NE, Salem 97301
Phone: 503-378-4830
Fax: 503-378-4861
Email: cjc@oregon.gov
Web: www.oregon.gov/cjc/Pages/default.aspx
Contact: Kenneth Sanchagrin, Executive Director
Statutory Authority: ORS 137.651–137.680
Duties and Responsibilities: Created in 1995, the commission serves as the policy development forum for state and local criminal justice systems. Twenty-one staff provide data analysis, planning and grant administration expertise to public safety officials and work with stakeholders to improve Oregon's criminal justice systems. The agency administers the statewide grant programs for specialty courts and justice reinvestment programs, administers Oregon's sentencing guidelines, serves as the State Administering Agency for the Byrne Justice Assistant Grant program and houses the Statistical Analysis Center. Nine commissioners direct the staff's work.

DENTISTRY, OREGON BOARD OF

Address: 1500 SW 1st Ave., Suite 770, Portland 97201
Phone: 971-673-3200
Fax: 971-673-3202
Email: information@oregondentistry.org
Web: www.oregon.gov/dentistry/Pages/index.aspx
Contact: Stephen Prisby, Executive Director
Statutory Authority: ORS Chapter 679, ORS 680.010–680.205, 680.990
Duties and Responsibilities: The board is the second oldest licensing board in Oregon, created by an act of the Legislature on February 23, 1887. The mission of the board is to promote high quality oral health care in Oregon by equitably regulating dental professionals.

The goals of the board are to protect the public from unsafe, incompetent or fraudulent practitioners and to encourage licensees to practice safely and competently in the best interests of their patients. The board does this by requiring the competency of applicants through written and clinical examinations, requiring continuing education, investigating complaints and enforcing the provisions of the Dental Practice Act and rules of the board, communicating board policies and other pertinent information on a regular basis, acting as a resource to consumers in determining the adequacy of their dental treatment, and working with other health care boards and associations to develop partnerships to forge a viable health care delivery system.

The Public Service Building in Salem houses the central offices of the Department of Education. (Oregon State Archives scenic photo)

EDUCATION, DEPARTMENT OF

Address: 255 Capitol St. NE, Salem 97310-0203
Phone: 503-947-5600
Fax: 503-378-5156
Email: ode.frontdesk@ode.state.or.us
Web: https://www.oregon.gov/ode/pages/default.aspx
Contact: Colt Gill, Director
Statutory Authority: ORS 326.111
Duties and Responsibilities: The Oregon Department of Education (ODE) oversees the education of over 582,000 students in Oregon's public kindergarten through grade 12 education system. ODE encompasses early learning, public preschool programs, the state School for the Deaf, regional programs for children with disabilities and education programs in Oregon youth corrections facilities.

While ODE is not in the classroom directly providing services, the agency (along with the State Board of Education) focuses on helping districts achieve both local and statewide goals and priorities through strategies such as developing policies and standards, providing accurate and timely data to inform instruction, training teachers how to use data effectively, administering state and federal grants, and sharing and helping districts implement best practices.

State Board of Education

Address: 255 Capitol St. NE, Salem 97310-0203
Phone: 503-947-5667
Fax: 503-378-5156
Email: StateBoard.PublicEmail@ode.state.or.us
Web: https://www.oregon.gov/ode/about-us/stateboard/Pages/default.aspx
Contact: Kimberly Howard, Chair
Statutory Authority: ORS 326.011–326.075
Duties and Responsibilities: The board provides leadership and vision for Oregon's public schools and districts by enacting equitable policies and

promoting educational practices that lead directly to the educational and life success of every student.

The Legislature created the board in 1951 to oversee the state's schools. The board sets policies and standards for Oregon's public school districts and educational service districts. All of these agencies have separate governing bodies responsible for transacting business within their jurisdictions. The board is also responsible for adopting administrative rules that the Department of Education implements.

The board is comprised of seven members appointed by the governor and confirmed by the Senate. Five members represent Oregon's five congressional districts, and two members represent the state at large. Members serve four-year terms and are limited to two consecutive terms. Board members elect their chair each year. The board holds public meetings at least six times per year.

Fair Dismissal Appeals Board
Address: 255 Capitol St. NE, Salem 97310-0203
Phone: 503-947-5915
Fax: 503-378-5156
Web: https://www.oregon.gov/ode/educator-resources/Pages/FairDismissalAppeals Board.aspx
Contact: Patricia Stoneroad, Complaint and Appeals Specialist
Statutory Authority: ORS 342.930
Duties and Responsibilities: The board consists of 24 members appointed by the governor from specific categories: six public school administrators, six contract teachers, six school board members and six who must have no occupational affiliation with a school district. Each category must be further distributed by size of school district.

The board was created to hear appeals of teacher and administrator dismissals by school districts. Once an appeal is filed, a three-member panel is selected by the board's executive secretary to hear the appeal and render a decision.

Quality Education Commission
Address: 255 Capitol St. NE, Salem 97310-0203
Phone: 503-947-5670
Fax: 503-378-5156
Web: https://www.oregon.gov/ode/reports-and-data/taskcomm/Pages/default.aspx
Contact: Brian Reeder, Assistant Superintendent
Statutory Authority: ORS 327.497–327.506
Duties and Responsibilities: The commission was created in 2001 with the charge to identify educational best practices and to estimate the level of funding required to ensure that the state system of kindergarten through grade 12 public education meets the goals established in statute. To fulfill that

charge, the commission researches educational best practices and estimates the costs of implementing them. The model used to estimate educational costs, known as the Quality Education Model, is maintained by the commission with assistance from the Department of Education.

Educator Advancement Council
Address: 255 Capitol St. NE, Salem 97310
Phone: 503-373-0053
Fax: 503-378-5156
Email: eacinfo@oregonlearning.org
Web: https://www.oregon.gov/EAC/Pages/default.aspx
Contact: Shadiin Garcia, Director
Statutory Authority: ORS 342.940, 342.943
Duties and Responsibilities: The council is an innovative partnership aimed at helping Oregon produce high-quality, well-supported and culturally-responsive public educators in every classroom. The Legislature created the council through the passage of Senate Bill 182. The council will expand Oregon's efforts to further support educators statewide by establishing a system of local educator networks that prioritize and enhance educators' access to professional learning and support services, combining state investment and other leveraged resources driven by educator need.

Early Learning Division
Address: 700 Summer St. NE, Suite 350, Salem 97301
Phone: 503-947-1400
Email: early.learning@state.or.us
Web: http://oregonearlylearning.com
Contact: Miriam Calderon, Director
Statutory Authority: ORS 326.425, 417.710, 417.727
Duties and Responsibilities: The mission of the division is to support all of Oregon's young children and families to learn and thrive. The values that guide the division's work include equity, dedication, integrity and collective wisdom to benefit children and families across Oregon. The division works as an integrated team to focus on child care, early learning programs, supporting the early childhood workforce, cross systems integration, policy and research, and equity.

Oregon School for the Deaf
Address: 999 Locust St. NE, Salem 97301-5254
Phone: 503-378-3825
Video phone: 503-400-6180
Fax: 503-378-4701
Web: www.osd.k12.or.us
Contact: Dr. Sharla Jones, Director
Duties and Responsibilities: Established in 1870, the Oregon School for the Deaf (OSD) educates Deaf and Hard of Hearing students (K-21) who require services and supports that are not provided

through their regular public school. OSD is funded by legislative appropriation and is governed by ODE. In the 2019–2020 school year, 120 students were enrolled at the school at no cost to their families.

Youth Development Council and Division

Address: 255 Capitol St. NE, Salem 97310-0203
Phone: 503-378-5148
Web: www.oregonyouthdevelopmentcouncil.org
Contact: Brian Detman, Director
Statutory Authority: ORS 417.847, 417.850, 417.852–417.854, 417.855
Duties and Responsibilities: The council, created in 2012, oversees the Youth Development Division, which supports the education system by developing state policy and administering funding for community and school-based youth development programs, services and initiatives for youth ages six to 24. The council advocates for youth through changes in state law, policy and funding for programs and services that support youth education, career/workforce development and juvenile crime prevention.

The Employment Building in Salem houses the central offices of the Employment Department. (Oregon State Archives scenic photo)

EMPLOYMENT DEPARTMENT

Address: 875 Union St. NE, Salem 97311
Phone: 503-947-1444; Toll-free: 1-800-237-3710
Fax: 503-947-1472
Web: Employment.Oregon.gov
Contact: David Gerstenfeld, Acting Director
Statutory Authority: ORS 657.601
Duties and Responsibilities: The mission of the department is to "Support Business and Promote Employment" by supporting economic stability for Oregonians and communities during times of unemployment through the payment of unemployment benefits, by matching qualified job seekers to businesses who need their skills and by providing quality workforce and economic information to promote informed decision-making.

With the passage of the Social Security Act in 1935, the federal government laid the groundwork for the unemployment insurance program, and the State Unemployment Compensation Commission was formed the same year. In 1957, a division was formed to research and collect unemployment and economic data. That Research Division was combined with the State Employment Service and the State Unemployment Compensation Commission to form the Department of Employment in 1959.

In 1971, the Legislature established the Department of Human Resources (DHR) with Employment as one of its divisions. The Employment Division operated within DHR until 1993 when Employment Department was created. Today, the department employs approximately 1,200 staff, providing services to approximately 140,700 Oregon businesses and over 382,000 Oregon citizens.

Unemployment Insurance Division

Address: 875 Union St. NE, Salem 97311
Phone: 503-947-1330
Fax: 503-947-1668
Contact: Lindsi Leahy, Director
Statutory Authority: ORS 657.601
Duties and Responsibilities: Unemployment insurance benefits replace part of the income lost when workers become unemployed through no fault of their own. The division is responsible for paying benefits to eligible claimants in an accurate and timely manner, deciding eligibility issues, discouraging fraud and collecting taxes to fund the program.

The money used to pay Oregon unemployment insurance benefits comes from Oregon employers' state payroll taxes, which are deposited in a trust fund to pay unemployment insurance benefits to unemployed Oregon workers.

Workforce and Economic Research Division

Address: 875 Union St. NE, Salem 97311
Phone: 503-947-1229
Fax: 503-947-1210
Web: www.QualityInfo.org
Contact: Bob Uhlenkott, Director
Statutory Authority: ORS 657.601
Duties and Responsibilities: The division's team of economists, workforce analysts and researchers collect, analyze and disseminate statewide and regional labor market information. They help organizations and businesses apply that information in their day-to-day operations. Analysts provide concise, up-to-date information about the local and state economies and their effects on the workforce. Research staff study the labor force and related topics, supply data and analysis to new and

expanding firms and analyze occupational supply and demand, which is gathered through surveys sent to employers.

In addition to offering general information, staff produces special reports and responds to requests. Businesses use this labor market information to identify challenges and opportunities. Economic development planners, educators and training providers, job applicants, legislators and the news media regularly rely on this information to learn about workforce issues that affect Oregonians and Oregon businesses.

Workforce Operations Division

Address: 875 Union St. NE, Salem 97311
Phone: 503-947-1277
Fax: 503-947-1658
Contact: Jim Pfarrer, Director
Statutory Authority: ORS 657.601
Duties and Responsibilities: This division of the Employment Department serves employers by recruiting workers with skills matching employers' needs.The department helps job seekers find jobs that match their skills, provides them with information about trends in occupations and refers job seekers to appropriate training programs.

The division partners with the Higher Education Coordinating Commission, local workforce development boards, local training providers and the Department of Human Services Self-Sufficiency and Vocational Rehabilitation programs to form the state's workforce system, WorkSource Oregon. The division also oversees programs aimed at assisting certain groups, such as military veterans, migrant seasonal farmworkers and workers adversely affected by foreign trade.

Other Groups:

Administrative Hearings, Office of
Address: 4600 25th Ave. NE, Suite 140, Salem 97301; Mail: PO Box 14020, Salem 97309-4020
Phone: 503-947-1515
Fax: 503-947-1920
Email: rema.a.bergin@oregon.gov
Web: www.oregon.gov/OAH/Pages/default.aspx
Contact: John Mann, Chief Administrative Law Judge
Statutory Authority: ORS 183.605
Duties and Responsibilities: The office was created by the Legislature in 1999 to provide an independent and impartial forum for citizens and businesses to dispute state agency actions against them. A Chief Administrative Law Judge is appointed by the governor and has independent statutory authority to manage the office. Fifty-nine

professional administrative law judges hold more than 24,000 hearings a year for approximately 70 state agencies. By statute, all administrative law judges are required to be "impartial in the performance of [their] duties and shall remain fair in all hearings." Oregon is one of 22 states with an independent central panel of administrative law judges.

Employment Appeals Board
Address: 875 Union St. NE, Salem 97311
Phone: 503-378-2077
Fax: 503-378-2129
Contact: Susana Alba, Interim Chair
Statutory Authority: ORS 657.685–657.690
Duties and Responsibilities: The three-member board is appointed by the governor to review orders issued in contested unemployment insurance claims cases. The board reviews 1,400 to 1,700 cases per year with authority to affirm, modify, reverse or remand for additional evidence the orders of administrative law judges at the Office of Administrative Hearings. Final written decisions of the board are subject to review by the Oregon Court of Appeals.

Employment Department Advisory Council
Address: 875 Union St. NE, Salem 97311
Phone: 503-947-1444
Fax: 503-947-1472
Contact: Jeannine Beatrice
Statutory Authority: ORS 657.695
Duties and Responsibilities: The council includes volunteer representatives from the public, employers and employees. Council members are appointed by the governor and assist the Employment Department director in the effective development of policies and programs with respect to unemployment insurance, employment services and labor market information.

Paid Family and Medical Leave Insurance Division
Address: 875 Union St. NE, Salem 97311
Contact: Gerhard Taeubel, Interim Director
Statutory Authority: ORS 657B
Duties and Responsibilities: ORS 657B was enacted in 2019, creating a Paid Family and Medical Leave Insurance program to be administered by the Oregon Employment Department. The program is expected to be fully operational by 2023, and it will provide employees with compensated time off from work to care for and bond with a child during the first year of the child's birth or arrival through adoption or foster care; to provide care for a family member who has a serious health condition; to recover from an employee's own serious health condition; and to take leave related to domestic

violence, stalking, sexual assault or harassment (safe leave).

The money used to pay Oregon paid family and medical leave insurance benefits comes from a payroll-based contribution shared by employers and employees. Contributions are deposited in a trust fund to pay for the insurance benefits and the administrative costs to run the program.

EMPLOYMENT RELATIONS BOARD

Address: 528 Cottage St. NE, Suite 400, Salem 97301-3807
Phone: 503-378-3807
Fax: 503-373-0021
Email: Emprel.Board@oregon.gov
Web: www.oregon.gov/ERB
Contact: Adam Rhynard, Chair
Statutory Authority: ORS Chapters 240, 663, ORS 243.650–243.795, 662.010–662.455
Duties and Responsibilities: The board resolves disputes concerning labor relations for an estimated 3,000 different employers and 250,000 employees in the public and private sectors under its jurisdiction. The board administers the collective bargaining law that covers public employees of the state of Oregon and its cities, counties, school districts and other local governments; hears and decides appeals from state employees concerning personnel actions; and administers the collective bargaining law that regulates private employers who are not covered by the National Labor Relations Act.

ENERGY, STATE DEPARTMENT OF

Address: 550 Capitol St. NE, Salem 97301
Phone: 503-378-4040; 1-800-221-8035 (Toll-free in Oregon)
Fax: 503-373-7806
Email: askenergy@oregon.gov
Web: www.oregon.gov/ENERGY
Contact: Janine Benner, Director
Statutory Authority: ORS Chapters 469, 470
Duties and Responsibilities: The department helps Oregonians make informed energy decisions and maintain a resilient and affordable energy system. It advances solutions to shape an equitable clean energy transition, protect the environment and public health, and responsibly balance energy needs and impacts for current and future generations.The department works with stakeholders across Oregon to help implement the state's energy goals and policies. The work is diverse—from helping Oregonians improve the energy efficiency of their homes, businesses and schools, to overseeing the state's interests in the cleanup project at the Hanford

nuclear site in Washington. The department provides policy expertise to prepare for Oregon's future energy needs and offers technical and financial resources to encourage adoption of and investment in energy efficiency and renewable energy resources. The department also staffs the Energy Facility Siting Council, which has jurisdiction over large energy-generating and transmission facilities within the state. This effort brings together project developers, local and regional governments, citizens and others to make sure proposed projects are approved, built, operated and decommissioned consistent with all applicable laws and regulations. The department was created in 1975 and has about 80 employees.

Energy Facility Siting Council

Address: 550 Capitol St. NE, Salem 97301
Phone: 503-378-4040; 1-800-221-8035 (Toll-free in Oregon)
Contact: Hanley Jenkins II, Chair

Global Warming Commission, Oregon

Address: 550 Capitol St. NE, Salem 97301
Phone: 503-378-4040; 1-800-221-8035 (Toll-free in Oregon)
Contact: Cathy Macdonald, Chair

Hanford Cleanup Board, Oregon

Address: 550 Capitol St. NE, Salem 97301
Phone: 503-378-4040; 1-800-221-8035 (Toll-free in Oregon)
Contact: Steve March, Chair

ENGINEERING AND LAND SURVEYING, STATE BOARD OF EXAMINERS FOR

Address: 670 Hawthorne Ave. SE, Suite 220, Salem 97301
Phone: 503-362-2666
Fax: 503-362-5454
Email: OSBEELS.info@oregon.gov
Web: www.oregon.gov/OSBEELS
Contact: Jason Barbee, Administrator
Statutory Authority: ORS 672.240
Duties and Responsibilities: Since 1919, the Oregon State Board of Examiners for Engineering and Land Surveying (OSBEELS) has regulated the practice of engineering. In 1945, regulation of the land surveying profession was added. In 1987, OSBEELS absorbed administrative oversight for Certified Water Right Examiners, and in 2005, legislation was passed to include authority to regulate the practice of photogrammetric mapping.

The 11-member board, along with 15 staff, ensure that registered professional engineers, land surveyors, photogrammetrists and certified water right examiners are qualified in fields in which technical and professional knowledge and skills are required. This is accomplished by setting standards of qualification for licensure, ensuring that individuals are fully qualified by education, experience and examination to practice in Oregon. The board also works to ensure that all licensed practitioners maintain competency by reviewing relevant laws and rules and revising them expeditiously, enforcing regulatory laws and rules by carefully investigating any complaints or information relating to violations, and effectively disseminating information regarding board goals and activities to licensees and the public.

OSBEELS transitioned to semi-independent status in 1999. It currently regulates more than 15,000 licensed professionals.

ENVIRONMENTAL QUALITY, DEPARTMENT OF

Address: 700 NE Multnomah St., Suite 600, Portland 97232
Phone: 503-229-5696; Toll-free (Oregon only): 1-800-452-4011; TTY: 800-735-2900
Fax: 503-229-6124
Web: www.oregon.gov/DEQ
Contact: Richard Whitman, Director; Leah Feldon, Deputy Director
Statutory Authority: ORS Chapters 454, 459, 466, 467, 468
Duties and Responsibilities: The Department of Environmental Quality (DEQ) is responsible for protecting and enhancing Oregon's water, air and land quality; managing the proper disposal of solid and hazardous wastes; providing assistance in cleaning up contaminated properties; and enforcing Oregon's environmental laws. The agency was formed in 1969 to replace the State Sanitary Authority, which was created in 1938 when citizens overwhelmingly supported an initiative to clean up the Willamette River.

With increasingly complex environmental problems, DEQ's role has expanded to fight climate change with policies to reduce greenhouse gas emissions, prevent toxic chemical releases and reduce risks from toxins already in the environment. DEQ encourages personal responsibility by providing communities with technical assistance. The agency director has the authority to issue civil penalties for violations of pollution laws and standards. DEQ relies on several citizen advisory committees and government officials to guide its decisions.

DEQ employs approximately 700 scientists, engineers, geologists, toxicologists, inspectors, legal and policy staff, technicians, managers and professional support staff across the state. DEQ's headquarters are located in Portland, with regional offices throughout the state.

Environmental Quality Commission
Address: 700 NE Multnomah St., Suite 600, Portland 97232
Phone: 503-229-5695
Fax: 503-229-6124
Contact: Stephanie Caldera
Duties and Responsibilities: The commission, DEQ's policy and rulemaking board, adopts administrative rules, issues orders and judges appeals of fines or other department actions and hires the DEQ director. Commission members are appointed to four-year terms by the governor.

Air and Water Quality Divisions
Address: 700 NE Multnomah St., Suite 600, Portland 97232
Contact: Ali Mirzakhalili, Air Quality Administrator, 503-229-5041; Justin Green, Water Quality Administrator, 503-229-2018
Duties and Responsibilities: DEQ's Air and Water Quality Programs work to keep Oregon's air and water clean and clear. Employees monitor air and water quality, and permit and inspect facilities—from major manufacturers to small shops—throughout the state to ensure compliance with environmental regulations. The programs provide valuable data showing long-term trends in Oregon's air and water quality as well as real-time conditions through tools such as the Air Quality Index, which provides snapshots of air quality conditions across Oregon.

The Water Quality Program ensures the state's waterways are safe for drinking water, fish and wildlife, recreation and irrigation. The program develops and implements water quality standards, regulates sewage treatment systems and industrial dischargers, collects and evaluates water quality data, provides grants and technical assistance to improve water quality and provides loans to communities to upgrade treatment facilities.

The Air Quality Program works to ensure Oregon's air meets the National Ambient Air Quality Standards required by the Federal Clean Air Act. The program monitors and analyzes air quality data, regulates emissions from a variety of sources and conducts vehicle emissions testing in Medford and the Portland metro area.

Land Quality Division
Address: 700 NE Multnomah St., Suite 600, Portland 97232
Phone: 503-229-6411
Contact: Lydia Emer, Administrator
Duties and Responsibilities: The division oversees agency programs in environmental cleanup and site assessment, hazardous and solid waste, spill response, underground storage tanks and materials management. DEQ inventories and assesses

sites contaminated with hazardous waste and supervises development and implementation of cleanup strategies. The emergency response program provides DEQ's round-the-clock capability to address releases of hazardous materials and oil to land and water, providing on-scene incident commanders for major cleanups. DEQ oversees Oregon's only hazardous waste landfill, regulates hazardous waste disposal and offers business pollution prevention assistance.

FILM AND VIDEO OFFICE, OREGON

Address: 123 NE 3rd Ave., Suite 210, Portland 97232
Phone: 971-254-4020
Email: shoot@oregonfilm.com
Web: www.oregonfilm.org
Contact: Tim Williams, Executive Director
Statutory Authority: ORS 284.305
Duties and Responsibilities: The office has been helping production companies find, secure and utilize Oregon locations since 1968. The office's mission is to promote the development of the film, television and multimedia industry in Oregon and to enhance the industry's revenues, profile and reputation within Oregon and internationally. The office administers the state's Oregon Production Investment Fund and Greenlight Oregon Labor Rebate programs that incentivize film, television and multimedia production in Oregon.

FISH AND WILDLIFE, OREGON DEPARTMENT OF

Address: 4034 Fairview Industrial Drive SE, Salem 97302
Phone: 503-947-6000; Toll-free: 1-800-720-6339 (ODFW); Licensing and Controlled Hunts Information: 503-947-6101
Email: odfw.info@state.or.us
Web: www.odfw.com; https://myodfw.com
Contact: Curt Melcher, Director
Statutory Authority: ORS 496.080–496.166
Duties and Responsibilities: The Oregon Department of Fish and Wildlife (ODFW) is responsible for sustainably managing fish and wildlife in Oregon. Through its commission, it sets regulations for recreational and commercial fishing, crabbing, clamming and hunting. It also manages species that are not hunted or fished, including state-listed endangered, threatened and sensitive species. ODFW operates more than 30 fish hatcheries raising trout, salmon and steelhead to supplement natural stocks and provide fishing opportunities. It also manages more than 20 wildlife areas providing habitat for fish and wildlife and hunting, fishing, viewing and other outdoor activities. The

Oregon State Police plays a key role in achieving ODFW's mission through enforcement of fish and wildlife regulations.

ODFW consists of the commission, a commission-appointed director and a statewide staff of approximately 1,000 permanent employees including field staff spread among offices throughout the state.

Fish and Wildlife Commission, Oregon

Address: 4034 Fairview Industrial Dr. SE, Salem 97302-1142
Phone: 503-947-6033
Web: www.dfw.state.or.us/agency/commission
Contact: Director's Office
Statutory Authority: ORS 496.090
Duties and Responsibilities: The commission consists of seven members appointed by the governor for staggered, four-year terms. One commissioner must be from each congressional district, one from east of the Cascades and one from west of the Cascades.

The commission was formed July 1, 1975, when the formerly separate fish and wildlife commissions were merged. Commissioners formulate general state programs and policies concerning management and conservation of fish and wildlife resources and establish seasons, methods and bag limits for recreational and commercial take.

Fish Division

Address: 4034 Fairview Industrial Dr. SE, Salem 97302-1142
Phone: 503-947-6201
Fax: 503-947-6200
Web: www.dfw.state.or.us/fish
Contact: Ed Bowles, Administrator
Statutory Authority: ORS 496.124, 506.142
Duties and Responsibilities: As part of ODFW's mission to protect and enhance Oregon's fish and wildlife and their habitats, the department is charged by statute to protect and propagate fish in the state. This includes direct responsibility for regulating the harvest, protection and enhancement of fish populations through habitat improvement and the rearing and release of fish into public waters. ODFW maintains hatcheries throughout the state to provide fish for program needs.

Restoration and Enhancement Board

Address: 4034 Fairview Industrial Dr. SE, Salem 97302-1142
Phone: 503-947-6232
Web: www.dfw.state.or.us/fish/RE
Contact: Kevin Herkamp, Coordinator
Statutory Authority: ORS 496.286–496.291

Duties and Responsibilities: On June 29, 1989, the Oregon Fisheries Restoration and Enhancement Act of 1989 was signed into law. The Act allows the Department of Fish and Wildlife to undertake a comprehensive program to restore state-owned fish hatcheries, enhance natural fish production, expand hatchery production and provide additional public access to fishing waters. The department's program provides increased recreational fishing opportunities and supports and improves the commercial salmon fishery.

Information and Education Division

Address: 4034 Fairview Industrial Dr. SE,
Salem 97302-1142
Phone: 503-947-6002
Fax: 503-947-6009
Contact: Roger Fuhrman, Administrator
Duties and Responsibilities: This division directs and/or provides all communications and education services for the department. These services include strategic outreach programs, informational campaigns, media and public relations communications, social media, public involvement activities, special events, hunter education programs, aquatic and angler education programs, additional education activities, creation of publications and videos, and website management.

Wildlife Division

Address: 4034 Fairview Industrial Dr. SE,
Salem 97302-1142
Phone: 503-947-6300
Fax: 503-947-6330
Web: www.dfw.state.or.us/wildlife
Contact: Doug Cottam, Administrator
Statutory Authority: ORS 496.124
Duties and Responsibilities: The division has direct responsibility for monitoring the numbers and health of wildlife species, setting population conservation and management objectives, overseeing wildlife habitat restoration and maintenance and regulating harvest of game animals. The Oregon Conservation Strategy is a key part of the division and guides voluntary actions to conserve wildlife on public and private land.

Access and Habitat Program

Address: 4034 Fairview Industrial Dr. SE,
Salem 97302-1142
Phone: 503-947-6087
Web: www.dfw.state.or.us/lands/AH
Contact: Travis Schultz
Statutory Authority: ORS 496.228
Duties and Responsibilities: In 1993, the Legislature created this incentive-based program to improve public hunting access and wildlife habitat on private lands in Oregon. The program's motto, "Landowners and Hunters Together for Wildlife," conveys its basic mission to foster partnerships between landowners and hunters for the benefit of the wildlife they value. The program also seeks to recognize and encourage the important contributions made by landowners to the state's wildlife resources.

FOREST RESOURCES INSTITUTE, OREGON

Address: 9755 SW Barnes Rd., Suite 210,
Portland 97225
Phone: 971-673-2944
Fax: 971-673-2946
Web: OregonForests.org; KnowYourForest.org; LearnForests.org; OregonForestLaws.org; OregonForestFacts.org; TheForestReport.org
Contact: Kathy Storm
Statutory Authority: ORS 526.600–526.675
Duties and Responsibilities: The Legislature created the Oregon Forest Resources Institute (OFRI) in 1991 to advance public understanding of forests, forest management and forest products and to encourage sound forestry through landowner education. OFRI is governed by a 13-member board of directors and is funded by a portion of the forest products harvest tax. OFRI's nine-member staff develops programs, publications and information-rich websites for the general public, family forest landowners and kindergarten through grade 12 teachers and students. OFRI helps the public understand the social, environmental and economic importance of Oregon's forests and the environmental benefits of forest products. The institute does this through its educational advertising and websites as well as through producing topical publications, videos and speaker presentations. OFRI is headquartered in Portland and has a satellite office and demonstration forest at The Oregon Garden in Silverton.

FORESTRY DEPARTMENT, STATE

Address: 2600 State St., Salem 97310
Phone: 503-945-7200
Email: forestry.information@oregon.gov
Web: www.oregon.gov/ODF/Pages/index.aspx
Statutory Authority: ORS Chapters 321, 477, 526, 527, 530, 532
Duties and Responsibilities: Since its inception in 1911, Oregon's Department of Forestry (ODF) has been committed to ensuring the sustainability of Oregon's forestlands by protecting them from wildfire, enforcing Oregon's Forest Practices Act and managing state-owned forests. ODF strives to accomplish its mission "to serve the people of Oregon by protecting, managing and promoting stewardship of Oregon's forests to enhance environmental, economic and community sustain-

ability" through the work of its four divisions and with oversight from the Oregon Board of Forestry. The department has more than 600 permanent and over 600 seasonal employees, who operate out of its Salem headquarters and 32 field offices throughout Oregon.

The Fire Protection Division protects just over half of Oregon's 30 million total acres of forestland—worth more than $60 billion—from wildfire. This includes all of Oregon's privately-owned forests, as well as state forests and some local and federal government forestlands.

The Private Forests Division administers Oregon's Forest Practices Act. Enacted in 1971, and modified many times since, the Act regulates stream and water quality protection, timber harvesting, reforestation, road construction and maintenance, and other forest practices on private, non-federal lands.

Through the State Forests Division, the agency manages approximately 745,000 acres of forestland owned by the state, or 3 percent of the state's forests. State-owned forests are found in the northern Coast and Cascade mountain ranges, in south-central Oregon, and scattered throughout the western part of the state. ODF manages these lands to achieve a balance of social, economic and environmental values. The agency also manages much of the state's Common School Fund forest lands, with the exception of the Elliott State Forest.

The Administrative Services Division provides support to the agency in the areas of Human Resources, Public Affairs, Procurement, Budget Management, Fiscal Services, Information Technology, Internal Audits and Safety/Risk Management. The division also includes the Partnership and Planning Program, which provides technical analysis and planning services to the department, as well as other state, federal and local agencies on a wide variety of forestry-related issues. Partnership and Planning is also responsible for supporting partner organizations' efforts to increase the pace, scale, and quality of restoration work on federal forestlands through the Federal Forest Restoration program.

Board of Forestry, State

Phone: 503-945-7200
Email: boardofforestry@oregon.gov
Contact: Hilary Olivos-Rood, Board
  Administrator
Statutory Authority: ORS Chapter 526
Duties and Responsibilities: The seven-member citizen board is appointed by the governor and confirmed by the Senate. Its mission is to lead Oregon in implementing policies and programs that promote sustainable management of Oregon's public and private forests. Its responsibilities are to supervise all matters of forest policy, appoint the state

forester, adopt rules regulating forest practices and provide general supervision of the state forester's agency-management responsibilities.

No more than three board members may derive a significant portion of their income from the forest products industry. There must be at least one member from each of the state's three major forest regions: northern, southern and eastern. The term of office is four years, and no member may serve more than two consecutive full terms. The state forester serves as secretary to the board.

Emergency Fire Cost Committee

Phone: 503-945-7200
Statutory Authority: ORS 477.750–477.775
Duties and Responsibilities: The Oregon Forest Land Protection Fund was established by the Legislature with the purpose of equalizing emergency fire suppression costs among the department's various protection districts. The emergency funding system is designed to operate as an "insurance policy," where all districts pay premiums into the fund so that money will be available to any individual district for fire suppression costs.

Family Forestlands, Committee for

Phone: 503-945-7200
Statutory Authority: ORS 526.016
Duties and Responsibilities: The committee researches policies impacting family forestland viability, resource protection and forestry benefits. The committee then makes recommendations to the Board of Forestry and state forester. The 13-member committee includes seven voting and six non-voting members. Voting members include four family forest owners and one representative each from the environmental community, forest products industry and general public. Non-voting ex officio members may include representatives from ODF, Oregon State University, Oregon small forestland groups, forestry-related industry associations and the Oregon Forest Resources Institute.

Stewardship Coordinating Committee

Phone: 503-945-7200
Statutory Authority: U.S. Cooperative Forestry
  Assistance Act, 16 U.S.C. 2101 et seq.
Duties and Responsibilities: The committee advises the state forester on policies and procedures for U.S. Forest Service, state and private forestry programs, such as Forest Legacy and Forest Stewardship. The committee consists of representatives from state and federal natural resource agencies, private forest landowners, consulting foresters and forest industry and conservation organizations.

The committee also serves as the forestry subcommittee to the Oregon Technical Advisory Committee, which advises both the U.S. Department of Agriculture (USDA) Farm Services Agency and USDA Natural Resource Conservation Service on federal farm and forestry assistance programs.

Forest Trust Land Advisory Committee

Phone: 503-945-7200
Statutory Authority: ORS 526.156
Duties and Responsibilities: The committee is comprised of the board of directors of the Council of Forest Trust Land Counties and advises the Board of Forestry and state forester on matters related to state forestlands managed by ODF. The counties that receive revenues from these forestlands are Benton, Clackamas, Clatsop, Columbia, Coos, Douglas, Josephine, Klamath, Lane, Lincoln, Linn, Marion, Polk, Tillamook and Washington.

Regional Forest Practice Committees

Phone: 503-945-7200
Statutory Authority: ORS 527.650
Duties and Responsibilities: Three Regional Forest Practice Committees, serving the northwest, southwest and eastern regions of the state, were created by the 1971 Oregon Forest Practices Act. Under Oregon law, a majority of committee members must be private forest landowners and persons involved with logging or forest operations. The committees advise the Board of Forestry on current forestry issues and forest management approaches.

Smoke Management Advisory Committee

Phone: 503-945-7200
Duties and Responsibilities: In 1989, the Legislature directed the state forester to establish the committee to provide advice and assistance to the department's Smoke Management Program. The state forester appoints three members: an industrial forestland owner representative, a nonindustrial forestland owner representative and a public representative. A U.S. Forest Service representative and a U.S. Bureau of Land Management representative are also invited to serve as members. Each member serves a two-year term that is renewable after the two-year period.

Committee members gather for public meetings in Salem twice a year to discuss and provide advice to the Smoke Management Program regarding current prescribed burning and smoke intrusion trends, program fund balance, implementation plan items and other current issues and projects of the program.

State Forests Advisory Committee

Phone: 503-945-7200
Duties and Responsibilities: The committee is comprised of interested citizens and representatives of forest industry, environmental and recreation

groups. It provides a forum to discuss issues, opportunities and concerns regarding state forestlands and offers advice and guidance to ODF on the implementation of the Northwest Oregon State Forests Management Plan. The plan provides guidance for managing 650,000 acres within the Tillamook, Clatsop and Santiam state forests, and several scattered state-owned forest tracts in Benton, Polk, Lincoln, Clackamas and Lane counties. The plan attempts to take a balanced approach to generating revenue, while prioritizing environmental and social benefits.

This is one of several historic buildings on the campus of the headquarters of the Department of Forestry. (Oregon State Archives scenic photo)

GEOLOGIST EXAMINERS, STATE BOARD OF

Address: 707 13th St. SE, Suite 114, Salem 97301
Phone: 503-566-2837
Fax: 503-485-2947
Email: osbge.info@oregon.gov
Web: www.oregon.gov/OSBGE/Pages/
   default.aspx
Contact: Christine Valentine, Administrator
Statutory Authority: ORS 672.505–672.705
Duties and Responsibilities: The mission of the board, established in 1977, is to safeguard the health, welfare and property of Oregonians with respect to geologic practice in Oregon. The board accomplishes this primarily through registration of geologists. The board also reviews complaints about geologist conduct and practice or unlicensed geologic practice and has authority to impose civil penalties, suspend, revoke or not renew registrations or seek other resolutions as appropriate. In addition, the board works to inform the public, government agencies and others about the practice of geology.

The board sets examination, education and experience standards for geologist registration and for a specialty certification in engineering geology, evaluates applications for examination and registration based on these standards and administers national and engineering geology specialty examinations. Geologists licensed in other states or jurisdictions can apply for registration in Oregon but must meet all of the board's standards.

Approximately 1,075 geologists are registered to practice in Oregon with about 225 also holding certification in engineering geology. The board is composed of four Oregon registered geologists, the state geologist (i.e., the Director of the Oregon Department of Geology and Mineral Industries) and a public member. The board is served by two staff, an executive director and registration specialist.

GEOLOGY AND MINERAL INDUSTRIES, STATE DEPARTMENT OF

Address: 800 NE Oregon St., Suite 965, Portland 97232
Phone: 971-673-1555
Fax: 971-673-1562
Web: www.oregon.gov/DOGAMI/Pages/index.aspx
Contact: Brad Avy, Director/State Geologist
Statutory Authority: ORS Chapters 516, 517, 520, 522, ORS 455.446, 455.447
Duties and Responsibilities: The department increases understanding of Oregon's geologic resources and hazards through science and stewardship. Established in 1937 as an independent state agency, its early focus on mining and rural economic development has expanded to include helping Oregonians understand and prepare for the natural hazards that accompany the state's geology.

Today, the department provides earth science information and regulation to make Oregon safe and prosperous. The Geological Survey & Services program develops maps, reports and data to help Oregon manage natural resources and prepare for natural hazards such as earthquakes, tsunamis, landslides, floods, volcanic eruptions and coastal erosion. The Mineral Land Regulation & Reclamation program oversees the state's mineral production and works to minimize impacts of natural resource extraction and to maximize the opportunities for land reclamation. The department has a staff of approximately 40 people.

Department of Geology and Mineral Industries Governing Board

Contact: Laura Maffei, Chair
Duties and Responsibilities: A five-member governing board of citizens, appointed by the governor and confirmed by the Senate, oversees the Department of Geology and Mineral Industries. The board sets policy, oversees general operations and adopts a strategic plan every six years to guide the department's mission and objectives.

GOVERNMENT ETHICS COMMISSION, OREGON

Address: 3218 Pringle Rd. SE, Rm. 220, Salem 97302-1680
Phone: 503-378-5105
Fax: 503-373-1456
Email: ogec.mail@oregon.gov
Web: www.oregon.gov/OGEC/Pages/default.aspx
Contact: Ronald A. Bersin, Executive Director
Statutory Authority: ORS 171.725–171.785, 192.660, 192.685, ORS Chapter 244
Duties and Responsibilities: The Oregon Government Ethics Commission (OGEC), established by vote of the people in 1974, is responsible for enforcement of government ethics laws which prohibit public officials from using their office for financial gain and require public disclosure of economic conflict of interest. The OGEC also enforces state laws that require lobbyists, and the entities they represent, to register and periodically report their lobbying expenditures. The third area of OGEC jurisdiction is the executive session provisions of the public meetings law.

The OGEC is a nine-member citizen commission served by nine staff members who focus on regulation and prevention through education.

The Barbara Roberts Human Services Building in Salem houses the central offices of the Oregon Health Authority. (Oregon State Archives scenic photo)

HEALTH AUTHORITY, OREGON

Address: 500 Summer St. NE, E20, Salem 97301-1097
Phone: 503-947-2340; 877-398-9238
Fax: 503-947-2341
Email: OHA.DirectorsOffice@dhsoha.state.or.us; OHPB.Info@dhsoha.state.or.us
Web: www.oregon.gov/OHA/Pages/index.aspx
Contact: Patrick Allen, Director
Statutory Authority: ORS 413.032
Duties and Responsibilities: The Oregon Health Authority (OHA) is responsible for improving the

lifelong health of Oregonians, improving quality and increasing access to health services, and containing and lowering health care costs. It was created by the 2009 Legislature to ensure that Oregonians have access to affordable, sustainable, high quality health care and to ensure health equity for all. One way it does this is through an innovative system of coordinated care organizations (CCOs) that serve most of the more than 1 million members of the Oregon Health Plan, Oregon's Medicaid program. The 15 CCOs work with partners in all 36 Oregon counties to provide better care at lower cost to ensure that their members' physical, behavioral and dental health needs are met.

OHA is overseen by the nine-member citizen Oregon Health Policy Board and carries out its work through several program areas.

Health Policy Board, Oregon

Address: 500 Summer St. NE, Salem 97301
Phone: 503-947-2340; 877-398-9238
Fax: 503-947-2341
Email: OHPB.Info@dhsoha.state.or.us
Web: www.oregon.gov/OHA/OHPB/Pages/
index.aspx
Statutory Authority: ORS 413.032
Duties and Responsibilities: The nine-member board serves as the policy making and oversight body for the Oregon Health Authority. The board is committed to providing access to high quality, affordable health care for all Oregonians and to improving population health.

The board was established by the Legislature in 2009, making the Oregon Health Authority responsible for most state health care services and for reforming the state's health care system.

Educators Benefit Board, Oregon

Address: 500 Summer St. NE, E-88, Salem 97301
Phone: 503-378-6610; Toll-free: 1-888-469-6322
Fax: 503-378-5832
Email: oebb.benefits@dhsoha.state.or.us
Web: www.oregon.gov/OHA/OEBB/Pages/
index.aspx
Contact: Ali Hassoun, Director
Statutory Authority: ORS 243.864
Duties and Responsibilities: The board provides a choice of benefit plans for employees in most of Oregon's kindergarten through grade 12 school districts, education service districts and community colleges, as well as a number of charter schools and local governments.

Equity and Inclusion, Office of

Address: 421 SW Oak St., Suite 750, Portland 97204

Phone: 971-673-1240; 971-673-1285 (Director); TTY: 711
Fax: 971-673-1128
Web: www.oregon.gov/OHA/OEI/Pages/
index.aspx
Contact: Leann Johnson, Director
Email: Leann.R.Johnson@dhsoha.state.or.us
Statutory Authority: ORS 431.137
Duties and Responsibilities: The office works with diverse communities throughout Oregon to eliminate health gaps and disparities by making health care more accessible and ensuring the delivery of care consistent with state and federal civil rights guidelines. It operates a Traditional Health Worker program to help ensure that culturally competent care is delivered by a diverse workforce. The office's Health Care Interpreter program trains and certifies bilingual persons to provide high-quality health care interpretation to Oregon's increasingly diverse populations.

Health Licensing Office (HLO)

Address: 700 Summer St. NE, Suite 320, Salem 97301-1287
Phone: 503-378-8667; TTY: 503-373-2114
Fax: 503-370-9004
Email: hlo.info@dhsoha.state.or.us
Web: www.oregon.gov/oha/ph/hlo/Pages/
index.aspx
Contact: Sylvie Donaldson, Director
Statutory Authority: ORS 676.600–676.992
Duties and Responsibilities: The office works with multiple boards, councils and programs to oversee a variety of health and health-related professions. It protects Oregonians' health and safety by ensuring that these professionals are trained and qualified to practice. The office tests people who apply for professional licenses, inspects facilities, responds to consumer complaints and disciplines practitioners who violate state requirements.

HLO Boards:

Athletic Trainers

Web: www.oregon.gov/OHA/PH/HLO/Pages/
Board-Athletic-Trainer.aspx
Statutory Authority: ORS 688.701–688.734
Duties and Responsibilities: The board oversees the practice of athletic trainers in Oregon. It has five members appointed by the governor.

Behavior Analysis Regulatory

Web: www.oregon.gov/OHA/PH/HLO/Pages/
Board-Behavior-Analysis-Regulatory.aspx
Statutory Authority: ORS 676.800–676.805
Duties and Responsibilities: The board oversees the licensing of behavior analysts and assistant behavior analysts and the registration of behavior

analysis interventionists, all of whom treat individuals with autism spectrum disorder. The board has nine members appointed by the governor and subject to confirmation by the Senate.

Certified Advanced Estheticians
Web: www.oregon.gov/OHA/PH/HLO/Pages/
Board-Certified-Advanced-Estheticians.aspx
Duties and Responsibilities: In July 2015, House Bill 2642 created the board to oversee the safe practice of advanced non-ablative esthetics in Oregon. The board has nine members appointed by the governor.

Cosmetology
Web: www.oregon.gov/OHA/PH/HLO/Pages/
Board-Cosmetology.aspx
Statutory Authority: ORS 690.005–690.992
Duties and Responsibilities: The board oversees the practice of cosmetologists in Oregon. It has seven members appointed by the governor and subject to confirmation by the Senate.

Denture Technology
Web: www.oregon.gov/OHA/PH/HLO/Pages/
Board-Denture-Technology.aspx
Statutory Authority: ORS 680.500–680.990
Duties and Responsibilities: The board oversees the practice of denturists in Oregon. It has seven members appointed by the governor and subject to confirmation by the Senate.

Direct Entry Midwifery
Web: www.oregon.gov/OHA/PH/HLO/Pages/
Board-Direct-Entry-Midwifery.aspx
Statutory Authority: ORS 687.405–687.991
Duties and Responsibilities: The board oversees the practice of licensed direct entry midwives in Oregon. It has seven members appointed by the governor and subject to confirmation by the Senate.

Electrologists and Body Art Practitioners
Web: www.oregon.gov/OHA/PH/HLO/Pages/
Board-Body-Art-Practitioners.aspx
Statutory Authority: ORS 690.350–690.992
Duties and Responsibilities: The board oversees the practices of tattoo artists, electrologists and body piercers, including specialty piercers and earlobe-only piercers. It has seven members appointed by the governor and subject to confirmation by the Senate.

Environmental Health Registration
Web: www.oregon.gov/OHA/PH/HLO/Pages/
Board-Environmental-Health-
Registration.aspx
Statutory Authority: ORS 700.005–700.995

Duties and Responsibilities: The board oversees the practices of environmental health specialists and waste water specialists in Oregon. It has seven members appointed by the governor.

Hearing Aids, Advisory Council on
Web: www.oregon.gov/OHA/PH/HLO/Pages/
Board-Advisory-Council-Hearing-Aids.aspx
Statutory Authority: ORS 694.015–694.991
Duties and Responsibilities: The council oversees the practice of hearing aid specialists in Oregon. It has seven members appointed by the governor and subject to confirmation by the Senate.

Licensed Dietitians
Web: www.oregon.gov/OHA/PH/HLO/Pages/
Board-Licensed-Dietitians.aspx
Statutory Authority: ORS 691.405
Duties and Responsibilities: The board oversees the practice of dietitians in Oregon. It has seven members appointed by the governor.

Long Term Care Administrators
Web: www.oregon.gov/OHA/PH/HLO/Pages/
Board-Nursing-Home-Administrators.aspx
Statutory Authority: ORS 678.800
Duties and Responsibilities: The board oversees the practice of Nursing Home Administrators and Residential Care Facility Administrators in the State of Oregon. It has nine members appointed by the governor and confirmed by the Senate.

Respiratory Therapist and Polysomnographic Technologist Licensing
Web: www.oregon.gov/oha/PH/HLO/Pages/
Board-RTPT.aspx
Statutory Authority: ORS 688.800–688.995
Duties and Responsibilities: The board oversees the practices of respiratory therapists and polysomnographic technologists in Oregon. It has seven members appointed by the governor and subject to confirmation by the Senate.

Sex Offender Treatment
Web: www.oregon.gov/OHA/PH/HLO/
Pages/Board-Sex-Offender-Treatment.aspx
Statutory Authority: ORS 675.360–675.410
Duties and Responsibilities: The board oversees the practices of clinical and associate sex offender therapists in Oregon. It has seven members appointed by the governor.

Health Policy and Analytics Division
Address: 421 SW Oak St., Suite 875, Portland, 97204
Phone: 503-947-2340; 877-398-9238

Fax: 971-673-3320
Web: www.oregon.gov/oha/HPA/Pages/
index.aspx
Contact: Jeremy Vandehey, Director
Duties and Responsibilities: The division collects and analyzes health data from throughout the state and makes reports and recommendations to OHA leaders, the governor and Legislature based on that data. The division also provides support to the Health Policy Board, Medicaid Advisory Committee, Health Care Workforce Committee and others. The chief medical officer supports the work of many programs and committees that are part of the health transformation effort, including the Patient Centered Primary Care Home program, Transformation Center and Health Evidence Review Commission.

Health Systems Division
Address: 500 Summer St. NE, E49, Salem 97301
Phone: 503-945-5772; 800-527-5772
Fax: 503-373-7327
Contact: Margie Stanton, Director
Duties and Responsibilities: The division manages the Oregon Health Plan, Oregon's Medicaid program, which covers more than 1.1 million Oregonians. It also manages the statewide behavioral health system, which works to integrate addiction services and mental health care with the state's physical health system. The division also oversees the Children's Wraparound Program, which works with the state's coordinated care organizations to ensure that children with special needs receive integrated care.

Public Employees' Benefit Board
Address: 500 Summer St. NE, E89, Salem 97301
Phone: 503-373-1102
Fax: 503-373-1654
Email: inquiries.pebb@dhsoha.state.or.us
Web: www.oregon.gov/OHA/PEBB/Pages/
index.aspx
Contact: Ali Hassoun, Director
Statutory Authority: ORS 243.125
Duties and Responsibilities: The board designs, contracts and administers benefits for state employees, including medical and dental coverage, life, accident, disability and long-term care insurance, and flexible spending accounts. The board also offers health care insurance options for retirees not yet eligible for Medicare.

Public Health Division
Address: 800 NE Oregon St., Suite 930, Portland 97232
Phone: 971-673-1222
Fax: 971-673-1299

Email: health.webmaster@dhsoha.state.or.us
Web: http://public.health.oregon.gov
Contact: Lillian Shirley, Public Health Director
Statutory Authority: ORS Chapters 97, 431–475, 624
Duties and Responsibilities: The division improves lifelong health for Oregonians by promoting health and preventing the leading causes of death, disease and injury in the state. The division assesses the public's health through data collection and uses that information to develop policies and programs that support improved health outcomes. The division oversees health promotion and prevention activities, health care facility licensing, environmental health regulation, public health emergency preparedness, epidemiological outbreak investigations and the Oregon State Public Health Laboratory.

The division works with local health departments, tribes, community organizations, health care providers, coordinated care organizations and other partners. The Public Health Advisory Board and other advisory committees provide guidance to the division.

State Hospital, Oregon
Salem Address: 2600 Center St. NE, Salem 97301
Phone: 503-945-2800; 800-544-7078;
TTY: 800-735-2900
Fax: 503-947-9022
Junction City Address: 29398 Recovery Way, Junction City 97448
Phone: 541-465-2554; 877-851-7330
Fax: 541-465-2777
Web: www.oregon.gov/oha/osh/pages/
index.aspx
Contact: Dolly Matteucci, Superintendent
Statutory Authority: ORS 179.321
Duties and Responsibilities: The hospital provides in-patient psychiatric care for adults from throughout the state. With two campuses, one in Salem and one in Junction City, the hospital's primary goal is to help people recover from their illnesses and return to the community.

Tribal Affairs
Address: 500 Summer St. NE, Salem 97301
Phone: 503-945-9703
Fax: 503-947-2341
Contact: Julie Johnson, Director
Statutory Authority: ORS 182.164
Duties and Responsibilities: Tribal Affairs develops, coordinates, monitors and evaluates OHA program activities to ensure that the relationship between OHA and the nine federally recognized tribes of Oregon is built on trust, mutual respect and an understanding of the relationship at a government-to-government level.

Tribal Affairs also supports programs that provide and coordinate physical, oral, behavioral and public health programs and services to tribal members so that the objectives of better care, better health and lower costs are met. These programs include Oregon Indian Health Service, Urban Indian Health Program, and tribal health services.

HIGHER EDUCATION COORDINATING COMMISSION

Address: 3225 25th St. SE, Salem 97302
Phone: 503-378-5690
Fax: 503-378-8395
Email: info.HECC@state.or.us
Web: https://www.oregon.gov/HigherEd
Contact: Ben Cannon, Executive Director;
Ramona Rodamaker, Deputy Director
Statutory Authority: ORS 351.735
Duties and Responsibilities: The Higher Education Coordinating Commission (HECC) is responsible for ensuring pathways to postsecondary opportunity and success for Oregonians statewide and serves as a convener of the groups and institutions working across the public and private higher education arena. HECC is a 14-member volunteer commission appointed by the governor. The HECC state agency supports the commission and is comprised of eight offices led by the executive director. Its authorities include advising the Legislature and governor, providing one strategic vision for Oregon higher education planning, funding and policy to meet state goals; authorizing postsecondary programs and degrees; administering key Oregon financial aid programs, collaborating with partners to oversee programs and administer funding to increase employment opportunities, workforce training and support for businesses; and evaluating and reporting success of higher education efforts.

In addition to the six offices listed below, the HECC has an Office of the Executive Director, responsible for executive leadership, commission administration, communications, legislative affairs, equity leadership, human resources and internal auditing; and an Office of Operations, responsible for support to all HECC offices in areas including budget, procurement, payroll, accounting and information technology.

Academic Policy and Authorization, Office of

Address: 3225 25th St. SE, Salem 97302
Phone: 503-378-5690
Fax: 503-378-8395
Web: https://www.oregon.gov/HigherEd/APA
Contact: Veronica Dujon, Director
Statutory Authority: ORS Chapter 345, 348.594–348.615, ORS Chapter 350

Duties and Responsibilities: This office oversees two primary areas: the quality, integrity and diversity of private postsecondary programs in Oregon for the benefit of students and consumers; and public university academic policy and program approval. The private postsecondary units consist of the Office of Degree Authorization (ODA) and the Private Career Schools Licensing Unit (PCS), responsible for policy and regulatory action that affect certain private institutions serving Oregonians. The ODA authorizes degree-granting private institutions, offering academic programs in Oregon or to Oregon students from outside the state. The PCS Licensing Unit licenses private career schools in Oregon. Both units also provide educational leadership, technical assistance, student and consumer protection and serve as conveners of private institutions and partners in Oregon. The office is also the portal entity for distance education offerings in Oregon through the multistate State Authorization Reciprocity Agreement. The public university academic policy unit provides academic coordination related to Oregon's seven public universities, including coordination of the academic program approval process, student complaints, statewide initiatives and legislative directives to enhance postsecondary pathways and student success.

Community Colleges and Workforce Development, Office of

Address: 3225 25th St. SE, Salem 97302
Phone: 503-378-8648
Fax: 503-378-8434
Email: ccwd.info@state.or.us
Web: https://www.oregon.gov/HigherEd/CCWD
Contact: Patrick Crane, Director
Statutory Authority: ORS 326.051
Duties and Responsibilities: The office provides coordination, leadership and resources to Oregon's network of 17 locally-governed community colleges, as well as adult basic skills providers, high school equivalency program providers and other partners. It has responsibility for coordinating community college programs and services, developing biennial budget recommendations for the community college funding and capital projects, allocation of state funding, coordination of the academic approval processes, and reporting to the Legislature. The office provides statewide administration of the Adult Education and Family Literacy components of the federally funded Workforce Investment and Opportunity Act; the Carl Perkins Career and Technical Education Act programs; and the Oregon High School Equivalency General Educational Development (GED®) programs.

Postsecondary Finance and Capital, Office of

Address: 3225 25th St. SE, Salem 97302
Phone: 503-378-5690
Fax: 503-378-8395
Email: info.HECC@state.or.us
Web: https://www.oregon.gov/HigherEd/PFC
Contact: Jim Pinkard
Statutory Authority: ORS Chapter 350
Duties and Responsibilities: This office provides fiscal coordination related to Oregon's public post-secondary institutions, including financial planning, fiscal reporting and analysis, capital bond funding administration, the allocation of state funding to public post-secondary institutions, and biennial budget recommendations. The office prepares budget recommendations to the commission for the Public University Support Fund, Public University State Programs, Public University Statewide Public Services, Community College Support Fund, as well as university and community college capital investments.

Research and Data, Office of

Address: 3225 25th St. SE, Salem 97302
Phone: 503-947-5701
Fax: 503-378-8395
Email: info.HECC@state.or.us
Web: http://www.oregon.gov/HigherEd/RD
Contact: Amy Cox, Director
Statutory Authority: ORS 351.735
Duties and Responsibilities: The office collects, analyzes and reports research and data on postsecondary education and training, including data on students and their characteristics, courses, enrollments, academic performance, completion and academic pathways to comply with state and federal reporting requirements and to inform decisions on the postsecondary education enterprise. The office also includes administration of the State Longitudinal Data System, which links data about students as they move from kindergarten through postsecondary education and employment.

Student Access and Completion, Office of

Address: 1500 Valley River Dr., Suite 100, Eugene 97401
Phone: 541-687-7400; Toll-free: 1-800-452-8807
Fax: 541-687-7414
Email: osac@hecc.oregon.gov
Web: www.OregonStudentAid.gov
Contact: Juan Báez-Arévalo, Director
Statutory Authority: ORS 341.522, ORS Chapter 348, 352.287
Duties and Responsibilities: The Office of Student Access and Completion (OSAC) administers several financial aid programs for students attending college or other postsecondary education

and training programs. These include state and federally-funded grants and privately-funded scholarships. In addition, OSAC promotes college access and affordability for Oregonians through ASPIRE, a college and career mentoring program, and statewide community outreach events.

OSAC's largest financial aid programs are the Oregon Opportunity Grant (OOG), the Oregon Promise Grant and the OSAC Scholarship application. The OOG is the state's largest need-based grant program and helps low-income students afford eligible Oregon colleges and universities. Oregon Promise is for recent high school and GED® test graduates to help cover tuition costs at any Oregon community college. The OSAC Scholarship application includes more than 600 scholarships, which students can access through the single application. These scholarships target a variety of student groups and are funded by private donors, foundations and employers. OSAC also administers grant programs supporting specific populations such as foster youth, students raising children and Oregon National Guard members.

Workforce Investments, Office of

Address: 3225 25th St. SE, Salem 97302
Phone: 503-947-5949
Fax: 503-947-1246
Email: info.HECC@state.or.us
Web: https://www.oregon.gov/HigherEd/OWI
Contact: Karen Humelbaugh, Director
Statutory Authority: ORS 660.300–660.364
Duties and Responsibilities: The Office of Workforce Investments (OWI) is one of several state entities focused on employment opportunities, skill attainment and work-related training statewide. OWI works in partnership with the Oregon's Employment Department, Department of Human Services, Commission for the Blind and others to provide leadership to Oregon's workforce system. It is responsible for convening partnerships, supporting and providing technical assistance to the Workforce and Talent Development Board (WTDB) and local workforce development boards, and implementing the governor's vision and the WTDB strategic plan.

The HECC is the administrative entity for federally-funded programs authorized by Titles I and II of the U.S. Workforce Innovation and Opportunity Act, including Youth, Adult and Dislocated Worker programs and Federal Discretionary grants, for which the HECC provides program and fiscal oversight as well as policy direction and technical assistance to state and local partners.

The OWI also administers and supports the Oregon Youth Corps, providing grant funding, training and resources to youth-serving agencies; Oregon Volunteers, supporting statewide service and volunteer efforts and providing funds for the state-based AmeriCorps program; and the STEM Investment Council, supporting STEM education initiatives

The North Capitol Mall Office Building in Salem houses the central offices of the Housing and Community Services Department. (Oregon State Archives scenic photo)

HOUSING AND COMMUNITY SERVICES DEPARTMENT

Address: 725 Summer St. NE, Suite B, Salem 97301-1266
Phone: 503-986-2000
Email: housinginfo@oregon.gov
Web: www.oregon.gov/OHCS/Pages/index.aspx
Contact: Margaret Salazar, Executive Director
Statutory Authority: ORS 456.555
Duties and Responsibilities: Oregon Housing and Community Services (OHCS) provides financial and program support to create and preserve opportunities for quality, affordable housing for Oregonians of lower and moderate income. OHCS administers programs that provide housing stabilization—from preventing and ending homelessness and assisting with utilities to keep someone stable, to financing multifamily, affordable housing and encouraging home ownership. It delivers these programs primarily through grants, contracts and loan agreements with local partners and community-based providers and has limited direct contact with low-income beneficiaries. Stewardship, compliance monitoring and asset management are all critical roles for OHCS.

Housing Stability Council, Oregon

Address: 725 Summer St. NE, Suite B, Salem 97301-1266
Phone: 503-986-2005
Fax: 503-986-2132
Email: housinginfo@oregon.gov
Web: www.oregon.gov/ohcs/hsc/pages/index.aspx
Contact: Cheyloa Chase, Executive Assistant to the Executive Director
Statutory Authority: ORS 456.567

Duties and Responsibilities: The council consists of nine members and is the governing body for OHCS. The council approves affordable housing projects, sets direction on statewide housing policy and serves as an advisory body to the agency. The council also serves as a public body for engagement with stakeholders, housing advocates and the public on affordable housing issues and policy decisions.

Deputy Director's Office

Address: 725 Summer St. NE, Suite B, Salem 97301-1266
Phone: 503-986-2000
Fax: 503-986-2020
Email: housinginfo@oregon.gov
Web: www.oregon.gov/OHCS/Pages/index.aspx
Contact: Caleb Yant, Deputy Director
Statutory Authority: ORS 456.555
Duties and Responsibilities: The office includes Human Resources, Administrative Services, Information Services, and the Finance and Budget Sections. It is responsible for the support services required to ensure that the business functions of OHCS are operating appropriately. This includes personnel development, information technology, research, facilities management, records management and auditing functions. It provides essential services to support OHCS' leadership and workforce to achieve the department's mission.

The Finance Section includes grants and monitoring, procurement, contracts and general accounting functions for all aspects of the department. Key program areas of the department rely on community partners for serving people with low incomes. Grants and contracts are critical for success in reaching low-income Oregonians. This section ensures accountability and stewardship of resources.

The Budget Section manages and reports on all aspects of the agency's budget. The section works closely with partners at the Legislative Fiscal Office and the Department of Administrative Services to provide needed reports and budget documents throughout the biennium.

Affordable Rental Housing Division

Address: 725 Summer St. NE, Suite B, Salem 97301-1266
Phone: 503-986-2000
Fax: 503-986-2020
Email: housinginfo@oregon.gov
Web: www.oregon.gov/OHCS/Pages/index.aspx
Contact: Julie Cody, Director
Statutory Authority: ORS 446.525–446.543, 456.515–456.723, 458.210–458.310, 458.600–458.650, 458.655–458.665

Duties and Responsibilities: The division administers federal and state-funded, multifamily rental housing resources to facilitate the increased availability of safe, decent and affordable housing for Oregonians with low incomes. This includes the development of new multifamily units and the acquisition and rehabilitation of existing multifamily units, support of homeownership for low- and moderate-income Oregonians through single family programs, long term maintenance of affordable multifamily housing through asset management and compliance, debt management, and foreclosure assistance under the Oregon Homeownership Stabilization Initiative.

Homeownership Division

Address: 725 Summer St. NE, Suite B, Salem 97301-1266
Phone: 503-986-2000
Fax: 503-986-2020
Email: housinginfo@oregon.gov
Web: www.oregon.gov/OHCS/Pages/index.aspx
Contact: Emese Perfecto, Director
Statutory Authority: ORS 456.587, 458.505–458.530, 458.600–458.650
Duties and Responsibilities: The division was established in 2019 and administers federal and state programs to increase homeownership among low- and moderate-income Oregonians. This includes resources for home buyer coaching, down payment assistance, home buyer interest rate advantage, home repair, foreclosure prevention and mortgage assistance.

Housing Stabilization Division

Address: 725 Summer St. NE, Suite B, Salem 97301-1266
Phone: 503-986-2000
Fax: 503-986-2020
Email: housinginfo@oregon.gov
Web: www.oregon.gov/OHCS/Pages/index.aspx
Contact: Andrea Bell, Director
Statutory Authority: ORS 456.587, 458.505–458.530, 458.600–458.650
Duties and Responsibilities: The division administers services for Oregonians with low and extremely low incomes to help stabilize their housing as well as achieve greater economic stability. Services include work to prevent and end homelessness, emergency rental assistance, energy bill payment assistance and weatherization assistance as well as other anti-poverty programs such as the Individual Development Accounts.

The division ensures that affordable housing projects across Oregon maintain compliance with state and federal regulations and are safe and healthy properties for the residents. The division's responsibilities also include contract administration on behalf of the U.S. Department of Housing and Urban Development, and human resources and facilities functions.

Public Affairs Division

Address: 725 Summer St. NE, Suite B, Salem 97301-1266
Phone: 503-986-2000
Fax: 503-986-2020
Email: housinginfo@oregon.gov
Web: www.oregon.gov/OHCS/Pages/index.aspx
Contact: Kenny LaPoint, Director
Statutory Authority: ORS 456.555
Duties and Responsibilities: The division includes Federal Planning, Housing Integrators and Government Relations and Communications. Public Affairs is the primary division that engages with the public, stakeholders, elected officials and the media.

HUMAN SERVICES, DEPARTMENT OF

Address: 500 Summer St. NE, Salem 97301
Phone: 503-945-5944
Fax: 503-581-6198
Email: communications.dhs@state.or.us
Web: www.oregon.gov/DHS
Contact: Fariborz Pakseresht, Director
Statutory Authority: ORS 409.010
Duties and Responsibilities: The Department of Human Services (DHS) works to help Oregonians in their own communities achieve safety, well-being and independence through services that protect, empower, respect choice and preserve dignity. The Director's Office is responsible for overall leadership, policy development and administrative oversight of programs, staff, and offices in DHS. These functions are coordinated with the Office of the Governor, Legislature, other state and federal agencies, partners and stakeholders, communities of color, local governments, advocacy and client groups and the private sector.

Key functions include Financial Services, Human Resources, Data and Research, Legislative Relations, Communications, Tribal Relations, Equity and Multicultural Services, Federal Financial Policy, Governor's Advocacy Office, and Internal Audits. The director's office also coordinates operations that support service delivery, including Contracts and Procurement, Facilities Services, Imaging and Records Management Services, Background Checks, Information Support Systems, Business Information Supports, Publications, Payment Accuracy and Recovery, Program Integrity, and Continuous Improvement.

Governor's Advocacy Office

Address: 500 Summer St. NE, E17, Salem 97301
Phone: 503-945-6904

Fax: 503-378-6532
Contact: Zachary Gehringer, Administrator
Duties and Responsibilities: The office handles client complaints related to DHS services. This office operates independently in investigations and reports directly to the governor by providing a quarterly report on the status of the complaints. Office staff works closely with field and central office staff, program staff, the Office of the Governor, key stakeholders and the DHS Director's Office.

Aging and People with Disabilities, Office of

Address: 500 Summer St. NE, E02, Salem 97301
Phone: 503-945-5600
Fax: 503-373-7823
Contact: Michael McCormick, Interim Director
Duties and Responsibilities: The Office of Aging and People with Disabilities (APD) assists older adults and people with disabilities to ensure that they experience person-centered services, supports and early interventions that are innovative and help maintain independence, promote safety, honor choice, respect cultural preferences and uphold dignity. This includes opportunities for community living, employment, family support and long-term services. The programs' goals are to achieve well-being, so older adults and people with disabilities feel safe and experience their best quality of life; accessibility, so they can readily and consistently access services and supports to meet their needs; quality outcomes, so they can engage in services that are preventive and evidence-informed; service equity, so that Oregonians experience programs, services and supports that are improved and responsive to historical inequities, current disparities and individual experiences; and engagement, so that consumers are empowered by information, communication and advocacy through strong, collaborative partnerships with stakeholders.

During the 2021–2023 biennium, APD expects to serve more than 5,000 people aged 60 and older through Oregon Project Independence; more than 36,450 older adults and people with physical disabilities per month with long-term care services paid through Medicaid; about 212,000 older individuals with Older Americans Act services; more than 172,860 Oregonians with direct financial support services; and more than 45,000 individuals who receive a Social Security Disability determination. In addition, about 40,000 Oregonians live in APD-licensed long-term care facilities. APD's Adult Protective Services (APS) unit investigates abuse in most of these long-term care settings as well as the community. In 2019, local APS offices received a total of 50,832 calls about potential abuse.

APD program units include the Aging and Disability Resource Connection (ADRC) of Oregon, which is a collaborative public-private partnership that streamlines consumer access to the aging and disability service delivery system. The ADRC is free and provides information and assistance that empowers people to make informed decisions. Through trained options counselors, Oregonians develop action plans to address long-term service and support needs that align with their preferences, financial situations, values and needs. Employees from both APD local offices and Area Agencies on Aging throughout Oregon are responsible for providing direct client services and for determining eligibility of the aging and people with disabilities for medical programs provided through the Oregon Health Authority.

APD is preparing for the demographic growth expected in the older adult population and is serving an increasingly diverse population. APD strives to identify disparities in outcomes and identify strategies to serve individuals in a culturally and linguistically appropriate manner.

Deaf and Hard of Hearing Services Program, Oregon

Address: 500 Summer St. NE, E02, Salem 97301
Email: odhhs.info@dhsoha.state.or.us
Web: www.oregon.gov/dhs/SENIORS-DISABILITIES/SPPD/Pages/ODHHS.aspx
Statutory Authority: ORS 410.740

Governor's Commission on Senior Services

Address: 500 Summer St. NE, E02, Salem 97301
Phone: 541-618-7854
Web: www.oregon.gov/DHS/SENIORS-DISABILITIES/ADVISORY/GCSS/Pages/index.aspx
Contact: Deb McCuin
Statutory Authority: ORS 410.320–410.340

Medicaid Long-Term Care Quality and Reimbursement Advisory Council

Address: 500 Summer St. NE, E02, Salem 97301
Phone: 503-945-6993
Web: www.oregon.gov/DHS/SENIORS-DISABILITIES/ADVISORY/Pages/mltcqrac.aspx
Contact: Max Brown
Statutory Authority: ORS 410.550–410.555

Oregon Disabilities Commission

Address: 500 Summer St NE, E02, Salem 97301
Phone: 971-239-6666

Web: www.oregon.gov/DHS/SENIORS-
DISABILITIES/ADVISORY/ODC/
Pages/index.aspx
Contact: Joseph Lowe
Statutory Authority: ORS 185.110–185.200
Duties and Responsibilities: The Oregon Disabilities Commission (ODC) is a governor-appointed commission within DHS. The commission is composed of 15 members broadly representative of major public and private agencies who are experienced in, or have demonstrated interest in, the needs of individuals with disabilities. Most of the members are individuals with disabilities. The ODC acts as a coordinating link between and among public and private organizations serving individuals with disabilities.

ODC works to secure economic, social, legal and political justice for individuals with disabilities through systems change. To carry this out, the commission identifies and hears the concerns of individuals with disabilities and uses the information to prioritize public policy issues which should be addressed; publicizes the needs and concerns of individuals with disabilities as they relate to the full achievement of economic, social, legal and political equity; and educates and advises the DHS, governor, Legislature and appropriate state agency administrators on how public policy can be improved to meet the needs of individuals with disabilities.

Child Welfare Programs

Address: 500 Summer St. NE, E48, Salem 97301
Phone: 503-945-5600
Fax: 503-373-7032
Web: www.oregon.gov/DHS/CHILDREN/
Pages/index.aspx
Contact: Rebecca Jones Gaston, Director
Duties and Responsibilities: The mission of DHS Child Welfare is to ensure that every child and family is empowered to live a safe, stable and healthy life. The program goals are to achieve safe and equitable reductions in the number of children experiencing foster care. This is accomplished by protecting children from abuse and neglect and safely maintaining them in their homes whenever possible and appropriate; finding safe, permanent, stable homes for children when needed; ensuring children in foster care are well cared for, remain connected to family, siblings and support networks and receive appropriate services; providing culturally appropriate and equitable treatment for all children served; and practicing quality assurance and improvement for defining, measuring and improving outcomes for children and families.

Child protection workers respond to all reports of child abuse and neglect. If a child cannot be safe at home, a foster care placement is made. The Child Welfare Program is committed to serving every child in foster care in Oregon in appropriate and culturally responsive placements that maintain their connection to communities. Child Welfare is focused on keeping children safe and reducing the number of children in foster care by supporting preventative measures for families, collaborating with community partners and ensuring a timely and safe return to families.

In federal fiscal year 2019, 10,887 children spent at least one day in foster care; 89,451 reports of abuse and neglect were received; 46,587 reports were referred for investigation; and 9,048 reports found abuse or neglect involving 13,674 victims. Of these, 42.1 percent of the victims were younger than six years old.

Child Welfare Advisory Committee
Address: 500 Summer St. NE, Salem 97301-1066
Phone: 503-945-8864
Fax: 503-373-7032
Contact: Lacey Andresen
Statutory Authority: ORS 418.005

Refugee Child Welfare Advisory Committee
Address: 500 Summer St. NE, E71, Salem 97301-1066
Phone: 503-947-5102
Fax: 503-945-6633
Contact: Angelica Quintero
Statutory Authority: ORS 418.941

Developmental Disabilities Programs

Address: 500 Summer St. NE, E09, Salem 97301
Phone: 503-945-5811; Toll-free:1-800-282-8096
Fax: 503-373-7274
Contact: Lilia Teninty, Director
Duties and Responsibilities: Intellectual and Developmental Disabilities (I/DD) Services programs provide leadership to support persons with intellectual and developmental disabilities to live as full participants in their communities. Oregon's system is built on critical partnerships among local governments, non-profits, provider agencies, self-advocates, and families. Its vision is that people and families access quality supports that are simple to use and responsive to their strengths, needs and choices, while they live and thrive as valued members of their community.

Individuals eligible for services must have an intellectual disability (IQ of 75 or below) that originates prior to age 18 or a developmental disability that originates prior to age 22. These disabilities must significantly impact a person's ability to function independently. Some persons with I/DD may also have significant medical or behavioral health needs. Most individuals with I/DD meet Medicaid financial eligibility requirements.

Most I/DD program services are administered under the Medicaid State Plan Community First Choice Option. Case management and employment services are available through traditional, home and community-based service waivers.

Oregon Council on Developmental Disabilities

Address: 2475 SE Ladd Ave., Portland 97214
Phone: 971-304-4191
Contact: Leslie Sutton, Executive Director
Statutory Authority: 42 USC 15001
Duties and Responsibilities: The council is made up of self-advocates, family members and representatives of community organizations that provide services and supports to people with developmental disabilities. Council members also include representatives of state agencies that receive federal funding on behalf of people with developmental disabilities. The governor appoints council members to serve up to two consecutive, four-year terms.

The purpose of the council is to ensure that people with developmental disabilities and family members are included in legislative and policy discussions about issues that impact their lives. Council members work together to determine goals and objectives in the five-year state plan, allocate funds to state plan activities and annually review the council's progress. The council is supported by five full-time staff who are charged with implementing the state plan. The council's mission is to advance social and policy change so people with developmental disabilities, their families and communities may live, work, play and learn together.

Self-Sufficiency Programs

Address: 500 Summer St. NE, E48, Salem 97301
Phone: 503-945-5600
Fax: 503-373-7032
Contact: Dan Haun, Director
Duties and Responsibilities: Self-Sufficiency Programs (SSP) provides low- or no-income Oregonians with benefits and services to help them find stability and stop multi-generational poverty. SSP focuses on equity, adapting services and policy to eliminate discrimination and disparities in how services are delivered. SSP benefits prioritize the safety and healthy development of children, the strength of the individual and family, and the prevention of abuse or neglect.

SSP works to achieve its mission by focusing on five foundational operating principles: family engagement, economic stability, collective impact, integrity and stewardship and professional

development. The benefits offered through SSP are Employment Related Day Care; Oregon Health Plan; Refugee Program; Supplemental Nutrition Assistance Program (SNAP); SNAP-related programs, such as its Employment and Training Program and Able-Bodied Adults without Dependents Program; Temporary Assistance for Domestic Violence Survivors; Temporary Assistance for Needy Families (TANF); TANF-related programs, such as the Job Opportunity and Basic Skills Program and Family Support and Connections; and Youth Services

Family Services Review Commission

Address: 500 Summer St. NE, E48, Salem 97301
Phone: 503-947-6071
Fax: 503-373-7032
Contact: Dan Haun, Self-Sufficiency Programs Director
Statutory Authority: ORS 411.075

LAND CONSERVATION AND DEVELOPMENT, DEPARTMENT OF

Address: 635 Capitol St. NE, Suite 150, Salem 97301-2540
Phone: 503-373-0050
Fax: 503-378-5518
Web: www.oregon.gov/LCD
Contact: Jim Rue, Director
Statutory Authority: ORS Chapters 92, 195, 196, 197, 215, 222, 227, 268, 308
Duties and Responsibilities: The Department of Land Conservation and Development (DLCD) is responsible for assisting with implementation of Oregon's statewide land use program in communities in all parts of the state. The program provides tools communities can employ to address climate change, equity and long term sustainability. DLCD provides help through technical assistance, partnerships with cities and counties, direct and applied grant assistance, and partnerships with state development agencies (Housing and Community Services, the Department of Transportation, and Business Oregon) and natural resource agencies (Agriculture, Forestry, Water Resources, State Lands, Environmental Quality and Fish and Wildlife) as well as Oregonians. The department is guided in policy development by the Land Conservation and Development Commission (LCDC) whose members are appointed by the governor.

Community Services Division

Address: 635 Capitol St. NE, Suite 150, Salem 97301-2540 (Regional Offices in Bend, Eugene, Medford and Portland)
Phone: 503-934-0034
Fax: 503-378-5518

Contact: Gordon Howard, Manager
Duties and Responsibilities: The division, formed in 2003, administers grant programs for local governments and provides technical land use planning assistance from several regional offices and Salem, to local government planners and officials, the general public and interest groups. The division reviews local comprehensive plan amendments and provides expertise on a wide range of subjects related to city and county comprehensive plans. Staff in this division include regional representatives serving local governments around the state as well as specialists in urban planning, rural resources, housing, and economic development.

Grants Advisory Committee

Address: 635 Capitol St. NE, Suite 150, Salem 97301-2540
Phone: 503-934-0034
Contact: Gordon Howard
Statutory Authority: ORS 197.639
Duties and Responsibilities: The committee is appointed by the Land Conservation and Development Commission. It advises the commission and the department on equitable and appropriate allocation of grants, technical assistance funding and other issues assigned by the commission.

Ocean and Coastal Services Division

Address: 635 Capitol St. NE, Suite 150, Salem 97301-2540 (Offices in Newport, Tillamook and Portland)
Phone: 503-373-0052
Fax: 503-378-6033
Web: www.oregon.gov/LCD/OCMP/Pages/index.aspx
Contact: Patty Snow, Manager
Duties and Responsibilities: The division, created in 1976, oversees Oregon's federally designated coastal program providing grants and technical assistance to coastal communities. The division provides assistance related to four statewide coastal planning goals and helps communities adopt local plans that address coastal hazards. The division also oversees development of Oregon's Territorial Sea Plan in cooperation with other agencies and conducts federal consistency reviews for federal projects and permits proposed in the Oregon coastal zone. Coastal staff also coordinate Oregon's Climate Change Adaptation Framework with 24 of Oregon's state agencies.

Planning Services Division

Address: 635 Capitol St. NE, Suite 150, Salem 97301-2540
Phone: 503-373-0046
Fax: 503-378-5518
Contact: Matt Crall, Manager

Duties and Responsibilities: The division oversees specialized planning programs, including the Transportation and Growth Management Program, Floodplain Management and Natural Hazards Planning, Measure 49 Services and the Oregon Sustainable Transportation Initiative. Staff in this division are chiefly responsible for supporting State Recovery Function 1: Community Planning in Oregon's Disaster Recovery Planning Process.

Other Groups:

Citizen Involvement Advisory Committee

Address: 635 Capitol St. NE, Suite 150, Salem 97301-2540
Phone: 503-373-0036
Contact: Sadie Carney
Statutory Authority: ORS 197.160
Duties and Responsibilities: The committee was established to advise LCDC and local governments on matters pertaining to public involvement in all phases of the land use planning process. It is an advisory body with no explicit or implied authority over any local government or state agency. The committee has up to eight volunteer members who serve four-year terms, including one from each of Oregon's five congressional districts and three who may be chosen at-large.

Local Officials Advisory Committee

Address: 635 Capitol St. NE, Suite 150, Salem 97301-2540
Phone: 503-373-0050
Contact: Esther Johnson
Statutory Authority: ORS 197.165
Duties and Responsibilities: LCDC appoints the committee for the purpose of promoting mutual understanding and cooperation between LCDC, DLCD and local governments in implementing and improving the statewide land use planning system. The committee is comprised of persons serving as city or county elected officials and reflects the geographic diversity of the state.

LAND USE BOARD OF APPEALS

Address: 775 Summer St. NE, Suite 330, Salem 97301-1283
Phone: 503-373-1265
Web: www.oregon.gov/luba/Pages/default.aspx
Contact: Michelle Rudd, Board Chair
Statutory Authority: ORS 197.810
Duties and Responsibilities: The 1979 Legislature created the Land Use Board of Appeals (LUBA) as an agency with exclusive jurisdiction to review

appeals of land use decisions made by cities, counties, districts and state agencies. Prior to LUBA's creation, appeals of land use decisions were heard in 36 different county circuit courts and sometimes before the Land Conservation and Development Commission. In creating LUBA, the Legislature intended to provide a simpler and faster process for resolving land use disputes and also to promote a consistent interpretation of state and local land use laws. LUBA's decisions are reviewable by appeal to the Court of Appeals. LUBA's secondary mission is to publish its orders and opinions which citizens, decision-makers and participants in land use processes can use to guide future land use decision-making.

LUBA is the first tribunal of its kind in the United States. It is a governor-appointed, three-member board, subject to confirmation by the Oregon Senate, serving four-year terms. Board members must be members of the Oregon State Bar, and the board is assisted by two administrative staff and a staff attorney.

LANDSCAPE ARCHITECT BOARD, STATE

Address: 707 13th St. SE, Suite 114, Salem 97301
Phone: 503-589-0093
Fax: 503-485-2947
Email: oslab.info@oregon.gov
Web: www.oregon.gov/LANDARCH/Pages/
default.aspx
Contact: Christine Valentine, Administrator
Statutory Authority: ORS 671.310–671.459
Duties and Responsibilities: Since 1981, the board has been charged with safeguarding Oregonians through the regulation of landscape architecture practice in the state. The board reviews complaints related to registrant practice and unlicensed practice and sets examination, education and experience standards for landscape architect licensure. The board is composed of four Oregon registered landscape architects and three public members, served by two staff filling the roles of executive director and registration specialist.

Landscape architects licensed in other states or jurisdictions can apply for registration in Oregon but must meet all of the board's standards. Firms that provide landscape architectural services must also be registered. More than 500 landscape architects are registered to practice in Oregon. Approximately 220 firms are registered with the board.

Landscape architects design, manage and protect the natural and built environment through the application of science and design expertise. They address various project components such as plantings, irrigation systems, site lighting, grading, drainage and erosion control, and settings for structures, roadways, walkways and similar features.

Landscape architects work on a wide array of private and public projects with goals to keep the public safe from hazards, protect and maximize natural resources and prevent damage to property due to changes in the built environment.

LANDSCAPE CONTRACTORS BOARD, STATE

Address: 2111 Front St. NE, Suite 2-101, Salem 97301
Phone: 503-967-6291
Fax: 503-967-6298
Email: lcb.info@oregon.gov
Web: www.oregon.gov/lcb
Contact: Elizabeth Boxall, Administrator
Statutory Authority: ORS 671.510–671.760
Duties and Responsibilities: The board was created in 1972, became semi-independent in 2002 and is responsible for regulating landscape construction work in Oregon. The agency is overseen by a board of seven individuals, appointed by the governor, who serve a maximum of six years. Five of the seven members are from the landscaping industry, and two represent the general public.

The board promotes consumer protection and contractor competency in the Oregon landscape contracting industry through five major program areas: Examinations, Licensing, Enforcement, Claims/Dispute Resolution and Education. The Board employs five staff who administer over 2,500 licensees.

The State Library Building in Salem houses the central offices of the Oregon State Library. (Oregon State Archives scenic photo)

LIBRARY, STATE

Address: 250 Winter St. NE, Salem 97301-3950
Phone: 503-378-4243
Fax: 503-585-8059
Web: www.oregon.gov/library
Contact: Jennifer Patterson, State Librarian
Statutory Authority: ORS Chapter 357

Duties and Responsibilities: The library provides information services to state government, library services to Oregonians who are print-disabled, and leadership, grants and other assistance to improve library service for all Oregonians. It was established as the Oregon Library Commission in 1905, becoming the Oregon State Library in 1913. The present State Library board consists of nine members from throughout the state who are appointed by the governor. The library is organized into an operations division and three program divisions.

The Government Information and Library Services Division provides research and reference assistance to state government and to persons on official state business. Collections include federal and state government publications and a comprehensive collection of materials about Oregon. The library also provides public access to Oregon state government documents.

The Library Support and Development Services Division includes planning for statewide library development; providing equal access to information resources for K–12 students through the Oregon School Library Information System; collecting and reporting library statistics; and administering state and federal library grant programs.

The Oregon Talking Book and Braille Library is the Oregon Regional Library for the Library of Congress' National Library Service for the Blind and Print Disabled. Oregonians with a print disability, which includes visual, physical and reading impairments, are eligible for free library services. Books and magazines are available in audio format and in braille.

LIQUOR CONTROL COMMISSION, OREGON

Address: 9079 SE McLoughlin Blvd., Portland 97222-7355
Phone: 503-872-5000; Toll-free: 1-800-452-6522
Fax: 503-872-5266
Web: www.oregon.gov/olcc/Pages/default.aspx
Contact: Steve Marks, Executive Director
Statutory Authority: ORS Chapters 471, 472, 473, 475B
Duties and Responsibilities: The Oregon Liquor Control Commission (OLCC) supports businesses, public safety and community livability through education and the enforcement of liquor and marijuana laws. OLCC places emphasis on addressing alcohol and marijuana sales to minors and visibly intoxicated people.

OLCC was created in 1933 by a special legislative session after national prohibition ended. The agency advocates responsible alcohol consumption by managing and distributing distilled spirits, licensing and regulating businesses that sell and serve alcohol and training and issuing permits for alcohol servers. In 2014, the agency took on added responsibilities of licensing, regulating and tracking Oregon's new recreational marijuana industry, as well as issuing marijuana worker permits. The OLCC is also responsible for administering Oregon's Bottle Bill.

Seven citizen commissioners set policy for the OLCC. The agency also relies on advisory committees, government officials and citizens to guide its decision-making. The agency employs 332 people and has four regional and numerous satellite offices throughout the state. Through the sale of distilled spirits and beer and wine privilege fees, OLCC is the third-largest revenue generator for the state, with a 2019–2021 biennium value of over $1.5 billion.

LONG-TERM CARE OMBUDSMAN, OFFICE OF THE

Address: 3855 Wolverine St. NE, Suite 6, Salem 97305-1251
Phone: 503-378-6533; Toll-free: 1-800-522-2602; TTY: 711
Fax: 503-373-0852
Email: ltco.info@oregon.gov
Web: www.oregon.gov/ltco
Contact: Fred Steele, Long-Term Care Ombudsman and Director
Statutory Authority: ORS 441.402–441.419
Duties and Responsibilities: The office includes three programs: Long-Term Care Ombudsman, the Residential Facilities Ombudsman and the Oregon Public Guardian. The office works to protect individual rights, promote independence and ensure quality of life for Oregonians living in long-term care and residential facilities and for Oregonians with decisional limitations.

The agency's two Ombudsman programs investigate and resolve complaints on behalf of residents, using a network of trained and certified volunteer ombudsmen. The Oregon Public Guardian program serves as a court-appointed, surrogate decision maker for adults incapable of making decisions about themselves and their affairs, and who have no one else to serve as their guardian or conservator.

LOTTERY, OREGON STATE

Address: PO Box 12649, Salem 97309
Phone: 503-540-1000; TTY: 503-540-1068
Fax: 503-540-1168
Email: lottery.webcenter@state.or.us
Web: www.oregonlottery.org
Contact: Barry Pack, Director
Statutory Authority: ORS Chapter 461
Duties and Responsibilities: As a result of two voter initiatives, Oregonians created the Oregon Lottery in 1984. The lottery's mission, "Operate a lottery with the highest standards of security and

integrity to earn maximum profits for the people of Oregon commensurate with the public good," directs the efforts of the over 500 statewide lottery employees. Oregon's lottery is both a public trust and a market-driven business. Lottery revenues—over $1 billion a year since 2006—result in transfers to the state to help fund public endeavors.

ORS 461.500 provides that at least 84 percent of total annual revenues be returned to the public, with at least 50 percent being returned as prizes and the remainder used for designated public purposes. The remaining 16 percent of annual revenues are available for the payment of administrative expenses. Lottery administrative expenses are currently at just under 4 percent of revenue, which makes the agency entirely self-funded.

Since it began selling tickets in 1985, the Oregon Lottery has grown to become the second largest revenue producer for the state, following income tax revenues. Since 1985, the lottery has transferred over $12 billion to help support public education, economic development, state parks and watershed enhancement, as well as veterans affairs and Outdoor School. It has also paid players over $40 billion in prizes and provided nearly $100 million for problem gambling treatment and awareness.

MARINE BOARD, STATE

Address: 435 Commercial St. NE, # 400, Salem 97301; Mail: PO Box 14145, Salem 97309-5065
Phone: 503-378-8587
Fax: 503-378-4597
Email: marine.board@state.or.us
Web: www.oregon.gov/OSMB/Pages/index.aspx
Contact: Larry Warren, Director
Statutory Authority: ORS Chapter 830
Duties and Responsibilities: The agency is responsible for titling and registering motorboats, registering outfitter/guides, co-managing aquatic invasive species inspection stations throughout the state, licensing charter boats, and issuing Waterway Access Permits for non-motorized boats 10 feet long and longer.

The five-member volunteer board adopts boating regulations to promote safety, reduce conflict, preserve traditional boat uses and protect the environment. The agency has 38 staff and four primary program areas: Boating Safety, Policy and Environmental, Registration, and Boating Facilities.

The revenue generated helps fund the agency and contracts with county sheriff's offices and the Oregon State Police for statewide marine patrol services. Funding also provides boating facility grants and engineering services to eligible applicants to develop and maintain boat ramps, parking, restrooms and temporary moorage facilities. Additionally, funding supports environmental and educational programs to promote environmental stewardship and boating safety.

MASSAGE THERAPISTS, STATE BOARD OF

Address: 728 Hawthorne Ave. NE, Salem 97301
Phone: 503-365-8657
Fax: 503-385-4465
Email: OBMT.info@state.or.us
Web: www.oregon.gov/OBMT/Pages/index.aspx
Contact: Robert Ruark, Executive Director
Statutory Authority: ORS 687.011–687.991
Duties and Responsibilities: The functions of the board date back to 1951 when the Legislature adopted a comprehensive bill for the Oregon State Board of Examiners, which was empowered to regulate conduct for massage establishments, issue licenses, refuse, revoke or suspend licenses and establish requirements for massage schools. In 1975, Senate Bill 390 passed, and the administration for licensing massage therapists changed to the State Board of Massage Therapists. The mission of the board is to protect the public by regulating and monitoring the practice of massage therapy in Oregon.

MEDICAL BOARD, OREGON

Address: 1500 SW 1st Ave., #620, Portland 97201-5847
Phone: 971-673-2700
Fax: 971-673-2670
Email: info@omb.oregon.gov
Web: www.oregon.gov/OMB
Contact: Nicole Krishnaswami, JD, Executive Director
Statutory Authority: ORS Chapter 677
Duties and Responsibilities: The board has been protecting Oregon citizens through the regulation of the practice of medicine since 1889. The agency now licenses and regulates medical doctors (MD), doctors of osteopathic medicine (DO), doctors of podiatric medicine (DPM), physician assistants (PA) and acupuncturists (LAc).

The 14-member board is composed of physicians, a physician assistant, and three members of the public. The board sets qualifications for licensure and grants licenses to applicants who meet those requirements. It investigates complaints and disciplines licensees who violate state law (the Medical Practice Act). The board also supports rehabilitation and education for licensees in an effort to promote access to quality care for all Oregonians. The board oversees more than 23,000 licensees and is staffed with 41 employees.

MEDICAL IMAGING, BOARD OF

Address: 800 NE Oregon St., Suite 1160A, Portland 97232
Phone: 971-673-0215

Fax: 971-673-0218
Email: OBMI.Info@state.or.us
Web: www.oregon.gov/OBMI/Pages/index.aspx
Contact: Stacy Katler. DVM, Executive Director
Statutory Authority: ORS 688.405–688.605, 688.915
Duties and Responsibilities: Created by legislation in 1977, the board currently licenses and oversees over 5,700 medical imaging technologists who are qualified to practice radiography, radiation therapy, sonography, nuclear medicine and magnetic resonance imaging (MRI). In addition, the board oversees the educational requirements and issues permits for over 400 limited x-ray machine operators. Licensure assures that imaging technologists are properly educated and trained. Accurate imaging procedures improve patient safety and help contain health costs by aiding in the prevention of health problems through effective diagnosis and treatment. Members of the board are appointed by the governor and confirmed by the Senate for three-year terms. There are twelve board members, including four physicians, three public members and five medical imaging licensees who represent each of the five medical imaging modalities. The board has four employees.

The State Office Building in Portland houses the central offices of the Board of Medical Imaging. (Oregon State Archives scenic photo)

MENTAL HEALTH REGULATORY AGENCY

Address: 3218 Pringle Rd. SE, Suite 130, Salem 97302-6309
Phone: 503-378-4154
Fax: 503-374-1904
Web: www.oregon.gov/MHRA
Contact: Charles J. Hill, Executive Director
Statutory Authority: ORS 675.160–675.178
Duties and Responsibilities: The agency was created to provide administrative and regulatory oversight to the Board of Psychology and the Board of Licensed Professional Counselors and Therapists. The agency performs the functions of budgeting, recordkeeping, staffing, contracting, procedure and policymaking, and performance and standard setting for the regulated boards. The boards maintain their own separate authority for complaint investigations, regulatory enforcement, establishment and collection of fees, licensing criteria and practice standards.

Counselors and Therapists, Oregon Board of Licensed Professional

Address: 3218 Pringle Rd. SE, Suite 120, Salem 97302-6312
Phone: 503-378-5499
Email: lpct.board@oregon.gov
Web: www.oregon.gov/OBLPCT/Pages/index.aspx
Contact: Charles Hill, Executive Director
Statutory Authority: ORS 675.705–675.835
Duties and Responsibilities: The board was created in 1989 to protect Oregon consumers seeking mental health counseling and marriage and family therapy services. The board determines if individuals meet initial and continuing education, training and examination standards for licensure and issues new and renewal licenses to those who are qualified. The board develops policies and standards for professional practice and enforces disciplinary action against counselors, therapists and interns who engage in misconduct or are incompetent. It also issues civil penalties to individuals practicing in Oregon without a license or engaging in misrepresentation. The eight members of the board are appointed by the governor and confirmed by the Senate for three-year terms.

Psychology, Oregon Board of

Address: 3218 Pringle Rd. SE, Suite 130, Salem 97302-6309
Phone: 503-378-4154
Email: psychology.board@oregon.gov
Web: www.oregon.gov/psychology
Contact: Charles J. Hill, Executive Director
Statutory Authority: ORS 675.010–675.150
Duties and Responsibilities: The board was created in 1963 to protect Oregon consumers of psychological services. The board determines if individuals meet initial and continuing education, training and examination standards for licensure and issues new and renewal licenses to those who are qualified. The board develops policies and standards for professional practice and enforces disciplinary action against psychologists, psychologist associates and residents who engage in misconduct or are incompetent. It also issues civil penalties to individuals practicing in Oregon without a license or engaging in misrepresentation. The nine members of the board are appointed by the

governor and confirmed by the Senate for three-year terms.

MILITARY DEPARTMENT, OREGON

Address: 230 Geer Dr. NE, Salem 97301;
Mail: PO Box 14350, Salem 97309-5047
Phone: 503-584-3985
Web: https://www.oregon.gov/OMD/Pages/Home.aspx
Statutory Authority: ORS 396.305
Duties and Responsibilities: The Oregon Military Department (OMD) was the first state agency created in Oregon. It administers, equips and trains the Oregon Army and Air National Guard. During peacetime and for natural disasters, the department responds to the governor in support of the citizens of Oregon. During wartime, the Oregon Army and Air National Guard can be federalized in support of national missions as directed by the U.S. president.

Command Group

Address: PO Box 14350, Salem 97309-5047
Phone: 503-584-3991
Email: tagor@mil.state.or.us
Web: https://www.oregon.gov/OMD/Pages/Home.aspx
Contact: Major General Michael E. Stencel, Adjutant General
Duties and Responsibilities: The Command Group consists of the Adjutant General Deputy Director; Joint Force Headquarters, including the Assistant Adjutants General for support and operations; and the Land and Air Component Commanders. The group administers all components of the Oregon Military Department/National Guard in cooperation with the governor and Legislature.

Deputy Director, State Affairs

Phone: 503-584-3884
Email: agdd@mil.state.or.us
Contact: Dave Stuckey, Deputy Director
Duties and Responsibilities: The deputy director functions as liaison to the governor's office, Oregon's senators, representatives, congressional delegates and other governmental agencies. This position provides supervisory oversight of the state division offices within OMD, including the Adjutant General's Comptroller, Installations, Personnel, Office of Emergency Management and Oregon's Youth Challenge Program.

Emergency Management, Office of

Address: 3225 State St., Rm. 115, Salem 97301;
Mail: PO Box 14370, Salem 97309-5062
Phone: 503-378-2911

Web: https://www.oregon.gov/OEM/Pages/default.aspx
Contact: Andrew Phelps, Director
Statutory Authority: ORS Chapter 401
Duties and Responsibilities: The office executes the governor's responsibilities to maintain an emergency services system to deal with emergencies or disasters that may present threats to the lives and property of Oregon's citizens. The office coordinates and facilitates emergency planning, preparedness, response and recovery activities with state and local emergency service agencies and organizations.

Installations Division

Address: PO Box 14350, Salem 97309-5047
Phone: 503-584-3914
Contact: Stan Hutchison, Director
Duties and Responsibilities: The division provides and maintains quality installations to support the missions of the Oregon National Guard. The division supports the Oregon National Guard and the citizens of Oregon by providing facilities for localized and statewide emergencies, training and housing soldiers and equipment and by providing environmental support for tactical training and the execution of federal and state missions. The division's rental program allows community groups and private parties to use armories on an as-available basis.

Public Affairs Office

Address: AGPA, PO Box 14350, Salem 97309-5047
Phone: 503-584-3917
Email: agpa@mil.state.or.us
Contact: Stephen Bomar, Director
Duties and Responsibilities: The office supports the Adjutant General's communication plan and is responsible to support information efforts for all Oregon Army and Air National Guard public, community and media relations including community outreach, social media, print, video and graphic design efforts.

Youth Challenge Program

Address: 23861 Dodds Rd., Bend 97701
Phone: 541-317-9623
Web: https://www.oycp.com/
Contact: Dan Radabaugh, Director
Duties and Responsibilities: The Oregon National Guard Youth Challenge Program is a statewide accredited, public, alternative high school that serves 16 to 18-year-old high school dropouts. The program is guided by military principles, structure and discipline and consists of two phases. During the residential phase, cadets (students) live on-site for five months and attend school, where

they earn credits to return to high school and earn their GED or high school diploma. The post-residential phase is a mandatory 12-month mentoring period during which cadets work with mentors from their home towns.

MORTUARY AND CEMETERY BOARD, STATE

Address: 800 NE Oregon St., Suite 430, Portland 97232-2195
Phone: 971-673-1500
Fax: 971-673-1501
Email: mortuary.board@state.or.us
Web: www.oregon.gov/MortCem/Pages/index.aspx
Contact: Chad Dresselhaus, Executive Director
Statutory Authority: ORS 97.170, 97.931, 692.300, 692.415
Duties and Responsibilities: The board was established on June 6, 1921. Its programs affect those who have suffered a loss, who make final arrangements and who provide death care goods and services. In order to protect the public, it is the board's responsibility to ensure that all of Oregon's death care facilities are properly licensed and to regulate the practice of individuals and facilities engaged in the care, preparation, processing, transportation and final disposition of human remains. Death care services are provided by approximately 2,400 licensed practitioners and facilities throughout the state. The board consists of 11 board members and seven employees.

NATUROPATHIC MEDICINE, OREGON BOARD OF

Address: 800 NE Oregon St., Suite 407, Portland 97232
Phone: 971-673-0193
Fax: 971-673-0226
Email: naturopathic.medicine@state.or.us
Web: www.oregon.gov/obnm
Contact: Mary-Beth Baptista, Executive Director
Statutory Authority: ORS Chapter 685
Duties and Responsibilities: The board was established by the 1927 Legislature to protect consumers of naturopathic medicine by enforcing practice standards. The profession has grown from 200 in 1998 to over 1,150 in 2019. The board is staffed with three full-time equivalent positions to support the seven-member board that includes two public members and five licensed naturopathic physicians. The board carries out the provisions of its authority by conducting background checks; examining, issuing and renewing licenses; approving educational opportunities for licensees; investigating

complaints; and taking action when discipline is appropriate.

NORTHWEST POWER AND CONSERVATION COUNCIL

Address: 851 SW 6th Ave., Portland 97204-1347
Phone: 503-229-5171
Fax: 503-229-5173
Email: info@nwcouncil.org
Contact: Richard Devlin, Ted Ferrioli, Oregon Council Members
Statutory Authority: ORS 469.805
Duties and Responsibilities: The council came into being with the passage of the Northwest Power Act of 1980. The Power Act established an interstate compact consisting of Oregon, Washington, Montana and Idaho, each state having two governor-appointed representatives. The council has two major planning functions under the Act: developing a fish and wildlife program to protect, mitigate and enhance fish and wildlife populations affected by the development of the federal Columbia River hydropower system; and developing a 20-year regional power plan. The council updates these plans on a roughly five-year rotation. The council strives to ensure, through public participation, an affordable and reliable energy system while enhancing fish and wildlife in the Columbia River Basin. In addition to the eight council members, there is a staff of approximately 50, located in offices spread throughout the four states.

NURSING, OREGON STATE BOARD OF

Address: 17938 SW Upper Boones Ferry Rd., Portland 97224-7012
Phone: 971-673-0685
Fax: 971-673-0684
Email: oregon.bn.info@state.or.us
Web: www.oregon.gov/OSBN/Pages/index.aspx
Contact: Ruby R. Jason, MSN, RN, NEA-BC, Executive Director
Statutory Authority: ORS 678.010–678.445
Duties and Responsibilities: Since 1911, the Oregon State Board of Nursing (OSBN) has regulated nursing practice and education to protect the public. It oversees the licensure, certification, and compliance of the approximately 90,000 registered nurses, licensed practical nurses, nursing assistants, and advanced practice nurses in Oregon.

The nine OSBN board members are appointed by the governor and include a mix of public members and nursing professionals. They represent a variety of nursing practice settings and geographic locations and serve three-year terms. The OSBN meets monthly and may hold special meetings if necessary. The OSBN employs a staff of about 50 who provide customer service and assist the board in carrying out its mission.

OCCUPATIONAL THERAPY LICENSING BOARD

Address: 800 NE Oregon St., Suite 407, Portland 97232
Phone: 971-673-0198
Fax: 971-673-0226
Email: nancy.schuberg@state.or.us
Web: www.oregon.gov/otlb
Contact: Nancy Schuberg, Executive Director
Statutory Authority: ORS 675.210–675.340
Duties and Responsibilities: The board was created in 1977 to regulate the practice of occupational therapy. The role of the board is to investigate complaints and take appropriate action, make and enforce laws and rules regarding occupational therapy practice, establish continuing education requirements, process applications and issue license and renewals and collect fees and authorize disbursements of funds. The mission of the board is to protect the public by supervising occupational therapy practice. The board is comprised of five volunteer members: two occupational therapists, one occupational therapy assistant and two public members. Each member is appointed by the governor and may serve up to two four-year terms.

OPTOMETRY, OREGON BOARD OF

Address: 1500 Liberty St. SE, Suite 210, Salem 97302
Phone: 503-399-0662
Fax: 503-914-5142
Email: shelley.g.sneed@oregon.gov
Web: www.oregon.gov/obo/Pages/index.aspx
Contact: Shelley Sneed, Executive Director
Statutory Authority: ORS Chapter 683
Duties and Responsibilities: The board was enacted in 1905 to protect Oregonians from the dangers of unqualified and improper practice of optometry. The board is comprised of five governor-appointed members: four are licensed optometrists, and one is a public member. Members serve three-year terms and oversee the agency and its functions. The board is assisted by two full-time staff who help board members enforce the agency's laws and rules. There are currently about 1,200 active and inactive licensed optometrists in Oregon. Oregonians can submit online complaints to the board for review if they believe an optometrist has breached Oregon law or given an improper

standard of care. The board does not handle fee disputes.

PARKS AND RECREATION DEPARTMENT, STATE

Address: 725 Summer St. NE, Suite C, Salem 97301
Phone: 503-986-0707;
Campground Reservations: 1-800-452-5687;
Parks Information: 1-800-551-6949
Fax: 503-986-0794
Email: Lisa.sumption@oregon.gov
Web: www.oregon.gov/OPRD/Pages/index.aspx
Contact: Lisa Sumption, Director
Statutory Authority: ORS Chapters 97, 358, 390
Duties and Responsibilities: The Oregon Parks and Recreation Department (OPRD) exists to protect and provide outstanding natural, scenic, recreational, cultural and historic places for the enjoyment and education of present and future generations. The state park tradition in Oregon began in 1922 with the first state park: a land donation on the Luckiamute River in the Willamette Valley became what is now Sarah Helmick State Recreation Site. Originally a division of the Highway Commission and later its successor, the Oregon Department of Transportation, the State Parks and Recreation Department was created as an independent agency in 1989.

As the state park system celebrates its centennial in 2022, OPRD continues to focus on protecting Oregon's outdoor and historic places, providing opportunities for great experiences and sustaining Oregon's quality outdoor recreation and heritage resources for the future. OPRD oversees one of the most popular state park systems in the nation—more than 250 properties providing more than 50 million visits a year—and manages other key recreation and heritage programs: Oregon's stunning public ocean shore, scenic waterways and bikeways, the State Historic Preservation Office, archaeological services, historic cemeteries and all-terrain vehicle safety certifications. OPRD programs serve Oregon communities directly with grants and advice related to outdoor recreation, museums and historic "Main Street" revitalization.

OPRD has about 595 full-time equivalent staff, with a large number of employees being seasonal. The governor-appointed State Parks and Recreation Commission sets OPRD's policy direction.

Historic Preservation Office, State

Address: 725 Summer St. NE, Suite C, Salem 97301
Phone: 503-986-0684
Fax: 503-986-0793

Email: chrissy.curran@oregon.gov
Web: www.oregon.gov/oprd/HCD/SHPO/
Pages/index.aspx
Contact: Christine Curran, Heritage Division
Manager and Deputy State Historic Preservation
Officer
Statutory Authority: ORS 358.612
Duties and Responsibilities: The office was
established in 1967, a year after the U.S. Congress
passed the National Historic Preservation Act.
Under federal and state mandates, the office
manages programs that create opportunities for
individuals, organizations and local governments to
become directly involved in the protection of significant historic and cultural resources. The office
creates these opportunities through archaeological
services, grant programs, planning assistance, tax
incentive programs and federal programs such as
the National Register of Historic Places. In addition, the Certified Local Government Program and
the Oregon Main Street Network collaborate with
communities to develop comprehensive revitalization strategies based on a community's unique
assets, character and heritage.
The OPRD director is Oregon's designated State
Historic Preservation Officer.

Historic Preservation, State Advisory Committee on

Address: 725 Summer St. NE, Suite C, Salem
97301
Phone: 503-986-0684
Fax: 503-986-0793
Email: chrissy.curran@oregon.gov
Web: www.oregon.gov/oprd/OH/Pages/
Commissions.aspx
Contact: Christine Curran, Deputy State Historic
Preservation Officer
Statutory Authority: ORS 358.622
Duties and Responsibilities: The committee is a
nine-member group that reviews nominations to
the National Register of Historic Places. The mem-
bers are professionally recognized in the fields of
history, architecture, archaeology and other
related disciplines. The committee holds public
meetings in February, June and October each year
at different locations within the state.

Heritage Commission, Oregon

Address: 725 Summer St. NE, Suite C, Salem
97301
Phone: 503-986-0671
Fax: 503-986-0793
Email: katie.henry@oregon.gov
Web: www.oregon.gov/oprd/OH/Pages/
Commissions.aspx
Contact: Katie Henry, Coordinator
Statutory Authority: ORS 358.570

Duties and Responsibilities: The commission,
established to secure, sustain, enhance and promote
Oregon's heritage, is a nine-member, governor-
appointed commission that has broad responsibilities as a connector and catalyst for hundreds of
organizations and thousands of Oregonians devoted to preserving and interpreting Oregon's heritage
resources. Its programs include the Heritage and
Museum Grant Programs, technical assistance for
heritage organizations and an annual conference. It
also gives annual Heritage Excellence Awards and
designates Oregon Heritage Traditions, All-Star
Communities and Statewide Celebrations.

Historic Cemeteries, Oregon Commission on

Address: 725 Summer St. NE, Suite C, Salem
97301
Phone: 503-986-0685
Fax: 503-986-0793
Email: kuri.gill@oregon.gov
Web: www.oregon.gov/oprd/OH/Pages/
Commissions.aspx
Contact: Kuri Gill, Coordinator
Statutory Authority: ORS 97.772–97.784
Duties and Responsibilities: Established in 1999,
the commission maintains a list of historic ceme-
teries and gravesites in Oregon. It works to promote
public education on the significance of historic
cemeteries and to provide financial and technical
assistance for restoring, improving and maintaining
their appearance.

Outdoor Recreation, Office of

Address: 725 Summer St. NE, Suite C, Salem
97301
Phone: 503-986-0740
Fax: 503-986-0792
Email: cailin.obrienfeeney@oregon.gov
Web: www.oregon.gov/OPRD/Pages/office-of-
outdoor-rec.aspx
Contact: Cailin O'Brien-Feeney
Statutory Authority: ORS 390.233
Duties and Responsibilities: Established in 2017,
the office was created to elevate the success of
outdoor recreation in every corner of the state.
Working at the policy level, the office pulls support
from public, nonprofit and commercial organizations to protect and expand access, promote participation and protect the natural resources upon
which outdoor recreation depends. Through policy
coordination, research and reporting, and development of common strategies across the public and
private sectors, the office works to ensure outdoor
recreation delivers personal, community and economic benefits in perpetuity.

PAROLE AND POST-PRISON SUPERVISION, STATE BOARD OF

Address: 1321 Tandem Ave. NE, Salem 97301
Phone: 503-945-9009
Fax: 503-373-7558
Web: https://www.oregon.gov/boppps
Contact: Dylan Arthur, Executive Director; Michael Hsu, Board Chair
Statutory Authority: ORS Chapters 144, 163A
Duties and Responsibilities: The board supports a safe and just Oregon by protecting citizens' rights and promoting positive offender change while maintaining accountability. The first State Parole board was created in 1911. In 1969, the board became a full-time agency with three board members. In 1975, the board was enlarged to five members, with the stipulation that at least one member must be a woman. The governor appoints members to four-year terms and also determines the chair and vice-chair. Members can serve a maximum of two terms. Staff consists of an executive director, a supervising executive assistant and 22 support staff. The board works closely with the Department of Corrections and local community corrections agencies to protect the public and reduce the risk of repeat criminal behavior through incarceration and community supervision decisions based on applicable laws, victims' interests, public safety and recognized principles of offender behavioral change.

The board imposes prison terms and makes release decisions on offenders whose criminal conduct occurred prior to November 1, 1989. It sets conditions of supervision for all offenders being released from prison, imposes sanctions for violations of supervision and determines whether discharge from parole supervision is compatible with public safety. Discharge from supervision for offenders sentenced under sentencing guidelines occurs automatically upon expiration of the statutory period of post-prison supervision.

In 2015, the board became responsible for assessing and classifying all registered sex offenders in Oregon into a notification level, based on risk to re-offend. This system improves community education and notification of high-risk registered sex offenders in Oregon (Level 3) and introduces opportunities for low risk offenders (Levels 2 and 1) to be reclassified to a lower notification level and receive relief from registration if they meet statutory requirements.

PATIENT SAFETY COMMISSION, OREGON

Address: PO Box 285, Portland 97207-0285
Phone: 503-928-6158

Fax: 503-224-9150
Email: info@oregonpatientsafety.org
Web: oregonpatientsafety.org
Contact: Heidi Steeves, Executive Director
Statutory Authority: ORS 442.820–442.835, Oregon Laws 2013, Chapter 5
Duties and Responsibilities: The Oregon Patient Safety Commission (OPSC) is a semi-independent state agency that supports healthcare facilities and providers in improving patient safety by encouraging broad information sharing, ongoing education, and open conversations to cultivate a more trusted healthcare system. OPSC also encourages all users and representatives of Oregon's healthcare system to work on shared goals that advance the mission—to reduce the risk of patient harm and encourage a culture of patient safety.

OPSC fulfills its mission through two main initiatives. The Patient Safety Reporting Program collects and analyzes information from healthcare facilities about serious patient harm or near misses. It shares the broader lessons learned to support facilities in refining their best practices and preventing future harm. The voluntary Early Discussion and Resolution process helps connect patients (or a family member) who experience harm and their healthcare provider so that they can speak candidly about the harm that occurred, work toward reconciliation and contribute to safeguarding others from similar harm.

OPSC's body of work is independent of any regulatory functions and seeks to advance, support, and encourage patient safety in Oregon.

PHARMACY, STATE BOARD OF

Address: 800 NE Oregon St., Suite 150, Portland 97232-2162
Phone: 971-673-0001
Fax: 971-673-0002
Email: pharmacy.board@oregon.gov
Web: www.oregon.gov/Pharmacy/Pages/index.aspx
Contact: Joseph Schnabel, Executive Director
Statutory Authority: ORS Chapters 475, 689
Duties and Responsibilities: The board was created in 1891 and consists of nine members appointed by the governor: five licensed pharmacists, two public members and two pharmacy technicians. There are also 22 staff members, led by the executive director. The duty of the board is to regulate the practice of pharmacy through licensure and compliance. Currently, there are 20,001 licensees, including individuals and drug outlets.

In 2018, the Public Health and Pharmacy Formulary Advisory Committee was established by law. This seven-member committee is appointed by the governor and consists of two physicians, two advanced practice nurses and three pharmacists.

The committee recommends to the Board of Pharmacy a formulary of drugs and devices that a pharmacist may prescribe and dispense to a patient pursuant to a diagnosis by a qualified health care practitioner.

PHYSICAL THERAPY, OREGON BOARD OF

Address: 800 NE Oregon St., Suite 407, Portland 97232-2187
Phone: 971-673-0200
Fax: 971-673-0226
Web: www.oregon.gov/PT
Contact: Michelle Sigmund-Gaines, Executive Director
Statutory Authority: ORS 688.160
Duties and Responsibilities: The board was created in 1971 to regulate the practice of physical therapy in Oregon. Its primary purpose is the protection of the public. The board achieves this by establishing and regulating professional standards of practice, which ensure that physical therapists and physical therapist assistants are properly educated, hold valid/current licenses, practice within their scope of practice and continue to receive ongoing training throughout their careers. Physical therapy practice is governed by state statutes and rules that define the scope of practice. The board issues licenses, promulgates rules, monitors continuing competency, investigates complaints, issues civil penalties for violations and may revoke, suspend or impose probation on a licensee or place limits on a licensee's practice.

The board regulates over 5,800 active licensees and is comprised of eight volunteer members: five physical therapists, one physical therapist assistant and two public members. Each member is appointed by the governor and confirmed by the Senate to serve a four-year term. A board member may be reappointed to one subsequent term.

The Oregon State Police Office Building in Salem houses the State Police and Fire Marshal. (Oregon State Archives scenic photo)

POLICE, DEPARTMENT OF STATE

Address: 3565 Trelstad Ave. SE, Salem 97317
Phone: 503-378-3720
Fax: 503-378-8282
Email: ask.osp@state.or.us
Web: www.oregon.gov/osp/Pages/index.aspx
Contact: Terri Davie, Superintendent
Statutory Authority: ORS 181A.015
Duties and Responsibilities: The department was created in 1931 to serve as a rural patrol and to assist local city police and sheriffs' departments. Some of the agency's specialized programs and services include transportation safety; major crime investigations; forensic services, including DNA identification, automated fingerprint identification and computerized criminal history files; drug investigation; fish and wildlife enforcement; gambling enforcement and regulation; state emergency response coordination; state Fire Marshal Service and Conflagration Act coordination; coordination of federal grants for public safety issues; coordination of Criminal Justice Information Standards; medical examiner services; Special Weapons and Tactics (SWAT); and serving as the point of contact to the National Office of Homeland Security.

The department employs more than 1,300 sworn and professional staff.

Criminal Investigations Division

Address: 3565 Trelstad Ave. SE, Salem 97317
Phone: 503-378-3720
Fax: 503-378-8282
Email: ask.osp@state.or.us
Web: www.oregon.gov/osp/programs/Pages/CID.aspx
Contact: Captain Jon Harrington
Statutory Authority: ORS 181A.145
Duties and Responsibilities: The division is the investigative resource of the Department of State Police and delivers statewide services in support of the agency's vision to provide "Premier Public Safety Services for Oregon." The division's Major Crimes Section, Drug Enforcement Section and Sex Offender Registration Unit work in conjunction with other state police divisions to enhance livability and safety by protecting the people, property and natural resources of Oregon.

Detectives are strategically located across the state to support local law enforcement with major criminal investigations and to serve on interagency teams. They also provide primary criminal investigative services on state property and at state institutions.

Criminal Justice Information Systems and Law Enforcement Data System

Address: 3565 Trelstad Ave. SE, Salem 97317
Phone: 503-378-5565
Fax: 503-378-2121
Email: Helpdesk.leds@state.or.us
Web: www.oregon.gov/osp/programs/cjis/
pages/default.aspx
Statutory Authority: ORS 181A.280
Duties and Responsibilities: The systems provide information-sharing services for security background checks and for assisting law enforcement and criminal justice agencies in their investigations. The unit also includes the Oregon State Athletic Commission that works to protect the public and participants involved in ring sports.

Fish and Wildlife Division

Address: 3565 Trelstad Ave. SE, Salem 97317
Phone: 503-378-3720
Fax: 503-378-8282
Email: osp.fwd@state.or.us
Web: www.oregon.gov/osp/programs/fw/
pages/default.aspx
Contact: Captain Casey Thomas
Statutory Authority: ORS 181A.015
Duties and Responsibilities: The division works to achieve compliance with the laws and regulations that protect and enhance the long-term health and equitable utilization of Oregon's fish and wildlife resources and the habitats upon which they depend. Other important services include public safety and enforcement of criminal and traffic laws.

Forensic Science & Pathology Bureau

Address: 3565 Trelstad Ave. SE, Salem 97317
Phone: 503-378-3720
Fax: 503-363-5475
Email: osp.forensics@state.or.us
Web: www.oregon.gov/osp/programs/forensics/
Pages/default.aspx
Contact: Major Alex Gardner
Statutory Authority: ORS 181A.150
Duties and Responsibilities: The bureau is a nationally-accredited, forensic laboratory system serving all state and local law enforcement agencies, medical examiners and prosecuting attorneys in Oregon. It also performs forensic analysis on criminal cases for the defense upon a court order. The bureau provides Oregon's only full service forensic laboratory system. Analysts provide technical assistance and training, evaluate and analyze evidence, interpret results and provide expert testimony related to the full spectrum of physical evidence recovered from crime scenes.

Gaming Division

Address: 3400 State St., G-750, Salem 97301
Phone: 503-378-6999
Fax: 503-378-6878
Email: ask.osp@state.or.us
Web: www.oregon.gov/osp/programs/Pages/
Gaming-Enforcement.aspx
Contact: Major Joel Lujan
Statutory Authority: ORS 181A.090
Duties and Responsibilities: The division consists of the Lottery Gaming Section and Tribal Gaming Section, both working to ensure that all gaming activities are conducted with fairness, integrity, honesty and security.

Medical Examiner Division

Address: 13309 SE 84th Ave., Suite 100,
Clackamas 97015
Phone: 971-673-8200
Email: osp.forensics@state.or.us
Web: www.oregon.gov/osp/programs/pages/
med.aspx
Contact: Dr. Sean Hurst, Medical Examiner
Statutory Authority: ORS Chapter 146
Duties and Responsibilities: The division provides direction and support to the state death investigation program. The medical examiner manages all aspects of the state medical examiner program and has responsibility for technical supervision of county offices in each of Oregon's 36 counties.

Patrol Services Division

Address: 3565 Trelstad Ave. SE, Salem 97317
Phone: 503-378-3720
Fax: 503-378-8282
Email: ask.osp@state.or.us
Web: www.oregon.gov/osp/programs/Pages/
PSD.aspx
Contact: Captain Stephanie Ingraham
Statutory Authority: ORS Chapter 181A
Duties and Responsibilities: The division provides a uniform presence and law enforcement services throughout the state with a primary responsibility for crash and crime reduction and other transportation safety issues, as well as to respond to emergency calls-for-service on Oregon's state and interstate highways.

State Fire Marshal, Office of

Address: 3565 Trelstad Ave. SE, Salem 97317
Phone: 503-378-3473
Fax: 503-373-1825
Email: oregon.sfm@state.or.us
Web: www.oregon.gov/osp/programs/sfm/
pages/default.aspx
Contact: Mariana Ruiz-Temple, State Fire
Marshal
Statutory Authority: ORS 476.020

Duties and Responsibilities: The office works to protect citizens, their property and the environment from fire and hazardous materials.

PSYCHIATRIC SECURITY REVIEW BOARD

Address: 610 SW Alder St., Suite 420, Portland 97204
Phone: 503-229-5596
Fax: 503-224-0215
Email: psrb@oregon.gov
Contact: Alison Bort, J.D., Ph.D., Executive Director
Statutory Authority: ORS 161.327, Chapter 163A, 426.701, 426.702, 419C.530
Duties and Responsibilities: The Psychiatric Security Review Board was originally established in 1977 to supervise individuals who successfully asserted the insanity defense (Guilty Except for Insanity or GEI) to a criminal charge. The board's responsibilities have expanded to supervise youth who successfully asserted the insanity defense (Responsible Except for Insanity or REI) and certain civil commitments. Additionally, it has been designated by the Legislature as the "relief" authority for two different populations: GEI sex offenders who request relief from sex offender registration and those who are barred from possessing a firearm due to a mental health determination (e.g. civil commitment, competency, GEI) who request restoration of firearm rights.

The board is comprised of adult and juvenile panels. Each consists of five members, appointed by the governor and confirmed by the Senate for four-year terms. The adult panel is comprised of a psychiatrist and a psychologist experienced in the criminal justice system, an experienced parole and probation officer, an attorney experienced in criminal trial practice and a member of the general public. The juvenile panel has a child psychiatrist, child psychologist, parole and probation officer experienced in juvenile criminal justice, an attorney experienced in juvenile criminal trial practice and a member of the general public. The agency employs 11 staff.

PUBLIC EMPLOYEES RETIREMENT SYSTEM

Address: 11410 SW 68th Pkwy., Tigard 97223; PO Box 23700, Tigard 97281-3700
Phone: 888-320-7377; TTY: 503-603-7766
Fax: 503-598-0561
Web: www.oregon.gov/PERS
Contact: Kevin Olineck, Director

Statutory Authority: ORS 237.350–237.980, 238.005–238.750, 238A.005–238A.475, 243.401–243.507
Duties and Responsibilities: The Public Employees Retirement System (PERS) has administered retirement benefits for Oregon's public sector workers (state, local government, and school district employees) since 1945. PERS serves more than 225,000 active/inactive members, 149,000 benefit recipients, and 906 employers. The system pays approximately $4.86 billion in benefits annually; about $4.08 billion is paid to Oregon residents. Those in-state payments support an estimated 36,914 jobs in Oregon. Investment income provided 73.9 percent of total PERS revenue since 1970, with member contributions providing 4.8 percent, and employer contributions providing 21.3 percent. Nearly 30 percent of PERS members are currently eligible to retire.

Public Employees Retirement Board
Address: PO Box 23700, Tigard 97281-3700
Phone: 888-320-7377
Contact: Sadhana Shenoy, Chair
Statutory Authority: ORS 238.630

Oregon Savings Growth Plan Advisory Committee
Address: 800 Summer St. NE, Salem 97310
Phone: 888-320-7377
Web: www.oregon.gov/PERS/OSGP
Contact: Colin Benson, Chair

PUBLIC SAFETY STANDARDS AND TRAINING, DEPARTMENT OF

Address: 4190 Aumsville Hwy. SE, Salem 97317
Phone: 503-378-2100
Fax: 503-378-4600
Web: www.oregon.gov/DPSST/Pages/default.aspx
Contact: Les Hallman, Interim Director
Statutory Authority: ORS 181A.355–181A.995, 206.010–206.015, 243.950–243.974, 703.010–703.325
Duties and Responsibilities: The mission of the Department of Public Safety Standards and Training (DPSST) is to promote excellence in public safety by delivering quality training and developing and upholding professional standards for police, fire, corrections, parole and probation and telecommunications personnel, in addition to licensing private security providers and private investigators in Oregon. DPSST also trains and certifies Oregon Liquor Control Commission regulatory specialists, regulates and licenses polygraph

examiners, determines sheriff candidates' eligibility to run for office and administers the Public Safety Memorial Fund. DPSST strives to provide resources and certification programs that public safety officers and organizations need to maintain the highest professional skill standards for service to Oregon's communities and citizens. These services are based at DPSST's 236-acre academy and extend across the state through a network of regional training coordinators.

DPSST is governed by a 24-member board and five discipline-specific policy committees. DPSST serves more than 42,000 public safety constituents across the state and employs 160 full-time staff and approximately 400 part-time employees and agency loaned instructors.

The functions of DPSST date back to 1961 with the establishment of the Board on Police Standards and Training. Since its inception, the addition of the corrections, parole and probation, telecommunications and emergency medical dispatch, fire, private security, private investigator and regulatory specialist disciplines expanded the board's oversight, and the name transitioned to the Board on Public Safety Standards and Training. The growth in scope of the board required the establishment of DPSST in 1997 as the agency to facilitate the standards and training requirements set forth by the board. DPSST also provides staffing for the board and policy committees and works with various board advisory committees and workgroups

DPSST's campus is home to the Fallen Law Enforcement Officers Memorial and the Fallen Firefighters Memorial. Memorial ceremonies for each are hosted annually to honor the officers and firefighters who have been killed in the line of duty.

Public Safety Standards and Training, Board on

Address: 4190 Aumsville Hwy. SE, Salem 97317
Phone: 503-378-2100
Web: www.oregon.gov/DPSST/BD/Pages/default.aspx
Contact: Darren Bucich, Chair; DaNeshia Barrett, Vice Chair
Statutory Authority: ORS 181A.360
Duties and Responsibilities: In addition to statutes set by the Legislature, DPSST's overall mission is guided by this board and five discipline-specific public safety policy committees. Membership of the board is outlined in ORS and provides a comprehensive representation of the constituent base.

The board and committees are integrally involved in setting standards for employment, training and certification or licensure of public safety professionals, fire service professionals, private security professionals, private investigators and polygraph examiners. Board and committee meetings are held

quarterly to review standards and curriculum, administrative rule changes, requests for waivers of the standards and cases addressing the denial or revocation of certification or licensure. In addition, the board and committees assist DPSST in setting the agency's goals for the future through guidance and input regarding policy direction and strategic planning.

PUBLIC UTILITY COMMISSION

Address: PO Box 1088, 201 High St. SE, #100, Salem 97308-1088
Phone: 503-378-6600
Fax: 503-378-5743
Email: puc.consumer@state.or.us
Web: www.oregon.gov/puc
Contact: Michael Dougherty, Chief Operating Officer
Statutory Authority: ORS Chapters 756, 757, 758, 759, 772
Duties and Responsibilities: The Oregon Public Utility Commission (PUC) is responsible for rate regulation of Oregon's investor-owned electric, natural gas, and telephone utilities, as well as select water companies. The rules governing PUC proceedings and the regulatory process are set forth in Oregon Administrative Rules Chapter 860, while the PUC's Internal Operating Guidelines inform the public of its decision-making process and describes the responsibilities of the PUC. Policy decisions are made by the three governor-appointed commissioners during regularly scheduled public meetings. These rules and guidelines help the PUC to ensure the safety, reliability and quality of essential utility services; scrutinize utility costs, risks and performance to ensure just and reasonable rates; manage customer and community choices to ensure value for all customers; encourage the community to be engaged and better informed on utility-related issues by participating in regular public meetings or submitting comments on topics of interest.

Through the Residential Service Protection Fund, the PUC supports the state's public policy that Oregonians have access to adequate and affordable telephone service through Oregon Relay, Oregon Telephone Assistance Program, Telecommunication Device Access Program and Emergency Medical Certificates. These programs provide assistance to low-income residents with a discount on monthly telephone or broadband service; individuals with disabilities who need adaptive telecommunications equipment to communicate effectively; Oregonians with hearing or speech disabilities who are provided the ability to place or receive calls through specially trained relay operators; and those with medical hardships who must maintain telephone service at all times.

Maritime Pilots, Oregon Board of

Address: 800 NE Oregon St., Portland 97232
Phone: 971-673-1530
Fax: 971-673-1531
Web: www.oregon.gov/puc/BMP
Contact: Tom Griffitts, Executive Director; Susan Johnson, Administrator
Statutory Authority: ORS Chapters 670, 776
Duties and Responsibilities: Part of the PUC for budget and administrative purposes, the board protects public health, safety and welfare by ensuring that only highly qualified and carefully trained persons are licensed to pilot vessels. The board directly supports at least $21 billion in cargo value that generates over 40,000 local jobs. Pilots are essential to Oregon's maritime industry. They are navigational and ship handling experts who direct the transit of vessels calling on the ports of Coos Bay, Yaquina Bay, Astoria, Kalama, Longview, Vancourver and Portland. Their functions have been regulated since 1846, making the Board of Maritime Pilots one of the oldest state agencies in Oregon.

RACING COMMISSION, OREGON

Address: 800 NE Oregon St., Suite 310, Portland 97232
Phone: 971-673-0207
Fax: 971-673-0213
Email: jack.mcgrail@oregon.gov
Web: www.oregon.gov/RACING/Pages/default.aspx
Contact: Jack McGrail, Executive Director
Statutory Authority: ORS 462.210
Duties and Responsibilities: Established in 1933, the commission regulates the pari-mutuel industry in Oregon, including racing, on- and off-track wagering for the good of the horses, the horsemen and women, the bettors, the licensees and the citizenry. The commission also regulates multi-jurisdictional account wagering hubs licensed in Oregon. By statute, 25 percent of the fees on wagering through these hubs goes to the state General Fund; the remaining 75 percent is used to support racing industry activities such as the commercial race meet in Grants Pass and the summer race meets in communities throughout the state.

The commission's five-member governing board is appointed by the governor and confirmed by the Senate. Terms are four years.

REAL ESTATE AGENCY

Address: 530 Center St. NE, Suite 100, Salem 97301
Phone: 503-378-4170
Fax: 503-378-2491
Email: orea.info@oregon.gov
Web: www.oregon.gov/rea
Contact: Steve Strode, Commissioner
Statutory Authority: ORS 696.375
Duties and Responsibilities: The agency is responsible for licensing, registering and regulating real estate brokers, principal real estate brokers, property managers, escrow agents, real estate marketing organizations and membership campgrounds. It also regulates aspects of condominium filings, timeshare filings and manufactured dwelling subdivisions. The agency is managed by a real estate commissioner appointed by the governor. The commissioner is advised by the nine-person Real Estate Board. The agency serves over 28,000 licensees and registrants.

Real Estate Board

Address: 530 Center St. NE, Suite 100, Salem 97301
Phone: 503-378-4170
Fax: 503-378-2491
Email: orea.board@oregon.gov
Web: www.oregon.gov/rea/about_us/Pages/Real_Estate_Board.aspx
Contact: Anna Higley, Deputy Commissioner
Statutory Authority: ORS 696.405
Duties and Responsibilities: The board consists of seven industry and two public members appointed by the governor. It meets at least six times a year. The board advises the real estate commissioner and the governor's office on real estate industry matters. It is also responsible for reviewing experience waiver requests and continuing education provider qualification petitions for approval.

REVENUE, DEPARTMENT OF

Address: 955 Center St. NE, Salem 97301-2555
Phone: 503-378-4988; Toll-free 800-356-4222; TTY: 800-886-7204
Fax: 503-945-8738
Email: questions.dor@oregon.gov
Web: www.oregon.gov/dor/Pages/index.aspx
Contact: Betsy Imholt, Director
Statutory Authority: ORS 305.025
Duties and Responsibilities: Started as the Oregon Tax Commission in 1909, the department has approximately 1,000 employees who help achieve its mission of making revenue systems work to fund the public services that preserve and enhance the quality of life for all citizens. The department administers nearly 40 tax programs, including personal income, corporate income and excise,

Executive

corporate activity, cigarette, tobacco and marijuana taxes. The department's tax programs provided 96 percent of Oregon's General Fund revenue for the 2017–19 biennium.

While the department does not collect property taxes, it ensures property tax laws are applied fairly and equitably across Oregon's 36 counties. The Property Tax Division administers the property tax deferral program, determines the value of industrial and centrally assessed properties and supports and trains county appraisers and assessors. Revenue also collects unpaid debt on behalf of more than 200 state agencies, courts, schools, municipalities, counties, boards and commissions.

The department is headquartered in Salem, with regional offices throughout the state.

The Revenue Building in Salem houses the central offices of the Department of Revenue. (Oregon State Archives scenic photo)

SOCIAL WORKERS, STATE BOARD OF LICENSED

Address: 3218 Pringle Rd. SE, Suite 240, Salem 97302-6310
Phone: 503-378-5735
Fax: 888-252-1046
Email: randy.harnisch@state.or.us
Web: www.oregon.gov/BLSW/Pages/index.aspx
Contact: Randy Harnisch, Executive Director
Statutory Authority: ORS 675.510–675.600
Duties and Responsibilities: Social workers in Oregon are licensed mental health professionals who work in a variety of settings from schools and social service agencies to hospitals and hospice facilities. The board was created to ensure that individuals serving the public as social workers have the education and skills to do the job safely, effectively and efficiently. Currently, there are over 6,000 licensed social workers in Oregon.

The board has seven members, four who are social workers and three who represent the public. The board has its office in Salem and has six staff members. Board meetings are held monthly in Salem and are open to the public.

The board was created in 1979 to set policy and adopt rules for social workers. Currently, the board offers four license types: Registered Baccalaureate Social Worker (RBSW), Licensed Master's Social Worker (LMSW), Clinical Social Work Associate (CSWA) and Licensed Clinical Social Worker (LCSW).

SPEECH-LANGUAGE PATHOLOGY AND AUDIOLOGY, STATE BOARD OF EXAMINERS FOR

Address: 800 NE Oregon St., Suite 407, Portland 97232-2162
Phone: 971-673-0220; TDD: 503-731-4031
Fax: 971-673-0226
Email: speechaud.board@state.or.us
Web: www.oregon.gov/BSPA/Pages/index.aspx
Contact: Erin K. Haag, Executive Director
Statutory Authority: ORS 681.205–681.505
Duties and Responsibilities: Audiologists and speech-language pathologists provide vital services to Oregonians in hospitals, home health settings, private practices, early intervention programs, early childhood special education programs and in Oregon's kindergarten through grade 12 school system. The board was established in 1973 to license and regulate the performance of audiologists, speech-language pathologists, and, as of 2013, speech-language pathology assistants to ensure consumer protection. The office is staffed by three employees (2.5 full-time equivalent) and overseen by the board, which is made up of two audiologists, two speech-language pathologists, one otolaryngologist and two public members.

STATE FAIR COUNCIL

Address: 2330 17th St. NE, Salem 97301
Phone: 971-701-6573
Fax: 503-947-3206
Web: http://oregonstatefaircouncil.org
Contact: Kim Grewe-Powell, Interim CEO
Statutory Authority: ORS 565.456
Duties and Responsibilities: The Legislature passed Senate Bill 7 in 2013 to create the council as a public corporation, and management of the fair and exposition center was transferred to this entity. The council oversees the Oregon State Fair and Exposition Center to showcase Oregon products and people; to educate and communicate to the citizens of Oregon about the needs, issues and context of the key industries of the state with emphasis on agriculture, forestry, technology and manufacturing; and to create an event that celebrates all of Oregon and Oregonians in an atmosphere of responsible community involvement

and citizenship. The exposition center hosts the annual state fair at the end of August through Labor Day and provides a venue for meetings, concerts, trade shows and other events the rest of the year from its location in Salem.

STATE LANDS, DEPARTMENT OF

Address: 775 Summer St. NE, Suite 100, Salem 97301-1279
Phone: 503-986-5200
Fax: 503-378-4844
Email: dsl@dsl.state.or.us
Web: www.oregon.gov/DSL/Pages/index.aspx
Contact: Vicki Walker, Director
Statutory Authority: ORS Chapter 273
Duties and Responsibilities: The Department of State Lands (DSL) is the administrative arm of the State Land Board, Oregon's oldest board. Established by the Oregon Constitution, the State Land Board has been composed of the governor (chair), secretary of state and state treasurer throughout its history.

At statehood in 1859, the federal government granted Oregon about 3.4 million acres of land for financing public education. The State Land Board oversees these state-owned "school lands" which now total only about a fifth of the original acreage. Revenues from these lands are dedicated to the Common School Fund, a trust fund for kindergarten through grade 12 public schools. Distributions from the fund's earnings are sent twice a year to the state's 197 school districts.

The State Land Board and the department also are charged with protecting public rights to use state-owned waterways for navigation, fishing, commerce and recreation.

Over time, the Oregon Legislature assigned various additional responsibilities to the agency, including administering the state's unclaimed property program (1957); protecting state wetlands and waterways (1967: removal-fill law; 1989: wetland conservation law); and serving as the state partner for the South Slough National Estuarine Research Reserve (1974). The department also administers the estates of people who die without a will and without known heirs.

DSL employs just over 100 people and is headquartered in Salem in a building that is an asset of the Common School Fund. The Eastern Region Office is located in Bend, and the South Slough National Estuarine Research Reserve is headquartered in Charleston on the south coast. In addition to the Director's Office and State Land Board, agency program areas operate under two divisions: Operations (Aquatic Resource Management and Real Property) and Administration (Business Operations and Support Services, and the South Slough).

South Slough National Estuarine Research Reserve

Address: PO Box 5417, 61907 Seven Devils Rd., Charleston 97420
Phone: 541-888-5558
Fax: 541-888-5559
Web: www.oregon.gov/DSL/SS/Pages/About.aspx
Contact: Bree Yednock, Manager
Statutory Authority: ORS 273.554
Duties and Responsibilities: The reserve is a 5,900-acre protected area located on the South Slough inlet of the Coos Estuary in Charleston, near Coos Bay. Established in 1974 by the Oregon Legislature, it is a partnership with the National Oceanic and Atmospheric Administration and DSL. The mission of the South Slough Reserve is to improve the understanding and management of estuaries and coastal watersheds in the Pacific Northwest. The South Slough was the first of 29 reserves nationwide and is the only program of its kind in Oregon.

The reserve has two core areas of service: education and science. Education staff provide classes and training for a wide variety of clients, including schoolchildren, science teachers, local decision-makers, and professionals involved in managing estuaries and coastal watersheds. The reserve's interpretive center offers informative displays and a system of hiking trails for tourists and area residents. Scientists provide research data for national and regional organizations.

The reserve is guided by an eight-member, governor-appointed, Management Commission, chaired by the director of DSL. The reserve employs 16 full-time staff, is supported by a large cadre of volunteers and hosts numerous student researchers and interns on an annual basis. The Friends of South Slough, a membership, all-volunteer nonprofit group, assists the reserve with its educational and research activities and obtains grants and other funding to promote and support the reserve's programs.

TAX PRACTITIONERS, STATE BOARD OF

Address: 3218 Pringle Rd. SE, Suite 250, Salem 97302-6308
Phone: 503-378-4034
Fax: 503-585-5797
Email: tax.bd@oregon.gov
Web: www.oregon.gov/OBTP/Pages/index.aspx
Contact: Howard Moyes, Executive Director; Glen Longworth, Chair

Statutory Authority: ORS 673.605–673.740

Duties and Responsibilities: The Oregon Legislature created the board in 1974 to protect consumers from incompetent and unethical tax return preparers, the first law and organization of its kind in the country. Today, the board licenses and regulates roughly 3,500 individual tax practitioners and more than 1,200 tax preparation businesses. The board is comprised of seven volunteer members who serve staggered three-year terms. Six of the members are licensed tax consultants, and the seventh member represents the general public. Two full-time staff administer day-to-day operations.

TEACHER STANDARDS AND PRACTICES COMMISSION

Address: 250 Division St. NE, Salem 97301
Phone: 503-378-3586
Fax: 503-378-4448
Email: contact.tspc@oregon.gov
Web: www.oregon.gov/tspc/Pages/index.aspx
Contact: Dr. Anthony Rosilez, Executive Director
Statutory Authority: ORS 342.350
Duties and Responsibilities: The commission was created by the 1965 Legislature to advise the State Board of Education on licensure, education and performance of teachers and other matters on which the board requested assistance. In 1973, the Legislature created a new state agency and transferred the full responsibility for educator licensure, educator licensure preparation programs and maintenance of professional standards of conduct to the commission. The commission processes approximately 20,000 licensure applications a year.

The 17 commission members are appointed to three-year terms by the governor and confirmed by the Senate.

TOURISM COMMISSION, OREGON

Address: 319 SW Washington St., Suite 700, Portland 97204
Phone: 971-717-6205
Fax: 971-717-6215
Email: info@traveloregon.com
Web: traveloregon.com; industry.traveloregon.com
Contact: Todd Davidson, CEO
Statutory Authority: ORS 284.101–284.146
Duties and Responsibilities: The commission, doing business as Travel Oregon, drives economic growth and job creation by strengthening tourism throughout the state. The commission works to enhance visitors' experiences by providing information, resources and trip-planning tools that inspire travel and consistently convey the exceptional qualities of Oregon.

Created in 1995 and made semi-independent by the Legislature in 2003, Travel Oregon is led by a nine-member governor-appointed board and employs 46 staff members, who market the state with advertising campaigns, publications, destination development and community enrichment, and who manage the state's Welcome Centers. Travel Oregon works with local communities, industry associations, government agencies and private businesses in the implementation of its industry and legislatively-approved biennial strategic plan.

The agency ensures broad economic impact throughout the state by partnering with Oregon's Regional Destination Management organizations in the state's seven tourism regions.

The Transportation Building in Salem houses the central offices of the Department of Transportation. (Oregon State Archives scenic photo)

TRANSPORTATION COMMISSION, OREGON

Address: MS 11, 355 Capitol St. NE, Salem 97301-3871
Phone: 503-986-3450
Fax: 503-986-3432
Web: www.oregon.gov/ODOT/Get-Involved/Pages/OTC_Main.aspx
Contact: Bob Van Brocklin, Chair
Statutory Authority: ORS 184.615–184.620
Duties and Responsibilities: The commission establishes state transportation policy. It is a five-member, volunteer citizen board. The governor appoints the members with the consent of the Senate. Members serve a four-year term and may be reappointed. The governor ensures that at least one member is a resident east of the Cascades and not more than three members belong to any one political party.

Transportation, Department of

Address: 355 Capitol St. NE, Salem 97301-3871
Phone: 503-986-3200; 1-888-ASK-ODOT (275-6368) for questions and concerns

Fax: 503-986-3432
Web: www.oregon.gov/ODOT/Pages/index.aspx
Contact: Kristopher Strickler, Director
Statutory Authority: ORS 184.615
Duties and Responsibilities: The Oregon Department of Transportation (ODOT) operates under the Transportation Commission, and works to provide a safe and reliable multimodal transportation system that connects people and helps Oregon's communities and economy thrive. ODOT is involved in developing Oregon's system of highways and bridges, public transit services, rail passenger and freight systems and bicycle and pedestrian paths. It is organized into four areas that manage driver licensing and vehicle registration programs, motor carrier operations and transportation safety programs: Operations; Revenue, Finance and Compliance; Government Relations; and Social Equity.

Operations

Address: MS 11, 355 Capitol St. NE, Salem 97301-3871
Phone: 503-986-3939
Fax: 503-986-3432
Contact: Cooper Brown, Assistant Director

Delivery and Operations Division

Address: 4040 Fairview Industrial Dr. SE, Salem 97302-1142
Phone: 503-986-2840
Fax: 503-986-3150
Contact: Karen Rowe, Administrator
Statutory Authority: ORS 184.615(3)
Duties and Responsibilities: The division is responsible for the design, maintenance, operation and construction of about 8,000 miles of state highways. The division's activities include identifying highway needs; maintaining state highway routes; acquiring rights of way; designing highways, bridges and related structures; evaluating environmental impacts of proposed projects; and conducting traffic studies.

Policy, Data and Analysis Division

Address: 555 13th St. NE, Suite 2, Salem 97301-4178
Phone: 503-986-3421
Fax: 503-986-4173
Web: www.oregon.gov/ODOT/Planning/Pages/SPR.aspx
Contact: Jerri Bohard, Administrator
Statutory Authority: ORS 184.615
Duties and Responsibilities: The division produces statewide transportation plans and policies, assists local governments in planning, collects and analyzes data to support strategic investment decisions, oversees transportation research, manages grant programs and coordinates statewide active

transportation and sustainability initiatives. The division also develops the Statewide Transportation Improvement Program, which is the state's four-year transportation capital improvement program.

Public Transportation Division

Address: 555 13th St. NE, Suite 3, Salem 97301-4179
Phone: 503-986-3412
Fax: 503-986-3183
Web: www.oregon.gov/odot/rptd/pages/index.aspx
Contact: Karyn Criswell, Administrator
Statutory Authority: ORS 184.615(3)
Duties and Responsibilities: Consisting of rail and public transit programs, the division works to encourage multimodal collaboration and gain additional efficiencies. The division supports intercity passenger bus and rail service and provides grants to local and regional governments and non-profit organizations for transportation services. Programs include Transit, Intercity Passenger Rail and Bus, and Rail and Transit Safety.

Transportation Safety Division

Address: MS 3, 4040 Fairview Industrial Dr. SE, Salem 97302-1142
Phone: 503-986-4190
Fax: 503-986-3143
Web: www.oregon.gov/odot/safety/pages/index.aspx
Contact: Troy E. Costales, Administrator
Statutory Authority: ORS 184.615(3), 802.300
Duties and Responsibilities: The division works with partners to organize, plan and implement statewide transportation safety programs that have helped reduce Oregon's highway fatality rate. The division conducts campaigns focused on driving behaviors, including use of safety belts and child safety seats, impaired drivers, speeding, young drivers and motorcycle safety. It partners with law enforcement, safety advocates and others to promote transportation safety. The division awards more than 500 grants and contracts to partners and other service providers each year.

Climate Office

Address: 555 13th St. NE, Suite 2, Salem 97301
Phone: 503-986-4227
Web: https://www.oregon.gov/odot/Programs/Pages/Climate-Office.aspx
Contact: Amanda Pietz, Administrator
Statutory Authority: Executive Order 20-04.
Duties and Responsibilities: The office was formed in recognition of the importance of reducing carbon emissions from transportation and the impacts climate is having on the Oregon transportation system's ability to move people and goods in the state. Climate is another critical

concern affecting ODOT's decisions and invest-ments, balanced alongside other important consid-erations. The office is tasked with consolidating efforts into a strategic approach to help Oregon achieve a cleaner transportation future.

Revenue, Finance and Compliance

Address: MS 11, 355 Capitol St, NE, Salem 97301
Phone: 503-986-3452
Fax: 503-986-3432
Web: www.oregon.gov/odot/
Contact: Travis Brouwer, Assistant Director
Statutory Authority: ORS 184.615(3)

Commerce and Compliance Division

Address: 3930 Fairview Industrial Dr. SE, Salem 97302-6351
Phone: 503-378-5849
Fax: 503-373-1940
Web: www.oregontruckingonline.com
Contact: Amy Ramsdell, Administrator
Statutory Authority: ORS Chapters 803, 810, 818, 823, 825, 826
Duties and Responsibilities: The Commerce and Compliance Division (CCD) ensures the safety of commercial trucks and buses and collects fees for their use of the roads. The division collects weight-mile tax and truck registration fees from trucking companies and also maintains a size and weight enforcement program to ensure that trucks follow size and weight requirements put in place to protect infrastructure and promote safety. CCD enforces commercial vehicle laws, including regu-lations on driver hours of service. Each year, CCD and its partner agencies inspect thousands of trucks to ensure that equipment is in good working order and that drivers meet all safety requirements.

Driver and Motor Vehicle Division

Address: 1905 Lana Ave. NE, Salem 97314-0100
Phone: 503-945-5000;
Toll-free (Portland): 503-299-9999
Fax: 503-945-0893
Web: www.oregon.gov/ODOT/DMV/Pages/index.aspx
Contact: Tom McClellan, Administrator
Statutory Authority: ORS 184.615(3)
Duties and Responsibilities: The Driver and Motor Vehicle Division (DMV) protects financial and ownership interests in vehicles, provides driv-er licenses and identification cards for Oregon res-idents and collects revenues for Oregon's highway system. DMV has been part of the Department of Transportation since 1969, but its core functions date back to 1905. The "D" in DMV stood for "department" only for about 12 years—from 1956

to 1969. For more than half a century before that, driver licensing and motor vehicle registration and titling were part of Oregon's Office of the Secretary of State.

There are currently more than 3.1 million licensed drivers and more than 4.5 million regis-tered vehicles in Oregon. DMV plays a major role in fraud prevention by enforcing strict identification standards in issuing driver licenses and ID cards and providing driver and vehicle data to law enforcement and courts electronically. DMV also regulates and inspects about 3,500 vehicle- and driver-related businesses, such as auto dealers and dismantlers.

Headquartered in Salem, DMV has 60 field offices throughout the state.

Budget and Finance Office

Address: MS 11, 355 Capitol St. NE, Salem 97301-3871
Phone: 503-986-3049
Contact: Stefan Hamlin, Budget Office Manager
Duties and Responsibilities: The office coordi-nates the department's legislative budget develop-ment process including all Emergency Board requests and program budget development. It pro-vides Sources and Uses chart preparation, allotment plans, Support Services assessment and permanent financing plans.

Government and External Relations

Address: MS 11, 355 Capitol St. NE, Salem 97301-3871
Phone: 503-986-2840
Fax: 503-986-3432
Contact: Lindsay Baker, Assistant Director
Duties and Responsibilities: The office consists of the Communications Section and the Government Relations Team. The Communications Section is responsible for coordinating ODOT's internal and external communications, including media rela-tions, public information and outreach. The Government Relations Team guides ODOT's par-ticipation in state and federal legislative efforts and intergovernmental relationships with tribal gov-ernments to advance ODOT's mission for the benefit of all Oregonians.

Social Equity

Address: MS 11, 355 Capitol St. NE, Salem 97301-3871
Phone: 503-986-4353
Fax: 503-986-3432
Contact: Nikotris Perkins, Assistant Director
Duties and Responsibilities: The office, which includes the Civil Rights Team, works to institu-tionalize equity, diversity and inclusion practices in ODOT's programs, policies, performance and priorities.

Other Groups:

Bicycle and Pedestrian Advisory Committee
Phone: 503-986-3555
Web: www.oregon.gov/odot/programs/pages/
bikeped.aspx
Contact: Jessica Horning, Program Manager
Statutory Authority: ORS 366.112

Governor's Advisory Committee on DUII (Driving under the Influence of Intoxicants)
Phone: 503-986-4188
Web: www.oregon.gov/ODOT/Safety/Pages/
GAC-DUII.aspx
Contact: Chuck Hayes, Chair

Oregon Freight Advisory Committee
Phone: 503-986-4128
Web: www.oregon.gov/ODOT/Get-Involved/
Pages/OFAC.aspx
Contact: Ray Drake, Senior Transportation
Planner
Statutory Authority: ORS 366.212

Oregon Transportation Safety Committee
Phone: 503-986-4188
Web: www.oregon.gov/ODOT/Safety/pages/
OTSC.aspx
Contact: Victor Hoffer, Chair

TRAVEL INFORMATION COUNCIL

Address: 1500 Liberty St. SE, Salem 97302
Phone: 503-378-4508
Fax: 503-378-6282
Web: https://oregontic.com/
Contact: Jim Denno, Executive Director
Statutory Authority: ORS 377.835
Duties and Responsibilities: The Oregon Travel Information Council (OTIC) is a semi-independent state agency formed by the Legislature in 1972. OTIC's programs enhance the public's motoring experience by helping travelers navigate to essential services, attractions and points of historic interest. The agency is responsible for the operation of 25 highway safety rest areas around the state under interagency agreements with the Oregon Department of Transportation and Oregon Parks and Recreation Department. OTIC administers the statewide "Blue Logo" Sign Program and information centers that identify gas, food, lodging and attractions on highways throughout Oregon and leads the Oregon Heritage Tree and Oregon Historical Marker programs.

The nine-member governing council, composed of eight volunteers appointed by the governor and one member of the Oregon Transportation Commission, guide the work of the agency. Members are selected for their knowledge of, experience with or interest in economic development, travel within Oregon, recreational opportunities in Oregon and Oregon's history and natural history.

The Veterans' Building in Salem houses the central offices of the Department of Veterans' Affairs. (Oregon State Archives scenic photo)

VETERANS' AFFAIRS, DEPARTMENT OF

Address: 700 Summer St. NE, Salem
97301-1285
Phone: 503-373-2000; Toll-free: 1-800-828-8801;
TTY: 503-373-2217
Fax: 503-373-2362
Web: www.oregon.gov/ODVA
Contact: Kelly Fitzpatrick, Director
Statutory Authority: ORS Chapters 406, 407,
408
Duties and Responsibilities: Established in 1945, the Oregon Department of Veterans' Affairs (ODVA) provides direct access to earned benefits and services to over 300,000 veterans and their families in Oregon. ODVA also provides special advocacy for veteran communities that have traditionally been underserved and builds partnerships with organizations to provide veteran-specific services for sustainable and supportive housing, access to health and behavioral health services and services to assist veterans in completing their educational goals. ODVA has four major program areas: aging veteran services, the veteran home loan program, statewide veteran services, and core operations to support and enhance the effectiveness and efficiency of the other program areas.

Advisory Committee to the Director of Veterans' Affairs
Address: 700 Summer St. NE, Salem 97301-
1285
Phone: 503-373-2383

Contact: John Howard, Chair
Statutory Authority: ORS 406.210
Duties and Responsibilities: The committee consists of nine people, all veterans appointed by the governor, who advise the director and staff of the ODVA on a wide variety of matters. The committee members act as advocates for veterans' issues and represent veterans' concerns across Oregon.

Aging Veteran Services Division

Address: 700 Summer St. NE, Salem 97301-1285
Phone: 503-373-2028
Fax: 503-373-2391
Contact: Ana Potter
Duties and Responsibilities: ODVA's Aging Veteran Services Division includes its Conservatorship and Representative Payee Programs, which help veterans, survivors and dependents who are legally designated "protected persons" to preserve and manage their estates and veterans benefits while providing income and assets for shelter, medical, personal and other needs. The division also operates two Oregon Veterans' Homes located in Lebanon and The Dalles where skilled nursing, rehabilitative care and Alzheimer's disease care are provided for veterans, spouses and Gold Star parents (parents whose children died while serving in the U.S. Armed Forces). Finally, the division trains and coordinates volunteers who aid and provide services to veterans.

Home Loan Program

Address: 700 Summer St. NE, Salem 97301-1285
Phone: 503-373-2051;
Toll-free: 1-800-828-8801; 1-888-673-8387 (within Oregon)
Fax: 503-373-2393
Contact: Cody Cox
Duties and Responsibilities: Administered by the ODVA since its inception, the Oregon Veteran (ORVET) Home Loan Program is designed to provide eligible veterans with home loans at the lowest possible interest rates.

Statewide Veteran Services Division

Address: 700 Summer St. NE, Salem 97301-1285
Phone: 503-373-2249
Contact: Sheronne Blasi
Duties and Responsibilities: The division is responsible for training Veteran Service Officers in the state of Oregon who provide free benefits counseling and claims services to veterans, survivors and dependents. The division serves the State Approving Agency and is responsible for the review, evaluation, approval, and oversight of schools and training facilities to ensure state and federal quality criteria are met for veterans using

their G.I. Bill® benefits. The division also includes Veteran Service Officers who provide services to underserved groups within Oregon's increasingly diverse veteran population, including women, tribal, incarcerated, LGBTQ and veterans currently enrolled in programs of higher education. Additionally, the division oversees the administration of several grant programs, including medical transportation for highly rural veterans, Campus Veteran Resource Programs and various Veteran Services Grants that range from working with homeless veterans, to aiding tribal veterans, to providing legal services for veterans.

VETERINARY MEDICAL EXAMINING BOARD

Address: 800 NE Oregon St., Suite 407, Portland 97232
Phone: 971-673-0224
Fax: 971-673-0226
Email: ovmeb.info@state.or.us
Web: www.oregon.gov/OVMEB/Pages/default.aspx
Contact: Cass McLeod-Skinner, Executive Director
Statutory Authority: ORS 686.210
Duties and Responsibilities: In 1903, the Legislature enacted the Veterinary Practice Act, which authorizes the board to regulate the practice of veterinary medicine in Oregon. The board works in the public interest by making and enforcing rules for competency, health, and safety standards for practitioners and facilities. The board licenses and investigates complaints against veterinarians, Certified Veterinary Technicians, euthanasia technicians and veterinary facilities to ensure compliance with the minimum standards of the Veterinary Practice Act. Facilities are regularly inspected for compliance with health, sanitation and drug safety requirements. Board members include five veterinarians, two members of the public and one Certified Veterinary Technician. Oregon's veterinary board was the first in the country to elect a Certified Veterinary Technician to serve as chair.

WATER RESOURCES DEPARTMENT

Address: 725 Summer St. NE, Suite A, Salem 97301
Phone: 503-986-0900
Fax: 503-986-0904
Web: www.oregon.gov/OWRD/Pages/index.aspx
Contact: Tom Byler, Director
Statutory Authority: ORS Chapters 536, 537, 538, 540, 541, 542, 543, 543A, 555
Duties and Responsibilities: The foundation of Oregon's water quantity laws go back to the

settlement of the West; however, establishment of a comprehensive set of water laws and an office to oversee the state's water resources did not occur until the office of State Engineer was created in 1905 and the Water Code was passed in 1909. The Water Code required that, with some exceptions, in order to use water in the state, an individual had to first obtain a water right. Over time, a variety of offices, boards and commissions managed water resources and the water rights system.

Today, the Water Resources Department (WRD) is the state agency charged with administration of the laws governing the management and distribution of surface and groundwater resources. The present form of the department was created in 1975, and the Water Resources Commission was established in 1985. The department protects existing water rights, processes water right transactions, facilitates voluntary streamflow restoration, increases understanding of demands on the state's water resources, provides accurate and accessible water resource data, and facilitates water supply solutions. The department also protects public health and safety through its dam safety and well construction programs.

Department headquarters and the Northwest Regional office are in Salem. The department also has four other regional offices and 15 small field offices throughout Oregon.

Water Resources Commission

Address: 725 Summer St. NE, Suite A, Salem 97301
Phone: 503-986-0876
Contact: Nirvana Cook, Commission Assistant
Statutory Authority: ORS 536.022
Duties and Responsibilities: The seven-member commission oversees department activities and sets policy consistent with state law.

Director's Office

Address: 725 Summer St. NE, Suite A, Salem 97301
Phone: 503-986-0876
Contact: Tom Byler
Duties and Responsibilities: The office develops and supervises policies and programs to ensure that water management practices follow Oregon Water Law, oversees implementation of the State's Integrated Water Resources Strategy and serves as the principal contact with the Legislature, tribes, stakeholder groups and Western States Water Council. In addition, the Water Resources Development Program administers grant and loan programs and provides funding and technical assistance to help individuals and communities meet their water needs.

Field Services Division

Address: 725 Summer St. NE, Suite A, Salem 97301
Phone: 503-986-0847
Contact: Ivan Gall, Administrator
Duties and Responsibilities: The division carries out the department's mission by enforcing the state's water laws and implementing the Water Resources Commission's policies in the field. The division has sole responsibility for the regulation of water uses based upon the water rights of record. Staff also inspects wells for protection of the groundwater resource, inspects dams for the protection of the public and collects streamflow and groundwater data for use by staff and the public.

Water Right Services Division

Address: 725 Summer St. NE, Suite A, Salem 97301
Phone: 503-986-0819
Contact: Dwight French, Administrator
Duties and Responsibilities: The division is responsible for processing water right permits to meet a variety of needs, including agriculture, drinking water, fish, wildlife, recreation and industry. In addition, the division processes transactions that allow water right holders to change how their existing water rights are used, including changes involving the transfer or lease of water instream. The division also adjudicates water right claims that predate the 1909 water code as well as federal and tribal rights.

Technical Services Division

Phone: 503-986-0900
Contact: Doug Woodcock, Agency Deputy Director
Duties and Responsibilities: The division includes groundwater and surface water scientists responsible for understanding the surface and groundwater resources of the state. The division also oversees the safety of dams, develops databases to share water resources information, licenses well drillers, enforces well construction standards and conducts enforcement proceedings for the department.

Groundwater Advisory Committee

Address: 725 Summer St. NE, Suite A, Salem 97301
Phone: 503-986-0933
Contact: Justin Iverson, Department Liaison; Kenneth Masten, Chair
Statutory Authority: ORS 536.090
Duties and Responsibilities: The committee's nine members, appointed by the Water Resources Commission, advise the commission and WRD on rules, legislation, groundwater public policy and the licensing of well constructors. The committee also reviews proposed expenditures of revenues

generated from start card fees associated with constructing wells.

Klamath River Basin Compact Commission

Address: 6600 Washburn Way, Klamath Falls 97603
Phone: 541-973-4431
Contact: Chrysten Lambert, Chair, Klamath Falls, federal government representative; Tom Byler, Oregon representative; Curtis Anderson, California representative
Statutory Authority: 542.610
Duties and Responsibilities: Members of the commission facilitate inter-governmental cooperation in development and proper use of the water resources of the Klamath River Basin.

WATERSHED ENHANCEMENT BOARD, OREGON

Address: 775 Summer St. NE, Suite 360, Salem 97301-1290
Phone: 503-986-0178
Fax: 503-986-0199
Email: april.mack@oregon.gov
Web: www.oregon.gov/OWEB/Pages/index.aspx
Contact: Meta Loftsgaarden, Executive Director
Statutory Authority: ORS Chapter 541
Duties and Responsibilities: The Oregon Watershed Enhancement Board (OWEB) provides grants to help Oregonians take care of local streams, rivers, wetlands and natural areas. Community members and landowners use scientific criteria to decide jointly what needs to be done to conserve and improve rivers and natural habitats in the places where they live. OWEB grants are funded from the Oregon Lottery, federal dollars and salmon license plate revenue. The agency, which was created in 1999, is led by an 18-member citizen board drawn from the public at large, tribes and federal and state natural resource agency boards and commissions. Headquartered in Salem, OWEB has approximately 30 staff, including six regional field representatives located in offices around the state.

WINE BOARD, OREGON

Address: 4640 SW Macadam Ave., Suite 240, Portland 97239
Phone: 503-228-8336
Fax: 503-228-8337
Email: info@oregonwine.org
Web: www.oregonwine.org; industry.oregonwine.org
Contact: Tom Danowski, Executive Director
Statutory Authority: ORS 576.753
Duties and Responsibilities: The board was established as a semi-independent state agency in 2003. It consists of nine volunteer members appointed by the governor for a term of three years. The board and eight staff members work on behalf of all Oregon wineries and independent growers throughout the state's diverse winegrowing regions, managing marketing, research and education initiatives that support and advance the Oregon wine and wine grape industry.

YOUTH AUTHORITY, OREGON

Address: 530 Center St. NE, Suite 500, Salem 97301-3777
Phone: 503-373-7205
Fax: 503-373-7622
Email: oya.info@oya.state.or.us
Web: www.oregon.gov/OYA
Contact: Joseph O'Leary, Director
Statutory Authority: ORS Chapters 419A, 419C, 420, 420A
Duties and Responsibilities: Established by the 1995 Legislature, the Oregon Youth Authority (OYA) protects the public and reduces crime by holding youth accountable for their behavior and providing opportunities for reformation in safe environments.

OYA provides treatment, education and job training services to youths aged 12 to 25. OYA exercises legal and physical custody over youths who commit offenses between the ages of 12 and 18 and have been committed to OYA by county juvenile courts, and physical custody over youths sentenced as adults to the legal custody of the Oregon Department of Corrections, but placed with OYA due to their young age.

OYA employs approximately 1,000 people throughout Oregon with central offices in Salem; provides probation and parole services in all 36 counties in Oregon; operates nine close-custody facilities; and contracts with a range of residential treatment providers and foster parents to ensure youth receive the most appropriate combination of placement, treatment and other services needed to leave OYA's custody ready to lead productive, crime-free lives.

Judicial

Oregon's judicial branch of government helps individuals, businesses and government groups resolve disputes, protect their rights and enforce their legal duties. Oregon judges review cases for compliance with federal, state and local laws. This section describes the judicial system and introduces Oregon's judges.

OREGON SUPREME COURT

Address: Supreme Court Bldg., 1163 State St., Salem 97301-2563
Records and Case Information: 503-986-5555; Oregon Relay 711
Fax: 503-986-5560

The Supreme Court of Oregon has seven justices elected by nonpartisan, statewide ballot to serve six-year terms. Justices elected to the Supreme Court must be United States citizens, members of the Oregon State Bar and residents of Oregon for at least three years. The court has its offices and courtroom in the Supreme Court Building, one block east of the State Capitol in Salem. The members of the court elect one of their number to serve as chief justice for a six-year term.

Powers and Authority

The Supreme Court was created, and its role largely defined, by Article VII of the Oregon Constitution, as amended. It is primarily a court of review in that it reviews, in selected cases, the decisions of the Court of Appeals. The Supreme Court usually selects cases with significant legal issues calling for interpretation of laws or legal principles affecting many citizens and institutions of society. When the Supreme Court decides not to review a Court of Appeals case, the Court of Appeals' decision becomes final. In addition to its discretionary review function, the Supreme Court hears direct appeals in death penalty, lawyer and judicial discipline, and Oregon Tax Court cases. It may accept original jurisdiction in mandamus, quo warranto and habeas corpus proceedings. It also reviews ballot measure titles, prison siting disputes, reapportionment of legislative districts and legal questions on Oregon law referred by federal courts.

Administrative Authority

The chief justice is the administrative head of the Judicial Department and exercises administrative authority over the appellate, circuit and tax courts. The chief justice makes rules and issues orders to carry out necessary duties and requires appropriate reports from judges and other officers and employees of the courts. As head of the Judicial Department, the chief justice appoints the chief judge of the Court of Appeals and the presiding judges of all state trial courts from the judges elected to those courts. The chief justice adopts certain rules and regulations respecting procedures for state courts. The chief justice also supervises a statewide plan for budgeting, accounting and fiscal management of the judicial department.

The chief justice and the Supreme Court have the authority to appoint lawyers, elected judges and retired judges to serve in temporary judicial assignments.

Admission and Discipline of Lawyers and Judges

The Supreme Court admits lawyers to practice law in Oregon and has the power to reprimand, suspend or disbar lawyers whose actions have been investigated and prosecuted by the Oregon State Bar. In admitting lawyers, the Supreme Court acts on the recommendation of the Board of Bar Examiners, which conducts examinations for lawyer applicants each February and July and screens applicants for character and fitness to practice law. The Supreme Court appoints at least 14 members to the Board of Bar Examiners. The board includes two public members who are not lawyers. The Supreme Court also has the power to censure, suspend or remove judges after investigation and recommendation by the Commission on Judicial Fitness and Disability.

OREGON COURT OF APPEALS

Address: Supreme Court Bldg., 1163 State St., Salem 97301-2563
Records and Case Information: 503-986-5555; Oregon Relay 771
Fax: 503-986-5865

Created in 1969 as a five-judge court, the Court of Appeals was expanded to six judges in 1973, to ten judges in 1977 and to 13 judges in 2012. The judges, otherwise elected on a statewide, nonpartisan basis for six-year terms, must be United States citizens, members of the Oregon State Bar and qualified electors of their county of residence. The chief justice of the Supreme Court appoints a chief judge from among the judges of the Court of Appeals.

Court of Appeals judges have their offices in the Justice Building in Salem and usually hear cases in the courtroom of the Supreme Court Building. The court ordinarily sits in panels of three judges. The Supreme Court has authority to appoint a Supreme Court justice, a circuit court judge or an Oregon Tax Court judge to serve as a judge pro tempore of the Court of Appeals. In 1995, the Court of Appeals established an Appellate Settlement Conference Program for mediation of cases in that court.

Jurisdiction

The Court of Appeals has jurisdiction to review appeals of most civil and criminal cases and most state administrative agency actions. The exceptions are appeals in death penalty, lawyer and judicial disciplinary, and Oregon Tax Court cases, which go directly to the Oregon Supreme Court.

Reviews and Decisions

A party aggrieved by a decision of the Court of Appeals may petition the Supreme Court for review within 35 days after the Court of Appeals issues its decision. The Supreme Court determines whether to review the case. The Supreme Court allows a petition for review whenever at least one fewer than a majority of the Supreme Court judges participating vote to allow it.

OREGON TAX COURT

Address: Robertson Bldg., 1241 State St., 4th Floor, Salem 97301-2563
Phone: 503-986-5645; TTY: 503-986-5651
Fax: 503-986-5507

The Oregon Tax Court has exclusive, statewide jurisdiction in all questions of law or fact arising under state tax laws, including income taxes, corporate excise taxes, property taxes, timber taxes, cigarette taxes, local budget law and property tax limitations.

The Oregon Tax Court consists of the Magistrate Division and the Regular Division.

Trials in the Magistrate Division are informal proceedings. Statutory rules of evidence do not apply, and the trials are not reported. The proceedings may be conducted by telephone or in person. A taxpayer may be represented by a lawyer, public accountant, real estate broker or appraiser.

All decisions of the magistrates may be appealed to the Regular Division of the Oregon Tax Court.

The judge of the Oregon Tax Court presides over trials in the Regular Division. The Regular Division is comparable to a circuit court and exercises equivalent powers. All trials are before the judge only, and are reported. The parties may either represent themselves or be represented by an attorney. Appeals from the judge's decision are made directly to the Oregon Supreme Court.

The judge serves a six-year term and is elected on the statewide, nonpartisan judicial ballot.

CIRCUIT COURTS

Each county has a circuit court, which is a state trial court of general jurisdiction. However, except for cases involving the termination of parental rights, Gilliam, Sherman and Wheeler Counties also have "county courts," which exercise jurisdiction in juvenile cases. In addition, Gilliam, Grant, Harney, Malheur, Sherman and Wheeler Counties' county courts exercise jurisdiction in probate, adoption, guardianship and conservatorship cases.

Circuit court judges are elected on a nonpartisan ballot for a term of six years. They must be citizens of the United States, members of the Oregon State Bar, residents of Oregon for at least three years and residents of their judicial district for a least one year, except Multnomah County judges who may reside within ten miles of the county. There are 177 circuit judges serving 36 counties. The circuit judges are grouped in 27 geographical areas called judicial districts. Of the 177, Multnomah County District has 38 circuit judges; Lane, Marion and Washington, 15; Clackamas, 11; Jackson, 10; Deschutes, 7; Coos/Curry, 6; Douglas, Josephine, Klamath, Linn and Umatilla/Morrow districts have 5; Yamhill and Hood River/Wasco/Sherman/Wheeler/Gilliam districts have 4; Benton, Clatsop, Columbia, Lincoln, Polk and Crook/Jefferson districts have 3; Malheur, Tillamook, Union/Wallowa districts have 2 and Baker, Lake, Grant/Harney districts have 1.

To expedite judicial business, the chief justice of the Supreme Court may assign any circuit judge to sit in any judicial district in the state.

Senior Judges

Under Oregon law, a judge who retires from the circuit court, Oregon Tax Court, Court of Appeals or Supreme Court, except a judge retired under the provisions of ORS 1.310, may be designated a

continued on page 87

Supreme Court

Walters, Martha Lee
Chief Justice
Position 7
Served since 2006
Term expires 1/2027

Balmer, Thomas A.
Associate Justice
Position 1
Served since 2001
Term expires 1/2027

Duncan, Rebecca A.
Associate Justice
Position 2
Served since 2017
Term expires 1/2025

Flynn, Meagan A.
Associate Justice
Position 3
Served since 2017
Term expires 1/2025

Garrett, Christopher L.
Associate Justice
Position 4
Served since 2019
Term expires 1/2027

Nakamoto, Lynn R.
Associate Justice
Position 6
Served since 2016
Term expires 1/2023

Nelson, Adrienne C.
Associate Justice
Position 5
Served since 2018
Term expires 1/2025

Judicial

Court of Appeals

Egan, James C.
Chief Judge
Position 6
Served since 2013
Term expires 1/2025

Aoyagi, Robyn R.
Associate Judge
Position 4
Served since 2017
Term expires 1/2025

Armstrong, Rex
Associate Judge
Position 10
Served since 1995
Term expires 1/2025

DeHoog, Roger J.
Associate Judge
Position 8
Served since 2016
Term expires 1/2023

DeVore, Joel S.
Associate Judge
Position 11
Served since 2013
Term expires 1/2027

James, Bronson D.
Associate Judge
Position 2
Served since 2017
Term expires 1/2025

Kamins, Jacqueline S.
Associate Judge
Position 9
Served since 2020
Term expires 1/2027

Lagesen, Erin C.
Associate Judge
Position 12
Served since 2013
Term expires 1/2027

Mooney, Josephine H.
Associate Judge
Position 1
Served since 2019
Term expires 1/2027

Ortega, Darleen
Associate Judge
Position 3
Served since 2003
Term expires 1/2023

Powers, Steven R.
Associate Judge
Position 7
Served since 2017
Term expires 1/2025

Shorr, Scott A.
Associate Judge
Position 5
Served since 2016
Term expires 1/2023

Tookey, Douglas L.
Associate Judge
Position 13
Served since 2013
Term expires 1/2027

Oregon Tax Court

Manicke, Robert T.
Tax Judge
Served since 2017
Term expires 1/2025

continued from page 84

senior judge of the state by the Supreme Court and is eligible for temporary assignment by the Supreme Court to any state court at or below the level in which he or she last served as a full-time judge. The current roster of senior judges follows:

From the Supreme Court: Richard Baldwin, David Brewer, Wallace P. Carson, Jr., Paul J. De Muniz, Robert D. Durham, W. Michael Gillette, Rives Kistler, Jack Landau, Susan M. Leeson, Virginia L. Linder, Edwin Peterson, R. William Riggs, George Van Hoomissen

From the Court of Appeals or Oregon Tax Court: Henry Breithaupt, Carl N. Byers, Mary J. Deits, Walter Edmonds, Rick T. Haselton, William L. Richardson, Timothy J. Sercombe

From the circuit courts: Pamela L. Abernethy, Ted Abram, A. Michael Adler, Daniel J. Ahern. Marshall L. Amiton, G. Philip Arnold, Fred Avera, Raymond Bagley, Glen D. Baisinger, Richard Barron, Gregory L. Baxter, Frank L. Bearden, Mary Ann Bearden, William Beckett, Douglas G. Beckman, Linda Bergman, Jack A. Billings, Carol Bispham, Alan C. Bonebrake, Alta J. Brady, Paula Brownhill, Claudia M. Burton, Nancy W. Campbell, Cynthia Carlson, H. Ted Carp, Joseph F. Ceniceros, Ronald E. Cinniger, Rita B. Cobb, Allan H. Coon, Patricia Crain, William D. Cramer, Jr., Deanne Darling, Ross Davis, Don A. Dickey, Henry R. Dickinson, Jr., Jim Donnell, Hugh C. Downer, Jr., Greg Foote, Stephen P. Forte, Kimberly C. Frankel, Julie Franz, Jackson L. Frost, Stephen A. Gallagher, Robert S. Gardner, Randolph L. Garrison, David Gernant, Michael J. Gillespie, James C. Goode, Dennis Graves, Joe Guimond, David Hantke, Daniel L. Harris, Wayne R. Harris, Barbara Haslinger, Eveleen Henry, Robert D. Herndon, Bryan T. Hodges, Janet S. Holcomb, William Horner, Robert J. Huckleberry, Don Hull, Thomas M. Hull, Rodger Isaacson, Mary M. James, Nely L. Johnson, Edward Jones, Donald Kalberer, Mitchell

A. Karaman, John V. Kelly, Rick Knapp, Karla J. Knieps, Frank D. Knight, Dale R. Koch, Thomas W. Kohl, Thomas Kolberg, Paula J. Kurshner, Jerome LaBarre, Kristena LaMar, Darryl Larson, Terry A. Leggert, Kip Leonard, Donald Letourneau, William O. Lewis, Paul J. Lipscomb, Jon B. Lund, Charles E. Luukinen, William S. Mackay, Jean K. Maurer, Steven Maurer, Robert B. McConville, John A. McCormick, Rick J. McCormick, Maureen McKnight, Keith E. Meisenheimer, Maurice K. Merten, Richard Mickelson, Eve Miller, Robert Millikan, Douglas Mitchell, Robert J. Morgan, Thomas Moultrie, Rudy M. Murgo, Gayle A. Nachtigal, George W. Neilson, Philip L. Nelson, Michael Newman, Robert F. Nichols, Jr., DeAnn Novotny, Joseph V. Ochoa, Loyd O'Neal, Rebecca Orf, Roxanne Osborne, Ronald J. Pahl, Dale W. Penn, J. Burdette Pratt, Steven Price, William G. Purdy, Keith R. Raines, Richard Rambo, Karsten H. Rasmussen, Robert Redding, Steven B. Reed, Garry L. Reynolds, Jamese Rhoades, Rick W. Roll, Ilisa Rooke-Lee, Don H. Sanders, Mark S. Schiveley, Joan G. Seitz, Robert Selander, Gregory F. Silver, Lane W. Simpson, Berkeley Smith, Bernard L. Smith, William C. Snouffer, Diana Stuart, Michael C. Sullivan, Patricia A. Sullivan, Ronald D. Thom, Gary S. Thompson, Kirsten Thompson, Carroll Tichenor, Stephen Tiktin, Suzanne Upton, Eric Valentine, Pierre Van Rysselberghe, Lyle Velure, Kenneth R. Walker, Elizabeth Welch, C. Gregory West, Russell West, Raymond B. White, Gary Williams, Janice R. Wilson, John Wilson, John Wittmayer, Merri Souther Wyatt, Jan Wyers, Frank J. Yraguen

From the district courts:* Richard J. Courson, Robert L. Gilliland, Charles H. Reeves

*Effective January 15, 1998, all district courts were abolished and the powers, functions and judges of the district courts were transferred to the circuit courts.

JUDICIAL CONFERENCE

The Oregon Judicial Conference, created under ORS 1.810, is composed of all judges of the Supreme Court, Court of Appeals, Tax Court, circuit courts and all senior judges certified under ORS 1.300. The chief justice of the Supreme Court is chair of the conference, and the state court administrator acts as executive secretary. Under

ORS 1.820, the conference may make a continuous survey and study of the organization, jurisdiction, procedure, practice and methods of administration and operation of the various courts within the state.

The Judicial Conference meets annually to conduct business, attend educational seminars, issue committee reports and adopt resolutions, if any.

STATE COURT ADMINISTRATOR, OFFICE OF THE

Source: Nancy J. Cozine, Administrator
Address: 510 Justice Bldg. Mail: Supreme Court Bldg., 1163 State St., Salem 97301-2563
Phone: 503-986-5500; Oregon Relay 711
Fax: 503-986-5503
Web: https://www.courts.oregon.gov/about/Pages/osca.aspx

The state court administrator position was created in 1971 to assist the chief justice in exercising administrative authority over the state courts. In 1983, with unification and state funding of the trial and appellate courts, the duties of the position expanded to include human resources, accounting, budget preparation, revenue, and collections, management of the legislative program, state court property inventory and procurement, internal audit, maintenance of a statewide automated information system, continuing education programs for judges and nonjudge staff, public information, and long-range planning for the future needs of the courts. (*See ORS 8.110 and 8.125*)

In addition, the state court administrator oversees staff responsible for managing records of all cases filed with the Supreme Court, Court of Appeals and Oregon Tax Court; publishes the opinions of the Supreme Court, Court of Appeals and Oregon Tax Court; oversees the State Law Library, and oversees the Office of the State Court Administrator; State Court Security, State Court Interpreter, Certified Shorthand Reporters and State Citizen Review Board programs. Under ORS 30.273, the state court administrator also calculates and posts the annual adjustment to the liability limitations under the Oregon Tort Claims Act.

Cases Filed in Oregon Courts 2014–2019

	2014	2015	2016	2017	2018	2019
Oregon Supreme Court	977	890	820	944	848	893
Oregon Court of Appeals	2,566	2,598	2,817	2,768	3,063	3,340
Oregon Tax Court, Regular	37	27	22	24	38	36
Oregon Tax Court, Magistrate	470	575	410	396	409	360
Circuit Courts	532,136	503,244	480,818	519,956	510,632	483,397

Circuit Court

(P) = Presiding Judge

Abar, Donald D.
District 3, Position 11

Adkisson, Marci (P)
District 13, Position 3

Albrecht, Cheryl
District 4, Position 31

Alexander, Steffan K.
District 4, Position 26

Allen, Beth
District 4, Position 34

Ambrosini, George
District 16, Position 5

Armstrong, Sean E
District 3, Position 7

Ashby, Wells B. (P)
District 11, Position 6

Bachart, Sheryl
District 17, Position 1

Baggio, Amy M.
District 4, Position 38

Bagley, Beth
District 11, Position 2

Bailey, D. Charles
District 20, Position 6

Bain, Robert S. (P)
District 14, Position 3

Barnack, Timothy
District 1, Position 6

Beaman, Cynthia
District 15, Position 6

Bennett, J. Channing
District 3, Position 1

Bergstrom, Eric
District 4, Position 8

Bloch, Eric J.
District 4, Position 20

Bloom, Benjamin M.
District 1, Position 7

Bottomly, Leslie G.
District 4, Position 6

Branford, Thomas (P)
District 17, Position 3

Brauer, Christopher
District 6, Position 5

Brown, Adrian L.
District 4, Position 12

Broyles, Audrey J.
District 3, Position 9

Buchér, Erik M.
District 20, Position 3

Buckley, Marcia L.
District 17, Position 2

Bunch, Dan
District 13, Position 5

Burge, Frances
District 16, Position 4

Bushong, Stephen (P)
District 4, Position 21

Butterfield, Eric
District 20, Position 4

Callahan, Cathleen B.
District 19, Position 1

Campbell, Monte
District 12, Position 2

Carlson, Charles D.
District 2, Position 2

Cascagnette, Bradley A.
District 2, Position 3

Caso, Rafael A.
District 12, Position 1

Chanti, Suzanne
District 2, Position 9

Chapman, Jennifer K.
District 25, Position 2

Charter, Joe
District 1, Position 8

Clarke, Michael T.
District 19, Position 3

Collins, John L.
District 25, Position 1

Collins, Robert
District 6, Position 1

Combs, Andrew E.
District 15, Position 2

Conover, R. Curtis
District 2, Position 12

Cromwell, Laura
District 1, Position 4

Judicial

Crutchley, Raymond
District 11, Position 1

Dahlin, Eric L.
District 4, Position 24

Dailey, Kathleen M.
District 4, Position 25

Delsman, David E.
District 23, Position 2

Demarest, Joan E.
District 21, Position 3

Donohue, Matthew J.
District 21, Position 2

**Easterday, Cynthia
(P)**
District 25, Position 3

Emerson, Alison M.
District 11, Position 7

Erwin, Andrew R.
District 20, Position 7

Flint, Bethany P.
District 11, Position 3

Fun, James Lee, Jr.
District 20, Position 13

Galli, Matthew
District 14, Position 5

Garcia, Oscar
District 20, Position 9

Gerking, Timothy
District 1, Position 5

Geyer, Courtland
District 3, Position 12

Greenlick, Michael A.
District 4, Position 19

Grove, Ted (P)
District 19, Position 2

Guptill, Rebecca D.
District 20, Position 2

Hart, Thomas M.
District 3, Position 13

Henry, Patrick W.
District 4, Position 35

Hill, Daniel J. (P)
District 6, Position 3

Hill, Jonathan R.
District 27, Position 1

Hill, Norman R. (P)
District 12, Position 3

Hillman, Annette (P)
District 22, Position 1

Hodson, Jerry
District 4, Position 3

Holland, Lauren S.
District 2, Position 11

Holmes Hehn, Amy
District 4, Position 14

Hoppe, David G.
District 1, Position 2

Hung, Lung S. (P)
District 9, Position 2

Jacquot, Megan L.
District 15, Position 4

Janney, Andrea M.
District 13, Position 1

Johnson, Kathleen E.
District 16, Position 3

Judicial

bar

y

w

b

d

f

h

j

n

p

r

t

Jones, Jeffrey S.
District 5, Position 1

Kane, Brendan J.
District 23, Position 4

Kapoor, Amit
District 2, Position 6

Karabeika, Heather
District 5, Position 8

Kersey, Alycia E.
District 13, Position 2

Kittson-MaQatish, Rachel
District 23, Position 3

Kochlacs, Charles G.
District 1, Position 10

Landis, Erin Keith
District 9, Position 1

Lavin, Andrew M.
District 4, Position 7

Leith, David E.
District 3, Position 8

Lemarr, Kelly D.
District 20, Position 5

Lieuallen, Jon S.
District 6, Position 2

Lininger, Ann
District 5, Position 2

Long, Morgan W
District 4, Position 13

Lopez, Angel
District 4, Position 22

Love, Valeri L.
District 2, Position 8

Loy, Michael S.
District 4, Position 33

Lucero, Angela Franco
District 4, Position 11

Margolis, Jesse
District 15, Position 3

Marshall, Christopher
District 4, Position 5

Marshall, William A. (P)
District 16, Position 2

Matarazzo, Judith H.
District 4, Position 28

Matyas, Cindee S.
District 18, Position 3

McAlpin, Jay A.
District 2, Position 7

McGlaughlin, Sarah
District 14, Position 4

McGuire, Patricia
District 4, Position 27

McHill, Thomas (P)
District 23, Position 5

McIntosh, Dawn (P)
District 18, Position 2

McIntyre, Kerrie K.
District 2, Position 13

McLane, Michael
District 22, Position 2

Mejia, Lorenzo A. (P)
District 1, Position 1

Menchaca, Ricardo
District 20, Position 8

Miller, Walter R., Jr.
District 11, Position 5

Moawad, Heidi
District 4, Position 36

Morgan, Stephen W.
District 2, Position 5

Norby, Susie
District 5, Position 11

Oden-Orr, Melvin
District 4, Position 23

Olson, John A.
District 7, Position 1

Orr, David J.
District 1, Position 9

Ostrye, Karen
District 7, Position 3

Pagán, Ramón A.
District 20, Position 14

Partridge, Lindsay R.
District 3, Position 10

Pellegrini, Cheryl
District 3, Position 3

Perez, Manuel
District 3, Position 15

Peterson, Beau V.
District 18, Position 1

Powers, Thomas B. (P)
District 10, Position 1

Prall, Tracy A. (P)
District 3, Position 2

Proctor, Kathleen
District 20, Position 15

Pruess, Brett A.
District 15, Position 5

Ramras, Christopher
District 4, Position 15

Raschio, Robert (P)
District 24, Position 1

Rastetter, Thomas
District 5, Position 10

Ravassipour, Kelly W.
District 1, Position 3

Rees, David
District 4, Position 9

Rigmaiden, Clara L.
District 2, Position 15

Photo
Not
Submitted

Roberts, Beth (P)
District 20, Position 12

Roberts, Leslie
District 4, Position 37

Russell, Shelley D.
District 4, Position 4

Ryan, Thomas
District 4, Position 18

**Shirtcliff, Matthew
(P)**
District 8, Position 1

Shugar, Kamala
District 2, Position 10

Photo
Not
Submitted

Simmons, Ann Marie
District 16, Position 1

Sims, Theodore E.
District 20, Position 1

Skye, Kelly
District 4, Position 17

Judicial

Souede, Benjamin N.
District 4, Position 30

Stauffer, Janet L. (P)
District 7, Position 2

Steele, Kathie F. (P)
District 5, Position 6

Stone, Martin E. (P)
District 15, Position 1

Svetkey, Susan M.
District 4, Position 16

Sykora, Alycia N.
District 11, Position 4

Temple, Eva J.
District 6, Position 4

Thompson, Brandon M.
District 20, Position 10

Thueson, Brandon S.
District 14, Position 1

Torres, Xiomara Y.
District 4, Position 32

Trevino, Mari (P)
District 27, Position 2

Tripp, Susan
District 3, Position 14

Troy II, Francis G.
District 4, Position 1

Van Dyk, Douglas V.
District 5, Position 4

**Van Rysselberghe,
Todd L.**
District 5, Position 7

**Vandenberg, David M.
(P)**
District 26, Position 1

Velure, Debra E.
District 2, Position 1

Villa-Smith, Kathryn
District 4, Position 29

Vitolins, Daina A.
District 22, Position 3

Vogt, Debra (P)
District 2, Position 14

**Von Ter Stegge,
Katharine**
District 4, Position 10

Waller, Nan G.
District 4, Position 2

Watkins, Ulanda L.
District 5, Position 9

Weber, Katherine
District 5, Position 5

Wetzel, Michael
District 5, Position 3

Wiles, Ladd
District 25, Position 4

**Williams, Locke A.
(P)**
District 21, Position 1

Williams, Wes
District 10, Position 2

Wipper, Janelle F.
District 20, Position 11

Wogan, Cameron F.
District 13, Position 4

Wolf, John A.
District 7, Position 4

Wolke, Pat
District 14, Position 2

Judicial

Wren, Daniel V.	**Wynhausen, Michael**	**Zennaché, Charles**
District 3, Position 5	District 23, Position 1	District 2, Position 4

CIRCUIT COURT JUDGES BY DISTRICT

District 1—Jackson
Jackson County Justice Bldg., Medford 97501

Barnack, Timothy
Pos. 6, Exp. 1-4-27, 541-776-7171 x6368

Bloom, Benjamin M.
Pos. 7, Exp. 1-6-25, 541-776-7171 x6707

Charter, Joe
Pos. 8, Exp. 1-4-27, 541-776-7171 x6631

Cromwell, Laura A.
Pos. 4, Exp. 1-6-25, 541-776-7171 x6657

Gerking, Timothy G.
Pos. 5, Exp. 1-6-25, 541-776-7171 x6672

Hoppe, David
Pos. 2, Exp. 1-4-27, 541-776-7171 x6000

Kochlacs, Charles G.
Pos. 10, Exp. 1-4-27, 541-776-7171 x6644

Mejia, Lorenzo A. (presiding judge)
Pos. 1, Exp. 1-4-27, 541-776-7171 x6689

Orr, David J.
Pos. 9, Exp. 1-6-25, 541-776-7171 x6690

Ravassipour, Kelly W.
Pos. 3, Exp. 1-4-27, 541-776-7171 x6751

District 2—Lane
Lane County Courthouse, Eugene 97401

Carlson, Charles D.
Pos. 2, Exp. 1-4-27, 541-682-4257

Cascagnette, Bradley A.
Pos. 3, Exp. 1-4-27, 541-682-4256

Chanti, Suzanne
Pos. 9, Exp. 1-2-23, 541-682-4254

Conover, R. Curtis
Pos. 12, Exp. 1-6-25, 541-682-4497

Holland, Lauren S.
Pos. 11, Exp. 1-2-23, 541-682-4415

Kapoor, Amit
Pos. 6, Exp. 1-2-27, 541-682-4258

Love, Valeri L.
Pos. 8, Exp. 1-6-25, 541-682-4753

McAlpin, Jay A.
Pos. 7, Exp. 1-6-25, 541-682-4240

McIntyre, Karrie K.
Pos. 13, Exp. 1-2-23, 541-682-4218

Morgan, Stephen
Pos. 5, Exp. 1-2-23, 541-682-4300

Rigmaiden, Clara L.
Pos. 15, Exp. 1-4-27, 541-682-4250

Shugar, Kamala
Pos. 10, Exp. 1-6-25, 541-682-3601

Velure, Debra E.
Pos. 1, Exp. 1-6-25, 541-682-4253

Vogt, Debra (presiding judge)
Pos. 14, Exp. 1-6-25, 541-682-4027

Zennaché, Charles
Pos. 4, Exp. 1-4-27, 541-682-4259

District 3—Marion

Marion County Courthouse, Salem 97309-0869

Abar, Donald D.
Pos. 11, Exp. 1-6-25, 503-588-8485

Armstrong, Sean E.
Pos. 7, Exp. 1-6-25, 503-588-5026

Bennett, J. Channing
Pos. 1, Exp. 1-6-25, 503-588-7950

Broyles, Audrey J.
Pos. 9, Exp. 1-2-23, 503-588-5492

Geyer, Courtland
Pos. 12, Exp. 1-6-25, 503-373-4445

Hart, Thomas M.
Pos. 13, Exp. 1-2-23, 503-584-7749

Leith, David E.
Pos. 8, Exp. 1-6-25, 503-588-5160

Partridge, Lindsay R.
Pos. 10, Exp. 1-6-25, 503-588-5028

Pellegrini, Cheryl
Pos. 3, Exp. 1-4-27, 503-588-4939

Perez, Manuel
Pos. 15, Exp. 1-6-27, 503-566-2974

Prall, Tracy A. (presiding judge)
Pos. 2, Exp. 1-4-27, 503-588-5030

Tripp, Susan
Pos. 14, Exp. 1-4-27, 503-373-4361

Wren, Daniel J.
Pos. 5, Exp. 1-6-25, 503-584-7765

Vacant
Pos. 4, Exp. 1-2-23, 503-584-7713

Vacant
Pos. 6, Exp. 1-2-23, 503-373-4303

District 4—Multnomah

Multnomah County Courthouse, Portland 97204

Albrecht, Cheryl
Pos. 31, Exp. 1-6-25, 971-274-0680

Alexander, Steffan K.
Pos. 26, Exp. 1-2-23, 971-274-0670

Allen, Beth
Pos. 34, Exp. 1-4-27, 971-274-0686

Baggio, Amy M.
Pos. 38, Exp. 1-4-27, 971-274-0694

Bergstrom, Eric
Pos. 8, Exp. 1-6-25, 971-274-0634

Bloch, Eric J.
Pos. 20, Exp. 1-2-23, 971-274-0658

Bottomly, Leslie G.
Pos. 6, Exp. 1-4-27, 971-274-0630

Brown, Adrian L.
Pos. 12, Exp. 1-4-27, 971-274-0642

Bushong, Stephen (presiding judge)
Pos. 21, Exp. 1-4-27, 971-274-0660

Dahlin, Eric L.
Pos. 24, Exp. 1-4-27, 971-274-0666

Dailey, Kathleen M.
Pos. 25, Exp. 1-2-23, 971-274-0668

Greenlick, Michael A.
Pos. 19, Exp. 1-4-27, 971-274-0656

Henry, Patrick W.
Pos. 35, Exp. 1-6-25, 971-274-0688

Hodson, Jerry
Pos. 3, Exp. 1-6-25, 971-274-0624

Holmes Hehn, Amy
Pos. 14, Exp. 1-4-27, 971-274-0646

Lavin, Andrew M.
Pos. 7, Exp. 1-6-25, 971-274-0632

Long, Morgan Wren
Pos. 13, Exp. 1-4-27 971-274-0644

Lopez, Angel
Pos. 22, Exp. 1-2-23, 971-274-0662

Loy, Michael S.
Pos. 33, Exp. 1-4-27, 971-274-0684

Lucero, Angela Franco
Pos. 11, Exp. 1-4-27, 971-274-0640

Marshall, Christopher J.
Pos. 5, Exp. 1-4-27, 971-274-0628

Matarazzo, Judith Hudson
Pos. 28, Exp. 1-6-25, 971-274-0674

McGuire, Patricia
Pos. 27, Exp. 1-6-25, 971-274-0672

Moawad, Heidi H.
Pos. 36, Exp. 1-4-27, 971-274-0690

Oden-Orr, Melvin
Pos. 23, Exp. 1-6-25, 971-274-0664

Ramras, Christopher A.
Pos. 15, Exp. 1-6-25, 971-274-0648

Rees, David
Pos. 9, Exp. 1-2-23, 971-274-0636

Roberts, Leslie
Pos. 37, Exp. 1-6-25, 971-274-0692

Russell, Shelley D.
Pos. 4, Exp. 1-6-25, 971-274-0626

Ryan, Thomas
Pos. 18, Exp. 1-4-27, 971-274-0654

Skye, Kelly
Pos. 17, Exp. 1-2-23, 971-274-0652

Souede, Benjamin N.
Pos. 30, Exp. 1-6-25, 971-274-0678

Svetkey, Susan M.
Pos. 16, Exp. 1-6-25, 971-274-0650

Torres, Xiomara Y.
Pos. 32, Exp. 1-6-25, 971-274 0682

Troy II, Francis G.
Pos. 1, Exp. 1-4-27, 971-274-0620

Villa-Smith, Kathryn L.
Pos. 29, Exp. 1-6-25, 971-274-0676

Von Ter Stegge, Katharine
Pos. 10, Exp. 1-6-25, 971-274-0638

Waller, Nan G.
Pos. 2, Exp. 1-4-27, 971-274-0622

District 5—Clackamas

Clackamas County Courthouse, Oregon City 97045

Jones, Jeffrey S.
Pos. 1, Exp. 1-6-25, 503-655-8687

Karabeika, Heather L.
Pos. 8, Exp. 1-4-27, 503-655-8643

Lininger, Ann
Pos. 2, Exp. 1-6-25, 503-655-2841

Norby, Susie
Pos. 11, Exp. 1-6-25, 503-650-8902

Rastetter, Thomas
Pos. 10, Exp. 1-2-23, 503-655-8432

Steele, Kathie F. (presiding judge)
Pos. 6, Exp. 1-4-27, 503-655-8678

Van Dyk, Douglas V.
Pos. 4, Exp. 1-2-23, 503-655-8688

Von Rysselberghe, Todd
Pos. 7, Exp. 1-6-25, 503-655-8644

Watkins, Ulanda
Pos. 9, Exp. 1-4-27, 503-557-8686

Weber, Katherine
Pos. 5, Exp. 1-2-23, 503-655-8233

Wetzel, Michael
Pos. 3, Exp. 1-6-25, 503-655-8685

District 6—Morrow, Umatilla

Umatilla County Courthouse, Pendleton 97801

Brauer, Christopher R.
Pos. 5, Exp. 1-6-25, 541-278-0341 x3222

Collins, Robert
Pos. 1, Exp. 1-6-25, 541-278-0341 x3232

Lieuallen, Jon S.
Pos. 2, Exp. 1-2-23, 541-278-0341 x3225

Stafford Hansell Gov't Center, Hermiston 97838

Hill, Daniel J. (presiding judge)
Pos. 3, Exp. 1-2-23, 541-667-3034

Temple, Eva J.
Pos. 4, Exp. 1-6-25, 541-667-3031

District 7—Gilliam, Hood River, Sherman, Wasco, Wheeler

Hood River Co. Courthouse, Hood River 97031

Olson, John A.
Pos. 1, Exp. 1-6-25, 541-387-6913

Ostrye, Karen
Pos. 3, Exp. 1-4-27, 541-387-6906

Wasco County Courthouse, The Dalles 97058

Stauffer, Janet L. (presiding judge)
Pos. 2, Exp. 1-2-23, 541-506-2710

Wolf, John A.
Pos. 4, Exp. 1-2-23, 541-506-2717

District 8—Baker

Baker County Courthouse, Baker City 97814

Shirtcliff, Matthew B. (presiding judge)
Pos. 1, Exp. 1-6-25, 541-523-6303

District 9—Malheur

Malheur County Courthouse, Vale 97918

Hung, Lung S. (presiding judge)
Pos. 2, Exp. 1-6-25, 541-473-5568

Landis, Erin Keith
Pos. 1, Exp. 1-2-23, 541-473-5568

District 10—Union, Wallowa

Union County Courthouse, La Grande 97850
Wallowa County Courthouse, Enterprise 97828

Powers, Thomas B. (presiding judge)
Pos. 1, Exp. 1-6-25, 541-962-9500 x2231;
541-426-4991

Williams, Wes
Pos. 2, Exp. 1-6-25, 541-962-9500 x2225;
541-426-4991

District 11—Deschutes

Deschutes County Courthouse, Bend 97701

Ashby, Wells B. (presiding judge)
Pos. 6, Exp. 1-2-23, 541-388-5300 x2520

Bagley, Beth
Pos. 2, Exp. 1-6-25, 541-388-5300 x2410

Crutchley, Raymond D.
Pos. 1, Exp. 1-6-25, 541-388-5300 x2450

Emerson, Alison M.
Pos. 7, Exp. 1-4-27, 541-388-5300 x2580

Flint, Bethany P.
Pos. 3, Exp. 1-2-23, 541-388-5300 x2370

Miller, Walter R., Jr.
Pos. 5, Exp. 1-4-27, 541-388-5300 x2550

Sykora, Alycia N.
Pos. 4, Exp. 1-2-23, 541-388-5300 x2490

District 12—Polk

Polk County Courthouse, Dallas 97338

Campbell, Monte S.
Pos. 2, Exp. 1-2-23, 503-623-9245

Caso, Rafael A.
Pos. 1, Exp. 1-6-25, 503-831-1776
Hill, Norman R. (presiding judge)
Pos. 3, Exp. 1-6-25, 503-623-5235

District 13—Klamath
Klamath Co. Courthouse, Klamath Falls 97601
Adkisson, Marci Warner (presiding judge)
Pos. 3, Exp. 1-2-23, 541-883-5503 x251
Bunch, Dan
Pos. 5, Exp. 1-2-23, 541-883-5503 x255
Janney, Andrea M.
Pos. 1, Exp. 1-4-27, 541-883-5503 x247
Kersey, Alycia Edgeworth
Pos. 2, Exp. 1-2-27, 541-883-5503 x257
Wogan, Cameron F.
Pos. 4, Exp. 1-2-23, 541-883-5503 x244

District 14—Josephine
Josephine County Courthouse, Grants Pass 97526
Bain, Robert S. (presiding judge)
Pos. 3, Exp. 1-6-25, 541-476-2309 x4541
Galli, Matthew
Pos. 5, Exp. 1-6-25, 541-476-2309 x4525
McGlaughlin, Sarah E.
Pos. 4, Exp. 1-2-23, 541-476-2309 x4539
Thueson, Brandon S.
Pos. 1, Exp. 1-6-25, 541-476-2309 x4543
Wolke, Pat
Pos. 2, Exp. 1-6-25, 541-476-2309 x7916

District 15—Coos, Curry
Coos County Courthouse, Coquille 97423
Beaman, Cynthia
Pos. 6, Exp. 1-4-27, 541-247-2742
29821 Ellensburg Ave., Gold Beach 97444
Combs, Andrew E.
Pos. 2, Exp. 1-6-25, 541-396-4095
Jacquot, Megan L.
Pos. 4, Exp. 1-2-23, 541-396-4115
Margolis, Jesse
Pos. 3, Exp. 1-6-25, 541-247-2742
29821 Ellensburg Ave., Gold Beach 97444
Pruess, Brett A.
Pos. 5, Exp. 1-6-25, 541-751-2337
PO Box 865, North Bend 97459
Stone, Martin E. (presiding judge)
Pos. 1, Exp. 1-2-23, 541-396-4117

District 16—Douglas
Douglas County Justice Bldg., Roseburg 97470
Ambrosini, George
Pos. 5, Exp. 1-6-25, 541-957-2422
Burge, Frances
Pos. 4, Exp. 1-2-23, 541-957-2420

Johnson, Kathleen
Pos. 3, Exp. 1-2-23, 541-957-2433
Marshall, William A. (presiding judge)
Pos. 2, Exp. 1-2-23, 541-957-2436
Simmons, Ann Marie G.
Pos. 1, Exp. 1-4-27, 541-957-2430

District 17—Lincoln
Lincoln County Courthouse, Newport 97365
Bachart, Sheryl
Pos. 1, Exp. 1-4-27, 541-265-4236 x8504
Branford, Thomas O. (presiding judge)
Pos. 3, Exp. 1-6-25, 541-265-4236 x8505
Buckley, Marcia L.
Pos. 2, Exp. 1-4-27, 541-574-8812

District 18—Clatsop
Clatsop County Courthouse, Astoria 97103
Matyas, Cindee S.
Pos. 3, Exp. 1-6-25, 503-325-8555 x301
McIntosh, Dawn M. (presiding judge)
Pos. 2, Exp. 1-2-23, 503-325-8555 x301
Peterson, Beau V.
Pos. 1, Exp. 1-4-27, 503-325-8555 x301

District 19—Columbia
Columbia County Courthouse, St. Helens 97051
Callahan, Cathleen B.
Pos. 1, Exp. 1-4-27; 503-397-2327 x302
Clarke, Michael T.
Pos. 3, Exp. 1-4-27, 503-397-2327 x322
Grove, Ted (presiding judge)
Pos. 2, Exp. 1-4-27, 503-397-2327 x314

District 20—Washington
Washington County Courthouse, Hillsboro 97124
Bailey, Charlie
Pos. 6, Exp. 1-6-25, 503-846-4403
Buchér, Erik M.
Pos. 3, Exp. 1-6-25, 503-846-2875
Butterfield, Eric
Pos. 4, Exp. 1-2-23, 503-846-8771
Erwin, Andrew R.
Pos. 7, Exp. 1-4-27, 503-846-8009
Fun, James Lee, Jr.
Pos. 13, Exp. 1-6-25, 503-846-3615
Garcia, Oscar
Pos. 9, Exp. 1-6-25, 503-846-4840
Guptill, Rebecca D.
Pos. 2, Exp. 1-4-27, 503-846-8308
Lemarr, Kelly D.
Pos. 5, Exp. 1-4-27, 503-846-6344
Menchaca, Ricardo J.
Pos. 8, Exp. 1-4-27, 503-846-6204
Pagán, Ramón A.
Pos. 14, Exp. 1-2-23, 503-846-3708

Proctor, Kathleen
Pos. 15, Exp. 1-6-25, 503-846-2808

Roberts, Beth (presiding judge)
Pos. 12, Exp. 1-4-27, 503-846-8642

Sims, Theodore E.
Pos. 1, Exp. 1-2-23, 503-846-8311

Thompson, Brandon M.
Pos. 10, Exp. 1-2-23, 503-846-2306

Wipper, Janelle F.
Pos. 11, Exp. 1-6-25, 503-846-3852

District 21—Benton
Benton County Courthouse, Corvallis 97330

Demarest, Joan E.
Pos. 3, Exp. 1-2-23, 541-243-7802

Donohue, Matthew J.
Pos. 2, Exp. 1-4-27, 541-243-7805

Williams, Locke A. (presiding judge)
Pos. 1, Exp. 1-4-27, 541-243-7822

District 22—Crook, Jefferson
Jefferson Co. Circuit Court, 129 SW E St., Suite 101, Madras 97741
Crook County Courthouse, Prineville 97754

Hillman, Annette (presiding judge)
Pos. 1, Exp. 1-6-25, 541-475-3317; 541-447-6541

McLane, Michael
Pos. 2, Exp. 1-4-27, 541-475-3317; 541-447-6541

Vitolins, Daina A.
Pos. 3, Exp. 1-4-27, 541-475-3317; 541-447-6541

District 23—Linn
Linn County Courthouse, Albany 97321

Delsman, David E
Pos. 2, Exp. 1-4-27, 541-967-3848

Kane, Brendan J.
Pos. 4, Exp. 1-6-25, 541-967-3848

Kittson-MaQatish, Rachel
Pos. 3, Exp. 1-6-25, 541-967-3848

McHill, Thomas (presiding judge)
Pos. 5, Exp. 1-2-23, 541-812-8765

Wynhausen, Michael
Pos. 1, Exp. 1-6-25, 541-812-8767

District 24—Grant, Harney
Grant County Courthouse, Canyon City 97820
Harney County Courthouse, Burns 97720

Raschio, Robert (presiding judge)
Pos. 1, Exp. 1-4-27, 541-573-5207; 541-575-1438

District 25—Yamhill
Yamhill County Courthouse, McMinnville 97128

Chapman, Jennifer K.
Pos. 2, Exp. 1-6-25, 503-434-7485

Collins, John L.
Pos. 1, Exp. 1-2-23, 503-434-7497

Easterday, Cynthia (presiding judge)
Pos. 3, Exp. 1-2-23, 503-434-7486

Wiles, Ladd
Pos. 4, Exp. 1-4-27, 503-434-3054

District 26—Lake
Lake County Courthouse, Lakeview 97630

Vandenberg, David M. (presiding judge)
Pos. 1, Exp. 1-4-27, 541-947-6051

District 27—Tillamook
Tillamook County Courthouse, Tillamook 97141

Hill, Jonathan R.
Pos. 1, Exp. 1-2-23, 503-842-2598 x112

Trevino, Mari (presiding judge)
Pos. 2, Exp. 1-4-27, 503-842-2598 x114

Circuit Judges Association:
President—Hon. Kathleen Johnson
President Elect—Hon. Rafael A. Caso
Secretary—Hon. Benjamin Souede
Treasurer—Hon. Beth Bagley
Immediate Past President—Hon. Benjamin M. Bloom

STATE OF OREGON LAW LIBRARY

Source: Cathryn Bowie, State Law Librarian
Address: 1163 State St., Supreme Court Bldg., Salem 97301-2563
Phone: 503-986-5640; TTY: 503-986-5561
Fax: 503-986-5623
Web: https://soll.libguides.com/index

The State of Oregon Law Library (SOLL) traces its origins to the organization of the territorial government of Oregon. The Territorial Act of 1848 provided for the establishment of a library "to be kept at the seat of government." An 1851 act provided for the appointment of a librarian and defined the librarian's duties. The library served a broad constituency from its beginnings: "Members of the legislature, and its clerks and officers; Judges of the Supreme and District Courts, and their clerks; Attorney-general and marshal of the Territory; attorneys-at-law, secretary of the Territory; and all other persons, shall have access to the library, and the privileges allowed by law." This inclusive policy was continued with statehood in 1859. Charge and control of the library was transferred to the Supreme Court in 1913.

Today, the library operates under the administrative authority of the office of the state court administrator with a mission to provide the comprehensive legal resources that the executive, legislative and judicial branches of state government require to serve the public effectively, and to afford all Oregonians access to legal information.

The library provides access to the largest collection of legal information resources in state government, including the primary law of all U.S. jurisdictions and secondary material in virtually all areas of law.

Related Organizations

BOARD OF BAR EXAMINERS

Source: Troy Wood, Regulatory Counsel
Address: 16037 SW Upper Boones Ferry Rd., PO Box 231935, Tigard 97281-1935
Phone: 503-620-0222
Web: www.osbar.org/admissions

Joanna T. Perini-Abbott, Chair, 2022; Hon. Kelly Skye, Vice-Chair, 2023; Todd Bofferding, Member, 2021; Dr. Randall Green, Ph.D., Public Member, 2021; Misha Isaak, Member, 2023; Lissa Kaufman, Member, 2022; Dr. Richard Kolbell, Ph. D., Public Member, 2021; Angela Franco Lucero, Member, 2021; Kendra Matthews, Member, 2022; Cassandra C. Skinner, Member, 2023; Michael Slauson, Member, 2021; Stephanie J. Tuttle, Member, 2021; Ernest Warren Jr., Member, 2022; Caroline Wong, Member, 2023

The Board of Bar Examiners, established in 1913, acts for the Supreme Court in evaluating an applicant's qualifications to practice law in Oregon. The Board determines an applicant's qualifications for admission to the Bar by administering and grading the Oregon bar examination twice a year; and investigating and evaluating the character and fitness of each applicant.

OREGON STATE BAR

Source: Helen Hierschbiel, Chief Executive Officer
Address: 16037 SW Upper Boones Ferry Rd., PO Box 231935, Tigard 97281-1935
Phone: 503-620-0222; Toll-free: 1-800-452-8260
Fax: 503-684-1366
Web: www.osbar.org

Board of Governors: David Wade, President, Eugene, 2022; Colin Andries, Portland, 2021; Christopher Cauble, Grants Pass, 2024; Gabriel Chase, Portland, 2024; Jenny Cooke; Portland, 2022; Katherine H. Denning, Salem, 2022; Kamron Graham, Portland, 2022; John E. Grant,

Portland, 2021; Bik-Na Han, Portland, 2022; Joseph Hesbrook, Public Member, 2022; Ryan Hunt, Salem, 2023; Matt McKean, Hillsboro, 2023; Rob Milesnick, Vancouver, 2023; Curtis Peterson, Portland, 2024; Joseph Piucci, Portland, 2023; Liani Reeves, Immediate Past-President, 2021; Michael Rondeau, Public Member, 2021; David Rosen, Bend, 2024; Tasha Winkler, Portland, 2023

Established in 1935, the Oregon State Bar is a public corporation and instrumentality of the Oregon Judicial Department that serves the public by regulating lawyers and improving access to justice and the delivery of legal services. The state bar oversees the admission and discipline of Oregon's lawyers. It also operates a lawyer referral service program, conducts continuing legal education programs, publishes legal and public service material, sponsors a legislative program to improve the laws and judicial system of Oregon, provides malpractice coverage for lawyers in private practice, distributes state funds allocated to legal service programs and monitors the programs for adherence to adopted standards.

COUNCIL ON COURT PROCEDURES

Source: Mark A. Peterson, Executive Director
Address: c/o Lewis & Clark Law School, 10015 SW Terwilliger Blvd., Portland 97219
Phone: 503-768-6505
Web: https://counciloncourtprocedures.org

Oregon's civil trial procedures were once found in laws passed by the Legislature and scattered among the Oregon Revised Statutes (ORS), until the Council on Court Procedures was established by the Legislature in 1977 (ORS 1.725 to 1.760).

The Council codified Oregon's requirements governing pleading, practice, and procedure in all civil proceedings in the circuit courts of the state – the Oregon Rules of Civil Procedure (ORCP) as the product of the Council, it is charged with the responsibility for maintaining the ORCP by promulgating amendments in odd-numbered years each biennium. The Council's promulgations amend the ORCP unless the Legislature by statute repeals, amends, or supplements a rule or a promulgation. See the Council's website and the above-referenced statutes for more detailed information.

Members with term-expiration dates:

Hon. Lynn R. Nakamoto, Oregon Supreme Court 2021; Hon. Douglas L. Tookey, Oregon Court of Appeals, 2021; Hon. D. Charles Bailey, Washington County Circuit Court, 2021; Hon. R. Curtis Conover, Lane County Circuit Court, 2021; Hon. Norman R. Hill, Polk County Circuit Court, 2021; Hon. David Euan Leith, Marion County Circuit Court, 2023; Hon. Thomas McHill, Linn County Circuit Court

2023; Hon. Susie L. Norby, Clackamas County Circuit Court, 2021; Hon. Leslie Roberts, Multnomah County Circuit Court, 2023; Hon. John A. Wolf, Gilliam, Hood River, Sherman, Wasco, & Wheeler County Circuit Courts, 2021; Kelly L. Andersen, Medford, 2021; Troy S. Bundy, Portland, 2023; Kenneth Crowley, Salem, 2023 (Vice Chair); Travis Eiva, Eugene, 2021; Jennifer Gates, Portland, 2021 (Chair); Barry Goehler, Lake Oswego, 2023; Meredith Holley, Eugene, 2021; Drake A. Hood, Hillsboro, 2023; Scott O'Donnell, Portland, 2021; Shenoa L. Payne, Portland, 2021; Tina Stupasky, 2023; Jeffrey Young, Portland, 2023; Margurite Weeks, Public Member, Portland, 2021 (Treasurer)

COMMISSION ON JUDICIAL FITNESS AND DISABILITY

Source: Rachel L. Mortimer, Executive Director
Address: PO Box 90398, Portland 97290
Phone: 503-626-6776
Fax: 503-626-6787
Web: https://www.courts.oregon.gov/programs/cjfd/Pages/default.aspx

Chair Jeffrey Wallace, Attorney, 2024; Vice-Chair Karyn Goodfriend, Public Member, 2024; Hon. Cheryl Albrecht, 2025; Hon. Monte S. Campbell, 2025; Roland Herrera, Public Member, 2024; Melanie Kebler, Attorney, 2023; Wilson Kenney, PhD, Public Member, 2023; Judith Parker, Attorney, 2023; Hon. Steven Powers, 2022;

Commission members are volunteers serving four-year terms. Three are judges appointed by the Supreme Court, three are lawyers appointed by the Oregon State Bar and three are citizens appointed by the governor and confirmed by the senate.

Pursuant to ORS 1.410 to 1.480, the Oregon Constitution and the Rules of Judicial Conduct, the commission investigates complaints regarding Oregon judges. If the commission believes there is substantial evidence of misconduct, a public hearing is held. The commission makes recommendations regarding disciplinary actions to the Supreme Court. A judge may be censured, suspended or removed from office by the Supreme Court. The commission cannot change the decision of a judge and does not have jurisdiction over arbitrators, mediators or municipal court judges.

COUNTY COURTS

At one time county courts existed in all 36 Oregon counties. The title "county judge" is retained in some counties as the title of the chair of the board of county commissioners. There is no requirement that county judges be members of the bar.

Where a county judge's judicial function still exists, it is limited to juvenile and probate matters and occupies only a portion of the judge's time, which is primarily devoted to nonjudicial administrative responsibilities as a member of the county board.

Today, only six counties, all east of the Cascades, have county judges who retain any judicial authority. Gilliam, Sherman and Wheeler have juvenile and probate jurisdiction, while Grant, Harney and Malheur have probate jurisdiction.

MUNICIPAL COURT

Oregon Municipal Judges Association

Source: A. Carl Myers, Director
Address: 1815 Commercial St. S., Salem 97302
Phone: 503-399-9219
Email: carl@feiblemancase.com
Web: www.omjaonline.com

The Oregon Municipal Judges Association (OMJA) participates in arranging continuing educational training sessions for municipal judges. It maintains a listserv system for judges to gain access to other municipal court judges and justices of the peace, whose two associations trade off on annual conferences in Oregon. OMJA coordinates with the Oregon Department of Transportation, which has its own annual conference for judges.

Many incorporated cities in Oregon have a municipal court as authorized by charter and state law. Municipal courts have concurrent jurisdiction with circuit and justice courts over all violations and misdemeanors committed or triable in the city in which the court is located. They do not have jurisdiction over felonies. Municipal courts primarily hear traffic violations and crimes; violations of municipal codes and ordinances, including animal, high grass and trash nuisances; vehicle impoundments and forfeitures; and parking and pedestrian violations. They also hear certain minor tobacco, liquor and drug violations.

Municipal courts may be a court of record, although most are not. Municipal court procedures are controlled to a large extent by state law.

A municipal judge need not be an attorney, although most are. Municipal judges are usually appointed by, and serve at the pleasure of, the city council. A few Oregon cities have elected judges. Qualifications for office are determined by the city council or charter. A municipal judge may perform weddings anywhere within the state of Oregon.

JUSTICE COURTS

Source: Damian Idiart, Justice of the Peace
Address: 4173 Hamrick Rd., Central Point 97502
Phone: 541-774-1286

Web: http://jacksoncountyor.org/Departments/
Justice-Court/Home

Justice court is held by a justice of the peace within the district for which he or she is elected. The county commissioners have power to establish justice court district boundaries. The justice of the peace is a remnant of territorial days when each precinct of the state was entitled to a justice court. Thirty-two justice courts currently administer justice in 21 counties.

Justice courts have jurisdiction within their county, concurrent with the circuit court, in all criminal prosecutions, except felony trials. Actions at law in justice courts are conducted using the mode of proceeding and rules of evidence similar to those used in the circuit courts, except where otherwise specifically provided.

Justice courts have jurisdiction over traffic, boating, wildlife and other violations occurring in their county. Justices of the peace also perform weddings at no charge if performed at their offices during regular business hours.

The justice court has small claims civil jurisdiction where the money or damages claimed do not exceed $7,500, except in actions involving title to real property, false imprisonment, libel, slander or malicious prosecution.

A justice of the peace must be a citizen of the United States, a resident of Oregon for three years, and a resident of the justice court district for one year prior to becoming a nonpartisan candidate for election to that office. They are elected to six-year terms. The names of the Oregon justices of the peace are listed by county in the Local Governments section.

OFFICE OF PUBLIC DEFENSE SERVICES

Source: Lane Borg, Executive Director; Per Ramfjord, Chair

Address: 1175 Court St. NE, Salem 97301-4030
Phone: 503-378-3349
Fax: 503-378-2163
Web: www.oregon.gov/OPDS

The Public Defense Services Commission (PDSC) is an independent body that governs the Office of Public Defense Services (OPDS). The chief justice of the Oregon Supreme Court appoints the seven commission members to four-year terms. The commission's primary charge is to establish "a public defense system that ensures the provision of public defense services in the most cost efficient manner consistent with the Oregon Constitution, the United States Constitution and Oregon and national standards of justice."

The PDSC appoints the executive director for OPDS. The OPDS has two divisions: Contract and Business Services (CBS) and the Appellate Division (AD), formerly known as the State Public Defender.

CBS is responsible for administering the public defense contracts that provide legal representation for financially eligible persons in criminal, civil commitment and juvenile proceedings and for processing requests and payments for non-contract fees and expenses. Contracts provide trial-level representation and appellate representation on cases not handled by AD.

AD is the appellate arm of OPDS. The division provides constitutionally mandated representation in the appellate courts to financially eligible persons in misdemeanor and felony criminal offenses, including capital offenses, parents in juvenile dependency cases, and inmates appealing administrative decisions from the State Board of Parole and Post-Prison Supervision.

Judicial

The Cove Palisades State Park

Jacob Hurd
Ms Campbell's 3rd Grade Class
Buff Elementary, Madras

This drawing by Jacob Hurd shows camping, boating, and hiking at The Cove Palisades State Park.

Note: The text is displayed as written.

I am writing about Cove Palisides. The Cove has two camp grounds and cabins. I piked it because there is a lake in the hight desert.

To start there is a lake in the high desert. Did you know you can do tons of stuff at the lake. You can water ski with your frinds. You can go fishing for kokahee, bull trout, bass and crayfish. And you can go swiming with your family.

Next you can explor in the hight desert. You can go camping and hiking. You can look at the nature. My favoret is the balancing rocks. My favoret hike is the Tamat'an trail. It is cool because it over looks the lake. They call the hight desert that because it is very dry.

Last I piked the cove because there is a lot to do at the cove like camping, boting, hiking and exploring. It is rilly cool because there is a lake in the hight desert.

Legislative

Oregon's Provisional Legislature first met formally in 1845 in Oregon City. They were a unicameral body that operated on an uncertain schedule. The present bicameral system—two houses with senators and representatives—was adopted in 1859 upon statehood. Today's legislators meet annually in Salem and deal with complex matters, by passing bills and appropriating funding. This section introduces the members of the Legislature and describes how the Legislature is organized.

OREGON'S LEGISLATIVE ASSEMBLY

Source: Legislative Administration
Address: 900 Court St. NE, Rm. 140-A, Salem 97301
Phone: 503-986-1848
Web: www.oregonlegislature.gov

President of the Senate

Peter Courtney, Senate President
Address: 900 Court St. NE, Rm. S-201, Salem 97301
Phone: 503-986-1600

The Senate president is elected by members of the Senate to select committee chairs and membership, preside over its daily sessions and coordinate its administrative operations. Subject to the rules of the Senate, the president refers measures to committees, directs Senate personnel and mediates questions on internal operations.

The Senate president's staff assists in carrying out official duties, helps coordinate Senate operations and provides a variety of public information services. In cooperation with the speaker of the House, the president coordinates and supervises the work product of the legislative branch of Oregon state government and represents that branch in contacts with the executive and judicial branches. The president's office works closely with all political parties to ensure that session goals are met.

Secretary of the Senate

Lori Brocker, Secretary of the Senate
Address: 900 Court St. NE, Rm. 233, Salem 97301
Phone: 503-986-1851

The secretary of the Senate is an elected officer of the state Senate. The secretary is responsible for and supervises Senate employees engaged in keeping measures, papers and records of proceedings and actions of the Senate. The secretary supervises preparation of the daily agenda, all measures, histories, journals and related publications and is in charge of publication of documents related to the Senate. In addition, the secretary has custody of all measures, official papers and records of the Senate, except when released to authorized persons

by signed receipt. The secretary also serves as parliamentary consultant to the Senate, advises officers of the Senate on parliamentary procedure and manages the Honorary Page program.

During the interim, the secretary receives messages from the governor announcing executive appointments requiring Senate confirmation, prepares the agenda for the convening of the Senate and supervises publication of the official record of proceedings.

Speaker of the House of Representatives

Tina Kotek, Speaker of the House
Address: 900 Court St. NE, Rm. 269, Salem 97301
Phone: 503-986-1200

The speaker of the House is elected by House members to preside over the deliberations of the House, preserve order and decorum and decide questions of order. The speaker appoints chairs and members to each committee and refers measures to appropriate committees in accordance with provisions of the rules of the House.

The House speaker's staff coordinates operations of the speaker's office, assists the presiding officer in performing official duties, provides research and policy support in issue areas, provides information to the news media and assists legislators in solving constituent problems. In conjunction with the Senate president's office, the speaker's office coordinates and supervises operations of the legislative branch of government, joint statutory committees and joint interim committees and task forces.

Chief Clerk of the House of Representatives

Timothy G. Sekerak, Chief Clerk
Address: 900 Court St. NE, Rm. H-271, Salem 97301
Phone: 503-986-1870

The chief clerk, elected by members of the House of Representatives, supervises and keeps a correct journal, and is the official custodian of all other records of House proceedings. The chief clerk notifies the Senate of all acts of the House, certifies and transmits all bills, resolutions and papers requiring Senate concurrence immediately upon their passage or adoption, and secures proper authentication of bills that have passed both houses and transmits them to the governor.

The chief clerk prepares the agenda, coordinates details for the organization of the House and acts as parliamentarian as directed by House rules. In addition, at the end of the legislative session, the chief clerk supervises and authenticates the revision and printing of the *House Journal* and prepares all legislative records that are to be permanently filed with the state archivist.

Caucus Offices

Rob Wagner (D), Senate Majority Leader
Address: 900 Court St. NE, Rm. S-223, Salem 97301
Phone: 503-986-1700

Fred Girod (R), Senate Republican Leader
Address: 900 Court St. NE, Rm. S-323, Salem 97301
Phone: 503-986-1950

Barbara Smith Warner (D), House Majority Leader
Address: 900 Court St. NE, Rm. H-295, Salem 97301
Phone: 503-986-1900

Christine Drazen (R), House Republican Leader
Address: 900 Court St. NE, Rm. H-395, Salem 97301
Phone: 503-986-1400

Caucus offices provide many services to their members during session and interim periods. Each office is directed by a leader chosen by the respective political party. The operations of the four offices are not identical, but typical services include conducting research, writing speeches and press releases, providing public information services, serving as liaison to state and federal agencies to help solve constituent problems, organizing caucus activities and circulating information about legislative business among caucus members during both session and interim periods.

Organization

Oregon's Legislative Assembly is composed of two chambers, House of Representatives and Senate. The Senate consists of 30 members elected to four-year terms. Half of the Senate seats are up for election every two years. The House consists of 60 representatives elected to two-year terms. Except in cases of persons selected to fill vacancies, legislators are elected in even-numbered years from single-member districts. Election by single-member district means that each Oregonian is represented by one senator and one representative. To qualify for a seat in the Legislature, one must be at least 21 years of age, a U.S. citizen and reside in the legislative district for at least one year prior to election. Each chamber elects presiding officers to oversee daily sessions and operations and perform other duties set by rule, custom and law. These officers are known as the president of the Senate and speaker of the House.

Functions

The Legislature enacts new laws and revises existing ones, makes decisions that keep the state in good economic and environmental condition and provides a forum for discussion of public issues.

The Legislature reviews and revises the governor's proposed budget and passes tax laws to provide needed revenue. The Oregon Constitution requires that the state must not spend money in excess of revenue.

The Legislature also influences executive and judicial branch decisions, enacting laws and adopting the budget and establishing state policy that directs all state agency activity and impacts the courts. The Senate confirms gubernatorial appointments to certain offices. Legislative Counsel Committee reviews state agency administrative rules to ensure that legislative intent is followed.

Legislative Process

During the 2019 Regular Session, 701 of 2,613 introduced bills became law. During the 2020 Regular Session, 3 of 258 introduced bills became law.

Most of the discussion and revisions of bills and other measures are done in committees. The process begins when a measure is introduced and referred to a committee. The committee may hear testimony on the measure, frequently from members of the public, and may amend the measure and send it to the floor of its respective chamber for debate. The committee can also table the

Senate and House District Numbers

Senate	House Dist.	Senate	House Dist.	Senate	House Dist.	Senate	House Dist.
1	1 and 2	9	17 and 18	17	33 and 34	25	49 and 50
2	3 and 4	10	19 and 20	18	35 and 36	26	51 and 52
3	5 and 6	11	21 and 22	19	37 and 38	27	53 and 54
4	7 and 8	12	23 and 24	20	39 and 40	28	55 and 56
5	9 and 10	13	25 and 26	21	41 and 42	29	57 and 58
6	11 and 12	14	27 and 28	22	43 and 44	30	59 and 60
7	13 and 14	15	29 and 30	23	45 and 46		
8	15 and 16	16	31 and 32	24	47 and 48		

measure and end its consideration. Unlike many state legislatures, Oregon does not amend measures during floor debate.

After a measure has been considered by a committee and passed by the chamber in which it was introduced, it is sent to the other chamber where a similar procedure is followed.

If both chambers pass a bill in identical form, including any amendments approved by the other chamber, it is enrolled (printed in final form) for the signatures of the presiding officers and governor. The governor may sign the bill, veto it or let it become law without signature. The governor may also veto line items of appropriation bills, but may not veto an act referred for a vote of the people or an act initiated by the people.

The Oregon Constitution and state law require that deliberations of the Legislative Assembly and

Chronology of Regular Legislative Sessions in Oregon

Leg. Assembly	Year	Dates	Length in Days	Leg. Assembly	Year	Dates	Length in Days
1	1860	Sept. 10–Oct. 19	40	46	1951	Jan. 8–May 3	116
2	1862	Sept. 8–Oct. 17	40	47	1953	Jan. 12–April 21	100
3	1864	Sept. 12–Oct. 22	41	48	1955	Jan. 10–May 4	115
4	1866	Sept. 10–Oct. 20	41	49	1957	Jan. 14–May 21	128
5	1868	Sept. 14–Oct. 28	44	50	1959	Jan. 12–May 6	115
6	1870	Sept. 12–Oct. 20	39	51	1961	Jan. 9–May 10	122
7	1872	Sept. 9–Oct. 23	45	52	1963	Jan. 14–June 3	141
8	1874	Sept. 14–Oct. 21	38	53	1965	Jan. 11–May 14	124
9	1876	Sept. 11–Oct. 20	40	54	1967	Jan. 9–June 14	157
10	1878	Sept. 9–Oct. 18	40	55	1969	Jan. 13–May 23	131
11	1880	Sept. 13–Oct. 23	41	56	1971	Jan. 11–June 10	151
12	1882	Sept. 11–Oct. 19	39	57	1973	Jan. 8–July 6	180
13	1885	Jan. 12–Feb. 21	40	58	1975	Jan. 13–June 14	153
14	1887	Jan. 10–Feb. 18	39	59	1977	Jan. 10–July 5	177
15	1889	Jan. 14–Feb. 22	39	60	1979	Jan. 8–July 4	178
16	1891	Jan. 12–Feb. 20	39	61	1981	Jan. 12–August 2	203
17	1893	Jan. 9–Feb. 17	39	62	1983	Jan. 10–July 16	188
18	1895	Jan. 14–Feb. 23	40	63	1985	Jan. 14–June 21	159
19	1897	Jan. 11–March 2	*	64	1987	Jan. 12–June 28	168
20	1899	Jan. 9–Feb. 18	40	65	1989	Jan. 9–July 4	177
21	1901	Jan. 14–March 4	50	66	1991	Jan. 14–July 1	168
22	1903	Jan. 12–Feb. 20	39	67	1993	Jan. 11–August 5	207
23	1905	Jan. 9–Feb. 17	40	68	1995	Jan. 9–June 10	153
24	1907	Jan. 14–Feb. 23	41	69	1997	Jan. 13–July 5	174
25	1909	Jan. 11–Feb. 20	41	70	1999	Jan. 11–July 24	195
26	1911	Jan. 9–Feb. 18	41	71	2001	Jan. 8–July 7	181
27	1913	Jan. 13–March 5	51	72	2003	Jan. 13–August 27	227
28	1915	Jan. 11–Feb. 20	41	73	2005	Jan. 10–August 5	208
29	1917	Jan. 8–Feb. 19	43	74	2007	Jan. 8–June 28	171
30	1919	Jan. 13–Feb. 27	46	75	2009	Jan. 12–June 29	169
31	1921	Jan. 10–Feb. 23	45	76	2011	Feb. 1–June 30	150
32	1923	Jan. 8–Feb. 22	46	76	2012	Feb. 1–March 5	34
33	1925	Jan. 12–Feb. 26	46	77	2013	Feb. 4–July 8	155
34	1927	Jan. 10–Feb. 25	47	77	2014	Feb. 3–March 7	33
35	1929	Jan. 14–March 5	50	78	2015	Feb. 2–July 6	155
36	1931	Jan. 12–March 6	54	78	2016	Feb. 1–March 3	32
37	1933	Jan. 9–March 9	60	79	2017	Feb. 1–July 7	157
38	1935	Jan. 14–March 13	59	79	2018	Feb. 5–March 3	27
39	1937	Jan. 11–March 8	57	80	2019	Jan. 22–June 30	160
40	1939	Jan. 9–March 15	66	80	2020	Feb. 3–March 8	35
41	1941	Jan. 13–March 15	62	81	2021	Jan. 19–	
42	1943	Jan. 11–March 10	59				
43	1945	Jan. 8–March 17	69				
44	1947	Jan. 13–April 5	83				
45	1949	Jan. 10–April 16	97				

The House of Representatives never formally convened because its members failed to reach agreement on organization.

Legislative

its committees be open to the public. The law also requires public notice of meetings and maintenance of public meeting records. These practices ensure that the legislative process is open to public scrutiny.

Effective Date of Laws

The regular effective date of a measure is January 1 of the year following passage of the measure. Some measures may contain a provision, such as an emergency clause, that specifies an earlier effective date.

The Oregon Constitution prohibits tax measures from having an emergency clause. This ensures that the people have the right to refer a tax measure for a vote by petition before it goes into effect.

Session Schedule

In 2010, voters approved a ballot measure referred by the Legislature requiring the Legislature to meet annually. Beginning in 2011, the Legislature convenes in February at the State Capitol in Salem, but sessions may not exceed 160 days in odd-numbered years and 35 days in even-numbered years. Five-day extensions are allowed by a two-thirds vote in both houses. In addition, the Legislature may hold an organizational session to swear in newly elected officials, elect legislative leaders, adopt rules, organize and appoint committees and begin introducing bills.

Special sessions to deal with emergencies may be called by the governor or by a majority of each chamber. For example, the Legislative Assembly called itself into a special session in 2002, 2006, 2008 and 2010, and Governor Kate Brown called for three special sessions in 2020 to deal with the COVID-19 pandemic.

Contacting a Legislator and Obtaining Legislative Information

During session, the following numbers are available to obtain legislative information:
• Outside Salem: 1-800-332-2313
• Within Salem: 503-986-1388

During the interim, individual legislators may be reached by calling the telephone numbers listed on pages 121–123 and 127–132. Legislative information may be obtained by calling Legislative Administration at 503-986-1848.

Session Interim

After adjournment of regular or special sessions, the work of the Legislature continues. Legislators study issues likely to be important during future sessions, become acquainted with new issues, prepare drafts of legislation and exercise legislative oversight.

Convening of the Senate to Act on Executive Appointments

The Legislative Assembly may require that appointments to state public office made by the governor, be subject to Senate confirmation.

During the legislative session, the Senate president refers executive appointments to a standing or special committee to review the background and qualifications of appointees, ensuring that statutory requirements are met. Appointees may be asked to come before the committee for personal interviews. The committee submits its recommendations to the full Senate for confirmation votes.

During the interim, the secretary of the Senate receives the governor's announcements of executive appointments requiring Senate confirmation. Generally, gubernatorial appointments made during a regular or special session of the Legislature are acted upon by the Senate prior to adjourning *sine die* or final adjournment.

History

Oregon's Provisional Legislature initially met formally in Oregon City, December 2 to December 19, 1845. An earlier pre-provisional committee met in August of 1845 after the formal ratification of Oregon's Organic Articles and Laws of 1843 and the inauguration of George Abernethy as governor. The first Provisional Legislature, a unicameral body with autonomous powers, conducted its sessions in a rather casual manner and frequently suspended its rules to take care of unexpected situations. It met at least annually until February 1849, five months before the first Territorial Legislature met during July 16 to July 24, 1849, also in Oregon City.

The Territorial Legislature was bicameral. It had an upper council of nine members and a lower house of 18 members elected from the eight existing counties that had regular annual meetings. Unlike the Provisional Legislature, its actions were subject to review in Washington, D.C. At the time of statehood and adoption of the constitution in 1859, the present bicameral system was adopted. The Legislature then met in the fall of even-numbered years until 1885 when the sessions were moved to the early winter months of odd-numbered years to accommodate members who farmed.

Statistical Summary of the Eightieth Legislative Assembly

Source: Legislative Counsel

Senate Total Membership	30
Democrats	18
Republicans	12
President: Peter Courtney (D), Salem	
House Total Membership	60
Democrats	38

Republicans   22
Speaker: Tina Kotek (D), Portland

2019 Regular Session

Session Length	160 Calendar Days
Convened	January 22, 2019
Adjourned	June 30, 2019

Bills Introduced	2,613
Other Measures	155
Total	2,768

Bills	House	Senate	Total
Introduced	1,509	1,104	2,613
Passed Both Houses	361	340	701
Vetoed	0	0	0
Became Law	360	340	700
Unsigned by Governor	1	0	1

Resolutions and Memorials

	House	Senate	Total
Introduced	73	82	155
Adopted	28	31	59

2020 Regular Session

Session Length	35 Calendar Days
Convened	February 3, 2020
Adjourned	March 8, 2020

Bills Introduced	258
Other Measures	25
Total	283

Bills	House	Senate	Total
Introduced	177	81	258
Passed Both Houses	3	0	3
Vetoed	0	0	0
Became Law	3	0	3
Unsigned by Governor	0	0	0

Resolutions and Memorials

	House	Senate	Total
Introduced	14	11	25
Adopted	1	2	3

STATUTORY COMMITTEES AND INTERIM OFFICES

Source: Legislative Administration
Address: 900 Court St. NE, Rm. 140-A, Salem 97301
Phone: 503-986-1848
Web: www.oregonlegislature.gov/la

Legislative Administration Committee

Brett Hanes, Interim Legislative Administrator

The Legislative Administration Committee provides services to the Legislative Assembly, its support staff and the public. The committee, authorized by ORS 173.710, includes the president of the Senate, speaker of the House, members of the Senate appointed by the president and members of the House appointed by the speaker.

Special Legislative Sessions

Year	Date	Length in Days
1860	Oct. 1–Oct. 2	2
1865	Dec. 5–Dec. 18	14
1885	Nov. 11–Nov. 24	14
1898	Sept. 26–Oct. 15	20
1903	Dec. 21–Dec. 23	3
1909	Mar. 15–Mar. 16	2
1920	Jan. 12–Jan. 17	6
1921	Dec. 19–Dec. 24	6
1933	Jan. 3–Jan. 7	5
1933	Nov. 20–Dec. 9	20
1935	Oct. 21–Nov. 9	20
1957	Oct. 28–Nov. 15	19
1963	Nov. 11–Dec. 2	13[1]
1965	May 21–May 25	5
1967	Oct. 30–Nov. 21	23
1971	Nov. 16–Nov. 22	7
1974	Jan. 24–Feb. 24	15
1975	Sept. 16–Sept. 16	1
1978	Sept. 5–Sept. 9	5[2]
1980	Aug. 4–Aug. 8	5
1981	Oct. 24–Oct. 24	1
1982	Jan. 18–Mar. 1	43
1982	June 14–June 14	1
1982	Sept. 3–Sept. 3	1
1983	Sept. 14–Oct. 4	21
1984	July 30–July 30	1
1990	May 7–May 7	1
1992	July 1–July 3	3
1995	July 28–Aug. 4	8
1996	Feb. 1–Feb. 2	2
2002	Feb. 8–Feb. 11	4
2002	Feb. 25–Mar. 2	6
2002	June 12–June 30	19
2002	Aug. 16–Aug. 20	5
2002	Sept. 1–Sept. 18	18
2006	April 20–April 20	1
2008	Feb. 4–Feb. 22	19
2010	Feb. 1–Feb. 25	25
2012	Dec. 14–Dec. 14	1
2013	Sept. 30–Oct. 2	3
2018	May 21–May 21	1
2020	June 24–June 26	3
2020	Aug. 10–Aug. 10	1
2020	Dec. 21–Dec. 21	1

[1]Nine-day recess, Nov. 22 to Dec. 2, due to death of President Kennedy.
[2]Does not include recess from Jan. 24 to Feb. 11.

The committee appoints an administrator to serve as its executive officer. The administrator's office coordinates and oversees the operation of the following administrative units:

Facility Services
Address: Room 49
Phone: 503-986-1360
Facility Services manages the infrastructure of the State Capitol Building, including maintenance, capital improvement projects, centralized purchasing, mail handling and distribution of legislative publications.

Visitor Services
Address: Capitol Kiosk and Room 148
Phone: 503-986-1388
Web: https://www.oregonlegislature.gov/capitol historygateway/Pages/Visit-the-Capitol.aspx
Visitor Services provides guided tours and information on the legislative process and Capitol history. It also operates the Capitol Gift Shop.

Employee Services
Address: Room 140-B
Phone: 503-986-1373

Financial Services
Address: Room 140-C
Phone: 503-986-1695

Information Services
Address: Room 40
Phone: 503-986-1914

Legislative Media
Address: Room 35
Phone: 503-986-1195

Legislative Counsel Committee and Office of Legislative Counsel
Dexter Johnson, Legislative Counsel
Address: 900 Court St. NE, Rm. S-101, Salem 97301
Phone: 503-986-1243
Fax: 503-373-1043
Web: www.oregonlegislature.gov/lc
The Legislative Counsel Committee, established by ORS 173.111, consists of the president of the Senate, senators appointed by the president, the speaker of the House of Representatives and representatives appointed by the speaker. The legislative counsel, selected by the committee, serves as executive officer.

The office drafts legislative measures for legislators, legislative committees, state agencies and statewide elected officials. The office provides legal opinions and other legal services to legislators, legislative committees and legislative staff. During legislative sessions, the office drafts amendments to measures and publishes the introduced, engrossed and enrolled measures.

The Office of the Legislative Counsel publishes *Oregon Laws*, the official compilation of that session's laws. The office also compiles and publishes *Oregon Revised Statutes* (ORS), the official codification of Oregon's statute laws, every two years. Each edition of ORS incorporates the new statutory provisions and amendments to statutory provisions passed by the Legislative Assembly or approved by the voters in the preceding two years. The ORS set includes a supplement of laws enacted during the even-year regular legislative session. The office also incorporates any new sections or amendments into its annual printing of the *Constitution of Oregon*.

Pursuant to ORS 183.710 to 183.725, the Office of the Legislative Counsel reviews all administrative rules adopted by state agencies to monitor whether an agency's rules are consistent with the agency's constitutional and statutory authority.

Oregon Law Commission
P.K. Runkles-Pearson, Chair
Sandy Weintraub, Executive Director
Address: University of Oregon School of Law, 1515 Agate St., Eugene 97403
Phone: 541-346-0042
Web: https://law-olc.uoregon.edu/
Established in 1997, the Oregon Law Commission, is the state's official law reform body. The commission and its work groups help to reform, correct and revise Oregon law based on suggestions for revision and its own review of Oregon's laws.

The commission consists of 15 commissioners: two appointed by the president of the Senate (one of whom must be a senator), two appointed by the speaker of the House of Representatives (one of whom must be a representative), the deans (or an appointee) from each of Oregon's three law schools, three appointed by the Oregon State Bar, the attorney general, the chief justice of the Supreme Court, the chief judge of the Court of Appeals, a circuit court judge and one appointed by the governor.

The commission submits a biennial report to the Legislative Assembly. Pursuant to ORS 173.335, the Office of the Legislative Counsel assists the commission in carrying out its duties.

Legislative Equity Office
Jackie Sandmeyer, Interim Director
Address: 900 Court St. NE, Rm. 62, Salem 97301
Phone: 503-986-1625
Web: https://www.oregonlegislature.gov/leo
The Legislative Equity Office created by House Bill 3377 (2019) and authorized by 2019 HCR 20, is a permanent, non-partisan office to prevent and respond to conduct at the Oregon State Capitol that is intimidating, hostile, offensive or retaliatory in nature.

Legislative Fiscal Office
Ken Rocco, Legislative Fiscal Officer

Address: 900 Court St. NE, Rm. H-178, Salem 97301
Phone: 503-986-1828
Web: https://www.oregonlegislature.gov/lfo

The Legislative Fiscal Office is a permanent, nonpartisan legislative agency created in 1959, pursuant to ORS 173.410 to 173.450, to serve legislators and committees on matters related to the state's fiscal affairs. The office provides research, analysis, evaluation and recommendations concerning state expenditures, budget issues, agency organization, program administration, audit findings and state information technology projects. It also provides fiscal impact assessments of proposed legislation and provides staff assistance to the Joint Legislative Committee on Information Management and Technology and the Joint Legislative Audit Committee. The office staffs the the Emergency Board and the Joint Committee on Ways and Means and any appointed budget committees during sessions.

Emergency Board

The Emergency Board, authorized by Article III, section 3, of the Oregon Constitution and by ORS 291.324, consists of the president of the Senate, the speaker of the House of Representatives, the co-chairs of the Joint Committee on Ways and Means and eight Senate and eight House members, totaling 20 members. Between sessions, the Emergency Board may allocate to state agencies, out of emergency funds appropriated to the board, additional monies to carry on activities required by law for which appropriations were not made. The board may authorize an agency to spend over the budgeted amount by accessing funds that are dedicated or continuously appropriated for the agency, approve a new budget for a new agency task and authorize transfers of funds between an agency's expenditure classifications.

Joint Committee on Ways and Means

The Joint Committee on Ways and Means, created under ORS 171.555, is the legislative appropriations committee that determines state budget policy. Staffed by the Legislative Fiscal Office and made up of both Senate and House members appointed by the president of the Senate and the speaker of the House, the committee works to determine state budget priorities. This joint appropriation process structure, employed in Oregon and a few other states, is especially effective in resolving budgetary differences.

Legislative Policy and Research Office

Misty Mason Freeman PhD., Director
Address: 900 Court St. NE, Rm. 453, Salem 97301

Phone: 503-986-1813
Web: https://www.oregonlegislature.gov/lpro

The Legislative Policy and Research Office (LPRO), established in 2016, provides professional and nonpartisan staffing, analysis and research that supports and informs the policy-making process. LPRO staff administer committee meetings, analyze legislative measures, provide policy research for legislators, support legislative task forces and work groups and produce committee meeting records. Staff also serve as a resource and additional communications link for legislators, legislative personnel, state agencies, the public and other participants in the legislative process.

The LPRO Director is selected by the Legislative Policy and Research Committee and is responsible for managing the office and its employees to execute the duties outlined in ORS 173.635.

Legislative Revenue Office

Christopher Allanach, Legislative Revenue Officer
Address: 900 Court St. NE, Rm. 160, Salem 97301
Phone: 503-986-1266
Web: https://www.oregonlegislature.gov/lro

Pursuant to ORS 173.810 to 173.850, the Legislative Revenue Office, established by the 1975 Legislature, provides nonpartisan analysis of tax and school finance issues.

The legislative revenue officer is appointed by, and responsible to, the House and Senate committees that deal with revenue and school finance.

The office staffs the House and Senate Revenue Committees, writes revenue impact statements for proposed legislation and researches tax and other revenue related issues.

Legislative Commission on Indian Services

Daniel P. Santos, Interim Executive Officer
Address: 900 Court St. NE, Rm. 167, Salem 97301
Phone: 503-986-1067
Web: www.oregonlegislature.gov/cis

The Legislative Commission on Indian Services consists of 14 members. Thirteen members are appointed by legislative leadership to two-year terms: one member from each of Oregon's nine federally-recognized tribal governments, two state senators and two state representatives. The commission may appoint one additional non-voting member from an area in which non-reservation Indians reside and who is associated with an Urban Indian Health Program under Title V of the federal Indian Health Care Improvement Act.

The commission works to improve services to American Indians in the state and to promote communication and relations between the State of Oregon and the nine federally-recognized tribes in Oregon.

Legislative

Senate Districts

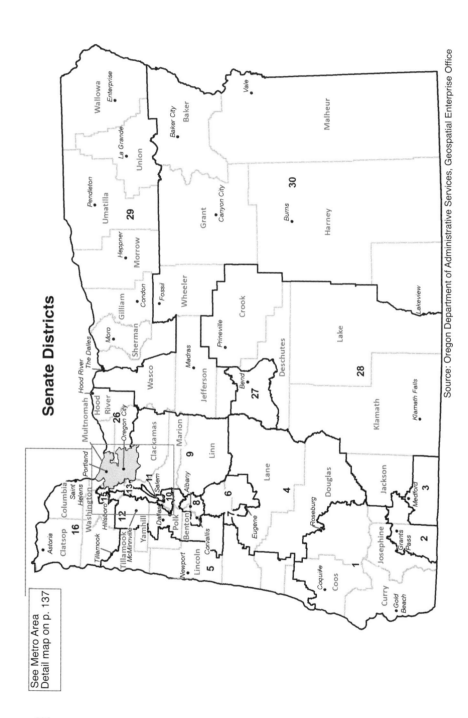

Source: Oregon Department of Administrative Services, Geospatial Enterprise Office

See Metro Area Detail map on p. 137

House Districts

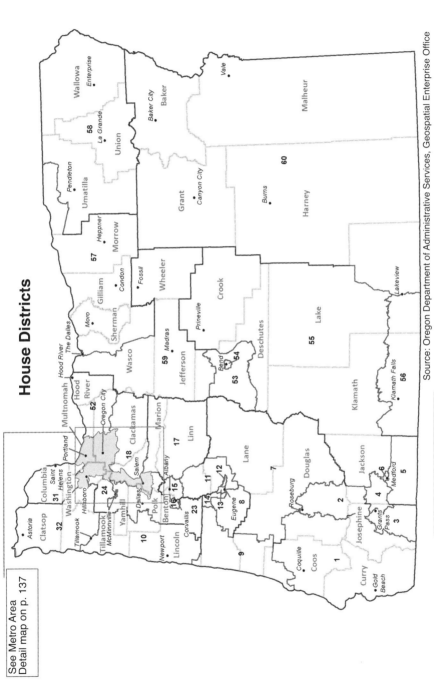

Legislative

See Metro Area
Detail map on p. 137

Metro Area Detail Maps

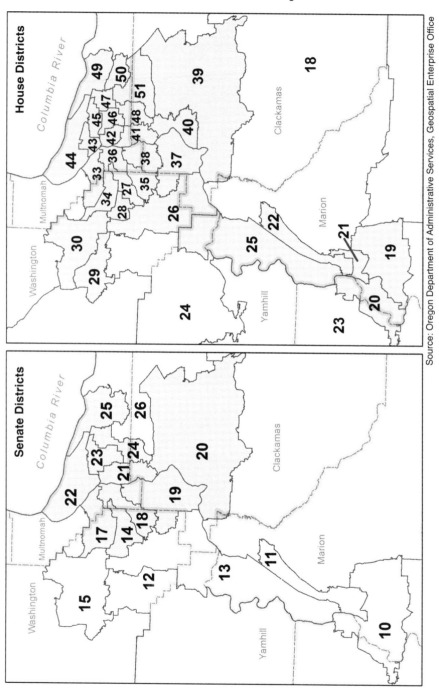

Source: Oregon Department of Administrative Services, Geospatial Enterprise Office

President of the Senate

Peter Courtney (Democrat, District 11) was born in Philadelphia, Pennsylvania, on June 18, 1943. He graduated with bachelor's and master's degrees from the University of Rhode Island and received a law degree from Boston University. Courtney was first elected to the Salem City Council in 1974, where he served until 1980. He began his legislative career in 1981 after his election to the House of Representatives and was first elected to the Senate in 1998. He has served as Senate President since 2003, when the Senate was evenly split. Since then, he has been elected as the Senate President for a record number of terms. Courtney is the longest serving Legislator in Oregon's history.

Courtney is retired from Western Oregon University, where he taught as an adjunct professor. He has worked as a political commentator for The 10 O'clock News at KPTV Channel 12, Portland and at KSLM Radio, Salem.

Peter Courtney

Courtney has served on the boards of Salem Area Mass Transit, Salem United Way, and Salem YMCA. He married his wife Margie in 1976. They have three sons, Peter, Sean, and Adam, three daughters-in-law, and five grandchildren.

Anderson, Dick
R—District 5

Beyer, Lee
D—District 6

Boquist, Brian
R—District 12

Burdick, Ginny
D—District 18

Courtney, Peter
D—District 11

Dembrow, Michael
D—District 23

Findley, Lynn P.
R—District 30

Frederick, Lew
D—District 22

Gelser, Sara
D—District 8

Girod, Fred
R—District 9

Golden, Jeff
D—District 3

Gorsek, Chris
D—District 25

Legislative

Hansell, Bill
R—District 29

Heard, Dallas
R—District 1

Jama, Kayse M.
D—District 24

Johnson, Betsy
D—District 16

Knopp, Tim
R—District 27

Lieber, Kate
D—District 14

Linthicum, Dennis
R—District 28

Manning, Jr., James
D—District 7

Patterson, Deb
D—District 10

Prozanski, Floyd
D—District 4

Riley, Chuck
D—District 15

Robinson, Art
R—District 2

Steiner Hayward, Elizabeth
D—District 17

Taylor, Kathleen
D—District 21

Thatcher, Kim
R—District 13

Thomsen, Chuck
R—District 26

Wagner, Rob
D—District 19

State Senators by District

District/Counties	Name/Address/Phone	Occupation/Yr. Elected*	Birthplace/Year
1. Curry and portions of Coos, Douglas, Jackson and Josephine	Dallas Heard (R) 900 Court St. NE, S-316 Salem 97301 541-673-1701	Landscape Contractor 2019/2021 (2015/2017)	Oregon 1985
2. Portions of Jackson and Josephine	Art Robinson (R) 900 Court St. NE, S-309 Salem 97301 503-986-1702	Scientist 2021	Illinois 1942
3. Portion of Jackson	Jeff Golden (D) 900 Court St., NE, S-421 Salem 97301 503-986-1703	Public Television Producer/Journalist 2019	California 1950
4. Portions of Douglas and Lane	Floyd Prozanski (D) PO Box 11511 Eugene 97440 541-342-2447	Attorney 2005/2009/2015/2019 (1995–2003)	Texas 1954
5. Lincoln and portions of Coos, Douglas, Lane, Polk, Tillamook and Yamhill	Dick Anderson (R) PO Box 263 Lincoln City 97367 503-986-1705	Real Estate Finance 2021	Ohio 1950
6. Portions of Lane and Linn	Lee Beyer (D) PO Box 131 Springfield 97477 541-726-2533	Retired Business Advisor 1999/2011/2015/2019 (1991–1997)	Nebraska 1948
7. Portion of Lane	James I. Manning, Jr. (D) 900 Court St. NE, S-205 Salem 97301 503-986-1707	Retired U.S. Army 2017/2021	Missouri 1953
8. Portions of Benton and Linn	Sara Gelser (D) 900 Court St. NE, S-405 Salem 97301 503-986-1708	Educator/Civil Servant 2015/2019 (2007–2015)	Nevada 1973
9. Portions of Clackamas, Linn and Marion	Fred Girod (R) 101 Fern Ridge Rd. SE Stayton 97383 503-769-4321	Dentist 2008/2009/2013/2017/ 2021 (1993–2007)	Oregon 1951
10. Portions of Marion and Polk	Deb Patterson (D) 900 Court St. NE, S-215 Salem 97301 503-986-1710	Ordained Clergy 2021	Alberta, Canada 1958
11. Portion of Marion	Peter Courtney (D) 900 Court St. NE, S-201 Salem 97301 503-986-1600	Retired from Western Oregon University 1999/2003/2007/2011/ 2015/2019 (1981–1997)	Pennsylvania 1943
12. Portions of Benton, Marion, Polk, Washington and Yamhill	Brian Boquist (R) 900 Court St. NE, S-311 Salem 97301 503-986-1712	Businessman/Rancher 2009/2013/2017/2021 (2005/2007)	Oregon 1958

Senate terms are four years, and House terms (in parentheses) are two years, unless appointed mid-term.

District/Counties	Name/Address/Phone	Occupation/Yr. Elected*	Birthplace/Year
13. Portions of Clackamas, Marion, Washington and Yamhill	Kim Thatcher (R) 900 Court St. NE, S-307 Salem 97301 503-986-1713	Small Business Owner 2015/2019 (2005/2007/2009/2011/ 2013)	Idaho 1964
14. Portion of Washington	Kate Lieber (D) 900 Court St. NE, S-417 Salem 97301 503-986-1714	Attorney 2021	Indiana 1966
15. Portion of Washington	Chuck Riley (D) 900 Court St. NE, S-207 Salem 97301 503-986-1715	Retired Computer Consultant 2015/2019 (2005/2007/2009)	Illinois 1939
16. Clatsop, Columbia and portions of Multnomah, Tillamook and Washington	Betsy Johnson (D) PO Box R Scappoose 97056 503-543-4046	Legislator/Former Com- mercial Helicopter Pilot 2007/2011/2015/2019 (2001/2003)	Oregon 1951
17. Portions of Multnomah and Washington	Steiner Hayward, Elizabeth (D) 3879 SW Hall Blvd. Beaverton 97005 503-277-2467	OHSU Associate Profes- sor of Family Medicine 2011/2015/2019	New York 1963
18. Portions of Multnomah and Washington	Ginny Burdick (D) 6227 SW 18th Dr. Portland 97239 503-986-1718	Communications Consultant/Legislator 1997/2001/2005/2009/ 2013/2017/2021	Oregon 1947
19. Portions of Clackamas, Multnomah and Washington	Rob Wagner (D) 900 Court St. NE, S-223 Salem 97301 503-986-1719	Legislator/Communica- tions Consultant 2019	California 1973
20. Portions of Clackamas and Marion	Position Vacant at press time		
21. Portions of Clackamas and Multnomah	Kathleen Taylor (D) 900 Court St. NE, S-423 Salem 97301 503-986-1721	Management Auditor 2017/2021	Wisconsin 1966
22. Portion of Multnomah	Lew Frederick (D) 900 Court St. NE, S-419 Salem 97301 503-231-2564	Communications Consultant 2017/2021 (2009–2015)	Washington 1951
23. Portion of Multnomah	Michael E. Dembrow (D) 900 Court St. NE, S-407 Salem 97301 503-986-1723	College Teacher 2013/2015/2017/2021 (2009/2011/2013)	Connecticut 1951
24. Portions of Clackamas and Multnomah	Kayse M. Jama (D) 900 Court St. NE, S-409 Salem 97301 503-986-1724	Legislator 2021	Somalia 1974
25. Portion of Multnomah	Chris Gorsek (D) 900 Court St. NE, S-403 Salem 97301 503-986-1725	Teacher 2021	Oregon 1958

District/Counties	Name/Address/Phone	Occupation/Yr. Elected*	Birthplace/Year
26. Hood River and portions of Clackamas and Multnomah	Chuck Thomsen (R) 900 Court St. NE, S-315 Salem 97301 503-986-1726	Orchardist 2011/2015/2019	Oregon 1957
27. Portion of Deschutes	Tim Knopp (R) 900 Court St. NE, S-425 Salem 97301 503-986-1727	Exec. Vice President Non-Profit Trade Assoc. 2013/2017/2021	Oregon 1965
28. Crook, Klamath and portions of Deschutes, Jackson and Lake	Dennis Linthicum (R) 900 Court St. NE, S-305 Salem 97301 503-986-1728	Software and Applications Developer 2017/2021	California 1956
29. Gilliam, Morrow, Sherman, Umatilla, Union and Wallowa and portion of Wasco	Bill Hansell (R) 900 Court St. NE, S-415 Salem 97301 503-986-1729	Former County Commissioner 2013/2017/2021	Washington 1945
30. Baker, Grant, Harney, Jefferson, Malheur, Wheeler and portions of Clackamas, Deschutes, Lake, Marion and Wasco	Lynn P. Findley (R) 900 Court St. NE, S-301 Salem 97301 503-986-1730	Retired Bureau of Land Mgmt, City Manager 2021	Oregon 1952

Senate terms are four years, and House terms (in parentheses) are two years, unless appointed mid-term.

MEMBERS OF THE OREGON HOUSE OF REPRESENTATIVES

Tina Kotek

Speaker of the House

Beginning with her work to win domestic partnership benefits for faculty and students at the University of Washington in the mid-1990s, Tina Kotek has worked to change the world and empower people to be part of that change.

She began her public service career as a policy advocate for Oregon Food Bank. She went on to serve as the policy director for Children First for Oregon before being elected to the Oregon House of Representatives in 2006.

In 2013, Speaker Kotek became the first openly lesbian speaker of any U.S. state house. Now the longest-serving speaker of the house in Oregon's history, she has led efforts to improve economic opportunity and promote equity for every Oregonian. She most recently guided the Oregon Legislature to pass the first statewide laws in the country to combat rent gouging and to re-legalize "missing middle" housing in areas previously solely reserved for detached single family housing. She also expanded funding and access to the state's Medicaid program, helped to create a paid family medical leave insurance program, and championed the Student Success Act to increase funding for the state's preK-12 public education system by $1 billion per year.

Alonso Leon, Teresa
D—District 22

Bonham, Daniel
R—District 59

Boshart Davis, Shelly
R—District 15

Breese-Iverson, Vikki
R—District 55

Bynum, Janelle
D—District 51

Campos, Wlnsvey
D—District 28

Cate, Jami
R—District 17

Clem, Brian L.
D—District 21

Dexter, Maxine E.
D—District 33

Drazan, Christine
R—District 39

Evans, Paul
D—District 20

Fahey, Julie
D—District 14

Gomberg, David
D—District 10

Grayber, Dacia
D—District 35

Hayden, Cedric
R—District 7

Helm, Ken
D—District 34

Hernandez, Diego
D—District 47

Holvey, Paul
D—District 8

Hudson, Zachary
D—District 49

Kotek, Tina
D—District 44

Kropf, Jason
D—District 54

Leif, Gary
R—District 2

Levy, Bobby
R—District 58

Lewis, Rick
R—District 18

Lively, John
D—District 12

Marsh, Pam
D—District 5

McLain, Susan
D—District 29

Meek, Mark
D—District 40

Moore-Green, Raquel
R—District 19

Mogan, Lily
R—District 3

Nathanson, Nancy
D—District 13

Nearman, Mike
R—District 23

Neron, Courtney
D—District 26

Noble, Ron
R—District 24

Nosse, Rob
D—District 42

Owens, Mark
R—District 60

Pham, Khanh
D—District 46

Post, Bill
R—District 25

Power, Karin
D—District 41

Prusak, Rachel
D—District 37

Rayfield, Dan
D—District 16

Reardon, Jeff
D—District 48

Reschke, E. Werner
R—District 56

Reynolds, Lisa
D—District 36

Ruiz, Ricki
D—District 50

Salinas, Andrea
D—District 38

Sanchez, Tawna
D—District 43

Schouten, Sheri
D—District 27

Smith, David Brock
R—District 1

Smith, Greg
R—District 57

Smith Warner, Barbara
D—District 45

Sollman, Janeen
D—District 30

Stark, Duane A.
R—District 4

Wallan, Kim
R—District 6

Weber, Suzanne
R—District 32

Wilde, Marty
D—District 11

Williams, Anna
D—District 52

Witt, Brad
D—District 31

**Wright, Gerald D.
"Boomer"**
R—District 9

Zika, Jack
R—District 53

State Representatives by District

District/Counties	Name/Address/Phone	Occupation/Yr. Elected*	Birthplace/Year

*House terms are two years, unless appointed mid-term.

District/Counties	Name/Address/Phone	Occupation/Yr. Elected*	Birthplace/Year
1. Curry and portions of Coos, Douglas and Josephine	David Brock Smith (R) 900 Court St. NE, H-379 Salem 97301 503-986-1401	Small Business 2017/2019/2021	California 1976
2. Portions of Douglas, Jackson and Josephine	Gary Leif (R) 900 Court St. NE, H-386 Salem 97301 503-986-1402	Retired Business Owner 2019/2021	Washington 1956

Legislative

District/Counties	Name/Address/Phone	Occupation/Yr. Elected*	Birthplace/Year

House terms are two years, unless appointed mid-term.

District/Counties	Name/Address/Phone	Occupation/Yr. Elected*	Birthplace/Year
3. Portion of Josephine	Lily Morgan (R) 900 Court St. NE, H-371 Salem 97301 503-986-1403	Parole/Probation Officer 2021	Oregon 1975
4. Portions of Jackson and Josephine	Duane A. Stark (R) 900 Court St. NE, H-372 Salem 97301 503-986-1404	Outreach Pastor 2015/2017/2019/2021	Oregon 1978
5. Portion of Jackson	Pam Marsh (D) 900 Court St. NE, H-474 Salem 97301 503-986-1405	Legislator 2017/2019/2021	Missouri 1954
6. Portion of Jackson	Kim Wallan (R) 900 Court St. NE, H-388 Salem 97301 503-986-1406	Lawyer 2019/2021	Oregon 1961
7. Portions of Douglas and Lane	Cedric Hayden (R) PO Box 459 Lowell 97452 503-986-1407	Dental Surgeon, Rancher 2015/2017/2019/2021	Oregon 1968
8. Portion of Lane	Paul Holvey (D) PO Box 51048 Eugene 97405 541-344-5636	Carpenters' Union Rep 2005/2007/2009/2011/ 2013/2015/2017/2019/ 2021	Oregon 1954
9. Portions of Coos, Douglas, Lane and Lincoln	Gerald D. "Boomer" Wright (R) 900 Court St. NE, H-476 Salem 97301 503-986-1409	Retired Educator 2021	California 1948
10. Portions of Lincoln, Polk, Tillamook and Yamhill	David Gomberg (D) 900 Court St. NE, H-480 Salem 97301 503-986-1410	Small Business Owner 2013/2015/2017/2019/ 2021	Oregon 1953
11. Portions of Lane and Linn	Marty Wilde (D) 3390 Potter St Eugene 97405 503-986-1411	Air Force Officer, Attorney 2019/2021	Oregon 1974
12. Portion of Lane	John Lively (D) 900 Court St. NE, H-488 Salem 97301 503-986-1412	Account Manager 2013/2015/2017/2019/ 2021	Oregon 1946
13. Portion of Lane	Nancy Nathanson (D) PO Box 41895 Eugene 97404 541-343-2206	Library Program Manager 2007/2009/2011/2013/ 2015/2017/2019/2021	Texas 1951
14. Portion of Lane	Julie Fahey (D) 900 Court St. NE, H-286 Salem 97301 503-986-1414	Business Consultant 2017/2019/2021	Illinois 1978

District/Counties	Name/Address/Phone	Occupation/Yr. Elected*	Birthplace/Year
15. Portions of Benton and Linn	Shelly Boshart Davis (R) 900 Court St. NE, H-389 Salem 97301 503-986-1415	Small Business Owner 2019/2021	Oregon 1980
16. Portion of Benton	Dan Rayfield (D) 900 Court St. NE, H-275 Salem 97301 503-986-1416	Attorney 2015/2017/2019/2021	California 1979
17. Portions of Linn and Marion	Jami Cate (R) 900 Court St. NE, H-378 Salem 97301 503-986-1417	Farmer 2021	Oregon 1987
18. Portions of Clackamas and Marion	Rick Lewis (R) 900 Court St. NE, H-484 Salem 97301 503-986-1418	Retired Law Enforcement 2017/2019/2021	Wyoming 1950
19. Portion of Marion	Raquel Moore-Green (R) 900 Court St. NE, H-385 Salem 97301 503-986-1419	Small Business Consultant 2019/2021	California 1955
20. Portions of Marion and Polk	Paul Evans (D) 900 Court St. NE, H-471 Salem 97301 503-986-1420	Educator, Small Business Owner 2015/2017/2019/2021	Oregon 1970
21. Portion of Marion	Brian L. Clem (D) 396 Hoyt St. SE Salem 97302 503-986-1421	Business Owner 2007/2009/2011/2013/ 2015/2017/2019/2021	Oregon 1972
22. Portion of Marion	Teresa Alonso Leon (D) 900 Court St. NE, H-272 Salem 97301 503-986-1422	State Representative 2017/2019/2021	Mexico 1975
23. Portions of Benton, Marion, Polk and Yamhill	Mike Nearman (R) 900 Court St. NE, H-381 Salem 97301 503-986-1423	Software Engineer 2015/2017/2019/2021	Wisconsin 1964
24. Portions of Washington and Yamhill	Ron Noble (R) 900 Court St. NE, H-380 Salem 97301 503-986-1424	Retired Law Enforcement 2017/2019/2021	California 1960
25. Portion of Marion	Bill Post (R) 900 Court St. NE, H-479 Salem 97301 503-986-1425	Radio Broadcaster 2015/2017/2019/2021	Arizona 1960
26. Portions of Clackamas, Washington and Yamhill	Courtney Neron (D) 900 Court St. NE, H-281 Salem 97301 503-986-1426	Teacher 2019/2021	California 1979
27. Portion of Washington	Sheri Schouten (D) 900 Court St. NE, H-280 Salem 97301 503-986-1427	Registered Nurse 2017/2019/2021	Oregon 1953

Legislative

District/Counties	Name/Address/Phone	Occupation/Yr. Elected*	Birthplace/Year
28. Portion of Washington	Wlnsvey E. Campos (D) 900 Court St. NE, H-285 Salem 97301 503-986-1428	Case Manager 2021	California 1995
29. Portion of Washington	Susan McLain (D) 900 Court St. NE, H-477 Salem 97301 503-986-1429	Retired Teacher 2015/2017/2019/2021	Oregon 1949
30. Portion of Washington	Janeen Sollman (D) 900 Court St. NE, H-487 Salem 97301 503-986-1430	Customer Service Specialist 2017/2019/2021	Philippines 1969
31. Columbia and portions of Multnomah and Washington	Brad Witt (D) 900 Court St. NE, H-382 Salem 97301 503-986-1431	Labor Official 2005/2007/2009/2011/ 2013/2015/2017/2019/ 2021	Massachusetts 1952
32. Clatsop and portions of Tillamook and Washington	Suzanne Weber (R) PO Box 892 Tillamook 97141 503-986-1432	Retired Teacher 2021	Minnesota 1946
33. Portions of Multnomah and Washington	Maxine E. Dexter (D) 900 Court St. NE, H-283 Salem 97301 503-986-1433	Physician 2021	Washington 1972
34. Portion of Washington	Ken Helm (D) 900 Court St. NE, H-490 Salem 97301 503-986-1434	Attorney 2015/2017/2019/2021	California 1965
35. Portions of Multnomah and Washington	Dacia Grayber (D) 900 Court St. NE, H-492 Salem 97301 503-986-1435	Firefighter 2021	New York 1975
36. Portion of Multnomah	Lisa Reynolds (D) 900 Court St. NE, H-485 Salem 97301 503-986-1436	Physician 2021	Illinois 1964
37. Portions of Clackamas and Washington	Rachel Prusak (D) 900 Court St. NE, H-489 Salem 97301 503-986-1437	Nurse Practitioner 2019/2021	Massachusetts 1975
38. Portions of Clackamas and Multnomah	Andrea Salinas (D) 900 Court St. NE, H-282 Salem 97301 503-986-1438	Lobbyist 2017/2019/2021	California 1969
39. Portion of Clackamas	Christine Drazan (R) PO Box 196 Canby 97013 503-986-1439	Nonprofit Executive 2019/2021	Oregon 1972
40. Portion of Clackamas	Mark Meek (D) 900 Court St. NE, H-478 Salem 97301 503-986-1440	Realtor 2017/2019/2021	California 1964

District/Counties	Name/Address/Phone	Occupation/Yr. Elected*	Birthplace/Year
41. Portions of Clackamas and Multnomah	Karin Power (D) 900 Court St. NE, H-274 Salem 97301 503-986-1441	Attorney 2017/2019/2021	New Jersey 1983
42. Portion of Multnomah	Rob Nosse (D) 900 Court St. NE, H-472 Salem 97301 503-986-1442	Labor Representative 2015/2017/2019/2021	Ohio 1967
43. Portion of Multnomah	Tawna Sanchez (D) 900 Court St. NE, H-273 Salem 97301 503-986-1443	Family Services Director 2017/2019/2021	Oregon 1961
44. Portion of Multnomah	Tina Kotek (D) 7930 N Wabash Ave. Portland 97217 503-986-1444	Policy Director 2007/2009/2011/2013/ 2015/2017/2019/2021	Pennsylvania 1966
45. Portion of Multnomah	Barbara Smith Warner (D) 900 Court St. NE, H-295 Salem 97301 503-986-1445	Labor Liaison to U.S. Senate 2013/2015/2017/2019/ 2021	Pennsylvania 1967
46. Portion of Multnomah	Khanh Pham (D) 900 Court St. NE, H-486 Salem 97301 503-986-1446	Community Organizer 2021	Oklahoma 1978
47. Portion of Multnomah	Diego Hernandez (D) 900 Court St. NE, H-373 Salem 97301 503-986-1447	Nonprofit Executive Director 2017/2019/2021	California 1987
48. Portions of Clackamas and Multnomah	Jeff Reardon (D) 900 Court St. NE, H-493 Salem 97301 503-986-1448	Teacher 2013/2015/2017/2019/ 2021	Washington 1947
49. Portion of Multnomah	Zachary Hudson (D) 900 Court St. NE, H-284 Salem 97301 503-378-1449	Teacher 2021	Oregon 1979
50. Portion of Multnomah	Ricki Ruiz (D) PO Box 171 Gresham 97030 503-986-1450	Community Coordinator 2021	Oregon 1994
51. Portions of Clackamas and Multnomah	Janelle Bynum (D) 900 Court St. NE, H-276 Salem 97301 503-986-1451	Restaurant Owner 2017/2019/2021	District of Columbia 1975
52. Hood River and portions of Clackamas and Multnomah	Anna Williams (D) 900 Court St. NE, H-473 Salem 97301 503-986-1452	Academic Advisor 2019/2021	Wyoming 1980
53. Portion of Deschutes	Jack Zika (R) PO Box 2077 Redmond 97756 503-986-1453	Realtor 2019/2021	Ohio 1977

Legislative

District/Counties	Name/Address/Phone	Occupation/Yr. Elected*	Birthplace/Year
54. Portion of Deschutes	Jason Kropf (D) 900 Court St. NE, H-491 Salem 97301 503-986-1454	Attorney 2021	Washington 1970
55. Crook and portions of Deschutes, Jackson, Klamath and Lake	Vikki Breese-Iverson (R) PO Box 249 Prineville 97754 541-233-4411	Realtor 2019/2021	Oregon 1974
56. Portions of Klamath and Lake	E. Werner Reschke (R) 900 Court St. NE, H-384 Salem 97301 503-986-1456	Online Marketing/Web Development 2017/2019/2021	California 1965
57. Gilliam, Morrow, Sherman and portions of Umatilla and Wasco	Greg Smith (R) PO Box 215 Heppner 97836 541-676-5154	Small Business Owner 2001/2003/2005/2007/ 2009/2011/2013/2015/ 2017/2019/2021	Oregon 1968
58. Union, Wallowa and portion of Umatilla	Bobby Levy (R) PO Box 69 Echo 97826 503-986-1458	Farmer, Small Business Owner 2021	Oregon 1953
59. Jefferson, Wheeler and portions of Deschutes and Wasco	Daniel Bonham (R) 900 Court St. NE, H-390 Salem 97310 503-986-1459	Small Business Owner 2017/2019/2021	California 1977
60. Baker, Grant, Harney, Malheur and portion of Lake	Mark Owens (R) 258 S Oregon St Ontario 97914 541-889-8866	Farmer 2021	California 1970

*House terms are two years, unless appointed mid-term.

State and Local Government Finance

Government finance—where government gets its money and how it spends it—affects all Oregonians. The connections between state and local government revenues and state and local government services are important. This section describes revenue sources and distribution.

Source: Department of Administrative Services, Chief Financial Office

State Government

Oregon operates under a biennial budget. Budgets begin July 1 of odd-numbered years and continue for two years. Oregon law requires all state and local governments to balance their budgets. How does the state government's budget work? The state receives money from a variety of sources which are grouped into funds. These funds are known as the General Fund, Lottery Fund, Other Funds and Federal Funds.

The total Legislatively Adopted Budget for the 2019–2021 biennium is $85.8 billion total funds.

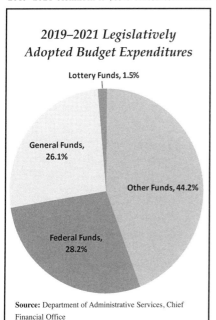

2019–2021 Legislatively Adopted Budget Expenditures

Lottery Funds, 1.5%

General Funds, 26.1%

Other Funds, 44.2%

Federal Funds, 28.2%

Source: Department of Administrative Services, Chief Financial Office

This is an increase of $7.8 billion, or 9.9 percent, from the 2017–2019 Legislatively Approved Budget of $78.0 billion. General and Lottery Funds portions amount to $23.7 billion, and Other Funds and Federal Funds are $37.9 billion and $24.2 billion respectively for the 2019–2021 budget.

General Fund

The 2019–2021 Legislatively Adopted Budget includes approximately $22.4 billion in General Fund expenditures—a 26.1 percent share of the total budget. As of the June 2020 revenue forecast, the gross General Fund revenues for the 2019–2021 biennium are expected to decrease by approximately $1,151 million from the 2019 close-of-session forecast due to the ongoing COVID-19 pandemic. With this updated economic forecast, General Fund revenues for the current biennium would be 10.9 percent smaller than they were during the 2017–2019 biennium budget. The General Fund is largely made up of personal and corporate income taxes collected by the Oregon Department of Revenue. The personal income tax makes up the largest share of General Fund revenue. It accounts for 86 percent of projected revenue for 2019–2021. Other sources make up the remainder. The largest of these other revenue sources are the cigarette tax, estate tax and the liquor apportionment transfer.

General Fund appropriations provide funding to agencies that do not generate revenues, receive federal funds or generate sufficient other funds to support their approved programs. Agencies do not actually receive money from the General Fund. Instead, they expend against an appropriation from the General Fund that is established for general government purposes up to the amount approved in their budget bill. General Fund monies are a scarce resource that can be used for any public purpose; therefore, allocations of monies are competitive and require fiscal oversight.

In 1990, voters approved Ballot Measure 5. This reduced local property tax rates, which reduced

Government Finance

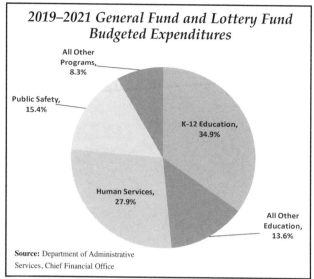

2019–2021 General Fund and Lottery Fund Budgeted Expenditures

- All Other Programs, 8.3%
- Public Safety, 15.4%
- K-12 Education, 34.9%
- Human Services, 27.9%
- All Other Education, 13.6%

Source: Department of Administrative Services, Chief Financial Office

and lottery expenses are paid, revenue flows to the Economic Development Fund. A portion of the Lottery Fund is constitutionally dedicated to be spent in specific ways. The remainder is distributed at the discretion of the Legislature for economic development.

The 2019–2021 Legislatively Adopted Budget includes $1.3 billion of expenditures from the Lottery Fund, which is 1.5 percent of the total budget. The Lottery Fund, distributes certain portions through three constitutionally dedicated transfers and five statutorily dedicated transfers. The total constitutionally dedicated transfers projected for the 2019-21 biennium amount

local revenue and, in turn, shifted much of the responsibility for funding public schools to the state's General Fund. The 2019–2021 Legislatively Adopted Budget has $8.249 billion, or 34.9 percent, of the General and Lottery Funds being spent kindergarten through twelfth grade education.

Lottery Fund

The Lottery Fund derives from the sale of lottery game tickets and from Video Lottery. After prizes

to $503.7 million, which accounts for 32.9 percent of total lottery resources and is a 2.5 percent increase over the previous biennium. As of the June 2020 economic and revenue forecast, the lottery outlook has lowered expectations considerably. Due to COVID-19 related social distancing measures and the recession, the forecast of available resources for the 2019-21 biennium have been lowered by $364.1 million, a 23.8 percent decrease.

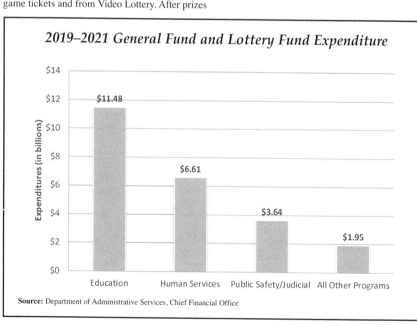

2019–2021 General Fund and Lottery Fund Expenditure

Expenditures (in billions)

- Education: $11.48
- Human Services: $6.61
- Public Safety/Judicial: $3.64
- All Other Programs: $1.95

Source: Department of Administrative Services, Chief Financial Office

Other Funds

The 2019–2021 Legislatively Adopted Budget includes $37.9 billion in Other Funds which is an 11 percent increase from the previous biennium. Other Funds revenue generally refers to monies collected by agencies in return for services. Legislative actions may allow an agency to levy taxes, provide services for a fee, license individuals, or otherwise earn revenues to pay for programs. These Other Funds are often separate and distinct from monies collected for general government purposes (General Fund), and they may be based on statutory language, federal mandate, legal requirements, or for specific business reasons. Some funds are "dedicated"— the income and disbursements are limited by the state's constitution or by another law (for example, the Highway Fund). Since Other Funds are typically for a specific program, competition for these monies is limited.

Federal Funds

The 2019–2021 Legislatively Adopted Budget includes $24.2 billion in Federal Funds for 6.1 percent increase from the previous biennium. Federal Funds are monies received from the federal government through entitlement programs, grants and aid awarded to various state agencies.

State Budget Process

Oregon state agencies develop biennial budgets according to instructions provided by the Department of Administrative Services, Chief Financial Office. This budget development process begins in even-numbered years, well before the Legislative Assembly convenes in January of the odd- numbered years. Agencies are required to prepare and submit their budget requests to the Chief Financial Office. These budget requests consist of narrative descriptions of agency programs, completed budgetary forms, and reports from the Oregon Budget Information and Tracking System (ORBITS). An agency budget request serves as a conduit to the governor and the Legislature that identifies the agency's needs and priorities.

Agencies begin by building a Current Service Level (CSL) budget, which is the amount of money needed in the upcoming biennium to continue existing authorized programs into the next biennium. An agency may request additions to their CSL budget through policy option packages, which describe the purpose and the amount needed. Agencies also must identify program reductions and key performance measure targets. For their 2021–2023 budget requests, agencies begin in March 2020 and submit their completed requests by September 2020. An agency's budget provides an outline of what an agency does, what it costs, and how many people are involved.

After analysis by the Governor's Office and the Chief Financial Office, the governor aligns her priorities with the agencies' requests resulting in the Governor's Recommended Budget. The governor has a legal obligation to submit a balanced budget for the entire state government; therefore, the Governor's Recommended Budget includes the proposed budgets for the Legislative Assembly and the Judicial Department. However, because of separation of power principles, the governor's budget recommendations are advisory only for the other two branches. The governor presents the Governor's Recommended Budget to the Legislative Assembly when it convenes in January of odd-numbered years.

When the Legislative Assembly is in session, a subcommittee of the Joint Committee on Ways and Means considers each agency's budget. At the budget hearings, an agency presents its budget request and answers questions asked by members of the committee. Staff members from the Legislative Fiscal Office and the Chief Financial Office are also present at the budget hearings. Members of the public may attend the hearings and request an opportunity to testify. At the end of an agency's budget hearings, the agency's budget goes to the full Joint Committee on Ways and Means for a vote and then on to the full House and Senate for a vote. The agency's budget may be amended at any point in this process, although changes typically occur during the subcommittee hearings. After passage by both chambers, an agency's budget becomes its Legislatively Adopted Budget for the biennium, and it goes into effect July 1 of odd-numbered years. If the Legislature makes changes to the adopted budget in legislative sessions or through the Emergency Board, it becomes known as the Legislatively Approved Budget.

Kicker Provision

The Oregon Constitution requires the governor to provide an estimate of biennial General Fund revenues. In 1979, the Legislature placed a condition on those revenue estimates that required excess funds to be "kicked back" to taxpayers if actual revenues exceeded estimated revenues by 2 percent or more of the close-of-session estimate.

For revenues from corporate income and excise taxes, the provision had required that the excess be returned to taxpayers who paid corporate income and excise taxes. However, this provision was amended in November 2012 by the citizen initiative process. Ballot Measure 85 requires that this excess be retained in the General Fund to provide additional funding for public education of kindergarten through twelfth grade. This measure is applicable to biennial estimates on or after July 1, 2013.

For General Fund revenues from all other sources where the actual revenues exceed the estimated revenues by 2 percent or more, the excess is "kicked back" to taxpayers who paid personal

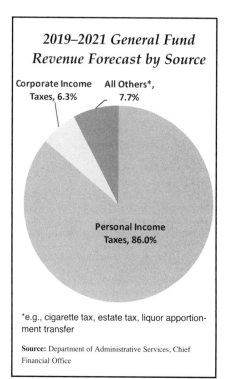

2019–2021 General Fund Revenue Forecast by Source

Corporate Income Taxes, 6.3%

All Others*, 7.7%

Personal Income Taxes, 86.0%

*e.g., cigarette tax, estate tax, liquor apportionment transfer

Source: Department of Administrative Services, Chief Financial Office

income tax. Ballot Measure 85 did not affect this provision. These taxpayers receive the refund as a tax credit in the following year's tax return. The refund is an identical proportion of each taxpayer's personal income tax liability for the prior year. Following the 2017-19 biennium, the personal income tax kicker reached a new high dollar amount of $1.7 billion. The corporate kicker also set a new high at $676 million, which is dedicated to the State School Fund for allocation during the 2019-21 biennium.

Rainy Day Fund and Education Stability Fund

Established in 2007, the Oregon Rainy Day Fund is essentially a savings account for state government. Withdrawals can be made, after a three-fifths vote of approval by the Legislature, if there is a decline in the General Fund for the current or subsequent biennium budgets, there is a prolonged employment decline or the governor declares an emergency. Given the economic conditions in 2009 and 2010, the fund needed to be utilized.

The Education Stability Fund (ESF) was created through a constitutional amendment approved by voters in 2002. The ESF receives 18 percent of net lottery proceeds deposited on a quarterly basis. The ESF has similar requirements as the Rainy Day Fund. Like the Rainy Day Fund, the ESF had been drawn down during the last economic downturn to balance budgets in the 2009–2011 and 2011–2013 biennia. At the beginning of the 2019–2021 biennium, the balance in the ESF was $621 million.

At the beginning of the 2019–2021 biennium, the two reserve funds had a combined balance total of $1.3 billion.

State Spending Limit

The state spending limit was first enacted by the 1979 Legislative Assembly. It limited the growth of General Fund appropriations to the growth of personal income in Oregon. The 2001 Legislative Assembly replaced this spending limit with one tying appropriations for a biennium to personal income for that biennium. The appropriations subject to this limit may not exceed eight percent of projected personal income for the same biennium. The limit may be exceeded if the governor declares an emergency and three-fifths of the members of both chambers vote to exceed it.

Local Government

Local government in Oregon is predominantly financed by the property tax, although there are other local taxes, such as hotel/motel taxes, transit taxes and, in Multnomah County, a business income tax.

Most local governments must prepare and adopt an annual budget. This includes schools, counties, cities, ports, rural fire protection districts, water districts, urban renewal agencies and special districts. Oregon's Local Budget Law establishes standard budget procedures and requires citizen participation in budget preparation and public disclosure of the budget before it is formally adopted. A budget officer must be appointed and a budget committee formed. The budget officer prepares a draft budget, and the budget committee reviews and revises it before it is approved. Notices are then published, copies of the budget are made available for public review, and at least two opportunities for public comment are provided.

Local government budgets are usually for a fiscal year beginning July 1 and ending June 30. However, local governments have the option of creating a two-year biennial budget like the state. The governing body must enact a resolution or an ordinance to formally adopt the budget, make appropriations, and levy and categorize any tax. This must be done no later than June 30. Budget revenues are divided into ensuing year property tax and non-property tax revenues.

The Oregon Constitution allows a local government to levy annually the amount that would be raised by its permanent rate limit without further authorization from the voters. When a local government has to increase the permanent rate limit or when the rate limit does not provide enough revenue to meet estimated expenditures, the government may request a local option levy from the voters. Approval requires a "double majority." This means that at least 50 percent of the registered voters must vote, and a majority of those who vote must approve the levy, unless the measure is submitted during an election held in any May or November, which are exempt from the "double majority" approval requirement. Since 1991, the Oregon Constitution has limited the maximum amount of taxes to support the public schools to $5 per $1,000 of real market value. The maximum amount to support other government operations is $10 per $1,000 of real market value.

Taxes

Personal Income Tax

Oregon residents and nonresidents who earn income in Oregon pay personal income tax. During the 2019 Legislative Session, the Legislature passed HB 3427, referred to as the Student Success Act, which created a Corporate Activity Tax (CAT) dedicated to school funding. As part of the legislation that created the CAT, and effective the beginning of the tax year 2020, the Legislature reduced Oregon's first three income tax brackets from 5 percent, 7 percent, and 9 percent, to 4.75 percent, 6.75 percent, and 8.75 percent respectively. After deductions and credits, the average effective tax rate is about 6.0 percent of adjusted gross income. Since 1993, the income tax brackets have been indexed to changes in the Consumer Price Index. The current standard deduction is $4,630 on joint returns, $2,315 on single and married filing separate returns, and $3,725 for a head of household return. Blind or elderly taxpayers, persons over the age of 65, will receive an additional $1,200 standard deduction on a single return and an additional $1,000 per eligible person on a joint return.

The personal income tax is the largest source of state tax revenue and is projected to comprise 86 percent of the total General Fund revenues in the 2019–2021 biennium. In January 2010, Oregon voters approved Ballot Measure 66, which made two changes to personal income tax calculations. First, it established new tax brackets for adjusted gross incomes above $125,000 (single filers) and $250,000 (joint filers) and phased out the federal tax subtraction for those same filers. Second, it allowed a one-year tax exclusion of the first $2,400 of unemployment benefits, as is permitted in federal tax law.

Business Taxes

Corporations that do, or are authorized to do, business in Oregon pay an excise tax. Corporations not doing, or that are not authorized to do, business

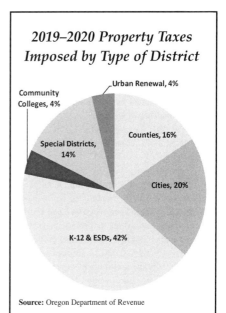

2019–2020 Property Taxes Imposed by Type of District

Urban Renewal, 4%
Community Colleges, 4%
Counties, 16%
Special Districts, 14%
Cities, 20%
K-12 & ESDs, 42%

Source: Oregon Department of Revenue

in Oregon, but that have income from an Oregon source, pay income tax. The tax rate is 6.6 percent on Oregon taxable income of $1 million or less and 7.6 percent on Oregon taxable income above $1 million. There is a minimum excise tax of $150.

The corporate excise and income tax is the second largest source of state tax revenue. Oregon voters approved Ballot Measure 67 in January 2010. The measure made three changes to Oregon corporate taxation. First, it increased the minimum corporate tax from $10 to $150. Second, it instituted a new corporate income tax rate structure that applied a marginal rate of 7.9 percent to corporate net income above $250,000 in tax years 2009 and 2010. For 2011 and 2012, the rate dropped to 7.6 percent. In 2013, the marginal rate was 7.6 percent for net income above $10 million and 6.6 percent for net income below $10 million. Third, it established higher rates for corporate filing fees with the secretary of state.

Property Tax

Property tax rates differ across Oregon. The rate depends on the tax rate approved by local voters and the limits established by the Oregon Constitution. Most properties are taxed by a number of districts, such as a city, county, school district, community college, fire district, or port. The total tax rate on any particular property is calculated by adding all the local taxing district rates in the area. The total tax rate is then multiplied by the assessed value of the property. The county assessor verifies the tax rates and levies submitted by each local taxing district on

Government Finance

an annual basis. The county tax collector collects the taxes and distributes the funds to the local districts.

Taxable property includes real property, mobile homes and some tangible personal property used by business. The state and each county assessor determine the value of property in each county. Measure 5, which was passed by the voters in November 1990, restricted non-school taxes on any property to $10 per $1,000 of real market value. It restricted school taxes on any property to $5 per $1,000 of real market value.

Measure 50 was passed by the voters in May 1997. Measure 50 added another limit to the Measure 5 limits. Now, each property has a real market value and an assessed value. Each taxing district has a fixed, permanent tax rate for operations. Districts may not increase this rate. Voters can approve local option levies for up to five years for operations and up to 10 years or the useful life of capital projects, whichever is less. Local option levies require a "double majority" for approval. Measure 50 established the 1997–1998 maximum assessed value as 90 percent of a property's 1995–1996 real market value. In subsequent tax years, the assessed value is limited to 3 percent annual growth until it reaches real market value. The assessed value can never exceed real market value. New property is assessed at the average county ratio of assessed to real market value of existing property of the same class. For 2008–2009, for all classes of property statewide, total assessed value was about 56 percent of real market value.

Resources

Department of Administrative Services, Chief Financial Office
https://www.oregon.gov/DAS/financial/Pages/Index.aspx
The Chief Financial Office publishes the "Budget Process Overview" and *Governor's Recommended Budget*.

Department of Administrative Services, Office of Economic Analysis
www.oregon.gov/DAS/oea/pages/index.aspx
The Office of Economic Analysis publishes Economic and Revenue Forecasts and related demographic data.

Department of Revenue
https://www.oregon.gov/DOR/pages/index.aspx
The Department of Revenue publishes information about taxes in Oregon.

Legislative Fiscal Office
www.oregonlegislature.gov/lfo
The Legislative Fiscal Office publishes detailed analyses of the *Legislatively Adopted Budget* and the *Governor's Recommended Budget*.

Legislative Revenue Office
www.oregonlegislature.gov/lro
The Legislative Revenue Office publishes reports on revenue-related issues including *Oregon Public Finance: Basic Facts,* which serves as an introduction to how Oregon government is financed.

Education

As Oregon's population grows and our economy evolves, the strength of our educational institutions is an important public policy issue. This section describes public education in Oregon and also lists independent colleges and universities.

PUBLIC EDUCATION IN OREGON

Oregon has 197 public school districts, operating a total of 1,326 public schools. For the school year 2018–2019, the teaching staff working in Oregon's public schools numbered the equivalent of 30,370 full-time positions. The average student/teacher classroom ratio was 19.4 to 1 (national average: 16.0 to 1).

Public schools enrolled 581,730 students from kindergarten through grade 12 (K–12), of which:

38.2 percent of students were students of color (national average: 52.9 percent);

46.3 percent of students qualified for free or reduced price lunches (national average: 51.3 percent);

13.3 percent of students were in Special Education (national average: 12.5 percent); and

8.8 percent of students were English Language Learners (national average: 10.1 percent). (2017–2018 data)

Oregon's combined state and local share of the K–12 education budget was $7.93 billion for the year ending June 30, 2018.

Sources:
U.S. Department of Education, National Center for Education Statistics, 2018–2019. The exception is for English Language Learners, where the latest data are for 2017–2018

Chief Education Office

The office was created in 2015 for the purpose of building a seamless system of education from birth to college and career. The office directs and coordinates multi-agency planning and stakeholder convening to eliminate barriers impeding student success and works to increase educational equity and opportunity for all students and education settings.

The office is focused on ensuring that every student in the state graduates from high school, and that Oregon reaches its "40-40-20" goal of 40 percent of students completing a two-year degree, 40 percent completing a four-year degree and 20 percent graduating from high school career ready. These goals reflect a shared commitment by the state and education groups to create the conditions for students to pursue an education and career path meaningful to them. A target date of 2025 has been set for reaching the "40-40-20" goal.

State Board of Education

The board sets educational policies and standards for Oregon's public school districts and educational service districts, providing leadership and vision by enacting equitable policies and promoting educational practices that help students achieve success in school and life.

The board has seven members appointed to four-year terms by the governor. Board members are Kimberly Howard, Chair (term ends 2024); Guadalupe Martinez Zapata, Vice-Chair (2024);

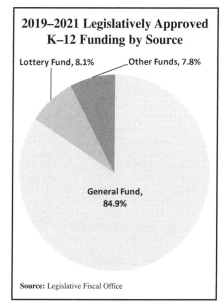

2019–2021 Legislatively Approved K–12 Funding by Source

Lottery Fund, 8.1% Other Funds, 7.8%

General Fund, 84.9%

Source: Legislative Fiscal Office

Bridgett Wheeler, Second Vice-Chair (2024); Jerome Colonna (2022); George Russell (2024); Jennifer Scurlock (2023) and Anthony Veliz (2021).

Department of Education

The governor acts as the superintendent of schools. The governor has authority to appoint a deputy superintendent of public instruction to run the Oregon Department of Education (ODE).

ODE oversees Oregon's public K–12 education system and encompasses the Early Learning Division, Youth Development Division, Oregon School for the Deaf and other programs.

For more information, see ODE's entry in the Executive section, pp. 38–40.

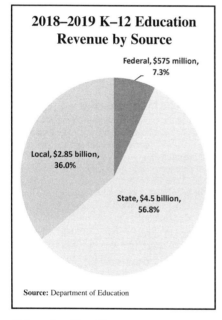

2018–2019 K–12 Education Revenue by Source

Federal, $575 million, 7.3%

Local, $2.85 billion, 36.0%

State, $4.5 billion, 56.8%

Source: Department of Education

Education Funding

Money to support public education in grades K–12 comes from state income taxes, the lottery fund, local revenues primarily consisting of property taxes, and federal funds. Historically, the largest source of funding had been local property taxes, but this changed dramatically in 1990 when voters passed Measure 5, which lowered the amount of property taxes dedicated to schools. By the 1995–1996 school year, local property taxes for education were limited to $5 per every $1,000 of a property's assessed real market value. In 1997, voters passed Measure 50, which further limited local property taxes for schools by placing restrictions on assessed valuation of property and property tax rates. The effect of these measures was to shift the bulk of public school funding from local property

taxes to Oregon's General Fund, which comes from state income taxes.

Oregon uses a formula to provide financial equity among school districts. Each school district receives (in combined state and local funds) an allocation per student, plus an additional amount for each student enrolled in more costly programs such as Special Education or English Language Learners.

The 2019–2021 legislatively adopted General Fund and Lottery Funds budget for the Education program area is $11.478 billion. This was an increase of $482 million (or 4.4%) from the 2017–2019 legislatively approved budget.

The 2020 Final Report from Oregon's Quality Education Commission (QEC) states, "The State School Fund requirement to fund K-12 schools at a level recommended by the QEC is estimated at $9.994 billion in the 2021–23 biennium, $833.6 million more than the funding required to maintain the Current Service Level—that is, to simply keep up with inflation and enrollment growth. This funding gap declined from the prior biennium (2019–2021), when it was $1.774 billion."

For more information see https://www.oregon.gov/ode/reports-and-data/taskcomm/Pages/QEMReports.aspx

HIGHER EDUCATION IN OREGON

Prospective students and families in Oregon can choose from a wide variety of postsecondary education options to earn degrees, certificates and training to build their futures and achieve their career goals. Oregon's higher education system enrolls hundreds of thousands of students in seven public universities, 17 community colleges, the Oregon Health & Science University, 42 private colleges and universities and many private career and trade schools.

Higher Education Coordinating Commission

Ben Cannon, Executive Director
Address: 3225 25th St. SE, Salem 97302
Phone: 503-378-5690
Email: info.HECC@state.or.us
Web: https://www.oregon.gov/HigherEd/Pages/index.aspx

For information about the HECC's duties and responsibilities, see entry in the Executive section, pp. 52–54.

Community Colleges

Oregonians are served by 17 community colleges with campuses and centers throughout the state, providing open access to advance their education and training. Providing certificates, two-year degrees and training programs, Oregon's community colleges prepare students with degrees and coursework to transfer to a four-year university and deliver customized workforce training programs designed to meet local labor market demand. The colleges are governed by locally-elected boards.

In 2018–2019, Oregon's community colleges awarded 10,978 Associate Degrees and 3,984 Certificates and Oregon Transfer Modules (OTMs).

Blue Mountain Community College
Dr. Dennis Bailey-Fougnier, President
Address: 2411 NW Carden Ave., PO Box 100, Pendleton 97801-1000
Phone: 541-276-1260
Web: www.bluecc.edu
　Fall 2019 Enrollment: 2,185
　Fall 2019 Tuition: $6,188

Central Oregon Community College
Dr. Laurie Chesley, President
Address: 2600 NW College Way, Bend 97703
Phone: 541-383-7700
Web: www.cocc.edu
　Fall 2019 Enrollment: 6,588
　Fall 2019 Tuition: $5,389

Chemeketa Community College
Dr. Jessica Howard, President, Salem
Jim Eustrom, President, Yamhill
Address: 4000 Lancaster Dr. NE, PO Box 14007, Salem 97309-7070
Phone: 503-399-5000
Web: www.chemeketa.edu

　Fall 2019 Enrollment: 11,869
　Fall 2019 Tuition: $5,175

Clackamas Community College
Dr. Tim Cook, President
Address: 19600 S Molalla Ave., Oregon City 97045-7998
Phone: 503-594-6000
Web: www.clackamas.edu
　Fall 2019 Enrollment: 10,561
　Fall 2019 Tuition: $5,079

Clatsop Community College
Chris Breitmeyer, President
Address: 1651 Lexington Ave., Astoria 97103
Phone: 503-325-0910
Web: www.clatsopcc.edu
　Fall 2019 Enrollment: 1,662
　Fall 2019 Tuition: $5,265

Columbia Gorge Community College
Dr. Marta Yera Cronin, President
Address: 400 E Scenic Dr., The Dalles 97058-3434
Phone: 541-506-6000
Web: www.cgcc.edu
　Fall 2019 Enrollment: 1,309
　Fall 2019 Tuition: $5,715

Klamath Community College
Roberto Gutierrez, President
Address: 7390 S 6th St., Klamath Falls 97603-7121
Phone: 541-882-3521

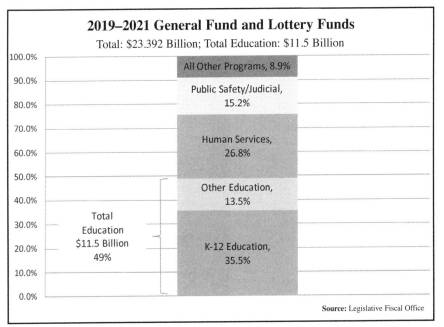

2019–2021 General Fund and Lottery Funds
Total: $23.392 Billion; Total Education: $11.5 Billion

- All Other Programs, 8.9%
- Public Safety/Judicial, 15.2%
- Human Services, 26.8%
- Other Education, 13.5%
- K-12 Education, 35.5%
- Total Education $11.5 Billion 49%

Source: Legislative Fiscal Office

Web: www.klamathcc.edu
Fall 2019 Enrollment: 2,161
Fall 2019 Tuition: $5,717

Lane Community College
Margaret Hamilton, President
Address: 4000 E 30th Ave., Eugene 97405-0640
Phone: 541-463-3000
Web: www.lanecc.edu
Fall 2019 Enrollment: 9,974
Fall 2019 Tuition: $5,957

Linn-Benton Community College
Dr. Lisa Avery, President
Address: 6500 Pacific Blvd. SW, Albany 97321
Phone: 541-917-4999
Web: https://www.linnbenton.edu
Fall 2019 Enrollment: 8,303
Fall 2019 Tuition: $5,486

Mount Hood Community College
Dr. Lisa Skari, President
Address: 26000 SE Stark St., Gresham 97030-3300
Phone: 503-491-6422
Web: www.mhcc.edu
Fall 2019 Enrollment: 8,897
Fall 2019 Tuition: $5,912

Oregon Coast Community College
Dr. Birgitte Ryslinge, President
Address: 400 SE College Way, Newport 97366
Phone: 541-867-8501
Web: www.oregoncoastcc.org
Fall 2019 Enrollment: 939
Fall 2019 Tuition: $5,895

Portland Community College
Mark Mitsui, President
Address: PO Box 19000, Portland 97280-0990
Phone: 971-722-6111
Web: www.pcc.edu
Fall 2019 Enrollment: 34,331
Fall 2019 Tuition: $5,672

Rogue Community College
Dr. Cathy Kemper-Pelle, President
Address: 3345 Redwood Hwy., Grants Pass 97527-9291
Phone: 541-956-7500
Web: www.roguecc.edu
Fall 2019 Enrollment: 6,148
Fall 2019 Tuition: $5,895

Southwestern Oregon Community College
Dr. Patty M. Scott, President
Address: 1988 Newmark Ave., Coos Bay 97420
Phone: 541-888-2525
Web: www.socc.edu
Fall 2019 Enrollment: 3,110
Fall 2019 Tuition: $5,859

Tillamook Bay Community College
Ross Tomlin, President
Address: 4301 Third St., Tillamook 97141
Phone: 503-842-8222
Web: www.tillamookbaycc.edu
Fall 2019 Enrollment: 929
Fall 2019 Tuition: $4,995

Treasure Valley Community College
Dana Young, President
Address: 650 College Blvd., Ontario 97914-3498
Phone: 541-881-8822
Web: www.tvcc.cc
Fall 2019 Enrollment: 2,215
Fall 2019 Tuition: $5,625

Umpqua Community College
Debra Thatcher, President
Address: 1140 Umpqua College Rd., Roseburg 97470
Phone: 541-440-4600
Web: www.umpqua.edu
Fall 2019 Enrollment: 3,923
Fall 2019 Tuition: $5,873

2018–2019 Community Colleges Revenue Components

LOCAL: Property Tax, 23%

STUDENTS: Tuition & Fees, 37%

STATE: General Fund, 40%

Source: Department of Education

Community college tuition figures are based on annualized in-district resident status. Enrollment numbers are based on fall, fourth-week headcount enrollment.

Public Universities

Oregon's public universities serve as educational, scholarly and research centers preparing students to succeed in the workforce and serve the needs of Oregon students and communities. Providing education at the baccalaureate level and beyond, the seven Oregon public universities include Eastern

Oregon University (EOU), La Grande; Oregon Institute of Technology (OIT), Klamath Falls and Wilsonville; Oregon State University (OSU), Corvallis and Bend; Portland State University (PSU), Portland; Southern Oregon University (SOU), Ashland; University of Oregon (UO), Eugene; and Western Oregon University (WOU), Monmouth.

In 2018–2019, the seven public universities collectively awarded a total of 23,675 degrees and certificates across the state, including 17,655 bachelor degrees and 5,990 advanced degrees and graduate certificates. The universities offer bachelor degrees in hundreds of majors and minors, certificate programs, professional programs, graduate programs, as well as research, scholarship, innovation and public service that directly serve Oregon's communities and industries and the needs of national and international constituents.

Eastern Oregon University
Tom Insko, President
Address: One University Blvd., La Grande 97850-2899
Phone: 541-962-3512; Toll-free: 1-800-452-8639
Web: www.eou.edu
Board of Trustees: www.eou.edu/governance
Fall 2019 Enrollment: 3,067
2019–2020 Tuition and Fees: $9,101

Oregon Institute of Technology
Dr. Nagi Naganathan, President
Address: 3201 Campus Dr., Klamath Falls 97601-8801
Phone: 541-885-1000
Web: www.oit.edu
Board of Trustees: www.oit.edu/trustees
Fall 2019 Enrollment: 5,319
2019–2020 Tuition and Fees: Klamath Falls campus, $10,719; Wilsonville campus, $9,180

Oregon State University
F. King Alexander, President
Address: 634 Kerr Administration Building, Corvallis 97331-2128
Phone: 541-737-4133
Web: www.oregonstate.edu; www.osucascades.edu
Board of Trustees: https://leadership.oregonstate.edu/trustees
Fall 2019 Enrollment: Corvallis campus, 31,719; OSU-Cascades Bend campus, 1,005
2019–2020 Tuition and Fees: Corvallis campus, $11,709; OSU-Cascades Bend campus, $10,638

Portland State University
Dr. Stephen Percy, President
Address: PO Box 751, Portland 97207-0751
Phone: 503-725-4419; Toll-free: 1-800-547-8887
Web: www.pdx.edu
Board of Trustees: www.pdx.edu/board
Fall 2019 Enrollment: 26,020
2019–2020 Tuition and Fees: $9,578

Southern Oregon University
Dr. Linda Schott, President

Address: 1250 Siskiyou Blvd., Ashland 97520
Phone: 541-552-7672
Web: www.sou.edu
Board of Trustees: https://governance.sou.edu
Fall 2019 Enrollment: 5,966
2019–2020 Tuition and Fees: $10,475

University of Oregon
Michael H. Schill, JD, President
Address: 110 Johnson Hall, Eugene 97403
Phone: 541-346-3036
Web: www.uoregon.edu
Board of Trustees: https://trustees.uoregon.edu
Fall 2019 Enrollment: 22,615
2019–2020 Tuition and Fees: $12,720

Western Oregon University
Dr. Rex Fuller, President
Address: 345 N Monmouth Ave., Monmouth 97361
Phone: 503-838-8888
Web: www.wou.edu
Board of Trustees: http://www.wou.edu/board/
Fall 2019 Enrollment: 4,929
2019–2020 Tuition and Fees: $9,768

Tuition and fee figures are based on 15 credit hours per term for undergraduate resident students. Certain programs are assessed at different rates than noted. Enrollment numbers are fall, fourth-week enrollment.

2018–2019 Public Universities Revenue Components

STATE: Appropriations, 26%

STUDENTS: Tuition & Fees, 65%

Other, 9%

Source: Department of Education

OREGON HEALTH & SCIENCE UNIVERSITY
Danny Jacobs, MD, President
Address: 3181 SW Sam Jackson Park Rd., Portland 97239-3098

Web: https://www.ohsu.edu/xd/
Board of Directors:
https://www.ohsu.edu/about/board-directors
Fall 2019 Enrollment: 3,017

The Oregon Health & Science University (OHSU) includes Oregon's only academic health center, and has schools of medicine, dentistry, nursing, public health (in partnership with PSU), and other health care professional programs. OHSU has been organized as a public corporation since 1995 and is governed by a board of directors, appointed by the governor and confirmed by the Senate. The state continues to support OHSU programs through grants and general funds that totaled $79.2 million in the 2019–2021 biennium.

Western Interstate Commission for Higher Education

Address: PO Box 3175, Eugene 97403
Phone: 541-346-5729
Web: https://www.wiche.edu

The Western Interstate Commission for Higher Education (WICHE) is a regional organization created by the Western Regional Education Compact, adopted in the 1950s. WICHE facilitates resource sharing among the higher education systems of the West. Fifteen states, including Oregon, are members of WICHE, which is governed by three governor-appointed commissioners from each state. Under terms of the compact, each state commits to support WICHE's basic operations through annual dues established by the full commission. Oregon's three commissioners are Ben Cannon, Salem; Camille Preus, Pendleton; and Hilda Rosselli, Salem.

Private and Independent Colleges and Universities

Oregon is home to many private colleges, universities and career schools providing a wide range of college and career training opportunities to Oregonians.

Northwest Commission on Colleges and Universities

Web: http://www.nwccu.org

The Northwest Commission on Colleges and Universities (NWCCU) recognizes higher education institutions for performance, integrity and quality to merit the confidence of the educational community and the public. The commission's accreditation of postsecondary institutions is a voluntary, non-governmental, self-regulatory process of quality assurance and institutional improvement.

Accreditation or preaccreditation by NWCCU also qualifies institutions and enrolled students for access to Title IV federal funds to support teaching, research and student financial aid.

Unless otherwise noted, the independent, non-profit higher education institutions listed below are accredited by NWCCU and have independent or exempt status from ongoing regulatory oversight by Oregon's Office of Degree Authorization.

Bushnell University, Eugene
Joseph Womack, President
Phone: 541-684-7241
Web: https://www.bushnell.edu

Corban University, Salem
Sheldon Nord, President
Phone: 503-581-8600
Web: www.corban.edu

Embry-Riddle Aeronautical University, Portland
Jennifer Stevens, Campus Director
Phone: 503-288-8690
Web: http://worldwide.erau.edu/locations/portland
– Accredited by the Southern Association of Colleges and Schools, Commission on Colleges

George Fox University, Newberg
Dr. Robin E. Baker, President
Phone: 503-554-2102
Web: www.georgefox.edu

Lewis & Clark College, Portland
Wim Wiewel, President
Phone: 503-768-7680
Web: www.lclark.edu

Linfield College, McMinnville
Dr. Miles K. Davis, President
Phone: 503-883-2234
Web: www.linfield.edu

Pioneer Hall on the campus of Linfield College in McMinnville. (Oregon State Archives scenic photo)

Mount Angel Seminary, Saint Benedict
Joseph Betschart, President
Phone: 503-845-3951
Web: www.mountangelabbey.org/seminary

Multnomah University, Portland
Dr. Craig Williford, President
Phone: 503-251-5352
Web: www.multnomah.edu

National University of Natural Medicine, Portland
Dr. Christine Girard, President
Phone: 503-552-1555
Web: https://nunm.edu

Northwest University, Salem
Dr. Debbie Lamm Bray, Program Dean
Phone: 503-304-0092
Web: https://oregon.northwestu.edu

Pacific Northwest College of Art, Portland
David Ellis, Interim President
Phone: 503-226-4391
Web: www.pnca.edu

Pacific University, Forest Grove
Lesley M. Hallick, President
Phone: 503-352-2123
Web: www.pacificu.edu

Reed College, Portland
Audrey Bilger, President
Phone: 503-777-7500
Web: www.reed.edu

Eliot Hall on the campus of Reed College in southeast Portland. (Oregon State Archives scenic photo)

University of Portland, Portland
Mark Poorman, President
Phone: 503-943-7101
Web: www.up.edu

University of Western States, Portland
Joseph Brimhall, President
Phone: 503-251-5712
Web: www.uws.edu

Walla Walla University
John McVay, President
Phone: 800-541-8900
Web: https://www.wallawalla.edu/

Warner Pacific University, Portland
Dr. Brian L. Johnson, President
Phone: 503-517-1238
Web: www.warnerpacific.edu

Egtvedt Hall on the campus of Warner Pacific University in southeast Portland. (Oregon State Archives scenic photo)

Western Seminary, Portland
Randal Roberts, President
Phone: 503-517-1860
Web: www.westernseminary.edu

Western University of Health Sciences, Lebanon
Dr. Paula M. Crone, Dean
Phone: 541-259-0200
Web: https://www.westernu.edu/northwest
– Accredited by the Western Association of Schools and Colleges

Willamette University, Salem
Stephen E. Thorsett, President
Phone: 503-370-6209
Web: www.willamette.edu

Silver Falls State Park

Emma Arvin
Jessica Sloan's 8th Grade Class
Duniway Middle School, McMinnville

This drawing by Emma Arvin shows a downed tree at Silver Falls State Park.

Silver Falls State Park is one of my all-time favorite state parks. There are many different trails you can explore, different sights to see. There are tall, green trees and plants littered along the ground. You can spot different types of animals, like deer, birds, insects, and some really cool slugs! It is a great place to go with my family. Everyone loves it! The trails range from easy to a bit more challenging, from a few miles to several miles! Along these trails you can see ten stunning waterfalls.

But my favorite part of Silver falls is hiking along the trail called South Falls and Maple Ridge Loop where you can walk behind the South Falls. When you are behind it, you can feel the spray of water against your face and the roaring of the rushing water is so loud you can't hear anyone talking. Walking behind it though can be sort of challenging though, there are gianormous puddles you have to skip around and a giant cliff above your head, but it makes it even more fun!

All in all, Silver Falls is a fantastic place to visit with the wildlife and the different trails, no matter if it is rainy or sunny, I guarantee it is the funnest State Park to visit!

Arts, History and Sciences

Through the organizations described in this section, we are fortunate to have many opportunities to gain greater understanding and appreciation for the arts and culture, history and heritage, Earth sciences and technology of Oregon.

ARTS AND CULTURE IN OREGON

Oregon Arts Commission
Brian Rogers, Executive Director
Address: 775 Summer St. NE, Suite 200, Salem 97301-1280
Phone: 503-986-0082
Fax: 503-581-5115
Web: https://www.oregonartscommission.org
The Oregon Arts Commission enhances the quality of life for all Oregonians through the arts by stimulating creativity, leadership and economic vitality.

The commission provides leadership, funding and arts programs through its grants, special initiatives and services. The commission works to improve access to the arts all around the state. The commission also supports the Oregon Folklife Network.

Oregon Cultural Trust
Brian Rogers, Executive Director
Address: 775 Summer St. NE, Suite 200, Salem 97301-1280
Phone: 503-986-0088
Fax: 503-581-5115
Web: https://culturaltrust.org
Founded in 2001, the Oregon Cultural Trust leads Oregon in cultivating, growing and valuing culture as an integral part of communities. Working with the Oregon Arts Commission, the Oregon Heritage Commission, the Oregon Historical Society, Oregon Humanities and the State Historic Preservation Office, the Cultural Trust inspires Oregonians to invest in a permanent fund that provides grants to cultural organizations. It is governed by a 13-member board of directors. Eleven voting members are appointed by the governor, and the president of the Senate and speaker of the House of Representatives each appoint a member of the Legislature as non-voting, advisory members.

Oregon Humanities
Adam Davis, Executive Director
Address: 921 SW Washington Ave., Suite 150, Portland 97205
Phone: 503-241-0543; Toll-free: 1-800-735-0543
Fax: 503-241-0024
Web: https://oregonhumanities.org
Oregon Humanities, formerly the Oregon Council for the Humanities, was established in 1971 as an independent, nonprofit affiliate of the National Endowment for the Humanities. It is one of five statewide partners of the Oregon Cultural Trust — programs that support an Oregon that invites diverse perspectives, explores challenging questions and strives for just communities.

Oregon's Major Arts Organizations

Oregon Shakespeare Festival
Nataki Garrett, Artistic Director; David Schmitz, Executive Director
Address: 15 S Pioneer St., PO Box 158, Ashland 97520
Phone: 1-800-219-8161
Fax: 541-482-0446
Web: https://www.osfashland.org
The Oregon Shakespeare Festival is one of the largest nonprofit theaters in the country. Established in 1935, it has an annual attendance of almost 400,000, presenting more than 760 performances of up to eleven plays in repertory from March through October on its three stages. The festival also offers backstage tours, classes, lectures, concerts and play readings.

Oregon Symphony Association
Scott Showalter, President and CEO
Address: 909 SW Washington St., Portland 97205
Phone: 503-228-1353; Toll Free: 1-800-228-7343
Web: https://www.orsymphony.org
Led by Music Director Carlos Kalmar, the Oregon Symphony is one of the largest performing arts organizations in the Pacific Northwest. Its many performances each year include the classical concert series, pops concerts, youth and educational concerts, family concerts and special performances at its home in Portland, as well as in Salem and elsewhere in Oregon.

Portland Art Museum

Brian Ferriso, Executive Director
Address: 1219 SW Park Ave., Portland 97205
Phone: 503-226-2811
Fax: 503-226-4842
Web: https://portlandartmuseum.org

The Portland Art Museum, founded in 1892, is the region's oldest and largest visual and media arts center and one of the state's greatest cultural assets. The museum is a premier venue for education in the visual arts and for the collection and preservation of art for the enrichment of present and future generations.

The internationally renowned museum presents special exhibitions drawn from the world's finest collections. The permanent collection showcases unique American tribal objects and Japanese, Chinese and Korean objects up to 3,000 years old. European, modern and contemporary art, Northwest art, photography and graphic arts round out the collection. Located in downtown Portland's cultural district, the museum offers lectures, tours and family activities.

Hallie Ford Museum of Art

John Olbrantz, Director
Address: 700 State St., Salem 97310
Phone: 503-370-6855
Web: https://willamette.edu/arts/hfma/index.html

The Hallie Ford Museum of Art (HFMA), which opened to the public in 1998, exists to support the liberal arts curriculum of Willamette University, and to serve as an intellectual and cultural resource for the City of Salem and beyond, through the collection, preservation, exhibition, and interpretation of historical and contemporary art with an emphasis on regional art.

The museum is a vibrant artistic hub offering access to historical, regional and contemporary art, and a wide variety of public programs.

Portland Opera

Sue Dixon, General Director
Address: 211 SE Caruthers St., Portland 97214
Administrative Offices: 503-241-1407
Patron Services: 503-241-1802
Web: https://www.portlandopera.org

Portland Opera presents classic and contemporary work. Public programming is held in Portland at the Keller Auditorium, the Newmark Theatre and at the company's artistic headquarters, The Hampton Opera Center, lending versatility in scale of production throughout Portland Opera's season—including grand works, intimate chamber pieces, new operas and standard repertoire. Regular ticket prices for performances start at $35. All performances are sung in the original language of the opera, presented with English captions.

Portland Opera supports the community with the Portland Opera To Go program, touring 50-minute adaptations of operas throughout the state and region. It also offers a resident artist program for emerging singers, a free simulcast performance each year, and community recitals and programs. Portland Opera also serenades Oregonians with its Opera a la Cart—a food truck that converts into a stage for free live pop-up performances.

The company also presents the Broadway In Portland series, connecting regional audiences with nationally touring Broadway productions.

OREGON HISTORY ORGANIZATIONS

Oregon's Major History and Heritage Organizations

State Archives

see Executive Section, page 13

National Historic Oregon Trail Interpretive Center

Sandra Tennyson, Acting Center Director
Address: 22267 OR Hwy. 86, Baker City 97814
Phone: 541-523-1843
Fax: 541-523-1834
Web: oregontrail.blm.gov

The National Historic Oregon Trail Interpretive Center portrays and interprets the Oregon Trail experience and its related themes, while preserving and protecting its historic and cultural heritage. Administrated by the Bureau of Land Management, the Interpretive Center offers living history demonstrations, interpretive programs, exhibits, multimedia presentations, special events, and more than four miles of interpretive trails to tell the stories of Oregon Trail pioneers, explorers, Native Americans, miners and settlers of the frontier west. The Interpretive Center is located on the Oregon National Historic Trail, and cultural features include wagon ruts from Oregon Trail migrations of the mid-19th century, and buildings and workings of a historic gold mine dating to the 1890s.

Oregon Geographic Names Board

Bruce J. Fisher, Board President
Address: 1200 SW Park Ave., Portland 97205
Phone: 503-319-1714
Web: https://www.ohs.org/about-us/affiliates-and-partners/oregon-geographic-names-board/index.cfm

Founded in 1908, the board is an advisor to the United States Board on Geographic Names and is associated with the Oregon Historical Society, which maintains the board's correspondence and records. It is composed of 25 appointed board members representing all geographic areas of the state and is served by advisors from government agencies and the private sector.

The board supervises the naming of all geographic features within the state to standardize geographic nomenclature, prevent confusion and duplication in naming geographic features, and correct previous naming errors. The board's recommendations are submitted to the U.S. board in Washington, D.C., for final action.

Oregon Heritage Commission, State Historic Preservation Office, Oregon Commission on Historic Cemeteries

see Executive Section, pages 66–67

Visitors view an exhibit at the Oregon Historical Society in Portland. (Oregon State Archives scenic photo)

Oregon Historical Society

Kerry Tymchuk, Executive Director
Address: 1200 SW Park Ave., Portland 97205
Phone: 503-222-1741; TDD: 503-306-5194
Fax: 503-221-2035
Web: https://www.ohs.org

For more than 100 years, the Oregon Historical Society (OHS) has provided a place for history — a home for Oregon heritage, culture, beginnings and future. The society has expanded far beyond its original mission of collecting, preserving, publishing and sharing Oregon's rich history. Attractions include exhibits covering a wide range of historical topics, lectures and special events, a museum store, its peer-reviewed journal, the *Oregon Historical Quarterly,* and research library with a wealth of books, maps, documents, oral histories, photographs and film footage. OHS also operates educational programs for children and adults, and provides smaller exhibits that travel around the state. Web site content is also available across the state through the OHS digital history projects, including the Oregon History Project, The Oregon Encyclopedia and Oregon TimeWeb. The museum is open Monday through Saturday,

10:00 a.m. to 5:00 p.m., and Sunday, 12:00 p.m. to 5:00 p.m. Admission covers entrance to both the museum and library (OHS members are free). Multnomah County residents are also admitted free due to a modest levy that was first approved by voters in November 2010 and renewed in May 2016.

Tamástslikt Cultural Institute

Roberta Conner, Director
Address: 47106 Wildhorse Blvd., Pendleton 97801
Phone: 541-429-7700
Fax: 541-429-7706
Web: https://www.tamastslikt.org

Tamástslikt Cultural Institute is dedicated to the accurate depiction and perpetuation of the culture and history of the Cayuse, Umatilla and Walla Walla Tribes. Located on the Umatilla Indian Reservation, Tamástslikt is the only tribally-owned and operated interpretive center along the National Historic Oregon Trail. Tamástslikt is a National Park Service certified interpretive site for both the Lewis and Clark and Oregon National Historic Trails and is wholly owned by the Confederated Tribes of the Umatilla Indian Reservation. The Institute is open Tuesday through Saturday from 10 a.m. to 5 p.m.

Visitors to Tamástslikt hear horses rumbling across a grassy plateau, Coyote saving the plants and animals from an ancient monster, generations'-old songs in the winter lodge and the bell and translated hymns in the church. They see the brilliant color of dancers at a competition powwow, poignant interviews with Tribal warriors and stories from families who have long participated in the Pendleton Round-Up. Ancient tools and art forms, ambient sounds and Tribal voices, along with historical photographs and contemporary video footage, combine to create an intriguing experience. One visit yields a new understanding of these contemporary Plateau people and their ancient ties to their Eastern Oregon and Southeastern Washington homeland.

Local native-made art and handcrafted goods and exclusive-to-Tamastslikt Pendleton Woolen Mills blankets are available in the spacious Museum Store. The Kinship Café offers lunch and spectacular views of the Blue Mountain foothills as well as Plateau-inspired menu for catering. The research library and archives are open to the public for on-site work, and three meeting rooms are available for daily/weekly rental. Admission is always free to Blue Star families, Inwai Circle of Friends, members of the CTUIR, Oregon Historical Society, Fort Walla Walla, and NARM. Group and family rates are available. All admissions are good for two successive business days.

Willamette Heritage Center

Michelle Cordova, Executive Director
Address: 1313 Mill St. SE, Suite 200, Salem 97301
Phone: 503-585-7012
Fax: 503-588-9902
Web: https://www.willametteheritage.org

The Willamette Heritage Center (WHC) connects generations by preserving and interpreting the history of the Mid-Willamette Valley. The 14 historic structures on the WHC's five-acre campus house permanent and changing exhibits, a research library and archives, textile learning center and event and office spaces.

Early settlement buildings take visitors back to the 1840s, when Euro-American missionaries and immigrants settled in the Mid-Willamette Valley, home of the Kalapuya. The 1841 Jason Lee House and Methodist Parsonage are the oldest standing wooden frame houses in the Pacific Northwest, featured along with the John D. Boon House (1847) and Pleasant Grove Church (1854), built by Oregon Trail immigrants. The 1896 Thomas Kay Woolen Mill, a National Park Service-designated American Treasure, vividly tells the story of industrialization in the Mid-Willamette Valley. Changing exhibits explore and highlight the rich and diverse cultural heritage of the region. The Research Library holds valuable photographs, records, and documents focused on Marion County. The WHC offers a variety of historical courses and tours as well as educational programs and events year-round. These include Sheep to Shawl in May, Oregon Trail Live in September, and Magic at the Mill in December.

The WHC is a private, 501(c)(3) nonprofit organization formed from the merger of Mission Mill Museum and the Marion County Historical Society. The WHC is open Monday through Saturday, 10:00 a.m. to 5:00 p.m. The Research Library is open Tuesday through Friday, 12:00 p.m. to 4:00 p.m. and by appointment.

See also Oregon Museums Association

Address: PO Box 8604, Portland 97207
Email: connect@oregonmuseums.org
Web: https://www.oregonmuseums.org

Regional Historical Societies and Heritage Organizations

Due to COVID-19, call ahead and verify hours before visiting

Aurora Colony Historical Society

Old Aurora Colony Museum
Address: 15018 Second St., NE, PO Box 202, Aurora 97002
Phone: 503-678-5754
Web: https://www.auroracolony.org

Baker Heritage Museum

Address: 2480 Grove St., Baker City 97814-2719
Phone: 541-523-9308
Web: www.bakerheritagemuseum.com

Benton County Historical Society & Museum

Address: 1101 Main St., PO Box 35, Philomath 97370
Phone: 541-929-6230
Fax: 541-929-6261
Web: https://www.bentoncountymuseum.org

The Benton County Historical Museum in Philomath. (Oregon State Archives scenic photo)

Cannon Beach History Center and Museum

Address: 1387 S Spruce St., Cannon Beach 97110
Phone: 503-436-9301
Web: https://cbhistory.org

Clackamas County Historical Society and Museum of the Oregon Territory

Address: 211 Tumwater Dr., PO Box 2211, Oregon City 97045
Phone: 503-655-5574
Fax: 503-655-0035
Web: http://clackamashistory.org

Clatsop County Historical Society

Address: 714 Exchange St., PO Box 88, Astoria 97103
Phone: 503-325-2203
Fax: 503-325-7727
Web: www.cumtux.org;
www.oregonfilmmuseum.org

Columbia River Maritime Museum

Address: 1792 Marine Dr., Astoria 97103
Phone: 503-325-2323
Fax: 503-325-2331
Web: http://www.crmm.org

Coos History Museum & Maritime Collection

Address: 1210 N Front St., Coos Bay 97420
Phone: 541-756-6320

Web: https://cooshistory.org

Crook County Historical Society and Bowman Museum

Address: 246 N Main St., Prineville 97754
Phone: 541-447-3715
Web: http://crookcountyhistorycenter.org

Curry Historical Society and Museum

Address: 29419 S Ellensberg Ave., PO Box 1598, Gold Beach 97444
Phone: 541-247-9396
Web: https://www.curryhistory.com

Deschutes County Historical Society and Museum

Address: 129 NW Idaho Ave., Bend 97703
Phone: 541-389-1813
Fax: 541-317-9345
Web: https://www.deschuteshistory.org

Douglas County Museum and Umpqua River Lighthouse Museum

Address: 123 Museum Dr., Roseburg 97471; 1020 Lighthouse Rd., Winchester Bay 97467
Phone: 541-957-7007; 541-271-4631
Web: http://www.umpquavalleymuseums.org

Five Oaks Museum

Address: 17677 NW Springville Rd., Portland 97229, PO Box 3790, Hillsboro 97123
Phone: 503-645-5353
Web: https://fiveoaksmuseum.org/

Four Rivers Cultural Center and Museum

Address: 676 SW Fifth Ave., Ontario 97914
Phone: 541-889-8191
Fax: 541-889-7628
Web: https://4rcc.com

Genealogical Forum of Oregon

Address: 2505 SE 11th Ave., Suite B18, Portland 97202-1061
Phone: 503-963-1932
Web: https://gfo.org

Gilliam County Historical Society

Address: Hwy. 19 at Burns Park, PO Box 377, Condon 97823
Phone: 541-384-4233
Web: http://www.co.gilliam.or.us/recreation/museums/index.php

Grant County Historical Museum

Address: 101 S Canyon City Blvd., Hwy 395, PO Box 464, Canyon City 97820
Phone: 541-575-0362
Web: https://grantcountyhistoricalmuseum.org

Gresham Historical Society

Address: 410 N Main Ave., Gresham 97030
Phone: 503-661-0347
Web: https://www.greshamhistoricalsociety.org

Harney County Historical Society

Address: 18 W D St., PO Box 388, Burns 97720
Phone: 541-573-5618
Email: harneymuseum@centurytel.net

The History Museum of Hood River County

Address: 300 E Port Marina Dr., PO Box 781, Hood River 97031
Phone/Fax: 541-386-6772
Web: https://www.hoodriverhistorymuseum.org

Josephine County Historical Society

Address: 512 SW Fifth St., Grants Pass 97526
Phone: 541-479-7827
Web: https://jocohistorical.org

Lake County Museum and Schminck Memorial Museum

Address: 118 S E St., PO Box 1222 Lakeview 97630; Open Thursday–Saturday, May–October
Phone: 541-947-2220
Web: https://www.lakecountyor.org/links/museum.php

Lane County Historical Society and Museum

Address: 740 W 13th Ave., Eugene 97402
Phone: 541-682-4242
Fax: 541-682-7361
Web: https://www.lchm.org

Lincoln County Historical Society

Address: 545 SW Ninth St., Newport 97365
Phone: 541-265-7509
Web: https://oregoncoasthistory.org

Linn County Historical Museum

Address: 101 Park Ave., PO Box 607, Brownsville 97327
Phone: 541-466-3390
Web: https://linnparks.com/museums/

Malheur Country Historical Society

Address: PO Box 691, Ontario 97914
Email: malheurcountryhist@gmail.com
Web: https://sites.google.com/site/malheurcountryhistorical/

North Lincoln County Historical Museum

Address: 4907 SW Hwy. 101, Lincoln City 97367
Phone: 541-996-6614
Web: http://www.northlincolncountyhistoricalmuseum.org

Oregon Black Pioneers

Zachary Stocks, Executive Director
Address: 117 Commercial St. NE., Suite 210, Salem 97301
Phone: 503-540-4063
Web: https://oregonblackpioneers.org

Oregon Jewish Museum and Center for Holocaust Education

Address: 724 NW Davis St., Portland 97209
Phone: 503-226-3600
Web: https://www.ojmche.org

Oregon Nikkei Legacy Center and Endowment

Address: 121 NW Second Ave., Portland 97209
Phone: 503-224-1458
Web: http://www.oregonnikkei.org

Polk County Historical Society

Address: 560 S Pacific Hwy., Rickreall 97371, PO Box 67, Monmouth 97361
Phone: 503-623-6251
Web: http://www.polkcountyhistoricalsociety.org

Rogue Valley Genealogical Society & Jackson County Genealogy Library

Address: 3405 S Pacific Hwy., Medford 97501
Phone: 541-512-2340
Web: https://rvgslibrary.org

Santiam Historical Society

Address: PO Box 326, Stayton 97383
Phone: 503-769-1406
Email: santiamhistoricalsociety@gmail.com

Sherman County Historical Society and Museum

Address: 200 Dewey St., PO Box 173, Moro 97039
Phone: 541-565-3232
Web: https://www.shermanmuseum.org

Southern Oregon Historical Society

Address: 106 N Central Ave., Medford 97501
Phone: 541-773-6536
Web: http://www.sohs.org

Talent Historical Society

Address: PO Box 582, Talent 97540
Phone: 541-512-8838
Web: http://talenthistory.org/about.html

Tillamook County Pioneer Museum

Address: 2106 Second St., Tillamook 97141
Phone: 503-842-4553
Web: http://www.tcpm.org

Troutdale Historical Society

Address: 732 E Historic Columbia River Hwy., Troutdale 97060
Phone: 503-661-2164
Web: https://www.troutdalehistory.org

Umatilla County Historical Society and Heritage Station Museum

Address: 108 SW Frazer Ave., PO Box 253, Pendleton 97801
Phone: 541-276-0012
Web: http://www.heritagestationmuseum.org

The Museum at Warm Springs

Address: 2189 Hwy. 26, PO Box 909, Warm Springs 97761
Phone: 541-553-3331
Fax: 541-553-3338
Web: https://museumatwarmsprings.org

Wasco County Museum

Address: 5000 Discovery Dr., The Dalles 97058
Phone: 541-296-8600
Web: https://www.gorgediscovery.org

Yaquina Pacific Railroad Historical Society

Address: 100 NW A St., Toledo 97391
Phone: 541-336-5256
Web: http://www.yaquinapacificrr.org

Yamhill County Museum and Library

Address: 605 Market St., PO Box 484, Lafayette 97127
Phone: 503-864-2308
Web: https://www.yamhillcountyhistory.org

EARTH SCIENCES AND TECHNOLOGY

Oregon's Major Industry, Science and Technology Organizations

Columbia Gorge Discovery Center

Carolyn Purcell, Executive Director
Address: 5000 Discovery Dr., The Dalles 97058
Phone: 541-296-8600
Fax: 541-298-8660
Web: https://www.gorgediscovery.org

The Columbia Gorge Discovery Center is the official interpretive center for the Columbia River Gorge National Scenic Area. Exhibits interpret Ice Age floods, 13,000 years of cultural history, Lewis and Clark, the Oregon Trail, transportation, agriculture and commerce of the region. Native plant restoration and live raptor programs promote conservation and stewardship. Open seven days a week, 9:00 a.m. to 5:00 p.m.

Evergreen Aviation & Space Museum

John Rasmussen, Interim Executive Director
Address: 500 NE Captain Michael King Smith Wy., McMinnville 97128
Phone: 503-434-4180
Web: https://www.evergreenmuseum.org

The Evergreen Aviation & Space Museum, a 501(c)3 non-profit organization, is home to the world's largest wooden aircraft, the Hughes Flying Boat *"Spruce Goose."* The museum collection also includes a rare SR-71 Blackbird spy plane, Titan II SLV Missile with its original lauch room, full-motion flight simulator ride and 3-D digital theater. The museum houses more than 150 historic aircraft, spacecraft and exhibits on display.

A plane at the Evergreen Aviation Museum in McMinnville. (Oregon State Archives scenic photo)

Located across from the McMinnville Airport, three miles southeast of McMinnville on Highway 18, the museum is open daily; closed Easter, Thanksgiving Day Christmas Eve and Christmas Day. Check the website for hours and admission prices.

High Desert Museum

Dr. Dana Whitelaw, Executive Director
Address: 59800 S Hwy. 97, Bend 97702-7963
Phone: 541-382-4754
Fax: 541-382-5256
Web: https://www.highdesertmuseum.org

The High Desert Museum is nationally acclaimed for its close-up wildlife encounters, living history experiences, Tribal and Western art, cultural exhibits and special programs for all ages. The museum features indoor and outdoor exhibits and natural animal habitats and is renowned for inspiring stewardship of high desert cultural and natural resources. Nature trails meander through the museum's 135 forested acres.

Major permanent exhibits include the Earle A. Chiles Hall of Exploration and Settlement,

the Henry J. Casey Hall of Plateau Indians and the Donald M. Kerr Birds of Prey Center, which is home to many raptors. Outdoor wildlife viewing areas include the "Fire in the Forest" interpretive fire trail. Three North American river otters can be found frolicking in the pond at the Autzen Otter Exhibit. Porcupines, badgers, a red fox and reptiles are also among the more than 100 animals in the museum's care.

The museum's turn-of-the-century working sawmill and replica High Desert Ranch provide authentic settings for its living history performers.

The museum, five minutes south of Bend, is open every day except Independence Day, Thanksgiving and Christmas, and is funded by visitors, members, donors and grants.

Malheur Field Station

Rose Garacci, Station Manager
Address: 34848 Sodhouse Ln., Princeton 97721
Phone: 541-493-2629
Email: malheurfieldstation@gmail.com
Web: https://malheurfieldstation.org

Malheur Field Station is an environmental education and research center in the northern Great Basin region in Southeastern Oregon, a diverse setting of marshlands, desert basins, alkali playas, upland desert scrub steppe, volcanic and glacial landforms and fault block mountains, 32 miles south of Burns on the Malheur National Wildlife Refuge. It provides a rich outdoor classroom for the biologist, geologist, archaeologist, astronomer, artist, or environmental science student. operated by the Great Basin Society, a 501(c)(3) organization founded in 1985. The field station provides public lectures, accredited and non-accredited courses, professional development workshops and scout projects. It also hosts individuals, groups, families, birding groups and K–12 school groups. A member-based consortium of northwest universities, colleges and education organizations guides the academic programs.

Accommodations, ranging from dormitories and kitchenettes to trailers and recreational vehicle hook-ups, can be arranged.

The field station's Natural History Museum exhibits and bookstore are open to the public.

Oregon Coast Aquarium

Carrie E. Lewis, President and CEO;
Kaety Jacobson, Board Chair
Address: 2820 SE Ferry Slip Rd., Newport 97365
Phone: 541-867-3474
Fax: 541-867-6846
Web: https://aquarium.org

No visit to Newport, Oregon is complete without a stop at the Oregon Coast Aquarium. The Aquarium strives to be a center of excellence for ocean literacy and fun, and it plays an active role in conservation, education and animal rehabilitation. The Aquarium's world-class indoor and outdoor exhibits have earned the facility consistent recognition as one of the top ten aquariums in the country.

The Aquarium's Passages of the Deep exhibit allows the visitor to literally immerse themselves in the ocean realm that exists right off the Oregon coast. A series of underwater walkways leads the visitor from the dark, quiet canyons of the Orford Reef, through the sparkling and teeming waters of Halibut Flats and finally into the vast blue expanse of the Open Sea. As you pass through these three ecosystems, you symbolically move further into the Pacific Ocean, encountering vastly different animals along the way. The sharks are particularly popular with Aquarium visitors, and all our species are native to Oregon coastal waters, including our largest specimen, the Broadnose Sevengill Shark.

The Oregon Coast Aquarium is a 501(c)(3) non-profit funded through ticket sales, grants and the support of Aquarium members.

Oregon Museum of Science and Industry (OMSI)

Erin Graham, President and CEO;
Alistair Firmin, Board Chair
Address: 1945 SE Water Ave., Portland 97214-3354
Phone: 503-797-4000
Web: https://omsi.edu

Founded in 1944, OMSI is one of the nation's leading science museums with an international reputation in science education. Today, the museum serves over 1 million visitors at the museum and through off-site education programs. OMSI is ranked as one of the top science centers in the United States and has an international reputation for its innovative exhibits and educational programs. Our mission is to inspire curiosity by creating engaging science-learning experiences for students of all ages and backgrounds. We foster experimentation and the exchange of ideas, and we help our community make smart, informed choices.

We are dedicated to helping people build the confidence and skills they need for whatever the future holds through hands-on, high-quality learning experiences in the museum, at our world-class resident camps and as part of the largest statewide science education program in the country.

OMSI is an independent, non-profit 501(c)(3) organization that receives no state or local tax support and relies on admissions, memberships, and donations to continue our educational mission, programs, and exhibit development.

OMSI is open Tuesday – Sunday and all holidays except Thanksgiving and Christmas.

Oregon State University Hatfield Marine Science Center

Bob Cowen, Director
Address: 2030 SE Marine Science Dr., Newport 97365

Phone: 541-867-0100
Fax: 541-867-0138
Web: https://hmsc.oregonstate.edu

The Hatfield Marine Science Center (HMSC) is Oregon State University's coastal research, teaching and marine extension hub, built on Yaquina Bay in 1965 with help from the Port of Newport and the federal government. HMSC was named in 1983 to honor Mark O. Hatfield, who served Oregon as a state legislator, Secretary of State and two-term governor before joining the U.S. Senate in 1966, where he served more than 30 years. Admission is by donation.

HMSC facilities accommodate over 300 researchers and students from OSU and six state and federal agencies. Facilities include a Visitor Center, research and teaching laboratories, including a seawater wet lab, and on-site housing for undergraduate and graduate students in residence and visiting scientists.

It is a base for oceanographic research vessels and is adjacent to the site of the National Oceanic and Atmospheric Administration (NOAA) Marine Operations Center, Pacific. As part of OSU's Marine Studies Initiative, HMSC has plans to expand academic programs at HMSC and build a new teaching and research building in Newport. See http://marinestudies.oregonstate.edu.

Agencies located at HMSC include the Oregon Department of Fish and Wildlife Marine Resources Program, the U.S. Environmental Protection Agency Pacific Coastal Ecology Branch, the U.S. Fish and Wildlife Service Oregon Coast National Wildlife Refuge Complex, the U.S. Geological Survey, the USDA's Agricultural Research Service, and NOAA, including elements of the Alaska Fisheries Science Center, the Northwest Fisheries Science Center and the Pacific Marine Environmental Laboratory.

HMSC research and education activities work to increase understanding of coastal and ocean ecosystems and foster sustainable management of marine resources.

Oregon Sea Grant manages HMSC Visitor Center, which has exhibit space for interactive, hands-on exhibits and aquaria including its beloved touch pool. A webcam features the giant Pacific octopus: http://hmsc.oregonstate.edu/visitor/octocam. Computer simulations and frequently changing exhibits enable visitors to experience being scientific explorers learning about some of the current research underway at the center.

Informal education programs and hands-on laboratories can be reserved by school and organized groups, and a dedicated corps of trained volunteers assists visitors with their individual explorations.

Oregon Zoo

Don Moore, PhD, Director
Address: 4001 SW Canyon Rd., Portland 97221
Phone: 503-220-2540
Fax: 503-226-6836

Nestled on 64 acres in the forested hills of Washington Park, the Oregon Zoo is just five minutes west of downtown Portland, easily accessible by public transit and just off Highway 26. Parking charges apply.

The Oregon Zoo, a service of Metro, is home to more than 2,000 animals from around the world. The Great Northwest area welcomes visitors to the zoo and includes the *Eagle Canyon* exhibit, which surrounds visitors with the splendors of a natural watershed. Visitors have a fish-eye view of salmon, sturgeon and other native fish. Farther up the trail, magnificent bald eagles appear. Visitors discover the importance of rivers and streams and the interconnectedness of animals and the ecosystem. The Great Northwest also features *Condors of the Columbia*—the home of an Oregon native brought back from near-extinction: the California condor. *The Family Farm*—a re-creation of an Oregon Century Farm—is complete with farmhouse and barn, allowing visitors of all ages a chance to interact with sheep, goats and chickens.

At the zoo, you can explore habitats of animals from around the world. *Red Ape Reserve* showcases orangutans and white-cheeked gibbons. *Predators of the Serengeti* houses lions and cheetahs, while the *Africa Savanna* is home to rhinos, hippos, giraffes and more. The *Africa Rainforest* features fruit bats, monkeys, crocodiles, and many bright and colorful birds, including flamingos. The *Amazon Flooded Forest* showcases some of the many animals living in the most diverse ecosystem in the world. At the Asian elephant habitat, visitors can connect with Portland's elephant family and learn about their care—the Oregon Zoo is recognized worldwide for its Asian elephant program, which has spanned more than 60 years. Other zoo residents include black bears, cougars, polar bears, penguins, Amur tigers and leopards, all living in lush exhibits recreating their natural habitats.

Visitors can hop aboard the Washington Park and Zoo Railway for a ride through the forested hillsides surrounding the zoo. In summer, visitors can enjoy the four-mile loop and get off at the International Rose Test Garden and take a stroll, enjoy city views, and catch a later train back to the zoo.

The zoo is and is dedicated to its mission of inspiring the community to create a better future for wildlife. Committed to conservation, the zoo is currently working to save endangered California condors, Oregon silverspot and Taylor's checkerspot butterflies, western pond turtles and Oregon spotted frogs. Other projects focused on saving animals from extinction include studies on Asian elephants, polar bears, orangutans and cheetahs.

University of Oregon Museum of Natural and Cultural History

Jon Erlandson, Executive Director
Address: 1680 E 15th Ave., Eugene 97403-1224
Phone: 541-346-3024
Fax: 541-346-5334
Web: https://mnch.uoregon.edu

Established by the 1935 Oregon Legislature, the Museum of Natural and Cultural History is the state's official repository for publicly owned anthropological and paleontological collections and is home to hundreds of thousands of cultural objects, fossils and biological specimens. It is an engine of scientific research and education, serving University of Oregon students and faculty, Native American tribes, the K-12 community, all Oregonians and visitors to the state.

The museum offers two signature exhibits: Explore Oregon is devoted to the state's natural history and geology, featuring the giant spike-toothed salmon and other paleontological wonders, and Oregon—Where Past is Present showcases 14,000 years of cultural history in the state, including 10,000-year-old sandals recovered from Oregon's Fort Rock Cave, as well as tools, coprolites, and other items from the Paisley Caves, Oregon's oldest cultural site.

In addition to these permanent offerings, visitors to the museum enjoy a diverse program of rotating exhibits emphasizing social justice and environmental stewardship.

Engaging hands-on displays await visitors of all ages throughout the museum with touchscreen displays, a curation station and a variety of other interactives. Children especially enjoy digging at a simulated archaeological site, sporting lab coats while interpreting their finds.

The museum is located on the University of Oregon campus near Hayward Field. Oregon Trail and other EBT cardholders receive admission discounts. Visit the museum's website for current hours and other admission information.

World Forestry Center

Joseph Furia, Executive Director
Address: 4033 SW Canyon Rd., Portland 97221
Phone: 503-228-1367
Fax: 503-228-4608
Web: https://www.worldforestry.org

Founded in 1966, World Forestry Center is dedicated to creating and inspiring champions of sustainable forestry. Based in Portland, Oregon, the organization is focused on shaping a society that values and takes action in support of the economic, ecological, and social benefits of forests. World Forestry Center's Discovery Museum was opened in 1971 to educate the general public about local and global forests and sustainable forestry. Through its professional programs, the nonprofit has hosted professionals from over 40 countries to learn about best forest practices in the northwest and to improve forest sustainability in other countries. A diverse roster of conferences and forums foster important discussions on natural resource issues for both the general public and professionals.

STUDENT ESSAY CONTEST WINNER
Harris Beach State Park

Ivy Elseth
Mrs. Thompson's Kindergarten Class
Lincoln Elementary School, Grants Pass

This drawing by Ivy Elseth shows a campsite at Harris Beach State Park.

Note: The text is displayed as written.

At Harris Beach State Park I like to walk by the water and roast mrshmelow by the fire and one time me and my sister and my uncle climd up a boulder. Me and my sister like to bick around the block. Sum time we go a difrit way. We like to invite my gramo and my grapo, my cusins to.

I like to invite to my capsite. We like to talk. My dad made hot dog and for breakfast, backin, eggs, pancakes. And for luch we sum time go out. Sum time we go to Zola's pizza and at Zola's we git to draw on the table and on every pizza box there is a difrit picsr. Wen we wit there was a Z on are pizza box. And sum times we breing chips – fredos. Are dog Kima always wit into the wotr. My sister, me and my dad wit into the water.

Economy

Historically, Oregon's economy was based on natural resources. Today, the economy is a mix of high-tech manufacturing and services in urban areas and the agricultural and forestry sectors in rural areas. Oregon's economy is now in a state of change and uncertainty as Oregonians respond to the spread of the COVID-19 virus.

OREGON'S ECONOMY

Source: Employment Department, Workforce and Economic Research Division

Oregon's economy entered the 2019–2021 biennium with job growth that was faster than the nation, and unemployment rates that were at historic lows. Oregon's job growth slowed in the autumn of 2019, however, and by the end of 2019 job growth was lagging behind the nation slightly. But Oregon's unemployment rate remained at record low levels and was down to 3.3 percent as 2020 began. In March 2020, Governor Kate Brown declared a state of emergency due to the novel coronavirus' threat to public health. Oregon's economic outlook changed dramatically in March 2020 as state and local governments implemented business restrictions to combat the spread of the COVID-19 virus. In April, Oregon's unemployment rate rose to 14.2 percent, and the state lost 253,400 nonfarm jobs. Both were record levels of loss.

The COVID-19 virus devastated Oregon's economy as over 90 percent of businesses across the state identified as having been negatively impacted by the pandemic during the peak of the crisis (U.S. Census Bureau, Small Business Pulse Survey). The most widely cited impact was a drop in revenue with nearly 70 percent of businesses seeing a decline in the demand for their goods or services during the first few months of pandemic restrictions. This loss in revenue led to a decrease in worker hours, business closures and mass layoffs. From the time of the first pandemic-related business closures through the end of 2020, more than 522,000 people (representing over 20% of the state's labor force) were paid unemployment benefits totaling $6.5 billion in Oregon.

The COVID-19 story and its impact on Oregon's economy is ongoing. As of early summer 2020 new cases of the virus continued to grow with many states across the nation reinstating restrictions to slow the spread of the virus. Although the full extent of the virus's impact here in Oregon is unknown, it is evident which sectors have been most impacted by these measures to slow the spread of the virus.

Counties with large accommodation and food service sectors and tourism destinations were the hardest hit by COVID-19 restrictions. The number of initial claims in Lincoln and Clatsop Counties on the Oregon Coast represented over 25 percent of the labor force. Deschutes County, a popular tourism and recreation destination, posted the highest share of unemployment insurance claims among Oregon's metropolitan counties, accounting for more than 20 percent of the Bend Metropolitan Statistical Area labor force.

Although COVID-related layoffs were spread across all industries, it became clear early on that the most vulnerable Oregonians were being impacted more significantly. Occupational groups with a median hourly rate of less than $20 an hour represented around 66 percent of total initial claims for unemployment insurance, but that group only accounted for 58 percent of statewide employment. Layoffs also disproportionally impacted younger workers in their 20s and 30s, as well as those with lower levels of educational attainment.

An economic recovery in Oregon is intricately tied to management and control of the public health crisis. Most forecasts and projections anticipate a strong recovery from our most recent recession once a reliable vaccine or treatment becomes available for COVID-19. However, a full recovery likely remains years down the road.

During the past three decades, Oregon made the transition from a resource-based economy to a more mixed manufacturing and marketing economy, with an emphasis on high technology. Oregon's hard times of the early 1980s signaled that structural changes had occurred in the traditional resource-based economy centered on timber. The state worked to develop new economic sectors to replace older ones. Most important, perhaps, was the state's growing high-tech sector, concentrated in the three counties around Portland. However, rural Oregon counties were generally left out of the shift to a new economy.

Oregon is one of the most trade dependent states in the nation, and to some extent, economic activity in other countries helps drive the state's economy. The value of exports from Oregon to foreign countries was $23.5 billion in 2019. The state's largest trading partners were China, Canada, Japan, Malaysia and South Korea. Of course, Oregon's trade with other U.S. states far exceeds its trade with foreign nations.

The aging population will factor into the future of Oregon's economy. Nationally, about half of the baby boom generation have already retired, and many of the remainder will in the next 10 years. Nearly one out of four workers in Oregon is already 55 years or older. As the generation ages, employers will need to find new workers with the skills to replace their retiring workforce. At the same time, the growing number of retirees will demand more leisure and health care services.

More people move to Oregon than move out of Oregon. This in-migration is a response to job opportunities and quality of life in the state, and it is a cause of job growth because the expanding population needs more goods and services. Oregon's population grew by 41,100 people in 2019 to a total of 4.2 million. Natural increase contributed just 5,600 to population growth, while net migration was responsible for 35,500 of the increase, a clear indication that Oregon's economic growth relies on people moving to the state.

Oregon's Top Ten Private Sector Industries by Employment in 2019:

1. Food services and drinking places (159,151)
2. Professional and technical services (99,626)
3. Administrative and support services (97,520)
4. Ambulatory health care services (94,284)
5. Specialty trade contractors (67,282)
6. Hospitals (59,591)
7. Social assistance (57,786)
8. Nursing & residential care facilities (52,313)
9. Management of companies and enterprises (50,467)
10. Food and beverage stores (43,304)

Employment

Oregon's labor force is 2.1 million strong. Three out of five of the state's working age residents were involved in the labor force in 2019. The total labor force includes unemployed people looking for a job, people who are self-employed, and employees working at the 161,000 business establishments and government entities across the state.

Total payroll employment reached a peak of 1,955,700 in February 2020, after the longest expansion in Oregon's history. Payroll employment fell by a few thousand jobs in March 2020, at the onset of the pandemic, and in April 2020 every major industry in Oregon lost jobs as the economy suffered the largest one-month contraction in history. The effect of COVID-19 control measures

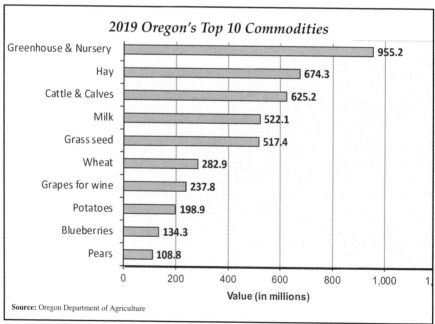

2019 Oregon's Top 10 Commodities

Commodity	Value (in millions)
Greenhouse & Nursery	955.2
Hay	674.3
Cattle & Calves	625.2
Milk	522.1
Grass seed	517.4
Wheat	282.9
Grapes for wine	237.8
Potatoes	198.9
Blueberries	134.3
Pears	108.8

Source: Oregon Department of Agriculture

on the economy of Oregon and the nation was more akin to a natural disaster than a business recession.

Leisure and hospitality suffered the brunt of the initial business closures. Payroll employment in the industry fell an astounding 54.6 percent in April. The industry had been growing steadily since 2010, adding roughly 46,000 jobs over the last 10 years. A drop of 6,000 industry jobs in March 2020 was followed by a collapse in April with the loss of 108,400 jobs. The reopenings of some restaurants and lodging that began in May offered an opportunity for some job gains in leisure and hospitality, but the industry is currently beset with uncertainty about its future.

Private education and health care is a large sector that historically added jobs consistently during recessions and expansions. Yet this sector shed the second-largest number of jobs in April 2020 when COVID-19 measures directly prohibited elective and non-urgent medical procedures and closed schools. Private-sector employers cut 30,300 jobs in April. Population growth, the aging of the population and increased access to health care means there is a growing need for workers in this sector, and it is expected to add more jobs over the next 10 years than any other sector. Private education and health care employment totaled 273,100 as of April 2020.

Oregon's manufacturing sector shrank about 20 percent during the Great Recession of 2008. The industry added back nearly 34,000 jobs since 2010 and seemed poised to return to its pre-recession level. Recent manufacturing job growth has been led by semiconductor and electronic component manufacturing, machinery manufacturing and food manufacturing. The industry shed about 11,000 jobs in April as businesses struggled to adapt their processes to COVID-19 requirements for social distancing and personal protective equipment for workers.

Oregon's high-tech sector is a crucial and dynamic piece of Oregon's economy that spans a number of industries. Taken together, Oregon's high-tech sector accounted for more than 94,000 jobs in 2019. This includes tech manufacturers such as computer and electronic product manufacturing, but it also includes computer system design; architectural, engineering, and related services; software publishers, and other high-tech industries.

The forestry sector is another crucial piece of Oregon's economy that supports employment in many private-sector industries and in government agencies. The combined categories of forest sector employment totaled 61,051 jobs in 2017. Employment in the sector has been stable in the previous two years. Forestry jobs have an outsized impact on the economies of rural counties and pay higher wages. The sector accounts for more than 7 percent

of jobs in some rural counties, but just 2 percent or fewer of jobs in urban counties.

While no industry sector was immune from the impacts of the restrictions and the drop in demand from the COVID-19 pandemic, the forest sector lost a lower percentage of jobs than the overall economy. Preliminary estimates show that in April 2020, Oregon lost roughly 13 percent of its jobs due to the pandemic while combined logging and wood product manufacturing lost about 5 percent.

Agricultural employment averaged 64,400 jobs in 2019. Agricultural employment is seasonal, so the number of jobs ranged from a low of 54,900 jobs in January and reached a high of 82,800 in July.

Oregon farms operated about 16 million acres of farm land in 2017 according to the 2017 Census of Agriculture. The market value of products sold reached $5 billion in 2017, ranking 28th in the U.S. Crops represented 66 percent of Oregon's sales or about $3.3 billion, while livestock, poultry and other animal products brought in 34 percent or $1.7 billion.

Wages

Oregon began a new three-tier minimum wage rate on July 1, 2020. The tiers vary by geography, with the highest rate of $13.25 per hour within the Portland urban growth boundary, a standard rate of $12.00 per hour in other areas of the state, and a rate of $11.50 per hour in designated nonurban counties. Oregon's minimum wage will increase by $0.50 or $0.75 each year through 2022, depending on the area. Starting in 2023, Oregon's minimum wage will be adjusted annually according to the increase in the U.S. Consumer Price Index.

Although Oregon's minimum wage is higher than most other states, private-sector workers in Oregon tend to work fewer hours per week and their average wage earnings are below the national level. Workers in Oregon earned an average of $1,058 weekly in 2019, which is below the national average of $1,139 per week.

Oregon workers earned an annual average of $55,027 in 2019, which varies widely by industry. The average annual pay in the information industry was $89,699, the most of any broad sector, followed by federal government ($76,990), professional and business services ($73,469), financial activities ($73,314) and manufacturing ($71,434). The lowest earnings were at jobs in leisure and hospitality, where pay averaged $23,798 per year.

Of course, the average wage for an industry does not reveal how many low- or high-wage jobs are in an industry. One-third of Oregon's jobs paid an average wage of less than $15 per hour in 2019 and another 22 percent were between $15 and $20 per hour. The remaining jobs paid at least $20 per hour.

Income

Per capita personal income, a broader measure of the income all Oregonians receive from all sources, was $52,937 per person in 2019. In addition to wages, personal income includes proprietors' income; income from dividends, interest, and rent; and transfer receipts.

The national per capita personal income reached $56,663 in 2019. Oregon's per capita personal income was just 93 percent of the nation's and ranked 26th among the states and Washington, D.C. Oregon's real per capita personal income, adjusted for inflation, grew 8.9 percent since 2015. That was the seventh fastest income growth among the states and faster than the national adjusted income growth rate of 7.6 percent.

Despite lower average incomes than the nation as a whole, Oregon's poverty rate is about the same as the nation. According to the U.S. Census Bureau, 12.6 percent of Oregon residents lived in families with incomes below the poverty threshold during 2018. The U.S. poverty rate was 13.1 percent. Oregon ranked 25th among the states with the lowest percentage of people living in poverty.

Revenue and Taxes

Oregon's state and local governments receive revenue from numerous sources including federal transfer payments; tuition, hospital and other charges; Lottery revenue; and taxes. Of all these sources, half of total state revenue is from taxation. Personal income tax and corporate excise tax are the most significant components of the state General Fund, and property tax is the most significant local tax in Oregon. These three taxes represent about 80 percent of all state and local taxes. Oregon does not have a general state sales tax. Beginning in 2020, the new corporate activity tax will provide additional funding for K-12 education.

The personal income tax is the largest source of state tax revenue, expected to account for 86 percent of the state's General Fund for the 2019–21 biennium. Oregon's taxable income is closely connected to federal taxable income. The state personal income tax rates range from 4.75 percent to 9.9 percent of taxable income. For tax year 2018, Oregon residents filed about 1.92 million Oregon personal income tax returns, representing about 2.6 million taxpayers, which includes spouses. Those taxpayers paid a final tax after adjustments, deductions and credits on average equal to about 6 percent of their total income. The top ten percent of taxpayers in income paid roughly half of Oregon's personal income tax, while the bottom half of taxpayers in income paid 9 percent of the total income tax.

The corporate excise and income tax is the second largest source of state tax revenue. The corporate tax rates are 6.6 percent and 7.6 percent of taxable business income. For tax year 2017, about 1 percent of corporate taxpayers accounted for almost 65 percent of income and excise tax revenue from C corporations (standard corporations). The minimum corporate excise tax ranges from $150 to $100,000, depending on the corporation's Oregon sales. More than 69 percent of all C corporations paid the minimum tax for tax year 2017, but minimum taxpayers accounted for less than 10 percent of the total tax paid by C corporations in 2017.

Local governments in Oregon began taxing property before statehood, but the current system is mainly the product of two statewide ballot measures passed in the 1990s, Measures 5 and 50. In Oregon's property tax system, each taxing district is limited to a fixed permanent tax rate, but voters can temporarily increase rates through local options levies or to repay bonds used to fund capital projects. Individual properties have a taxable assessed value equal to, or less than, the real market value. The taxable assessed value generally cannot increase by more than 3 percent per year, and it cannot exceed the real market value. Taxes for an individual property are calculated by applying the tax rates of the local districts to the taxable assessed value of each property and are generally limited to no more than $5 per $1,000 of real market value for education districts and $10 per $1,000 of real market value for all other taxing districts. Levies to repay bonds are outside of this limit.

Additional Information

Department of Agriculture
www.oregon.gov/ODA/Pages/default.aspx

Bureau of Labor and Industries – Minimum Wage
www.oregon.gov/boli/WHD/OMW/Pages/Minim um-Wage-Rate-Summary.aspx

Employment Department – Labor Market Information
www.QualityInfo.org

Department of Revenue
https://www.oregon.gov/DOR/Pages/index.aspx

U.S. Department of Labor, Bureau of Labor Statistics
www.bls.gov/home.htm

Media Directories

Oregon's long tradition of open government and citizen involvement depends in part on its citizens receiving accurate and timely information. The media play an important role in providing this information to Oregonians. This section lists Oregon's media resources.

NEWSPAPERS PUBLISHED IN OREGON

The following newspapers are published at least once a week. See "Selected Periodicals" following this section for other magazines and journals.

Key: (P) = Publisher, (E) = Editor, (GM) = General Manager

Albany
Albany Democrat-Herald
Mon–Sun a.m.; Shanna Cannon (P); Bennet Hall (E); Estab. 1865
PO Box 130, Albany 97321; 541-926-2211;
Web: https://democratherald.com/

Ashland
Ashland Daily Tidings
Mon–Sat a.m.; Steven Saslow (P); Justin Umberson (E); Estab. 1876
PO Box 1108, Medford 97501; 541-776-4411;
Web: https://ashlandtidings.com/

Astoria
The Daily Astorian
Mon–Fri a.m.; Kari Borgen (P) Derrick DePledge (E); Estab. 1873
PO Box 210, Astoria 97103; 503-325-3211; 800-781-3211; Fax: 503-325-6573
Web: https://www.dailyastorian.com/

Baker City
Baker City Herald
Mon, Wed, Fri p.m.; Karrine Brogiotto (P); Estab. 1870
PO Box 807, Baker City 97814; 541-523-3673; Fax: 541-833-6414
Web: https://www.bakercityherald.com/

Bandon
Bandon Western World
Wed; Ben Kenfield (P); Estab. 1912
PO Box 248, Bandon 97411; 541-266-6047
Web: https://theworldlink.com/

Beaverton
Beaverton Valley Times
Thur; Christine Moore (P); Mark Miller (E); Estab. 1921
6605 SE Lake Rd, Portland 97222; 971-204-7735
Web: https://pamplinmedia.com/beaverton-valley-times-home

Bend
The Bulletin
Mon–Sun a.m.; Heidi Wright (P); Gerard O'Brien (E); Estab. 1903
PO Box 6020, Bend 97708-6020; 541-382-1811; Fax: 541-385-5804
Web: https://www.bendbulletin.com/

Brookings
Curry Coastal Pilot
Wed, Sat; Ben Kenfield (P); Brian Williams (E); Estab. 1946
PO Box 700, Brookings 97415; 541-813-1717; Fax: 541-813-1931
Web: https://www.currypilot.com/

Brownsville
The Times
Wed; Vance and Holly Parrish (P); Vance Parrish (E); Estab. 1888
PO Box 278, Brownsville 97327; 541-466-5311
Web: https://thebrownsvilletimes.com/

Burns
Burns Times-Herald
Wed; Randy Parks (E); Estab. 1887
355 N. Broadway Ave., Burns 97720; 541-573-2022; Fax: 541-573-3915
Web: http://btimesherald.com/

Canby
Canby Herald
Wed; John Baker (E); Sandy Storey (GM); Estab. 1906
911 SW Fourth, Canby 97013; 503-266-6831; Fax: 503-266-6836
Web: https://pamplinmedia.com/canby-herald-news/

Cave Junction

Illinois Valley News
Wed; Dan Mancuso (P); Laura Mancuso (E); Estab. 1937
PO Box 1370, Cave Junction 97523; 541-592-2541
Web: http://www.illinois-valley-news.com/

Clatskanie

The Chief
Wed; Jeremy Ruark (P) & (E); Estab. 1891
1805 Columbia Blvd, St Helens 97051; Phone: 503-397-0116; Fax: 503-397-4093
Web: https://www.thechiefnews.com/

The Hotel Condon in downtown Condon. (Oregon State Archives scenic photo)

Condon

The Times-Journal
Thur; Stephen and Renee Allen (P) & (E); Estab. 1886
PO Box 746, Condon 97823; 541-384-2421; Web: https://timesjournal1886.com/

Coos Bay

The World
Mon–Thur, Sat; Ben Kenfield (P); Amy Moss Strong (E); Estab. 1878
350 Commercial St., Coos Bay 97420; 541-269-1222
Web: https://theworldlink.com

Coquille

The Sentinel
Wed; Matt Hall (P) & (E); Estab. 1882
61 E. First St., Coquille 97423; 541-396-3191; Fax: 541-396-3624

Corvallis

Corvallis Gazette-Times
Mon–Sun a.m.; Shanna Cannon (P); Bennett Hall (E); Estab. 1862
PO Box 130, Albany 97321; 541-926-2211; Web: https://www.gazettetimes.com

Cottage Grove

Cottage Grove Sentinel
Wed; Jenna Bartlett (P); Ned Hickson (E); Gary Manly (GM); Estab. 1889
116 N. Sixth St., Cottage Grove 97424; 541-942-3325; Fax: 541-942-3328
Web: https://www.cgsentinel.com

Creswell

The Creswell Chronicle
Thur; Noel Mash (P); Erin Tierney (E); Estab. 1909
PO Box 428, Creswell 97426; 541-895-2197; Web: https://www.chronicle1909.com

Dallas

Polk County Itemizer-Observer
Wed; Scott Olson (P); Jolene Guzman (E); Estab. 1875
PO Box 108, Dallas 97338; 503-623-2373; Fax: 503-623-2395
Web: https://www.polkio.com

Drain

The Drain Enterprise
Thur; Sue Anderson (P) & (E); Estab. 1951
PO Box 26, Drain 97435; 541-836-2241; Fax: 541-836-2243

Enterprise

Wallowa County Chieftain
Wed; Chris Rush (P); Ellen Morris Bishop (E); Jennifer Cooney (GM); Estab. 1884
209 NW First St., Enterprise 97828; 541-426-4567; Fax: 541-426-3921
Web: https://www.wallowa.com

Estacada

Estacada News
Thur; Steve Brown (P) & (E); Estab. 1904
307 SW Hwy 224, Estacada 97023; 503-630-3241
Web: https://pamplinmedia.com/estacada-news-home/

Eugene

Eugene Weekly
Thur; Camilla Mortensen (E); Estab. 1982
1251 Lincoln St., Eugene 97401; 541-484-0519; Fax: 541-484-4044
Web: https://www.eugeneweekly.com

The Register-Guard
Mon–Sun a.m.; Shanna Cannon (P); Michelle Maxwell (E); Estab. 1862
3500 Chad Dr., Suite 600, Eugene 97408; 541-485-1234
Web: https://www.registerguard.com

Florence

Siuslaw News

Wed, Sat; Jenna Bartlett (P); Ned Hickson (E); Estab. 1890

148 Maple St., Florence 97439; 541-997-3441; Web: https://www.thesiuslawnews.com

Forest Grove

News-Times

Wed; Nikki DeBuse (P); Mark Miller (E); Estab. 1886

2004 Main St., Suite 309; Forest Grove 97116; 503-357-3181

Web: https://pamplinmedia.com/forest-grove-news-times-news/

Gold Beach

Curry County Reporter

Wed; Matt Hall (P) & (E); Estab. 1914

PO Box 766, Gold Beach 97444; 541-332-6397

Web: https://www.currycountyreporter.com

Grants Pass

Grants Pass Daily Courier

Tue–Fri, Sun; Travis Moore (P); Scott Stoddard (E); Estab. 1885

409 SE Seventh St, Grants Pass 97526; 541-474-3700; Fax: 541-247-6644

Web: http://www.thedailycourier.com

Gresham

Outlook

Tue, Fri; J. Mark Garber (Pres.); Steve Brown (E); Don Atwell (GM); Estab. 1911

PO Box 747, Gresham 97030; 503-665-2181; Fax: 503-665-2187

Web: https://pamplinmedia.com/gresham-outlook-home/

Halfway

Hells Canyon Journal

Wed; Steve Backstrom (P) & (E); Estab. 1984

PO Box 646, Halfway 97834; 541-742-7900; Fax: 541-742-7900

Heppner

Heppner Gazette-Times

Wed; David Sykes (P); Bobbi Gordon (E); Estab. 1883

PO Box 337, Heppner 97836; 541-676-9228; Fax: 541-676-9211

Web: http://heppner.net/heppner-gazette-times

Hermiston

Hermiston Herald

Wed; Christopher Rush (P); Jade McDowell (E); Estab. 1906

333 E. Main St., Hermiston 97838; 541-567-6457

Web: https://www.hermistonherald.com

Hood River

Columbia Gorge News

Wed & Sat; Chelsea Marr (P); Kirby Neumann-Rea (E); Estab. 1905

PO Box 390, Hood River 97031; 541-386-1234

Web: https://www.columbiagorgenews.com

John Day

Blue Mountain Eagle

Wed; Chris Rush (P); Sean Hart (E); Estab. 1898

195 N. Canyon Blvd., John Day 97845; 541-575-0710; Fax: 541-575-1244

Web: https://www.bluemountaineagle.com

Keizer

Keizertimes

Fri; Lyndon Zaitz (P); Eric Howald (E); Estab. 1979

142 Chemawa Rd. N, Keizer 97303; 503-390-1051; Fax: 503-390-8023

Web: https://www.keizertimes.com

Klamath Falls

Herald and News

Tue, Wed, Fri & Sun a.m.; Mark Dobie (P); Kurt Liedtke (E); Joe Hudon (GM); Estab. 1906

PO Box 788, Klamath Falls 97601; 800-275-0982

Web: https://www.heraldandnews.com

La Grande

The Observer

Mon, Wed, Fri; Karrine Brogoitti (P); Phil Wright (E); Estab. 1896

1406 Fifth St., La Grande 97850; 541-963-3161; Fax: 541-963-7804

Web: https://www.lagrandeobserver.com

Lake Oswego

Lake Oswego Review

Thur; J. Brian Monihan (P); Gary Stein (E); Estab. 1920

PO Box 548, Lake Oswego 97034; 503-635-8811; Fax: 503-635-8817

Web: https://pamplinmedia.com/lake-oswego-review-home/

Lakeview

Lake County Examiner

Wed; Tillie Flynn (GM); Estab. 1880

739 N. Second St., Lakeview 97630; 541-947-3378; Fax: 541-947-4359

Web: http://www.lakecountyexam.com

Lebanon

Lebanon Express

Wed; Jeff Precourt (P); Les Gehrett (E); Estab. 1887

90 E. Grant St., Lebanon 97355; 541-258-3151; Web: https://www.lebanon-express.com

Lincoln City

The News Guard
Wed; Frank Perea (P); Max Kirkendall (E); Estab. 1927
PO Box 848, Lincoln City 97367; 541-994-2178
Web: https://www.thenewsguard.com

Madras

The Madras Pioneer
Wed; Tony Ahern (P); Teresa Jackson (E); Estab. 1904
345 SE Fifth St., Madras 97741; 541-475-2275; Fax: 541-475-3710
Web: https://pamplinmedia.com/madras-pioneer-home/

McKenzie Bridge

McKenzie River Reflections
Thur; Ken Engelman (P); Louise Engelman (E); Estab. 1978
59059 Old McKenzie Hwy., McKenzie Bridge 97413; 541-822-3358; Fax: 541-663-4550
Web: https://www.mckenzieriverreflectionsnewspaper.com

McMinnville

News-Register
Tue, Fri; Jeb Bladine (P); Ossie Bladine (E); Estab. 1866
PO Box 727, McMinnville 97128; 503-472-5114; 800-472-1198; Fax: 503-472-9151
Web: https://newsregister.com

Medford

Mail Tribune
Mon–Sun a.m.; Gail Whiting (P); Justin Umberson (E); Estab. 1907
111 N. Fir St., Medford 97501; 541-776-4411; Web: https://mailtribune.com

Milton-Freewater

Valley Herald
Fri; Sherrie Widmer (P) & (E); Estab. 2001
PO Box 664, Milton-Freewater 97862; 541-938-6688
Web: http://www.mfvalleyherald.net/home.html

Molalla

Molalla Pioneer
Wed; Sandy Storey (GM); Joe Baker (E); Estab. 1913
911 SW Fourth Ave., Canby 97013; 503-829-2301
Web: https://pamplinmedia.com/molalla-pioneer-home/

Myrtle Creek

The Douglas County Mail
Thur; Robert L. Chaney, Sr. (P) & (E); Estab. 1902
PO Box 729, Myrtle Creek 97457; 541-863-5233; Fax: 541-863-5234

Newberg

The Newberg Graphic
Wed; Allen Herriges (P); Gary Allen (E); Estab. 1888
1505 Portland Rd., Suite 210, Newberg 97132; 503-538-2181; Fax: 503-538-1632
Web: https://pamplinmedia.com/newberg-graphic-home/

Newport

News-Times
Wed, Fri; Jeremy Burke (P); Steve Card (E); Estab. 1882
831 NE Avery St., Newport 97365; 541-265-8571; Fax: 541-265-3862
Web: https://newportnewstimes.com

Oakridge

Dead Mountain Echo
Thur; Viki Burns (P) & (E); Estab. 1973
PO Box 406, Oakridge 97463; 541-782-4241

Ontario

The Argus Observer
Tue–Fri p.m., Sun a.m.; Stephanie Spiess (P); Leslie Thompson (E); Estab. 1897
1160 SW Fourth St., Ontario 97914; 541-889-5387; Fax: 541-889-3347
Web: https://www.argusobserver.com

Pendleton

East Oregonian
Tue–Sat; Christopher Rush (P); Andrew Cutler (E); Estab. 1875
211 SE Byers Ave., Pendleton 97801; 541-276-2211; 800-522-0255
Web: https://www.eastoregonian.com

Port Orford

Port Orford News
Wed; Matt Hall (P) & (E); Estab. 1958
PO Box 5, Port Orford 97465; 541-332-6397
Web: https://www.portorfordnews.net

Portland

Daily Journal of Commerce
Mon, Wed, Fri; Nick Bjork (P) Joe Yovino (E); Estab. 1872
11 NE Martin Luther King Jr. Blvd. Ste 201, Portland 97232; 503-226-1311
Web: https://djcoregon.com

Portland Tribune
Tue, Thur; Mark Garber, President (P); John Schrag (E); Estab. 2001
6605 SE Lake Rd., Portland 97222-2161; 503-226-6397; Fax: 503-226-7042
Web: https://pamplinmedia.com

The Asian Reporter
Bi-monthly (1st and 3rd Mon); Jaime Lim (P); Ronalt Catalani & Jeff Wenger (E); Estab. 1991
922 N. Killingsworth St., Portland 97217; 503-283-4440; Fax: 503-283-4445
Web: http://www.asianreporter.com

The Oregonian
Mon–Sun digital (Wed, Fri, Sat, Sun print a.m.); John Maher (Pres.); Therese Bottomly (VP Content); Estab. 1850
1500 SW First Ave., Portland 97201; 503-221-8327
Web: http://www.oregonlive.com

The Skanner
Bernie Foster (P); Bobbie Foster (E); Estab. 1975
415 N. Killingsworth St., Portland 97217; 503-285-5555; Fax: 503-285-2900
Web: https://www.theskanner.com

Willamette Week
Wed; Mark Zusman (P) & (E); Estab. 1974
2220 NW Quimby St., Portland 97210; 503-243-2122
Web: https://www.wweek.com

A statue by Greg Congleton in Prineville. (Oregon State Archives scenic photo)

Prineville
Central Oregonian
Tue, Fri; Tony Ahern (P); Jason Cheney (E); Teresa Tooley (GM); Estab. 1881
558 N. Main St., Prineville 97754; 541-447-6205; Fax: 541-447-1754
Web: https://pamplinmedia.com/central-oregon-ian-home/

Redmond
The Redmond Spokesman
Heidi Wright (P); Gerry O'Brien (E); Estab. 1910
PO Box 6020, Bend 97708; 541-548-2184; Fax: 541-548-3203
Web: https://www.redmondspokesman.com

Rogue River
Rogue River Press
Wed; Teresa Pearson (P) & (E); Estab. 1915
PO Box 1485, Rogue River 97537; 541-582-1707
Web: http://www.rogueriverpress.com

Roseburg
The News-Review
Tue–Sun a.m.; Rachelle Carter (P); Ian Campbell (E); Estab. 1867
345 NE Winchester St., Roseburg 97470; 541-672-3321
Web: https://www.nrtoday.com

Saint Helens
The Chronicle
Wed; Jeremy Ruark (P) & (E); Estab. 1881
PO Box 1153, Saint Helens 97051; 503-397-0116; Fax: 503-397-4093
Web: https://www.thechronicleonline.com

Salem
Capital Press
Fri; Joe Beach (P) & (E); Estab. 1928
PO Box 2048, Salem 97308; 503-364-4431; 800-882-6789
Web: https://www.capitalpress.com

Statesman Journal
Mon–Sun a.m.; Cherrill Crosby (E); Estab. 1851
340 Vista Ave SE, Suite 200, Salem 97302; 503-399-6773; 800-452-2511
Web: https://www.statesmanjournal.com

Sandy
Sandy Post
Wed; J. Mark Garber (Pres.); Steve Brown (P) & (E); Estab. 1937
PO Box 68, Sandy 97055; 503-665-2181; Fax: 503-665-2187
Web: https://pamplinmedia.com/sandy-post-home/

Scappoose
Columbia County Spotlight
Fri a.m.; Nikki DeBuse (P); Mark Miller (E); Estab. 1961
52490 SE Second St., Suite 140, Scappoose 97056; 503-543-6387; Fax: 503-543-6380
Web: https://pamplinmedia.com/south-county-spotlight-home/

Seaside
Seaside Signal
Every other Fri; Kari Borgen (P); Richard Marx (E); Estab. 1905
1555 N. Roosevelt Dr., Seaside 97138; 503-738-5561
Web: https://www.seasidesignal.com

Silverton

Appeal Tribune
Wed; Cherrill Crosby (E); Estab. 1880
340 Vista Ave., SE, Salem 97302; 503-399-6773
Web: https://www.statesmanjournal.com/news/silverton/

Stayton

The Stayton Mail
Wed; Cherrill Crosby (E); Estab. 1894
340 Vista Ave., SE, Salem 97302; 503-399-6773
Web: https://www.statesmanjournal.com/news/stayton/

Sweet Home

The New Era
Wed; Scott Swanson (P) & (E); Estab. 1929
PO Box 39, Sweet Home 97386; 541-367-2135
Web: https://www.sweethomenews.com

The Dalles

Columbia Gorge News
Wed & Sat; Chelsea Marr (P) Mark Gibson (E); Estab. 1890
PO Box 1910, The Dalles 97058; 541-296-2141
Web: https://www.columbiagorgenews.com

The Wasco County Courthouse in The Dalles. (Oregon State Archives scenic photo)

Tigard/Tualatin/Sherwood

The Times
Thur; Christine Moore (P); Mark Miller (E); Estab. 1956
PO Box 22109, Portland 97269; 971-204-7735
Web: https://pamplinmedia.com/the-times-home

Tillamook

Headlight Herald
Wed; Joe Warren (P) & (E); Estab. 1888
1906 Second St., Tillamook 97141; 503-842-7535; Fax: 503-842-8842
Web: www.tillamookheadlightherald.com

Vale

Malheur Enterprise
Wed; Les Zaitz (P) & (E); Howard Benson (GM); Estab. 1909
PO Box 310, Vale 97918; 541-473-3377
Web: https://www.malheurenterprise.com

Warrenton

The Columbia Press
Fri; Cindy Yingst (P) & (E); Estab. 1922
5 N. Hwy. 101, Suite 500, Warrenton 97146; 503-861-3331; Fax: 503-861-7039
Web: https://www.thecolumbiapress.com

West Linn

West Linn Tidings
Thur; J. Brian Monihan (P); Patrick Malee (E); Estab. 1981
PO Box 548, Lake Oswego 97034; 503-635-8811
Web: https://pamplinmedia.com/west-linn-tidings-home/

Wilsonville

Wilsonville Spokesman
Wed; J. Brian Monihan (P); Patrick Malee (E); Estab. 1985
PO Box 548, Lake Oswego 97034; 503-635-8811; Fax: 503-635-8817
Web: https://pamplinmedia.com/wilsonville-spokesman-home/

Woodburn

Woodburn Independent
Wed; Allen Herriges (P); Phil Hawkins (E); Estab. 1888
1585 N Pacific Hwy., Suite H, Woodburn 97071; 503-981-3441
Web: https://pamplinmedia.com/woodburn-independent-home/

Oregon Newspaper Publishers Association

Executive Director: Laurie Hieb
Address: 400 Second St., Suite 100, Lake Oswego 97034
Phone: 503-624-6397
Fax: 503-639-9009
Email: http://www.orenews.com

Selected Periodicals Published in Oregon

The State Library has compiled a representative sample of the many periodicals published in Oregon. The first year of each periodical's publication follows its title and publication schedule.

Key: A = Annual; BM = Bi-monthly; BW = Bi-weekly; M = Monthly; Q = Quarterly; SA = Semi-annual; SM = Semi-monthly; W = Weekly

1859: Oregon's magazine (BM) 2009: Statehood Media, 70 SW Century Dr., Suite 100-218, Bend 97702; 541-728-2764;

Web: https://1859oregonmagazine.com

Agri-Times Northwest (SM) 1984: Sterling Ag, LLC, PO Box 1626, Pendleton 97801-0189; 541-276-6202; Fax: 541-278-4778;

Web: www.agritimesnw.com

Animal Law Review (SA) 1995: Lewis & Clark Law School, 10015 SW Terwilliger Blvd., Portland 97219; 503-768-6798;

Web: https://law.lclark.edu/law_reviews/animal_law_review

Backwoods Home Magazine (BM) 1989: PO Box 712, Gold Beach 97444; 541-250-5134;

Web: www.backwoodshome.com

basalt (A)(2005): One University Boulevard, College of Arts & Science—Loso Hall, Eastern Oregon University, La Grande, Oregon 97850; 541-962-3633;

Web: https://www.eou.edu/basalt/

Book Dealers World (Q) 1980: National Association of Book Entrepreneurs, PO Box 606, Cottage Grove 97424; Phone/Fax: 541-942-7455;

Web: www.bookmarketingprofits.com

Calyx (SA) 1976: PO Box B, Corvallis 97339; 541-753-9384;

Web: https://www.calyxpress.org

Digger (M) 1988: Oregon Association of Nurseries, 29751 SW Town Center Loop W. Wilsonville 97070; 503-682-5089; 888-283-7219; Fax: 503-682-5099;

Web: www.diggermagazine.com

Environmental Law (Q) 1970: Lewis & Clark Law School, 10015 SW Terwilliger Blvd., Portland 97219; 503-768-6700; Fax: 503-768-6783;

Web: https://law.lclark.edu/law_reviews/environmental_law/

Eugene Magazine (Q) 2006: Olive Tree, LLC, 1255 Railroad Blvd., Eugene 97401; 541-686-6608;

Web: https://eugenemagazine.com

Flyfishing and Tying Journal (Q) 1978: Frank Amato Publications, PO Box 82112, Portland 97282; 503-653-8108; 800-541-9498;

Web: https://amatobooks.com

Journal of Environmental Law and Litigation (SA) 1985: 138 Knight Law Center, 1221 University of Oregon, Eugene 97403; 541-346-1559;

Web: https://law.uoregon.edu/explore/JELL

El Latino de Hoy: Semanario Latinoamericano de Oregon (W) 1991: 2318 SW 18th Ave., Portland 97201; 503-493-1106; Fax: 503-753-1183;

Web: www.ellatinodehoy.com.

Metroscape (SA) 1995: Institute of Portland Metropolitan Studies, Portland State University, PO Box 751, Portland 97207-0751; 503-725-5170; Fax: 503-725-5199;

Web: https://metroscape.imspdx.org

Midwifery Today (Q) 1987: PO Box 2672, Eugene 97402; 541-344-7438;

Web: https://midwiferytoday.com/magazine/

Northwest Labor Press (SM) 1987: PO Box 13150, Portland 97213; 503-288-3311;

Web: http://nwlaborpress.org

Noticias Latinas! Latin News! (Q) 1995: Latin Media Northwest, 16239 SE McLoughlin Blvd., Suite 209, Milwaukie 97267; 503-827-5507; Fax: 503-227-7790;

Web: www.latinmedianw.com

OLA Quarterly (Q) 1995: Oregon Library Association, PO Box 3067, La Grande 97850; 541-962-5824;

Web: http://journals3.library.oregonstate.edu/olaq

Oregon Business Magazine (M) 1981: MIF Publications, Inc., 715 SW Morrison St., Suite 800, Portland 97205; 503-445-8811;

Web: https://www.oregonbusiness.com

Oregon Coast (BM) 1982: Northwest Regional Magazines, 88906 Highway 101, Suite #2, PO Box 119, Florence 97439; 541-997-8401; 800-348-8401;

Web: https://oregoncoastmagazine.com

Oregon Grange Bulletin (BM) 1990: Oregon State Grange, 643 Union St. NE, Salem 97301; 503-316-0106; Fax: 503-316-0109;

Web: http://orgrange.org/osg-bulletin/

Oregon Historical Quarterly (Q) 1900: Oregon Historical Society, 1200 SW Park Ave., Portland 97205; 503-222-1741;

Web: https://www.ohs.org/research-and-library/oregon-historical-quarterly/

Media Directories

Oregon Home (Q) 1997: MediAmerica, 715 SW Morrison, Suite 800, Portland 97205; 888-881-5861;

Web: https://www.oregonhomemagazine.com

Oregon Humanities (Q) 1983: Oregon Humanities, 921 SW Washington St., Suite 150, Portland 97205; 503-241-0543; 800-735-0543; Fax: 503-241-0024;

Web: https://www.oregonhumanities.org/rll/magazine/

Oregon Hunter (BM) 1983: Oregon Hunters Association, PO Box 1706, Medford 97501; 541-772-7313; Fax: 541-772-0964;

Web: https://oregonhunters.org/publications

Oregon Law Review (Q) 1921: University of Oregon, 1515 Agate St., 1221 University of Oregon, Eugene 97403; 541-346-3844; Fax 541-346-1596;

Web: https://law.uoregon.edu/explore/OLR

Oregon Small Farm News (Q) 2007: Oregon State University, Small Farms Program, Corvallis, 97331;

Web: https://smallfarms.oregonstate.edu/small-farms/oregon-small-farm-news

Oregon Wheat (BM) 1962: Oregon Wheat Growers League, 115 SE 8th St., Pendleton 97801-2319; 541-276-7330; Fax 541-276-1723;

Web: https://www.owgl.org

Oregon's Agricultural Progress (SA) 1953: Oregon State University, Agricultural Experiment Station, 422 Kerr Admin. Bldg., Corvallis 97331-2119; 541-737-3311;

Web: https://oap.oregonstate.edu

Peaceworker (M) 2003: 1850 Saginaw St. S, Salem 97302; 503-428-4280;

Web: http://peaceworker.org

Portland Monthly (M) 2003: SagaCity Media, 921 SW Washington St., Suite 750, Portland 97205; 503-222-5144; Fax: 503-227-8777;

Web: https://www.pdxmonthly.com

Random Lengths (W) 1944: PO Box 867, Eugene 97440-0867; 541-686-9925/888-686-9925; Fax; 800-874-7979; 541-686-9629;

Web: www.randomlengths.com

Resource Recycling (M) 1982: Resource Recycling, PO Box 42270, Portland 97242-0270; 503-233-1305; Fax: 503-233-1356;

Web: https://resource-recycling.com

Rubberstampmadness (Q) 1980: RSM Enterprises, Inc., PO Box 610, Corvallis 97339-0610; 541-752-0075; 877-782-6762;

Web: www.rsmadness.com

Ruralite (M) 1953: Ruralite Services, Inc., 5605 NE Elam Young Pkwy., Hillsboro 97124; 503-357-2105;

Web: www.ruralite.org

The Scribe: (M) Medical Society of Metropolitan Portland. 1983: PO Box 19388, Portland 97280; 503-222-9977; Fax: 503-222-3164;

Web: https://msmp.org/The-Scribe

Skipping Stones (Q) 1988: PO Box 3939, Eugene 97403-0939; 541-342-4956;

Web: http://www.skippingstones.org/wp/

Small Farmers Journal (Q) 1976: PO Box 1627, Sisters 97759-1627; 541-549-2064; 800-876-2893;

Web: https://smallfarmersjournal.com

Spot Magazine (BM) 2005: PO Box 16667, Portland 97292; 503-261-1162;

Web: https://www.spotmagazine.net

Take Root (Q) 2011: Duhn & Associates, PO Box 636, Junction City 97448-0636; 541-952-0300;

Web: http://www.takerootmagazine.com/index.html

The Timberline Review (A) 2015: Willamette Writers, 5331 SW Macadam Ave., Suite 258, PMB 215, Portland 97239; Web: http://timberlinereview.com/

True Parent (M) 2014: Index Newspapers, 115 SW Ash, Suite 600, Portland 97204; 503-294-0840; Fax: 503 294-0844; Web: https://www.portlandmercury.com/true-parent-10

We'Moon (A) 1981: Mother Tongue Ink, PO Box 187, Wolf Creek 97497; 541-956-6052; Web: https://wemoon.ws

West Wind Review (A) 1982: Southern Oregon University, 1250 Siskiyou Blvd. Ashland 97520; Web: http://westwindreview.blogspot.com/

Willamette Journal of International Law and Dispute Resolution (A) 1997: Willamette University College of Law, 245 Winter St. SE, Salem 97301; 503-370-6632;

Web: https://willamette.edu/law/resources/journals/wjildr/

Willamette Law Review (Q) 1978: Willamette University College of Law, 245 Winter St. SE, Salem 97301; 503-370-6186; Fax: 503-375-5463;

Web: https://willamette.edu/law/resources/journals/review/

One Hundred Years of Oregon State Parks

Celebrating the Best of Oregon

Nehalem Bay State Park. *(Oregon State Archives)*

Colorful 1958 artwork promoted tourism to Vista House, part of the state park system in the Columbia River Gorge. Illustrations from this period typically idealized families visiting state parks. *(All artwork: Oregon State Library, Oregon Highway Department Tourism Promotion Campaign Review)*

One Hundred Years of Oregon State Parks

State parks represent the best of Oregon: from the dramatic vistas of the rugged coastline to the tranquil beauty of mountain lakes; from important historical sites to fascinating natural wonders. These are all under the umbrella of the Oregon State Parks and Recreation Department. While the department in its current form is a more recent organization, the state park system is celebrating its centennial in 2022, a century after Oregon Trail pioneer Sarah Helmick donated land for the first state park (Sarah Helmick State Park, near Monmouth).

Of course, the large and impressive system of 256 state parks, heritage sites, natural areas, and related resources in every part of Oregon didn't happen by accident. It was the product of foresight, persistence, and a bit of luck over the decades. Civic leaders in the early 1900s focused their attention on developing highways to "get Oregon out of the mud," a reference to the typical condition of the state's road system. As highways developed and provided better access, public interest grew in exploring the natural beauty of the state through visits to roadside parks, camping and related recreation.

The golden age of expansion for the state park system came while Samuel H. Boardman served as the first state parks superintendent from 1929 to 1950. He was remarkably successful at convincing Oregonians to donate land for parks. Boardman used his powers of persuasion while appealing to the Oregon State Highway Commission to fund key purchases, such as Silver Falls State Park and many of the coastal state parks. Without his visionary efforts, many of Oregon's most treasured parks would have been developed into residential or commercial properties.

Although funding continues to present challenges, the State Parks and Recreation Department is still growing and succeeding at its mission "to provide and protect outstanding natural, scenic, cultural, historic and recreational sites for the enjoyment and education of present and future generations." We hope you enjoy this centennial state parks photo exhibit. You can read about interesting and quirky state parks in the essay on page 312.

Samuel Boardman's first park land purchase was a parcel that became the basis for Silver Falls State Park, which is considered to be a flagship site in the state park system. Shown here is South Falls. *(Oregon State Archives)*

Young people on the shore of Wallowa Lake wave at a passing boat in 1967. Wallowa Lake State Park sits on the southern shore of the lake beneath towering peaks known as the Swiss Alps of Oregon. *(Oregon State Archives, Highway Photo 7553)*

State Parks Ranger Kevin Price leads students on a field trip to state parks in the Columbia River Gorge. *(Courtesy of State Parks and Recreation Department)*

The Fort Rock State Natural Area, which is managed by the State Parks and Recreation Department, preserves and interprets this geological wonder southeast of La Pine. The tuff ring rises 200 feet above an Ice Age lake bed. Learn more on page 313. *(Oregon State Archives)*

Thompson's Mills State Heritage Site near Shedd in the heart of the Willamette Valley helps preserve and interpret the agricultural history of the Oregon. Situated along the Calapooya River, it is the oldest existing water-powered grain mill in the state. Learn more on page 316. *(Oregon State Archives)*

The Darlingtonia State Natural Site just north of Florence on the coast preserves a bog containing *Darlingtonia californica* plants, also known as cobra lilies. The carnivorous plants trap insects in hollow tubes with downward facing hairs. Insects then fall into water at the bottom of the plant and are decomposed by bacteria into nitrogen used by the plant. See page 316. *(Oregon State Archives)*

Campers relax by their travel trailer at Sunset Bay State Park in 1962. As more Americans entered the middle class in the years after World War II, they took to the highways to explore the country. In response, state parks in Oregon expanded camping facilities. *(Oregon State Archives, Highway Photo 7072)*

The Kam Wah Chung State Heritage Site in John Day preserves and interprets the story of two Chinese immigrants, Ing "Doc" Hay, who practiced herbal medicine, and Lung On, who ran the general store. Beginning in the late 1800s, the building served as a center of social, religious and medical life for Oregon's Chinese community for over 60 years. Learn more on page 314. *(Oregon State Archives)*

The Portland Women's Forum State Scenic Viewpoint offers a stunning view of the Columbia River Gorge. This photo looks east showing sunrise over Vista House to the right. *(Oregon State Archives)*

A family picnics at Shore Acres State Park southwest of Coos Bay in the 1950s. The setting offers visitors striking views of the sandstone cliffs and easy access to the Oregon Coast Trail. It's also a great place to watch migrating whales. *(Oregon State Library, Oregon Highway Department 1958 Tourism Promotion Campaign Review)*

A car hugs a narrow passage along a cliff on the aptly named Hug Point in 1938. Today, Hug Point State Recreation Site gives visitors access to beaches and scenic views. Before the coast highway was built, the beach was the only way to travel on this part of the coast. *(Oregon State Archives, Highway Photo G565)*

The Pete French Round Barn State Heritage Site southeast of Burns preserves the history of ranching in the region. The barn was built by cattle baron Peter French in the late 1800s to provide covered space to train and exercise horses during the winter. Learn more on page 314. *(Oregon State Archives)*

Tourists take in the scenery at Wallowa Lake State Park in the 1950s. The lake is a vestige of glaciation. *(Oregon State Library, Oregon Highway Department 1958 Tourism Promotion Campaign Review)*

The evening light hits the rugged cliffs at Otter Point State Recreation Site north of Gold Beach. Despite its striking beauty, the park is less visited than many other coastal state parks. *(Oregon State Archives)*

A man and woman roast hot dogs on the beach next to Heceta Head at sunset in 1938. The Heceta Head Lighthouse State Scenic Viewpoint is best known for its iconic lighthouse and assistant lightkeeper's house. *(Oregon State Archives, Highway Photo G485)*

Clouds roll over a pond at Hat Rock State Park. The park is named for a basalt outcropping that was the first distinctive landmark passed by the Lewis and Clark Expedition in 1805 as it traveled west on the Columbia River to the Pacific Ocean. *(Oregon State Archives)*

The John Day River wanders through the rugged landscape at Cottonwood Canyon State Park. Established in 2013, the park is the second largest in the state park system behind only Silver Falls State Park. In additon to its scenic beauty, the park interprets the ranching history of Oregon and features camping and miles of hiking trails. *(Oregon State Archives)*

The Wolf Creek Inn State Heritage Site, built in 1883 along the Applegate Trail, is the oldest continuously operating inn in the Pacific Northwest. The historic building hosted some of Hollywood's biggest stars, such as Clark Gable, Orson Welles, and Carole Lombard, who came seeking a quiet refuge from film studio life. Learn more on page 314. *(Oregon State Archives)*

Travelers along Mountain View Drive are rewarded with great views of Lake Billy Chinook at Cove Palisades State Park. Shown above is the confluence of the Crooked River on the left and the Deschutes River on the right. Camping, boating and hiking are features of the park. *(Oregon State Archives)*

Early morning clouds mirror the coastline along the beach at Seven Devils State Recreation Site. This out of the way park north of Bandon offers access to miles of beach and is a good place for beachcombing and agate hunting. *(Oregon State Archives)*

Tourists take in sweeping views of the coast at Neahkanie Viewpoint along Highway 101 in the 1950s. The viewpoint is part of Oswald West State Park. *(Oregon State Library, Oregon Highway Department 1958 Tourism Promotion Campaign Review)*

People take advantage of picnic facilities at the present-day Yaquina Bay State Recreation Site in Newport along the north shore of Yaquina Bay in 1947. *(Oregon State Archives, Highway Photo 142)*

The State Parks and Recreation Department has managed the grounds around the Oregon State Capitol as a park since 2008. The park is famous for the cherry blossoms that peak in late March. *(Oregon State Archives)*

The Erratic Rock State Natural Site off Highway 18 near McMinnville is focused on a 90-ton glacial erratic from the Missoula Floods 12,000 to 17,000 years ago. The rock floated over 500 miles in an iceberg following the path of the Columbia River. Learn more on page 315 *(Oregon State Archives)*

Tourists stop at a viewpoint for pictures in the 1950s. This location is now part of the Cape Sebastian State Scenic Corridor south of Gold Beach. *(Oregon State Library, Oregon Highway Department 1958 Tourism Promotion Campaign Review)*

A kayaker prepares to launch into the Clackamas River at Milo McIver State Park near Estacada. *(Courtesy of State Parks and Recreation Department)*

Smith Rock State Park near Terrebonne is a world-class destination for rock climbers. The striking rock formations have a volcanic history. Over the millennia, the Crooked River has cut a channel through the roughly 600-foot high cliffs. Hikers can also explore miles of park trails with impressive scenic vistas. *(Oregon State Archives)*

The snow-covered Wallowa Mountains reflect in the placid spring waters of Wallowa Lake. Wallowa Lake State Park is nestled amid the mountains at the far end of the lake. *(Oregon State Archives)*

Two women take in the view of Prineville from the Ochoco State Scenic Viewpoint in 1949. The viewpoint is located on top of rimrock to the west of Prineville. *(Oregon State Archives, Highway Photo 4180)*

Reflections on a peaceful morning highlight the serene beauty of the Illinois River Forks State Park located at the confluence of the east and west forks of the Illinois River. *(Oregon State Archives)*

The Travel Information Division of the Oregon Highway Department used photos such as this one taken in 1938 to attract tourists to the state. Here women relax and practice archery next to a waterfall at Hug Point, now part of the Hug Point State Recreation Site. *(Oregon State Archives, Highway Photo G541)*

The Collier Memorial State Park north of Klamath Falls features an outdoor museum of historic logging equipment and a relocated pioneer village. The park, set in a pine forest, also offers camping, fishing and hiking. *(Oregon State Archives)*

Set in the rugged canyonlands of southeast Oregon, Lake Owyhee State Park rewards visitors looking to escape the crowds with boating, fishing, camping and scenic views of dramatic rock formations along the 53-mile-long lake. *(Oregon State Archives)*

The Heceta Head Lighthouse, first illuminated in 1894, is preserved as part of a state scenic view-point. In addition to taking in the sweeping views, visitors can hike along the Oregon Coast Trail, tour the historic lighthouse, and stay at a bed and breakfast room in the assistant lightkeeper's house. *(Oregon State Archives)*

An artillery gun from a military ship is on display near the mouth of the Columbia River at Fort Stevens State Park. The park preserves the military history of Fort Stevens, which was shelled by a Japanese submarine during World War II. Learn more on page 316. *(Oregon State Archives)*

A fishing pier extends over Prineville Reservoir at Prineville Reservoir State Park. The park is known for water sports, fishing, hiking and camping. *(Oregon State Archives)*

A family enjoys the view from the rim of South Falls at Silver Falls State Park. The park is one of the most popular in the state park system. *(Courtesy of State Parks and Recreation Department)*

The Sumpter Valley Dredge State Heritage Area features one of the largest and most accessible gold dredges in the country. Built in 1935, the dredge operated for 20 years on the Powder River at Sumpter and left miles of tailings (waste rocks) in its wake. The site offers guided and self-guided tours inside this relic of gold mining on an industrial scale. Learn more on page 314. *(Oregon State Archives)*

Cape Blanco State Park sits at the westernmost point of Oregon. *(Oregon State Archives)*

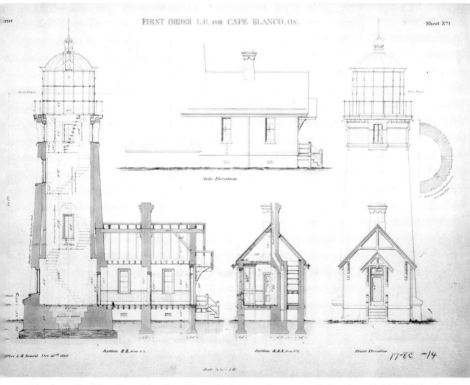

FIRST ORDER L.H. FOR CAPE BLANCO, OR.

Sheet Nº1

Side Elevation

Section B.B. from Nº 1.

Section A.A.A. from Nº 2.

Front Elevation

This vintage building plan of the Cape Blanco Lighthouse shows several elevations. Built in 1870, the structure is the oldest standing lighthouse on the Oregon coast. *(Courtesy of State Parks and Recreation Department)*

The Deschutes River flows into the Columbia River at Heritage Landing. The site is part of the state park system and offers boating, fishing and hiking. *(Oregon State Archives)*

In 1938, tourists take in the view at Cleawox Lake, now part of Jessie M. Honeyman Memorial State Park, south of Florence. *(Oregon State Archives, Highway Photo G488)*

Beverly Beach State Park north of Newport is a popular place to watch sunsets. *(Oregon State Archives)*

End of exhibit. Learn more in an expanded Web exhibit at **bluebook.state.or.us**

Oregon State Symbols

State Flag: The front of the Oregon ceremonial flag. Navy blue and gold are the state colors.
(Oregon State Archives)

State Flag: The reverse of the ceremonial flag. Oregon is the only state to have different designs on two sides of the flag.
(Oregon State Archives)

State Seal: The seal of the State of Oregon.
(Oregon State Archives)

State Animal: American Beaver *(Castor canadensis)* *(Oregon Department of Fish and Wildlife)*

State Gemstone: Oregon Sunstone *(Oregon Department of Geology and Mineral Industries)*

State Insect: Oregon Swallowtail *(Papilio oregonius)* *(Oregon State Capitol)*

State Mushroom: Pacific Golden Chanterelle *(Cantharellus formosus)* *(Richard F. Bishop)*

State Nut: Hazelnut *(Corylus avellana)* *(Oregon State Archives)*

State Shell: Hairy Triton *(Fusitriton oregonesis)* *(Bill Hanshumaker, Hatfield Marine Science Center)*

State Crustacean: Dungeness Crab
(Metacarcinus magister)
(Dungeness Crab Commission)

State Bird: Western Meadowlark *(Sturnella neglecta)*
(Jim Leonard)

State Rock: Thunderegg (geode)
(Oregon Department of Geology and Mineral Industries)

State Fruit: Pear *(Pyrus communis)*
(Pear Bureau Northwest)

State Flower: Oregon Grape
(Mahonia Aquifolium)
(Oregon State Archives)

State Fossil: Dawn Redwood
(Metasequoia glyptostroboides)
(National Park Service, John Day Fossil Be[...]
National Monument)

State Fish: Chinook Salmon *(Oncorhynchus tshawytscha)*
(Oregon Department of Fish and Wildlife)

State Raptor: Osprey *(Pandion haliaetus)*
(Jim Leonard)

State Tree: Douglas Fir *(Pseudotsuga menziesii)*
(Oregon State Archives)

The State Capitol decorated with special lighting to celebrate the 75th Anniversary of the building in 2013. *(Oregon State Archives)*

Physical Features Map

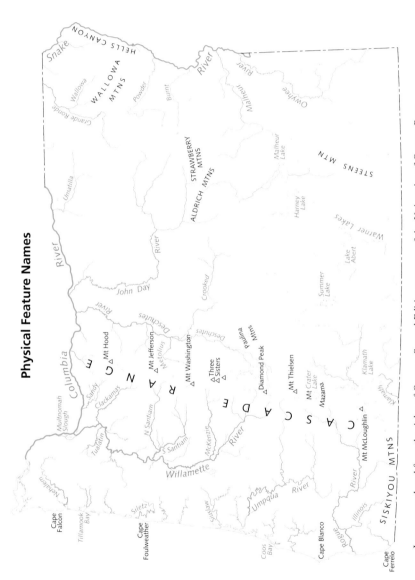

Physical Feature Names

Snake *River*

HELLS CANYON

WALLOWA MTNS

Wallowa

Grande Ronde

Powder

Burnt

River

Malheur

Owyhee *River*

Malheur Lake

STEENS MTN

STRAWBERRY MTNS

ALDRICH MTNS

Umatilla

Harney Lake

Warner Lakes

Lake Abert

John Day

River

Crooked

Summer Lake

Columbia *River*

Multnomah Slough

Sandy

Clackamas

Deschutes

Metolius

Deschutes

Paulina Mtns

Klamath Lake

Mt Hood △

CASCADE

Mt Jefferson △

Mt Washington △

△ Three Sisters △

△ Diamond Peak

Mt Thielsen △

Mt Crater Lake

Mazama

Klamath

Tualatin

N Santiam

S Santiam

McKenzie

River

Mt McLoughlin △

SISKIYOU MTNS

Willamette

Nehalem

Cape Falcon

Tillamook Bay

Siletz

Cape Foulweather

Siuslaw

Umpqua *River*

Coos Bay

Cape Blanco

Rogue

River

Illinois

Cape Ferrelo

National, International and Tribal

The citizens of the United States, through our federal government, own more than half the land in Oregon. Oregon's position on the Pacific Rim has resulted in strong ties between Oregon and other nations. Oregon has nine federally recognized tribes, who have distinct relationships with state government. This section contains information about the federal government, representatives of other nations, and tribes in Oregon.

U.S. SENATORS

Jeff Merkley

Democrat. Born in Myrtle Creek, October 24, 1956. Stanford University, B.A., 1979; master's degree in Public Policy from Woodrow Wilson School at Princeton University, 1982. He was Executive Director of Portland Habitat for Humanity before serving as President of the World Affairs Council of Oregon for seven years, where he continues to serve on the Board of Trustees. He and his wife Mary have two children.

Elected to the Oregon House of Representatives, 1999; became speaker of the House in 2007. Elected to the U.S. Senate, 2008; reelected 2014 and 2020.

Committee member: Appropriations, Ranking member on Agriculture, Rural Development & FDA Subcommitte; Budget; Environment and Public Works; Foreign Relations. Term expires 2027.

Washington, D.C., Office: 313 Hart Senate Office Bldg., Washington, D.C. 20510; 202-224-3753; Fax: 202-228-3997; Web/email: https://www.merkley.senate.gov

District Offices: Bend: 131 NW Hawthorne Ave., Suite 208, Bend 97701; 541-318-1298
Eugene: 405 E Eighth Ave., Suite 2010, Eugene 97401; 541-465-6750
Medford: 10 S Bartlett St., Suite 201, Medford 97501; 541-608-9102
Pendleton: 310 SE Second St., Suite 105, Pendleton 97801; 541-278-1129
Portland: One World Trade Center, 121 SW Salmon St., Suite 1400, Portland 97204; 503-326-3386
Salem: 500 Liberty St. SE, Suite 320, Salem 97301; 503-362-8102

Ron Wyden

Democrat. Born in Wichita, Kansas, May 3, 1949. Stanford University, A.B. in Political Science, 1971; University of Oregon School of Law, J.D., 1974. Co-director, Oregon Gray Panthers, 1974–1980; director, Oregon Legal Services for the Elderly, 1977–1979; public member, Oregon Board of Examiners of Nursing Home Administrators, 1978–1979.

Elected to the U.S. House of Representatives, 1980; reelected 1982, 1984, 1986, 1988, 1990, 1992 and 1994. Elected to the U.S. Senate, 1996; reelected 1998, 2004, 2010 and 2016.

Chairman of Finance Committee; Committee member: Budget; Energy and Natural Resources; Select Committee on Intelligence; Joint Committee on Taxation. Term expires 2023.

Washington, D.C., Office: 221 Dirksen Senate Office Bldg., Washington, D.C. 20510-3703; 202-224-5244; Fax: 202-228-2717; Web/email: https://www.wyden.senate.gov

District Offices: Bend: Jamison Bldg., 131 NW Hawthorne Ave., Suite 107, Bend 97701; 541-330-9142; Fax: 541-330-6266
Eugene: Wayne Morse Federal Courthouse, 405 E Eighth Ave., Suite 2020, Eugene 97401; 541-431-0229; Fax: 541-431-0610
La Grande: SAC Annex Bldg., 105 Fir St., Suite 201, La Grande 97850; 541-962-7691; Fax: 541-963-0885
Medford: The Federal Courthouse, 310 W Sixth St., Rm. 118, Medford 97501; 541-858-5122; Fax: 541-858-5126
Portland: 911 NE 11th Ave., Suite 630, Portland 97232; 503-326-7525; Fax: 503-326-7528
Salem: 707 13th St. SE, Suite 285, Salem 97301; 503-589-4555; Fax: 503-589-4749

U.S. REPRESENTATIVES

Suzanne Bonamici—First District

Counties: Clatsop, Columbia, Washington, Yamhill and part of Multnomah

Democrat. Born in Detroit, Michigan, October 14, 1954. University of Oregon, B.A., 1980; University of Oregon School of Law, J.D., 1983. Before going into private practice in Portland, she was a consumer protection attorney for the Federal Trade Commission in Washington, D.C. She and her husband Michael Simon have two children.

Elected to the Oregon House of Representatives, 2006. Appointed to the Oregon State Senate, 2008; elected 2008; reelected 2010. Elected to the U.S. House of Representatives, 2012; reelected 2014, 2016, 2018 and 2020.

Committee member: Education and Labor; and Science, Space and Technology. Term expires 2023.

Washington, D.C., Office: 2231 Rayburn House Office Bldg., Washington, D.C. 20515; 202-225-0855; Fax: 202-225-9497; Web and email: https://bonamici.house.gov

District Office: 12725 SW Millikan Way, Suite 220, Beaverton 97005; 503-469-6010; Toll-free: 800-422-4003; Fax: 503-469-6018

Cliff Bentz—Second District

Counties: Baker, Crook, Deschutes, Gilliam, Grant, Harney, Hood River, Jackson, Jefferson, Grants Pass area of Josephine, Klamath, Lake, Malheur, Morrow, Sherman, Umatilla, Union, Wallowa, Wasco and Wheeler

Republican. Born January 12, 1952, in Salem, Oregon. Eastern Oregon State College, B.S., 1974; Lewis & Clark Law School, J.D., 1977. Attorney and farmer. Served in the Oregon Legislature. He and his wife Lindsay, a veterinarian, live in Ontario and have two children.

Served in the Oregon House of Representatives, 2008–2018; Served in the Oregon Senate, 2018–2019

Elected to the U.S. House of Representatives, 2020

Committee memberships not yet assigned at press time. Term expires 2023.

Washington, D.C., Office: 1239 Longworth House Office Bldg., Washington, D.C. 20515; 202-225-6730; Fax: 202-225-5774; Web and email: https://bentz.house.gov

District Offices: Medford: 14 N Central Ave., Suite 112, Medford 97501; 541-776-4646; Fax: 541-779-0204

Earl Blumenauer—Third District

Counties: Most of Multnomah and the northern part of Clackamas

Democrat. Born in Portland, August 16, 1948. Attended Lewis & Clark College and Law School, and Harvard University's Kennedy School of Government. Received B.A. degree, political science, 1970; law degree, 1976.

Elected to Oregon House of Representatives, 1972; reelected 1974 and 1976. Elected to Multnomah County Board of Commissioners, 1978; reelected 1982. Elected to Portland City Council, 1986; reelected 1990 and 1994.

Elected to Congress, 1996; reelected 1998, 2000, 2002, 2004, 2006, 2008, 2010, 2012, 2014, 2016, 2018 and 2020.

Committee member: Ways and Means, and its Subcommittees on Health and Trade. Term expires 2023.

Washington, D.C., Office: 1111 Longworth House Office Bldg., Washington, D.C. 20515; 202-225-4811; Fax: 202-225-8941; Web and email: https://blumenauer.house.gov

District Office: 911 NE 11th Ave., Suite 200, Portland 97232; 503-231-2300; Fax: 503-230-5413

Peter DeFazio—Fourth District

Counties: Coos, Curry, Douglas, Lane, Linn and most of Benton and Josephine

Democrat. Born in Needham, Massachusetts, May 27, 1947. Tufts University, B.A., 1969; University of Oregon, M.A., 1977. Honorable discharge, U.S. Air Force Reserve, 1971. Aide to Congressman Jim Weaver, 1977–1982; elected to Lane County Board of Commissioners, 1982. He and his wife Myrnie Daut live in Springfield.

Elected to the U.S. House of Representatives, 1986; reelected 1988, 1990, 1992, 1994, 1996, 1998, 2000, 2002, 2004, 2006, 2008, 2010, 2012, 2014, 2016, 2018 and 2020.

Chairman of Transportation and Infrastructure Committee. Term expires 2023.

Washington, D.C., Office: 2134 Rayburn House Office Bldg., Washington, D.C. 20515; 202-225-6416; Fax: 202-225-0032; Web and email: https://defazio.house.gov

District Offices: Coos Bay: 125 Central Ave., Suite 350, Coos Bay 97420; 541-269-2609; Fax: 541-465-6458

Eugene: 405 E Eighth Ave., Suite 2030, Eugene 97401; 541-465-6732; Toll-free: 800-944-9603; Fax: 541-465-6458

Roseburg: 612 SE Jackson, Rm. 9, Roseburg 97470; 541-440-3523; Fax: 541-465-6458

Kurt Schrader—Fifth District

Counties: Lincoln, Marion, Polk, Tillamook, parts of northern Benton, most of Clackamas and parts of southwestern Multnomah

Democrat. Born in Bridgeport, Connecticut, October 19, 1951. Cornell University, NY, B.A., 1973; University of Illinois, D.V.M., 1977. Owner, Clackamas County Veterinary Clinic. He has five grown children.

Elected to Oregon House of Representatives, 1996; served through 2002; elected to Oregon Senate, 2002; served through 2008.

Elected to the U.S. House of Representatives, 2008; reelected 2010, 2012, 2014, 2016, 2018 and 2020.

Committee member: Energy and Commerce; Subcommittee on Health; Subcommittee on Energy; Subcommittee on Communications and Technology. Term expires 2023.

Washington, D.C., Office: 2431 Rayburn House Office Bldg., Washington, D.C. 20515; 202-225-5711; Fax: 202-225-5699; Web and email: https://schrader.house.gov

District Offices: Oregon City: 621 High St., Oregon City 97045; 503-557-1324; Fax: 503-557-1981

Salem: 530 Center St NE, Suite 415, Salem 97301; 503-588-9100; Toll Free: 877-301-KURT (5878); Fax: 503-588-5517

National/International/Tribal

Congressional Districts

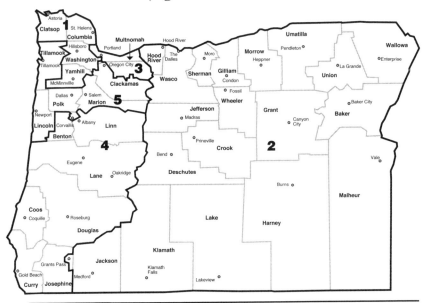

U.S. GOVERNMENT IN OREGON

For information about U.S. Government, contact the Federal Government Information Line at 1-800-FED-INFO (1-800-333-4636), or go to: http://www.loc.gov/rr/news/fedgov.html

U.S. DISTRICT COURTS

https://ord.uscourts.gov/index.php/211-divisions

Main Office:

U.S. Courthouse
Address: 1000 SW Third Ave., Suite 740, Portland 97204; 503-326-8000

Eugene Divisional Office:

Wayne L. Morse U.S. Courthouse
Address: 405 E Eighth Ave., Suite 2100, Eugene 97401; 541-431-4100

Medford Divisional Office:

James A. Redden U.S. Courthouse
Address: 310 W Sixth St., Room 201, Medford 97501; 541-608-8777

Pendleton Divisional Office:

John F. Kilkenny U.S. Courthouse
Address: 104 SW Dorian Ave., Pendleton 97801; 541-278-4053

MAJOR POLITICAL PARTIES

Democratic National Committee

Address: 430 S Capitol St. SE, Washington, D.C. 20003
Phone: 202-863-8000
Web: https://democrats.org

Democratic State Central Committee of Oregon

Address: 232 NE Ninth Ave., Portland 97232-2915
Phone: 503-224-8200
Web: https://dpo.org

Independent Party of Oregon

Address: 9220 SW Barbur Blvd., Suite 119, Portland 97219
Phone: 503-687-1206
Web: www.indparty.com

Republican National Committee

Address: 310 First St. SE, Washington, D.C. 20003
Phone: 202-863-8500
Web: https://gop.com

Republican State Central Committee of Oregon

Address: 25375 SW Parkway Ave., #200, Wilsonville 97070
Phone: 503-595-8881
Web: https://oregon.gop

NATIVE PEOPLES OF OREGON

Source: Legislative Commission on Indian Services
Contact: Daniel P. Santos, Interim Executive Officer
Address: 900 Court St. NE, Rm. 167, Salem 97301
Phone: 503-986-1067
Web: https://www.oregonlegislature.gov/cis

Oregon's total "American Indian" population, according to the 2010 U.S. Census, included 109,223 people as "American Indian or Alaskan Native." Oregon's "American Indians" live in all 36 counties and are about 3 percent of Oregon's total population. In addition to members of the nine federally recognized tribes in Oregon, there are a significant number of enrolled members of many Tribes based outside of Oregon who also reside within our state.

Members of Oregon's nine federally recognized tribes speak of being in this area from time immemorial. Village sites and traditional ways are known to date back many thousands of years.

Tribal governments are separate and unique sovereign nations with powers to protect the health, safety and welfare of their enrolled members and to govern their lands. This tribal sovereignty predates the existence of the U.S. government and the State of Oregon. The members residing in Oregon are citizens of their tribes, citizens of Oregon, and since 1924, citizens of the United States of America.

The U.S. Department of the Interior, Bureau of Indian Affairs, oversees tribal interests and administers the federal government's trust obligations. At times, the federal government has been supportive of tribal self-determination, and in other periods, has adopted policies and passed legislation having a negative impact on the ability of tribes to govern as sovereigns. "Termination," one such policy in the 1950s, was an attempt to sever federal trusteeship and support for tribal sovereignty. Of the 109 tribes and bands terminated nationwide, 62 were in Oregon. In 1975, the federal government recognized the failure of its termination policy and passed the Indian Self-Determination and Education Assistance Act, and later, the Tribal Self-Governance Act.

Several tribes began the process to restore their status as sovereign nations. In 1977, The Confederated Tribes of Siletz was the second tribe in the nation to achieve restoration. Following Siletz was the Cow Creek Band of the Umpqua Tribe of Indians in 1982, the Confederated Tribes of Grand Ronde in 1983, the Confederated Tribes of Coos, Lower Umpqua and Siuslaw in 1984, the Klamath Tribes in 1986 and the Coquille Indian Tribe in 1989.

Another three federally recognized tribal governments exist in Oregon: the Confederated Tribes of Warm Springs (Treaty of 1855), the Confederated Tribes of Umatilla (Treaty of 1855) and the Burns Paiute Tribe (1972 Executive Order). Fort McDermitt Paiute Shoshone Tribe is a federally-recognized tribe with reservation lands straddling Oregon and Nevada, but the tribe's population center is in Nevada. Celilo Village is a federally-recognized tribal entity near The Dalles, jointly administered by the Confederated Tribes of Warm Springs, the Confederated Tribes of Umatilla and the Yakama Indian Nation (Washington).

All Oregon tribal governments have reservation or trust lands created by treaties, statutes or executive branch actions. Tribal governments have regulatory authority over these lands, unless that authority has been removed by Congress. Nearly 904,000 acres, or at least 1.6 percent of land within Oregon's boundaries, are held in trust by the federal government or are designated reservation lands. Tribal governments have the authority to decide their own membership qualifications and have a right to exclude individuals from their reservations. Just as Oregon does not collect tax on federal lands nor tax federal or local governments or non-profit corporations, Oregon does not tax tribal governments, but all tribal members as individual citizens pay federal taxes and most pay state taxes, with the exception of those who live and work on a reservation or earn money on reservation or trust lands or from trust resources.

Public Law 280 gave the state certain civil and criminal jurisdiction over tribes with the exception of the Confederated Tribes of Warm Springs, the Confederated Tribes of Umatilla and the Burns Paiute Tribe, which are "non Public Law 280" tribes. Notwithstanding Public Law 280, all Oregon tribes have the authority to elect their own governments and adopt laws and ordinances. Oregon tribal governments have their own departments dealing with governmental services, including law enforcement and tribal court systems. In addition, each tribal government operates programs in the areas of natural resources, cultural resources, education, health and human services, public safety, housing, economic development and other areas to serve their members. Oregon maintains a government-to-government relationship with the tribal governments as directed in ORS 182.162 to 182.168.

Passage of the National Indian Gaming Regulatory Act in 1988 created the opportunity to build gaming centers on reservation and trust lands. Besides providing employment opportunities for tribal members and citizens of surrounding communities, revenues from these tribal enterprises fund health clinics, education, scholarships, housing and other services. Gaming and other enterprises have made these tribal governments some of the largest employers in their counties—generating employment for tax-paying employees, benefiting local communities and the entire state. All Oregon tribal governments are striving to diversify their revenue streams and are actively pursuing other avenues of generating revenue.

Most Oregon tribes are "confederations" of three or more tribes and bands. Each tribe's area of interest may extend far beyond its tribal governmental center or reservation location.

Burns Paiute Tribe

Address: 100 Pasigo St., Burns 97720
Phone: 541-573-2088
Email: Beverly.Beers@burnspaiute-nsn.gov
Web: https://www.burnspaiute-nsn.gov
Restoration: by Executive Order, October 13, 1972
Number of
Members: 420
Land Base Acreage:
13,736 acres
Number of people
employed by the
Tribe: 54

Economy: Burns
Paiute Tribe Old
Camp RV Park, Burns
Paiute Foundation

Points of Interest: Steens Mountain recreational area; Malheur National Wildlife Refuge; Reservation Day Powwow occurs two days each fall about October 13; annual Mother's Day Powwow

History and Culture: The Burns Paiute Reservation is located north of Burns in Harney County. Today's tribal members are primarily the descendants of the "Wadatika" band of Paiutes of central and southern Oregon. The Wadatika, named for the wada seeds collected near Malheur Lake shores, lived on seeds, berries, roots and vegetation they gathered and wild animals they hunted. Their territory included the area from the Cascade Mountains to Boise, Idaho, and the Blue Mountains to Steens Mountain. Paiute legends say that the Paiutes have lived in this area since before the Cascade Mountains were formed, coming from the south as part of a migration through the Great Basin. People of the Burns Paiute Tribe were basket makers who used fibers of willow, sagebrush, tule plant and Indian hemp to weave baskets, sandals, fishing nets and traps. Archeologists have found clothing made from animal and bird hides and sandals made from sagebrush fibers believed to be close to 10,000 years old. The tribe continues to hunt, gather food and do beadwork and drum-making in traditional ways.

Tribal Court: Tribal Judge Christie Timko; Associate Judge Patricia Davis, 100 Pasigo St., Burns 97720; 541-573-2793

Tribal Council 2021: Chairperson Jody Richards, Vice-Chair Diane Teeman, Secretary Tracy Kennedy, Sergeant at Arms Lucas Samor, Members at Large: Cecil Dick, Brenda Sam and Margarita Zacarias

Confederated Tribes of Coos, Lower Umpqua and Siuslaw

Address: 1245 Fulton Ave., Coos Bay 97420
Phone: 541-888-9577, 888-280-0726
Email: abarry@ctclusi.org
Web: https://ctclusi.org
Restoration Date:
October 17, 1984
Number of
Members: 1,271
Land Base Acreage:
about 415 acres
Number of people
employed by the
Tribes: 692

Economy: Three Rivers Casino & Hotel, Ocean Dunes Golf Course, Restoration Forest Plan

Points of Interest: Three Rivers Casino & Hotel; Salmon Ceremony held on the first Sunday in August at the Tribal Hall in Coos Bay; Annual Restoration Day celebrated on or about October 17 each year. The tribes sponsor seasonal hunting and gathering events and observe summer and winter solstices.

History and Culture: The tribal ancestors understood the land to be the Spirit expressing itself in the natural world. The people were connected to the land with certainty and gratitude. It sustained, nurtured and made life possible, while supporting all the spirits sharing this world. The tribal economy reflected the relationship of the Creator to the People. Acquiring objects of both aesthetic and utilitarian value was a measure of an individual's wealth and status, yet acquisition was not an end in itself. The annual Potlatch became the setting for individuals to give their possessions to others, further mirroring the Creator's relationship to the People. The spiritual act of gifting your possessions to others remains a powerful personal experience and a statement of faith and trust.

The tribes administered laws with transparency and a focus on the collective rights of the people. Individualism at the expense of community was not tolerated. Victims of an offense participated in the forming of appropriate punishments in the public arena where justice and fairness were, like other decision-making processes, a group affair.

By 1854, white settlers began taking Donation Land Claims around Coos Bay. In 1856, the U.S. Army forcibly removed the tribal people to the new 18,000 acre Great Coast Reservation established on a windswept spit on the north side of the mouth of the Umpqua River.

Tribal Court: Tribal Judge J. D. Williams, 1245 Fulton Ave., Coos Bay 97420; 541-888-9577

Tribal Council: Chief Doc Slyter (2030), Chair Debbie Bossley (2022), Vice-Chair Mark Petrie (2023), Doug Barrett (2022), Enna Helms (2023), Josh Davies (2022), Iliana Montiel (2023)

Coquille Indian Tribe

Address: 3050 Tremont St., North Bend 97459
Phone: 541-756-0904
Email: cit@coquilletribe.org
Web: http://www.coquilletribe.org
Restoration Date:
June 28, 1989
Number of Members: 1,113
Land Base Acreage:
6,552 acres (in trust)
Free Land: 3,456 acres (three separate parcels)

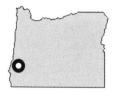

Number of people employed by the Tribe: 544

Economy: The tribe contributes to the economy of Coos County and its other service area counties, Curry, Douglas, Jackson and Lane, through business ventures, including timber operations; the Mill Casino, Hotel and RV Park; the Laundry Mill; Tribal One Broadband Technologies, LLC; and Sek-wet-Se Nonprofit Corporation. The tribe is the second largest employer in Coos County.

Points of Interest: Dune rides and shipwrecks at Oregon Dunes National Recreation Area, Charleston Harbor, charter fishing for tuna and salmon, crabbing; storm watching, beachcombing, tide pooling, canoeing, and the holiday lights showcase at Shore Acres State Park

History and Culture: The Coquilles' ancestral homelands, more than one million acres of lower Coos Bay and the Coquille River watershed, were ceded by treaties to the U.S. government in 1851 and 1855 in exchange for reservation land that never materialized because the treaties were never ratified by the U.S. Senate. No permanent tribal land existed until 1989, when Congress passed Public Law 101-42 re-establishing the Coquilles as a federally-recognized tribe.

After regaining federal recognition, the Coquille tribal government created programs to provide housing, health care, education, elder care, law enforcement and judicial services to its members. Cultural preservation efforts include learning and teaching oral histories and traditions to members of the tribe.

A congressional act in 1996 restored 5,410 acres of forest land to the tribe. The tribe operates a multi-discipline, natural resources program to manage its forest lands under certification standards of the Forest Stewardship Council.

Tribal Court: Chief Judge Melissa Cribbins, 3050 Tremont St., North Bend 97459; 541-756-0904

Tribal Council: Chief Donald B. Ivy (2022), Chairperson Brenda Meade (2021), Vice-Chair Jon Ivy (2023), Secretary/Treasurer Linda Mecum (2021), Representatives: Laurabeth Barton (2021), Don Garrett (2023) and Randy Hunter (2022)

Cow Creek Band of Umpqua Tribe of Indians

Address: 2371 NE Stephens St., Suite 100, Roseburg 97470
Phone: 541-672-9405, 800-929-8229
Email: dfields@cowcreek.com
Web: https://www.cowcreek.com
Treaty Date: September 19, 1853
Restoration Date:
December 29, 1982
Number of Members: 1,760
Land Base Acreage:
1,840 acres (in trust)
Number of people employed by the Tribe: 1,100

Economy: The tribe was restored without reservation land in 1982. All land held by the tribe has been by purchase. The Seven Feathers Casino Resort in Canyonville, including hotels, restaurants and entertainment venues, is the tribe's main income source. Other businesses, such as the K-BAR cattle ranch in Rogue River, have been acquired in their economic diversification program. Since recognition, the tribe has developed housing, education and social services programs, business corporations, a utility cooperative, charitable foundation and tribal court system. The tribe is one of the largest employers in Douglas County.

Points of Interest: Oregon's Interstate-5 passes through Canyonville, the Seven Feathers Resort and the heart of Cow Creek's homeland. The area includes the Umpqua River, the Cascade Mountains, the Pacific Ocean and dunes and a growing wine industry.

History and Culture: The Cow Creeks lived between the Cascade and Coast Ranges in southwestern Oregon, along the South Umpqua River. They hunted deer and elk and fished silver salmon and steelhead as far north as the Columbia River, east to Crater Lake, and south to the Klamath Marsh.

Except for the purpose of the Termination Act in 1954, which called for the immediate termination of federal relations with more than 60 tribes in western Oregon, the Cow Creek's Treaty of 1853 was ignored by the U.S. government for over 128 years until federal recognition in 1982.

Tribal Court: Tribal Judge Ronald Yockim, 2371 NE Stephens St., Suite 100, Roseburg 97470; 541-672-9405

2021–2022 Tribal Council: Chairman Daniel Courtney, Vice-Chair Gary Jackson, Secretary Yvonne Dumont-McCafferty, Treasurer Robert VanNorman, Members: Jessica Bochart, Tom Cox, Rob Estabrook, Carla Keene, Gerald Rainville, Kathleen Steward and Luann Urban

Confederated Tribes of The Grand Ronde Community

Address: 9615 Grand Ronde Rd., Grand Ronde 97347
Phone: 503-879-5211, 1-800-422-0232
Email: publicaffairs@grandronde.org
Web: https://www.grandronde.org
Restoration Date:
November 22, 1983
Number of Members: 5,567
Land Base Acreage: about 11,288 acres
Number of people employed by the Tribes: 1,660

Economy: Spirit Mountain Casino, over 10,000 acres of forest lands and wildfire fighting crew

Points of Interest: Spirit Mountain Casino is Oregon's most successful casino, and the tribe dedicates 6 percent of the profits to its Spirit Mountain Community Fund, which supports charitable organizations in an 11-county area of western Oregon. The fund has given more than $55 million to area charities since 1997. The West Valley Veterans' Memorial, four granite pillars representing the four branches of the armed services, holds the names of tribal members and area veterans who fought and served their country.

The tribe hosts a Veterans' Powwow each July and a Competition Powwow on the third weekend of August. Fort Yamhill Heritage Area nearby tells the story of the relocation, transition and sadness for Grand Ronde's people when they were forced from their ancestral homelands, which extended from the banks of the Columbia River to the Oregon–California border, on to the Grand Ronde Reservation under military guard.

History and Culture: The tribes include Athabaskan-speaking Chasta from Rogue River and Upper Umpqua from southern Oregon. Molalla tribes are from the western Cascade Mountains, Kalapuya Tribes are from the Willamette Valley, and Chinookan-speaking Tumwater, Clackamas, Watlala and Multnomah are from the lower Willamette and Columbia Rivers. Chinuk Wawa became the tribes' common language. Traditional basket making and weaving, skills still practiced today, were important tribal utility and cultural skills.

Tribal Court: Tribal Judge Cynthia Kaufman-Noble, 9615 Grand Ronde Rd., Grand Ronde 97347; 503-879-2303

Tribal Council 2021: Chair Cheryle J. Kennedy, Vice-Chair Chris Mercier, Secretary Jon A. George, Steve Bobb Sr., Kathleen George, Jack Giffen Jr., Denise Harvey, Michael Langley and Lisa Leno

Klamath Tribes

Address: PO Box 436, 501 Chiloquin Blvd., Chiloquin 97624
Phone: 541-783-2219, 800-524-9787
Email: taylor.tupper@klamathtribes.com
Web: http://klamathtribes.org
Restoration Date:
August 27, 1986
Number of Members: 5,200
Land Base Acreage: no reservation land
Number of people employed by the Tribes: Over 350

Economy: Kla-Mo-Ya Casino, Crater Lake truck stop, travel center and hotel, wellness center

Points of Interest: Kla-Mo-Ya Casino, Crater Lake National Park, Lava Beds National Monument and Tulelake History Museum. Named by *Sunset Magazine* as one of the nation's five best birding hotspots, the Klamath Basin in the Pacific Flyway is a migratory flyway for more than 350 species of birds, including Bald Eagles, Clarke's Grebes and Black Terns

History and Culture: Traditionally, every March, the c'waam (Lost River Suckerfish) swims up the Sprague River to spawn. A certain snowfall at this time of year heralds the c'waam's return, and the evening sky reveals the fish constellation (three stars in line making "Orion's Belt") on the southwestern horizon. Klamath traditions state that watchmen, or swaso.llalalYampgis, monitored the riverbanks to see exactly when the fish would return. The head "shaman" would then give thanks for their return. Tribal elders continue this ceremony to ensure the survival of a species, tribal traditions, and mankind. The celebration includes traditional dancing, drumming, feasting and releasing of a pair of c'waam into the river. Other annual events include the Restoration Celebration held the fourth weekend in August and the New Year's Eve Sobriety Powwow.

The Klamath Tribes, the Klamath, Modoc and Yahooskin Paiute people, have lived in the Klamath Basin from time beyond memory. Legends and oral history tell about when the world and the animals were created, when the animals and gmok'am'c, the Creator, sat together and discussed the creation of man. According to tribal sayings, if stability defines success, their presence here has been, and always will be, essential to the economic well-being of their homeland.

Tribal Court: Tribal Judge Patricia Davis Gibson 118 W. Chocktoot St., PO Box 1260, Chiloquin 97624; 541-783-3020

2021–2022 Tribal Council: Chairman Don Gentry, Vice-Chair Gail Hatcher, Secretary Roberta Frost, Treasurer Brandi Hatcher, council members Jeannie McNair, Jessie Hecocta, Rosemary Treetop, Ellsworth Lang, Willa Powless and Clayton Dumont

Confederated Tribes of Siletz Indians

Address: 201 SE Swan Ave. PO Box 549, Siletz 97380
Phone: 541-444-2532
Email: sharone@ctsi.nsn.us
Web: http://www.ctsi.nsn.us
Restoration Date: November 18, 1977
Number of Members: 5,080
Land Base Acreage: 15,265 acres
Reservation Land: 4,010 acres
Number of people employed by the Tribes: 1,121

Economy: The Tribes own and operate the Chinook Winds Casino Resort in Lincoln City. The Siletz Tribal Business Corporation manages other businesses, including RV Parks and Siletz Tribal Prints & Gifts, and leases office space in Lincoln City, Eugene, Salem and Portland.

Points of Interest: Chinook Winds Casino and Resort, including ocean-front hotel, restaurants, arcade and childcare; 18-hole golf course in Lincoln City; Nesika Illahee Powwow each August; and the Tribes' Restoration Powwow each November

History and Culture: The Confederated Tribes of Siletz Indians is a diverse confederation of 27 Western Oregon, Northern California and Southern Washington bands. A 1.1 million-acre reservation was established by President Franklin Pierce on November 9, 1855, fulfilling the stipulations of eight treaties. Over time, reservation lands were taken away, and the CTSI were terminated as a tribe in 1954. In 1977, the CTSI was the second tribe in the nation to achieve restoration. In 1980, some reservation lands were re-established. In spite of mistreatment and displacement, the CTSI continues work to recover as much as possible of what was lost.

Since 1980, the tribe has increased its land base to 15,265 acres, which includes 14,666 acres of timberland and 599 acres for cultural preservation, housing, economic purposes, and wildlife habitat enhancement. About 58 percent (9,045 acres) of the land base is in Lincoln County. The tribe provides homes for nearly 192 members and families and over 1,000 jobs.

Tribal Court: Tribal Chief Judge Calvin E. Gantenbein, PO Box 549, Siletz 97380; 541-444-8228

Tribal Council: Chairperson Delores Pigsley (2022), Vice-Chair Alfred "Bud" Lane III (2022), Treasurer Robert Kentta (2023), Secretary Sharon Edenfield (2021), Members: Lillie Butler (2022), Loraine Butler (2023), Reggie Butler, Sr. (2021), Angela Ramirez (2021) and Selene Rilatos (2023)

Confederated Tribes of the Umatilla Indian Reservation

Address: 46411 Ti'mine Way, Pendleton 97801
Phone: 541-276-3165
Email: info@ctuir.org
Web: http://ctuir.org
Treaty Date: June 9, 1855; 12 Stat. 945
Number of Members: 3,152
Land Base Acreage: 172,000 acres
Number of people employed by the Tribes: 1,645

Economy: Prior to the 1855 Treaty, the tribes' economy consisted of intertribal trade, trade with fur companies, hunting, fishing and livestock. Today, the economy includes agriculture, livestock, tourism, a travel plaza, grain elevator, the Wildhorse Resort (casino, hotel, RV Park, golf course), Tamástslikt Cultural Institute, Cayuse Technologies, and Coyote Business Park, a 520-acre commercial and light industrial business development on the Interstate 84 Highway. The reservation is also home to the Umatilla National Forest Supervisor's Office.

Points of Interest: Tamástslikt Cultural Institute, Wildhorse Resort & Casino, Wildhorse Golf Course, Nix-yá-wii Warriors Memorial, Crow's Shadow Institute of the Arts, Indian Lake Recreation Area, seasonal upland gamebird and turkey hunting

History and Culture: Three tribes make up the CTUIR: Cayuse, Umatilla and Walla Walla. They have lived on the Columbia River Plateau for over 10,000 years, an area of about 6.4 million acres in what is now northeastern Oregon and southeastern Washington. In 1855, the tribes and the United States government negotiated a treaty in which the tribes ceded 6.4 million acres, while reserving a section of land for their exclusive use in the form of a reservation. The CTUIR reserved rights in the treaty, including fishing and hunting rights and the right to gather traditional foods and medicines within the ceded areas.

The traditional religion of the tribes is called "Washat" or "Seven Drums." Native languages are still spoken, and a language preservation program is helping to re-establish the languages.

Tribal Court: Tribal Judge William Johnson, 46411 Ti'mine Way, Pendleton 97801; 541-276-2046

Board of Trustees 2020–2021: Chair Kat Brigham, General Council Chair Lindsey Watchman, Vice-Chair Jeremy Wolf, Treasurer Sandra Sampson, Secretary Sally Kosey, Members at Large: Jill-Marie Gavin, Armand Minthorn, Boots Pond and Corinne Sams

Confederated Tribes of Warm Springs Reservation

Address: PO Box C, Warm Springs 97761
Phone: 541-553-3257
Email:michele.stacona@wstribes.org
Web: https://warmsprings-nsn.gov
Treaty Date: June 25, 1855
Number of Members: 5,363
Land Base Acreage: 644,000 acres
Number of people employed by the Tribes: 1,012

Economy: The tribes have established a number of enterprises under the Corporate Charter that are operated independently of tribal government, but contribute to the economy of the reservation, including Warm Springs Power & Water, Warm Springs Forest Products, Warm Springs Composite Products and Indian Head Casino.

Points of Interest: Indian Head Casino and the Museum at Warm Springs; the annual April Welcome Home Vietnam Veterans' Parade and Expo

History and Culture: Long before Europeans set foot on the North American continent, the three tribes of the Warm Springs Reservation – the Wasco, the Walla Walla (later called the Warm Springs), and the Paiute – had developed societies beside the Columbia River, Cascade Mountains, and other parts of Oregon. Prior to settling on the reservation, natural food resources were so plentiful that agriculture was unnecessary. Salmon from the nearby Columbia was a staple for the Wasco and Warm Springs bands. The high-plains Paiutes depended more on deer and other large game. All three tribes took advantage of assorted roots, fruits and other plant life. Salmon were hauled out of the Columbia with long-handled dip nets. Roots were pulled from the ground with specialized digging sticks called kapns. Berries were gathered in ornately-woven baskets. Centuries of practice perfected these methods.

Tribal Court: Chief Tribal Judge Lisa Lomis, PO Box 850, Warm Springs 97761; 541-553-3454

Tribal Council 2021: Chairman Raymond Tsumpti, Jr.; Paiute Chief Joe Moses; Warm Springs Chief Delvis Heath; Wasco Chief Alfred Smith, Jr.; Representatives: Anita Jackson, Brigette McConville, Raymond "Captain" Moody, Glendon Smith, Lola Sohappy, Lincoln Suppah, Wilson Wewa, Jr.

OREGON CONSULAR CORPS

Many foreign nations maintain consulates in Oregon. Consuls, officials appointed by a government to live in a foreign city to look after the business and interests of the home country and to assist and protect its nationals within the consular territory, promote a country's trade within the assigned area, assist and protect shipping interests, assist native seamen in distress, may adjudicate shipping matters, administer oaths, legalize ships' papers and foreign documents as required by a country's laws, issue passports and visas and explain a country's policies, cultural achievements and its attractions for tourism.

See this listing by country below.

Barbados
H. Desmond Johnson, M.D., Honorary Consul
Address: 4750 SW Trail Rd., Tualatin 97062
Phone: 503-805-5886
Email: bajandoc@hotmail.com

Belgium
Cyrille Michel, Honorary Consul
Address: 7912 NE 69th St., Vancouver, WA 98662
Phone: 503-803-7534
Email: cyrillebmichel@gmail.com

Canada
Barton Eberwein, Honorary Consul
Address: 805 SW Broadway, Ste 2100, Portland 97205
Phone: 503-880-7877
Email: bart-eberwein@hoffmancorp.com

Czech Republic
Marie Amicci, Honorary Consul
Address: 12520 SW 68th Ave., Ste B, Tigard 97223
Phone: 503-293-9545
Email: cz_consul_pdx@msn.com

Denmark
Ingolf Noto, Honorary Consul
Address: 888 SW Fifth Ave., Ste 1600, Portland 97204
Phone: 503-802-2131
Email: ingolf.noto@tonkon.com

France
Dominiqe Geulin, Honorary Consul
Address: 2340 NW Thurman St., Suite 203, Portland 97210
Phone: 503-941-8173
Email: consulhonorairePDX@gmail.com

Germany
Blake Peters, Honorary Consul
Address: 3900 SW Murray Blvd., Beaverton 97005
Phone: 503-626-9089
Email: blakepeters.hk@gmail.com

Guatemala
Marta Guembes-Herrera, Honorary Consul
Please contact by email
Phone: 503-530-0046
Email: consulguatemala.or@gmail.com

Italy
Andrea Bartoloni, Honorary Consul
Address: 1331 NW Lovejoy Ste 900, Portland 97209
Phone: 503-226-8622
Email: ab@aterwynne.com

Japan
Masaki Shiga, Consul General
Address: 1300 SW Fifth Ave., Ste. 2700, Portland 97201
Phone: 503-221-1811
Email: masaki.shiga@mofa.go.jp

Korea, Republic of
Greg Caldwell, Honorary Consul
Address: 8433 SW 10th Ave., Portland 97219
Phone: 503-768-7457
Email: caldwell@lclark.edu

Susan Soonkeum Cox, Honorary Consul
Address: PO Box 2880, Eugene 97402
Phone: 541-687-2202
Email: coxkoreanconsulate.eug@gmail.com

Latvia, Republic of
Uldis J. Berzins, M.D., Honorary Consul
Address: 655 Medical Center Dr. NE, Salem 97301
Phone: 503-581-5287
Email: ujberzins@aol.com

Lithuania
Randolph L. Miller, Honorary Consul
Address: 333 SE Second Ave., Portland 97214
Phone: 503-234-5000
Email: Randy@ProduceRowLLC.com

Luxembourg
Bill Failing, Honorary Consul
Address: 2649 SW Georgian Pl., Portland 97201
Phone: 503-309-2768
Email: wlfailing@gmail.com

Malaysia
John L. Blackwell, Honorary Consul
Address: 4708 SW Fairview Blvd., Portland 97221
Phone: 503-740-8404
Email: johnlblackwell1@gmail.com

Malta
Joseph Micallef, Honorary Consul
Address: 22233 SW Antioch Downs Ct., Tualatin 97062
Phone: 503-638-3949
Email: maltaconsul.portland@gov.mt

Mexico
Carlos Quesnel, Consul General
Address: 1305 SW 12th Ave., Portland 97201
Phone: 503-274-1442
Email: portland@sre.gob.mx

Micronesia
Joe B. Enlet, Consul General
Address: 7931 NE Halsey St., Ste 201, Portland 97213
Phone: 503-954-3710
Email: Joe.enlet@gov.fm

The Netherlands
D.J. van Hameren, Honorary Consul
Address: 2806 NW Fairfax Terrace, Portland 97210
Phone: 503-686-3595
Email: portland@nlconsulate.com

New Zealand
Charles Swindells, Honorary Consul
Address: NW 23 Pl., Ste 6, PMB 481, Portland 97210-5580
Phone: 503-803-7129
Email: cjs@theswindells.org

Norway
Larry K. Bruun, Honorary Consul
Address: 4380 SW Macadam, Ste 120, Portland 97239
Phone: 503-221-0870
Email: lbruun@wbgatty.com

Romania
James H. Rudd, Honorary Consul
Address: 888 SW Fifth Ave., Ste. 1200, Portland 97204
Phone: 503-382-5165
Email: rudd@fergwell.com

Taiwan
Daniel K.C. Chen, Director General
Address: 600 University St., Ste 2020, Seattle, WA 98101
Phone: 206-441-4586
Email: infoseattle@mofa.gov.tw

Thailand
Nicholas J. Stanley, Honorary Consul
Address: 1136 NW Hoyt, Ste. 210, Portland 97209
Phone: 503-221-0440
Email: thai@siaminc.com

Ukraine
Valeriy V. Goloborodko, Honorary Consul
Address: 600 1st Ave., Seattle, WA 98104
Phone: 425-209-0209
Email: hc@uaconsulate.org

United Kingdom
Wilfred Pinfold, Honorary Consul
Address: 2004 NW Irving St., #3, Portland 97209
Phone: 503-709-2975
Email: wp@wilfredpinfold.com

Source: Michou Jardini, Oregon Consular Corps, 503-808-0974; www.oregonconsularcorps.us

Tumalo State Park

Luther Lawson
Kellie Eldridge's 6th Grade Class
Elton Gregory Middle School, Redmond

This impressionistic drawing by Luther Lawson shows the Deschutes River at Tumalo State Park.

My favorite State Park is Tumalo State Park because I love swimming through the river and fighting against the rapids. Also I like walking up the trails to the bridge and putting my donut shaped float tube into the water and going through the rapids and usually falling off and hitting my butt on the rocks because I slip off the donut shaped float tube all the time.

Another thing that I enjoy doing at Tumalo is bringing my dogs, Ruby a German Pointer who is extremely energetic. I've had Ruby for 3 years and she doesn't like the water, but when there's a bird she does not care if she gets wet are not.

Then when my friends come to Tumalo with me we get our donut float tubes and go to the bridge and tie all of our tubes together, then go down the rapids. We all usually fall off because the rope gets stuck on a rock and we have to swim up the rapids to get the tubes that got stuck on the rock. Also, sometimes we try to block off the rapids with rocks. Also we try to get to this picnic table that is on the side of the river somewhere, I don't know if it's still there, but we just sit there and talk, while people going down the rapids look at us like we are crazy people.

And that's my favorite state park and probably always will be because it requires the least amount of hiking.

Local Governments

Oregon offers us a place of rich geographic diversity to establish our communities—from the Pacific Ocean beaches and Coast Range eastward to the Willamette Valley, Klamath Mountains and southwest valleys; on to the Cascade Range; then further east to the Columbia River Plateau, Blue Mountains, the southeast Basin and ranges; and on to the Snake River at our eastern border. This section identifies incorporated cities and towns, counties, regional governments and special districts.

SALEM— OREGON'S CAPITAL

Salem, with a population of 168,970 is Oregon's state capital and the third largest city. Salem is also the county seat of Marion County, but a small portion contained within its corporate limits of 44 square miles lies across the Willamette River in Polk County. Salem is situated on the 45th geographic parallel in the center of the Willamette Valley—one of the most fertile and agriculturally productive regions in the world—47 miles south of Portland and 64 miles north of Eugene.

Salem serves as the hub of both state government and the surrounding farming communities. State government is the largest employer, with approximately 17,958 state employees and offices for 69 state agencies located in Salem. Salem is also one of the largest food-processing centers in the United States.

In addition, Salem is one of Oregon's oldest cities. The tribal name for the locality was Chemeketa, said to mean "meeting or resting place." It may also have been the name of one of the bands of the Kalapuya Tribe. In 1840–1841, the Jason Lee Mission was moved from the banks of the Willamette River, upstream to a site on Mill Creek. In 1842, the missionaries established the Oregon Institute. When the mission was dissolved in 1844, it was decided to lay out a townsite on the Oregon Institute lands. Either David Leslie, one of the trustees who came to Oregon from Salem, Massachusetts, or W. H. Willson, who filed plats in 1850–1851 for what is now the main part of the city, selected the name "Salem." Salem is the Anglicized form of the Hebrew word shalom, meaning peace.*

The location of the Oregon capital caused a spirited contest that lasted nearly 15 years. By a legislative act in 1851, the territorial government moved the capital to Salem from Oregon City. In 1855, it was moved to Corvallis, only to move back to Salem the same year. Destruction of the Capitol Building at Salem on December 31, 1855, was considered an incendiary part of this controversy.

The close proximity of government provides Salem citizens with a distinct opportunity to be involved in the decision-making processes of the state. The citizens of Salem also have a long history of commitment to community improvement, a commitment recognized nationally through the presentation of two All-America City Awards in 1960–1961 and 1982–1983.

*Early Salem history from *Oregon Geographic Names* by Lewis A. McArthur.

INCORPORATED CITIES AND TOWNS

Source: Michael McCauley, Executive Director, League of Oregon Cities
Address: 1201 Court St. NE, Suite 200, Salem 97301, PO Box 928, Salem 97308
Phone: 503-588-6550
Fax: 503-399-4863
Email: loc@orcities.org
Web: http://www.orcities.org

There are 241 incorporated cities in Oregon. Cities are centers of population, commerce, education and services. Seventy percent of Oregonians live in cities. Nearly 70 percent of Oregon's property value is in cities. Economic activity within cities generates 83 percent of the state's income tax receipts as more than 82 percent of jobs are located in cities. There are more than 16,000 miles of city roads. Cities employ more than 3,600 police officers, comprising 60 percent of all law enforcement officers in Oregon. All of the public institutions of higher education are located in cities, as well as all but two private colleges. All but one of Oregon's 60 hospitals are located within a city. Cities form the heart of Oregon's cultural, educational, service and economic activity.

Among the services city governments typically provide are fire and police protection, streets and street maintenance, sewer and water treatment and collection systems, building permit activities, libraries, parks and recreation activities, and other numerous social services determined locally. Cities also have considerable responsibilities for land use planning within their city limits and urban growth boundaries.

City councils serve as the highest authority within city governments in deciding issues of public policy. In open public forums, city councils pass laws (ordinances), adopt resolutions and generally conduct discussions involving the governance of their communities and the welfare of their citizens.

Four forms of city government determine the administrative role of any city council. Most Oregon cities with populations over 2,500 have the council/manager or council/administrator form, in which the council hires a chief executive officer to be responsible for the daily supervision of city affairs. Portland has a commission form of government, where the elected commissioners function collectively as the city council and serve as administrators of city departments. Smaller Oregon cities typically have the mayor/council form, in which the legislative and policy-making body is a popularly-elected council.

City administrators and other city employees often participate in the policy development process but are primarily responsible for effective delivery of municipal services and programs. Under home rule, cities have latitude in managing their affairs, except where the subject matter has been preempted by state government.

Regardless of the form of government, cities find their strength in a cooperative relationship between the citizens, city officials, the private sector and other government entities. Cities recognize the positive impact of working together, both regionally and on a statewide basis, to enhance community livability.

City name origins are available from *Oregon Geographic Names* by Lewis A. McArthur.

Incorporation dates listed below are based on information available.

*County seat

Adair Village
County: Benton
Address: 6030 NE Wm. R. Carr Ave., 97330
Phone: 541-745-5507
Fax: 541-230-5219
Web: http://adairvillage.org
Elevation: 330'
Incorporated: 5/25/1976
Mayor: William "Bill" Currier

Adams
County: Umatilla
Address: PO Box 20, 97810
Phone: 541-566-9380
Fax: 541-566-2077
Web: http://www.cityofadamsoregon.com
Elevation: 1,526'
Incorporated: 2/10/1893
Mayor: Colton J. Chase

Adrian
County: Malheur
Address: PO Box 226, 97901
Phone: 541-372-2179
Email: cityofadrian@hotmail.com
Elevation: 2,225'
Incorporated: 7/10/1972
Mayor: Bill Currier

*Albany
County: Benton/Linn
Address: PO Box 490, 333 Broadalbin St. SW, 97321
Phone: 541-917-7500
Fax: 541-917-7511
Web: https://www.cityofalbany.net
Elevation: 210'
Incorporated: 10/10/1864
Mayor: Alex Johnson II

Amity
County: Yamhill
Address: PO Box 159, 109 Maddox Ave., 97101
Phone: 503-835-3711
Fax: 503-835-3780
Web: https://www.cityofamityoregon.org
Elevation: 162'
Incorporated: 10/19/1880
Mayor: Joshua Clark

Antelope
County: Wasco
Address: PO Box 105, 97001
Phone: 541-489-3201
Web: https://www.cityofantelope.us/
Elevation: 2,654'
Incorporated: 11/12/1896
Mayor: Peggy Sue Tucker

Arlington
County: Gilliam
Address: PO Box 68, 97812
Phone: 541-454-2743
Fax: 541-454-2753
Web: http://www.cityofarlingtonoregon.com
Elevation: 285'
Incorporated: 11/20/1885
Mayor: Jeffery C. Bufton

Ashland
County: Jackson
Address: 20 E Main St., 97520
Phone: 541-488-6002
Fax: 541-488-5311
Web: http://www.ashland.or.us
Elevation: 1,949'
Incorporated: 10/13/1874
Mayor: Julie Akins

*Astoria
County: Clatsop
Address: 1095 Duane St., 97103
Phone: 503-325-5821
Fax: 503-325-2997
Web: http://www.astoria.or.us
Elevation: 23'

Incorporated: 10/20/1876
Mayor: Bruce Jones

Athena
County: Umatilla
Address: PO Box 686, 302 E Current St., 97813
Phone: 541-566-3862
Fax: 541-566-2781
Web: http://www.cityofathena.com
Elevation: 1710'
Incorporated: 2/20/1889
Mayor: Rebecca Schroeder

Aumsville
County: Marion
Address: 595 Main St., 97325
Phone: 503-749-2030
Fax: 503-749-1852
Web: http://www.aumsville.us
Elevation: 366'
Incorporated: 8/3/1911
Mayor: Derek Clevenger

Aurora
County: Marion
Address: 21420 Main St. NE, 97002
Phone: 503-678-1283, ext. 2
Fax: 503-678-2758
Web: https://www.ci.aurora.or.us
Elevation: 136'
Incorporated: 2/20/1893
Mayor: Brian Asher

*Baker City
County: Baker
Address: PO Box 650, 1655 First St., 97814
Phone: 541-523-6541
Fax: 541-524-2024
Web: http://www.bakercity.com
Elevation: 3,451'
Incorporated: 10/13/1874
Mayor: Kerry McQuisten

Bandon
County: Coos
Address: PO Box 67, 555 Hwy. 101, 97411
Phone: 541-347-2437
Fax: 541-347-1415
Web: http://www.cityofbandon.org
Elevation: 20'
Incorporated: 2/18/1891
Mayor: Mary Schamehorn

Banks
County: Washington
Address: 13680 NW Main St., 97106
Phone: 503-324-5112
Fax: 503-324-6674
Web: https://www.cityofbanks.org
Elevation: 250'
Incorporated: 1/16/1920
Mayor: Stephanie Jones

Barlow
County: Clackamas
Address: 106 N Main St., 97013-9191
Phone: 503-266-1330

Elevation: 103'
Incorporated: 2/13/1903
Mayor: Michael E. Lundsten

Bay City
County: Tillamook
Address: PO Box 3309, 5525 B St., 97107
Phone: 503-377-2288
Fax: 503-377-4044
Web: http://www.ci.bay-city.or.us
Elevation: 17'
Incorporated: 9/13/1910
Mayor: David McCall

Beaverton
County: Washington
Address: PO Box 4755, 12725 SW Millikan Way, 97005
Phone: 503-526-2222
Fax: 503-526-2479
Web: https://www.beavertonoregon.gov
Elevation: 189'
Incorporated: 2/10/1893
Mayor: Lacey Beaty

*Bend
County: Deschutes
Address: PO Box 431, 710 NW Wall St., 97709
Phone: 541-388-5505
Fax: 541-385-6676
Web: https://www.bendoregon.gov
Elevation: 3,628'
Incorporated: 1/19/1905
Mayor: Sally Russell

The Tower Theatre in downtown Bend was constructed in 1940. (Oregon State Archives scenic photo)

Boardman
County: Morrow
Address: PO Box 229, 200 City Center Cir., 97818
Phone: 541-481-9252
Fax: 541-481-3244
Web: http://www.cityofboardman.com
Elevation: 308'
Incorporated: 5/20/1921
Mayor: Paul Keefer

Bonanza

County: Klamath
Address: PO Box 297, 97623
Phone: 541-545-6566
Fax: 732-453-7252
Web: http://www.townofbonanza.com
Elevation: 4,127'
Incorporated: 2/20/1901
Mayor: Betty Tyree

Brookings

County: Curry
Address: 898 Elk Dr., 97415
Phone: 541-469-2163
Fax: 541-469-3650
Web: https://www.brookings.or.us
Elevation: 129'
Incorporated: 10/15/1951
Mayor: Jake Pieper

Brownsville

County: Linn
Address: PO Box 188, 255 N Main St., 97327
Phone: 541-466-5666
Fax: 541-466-5118
Web: https://www.ci.brownsville.or.us
Elevation: 265'
Incorporated: 10/19/1876
Mayor: Don Ware

*Burns

County: Harney
Address: 242 S Broadway Ave., 97720
Phone: 541-573-5255
Fax: 541-573-5622
Web: http://www.ci.burns.or.us
Elevation: 4,148'
Incorporated: 2/18/1891
Mayor: Jerry Woodfin

Butte Falls

County: Jackson
Address: PO Box 268, 431 Broad St., 97522
Phone: 541-865-3262
Fax: 541-865-3777
Email: bfcityhall@gmail.com
Elevation: 2,536'
Incorporated: 8/21/1911
Mayor: Linda Spencer

Canby

County: Clackamas
Address: PO Box 930, 222 NE 2nd Ave., 97013
Phone: 503-266-4021
Fax: 503-266-7961
Web: http://www.canbyoregon.gov
Elevation: 154'
Incorporated: 2/15/1893
Mayor: Brian Hodson

Cannon Beach

County: Clatsop
Address: PO Box 368, 163 E Gower St., 97110
Phone: 503-436-1581
Fax: 503-436-2050
Web: https://www.ci.cannon-beach.or.us

Elevation: 30'
Incorporated: 3/5/1957
Mayor: Sam Steidel

*Canyon City

County: Grant
Address: PO Box 276, 123 S Washington St., 97820
Phone: 541-575-0509
Fax: 541-575-0515
Email: tocc1862@centurylink.net
Elevation: 3,194'
Incorporated: 10/19/1864
Mayor: Steve Fischer

Canyonville

County: Douglas
Address: PO Box 765, 250 N Main, 97417
Phone: 541-839-4258
Fax: 541-839-4680
Web: https://cityofcanyonville.com
Elevation: 766'
Incorporated: 1/29/1901
Mayor: Jake Young

Carlton

County: Yamhill
Address: 191 E Main St., 97111
Phone: 503-852-7575
Fax: 503-852-7761
Web: https://www.ci.carlton.or.us
Elevation: 198'
Incorporated: 2/17/1899
Mayor: Linda Watkins

Cascade Locks

County: Hood River
Address: PO Box 308, 140 SW Wa Na Pa St., 97014
Phone: 541-374-8484
Fax: 541-374-8752
Web: https://www.cascade-locks.or.us
Elevation: 170'
Incorporated: 6/19/1935
Mayor: Bobby Dale Walker

Cave Junction

County: Josephine
Address: PO Box 1396, 222 W Lister St., 97523
Phone: 541-592-2156
Fax: 541-592-6694
Web: https://www.cavejunctionoregon.us
Elevation: 1,575'
Incorporated: 9/23/1946
Mayor: Meadow Martell

Central Point

County: Jackson
Address: 140 S Third St., 97502
Phone: 541-664-3321
Fax: 541-664-6384
Web: http://www.centralpointoregon.gov
Elevation: 1,272'
Incorporated: 2/25/1889
Mayor: Henry Williams

Chiloquin

County: Klamath
Address: PO Box 196, 127 S First Ave., 97624
Phone: 541-783-2717
Fax: 541-783-2035
Email: chiloquin@centurylink.net
Elevation: 4,180'
Incorporated: 3/3/1926
Mayor: Julie Bettles

Clatskanie

County: Columbia
Address: PO Box 9, 75 S Nehalem St., 97016
Phone: 503-728-2622
Fax: 503-728-3297
Web: http://www.cityofclatskanie.com
Elevation: 45'
Incorporated: 2/18/1891
Mayor: Robert "Bob" Brajcich

Coburg

County: Lane
Address: PO Box 8316, 91136 N Willamette St., 97408
Phone: 541-682-7850
Web: http://www.coburgoregon.org
Elevation: 398'
Incorporated: 2/10/1893
Mayor: Ray Smith

Columbia City

County: Columbia
Address: PO Box 189, 1840 Second St., 97018
Phone: 503-397-4010
Fax: 503-366-2870
Web: http://www.columbia-city.org
Elevation: 75'
Incorporated: 6/7/1926
Mayor: Casey Wheeler

*Condon

County: Gilliam
Address: PO Box 445, 128 S Main St., 97823
Phone: 541-384-2711
Fax: 541-384-2700
Web: http://cityofcondon.com
Elevation: 2,831'
Incorporated: 2/10/1893
Mayor: Jim Hassing

Coos Bay

County: Coos
Address: 500 Central Ave., 97420
Phone: 541-269-1181
Fax: 541-267-5912
Web: http://coosbay.org
Elevation: 10'
Incorporated: 10/24/1874
Mayor: Joe Benetti

*Coquille

County: Coos
Address: 851 N Central Blvd., 97423
Phone: 541-396-2115
Fax: 541-396-5125
Web: http://www.cityofcoquille.org

Elevation: 40'
Incorporated: 2/25/1885
Mayor: Sam Flaherty

Cornelius

County: Washington
Address: 1355 N Barlow St., 97113
Phone: 503-357-9112
Fax: 503-357-7775
Web: http://www.ci.cornelius.or.us
Elevation: 179'
Incorporated: 2/10/1893
Mayor: Jeffrey C. Dalin

*Corvallis

County: Benton
Address: PO Box 1083, 97339, 501 SW Madison Ave., 97333
Phone: 541-766-6900
Fax: 541-766-6946
Web: https://www.corvallisoregon.gov
Elevation: 230'
Incorporated: 1/28/1857
Mayor: Biff Traber

Cottage Grove

County: Lane
Address: 400 E Main St., 97424
Phone: 541-942-5501
Fax: 541-942-1267
Web: https://www.cottagegrove.org
Elevation: 640'
Incorporated: 2/11/1887
Mayor: Jeff Gowing

Cove

County: Union
Address: PO Box 8, 504 Alder St., 97824
Phone: 541-568-4566
Fax: 541-568-7747
Web: http://cityofcove.org
Elevation: 2,870'
Incorporated: 3/10/1904
Mayor: Sherry Haeger

Creswell

County: Lane
Address: PO Box 276, 97426
Phone: 541-895-2531
Fax: 541-895-3647
Web: http://www.ci.creswell.or.us
Elevation: 542'
Incorporated: 7/16/1909
Mayor: Amy Knudsen

Culver

County: Jefferson
Address: PO Box 368, 200 First Ave., 97734
Phone: 541-546-6494
Fax: 541-546-3624
Web: https://www.cityofculver.net
Elevation: 2,640'
Incorporated: 6/27/1946
Mayor: Jake Schwab

*Dallas

County: Polk
Address: 187 SE Court St., 97338
Phone: 503-623-2338
Fax: 503-623-2339
Web: https://www.dallasor.gov
Elevation: 325'
Incorporated: 2/20/1874
Mayor: Brian Dalton

Dayton

County: Yamhill
Address: PO Box 339, 416 Ferry St., 97114
Phone: 503-864-2221
Fax: 503-864-2956
Web: http://www.ci.dayton.or.us
Elevation: 280'
Incorporated: 10/15/1880
Mayor: Elizabeth "Beth" Wytoski

Dayville

County: Grant
Address: PO Box 321, 3 Park Ln., 97825
Phone: 541-987-2188
Email: dville@ortelco.net
Elevation: 2,369'
Incorporated: 10/25/1913
Mayor: Ilah Bennett

Depoe Bay

County: Lincoln
Address: PO Box 8, 570 SE Shell Ave., 97341
Phone: 541-765-2361
Fax: 541-765-2129
Web: http://www.cityofdepoebay.org
Elevation: 56'
Incorporated: 12/14/1973
Mayor: Kathy M. Short

Detroit

County: Marion
Address: PO Box 589, 160 Detroit Ave., 97342
Phone: 503-854-3496
Fax: 503-854-3232
Web: http://detroitoregon.us
Elevation: 1,595'
Incorporated: 9/29/1952
Mayor: James R. Trett

Donald

County: Marion
Address: PO Box 388, 10710 Main St. NE, 97020
Phone: 503-678-5543
Fax: 503-678-2750
Web: https://www.donaldoregon.gov
Elevation: 198'
Incorporated: 12/6/1912
Mayor: Rick Olmsted

Drain

County: Douglas
Address: PO Box 158, 129 West C Ave., 97435
Phone: 541-836-2417
Fax: 541-836-7330
Web: https://www.cityofdrain.org

Elevation: 303'
Incorporated: 2/9/1887
Mayor: Justin Cobb

Dufur

County: Wasco
Address: PO Box 145, 175 NE Third St., 97021
Phone: 541-467-2349
Fax: 541-467-2353
Web: https://www.cityofdufur.org
Elevation: 1,345'
Incorporated: 2/10/1893
Mayor: Merle Keys

The historic Balch Hotel in Dufur preserves the charms of another era. (Oregon State Archives scenic photo)

Dundee

County: Yamhill
Address: PO Box 220, 620 SW Fifth St., 97115
Phone: 503-538-3922
Fax: 503-538-1958
Web: www.dundeecity.org
Elevation: 189'
Incorporated: 2/21/1895
Mayor: David Russ

Dunes City

County: Lane
Address: PO Box 97, Westlake, 82877 Spruce St., 94793
Phone: 541-997-3338
Fax: 541-997-5751
Web: https://www.dundeecity.org
Elevation: 39'
Incorporated: 6/13/1963
Mayor: Robert Forsythe

Durham

County: Washington
Address: 17160 SW Upper Boones Ferry Rd., 97224
Phone: 503-639-6851
Fax: 503-598-8595
Web: https://durham-oregon.us
Elevation: 197'
Incorporated: 7/20/1966
Mayor: Gery Schirado

Eagle Point

County: Jackson
Address: PO Box 779, 17 Buchanan Ave., 97524

Phone: 541-826-4212
Fax: 541-826-6155
Web: http://www.cityofeaglepoint.org
Elevation: 1,310'
Incorporated: 2/16/1911
Mayor: Ruth Jenks

Echo

County: Umatilla
Address: PO Box 9, 20 S Bonanza St., 97826
Phone: 541-376-8411
Fax: 541-376-8218
Web: http://www.echo-oregon.com
Elevation: 635'
Incorporated: 3/9/1904
Mayor: Chad Ray

Elgin

County: Union
Address: PO Box 128, 180 N Eighth Ave., 97827
Phone: 541-437-2253
Fax: 541-437-0131
Web: https://cityofelginor.org
Elevation: 2,670'
Incorporated: 2/18/1891
Mayor: Allan L. Duffy

Elkton

County: Douglas
Address: PO Box 508, 366 First St., 97436
Phone: 541-584-2547
Fax: 541-584-2547
Web: http://elkton-oregon.com
Elevation: 132'
Incorporated: 11/4/1948
Mayor: Daniel Burke

*Enterprise

County: Wallowa
Address: 117 E Main St., 97828
Phone: 541-426-4196
Fax: 541-426-3395
Web: http://www.enterpriseoregon.org
Elevation: 3,757'
Incorporated: 2/21/1889
Mayor: Ashley Sullivan

Estacada

County: Clackamas
Address: PO Box 958, 475 SE Main St., 97023
Phone: 503-630-8270
Fax: 503-630-8280
Web: https://www.cityofestacada.org
Elevation: 468'
Incorporated: 1/31/1905
Mayor: Sean Drinkwine

*Eugene

County: Lane
Address: 125 E Eighth Ave., 2nd Floor, 97401
Phone: 541-682-5010
Fax: 541-682-5414
Web: https://www.eugene-or.gov
Elevation: 430'
Incorporated: 10/17/1862 or 10/22/1864
Mayor: Lucy Vinis

Fairview

County: Multnomah
Address: PO Box 337, 1300 NE Village St., 97024
Phone: 503-665-7929
Fax: 503-666-0888
Web: http://www.fairvieworegon.gov
Elevation: 114'
Incorporated: 5/11/1908
Mayor: Brian Cooper

Falls City

County: Polk
Address: 299 Mill St., 97344
Phone: 503-787-3631
Fax: 503-787-3023
Web: https://www.fallscityoregon.gov
Elevation: 370'
Incorporated: 2/13/1893
Mayor: Jeremy Gordon

Florence

County: Lane
Address: 250 Hwy. 101, 97439
Phone: 541-997-3437
Fax: 541-997-6814
Web: https://www.ci.florence.or.us
Elevation: 14'
Incorporated: 2/10/1893
Mayor: Joe Henry

Forest Grove

County: Washington
Address: PO Box 326, 1924 Council St., 97116
Phone: 503-992-3200
Fax: 503-992-3207
Web: https://www.forestgrove-or.gov
Elevation: 210'
Incorporated: 10/5/1872
Mayor: Peter B. Truax

*Fossil

County: Wheeler
Address: PO Box 467, 401 Main St., 97830
Phone: 541-763-2698
Fax: 541-763-2124
Web: http://cityoffossil.com
Elevation: 2,673'
Incorporated: 2/18/1891
Mayor: Carol E. MacInnes

Garibaldi

County: Tillamook
Address: PO Box 708, 107 Sixth St., 97118
Phone: 503-322-3327
Fax: 503-322-3737
Web: http://www.ci.garibaldi.or.us
Elevation: 22'
Incorporated: 4/8/1946
Mayor: Tim Hall

Gaston

County: Washington
Address: PO Box 129, 116 Front St., 97119
Phone: 503-985-3340
Fax: 503-985-1014
Email: gaston.city@comcast.net

Elevation: 300'
Incorporated: 12/7/1911
Mayor: Jerry Spaulding

Gates
County: Marion
Address: 101 Sorbin Ave. W, 97346
Phone: 503-897-2669
Email: ctygtes@wbcable.net
Elevation: 945'
Incorporated: 7/7/1955
Mayor: Ronald Carmickle

Gearhart
County: Clatsop
Address: PO Box 2510, 698 Pacific Way, 97138
Phone: 503-738-5501
Fax: 503-738-9385
Web: https://www.cityofgearhart.com
Elevation: 16'
Incorporated: 1/28/1918
Mayor: Paulina Cockrum

Gervais
County: Marion
Address: PO Box 329, 592 Fourth St., 97026
Phone: 503-792-4900
Fax: 503-792-3791
Web: http://www.gervaisoregon.org
Elevation: 184'
Incorporated: 10/29/1874
Mayor: Andrea (Annie) Gilland

Gladstone
County: Clackamas
Address: 525 Portland Ave., 97027
Phone: 503-656-5225
Fax: 503-557-2761
Web: https://www.ci.gladstone.or.us
Elevation: 61'
Incorporated: 1/5/1911
Mayor: Tammy Stempel

Glendale
County: Douglas
Address: PO Box 361, 124 Third St., 97442
Phone: 541-832-2106
Fax: 541-832-3221
Web: http://cityofglendaleor.com
Elevation: 1,443'
Incorporated: 2/23/1901
Mayor: Lucille Martin

*Gold Beach
County: Curry
Address: 29592 Ellensburg Ave., 97444
Phone: 541-247-7029
Fax: 541-247-2212
Web: https://www.goldbeachoregon.gov
Elevation: 50'
Incorporated: 9/24/1945
Mayor: Tamie Kaufman

Gold Hill
County: Jackson
Address: PO Box 308, 420 Sixth Ave., 97525

Phone: 541-855-1525
Fax: 541-855-4501
Web: https://www.ci.goldhill.or.us
Elevation: 1,085'
Incorporated: 2/12/1895
Mayor: Brad Studebaker

Granite
County: Grant
Address: 1378 Main St., 97877
Phone: 541-755-5100
Fax: 541-755-5100
Email: granitecity@pinetel.com
Elevation: 4,695'
Incorporated: 5/17/1900
Mayor: David Mosteit

*Grants Pass
County: Josephine
Address: 101 NW A St., 97526
Phone: 541-450-6000
Fax: 541-479-0812
Web: https://www.grantspassoregon.gov
Elevation: 960'
Incorporated: 2/18/1891
Mayor: Sara Bristol

Grass Valley
County: Sherman
Address: PO Box 191, 97029
Phone: 541-333-2434
Fax: 541-333-2276
Email: cityofgv@embarqmail.com
Elevation: 2,275'
Incorporated: 10/8/1900
Mayor: Neil Pattee

Greenhorn
County: Baker
Address: 28932 S Cramer Rd., Molalla 97038
Phone: 503-310-0913
Email: dalemclouth@molalla.net
Elevation: 6,300'
Incorporated: 2/20/1903
Mayor: Dale McLouth

Gresham
County: Multnomah
Address: 1333 NW Eastman Pkwy., 97030
Phone: 503-661-3000
Fax: 503-618-3301
Web: https://greshamoregon.gov
Elevation: 301'
Incorporated: 6/3/1904
Mayor: Travis Stovall

Haines
County: Baker
Address: PO Box 208, 819 Front St., 97833
Phone: 541-856-3366
Fax: 541-856-3812
Web: https://www.cityofhainesor.org
Elevation: 3,341'
Incorporated: 3/11/1902
Mayor: James H. Brown

Halfway
County: Baker
Address: PO Box 738, 97834-0738
Phone: 541-742-4741
Fax: 541-742-4741
Email: halfwaycity@gmail.com
Elevation: 2,651'
Incorporated: 5/27/1909
Mayor: Nik Melchior

Halsey
County: Linn
Address: PO Box 10, 100 W Halsey St., 97348
Phone: 541-369-2522
Fax: 541-369-2521
Web: http://ww.cityofhalsey.com
Elevation: 213'
Incorporated: 10/20/1876
Mayor: Jerry Lachenbruch

Happy Valley
County: Clackamas
Address: 16000 SE Misty Dr., 97086-6299
Phone: 503-783-3800
Fax: 503-658-5174
Web: https://www.happyvalleyor.gov
Elevation: 377'
Incorporated: 12/4/1965
Mayor: Tom Ellis

Harrisburg
County: Linn
Address: PO Box 378, 120 Smith St., 97446
Phone: 541-995-6655
Fax: 541-995-9244
Web: http://www.ci.harrisburg.or.us
Elevation: 309'
Incorporated: 10/24/1866
Mayor: Robert "Bobby" Duncan

Helix
County: Umatilla
Address: PO Box 323, 97835
Phone: 541-457-2521
Email: cityofhelix@gmail.com
Elevation: 1,754'
Incorporated: 1/9/1903
Mayor: Kim Herron

The historic Morrow County Courthouse in Heppner was built in 1903. (Oregon State Archives scenic photo)

*Heppner
County: Morrow
Address: PO Box 756, 111 N Main St., 97836
Phone: 541-676-9618
Fax: 541-676-9650
Web: https://cityofheppner.com
Elevation: 2,192'
Incorporated: 2/9/1887
Mayor: Jim Kindle

Hermiston
County: Umatilla
Address: 180 NE Second St., 97838
Phone: 541-567-5521
Fax: 541-567-5530
Web: https://hermiston.or.us
Elevation: 643'
Incorporated: 7/23/1907
Mayor: David A. Drotzmann

*Hillsboro
County: Washington
Address: 150 E Main St., 97123
Phone: 503-681-6100
Fax: 503-681-6213
Web: https://www.hillsboro-oregon.gov
Elevation: 196'
Incorporated: 10/19/1876
Mayor: Steve Callaway

Hines
County: Harney
Address: PO Box 336, 101 E Barnes Ave., 97738
Phone: 541-573-2251
Fax: 541-573-5827
Web: http://www.ci.hines.or.us
Elevation: 4,155'
Incorporated: 12/13/1930
Mayor: Nikki Morgan

*Hood River
County: Hood River
Address: 211 Second St., 97031
Phone: 541-386-1488
Fax: 541-387-5289
Web: http://ci.hood-river.or.us
Elevation: 160'
Incorporated: 2/15/1895
Mayor: Kate McBride

Hubbard
County: Marion
Address: PO Box 380, 3720 Second St., 97032
Phone: 503-981-9633
Fax: 503-981-8743
Web: http://www.cityofhubbard.org
Elevation: 181'
Incorporated: 2/18/1891
Mayor: Charles Rostocil

Huntington
County: Baker
Address: PO Box 369, 50 E Adams, 97907
Phone: 541-869-2202
Fax: 541-869-2550
Email: Huntingtoncityof@gmail.com

Elevation: 2,110'
Incorporated: 2/18/1891
Mayor: Richard Cummings

Idanha
County: Linn/Marion
Address: PO Box 430, 111 Hwy. 22 NW, 97350
Phone: 503-854-3313
Fax: 503-854-3114
Email: cityofid@bmi.net
Elevation: 1,718'
Incorporated: 3/15/1950
Mayor: Robert Weikum

Imbler
County: Union
Address: PO Box 40, 180 Ruckman Ave., 97841
Phone: 541-534-6095
Fax: 541-534-2343
Email: imblercity@oregonwireless.net
Elevation: 2,725'
Incorporated: 3/20/1922
Mayor: Jason M.L. Berglund, Sr.

Independence
County: Polk
Address: PO Box 7, 555 S Main St., 97351
Phone: 503-838-1212
Fax: 503-606-3282
Web: https://www.ci.independence.or.us
Elevation: 168'
Incorporated: 10/20/1874
Mayor: John McArdle

A Riverview Park fountain in Independence on the Willamette River. (Oregon State Archives scenic photo)

Ione
County: Morrow
Address: PO Box 361, 385 W Second St., 97843
Phone: 541-422-7414
Fax: 541-422-7179
Web: http://www.cityofioneoregon.com
Elevation: 1,089'
Incorporated: 7/14/1899
Mayor: Rod Taylor

Irrigon
County: Morrow
Address: PO Box 428, 500 NE Main St., 97844
Phone: 541-922-3047

Fax: 541-922-9322
Web: https://ci.irrigon.or.us
Elevation: 297'
Incorporated: 2/28/1957
Mayor: Margaret Anderson

Island City
County: Union
Address: 10605 Island Ave., 97850
Phone: 541-963-5017
Fax: 541-963-3482
Web: https://islandcityoregon.com
Elevation: 2,743'
Incorporated: 2/12/1904
Mayor: Dan Comfort

Jacksonville
County: Jackson
Address: PO Box 7, 206 N Fifth St., 97530
Phone: 541-899-1231
Fax: 541-899-7882
Web: http://www.jacksonvilleor.us
Elevation: 1,569'
Incorporated: 10/19/1860
Mayor: Donna Bowen

Jefferson
County: Marion
Address: PO Box 83, 150 N Second St., 97352
Phone: 541-327-2768
Fax: 541-327-3120
Web: https://www.jeffersonoregon.org
Elevation: 240'
Incorporated: 10/29/1870
Mayor: Michael Myers

John Day
County: Grant
Address: 450 E Main St., 97845
Phone: 541-575-0028
Fax: 541-575-3668
Web: http://www.cityofjohnday.com
Elevation: 3,087'
Incorporated: 5/9/1900
Mayor: Ron Lundbom

Johnson City
County: Clackamas
Address: 16121 SE 81st Ave., 97267
Phone: 503-655-9710
Fax: 503-723-0317
Email: johnson.city@hotmail.com
Elevation: 114'
Incorporated: 6/23/1970
Mayor: Vincent O. Whitehead, Jr.

Jordan Valley
County: Malheur
Address: PO Box 187, 306 Blackaby St., 97910
Phone: 541-586-2460
Fax: 541-586-2460
Web: http://www.cityofjordanvalley.com
Elevation: 4,389'
Incorporated: 3/21/1911
Mayor: Lee Ann Conro

Joseph
County: Wallowa
Address: PO Box 15, 201 N Main St., 97846
Phone: 541-432-3832
Fax: 541-432-3833
Web: http://www.josephoregon.org
Elevation: 4,200'
Incorporated: 2/9/1887
Mayor: Belinda Buswell

Junction City
County: Lane
Address: PO Box 250, 680 Greenwood St., 97448
Phone: 541-998-2153
Fax: 541-998-3140
Web: https://www.junctioncityoregon.gov
Elevation: 325'
Incorporated: 10/29/1872
Mayor: Beverly Ficek

Keizer
County: Marion
Address: PO Box 21000, 930 Chemawa Rd. NE, 97303
Phone: 503-390-3700
Fax: 503-393-9437
Web: https://www.keizer.org
Elevation: 132'
Incorporated: 11/16/1982
Mayor: Cathy Clark

King City
County: Washington
Address: 15300 SW 116th Ave., 97224-2693
Phone: 503-639-4082
Fax: 503-639-3771
Web: http://www.ci.king-city.or.us
Elevation: 213'
Incorporated: 7/14/1966
Mayor: Ken Gibson

*Klamath Falls
County: Klamath
Address: PO Box 237, 500 Klamath Ave., 97601
Phone: 541-883-5316
Fax: 541-883-5399
Web: https://www.klamathfalls.city
Elevation: 4,099'
Incorporated: 2/6/1893
Mayor: Carol Westfall

*La Grande
County: Union
Address: PO Box 670, 1000 Adams Ave., 97850
Phone: 541-962-1309
Fax: 541-963-3333
Web: http://www.cityoflagrande.org/
Elevation: 2,785'
Incorporated: 12/18/1865
Mayor: Steve Clements

La Pine
County: Deschutes
Address: PO Box 2460, 16345 Sixth St., 97739
Phone: 541-536-1432
Fax: 541-536-1462
Web: https://www.lapineoregon.gov
Elevation: 4,236'
Incorporated: 12/11/2006
Mayor: Daniel L. Richer

Lafayette
County: Yamhill
Address: PO Box 55, 486 Third St., 97127
Phone: 503-864-2451
Fax: 503-864-4501
Web: https://www.ci.lafayette.or.us
Elevation: 160'
Incorporated: 10/17/1878
Mayor: Wade Witherspoon

Lake Oswego
County: Clackamas
Address: PO Box 369, 380 A Ave., 97034
Phone: 503-635-0290
Fax: 503-635-0269
Web: http://www.ci.oswego.or.us
Elevation: 146'
Incorporated: 1/15/1910
Mayor: Joe Buck

Lakeside
County: Coos
Address: PO Box L, 915 North Lake Rd., 97449
Phone: 541-759-3011
Fax: 541-759-3711
Web: https://www.cityoflakeside.org
Elevation: 23'
Incorporated: 6/26/1974
Mayor: James Edwards

*Lakeview
County: Lake
Address: 525 N First St., 97630
Phone: 541-947-2029
Fax: 541-947-2952
Web: https://townoflakeview.org
Elevation: 4,802'
Incorporated: 2/10/1893
Mayor: Ray Turner

Lebanon
County: Linn
Address: 925 S Main St., 97355
Phone: 541-258-4900
Fax: 541-258-4950
Web: https://www.ci.lebanon.or.us
Elevation: 351'
Incorporated: 10/17/1878
Mayor: Paul Aziz

Lexington
County: Morrow
Address: PO Box 416, 97839
Phone: 541-989-8515
Fax: 541-989-8515
Web: http://www.lexingtonoregon.com
Elevation: 1,450'
Incorporated: 2/3/1903
Mayor: Juli A. Kennedy

Lincoln City
County: Lincoln
Address: PO Box 50, 801 SW Hwy. 101, 97367
Phone: 541-996-2152
Fax: 541-994-7232
Web: https://www.lincolncity.org
Elevation: 11'
Incorporated: 2/24/1965
Mayor: Dick Anderson

Lonerock
County: Gilliam
Address: Lonerock Rte., 104 SE Main St., Condon 97823
Phone: 541-384-2241
Email: lonerock@reagan.com
Elevation: 2,800'
Incorporated: 2/20/1901
Mayor: Shannon N. Hill

Long Creek
County: Grant
Address: PO Box 489, 250 Hardisty St., 97856
Phone: 541-421-3601
Fax: 541-421-3075
Web: http://www.cityoflongcreek.com
Elevation: 3,754'
Incorporated: 2/18/1891
Mayor: Don Porter

Lostine
County: Wallowa
Address: PO Box 181, 97857
Phone: 541-569-2415
Web: https://www.cityoflostine.com
Elevation: 3,200'
Incorporated: 12/28/1903
Mayor: Dusty Tippet

Lowell
County: Lane
Address: PO Box 490, 107 E Third St., 97452
Phone: 541-937-2157
Fax: 541-937-2936
Web: https://www.ci.lowell.or.us
Elevation: 742'
Incorporated: 11/24/1954
Mayor: Don Bennett

Lyons
County: Linn
Address: 449 Fifth St., 97358
Phone: 503-859-2167
Fax: 503-859-5167
Web: https://www.cityoflyons.org
Elevation: 660'
Incorporated: 12/17/1958
Mayor: Lloyd R. Valentine, Jr.

*Madras
County: Jefferson
Address: 125 SW E St., 97741
Phone: 541-475-2344
Fax: 541-475-7061
Web: https://www.ci.madras.or.us
Elevation: 2,242'

Incorporated: 3/29/1910
Mayor: Richard Ladeby

Malin
County: Klamath
Address: PO Box 61, 2432 Fourth St., 97632
Phone: 541-723-2021
Fax: 541-723-2011
Web: http://www.cityofmalin.org
Elevation: 4,062'
Incorporated: 2/22/1922
Mayor: Gary R. Zieg

Manzanita
County: Tillamook
Address: PO Box 129, 543 Laneda Ave., 97130
Phone: 503-368-5343
Fax: 503-368-4145
Web: https://ci.manzanita.or.us
Elevation: 78'
Incorporated: 4/15/1946
Mayor: Mike Scott

Maupin
County: Wasco
Address: PO Box 308, 408 Deschutes Ave., 97037
Phone: 541-395-2698
Fax: 541-395-2499
Web: http://cityofmaupin.org
Elevation: 1,047'
Incorporated: 4/17/1922
Mayor: Lynn Ewing

Maywood Park
County: Multnomah
Address: 10100 NE Prescott St., Suite 147, Portland 97220
Phone: 503-255-9805
Web: https://cityofmaywoodpark.com
Elevation: 77'
Incorporated: 10/25/1967
Mayor: Michelle Montross

*McMinnville
County: Yamhill
Address: 230 NE Second St., 97128
Phone: 503-435-5702
Fax: 503-472-4104
Web: https://www.mcminnvilleoregon.gov
Elevation: 157'
Incorporated: 10/20/1876
Mayor: Scott A. Hill

*Medford
County: Jackson
Address: 411 W Eighth St., Suite 310, 97501
Phone: 541-774-2000
Fax: 541-618-1700
Web: http://www.ci.medford.or.us
Elevation: 1,382'
Incorporated: 2/24/1885
Mayor: Randy Sparacino

Merrill
County: Klamath
Address: PO Box 487, 301 E Second St., 97633

Phone: 541-798-5808
Fax: 541-798-0145
Web: http://www.cityofmerrill.org
Elevation: 4,071'
Incorporated: 7/16/1908
Mayor: William V. Carlson, Sr.

Metolius
County: Jefferson
Address: 636 Jefferson Ave., 97741
Phone: 541-546-5533
Fax: 541-546-8809
Web: https://www.cityofmetolius.org
Elevation: 2,530'
Incorporated: 12/16/1912
Mayor: Patty Wyler

Mill City
County: Linn/Marion
Address: PO Box 256, 444 S First Ave., 97360
Phone: 503-897-2302
Fax: 503-897-3499
Web: http://www.ci.mill-city.or.us
Elevation: 862'
Incorporated: 10/15/1947
Mayor: Tim Kirsch

Millersburg
County: Linn
Address: 4222 NE Old Salem Rd., Albany 97321
Phone: 541-928-4523
Fax: 541-928-8945
Web: http://cityofmillersburg.org
Elevation: 235'
Incorporated: 11/4/1974
Mayor: Jim Lepin

Milton-Freewater
County: Umatilla
Address: PO Box 6, 722 S Main St., 97862
Phone: 541-938-5531
Fax: 541-938-8224
Web: https://www.mfcity.com
Elevation: 1,071'
Incorporated: 12/4/1950
Mayor: Lewis S. Key

The Milwaukie Masonic Lodge in Milwaukie.was constructed in 1925. (Oregon State Archives scenic photo)

Milwaukie
County: Clackamas
Address: 10722 SE Main St., 97222
Phone: 503-786-7555
Web: https://www.milwaukieoregon.gov
Elevation: 50'
Incorporated: 2/4/1903
Mayor: Mark Gamba

Mitchell
County: Wheeler
Address: PO Box 97, 97750
Phone: 541-462-3121
Fax: 541-462-3121
Web: mitchelloregon.us
Elevation: 2,894'
Incorporated: 2/18/1891
Mayor: Steven Trip

Molalla
County: Clackamas
Address: PO Box 248, 117 N Molalla Ave., 97038
Phone: 503-829-6855
Fax: 503-829-3676
Web: https://www.cityofmolalla.com
Elevation: 375'
Incorporated: 8/23/1913
Mayor: Scott Keyser

Monmouth
County: Polk
Address: 151 W Main St., 97361
Phone: 503-838-0722
Fax: 503-838-0725
Web: http://www.ci.monmouth.or.us
Elevation: 214'
Incorporated: 10/19/1880
Mayor: Cecelia Koontz

Monroe
County: Benton
Address: PO Box 486, 664 Commercial St., 97456
Phone: 541-847-5175
Fax: 541-847-5177
Web: https://ci.monroe.or.us
Elevation: 298'
Incorporated: 5/16/1913
Mayor: Daniel Sheets

Monument
County: Grant
Address: PO Box 426, 291 Main St., 97864
Phone: 541-934-2025
Fax: 541-934-2025
Email: cityofmonument@centurytel.net
Elevation: 2,000'
Incorporated: 3/6/1905
Mayor: Sahara Hyder

*Moro
County: Sherman
Address: PO Box 231, 97039
Phone: 541-565-3535
Fax: 541-565-3535

Web: http://www.cityofmoro.net
Elevation: 1,870'
Incorporated: 2/17/1899
Mayor: Bert Perisho

Mosier
County: Wasco
Address: PO Box 456, 208 Washington St., 97040
Phone: 541-478-3505
Fax: 541-478-3810
Web: https://cityofmosier.com
Elevation: 164'
Incorporated: 10/14/1914
Mayor: Arlene Burns

Mount Angel
County: Marion
Address: PO Box 960, 5 N Garfield St., 97362
Phone: 503-845-9291
Fax: 503-845-6261
Web: http://www.ci.mt-angel.or.us
Elevation: 168'
Incorporated: 2/10/1893
Mayor: Don R. Fleck

Mount Vernon
County: Grant
Address: PO Box 647, 97865
Phone: 541-932-4688
Fax: 541-932-4222
Email: cmtv@ortelco.net
Elevation: 2,865'
Incorporated: 5/13/1949
Mayor: Kenny Delano

Myrtle Creek
County: Douglas
Address: PO Box 940, 207 NW Pleasant St., 97457
Phone: 541-863-3171
Fax: 541-863-6851
Web: http://www.cityofmyrtlecreek.com
Elevation: 650'
Incorporated: 2/13/1893
Mayor: Matthew Hald

An antique car in downtown Myrtle Creek. (Oregon State Archives scenic photo)

Myrtle Point
County: Coos
Address: 424 Fifth St., 97458
Phone: 541-572-2626
Fax: 541-572-3838
Web: http://www.ci.myrtlepoint.or.us
Elevation: 131'
Incorporated: 2/4/1887
Mayor: Mike West

Nehalem
County: Tillamook
Address: PO Box 143, 35900 Eighth St., 97131
Phone: 503-368-5627
Fax: 503-368-4175
Web: https://www.ci.nehalem.or.us
Elevation: 11'
Incorporated: 2/2/1899
Mayor: William L. Dillard, Jr.

Newberg
County: Yamhill
Address: PO Box 970, 414 E First St., 97132
Phone: 503-538-9421
Fax: 503-537-5013
Web: https://www.newbergoregon.gov
Elevation: 175'
Incorporated: 2/21/1889
Mayor: Rick Rogers

*Newport
County: Lincoln
Address: 169 SW Coast Hwy., 97365
Phone: 541-574-0603
Fax: 541-574-0609
Web: http://www.newportoregon.gov
Elevation: 134'
Incorporated: 10/23/1882
Mayor: Dean H. Sawyer

North Bend
County: Coos
Address: PO Box B, 835 California St., 97459
Phone: 541-756-8500
Fax: 541-756-8527
Web: http://www.northbendoregon.us
Elevation: 41'
Incorporated: 7/6/1903
Mayor: Jessica Engelke

North Plains
County: Washington
Address: 31360 NW Commercial St., 97133
Phone: 503-647-5555
Fax: 503-647-2031
Web: https://www.northplains.org
Elevation: 176'
Incorporated: 10/1/1963
Mayor: Teri Lenahan

North Powder
County: Union
Address: PO Box 309, 635 Third St., 97867
Phone: 541-898-2185
Fax: 541-898-2647
Email: cityofnp@eoni.com

Elevation: 3,256'
Incorporated: 7/28/1902
Mayor: Mike Wisdom

Nyssa
County: Malheur
Address: 301 Main St., 97913
Phone: 541-372-2264
Fax: 541-372-3737
Web: https://www.nyssacity.org
Elevation: 2,192'
Incorporated: 2/24/1903
Mayor: Betty Holcomb

Oakland
County: Douglas
Address: 637 NE Locust St., 97462
Phone: 541-459-4531
Fax: 541-459-4472
Web: http://www.oaklandoregon.org
Elevation: 484'
Incorporated: 10/17/1878
Mayor: Thomas Hasvold

Oakridge
County: Lane
Address: PO Box 1410, 48318 E First St., 97463
Phone: 541-782-2258
Fax: 541-782-1081
Web: https://www.ci.oakridge.or.us
Elevation: 1,240'
Incorporated: 1/22/1934
Mayor: Kathy Holston

Ontario
County: Malheur
Address: 444 SW Fourth St., 97914
Phone: 541-889-7684
Fax: 541-889-7121
Web: http://www.ontariooregon.org
Elevation: 2,150'
Incorporated: 9/9/1896
Mayor: Riley J. Hill

*Oregon City
County: Clackamas
Address: 625 Center St., 97045
Phone: 503-657-0891
Fax: 503-657-3339
Web: https://www.orcity.org
Elevation: 167'
Incorporated: 12/24/1844
Mayor: Rocky Smith, Jr. Commission President

Paisley
County: Lake
Address: PO Box 100, 705 Chewaucan St., 97636
Phone: 541-943-3173
Fax: 541-943-3982
Web: http://www.cityofpaisley.net
Elevation: 4,369'
Incorporated: 11/18/1911
Mayor: Ralph Paull

*Pendleton
County: Umatilla
Address: 500 SW Dorion Ave., 97801
Phone: 541-966-0200
Fax: 541-966-0231
Web: https://pendleton.or.us
Elevation: 1,200'
Incorporated: 10/25/1880
Mayor: John Turner

Philomath
County: Benton
Address: PO Box 400, 980 Applegate St., 97370
Phone: 541-929-6148
Fax: 541-929-3044
Web: https://www.ci.philomath.or.us
Elevation: 270'
Incorporated: 10/20/1882
Mayor: Chas Jones

Phoenix
County: Jackson
Address: PO Box 330, 112 W Second St., 97535
Phone: 541-535-1955
Fax: 541-535-5769
Web: http://www.phoenixoregon.gov
Elevation: 1,543'
Incorporated: 10/13/1910
Mayor: Terry Baker

Pilot Rock
County: Umatilla
Address: PO Box 130, 144 N Alder Pl., 97868
Phone: 541-443-2811
Fax: 541-443-2253
Web: https://cityofpilotrock.org
Elevation: 1,637'
Incorporated: 1/10/1902
Mayor: Virginia Carol Carnes

Port Orford
County: Curry
Address: PO Box 310, 555 W 20th St., 97465
Phone: 541-332-3681
Fax: 877-281-5307
Web: http://www.portorford.org
Elevation: 59'
Incorporated: 12/21/1911
Mayor: Pat Cox

*Portland
County: Clackamas/Multnomah/Washington
Address: 1221 SW Fourth Ave., Rm. 110, 97204
Phone: 503-823-4000
Fax: 503-823-3050
Web: https://www.portlandoregon.gov
Elevation: 77'
Incorporated: 1/23/1851
Mayor: Ted Wheeler

Powers
County: Coos
Address: PO Box 250, 275 Fir St., 97466
Phone: 541-439-3331
Email: admin@cityofpowers.com
Elevation: 286'

Incorporated: 12/26/1945
Mayor: Robert Kohn

Prairie City
County: Grant
Address: PO Box 370, 133 S Bridge St., 97869
Phone: 541-820-3605
Fax: 541-820-3566
Web: http://cityofprairiecity.com
Elevation: 3,548'
Incorporated: 2/19/1891
Mayor: Jim Hamsher

Prescott
County: Columbia
Address: 72742 Blakely St., Rainier 97048
Phone: 503-369-0281
Email: jl.oswald@hotmail.com
Elevation: 30'
Incorporated: 5/9/1949
Mayor: Larry Hudnall

*Prineville
County: Crook
Address: 387 NE Third St., 97754
Phone: 541-447-5627
Fax: 541-447-5628
Web: https://www.cityofprineville.com
Elevation: 2,868'
Incorporated: 10/23/1880
Mayor: Rodney Jason Beebe

Rainier
County: Columbia
Address: PO Box 100, 106 West B St., 97048
Phone: 503-556-7301
Fax: 503-556-3200
Web: http://www.cityofrainier.com
Elevation: 45'
Incorporated: 11/25/1885
Mayor: Jerry Cole

Redmond
County: Deschutes
Address: 411 SW 9th St., 97756
Phone: 541-923-7710
Web: https://www.ci.redmond.or.us
Elevation: 3,077'
Incorporated: 7/16/1910
Mayor: George Endicott

Reedsport
County: Douglas
Address: 451 Winchester Ave., 97467
Phone: 541-271-3603
Web: https://www.cityofreedsport.org
Elevation: 36'
Incorporated: 8/6/1919
Mayor: Linda R. McCollum

Richland
County: Baker
Address: PO Box 266, 89 Main St., 97870
Phone: 541-893-6141
Fax: 541-893-6267
Email: richcity@eagletelephone.com

Elevation: 2,231'
Incorporated: 8/8/1902
Mayor: Patrick Lattin

Riddle
County: Douglas
Address: PO Box 143, 647 E First Ave., 97469
Phone: 541-874-2571
Fax: 541-874-2625
Email: coriddle@frontiernet.net
Elevation: 685'
Incorporated: 1/30/1893
Mayor: William "Bill" G. Duckett

Rivergrove
County: Clackamas/Washington
Address: PO Box 1104, Lake Oswego 97035
Phone: 503-639-6919
Web: https://www.cityofrivergrove.org
Elevation: 140'
Incorporated: 3/11/1971
Mayor: Walt Williams

Rockaway Beach
County: Tillamook
Address: PO Box 5, 276 S Hwy. 101, 97136
Phone: 503-355-2291
Fax: 503-355-8221
Web: https://rockawaybeachor.us
Elevation: 17'
Incorporated: 7/14/1943
Mayor: Susan Wilson

Rogue River
County: Jackson
Address: PO Box 1137, 133 Broadway, 97537
Phone: 541-582-4401
Fax: 541-582-0937
Web: https://www.cityofrogueriver.org
Elevation: 1,004'
Incorporated: 10/8/1910
Mayor: Wayne Stuart

*Roseburg
County: Douglas
Address: 900 SE Douglas Ave., 97470-3397
Phone: 541-492-6700
Web: http://www.cityofroseburg.org
Elevation: 475'
Incorporated: 10/26/1868
Mayor: Larry Rich

Rufus
County: Sherman
Address: PO Box 27, 304 W Second St., #100, 97050
Phone: 541-739-2321
Fax: 541-739-8229
Email: rufuscityhall@gmail.com
Elevation: 235'
Incorporated: 11/3/1964
Mayor: Dowen Jones

*Saint Helens
County: Columbia
Address: PO Box 278, 265 Strand St., 97051

Phone: 503-397-6272
Fax: 503-397-4016
Web: https://www.ci.st-helens.or.us
Elevation: 42'
Incorporated: 2/25/1889
Mayor: Rick Scholl

The St. Helens Marina on the Columbia River in Saint Helens. (Oregon State Archives scenic photo)

Saint Paul
County: Marion
Address: PO Box 7, 20239 Main St., 97137
Phone: 503-633-4971
Fax: 503-633-4972
Email: stpaulcity@stpaultel.com
Elevation: 169'
Incorporated: 2/16/1901
Mayor: Marty Waldo

*Salem
County: Marion/Polk
Address: 555 Liberty St. SE, 97301
Phone: 503-588-6255
Fax: 503-588-6354
Web: https://www.cityofsalem.net
Elevation: 154'
Incorporated: 1/13/1857
Mayor: Chuck Bennett

Sandy
County: Clackamas
Address: 39250 Pioneer Blvd., 97055
Phone: 503-668-5533
Fax: 503-668-8714
Web: https://www.ci.sandy.or.us
Elevation: 992'
Incorporated: 9/11/1911
Mayor: Stan P. Pulliam

Scappoose
County: Columbia
Address: 33568 E Columbia Ave., 97056
Phone: 503-543-7146
Fax: 503-543-7182
Web: http://www.ci.scappoose.or.us
Elevation: 64'
Incorporated: 8/13/1921
Mayor: Scott Burge

Scio
County: Linn
Address: PO Box 37, 97374-0037
Phone: 503-394-3342
Fax: 503-394-2340
Web: http://ci.scio.or.us/home%20page.htm
Elevation: 317'
Incorporated: 10/24/1866
Mayor: Gary Chad Weaver

Scotts Mills
County: Marion
Address: 265 Fourth St., PO Box 220, 97375
Phone: 503-873-5435
Fax: 503-874-4540
Web: https://www.scottsmills.org
Elevation: 426'
Incorporated: 8/2/1916
Mayor: Paul Brakeman

Seaside
County: Clatsop
Address: 989 Broadway, 97138
Phone: 503-738-5511
Fax: 503-738-5514
Web: http://www.cityofseaside.us
Elevation: 17'
Incorporated: 2/17/1899
Mayor: Jay Barber

Seneca
County: Grant
Address: PO Box 208, 106 A Ave., 97873
Phone: 541-542-2161
Fax: 877-688-0015
Email: admin@senecaoregon.com
Elevation: 4,690'
Incorporated: 8/6/1970
Mayor: Brad Smith

Shady Cove
County: Jackson
Address: PO Box 1210, 97539
Phone: 541-878-2225
Fax: 541-878-2226
Web: http://www.shadycove.net
Elevation: 1,406'
Incorporated: 11/8/1972
Mayor: Shari Tarvin

Shaniko
County: Wasco
Address: PO Box 17, 97057
Phone: 541-489-3447
Web: http://www.shanikooregon.com
Elevation: 3,344'
Incorporated: 3/13/1901
Mayor: Don Treanor

Sheridan
County: Yamhill
Address: 120 SW Mill St., 97378
Phone: 503-843-2347
Fax: 503-843-3661
Web: https://www.cityofsheridanor.com
Elevation: 189'

Incorporated: 10/25/1880
Mayor: Harry F. Cooley

Sherwood
County: Washington
Address: 22560 SW Pine St., 97140
Phone: 503-625-5522
Fax: 503-625-5524
Web: http://www.sherwoodoregon.gov
Elevation: 193'
Incorporated: 2/10/1893
Mayor: Keith Mays

Siletz
County: Lincoln
Address: PO Box 318, 215 W Buford Ave., 97380
Phone: 541-444-2521
Fax: 541-444-7371
Web: http://www.cityofsiletz.org
Elevation: 130'
Incorporated: 3/31/1947
Mayor: Will Worman

Silverton
County: Marion
Address: 306 S Water St., 97381
Phone: 503-873-5321
Fax: 503-873-3210
Web: http://www.silverton.or.us
Elevation: 252'
Incorporated: 2/16/1885
Mayor: Kyle B. Palmer

*Buildings overlook Silver Creek in downtown Silverton.
(Oregon State Archives scenic photo)*

Sisters
County: Deschutes
Address: PO Box 39, 520 E Cascade Ave., 97759
Phone: 541-549-6022
Fax: 541-549-0561
Web: https://www.ci.sisters.or.us
Elevation: 3,182'
Incorporated: 4/9/1946
Mayor: Michael Preedin

Sodaville
County: Linn
Address: 30723 Sodaville Rd., 97355
Phone: 541-258-8882

Fax: 541-258-8882
Web: http://www.sodaville.org
Elevation: 492'
Incorporated: 10/25/1880
Mayor: Lori McAllen

Spray
County: Wheeler
Address: PO Box 83, 300 Park Ave., 97874
Phone: 541-468-2069
Fax: 541-468-2044
Web: http://sprayoregon.us
Elevation: 1,801'
Incorporated: 9/18/1958
Mayor: Valerie Howell

Springfield
County: Lane
Address: 225 Fifth St., 97477
Phone: 541-726-3700
Fax: 541-726-2363
Web: http://www.springfield-or.gov
Elevation: 456'
Incorporated: 2/25/1885
Mayor: Christine Lundberg

Stanfield
County: Umatilla
Address: PO Box 369, 160 S Main St., 97875
Phone: 541-449-3831
Fax: 541-449-1828
Web: https://cityofstanfield.com
Elevation: 592'
Incorporated: 5/13/1910
Mayor: Thomas J. McCann

Stayton
County: Marion
Address: 362 N Third Ave., 97383
Phone: 503-769-3425
Fax: 503-769-1456
Web: http://www.staytonoregon.gov
Elevation: 452'
Incorporated: 2/13/1901
Mayor: Henry (Hank) A. Porter

Sublimity
County: Marion
Address: PO Box 146, 245 NW Johnson St., 97385
Phone: 503-769-5475
Fax: 503-769-2206
Web: http://www.cityofsublimity.org
Elevation: 551'
Incorporated: 2/3/1903
Mayor: James Kingsbury

Summerville
County: Union
Address: 301 Main St., 97876
Phone: 541-534-6701
Email: sherirogers46@gmail.com
Elevation: 2,705'
Incorporated: 11/24/1885
Mayor: Sheri Rogers

Sumpter
County: Baker
Address: PO Box 68, 240 N Mill St., 97877
Phone: 541-894-2314
Fax: 541-894-2375
Email: cityofsumpter@qwestoffice.net
Elevation: 4,429'
Incorporated: 5/5/1898
Mayor: Greg Lucas

Sutherlin
County: Douglas
Address: 126 E Central Ave., 97479
Phone: 541-459-2856
Fax: 541-459-9363
Web: http://www.ci.sutherlin.or.us
Elevation: 516'
Incorporated: 5/4/1911
Mayor: Todd McKnight

Sweet Home
County: Linn
Address: 1140 12th Ave., 97386
Phone: 541-367-5128
Fax: 541-367-5113
Web: https://www.sweethomeor.gov
Elevation: 537'
Incorporated: 2/10/1893
Mayor: Greg Mahler

Talent
County: Jackson
Address: PO Box 445, 110 E Main St., 97540
Phone: 541-535-1566
Fax: 541-535-7423
Web: www.cityoftalent.org
Elevation: 1,635'
Incorporated: 11/25/1910
Mayor: Darby Ayers-Flood

Tangent
County: Linn
Address: PO Box 251, 32166 Old Oak Dr., 97389
Phone: 541-928-1020
Fax: 541-928-4920
Web: http://www.cityoftangent.org
Elevation: 245'
Incorporated: 2/10/1893
Mayor: Loel E. Trulove, Jr.

*The Dalles
County: Wasco
Address: 313 Court St., 97058
Phone: 541-296-5481
Fax: 541-296-6906
Web: http://www.thedalles.org
Elevation: 109'
Incorporated: 1/26/1857
Mayor: Rich Mays

Tigard
County: Washington
Address: 13125 SW Hall Blvd., 97223
Phone: 503-639-4171
Fax: 503-684-7297
Web: http://www.tigard-or.gov
Elevation: 300'
Incorporated: 10/3/1961
Mayor: Jason B. Snider

*Tillamook
County: Tillamook
Address: 210 Laurel Ave., 97141
Phone: 503-842-2472
Fax: 503-842-3445
Web: http://tillamookor.gov
Elevation: 24'
Incorporated: 2/18/1891
Mayor: Suzanne Weber

Toledo
County: Lincoln
Address: PO Box 220, 206 N Main St., 97391
Phone: 541-336-2247
Fax: 541-336-3512
Web: http://www.cityoftoledo.org
Elevation: 59'
Incorporated: 10/11/1893
Mayor: Rod Cross

Troutdale
County: Multnomah
Address: 219 E Historic Columbia River Hwy., 97060
Phone: 503-665-5175
Fax: 503-667-6403
Web: https://www.troutdaleoregon.gov
Elevation: 30'–200'
Incorporated: 10/3/1907
Mayor: Randy Lauer

Tualatin
County: Clackamas/Washington
Address: 18880 SW Martinazzi Ave., 97062
Phone: 503-692-2000
Fax: 503-692-5421
Web: https://www.tualatinoregon.gov
Elevation: 123'
Incorporated: 5/8/1913
Mayor: Frank Bubenik

Turner
County: Marion
Address: PO Box 456, 5255 Chicago St., SE, 97392
Phone: 503-743-2155
Fax: 503-743-4010
Web: https://www.cityofturner.org
Elevation: 287'
Incorporated: 2/10/1905
Mayor: Steve Horning

Ukiah
County: Umatilla
Address: PO Box 265, 97880
Phone: 541-427-3900
Fax: 541-427-3902
Web: http://www.cityofukiahoregon.com
Elevation: 3,400'
Incorporated: 5/23/1972
Mayor: Clinton Barber

Umatilla

County: Umatilla
Address: PO Box 130, 700 Sixth St., 97882
Phone: 541-922-3226
Fax: 541-922-5758
Web: https://www.umatilla-city.org
Elevation: 322'
Incorporated: 10/24/1864
Mayor: Mary Dedrick

Union

County: Union
Address: PO Box 529, 342 S Main, 97883
Phone: 541-562-5197
Fax: 541-562-5196
Web: https://www.cityofunion.com
Elevation: 2,791'
Incorporated: 10/19/1878
Mayor: Leonard L. Flint

Unity

County: Baker
Address: 1995 Third St., Baker City 97814
Phone: 541-523-8200
Fax: 541-523-8201
Web: https://www.bakercounty.org
Elevation: 4,040'
Incorporated: 7/31/1972
General Manager: Mark Bennett

*Vale

County: Malheur
Address: 252 B St. W, 97918
Phone: 541-473-3133
Fax: 541-473-3895
Web: https://www.cityofvale.com
Elevation: 2,343'
Incorporated: 2/21/1889
Mayor: Tom Vialpendo

Veneta

County: Lane
Address: PO Box 458, 88184 Eighth St., 97487
Phone: 541-935-2191
Fax: 541-935-1838
Web: https://www.venetaoregon.gov
Elevation: 418'
Incorporated: 5/4/1962
Mayor: Keith Weiss

Vernonia

County: Columbia
Address: 1001 Bridge St., 97064
Phone: 503-429-5291
Fax: 503-429-4232
Web: http://www.vernonia-or.gov
Elevation: 635'
Incorporated: 2/18/1891
Mayor: Rick Hobart

Waldport

County: Lincoln
Address: PO Box 1120, 125 Alsea Hwy., 97394
Phone: 541-264-7417
Fax: 541-264-7418
Web: http://www.waldport.org

Elevation: 12'
Incorporated: 3/11/1911
Mayor: Greg L. Holland

Wallowa

County: Wallowa
Address: PO Box 487, 97885
Phone: 541-886-2422
Fax: 541-886-4215
Web: https://cityofwallowa.weebly.com
Elevation: 2,950'
Incorporated: 1/18/1909
Mayor: Gary Lee Hulse

Warrenton

County: Clatsop
Address: PO Box 250, 225 S Main Ave., 97146
Phone: 503-861-2233
Fax: 503-861-2351
Web: http://www.ci.warrenton.or.us
Elevation: 8'
Incorporated: 2/11/1899
Mayor: Henry Balensifer, III

Wasco

County: Sherman
Address: PO Box 26, 1017 Clark St., 97065
Phone: 541-442-5515
Fax: 541-442-5001
Web: http://www.wascooregon.com
Elevation: 1,281'
Incorporated: 4/14/1898
Mayor: Beth McCurdy

Waterloo

County: Linn
Address: PO Box 1066, 31140 First St., Lebanon 97355
Phone: 541-451-2245
Fax: 541-451-3133
Email: main@waterlooor.com
Elevation: 402'
Incorporated: 2/15/1893
Mayor: Justin Cary

West Linn

County: Clackamas
Address: 22500 Salamo Rd., #100, 97068
Phone: 503-657-0331
Fax: 503-650-9041
Web: https://westlinnoregon.gov
Elevation: 642'
Incorporated: 8/15/1913
Mayor: Jules Walters

Westfir

County: Lane
Address: PO Box 296, 47441 Westoak Rd., 97492
Phone: 541-782-3983
Web: http://www.westfir-oregon.com
Elevation: 1,075'
Incorporated: 2/6/1979
Mayor: Melody Cornelius

Weston
County: Umatilla
Address: PO Box 579, 114 Main St., 97886
Phone: 541-566-3313
Fax: 541-566-2792
Web: http://www.cityofwestonoregon.com
Elevation: 1,796'
Incorporated: 10/19/1878
Mayor: Duane Thul

Wheeler
County: Tillamook
Address: PO Box 177, 97147
Phone: 503-368-5767
Fax: 503-368-4273
Web: https://ci.wheeler.or.us
Elevation: 37'
Incorporated: 6/11/1913
Mayor: Doug Honeycutt

An Oregon Coast Scenic Railroad stop in Wheeler. (Oregon State Archives scenic photo)

Willamina
County: Polk/Yamhill
Address: 411 NE C St., 97396
Phone: 503-876-2242
Fax: 503-876-1121
Web: https://www.willaminaoregon.gov
Elevation: 225'
Incorporated: 2/13/1903
Mayor: Bob Burr

Wilsonville
County: Clackamas/Washington
Address: 29799 SW Town Center Lp. E, 97070
Phone: 503-682-1011
Fax: 503-682-1015
Web: https://www.ci.wilsonville.or.us
Elevation: 179'
Incorporated: 10/10/1968
Mayor: Julie Fitzgerald

Winston
County: Douglas
Address: 201 NW Douglas Blvd., 97496
Phone: 541-679-6739
Fax: 541-679-0794
Web: https://winstoncity.org
Elevation: 534'
Incorporated: 6/29/1953
Mayor: D. Scott Rutter

Wood Village
County: Multnomah
Address: 2055 NE 238th Dr., 97060
Phone: 503-667-6211
Fax: 503-669-8723
Web: https://www.woodvillageor.gov
Elevation: 90'–330'
Incorporated: 2/9/1951
Mayor: T. Scott Harden

Woodburn
County: Marion
Address: 270 Montgomery St., 97071
Phone: 503-982-5222
Fax: 503-982-5243
Web: http://www.woodburn-or.gov
Elevation: 197'
Incorporated: 2/20/1889
Mayor: Eric Swenson

Yachats
County: Lincoln
Address: PO Box 345, 441 Hwy. 101 N, #2, 97498
Phone: 541-547-3565
Fax: 541-547-3063
Web: https://yachatsoregon.org
Elevation: 45'
Incorporated: 7/18/1966
Mayor: Leslie Vaaler

Yamhill
County: Yamhill
Address: PO Box 9, 205 S Maple St., 97148
Phone: 503-662-3511
Fax: 503-662-4589
Web: https://cityofyamhill.org
Elevation: 182'
Incorporated: 2/20/1891
Mayor: Yvette Potter

Yoncalla
County: Douglas
Address: PO Box 508, 2640 Eagle Valley Rd., 97499
Phone: 541-849-2152
Fax: 541-849-2552
Web: https://www.cityofyoncalla.org
Elevation: 367'
Incorporated: 2/27/1901
Mayor: Stacey L. Atwell-Keister

CITY POPULATIONS: 1980–2020

Source: Population Research Center, Portland State University
Phone: 503-725-3922

*Change in population between 2010 and 2020

Cities or counties that share rank numbers are tied in rank.

Rank	City	% Change*	2020	2010	2000	1990	1980
158	Adair Village	31.5	1,105	840	536	554	589
204	Adams	2.7	375	365	297	223	240
224	Adrian	8.6	190	175	147	131	162
11	Albany	9.2	54,935	50,325	40,852	29,540	26,511
135	Amity	5.6	1,705	1,615	1,478	1,175	1,092
237	Antelope	11.1	50	45	59	34	39
186	Arlington	5.1	615	585	524	425	521
28	Ashland	5.0	21,105	20,095	19,522	16,252	14,943
54	Astoria	2.1	9,675	9,475	9,813	10,069	9,996
152	Athena	4.0	1,170	1,125	1,221	997	965
83	Aumsville	16.9	4,215	3,605	3,003	1,650	1,432
163	Aurora	7.1	985	920	655	523	306
50	Baker City	1.8	10,010	9,830	9,860	9,140	9,471
98	Bandon	4.9	3,225	3,075	2,833	2,215	2,311
122	Banks	11.5	1,980	1,775	1,286	563	489
233	Barlow	0.0	135	135	140	118	105
145	Bay City	5.0	1,355	1,290	1,149	1,027	986
6	Beaverton	10.3	99,225	89,925	76,129	53,307	31,962
7	Bend	21.0	92,840	76,740	52,029	20,447	17,260
80	Boardman	42.2	4,580	3,220	2,855	1,387	1,261
195	Bonanza	-3.4	455	471	415	323	270
67	Brookings	5.0	6,670	6,350	5,447	4,400	3,384
133	Brownsville	3.6	1,730	1,670	1,449	1,281	1,261
104	Burns	1.1	2,835	2,805	3,064	2,913	3,579
194	Butte Falls	8.2	460	425	439	252	428
34	Canby	8.7	17,210	15,830	12,790	8,990	7,659
132	Cannon Beach	2.7	1,740	1,695	1,588	1,221	1,187
178	Canyon City	0.0	705	705	669	648	639
121	Canyonville	5.3	1,985	1,885	1,293	1,219	1,288
111	Carlton	13.6	2,290	2,015	1,514	1,289	1,302
141	Cascade Locks	24.0	1,420	1,145	1,115	930	838
124	Cave Junction	4.8	1,975	1,885	1,363	1,126	1,023
32	Central Point	9.1	18,755	17,185	12,493	7,512	6,357
176	Chiloquin	0.7	740	735	716	673	778
129	Clatskanie	3.5	1,795	1,735	1,528	1,629	1,648
143	Coburg	32.2	1,375	1,040	969	763	699
122	Columbia City	1.8	1,980	1,945	1,571	1,003	678
181	Condon	0.0	685	685	759	635	783
36	Coos Bay	5.3	16,810	15,970	15,374	15,076	14,424
87	Coquille	1.4	3,920	3,865	4,184	4,121	4,481
42	Cornelius	6.4	12,635	11,875	9,652	6,148	4,402
10	Corvallis	9.7	59,730	54,460	49,322	44,757	40,960

Rank	City	% Change*	2020	2010	2000	1990	1980
49	Cottage Grove	4.6	10,155	9,705	8,445	7,403	7,148
188	Cove	0.9	555	550	594	507	451
74	Creswell	11.0	5,585	5,030	3,579	2,431	1,770
136	Culver	15.0	1,570	1,365	802	570	514
37	Dallas	13.5	16,555	14,590	12,459	9,422	8,530
105	Dayton	8.3	2,745	2,535	2,119	1,526	1,409
230	Dayville	3.3	155	150	138	144	199
140	Depoe Bay	3.6	1,450	1,400	1,174	870	723
219	Detroit	0.0	205	205	262	331	367
162	Donald	1.5	995	980	625	316	267
153	Drain	0.9	1,165	1,155	1,021	1,086	1,148
185	Dufur	3.3	625	605	588	527	560
96	Dundee	3.6	3,285	3,170	2,598	1,663	1,223
144	Dunes City	4.6	1,365	1,305	1,241	1,081	1,124
127	Durham	39.1	1,885	1,355	1,382	748	707
58	Eagle Point	10.7	9,375	8,470	4,797	3,008	2,764
177	Echo	2.9	720	700	650	500	624
133	Elgin	1.2	1,730	1,710	1,654	1,586	1,701
219	Elkton	5.1	205	195	147	172	155
120	Enterprise	2.8	1,995	1,940	1,895	1,905	2,003
86	Estacada	47.8	4,035	2,730	2,371	2,016	1,419
2	Eugene	11.1	173,620	156,295	137,893	112,733	105,664
56	Fairview	5.8	9,440	8,920	7,561	2,391	1,749
161	Falls City	5.8	1,000	945	966	818	804
59	Florence	5.4	8,925	8,465	7,263	5,171	4,411
22	Forest Grove	20.4	25,435	21,130	17,708	13,559	11,499
193	Fossil	0.0	475	475	469	399	535
171	Garibaldi	6.4	830	780	899	886	999
182	Gaston	3.1	655	635	600	563	471
189	Gates	13.7	540	475	471	499	455
138	Gearhart	5.5	1,545	1,465	995	1,027	967
106	Gervais	4.4	2,620	2,510	2,009	992	799
43	Gladstone	3.9	11,945	11,495	11,438	10,152	9,500
168	Glendale	-1.7	860	875	855	707	712
109	Gold Beach	2.4	2,310	2,255	1,897	1,546	1,515
148	Gold Hill	1.6	1,240	1,220	1,073	964	904
238	Granite	0.0	40	40	24	8	17
15	Grants Pass	9.2	37,725	34,555	23,003	17,503	15,032
227	Grass Valley	0.0	165	165	171	160	164
241	Greenhorn	0.0	2	2	0	0	0
4	Gresham	6.7	112,660	105,595	90,205	68,249	33,005
201	Haines	0.0	415	415	426	405	341
209	Halfway	3.4	300	290	337	311	380
165	Halsey	3.8	945	910	724	667	693
26	Happy Valley	58.9	22,400	14,100	4,519	1,519	1,499
88	Harrisburg	3.6	3,695	3,565	2,795	1,939	1,881
221	Helix	8.1	200	185	183	150	155
146	Heppner	0.4	1,295	1,290	1,395	1,412	1,498

Rank	City	% Change*	2020	2010	2000	1990	1980
31	Hermiston	11.8	18,775	16,795	13,154	10,047	8,408
5	Hillsboro	13.8	104,670	91,970	70,186	37,598	27,664
137	Hines	0.0	1,565	1,565	1,623	1,452	1,632
61	Hood River	19.3	8,565	7,180	5,831	4,632	4,329
94	Hubbard	4.4	3,315	3,175	2,483	1,881	1,640
196	Huntington	1.1	445	440	515	522	539
230	Idanha	14.8	155	135	232	289	319
208	Imbler	0.0	305	305	284	299	292
54	Independence	12.5	9,675	8,600	6,035	4,425	4,024
207	Ione	0.0	330	330	321	255	345
118	Irrigon	11.8	2,040	1,825	1,702	737	700
155	Island City	14.0	1,140	1,000	916	696	477
102	Jacksonville	9.2	3,040	2,785	2,235	1,896	2,030
97	Jefferson	5.3	3,280	3,115	2,487	1,805	1,702
130	John Day	0.0	1,750	1,750	1,821	1,836	2,012
187	Johnson City	0.0	565	565	634	586	378
225	Jordan Valley	-2.8	175	180	239	364	473
156	Joseph	3.2	1,120	1,085	1,054	1,073	999
71	Junction City	14.2	6,200	5,430	4,721	3,670	3,320
14	Keizer	5.5	38,585	36,570	32,203	21,884	--
81	King City	37.4	4,280	3,115	1,949	2,060	1,853
27	Klamath Falls	4.9	21,940	20,925	19,460	17,737	16,661
41	La Grande	2.8	13,460	13,095	12,327	11,766	11,354
119	La Pine	20.8	2,005	1,660	--	--	--
85	Lafayette	11.1	4,155	3,740	2,586	1,292	1,215
13	Lake Oswego	7.8	39,480	36,620	35,278	30,576	22,527
130	Lakeside	3.2	1,750	1,695	1,421	1,437	1,453
110	Lakeview	0.2	2,300	2,295	2,474	2,526	2,770
33	Lebanon	11.7	17,335	15,525	12,950	10,950	10,413
213	Lexington	10.4	265	240	263	286	307
60	Lincoln City	11.7	8,865	7,935	7,437	5,908	5,469
240	Lonerock	0.0	20	20	24	11	26
223	Long Creek	0.0	195	195	228	249	252
217	Lostine	0.0	215	215	263	231	250
159	Lowell	4.3	1,090	1,045	880	785	661
150	Lyons	3.4	1,200	1,160	1,008	938	877
70	Madras	6.9	6,470	6,050	5,078	3,443	2,235
173	Malin	1.9	820	805	640	725	539
183	Manzanita	7.5	645	600	564	513	443
199	Maupin	3.6	435	420	411	456	495
175	Maywood Park	0.0	750	750	777	781	845
17	McMinnville	7.4	34,615	32,240	26,499	17,894	14,080
8	Medford	10.8	83,115	74,980	63,687	47,021	39,746
169	Merrill	0.0	845	845	897	837	822
172	Metolius	16.2	825	710	729	450	451
126	Mill City	3.2	1,915	1,855	1,537	1,555	1,565
103	Millersburg	111.9	2,850	1,345	651	715	562
66	Milton-Freewater	2.3	7,210	7,045	6,470	5,533	5,086

Rank	City	% Change*	2020	2010	2000	1990	1980
29	Milwaukie	1.5	20,600	20,290	20,490	18,670	17,931
228	Mitchell	23.1	160	130	170	163	183
53	Molalla	22.2	9,910	8,110	5,647	3,651	2,992
52	Monmouth	4.1	9,940	9,545	7,741	6,288	5,594
184	Monroe	4.1	640	615	607	448	412
234	Monument	0.0	130	130	151	162	192
206	Moro	4.6	340	325	337	292	336
192	Mosier	12.6	490	435	410	244	340
90	Mount Angel	7.2	3,520	3,285	3,121	2,778	2,876
190	Mount Vernon	0.0	525	525	595	549	569
89	Myrtle Creek	4.7	3,600	3,440	3,419	3,063	3,365
107	Myrtle Point	0.8	2,535	2,515	2,451	2,712	2,859
212	Nehalem	5.6	285	270	203	232	258
25	Newberg	9.1	24,120	22,110	18,064	13,086	10,394
47	Newport	3.7	10,400	10,030	9,532	8,437	7,519
51	North Bend	2.9	9,975	9,695	9,544	9,614	9,779
92	North Plains	70.6	3,360	1,970	1,605	997	715
196	North Powder	1.1	445	440	489	448	430
93	Nyssa	2.3	3,340	3,265	3,163	2,629	2,862
164	Oakland	4.3	965	925	954	844	886
95	Oakridge	3.3	3,310	3,205	3,172	3,063	3,680
45	Ontario	1.3	11,515	11,365	10,985	9,394	8,814
16	Oregon City	12.2	35,885	31,995	25,754	14,698	14,673
209	Paisley	22.4	300	245	247	350	343
35	Pendleton	2.5	17,025	16,605	16,354	15,142	14,521
75	Philomath	17.0	5,370	4,590	3,838	2,983	2,673
79	Phoenix	2.6	4,660	4,540	4,060	3,239	2,309
139	Pilot Rock	0.0	1,505	1,505	1,532	1,478	1,630
154	Port Orford	1.3	1,150	1,135	1,153	1,025	1,061
1	Portland	13.8	664,605	583,775	529,121	438,802	366,383
179	Powers	1.4	700	690	734	682	819
167	Prairie City	0.5	915	910	1,080	1,117	1,106
236	Prescott	0.0	55	55	72	63	73
48	Prineville	11.8	10,355	9,260	7,358	5,355	5,276
125	Rainier	2.4	1,940	1,895	1,687	1,674	1,655
18	Redmond	22.8	32,215	26,225	13,481	7,165	6,452
82	Reedsport	1.9	4,230	4,150	4,378	4,796	4,984
225	Richland	12.9	175	155	147	161	181
151	Riddle	0.4	1,190	1,185	1,014	1,143	1,265
191	Rivergrove	75.9	510	290	324	294	314
142	Rockaway Beach	5.7	1,390	1,315	1,267	970	906
114	Rogue River	5.4	2,250	2,135	1,851	1,759	1,308
24	Roseburg	15.0	24,915	21,660	20,017	17,069	16,644
211	Rufus	16.0	290	250	268	295	352
40	Saint Helens	7.8	13,915	12,905	10,019	7,535	7,064
198	Saint Paul	4.8	440	420	354	322	312
3	Salem	8.9	168,970	155,100	136,924	107,793	89,091
44	Sandy	20.7	11,650	9,655	5,385	4,152	2,905

Rank	City	% Change*	2020	2010	2000	1990	1980
65	Scappoose	11.0	7,360	6,630	4,976	3,529	3,213
166	Scio	11.9	940	840	695	623	579
203	Scotts Mills	8.5	385	355	312	283	249
68	Seaside	1.6	6,565	6,460	5,900	5,359	5,193
221	Seneca	0.0	200	200	223	191	285
100	Shady Cove	8.1	3,140	2,905	2,307	1,351	1,097
239	Shaniko	0.0	35	35	26	26	30
72	Sheridan	-0.4	6,100	6,125	5,561	3,979	2,249
30	Sherwood	9.2	19,885	18,205	11,791	3,093	2,386
149	Siletz	2.1	1,235	1,210	1,133	992	1,001
46	Silverton	14.0	10,520	9,230	7,414	5,635	5,168
99	Sisters	57.8	3,220	2,040	959	708	696
205	Sodaville	14.5	355	310	290	192	171
228	Spray	0.0	160	160	140	149	155
9	Springfield	3.6	61,535	59,425	52,864	44,664	41,621
112	Stanfield	11.5	2,280	2,045	1,979	1,568	1,568
63	Stayton	3.1	7,880	7,645	6,816	5,011	4,396
101	Sublimity	13.8	3,050	2,680	2,148	1,491	1,077
233	Summerville	0.0	135	135	117	142	143
218	Sumpter	2.4	210	205	171	119	133
62	Sutherlin	5.4	8,260	7,840	6,669	5,020	4,560
57	Sweet Home	5.3	9,415	8,945	8,016	6,850	6,921
69	Talent	7.6	6,530	6,070	5,589	3,274	2,577
147	Tangent	8.6	1,265	1,165	933	556	478
39	The Dalles	8.9	14,845	13,630	12,156	11,021	10,820
12	Tigard	13.4	54,520	48,090	41,223	29,435	14,799
77	Tillamook	0.2	4,930	4,920	4,352	4,001	3,991
90	Toledo	1.4	3,520	3,470	3,472	3,174	3,151
38	Troutdale	1.3	16,180	15,980	13,777	7,852	5,908
19	Tualatin	4.4	27,195	26,060	22,791	14,664	7,483
108	Turner	29.9	2,410	1,855	1,199	1,281	1,116
215	Ukiah	29.7	240	185	255	250	249
64	Umatilla	10.1	7,605	6,905	4,978	3,046	3,199
115	Union	2.1	2,175	2,130	1,926	1,847	2,062
235	Unity	7.1	75	70	131	87	115
128	Vale	0.0	1,875	1,875	1,976	1,491	1,558
78	Veneta	6.1	4,845	4,565	2,762	2,519	2,449
117	Vernonia	-2.1	2,110	2,155	2,228	1,808	1,785
116	Waldport	4.4	2,125	2,035	2,050	1,595	1,274
170	Wallowa	3.7	840	810	869	748	847
76	Warrenton	7.0	5,350	5,000	4,096	2,681	2,493
200	Wasco	3.7	425	410	381	374	415
216	Waterloo	2.2	235	230	239	191	211
20	West Linn	3.3	25,975	25,150	22,261	16,389	11,358
213	Westfir	3.9	265	255	280	278	312
180	Weston	3.0	690	670	717	606	719
202	Wheeler	-3.6	400	415	391	335	319
113	Willamina	12.1	2,270	2,025	1,844	1,748	1,749
21	Wilsonville	32.7	25,915	19,525	13,991	7,106	2,920

Rank	City	% Change*	2020	2010	2000	1990	1980
73	Winston	4.4	5,620	5,385	4,613	3,773	3,359
84	Wood Village	8.1	4,190	3,875	2,860	2,814	2,253
23	Woodburn	4.6	25,185	24,085	20,100	13,404	11,196
174	Yachats	13.0	780	690	617	533	482
157	Yamhill	8.8	1,110	1,020	794	867	690
160	Yoncalla	2.4	1,075	1,050	1,052	919	805

COUNTY POPULATIONS: 1980–2020

Rank	County	% Change*	2020	2010	2000	1990	1980
28	Baker	4.5	16,910	16,185	16,741	15,317	16,134
11	Benton	10.4	94,665	85,735	78,153	70,811	68,211
3	Clackamas	13.2	426,515	376,780	338,391	278,850	241,911
19	Clatsop	6.4	39,455	37,070	35,630	33,301	32,489
17	Columbia	7.8	53,280	49,430	43,560	37,557	35,646
16	Coos	0.4	63,315	63,035	62,779	60,273	64,047
26	Crook	11.5	23,440	21,020	19,182	14,111	13,091
27	Curry	2.9	23,005	22,355	21,137	19,327	16,992
7	Deschutes	24.8	197,015	157,905	115,367	74,958	62,142
9	Douglas	4.5	112,530	107,690	100,399	94,649	93,748
34	Gilliam	6.4	1,990	1,870	1,915	1,717	2,057
31	Grant	-1.9	7,315	7,460	7,935	7,853	8,210
32	Harney	-2.2	7,280	7,445	7,609	7,060	8,314
24	Hood River	14.5	25,640	22,385	20,411	16,903	15,835
6	Jackson	9.8	223,240	203,340	181,269	146,389	132,456
25	Jefferson	10.8	24,105	21,750	19,009	13,676	11,599
12	Josephine	4.6	86,560	82,775	75,726	62,649	58,855
15	Klamath	2.4	68,075	66,505	63,775	57,702	59,117
30	Lake	2.3	8,075	7,890	7,422	7,186	7,532
4	Lane	8.3	381,365	352,010	322,959	282,912	275,226
18	Lincoln	4.7	48,305	46,135	44,479	38,889	35,264
8	Linn	9.0	127,320	116,840	103,069	91,227	89,495
20	Malheur	2.4	32,105	31,345	31,615	26,038	26,896
5	Marion	10.5	349,120	315,900	284,834	228,483	204,692
29	Morrow	14.8	12,825	11,175	10,995	7,625	7,519
1	Multnomah	12.6	829,560	736,785	660,486	583,887	562,647
13	Polk	11.0	83,805	75,495	62,380	49,541	45,203
35	Sherman	1.7	1,795	1,765	1,934	1,918	2,172
23	Tillamook	5.0	26,530	25,260	24,262	21,570	21,164
14	Umatilla	7.2	81,495	76,000	70,548	59,249	58,861
22	Union	4.0	26,840	25,810	24,530	23,598	23,921
33	Wallowa	2.2	7,160	7,005	7,226	6,911	7,273
21	Wasco	8.2	27,295	25,235	23,791	21,683	21,732
2	Washington	16.8	620,080	531,070	445,342	311,554	245,860
36	Wheeler	0.0	1,440	1,440	1,547	1,396	1,513
10	Yamhill	9.3	108,605	99,405	84,992	65,551	55,332
	Oregon	**11.2**	**4,268,055**	**3,837,300**	**3,421,399**	**2,842,321**	**2,633,156**

*Change in population between 2010 and 2018

COUNTY GOVERNMENT

The word "county" is from the Middle English word *conte*, meaning the office of a count. However, a county within the United States, defined by Merriam-Webster's dictionary as "the largest territorial division for local government within a state," is based on the Anglo-Saxon shire, which corresponds to the modern county. Counties were brought to the United States by the English colonists and were established in the central and western parts of the United States by the pioneers as they moved westward.

Early county governments in Oregon were very limited in the services they provided. Their primary responsibilities were forest and farm-to-market roads, law enforcement, courts, care for the needy and tax collections. In response to demands of a growing population and a more complex society, today's counties provide a wide range of important public services, including, public health, mental health, juvenile services, criminal prosecution, hospitals, nursing homes, airports, parks, libraries, land-use planning, building regulations, refuse disposal, elections, air pollution control, veterans services, economic development, urban renewal, public housing, vector control, county fairs, museums, dog control, civil defense and senior services.

Originally, counties functioned almost exclusively as agents of the state government. Their every activity had to be either authorized or mandated by state law. However, in 1958, an amendment to the Oregon Constitution authorized counties to adopt "home rule" charters, and a 1973 state law granted all counties power to exercise broad "home rule" authority. As a result, the national Advisory Commission on Intergovernmental Relations has identified county government in Oregon as having the highest degree of local discretionary authority of any state in the nation.

Nine counties have adopted "home rule" charters, wherein voters have the power to adopt and amend their own county government organization. Lane and Washington were the first to adopt "home rule" in 1962, followed by Hood River (1964), Multnomah (1967), Benton (1972), Jackson (1978), Josephine (1980), Clatsop (1988) and Umatilla (1993).

Twenty-eight of Oregon's 36 counties, including the nine with charters, are governed by a board of commissioners comprised of three to five elected members. The remaining eight less populated counties are governed by a "county court" consisting of a county judge and two commissioners.

Baker County

County Seat: 1995 Third St., Baker City 97814
Phone: 541-523-8203 (General); 541-523-8207 (County Clerk)
Fax: 541-523-8240
Email: skirby@bakercounty.org
Web: https://www.bakercounty.org
Established:
Sept. 22, 1862
Elev. at Baker City: 3,471'
Area: 3,089 sq. mi.

Average Temp.:
January 25.2°
July 66.6°
Assessed Value:
$1,767,103,520
Real Market Value: $2,985,366,510
(includes the value of non-taxed properties)
Annual Precipitation: 10.63"
Economy: Agriculture, forest products, manufacturing and recreation
Points of Interest: The Oregon Trail Interpretive Center and Old Oregon Trail, Sumpter Gold Dredge Park and ghost towns, Sumpter Valley Railroad, Baker City Restored Historic District (including Geiser Grand Hotel), Anthony Lakes Ski Resort, Eagle Cap Wilderness area, Brownlee, Oxbow and Hells Canyon Reservoirs, Hells Canyon

Baker County was established from part of Wasco County and named after Colonel Edward D. Baker, a U.S. Senator from Oregon. A Union officer and close friend of President Lincoln, Colonel Baker was the only member of Congress to die in the Civil War. He was killed at Ball's Bluff, Virginia. Auburn, which no longer exists, was the first county seat. Baker City became the county seat in 1868 and was incorporated in 1874.

Before 1861, the majority of immigrants only paused in Baker County on their way west, unaware of its vast agricultural and mineral resources. Then the great gold rush began, and Baker County became one of the Northwest's largest gold producers. Farming, ranching, logging and recreation have become the chief economic bases for an area that displays spectacular scenery, including the world's deepest gorge Hells Canyon; an outstanding museum with the famous Cavin-Walfel rock collection; and numerous historic buildings with interesting architectural features.

County Officials: Commissioners—Chair William "Bill" E. Harvey 2023; Mark E. Bennett 2023, Bruce Nichols 2025, Dist. Atty. Greg M. Baxter 2025; Assess. Kerry Savage 2025; Clerk Stefanie Kirby 2023; Justice of the Peace Brent Kerns 2023; Sheriff Travis Ash 2025; Surv. Tom Hanley 2025; Treas. Alice Durflinger 2023; Co. Admin. Christena Cook; Chief Information Officer Bill Lee

Benton County

County Seat: 205 NW Fifth St., Corvallis 97330
Phone: 541-766-6800 (General); 541-766-6859 (Trial Court Administrator)
Fax: 541-766-6893
Email: webmaster@co.benton.or.us
Web: https://www.co.benton.or.us
Established: Dec. 23, 1847

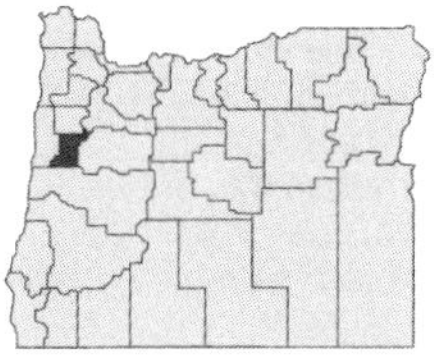

Elev. at Corvallis: 224'
Area: 679 sq. mi.
Average Temp.: January 39.3° July 65.6°
Assessed Value: $9,545,994,419
Real Market Value: $18,822,318,695 (includes the value of non-taxed properties)
Annual Precipitation: 42.71"
Economy: Agriculture, forest products, research and development, electronics and wineries
Points of Interest: Benton County Courthouse, Oregon State University Campus, Benton County Museum (Philomath), Alsea Falls, Mary's Peak, William L. Finley National Wildlife Refuge, Peavy Arboretum, McDonald Forest, Jackson-Frazier Wetland, Beazell Memorial Forest & Education Center

Benton County was created from Polk County by an act of the Provisional Government of Oregon in 1847. It is one of seven counties in the United States to be named after Senator Thomas Hart Benton of Missouri, a longtime advocate of the development of the Oregon Territory. The county is located in an area originally inhabited by the Klickitat Tribe, who rented the area from the Kalapuya Tribe for use as hunting grounds. At that time, the boundaries began at the intersection of Polk County and the Willamette River, ran as far south as the California border and as far west as the Pacific Ocean. Later, portions of Benton County were taken to form Coos, Curry, Douglas, Jackson, Josephine, Lane and Lincoln Counties, leaving it in its present form with 679 square miles of land area.

A substantial portion of the nation's research in forestry, agriculture, engineering, education and the sciences takes place at OSU located at the county seat in Corvallis.

County Officials: Commissioners—Xanthippe "Xan" Augerot (D) 2025, Nancy Wyse (D) 2025, Pat Malone (D) 2023; Dist. Atty. John Haroldson 2025; Assess. Tami Tracy; Clerk James Morales; Sheriff Scott Jackson 2023; Surv. Joe Mardis; Tax Collector Mary Otley; Public Information Officer Alyssa Rash

Clackamas County

County Seat: County Courthouse, 807 Main St., Oregon City 97045
Phone: 503-655-8581 (General); 503-655-8447 (Court Administrator) 503-655-8447 ext 6 (Records)
Email: bcc@co.clackamas.or.us
Web: https://www.clackamas.us
Established: July 5, 1843

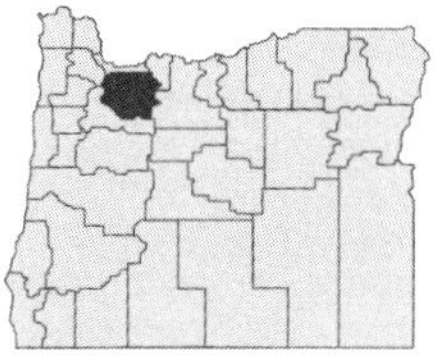

Elev. at Oregon City: 55'
Area: 1,884 sq. mi.
Average Temp.: January 40.2° July 68.4°
Assessed Value: $55,820,612,468
Real Market Value: $100,737,591,399 (includes the value of non-taxed properties)
Annual Precipitation: 48.40"
Economy: Agriculture, metals manufacturing, trucking and warehousing, nursery stock, retail services, wholesale trade and construction
Points of Interest: Mount Hood and Timberline Lodge, Willamette Falls and navigation locks, McLoughlin House, Canby Ferry, Molalla Buckaroo, driving tour of Old Barlow Road, Clackamas Town Center, Museum of the Oregon Territory, North Clackamas Aquatic Park

Clackamas County was named for the resident Clackamas Tribe and was one of the four original Oregon counties created in 1843. Oregon City, the county seat, was the first incorporated city west of the Rocky Mountains, the first capital of the Oregon Territory and the site of the first legislative session.

In 1849, when the city of San Francisco was platted, Oregon City was the site of the only federal court west of the Rockies. The plat was filed in 1850 in the first plat book of the first office of records on the West Coast and are still in Oregon City. The area's early history is featured at the Clackamas County Historical Society and Museum of the Oregon Territory.

From its 55-foot elevation at Oregon City, the county rises to 11,235 feet at the peak of Mount Hood, the only year-round ski resort in the United States and the site of the Timberline Lodge National Historical Landmark. The mountains, rivers and forests offer excellent outdoor recreation activities, from skiing and rafting to fishing and camping.

County Officials: Commissioners—Chair Tootie Smith 2025, Mark Shull 2025, Sonya Fischer 2023, Paul Savas 2023, Martha Schrader 2025; Dist. Atty. John D. Wentworth 2025; Assess. Tami Little 2023; Clerk Sherry Hall 2023; Justice of the Peace Karen Brisbin 2023; Sheriff Angela Brandenburg 2025; Surv. Ray Griffin; Treas. Brian T. Nava 2023; Co. Admin. Gary Schmidt

Clatsop County

County Seat: 800 Exchange St., Suite 410, Astoria 97103
Phone: 503-325-1000 (General); 503-325-8555 (Court Administrator)
Fax: 503-325-8325
Email: clerk@co.clatsop.or.us
Web: https://www.co.clatsop.or.us
Established:
June 22, 1844
Elev. at Astoria:
19'
Area: 1085 sq. mi.
Average Temp.:
January 41.9°
July 60.1°
Assessed Value:
$6,832,654,797
Real Market Value: $10,593,072,191
(includes the value of non-taxed properties)
Annual Precipitation: 66.40"
Economy: Fishing, tourism and forest products
Points of Interest: Astoria Column, Port of Astoria, Flavel Mansion Museum, Lewis and Clark Expedition Salt Cairn, Fort Clatsop, Fort Stevens, Columbia River Maritime Museum

Clatsop County was created from the original Tuality District in 1844 and named for the Clatsop Tribe, one of the many Chinook tribes living in Oregon. *The Journals of Lewis and Clark* mention the tribe. Fort Clatsop, Lewis and Clark's winter headquarters in 1805 and now a national memorial near the mouth of the Columbia River, also took the tribe's name.

Astoria, Oregon's oldest city, was established as a fur trading post in 1811 and named after John Jacob Astor. The first U.S. Post Office west of the Rocky Mountains was also established in Astoria in 1847. The first county courthouse was completed in 1855, and the present courthouse was erected in 1904. Records show that the summer resort of Seaside was founded by Ben Holladay, pioneer Oregon railroad builder, in the early 1870s when he constructed the Seaside House, a famous luxury hotel for which the city was finally named. The Lewis and Clark Expedition reached the Pacific Ocean at this spot.

County Officials: Commissioners—Chair Mark Kujala 2023, John Toyooka 2025, Courtney Bangs 2025, Pamela Wev 2023, Lianne Thompson 2023; Dist. Atty. Ron L. Brown 2023; Assess. Suzanne Johnson; Clerk Tracie Krevanko; Sheriff Matt Phillips 2025; Surv. Vance Swenson; Treas. Jennifer Carlson; County Manager Don Bohn

Columbia County

County Seat: Courthouse, 230 Strand St., Saint Helens 97051
Phone: 503-397-3796 (General); 503-397-7210 (Court Administrator)
Fax: 503-397-7266
Email: Betty.Huser@columbiacountyor.gov
Web: https://www.columbiacountyor.gov
Established:
Jan. 16, 1854
Elev. at Saint Helens: 42'
Area: 687 sq. mi.
Average Temp.:
January 39.0°
July 68.4°
Assessed Value:
$5,801,856,701
Real Market Value: $9,861,813,787
(includes the value of non-taxed properties)
Annual Precipitation: 44.60"
Economy: Agriculture, forest products, manufacturing, surface mining and tourism
Points of Interest: Lewis and Clark Heritage Canoe Trail, Vernonia–Banks State Trail, Jewell Elk Refuge, Sauvie Island Wildlife Area, Sand Island Park, Jones Beach near Clatskanie, Prescott Beach Park, Dibblee Beach, Camp Wilkerson, CZ Trail, Big Eddy Park, Vernonia Golf Course, Lewis and Clark Bridge at Rainier, Columbia County Fairgrounds

Chinook and Clatskanie Tribes inhabited this bountiful region centuries before Captain Robert Gray, commanding the *Columbia Rediviva*, landed on Columbia County's timbered shoreline in 1792. The Corps of Discovery expedition, led by Lewis and Clark, traveled and camped along the Columbia River shore in the area later known as Columbia County in late 1805 and early 1806.

The county has 62 miles of Columbia riverfront with deep water ports and premium industrial property. The Columbia River is a major route for ocean-going vessels and is a popular playground for fishing, boating, camping and windsurfing. The county has two marine parks, Sand Island and J. J. Collins Memorial Marine Park. Columbia County's strong economic and cultural heritage is centered on industries such as forest products, shipbuilding, mining and agriculture. Residents enjoy the rural lifestyle and scenic beauty of Columbia County, coupled with its proximity to Portland.

County Officials: Commissioners—Henry Heimuller 2023, Margaret Magruder 2025, Casey Garrett 2025; Dist. Atty. Jeffrey D. Auxier 2023; Assess. Sue Martin 2023; Clerk Betty Huser 2023; Justice of the Peace Diana M. Shera Taylor 2025; Sheriff Brian Pixley 2023; Surv. Nathan Woodward; Treas. Mary Ann Guess 2025

Coos County

County Seat: Courthouse, 250 N Baxter, Coquille 97423
Phone: 541-396-7500 (General)
Fax: 541-396-1010
Email: dheller@co.coos.or.us
Web: http://www.co.coos.or.us
Established:
Dec. 22, 1853
Elev. at Coquille:
40'
Area: 1,629 sq. mi.
Average Temp.:
January 44.2°
July 60.9°
Assessed Value:
$6,010,472,708
Real Market Value: $8,613,473,396
(includes the value of non-taxed properties)
Annual Precipitation: 56.8"
Economy: Forest products, tourism, fishing and agriculture dominate the Coos County economy. Boating, dairy farming, myrtlewood manufacturing, shipbuilding and repair, and agriculture specialty products, including cranberries, also play an important role.
Points of Interest: Lumber port, myrtlewood groves, Shore Acres State Park and Botanical Gardens, beaches, Oregon Dunes National Recreation Area, museums, fishing fleets, boat basins, scenic golf courses

Coos County was created by the Territorial Legislature from parts of Umpqua and Jackson counties in 1853 and included Curry County until 1855. The county seat was Empire City until 1896 when it was moved to Coquille. Although trappers had been in the area a quarter century earlier, the first permanent settlement in present day Coos County was established at Empire City, now part of Coos Bay, by members of the Coos Bay Company in 1853. The name "Coos" derives from the Coos Tribe.

The International Port of Coos Bay, considered the best natural harbor between Puget Sound and San Francisco, is the world's largest forest products shipping port.

County Officials: Commissioners—Chair John Sweet 2023, Melissa Cribbins 2023, Robert "Bob" Main 2025; Dist. Atty. Paul R. Frasier 2025; Assess. Steve Jansen 2025; Clerk Debbie Heller 2023; Sheriff Craig Zanni 2023; Surv. Michael Dado 2025; Treas. Megan Simms 2025

Crook County

County Seat: Courthouse, 300 NE Third St., Room 23, Prineville 97754
Phone: 541-447-6553 (General); 541-447-6555 (Court Administrator)
Fax: 541-416-2145
Email: cheryl.seely@co.crook.or.us
Web: https://www.co.crook.or.us
Established:
Oct. 24, 1882
Elev. at Prineville:
2,868'
Area: 2,991 sq. mi.
Average Temp.:
January 31.8°
July 64.5°
Assessed Value:
$2,498,973,653
Real Market Value: $3,907,405,991
(includes the value of non-taxed properties)
Annual Precipitation: 10.50"
Economy: Forest products, agriculture, livestock raising, recreation/tourism services, manufacturing and wholesale trade constitute most of Crook County's economy.
Points of Interest: Pine Mills, Crooked River Canyon, Ochoco Mountains, Prineville and Ochoco Reservoirs, rockhound areas, county courthouse, Steins Pillar, Wildland Firefighters Monument, and geological formations

Crook County was formed from Wasco County in 1882 and named for Major General George Crook, U.S. Army. Geographically, the county is in the center of Oregon. It is unique in that it has only one incorporated population center, the city of Prineville founded in 1868. Prineville's colorful past was the scene of tribal raids, range wars between sheep and cattle ranchers and vigilante justice. Other communities in this sparsely settled region are Powell Butte, Post and Paulina.

Thousands of hunters, fishers, boaters, sightseers and rockhounds are annual visitors to its streams, reservoirs and the Ochoco Mountains. Rockhounds can dig for agates, limb casts, jasper and thundereggs on more than 1,000 acres of mining claims provided by the Prineville Chamber of Commerce. Major annual events include the Prineville Rockhound Powwow, Crooked River Roundup, Crook County Fair, Old Fashioned Fourth of July Celebration, High Desert Celtic Festival and the Lord's Acre Sale.

County Officials: County Court—Judge Seth Crawford 2025, Brian Barney 2023, Jerry Brummer 2025; Dist. Atty. Wade L. Whiting 2023; Assess. Jon Soliz 2023; Clerk Cheryl Seely 2023; Sheriff John Gautney 2025; Surv. Greg Kelso 2025; Treas. Galan Carter 2023

❖❖❖

❖❖❖

Curry County

County Seat: 94235 Moore St., Suite 212, Gold Beach 97444
Phone: 541-247-3295 (General); 541-247-4511 (Court Administrator)
Fax: 541-247-6440 (Elections Division)
Email: kolenr@co.curry.or.us
Web: http://www.co.curry.or.us
Established:
  Dec. 18, 1855
Elev. at
  Gold Beach: 60'
Area: 1,648 sq. mi.
Average Temp.:
  January 45.0°
  July 65.0°
Assessed Value:
  $3,357,415,314
Real Market Value: $4,936,691,246
(includes the value of non-taxed properties)
Annual Precipitation: 82.67"
Economy: Forest products, agriculture, commercial and sport fishing, recreation and tourism
Points of Interest: Coastal ports, Cape Blanco Lighthouse, Cape Sebastian and Samuel H. Boardman State Parks, Rogue River Japanese Bomb Site, Thomas Creek Bridge near Brookings – Oregon's highest bridge at 345 feet

Named after Territorial Governor George L. Curry, the county was a part of "Coose" County until it was created in 1855. Port Orford was the county seat until 1859 when it was replaced by Ellensburg (later renamed Gold Beach).

Curry County contains valuable standing timber and also offers spectacular coastal scenery, clamming and crabbing, excellent fishing (freshwater and saltwater), upriver scenic boat trips, hiking trails, and gold for the fun of panning. The Port of Brookings is considered one of the safest harbors on the coast.

Agricultural products include sheep and cattle, cranberries, blueberries, Easter lilies and horticultural nursery stock. Curry County is also a prolific producer of myrtlewood.

County Officials: Commissioners—Court Boice 2025, John Herzog 2025, Christopher Paasch 2023; Dist. Atty. Joshua A. Spansail 2025; Assess. Jim Kolen 2025; Clerk Reneé Kolen 2025; Sheriff John Ward 2025; Treas. Terry Hanscam 2025

Deschutes County

County Seat: 1300 NW Wall St., Suite 206, Bend 97703
Phone: 541-388-6570 (County Administrator)
Fax: 541-385-3202
Email: Elections@deschutes.org
Web: https://www.deschutes.org
Established:
  Dec. 13, 1916
Elev. at Bend:
  3,628'
Area: 3,055 sq. mi.
Average Temp.:
  January 30.5°
  July 65.5°
Assessed Value:
  $27,313,891,829
Real Market Value: $48,810,447,180
(includes the value of non-taxed properties)
Annual Precipitation: 12"
Economy: Tourism, retail trade, forest products, recreational equipment, aviation, software and high technology
Points of Interest: Smith Rock State Park, Mount Bachelor ski area, High Desert Museum, Lava Lands, Cascade Lakes Highway, Lava River Caves State Park, Lava Cast Forests, Newberry Crater, Pilot Butte, Three Sisters Wilderness, Central Oregon Community College, Deschutes County Fairgrounds, Redmond Airport, Pine Mountain Observatory

French-Canadian fur trappers of the Hudson's Bay Company gave the name Riviere des Chutes (River of the Falls) to the Deschutes River, from which Deschutes County took its name. In 1916, Deschutes County was created from a part of Crook County.

Deschutes County, outdoor recreation capital of Oregon, with snow-capped peaks dominating the skyline to the west and the wide-open high desert extending to the east, captivates locals and visitors alike.

Deschutes County has experienced rapid growth largely due to its climate and year-round recreation activities. Central Oregon offers downhill and cross-country skiing, snowboarding, fishing, hunting, hiking, rock climbing, whitewater rafting and golf, among many other opportunities. Deschutes County is the host of diverse annual events, including the Cascade Festival of Music, the Art Hop, Cascade Children's Festival, Pole Pedal Paddle, Sisters Rodeo, Sunriver Sunfest and the Cascade Cycling Classic.

County Officials: Commissioners—Chair Patti Adair (R) 2023, Anthony "Tony" DeBone (R) 2023, Phil Chang (D) 2025; Dist. Atty. John Hummel 2023; Assess. Scot Langton 2023; Clerk Nancy Blankenship 2023; Sheriff L. Shane Nelson 2025; Surv. Kevin Samuel; Treas. Greg Munn 2025; Justice of the Peace Charles Fadeley 2023; Co. Admin. Tom Anderson

Douglas County

County Seat: Courthouse, 1036 SE Douglas Ave., Roseburg 97470
Phone: 541-672-3311 (General); 541-957-2409 (Court Administrator)
Fax: 541-440-6292
Email: HR@co.douglas.or.us
Web: http://www.co.douglas.or.us
Established:
Jan. 7, 1852
Elev. at Roseburg:
475'
Area: 5,071 sq. mi.
Average Temp.:
January 41.2°
July 68.4°
Assessed Value:
$10,450,297,513
Real Market Value: $17,210,293,664
(includes the value of non-taxed properties)
Annual Precipitation: 33.35"
Economy: Forest products, mining, agriculture, fishing and recreation
Points of Interest: Winchester Bay, Salmon Harbor, Oregon Dunes National Recreation Area, North Umpqua River, Diamond Lake, historic Oakland, Wildlife Safari, Douglas County Museum, wineries

Douglas County was named for U.S. Senator Stephen A. Douglas, Abraham Lincoln's opponent in the presidential election of 1860 and an ardent congressional advocate for Oregon. Douglas County was created in 1852 from the portion of Umpqua County which lay east of the Coast Range summit. In 1862, Douglas County absorbed what remained of Umpqua County.

Douglas County extends from sea level at the Pacific Ocean to 9,182-foot Mount Thielsen in the Cascade Range. The Umpqua River marks the dividing line between northern and southern Oregon, and its entire watershed lies within the county's boundaries. The county contains nearly 2.8 million acres of commercial forest lands and the largest stand of old growth timber in the world, which still provides the region's main livelihood. Approximately 25 percent of the labor force is employed in the forest products industry. Agriculture includes field crops, orchards and livestock. Over 50 percent of the land area of the county is federal public land.

County Officials: Commissioners—Chris Boice 2023, Tim Freeman 2023, Tom Kress 2023; Dist. Atty. Richard Wesenberg 2025; Assess. Heather Coffel 2023; Clerk Daniel J. Loomis 2025; Justices of the Peace Machelle Briggs-Mayfield 2025 & Kathleen Miller 2025; Sheriff John Hanlin 2025; Surv. Kris DeGroot 2023; Treas. Samuel W. Lee 2025

Gilliam County

County Seat: Courthouse, 221 S Oregon St., Condon 97823-0427
Phone: 541-384-2311 (County Clerk); 541-384-3303 (Court Administrator)
Fax: 541-384-2166 (County Clerk); 541-384-3304 (Courthouse)
Email: ellen.wagenaar@co.gilliam.or.us
Web: http://www.co.gilliam.or.us
Established:
Feb. 25, 1885
Elev. at Condon:
2,844'
Area: 1,223 sq. mi.
Average Temp.:
January 31.9°
July 71.3°
Assessed Value:
$1,024,617,682
Real Market Value: $2,447,620,315
(includes the value of non-taxed properties)
Annual Precipitation: 11.39"
Economy: Agriculture, recreation, environmental services, wind power generation, waste management and waste disposal landfills. Hunting, fishing and tourism are secondary industries. The largest individual employers in the county are Chemical Waste Management of the Northwest and Oregon Waste Systems.
Points of Interest: Old Oregon Trail, Arlington Bay and Marina, Lonerock area, Condon historic district, tribal pictographs

Gilliam County was established in 1885 from a portion of Wasco County, and named for Colonel Cornelius Gilliam, a veteran of the Cayuse Indian War. Alkali, now Arlington, was the first county seat. In 1890, voters moved the county seat to Condon, then named "Summit Springs." A brick courthouse was built in Condon in 1903 which was destroyed by fire in 1954. The present courthouse was built on the same site in 1955.

In the heart of the Columbia Plateau wheat area, Gilliam County has an average farm size of about 4,200 acres, principally raising wheat, barley and beef cattle.

With elevations of over 3,000 feet near Condon in the south of the county, and 285 feet at Arlington, 38 miles north, the county offers a variety of climates. Two major rivers, the John Day and Columbia, and Interstate 84 traverse the area east to west. Highway 19 connects the county's major cities north to south and serves as the gateway to the John Day Valley.

County Officials: County Court—Judge Elizabeth A. Farrar 2023, Sherrie Wilkins 2023, Pat Shannon 2025; Dist. Atty. Marion Weatherford 2023; Clerk Ellen Wagenaar 2023; Justice of the Peace Cris Patnode 2027; Sheriff Gary Bettencourt 2023; Surv. Todd Catterson 2023; Treas. Nathan Hammer 2023; Assess. Chet Wilkins 2025

Grant County

County Seat: Courthouse, 201 S Humbolt St., Suite 290, Canyon City 97820
Phone: 541-575-1675 (General); 541-575-0509 (Court Administrator)
Fax: 541-575-2248
Email: percyb@grantcounty-or.gov
Web: https://www.grantcountyoregon.net
Established:
  Oct. 14, 1864
Elev. at Canyon City: 3,194'
Area: 4,528 sq. mi.
Average Temp.:
  January 30.7°
  July 68.4°
Assessed Value:
  $631,245,091
Real Market Value: $1,623,449,270
(includes the value of non-taxed properties)
Annual Precipitation: 14.28"
Economy: Forest products, agriculture, hunting, livestock and recreation
Points of Interest: John Day Fossil Beds National Monument, Veterans Memorial, Kam Wah Chung Museum, Joaquin Miller Cabin, Grant County Historical Museum, Sacred Totem Pole, Grant County Historical Mural, Dewitt Museum, Depot Park, Sumpter Valley Railroad, Strawberry Mountain Wilderness, North Fork John Day River Wilderness

Grant County was created in 1864 from Wasco and Umatilla counties and was named for General Ulysses S. Grant. It shares boundaries with more counties (eight) than any other county in Oregon.

Grant County contains the headwaters of the John Day River, which has more miles of Wild and Scenic designation than any other river in the United States. More than 60 percent of the land in the county is in public ownership.

County Officials: County Court—Judge Scott Myers 2025, Commissioners Sam Palmer 2023, Jim Hamsher 2025; Dist. Atty. Jim Carpenter 2023; Assess. David Thunell 2025; Clerk Brenda Percy 2023; Justice of the Peace Kathleen Stinnett 2025; Sheriff Todd McKinley 2025; Surv. Mike Springer 2025; Treas. Julie Ellison 2025

Harney County

County Seat: Courthouse, 450 N Buena Vista Ave., Burns 97720
Phone: 541-573-6641 (General); 541-573-5207 (Court Administrator)
Fax: 541-573-8370
Email: derrin.robinson@co.harney.or.us
Web: https://www.co.harney.or.us
Established:
  Feb. 25, 1889
Elev. at Burns:
  4,118'
Area: 10,228 sq. mi.
Average Temp.:
  January 27.5°
  July 69.4°
Assessed Value:
  $640,912,855
Real Market Value: $1,803,767,209
(includes the value of non-taxed properties)
Annual Precipitation: 10.13"
Economy: Forest products, manufacturing, livestock and agriculture
Points of Interest: Steens Mountain, Malheur National Wildlife Refuge, Alvord Desert, Alvord Hot Springs, Eastern Oregon Agricultural Research Center, "P" Ranch Round Barn, Frenchglen, Wild Horse Corrals, Delintment Lake, Yellowjacket Lake

In 1826, Peter Skene Ogden became the first white man to explore this area when he led a fur brigade for the Hudson's Bay Company. In 1889, Harney, the largest county in Oregon, was carved out of Grant County and named for Major General William S. Harney, commander of the Department of Oregon, U.S. Army, from 1858–1859. Harney was instrumental in opening areas of Eastern Oregon for settlement.

A fierce political battle, with armed night riders who spirited county records from Harney to Burns, ended with Burns as the county seat in 1890. The courthouse was constructed five years later. Burns' first newspaper was established in 1884, and its first church was established in 1887.

Harney County shares the largest ponderosa pine forest in the nation with Grant County and has more than 100,000 beef cattle on its vast ranges. Its abundance of game, campsites, excellent fishing and bird watching have stimulated fast-growing recreational activities.

County Officials: County Court—Judge Peter Runnels 2023, Commissioners Mark Owens 2025, Kristen Shelman 2025; Dist. Atty. Ryan Hughes 2025; Assess. Karen Zabala 2025; Clerk Derrin "Dag" Robinson 2025; Justice of the Peace Vicky Clemens 2025; Sheriff Dan Jenkins 2025; Surv. Kenny Delano; Treas. Bobbi Jo Heany 2023

Hood River County

County Seat: 601 State St., Hood River 97031-2093

Phone: 541-386-3970 (General); 541-386-3535 (Court Administrator)

Fax: 541-387-6864

Email: brian.beebe@co.hood-river.or.us

Web: https://www.co.hood-river.or.us

Established:
June 23, 1908

Elev. at Hood River: 154'

Area: 533 sq. mi.

Average Temp.:
January 33.6°
July 72°

Assessed Value:
$2,911,182,045

Real Market Value: $5,223,768,139
(includes the value of non-taxed properties)

Annual Precipitation: 30.85"

Economy: Agriculture, industry, tourism and services including health care

Points of Interest: Bridge of the Gods, Cloud Cap Inn, Mount Hood Recreation Area, Mount Hood Meadows Ski Area, Lost Lake, Hood River Valley Fruit Loop Tour

The first white settlers in Hood River County filed a donation land claim in 1854. The first school was built in 1863, and a road from The Dalles was completed in 1867. By 1880, there were 17 families living in the valley. Hood River County was created in 1908 from Wasco County.

Fruit grown in the fertile valley is of such exceptional quality that the county leads the world in Anjou pear production. There are more than 14,000 acres of commercial orchards growing pears, apples, cherries and peaches. Hood River County also has two ports and two boat basins. Windsurfing and kiteboarding on the Columbia River are very popular sports that attract visitors from all over the world.

County Officials: Commissioners—Chair Mike Oates 2025, Bob Benton 2023, Karen Joplin 2023, Arthur Babitz 2025, Les Perkins 2025; Dist. Atty. Carrie Rassmussen 2025; Justice of the Peace John Harvey 2023; Sheriff Matt English 2025; Assess./Clerk Brian Beebe; Surv. Bradley Cross; Co. Admin. Jeff Hecksel; Treas. Montina Ruffin

Jackson County

County Seat: Courthouse, 10 S Oakdale Ave., Medford 97501

Phone: 541-774-6029 (General); 541-776-7171 (Court Administrator - Justice Bldg., 100 S Oakdale Ave., Medford 97501)

Fax: 541-774-6455

Email: walkercd@jacksoncounty.org

Web: https://jacksoncountyor.org

Established:
Jan. 12, 1852

Elev. at Medford:
1,382'

Area: 2,801 sq. mi.

Average Temp.:
January 37.6°
July 72.5°

Assessed Value:
$22,786,215,178

Real Market Value: $34,601,251,454
(includes the value of non-taxed properties)

Annual Precipitation: 19.84"

Economy: Medical, retail, tourism, agriculture, manufacturing and forest products

Points of Interest: Mount Ashland Ski Resort, Historic Jacksonville, Oregon Shakespeare Festival, Peter Britt Music Festival, Southern Oregon University, Pear orchards, Howard Prairie Lake, Emigrant Lake, Hyatt Lake, Fish Lake, Rogue River, Lithia Park, Lost Creek Dam, Butte Creek Mill, Crater Lake Highway, wineries, Rogue Community College

Named for President Andrew Jackson, Jackson County was formed in 1852 from Lane County and the unorganized area south of Douglas and Umpqua Counties. It included lands which now lie in Coos, Curry, Josephine, Klamath and Lake counties. The discovery of gold near Jacksonville in 1852 and completion of a wagon road, which joined the county with California to the south and Douglas County to the north, brought many pioneers.

County Officials: Commissioners—Chair Rick Dyer (R) 2023, Colleen Roberts (R) 2023; Dave Dotterrer (R) 2025; Dist. Atty. Beth Heckert 2025; Assess. David Arrasmith 2025; Clerk Chris Walker 2023; Justice of the Peace Damian Idiart 2027; Sheriff Nathan Sickler 2023; Surv. Scott Fein 2025; Finance Director/Treas. Shannon Bell; Co. Admin. Danny Jordan

Jefferson County

County Seat: 66 SE D St., Madras 97741
Phone: 541-475-4451 (General); 541-475-3317 (Court Administrator)
Fax: 541-325-5018
Email: KZemke@jeffco.net
Web: https://www.jeffco.net
Established:
  Dec. 12, 1914
Elev. at Madras:
  2,242'
Area: 1,791 sq. mi.
Average Temp.:
  January 37.4°
  July 70.1°
Assessed Value:
  $1,990,624,730
Real Market Value: $3,994,849,986
(includes the value of non-taxed properties)
Annual Precipitation: 10.2"
Economy: Agriculture, forest products and recreation
Points of Interest: Mount Jefferson, Warm Springs Indian Reservation, Metolius River, Black Butte, Suttle Lake, Blue Lake, Santiam Summit, Lake Billy Chinook behind Round Butte Dam, Haystack Reservoir, Priday Agate Beds

Jefferson County was established in 1914 from a portion of Crook County. It was named for Mount Jefferson on its western boundary. The county owes much of its agricultural prosperity to the railroad, which arrived in 1911 and to the development of irrigation projects in the late 1930s. The railroad, which links Madras with the Columbia River, was completed after constant feuds and battles between two lines working on opposite sides of the Deschutes River.

Vegetable, grass and flower seeds, garlic, mint and sugar beets are cultivated on some 60,000 irrigated acres. Jefferson County also has vast acreages of rangelands and a healthy industrial base related to forest products. The Warm Springs Forest Products Industry, a multi-million dollar complex owned by the Confederated Tribes of the Warm Springs Reservation—partially located in the northwestern corner of the county—is the single biggest industry. With 300 days of sunshine and a low yearly rainfall, fishing, hunting, camping, boating, water-skiing and rock hunting are popular recreations.
County Officials: Commissioners—Chair Kelly Simmelink 2023, Wayne Fording 2025, Mae Huston 2023; Dist. Atty. Steven Leriche 2025; Assess. Jean McCloskey 2025; Clerk Kate Zemke 2023; Sheriff Jim Adkins 2023; Treas. Brandie McNamee 2025; Surv. Gary L. DeJarnatt

Josephine County

County Seat: Courthouse, 500 NW Sixth St., Grants Pass; PO Box 69, Grants Pass 97526
Phone: 541-474-5243 (General); 541-476-2309 (Court Administrator)
Fax: 541-474-5246
Email: clerk@co.josephine.or.us
Web: http://www.co.josephine.or.us
Established:
  Jan. 22, 1856
Elev. at Grants Pass: 948'
Area: 1,641 sq. mi.
Average Temp.:
  January 39.9°
  July 71.6°
Assessed Value:
  $8,466,532,267
Real Market Value: $13,299,483,633
(includes the value of non-taxed properties)
Annual Precipitation: 32.31"
Economy: Tourism, recreation, forest products, electronics and software
Points of Interest: Oregon Caves National Monument, Wolf Creek Tavern, Sunny Valley Covered Bridge and Interpretive Center, Hellgate Canyon-Rogue River, Grants Pass Historic District, Growers Market, Kalmiopsis Wilderness, Rogue Community College, Barnstormers Theater, Rogue Music Theater

Josephine County, named for Virginia "Josephine" Rollins, the first white woman to make this county her home, was established in 1856 out of the western portion of Jackson County. The county seat was originally located in Sailor Diggings (later, Waldo), but in July of 1857 was relocated to Kerbyville, situated on the main route between the port of Crescent City, California and the gold fields.

The discovery of rich placers at Sailor Diggings in 1852 and the resulting gold rush brought the first settlers to this region. Several U.S. Army forts were maintained in the county, and many engagements during the Rogue River Indian War (1855–1858) took place within its boundaries. In 1886, the county seat was finally relocated to Grants Pass, a new town on the railroad that was completed through Oregon that same year. Grants Pass is now the departure point for most Rogue River scenic waterway guided fishing and boat trips. The Illinois River, one of the Rogue's tributaries, has also been designated a scenic waterway.
County Officials: Commissioners—Dan DeYoung 2025, Darin Fowler 2023, Herman Baertschiger 2025; Dist. Atty. Joshua J. Eastman 2025; Assess. Connie Roach 2025; Clerk Rhiannon Henkels 2023; Sheriff Dave R. Daniel 2023; Surv. Peter D. Allen 2025; Treas. Eva Arce 2025

Klamath County

County Seat: 305 Main St., Klamath Falls 97601-6391
Phone: 541-883-5134 (General); 541-883-5503 (Court Administrator)
Fax: 541-885-6757
Email: rlong@co.klamath.or.us
Web: http://www.klamathcounty.org
Established:
Oct. 17, 1882
Elev. at Klamath Falls: 4,105'
Area: 6,135 sq. mi.
Average Temp.:
January 29.8°
July 68.0°
Assessed Value:
$6,341,433,096
Real Market Value: $9,394,110,786
(includes the value of non-taxed properties)
Annual Precipitation: 14.31"
Economy: Agriculture, renewable energy, tourism/recreation, technology, forest products, and medical services
Points of Interest: Crater Lake National Park, Klamath Lake (Oregon's largest lake), Collier Memorial State Park and Logging Museum, seven National Wildlife Refuges, Oregon Institute of Technology (Oregon Tech), Klamath Community College, Klamath County Museum, Favell Museum of Western Art, Ross Ragland Theatre, Spence Mountain and Moore Park trail systems

Klamath County is the proud home of Kingsley Air Base, that trains F-15 fighter pilots and employs more than 1000 people, making it the third largest employer in the county.

The Klamath or "Clamitte" Tribe, for which Klamath County was named, has had a presence for thousands of years. The Legislature created Klamath County by dividing Lake County in 1882. Linkville was named county seat, and its name was changed to Klamath Falls in 1893. The railroad came in the early 1900s. Also, work began on the federal Klamath Project, a reclamation which drained much of the 128 square mile Lower Klamath Lake to provide 188,000 acres of irrigable land for agriculture, a major contributor to the basin's economy, despite competing with the tribes and fish for available water.

Klamath boasts more than 300 sunny days a year and is home to dozens of large-scale solar projects. Natural geothermal hot wells provide heat for many homes, businesses and the Oregon Tech campus. Oregon Tech was the first University in the country to be powered completely by renewable energy and is home to Oregon Renewable Energy Center.
County Officials: Commissioners—Donnie Boyd 2025, Derrick DeGroot 2025, Kelley Minty Morris 2023; Dist. Atty. Eve A. Costello 2023; Assess. Nathan Bigby 2023; Clerk Rochelle Long 2023; Justice of the Peace Karen Oakes 2023; Sheriff Chris Kaber 2025; Surv. Sheryl Hatcher 2025; Treas. Vickie Noel 2023

Lake County

County Seat: Courthouse, 513 Center St., Lakeview 97630
Phone: 541-947-6006 (General); 541-947-6051 (Court Administrator)
Fax: 541-947-6015
Email: sgeaney@co.lake.or.us
Web: http://www.lakecountyor.org
Established:
October 24, 1874
Elev. at Lakeview: 4,800'
Area: 8,359 sq. mi.
Average Temp.:
January 28.4°
July 67.0°
Assessed Value:
$1,001,082,834
Real Market Value: $2,023,089,229
(includes the value of non-taxed properties)
Annual Precipitation: 15.80"
Economy: Livestock, forest products, agriculture and recreation
Points of Interest: Hart Mountain Antelope Refuge, Fort Rock and Fort Rock Homestead Village Museum, Abert Lake and Rim, Goose Lake, Hunter's Hot Springs, Old Perpetual Geyser, Schminck Memorial Museum and Lake County Museum, Lake County Round-Up Museum, Warner Canyon Ski Area, Gearhart Wilderness, Lost Forest, Crack-in-the-Ground, Sheldon National Wildlife Refuge, Summer Lake Hot Springs, Hole-in-the-Ground, sunstones (Oregon's state gemstone) near Plush, Warner Wetlands, Summer Lake Wildlife Area

Lake County was created from Jackson and Wasco Counties by the 1874 Legislature. It then included the present Klamath County and all of the present Lake County except Warner Valley. In 1882, Klamath was removed, and in 1885, the Warner area from Grant County was added.

Linkville, now Klamath Falls, was the first county seat. M. Bullard gave 20 acres as the Lakeview townsite. In the 1875 election, the county seat was moved to Lakeview. The Hart Mountain Antelope Refuge is a 270,000 acre wildlife haven for antelope, mule deer, bighorn sheep and upland birds. A number of migratory waterfowl flyways converge on Goose Lake, south of Lakeview, the Warner Wetlands near Plush and the Summer Lake Wildlife area. Lakeview has been deemed the hang gliding capital of the West.
County Officials: Commissioners—Chair James Williams 2023, Mark Albertson 2023, Barry Shullenberger 2025; Dist. Atty. Ted K. Martin 2025; Assess. Dave Knowles 2025; Clerk Stacie Geaney 2025; Sheriff Michael Taylor 2023; Surv. Darryl Anderson 2023; Treas. Ann Crumrine 2025

Lane County

County Seat: Courthouse, 125 E Eighth Ave.,
Eugene 97401
Phone: 541-682-4203 (General); 541-682-4166
(Court Administrator)
Fax: 541-682-4616
Web: https://www.lanecounty.org
Established:
Jan. 28, 1851
Elev. at Eugene:
422'
Area: 4,620 sq. mi.
Average Temp.:
January 40°
July 70°

Assessed Value:
$36,851,311,671
Real Market Value: $70,040,274,892
(includes the value of non-taxed properties)
Annual Precipitation: 46"
Economy: Agriculture, higher education, high
technology, forest products, recreation, recreational
vehicle manufacturing and tourism
Points of Interest: Twenty historic covered bridges,
Bohemia Mines, coastal sand dunes, Darlingtonia
Botanical Wayside, Fern Ridge Reservoir, Heceta
Head Lighthouse, Hendricks Park Rhododendron
Garden, hot springs, Hult Center for the Performing
Arts, Lane Community College, Lane ESD Plane-
tarium, Martin Rapids whitewater, McKenzie
Pass, Mt. Pisgah Arboretum, Old Town Florence,
Pac-12 sports events, Proxy Falls, Sea Lion Caves,
University of Oregon, vineyards and wineries,
Waldo Lake, Carl G. Washburne State Park tide
pools, Willamette Pass ski area

Lane County was named for General Joseph
Lane, a rugged frontier hero who was Oregon's first
territorial governor. Pioneers traveling the Oregon
Trail in the late 1840s came to Lane County mainly
to farm. The county's first district court met under
a large oak tree until a clerk's office could be built
in 1852. A few years later, the first courthouse
opened in what is now downtown Eugene. With the
building of the railroads, the market for timber
opened in the 1880s. Today, wood products are still
an important part of the economy in addition to
high-technology manufacturing and tourism. Lane
County government operates under a home rule
charter approved by voters in 1962.

Although 90 percent of Lane County is forest
land, Eugene and Springfield comprise the second
largest urban area in Oregon.

County Officials: Commissioners—Jay Bozievich
2023, Pat Farr 2025, Joe Berney 2023, Laurie
Trieger 2025, Heather Buch 2023; Dist. Atty.
Patricia Perlow 2023; Assess. Mike Cowles 2023;
Clerk Cheryl Betschart; Justice of the Peace Rick
Brissenden 2023; Sheriff Clifton Harrold 2025;
Surv. Jay Blomme; Co. Admin. Steve Mokrohisky

Lincoln County

County Seat: Courthouse, 225 W Olive St.,
Newport 97365
Phone: 541-265-6611 (General); 541-265-4236
(Court Administrator)
Fax: 541-265-4176
Email: djenkins@co.lincoln.or.us
Web: https://www.co.lincoln.or.us
Established:
Feb. 20, 1893
Elev. at Newport:
134'
Area: 992 sq. mi.
Average Temp.:
January 44.4°
July 57.6°
Assessed Value:
$8,545,581,420
Real Market Value: $12,908,014,658
(includes the value of non-taxed properties)
Annual Precipitation: 71.93"
Economy: Tourism, government, services and
retail, forest products and fishing
Points of Interest: Agate Beach, Alsea Bay
Interpretive Center, Beverly Beach State Park,
Boiler Bay, Cape Perpetua Visitors' Center, Cascade
Head, Connie Hansen Garden Conservancy, Devils
Lake, Lincoln County Historical Museum, Newport
Performing and Visual Arts Centers, OSU Hatfield
Marine Science Center and Interpretive Center,
Oregon Coast Aquarium, Otter Crest Viewpoint,
Seal Rock Park, South Beach State Park, Yaquina
Arts Center, Yaquina Bay State Park and Light-
house, Yaquina Head Outstanding Natural Area

With miles of beach and coastline, Lincoln
County is one of the most popular visitor destinations on the Oregon Coast. Named for President
Abraham Lincoln, Lincoln County was created by
the Oregon Legislature in 1893. Lincoln County has
a very temperate climate and a short, but productive,
growing season.

Depoe Bay is known as "the whale watching
capital of the world." Lincoln City offers more than
2,000 hotel, motel and bed and breakfast rooms and
resorts, as well as the Siletz Tribe's Chinook Winds
Casino. Newport, known as Oregon's oceanography
research center, features numerous interpretive
centers and the Oregon Coast Aquarium, along with
a large fishing fleet and working bay front. Siletz is
the home of the Administration Center and reservation of the Confederated Tribes of Siletz Indians
of Oregon. Toledo is known as Lincoln County's
industrial center. Waldport features the Alsea Bay
Interpretive Center. Yachats is known as the "Gem
of the Oregon Coast."

County Officials: Commissioners—Kaety
Jacobson (D) 2023, Claire Hall (D) 2025, Doug
Hunt (D) 2023; Dist. Atty. Lanee Danforth 2025;
Assess. Joe Davidson 2025; Clerk Dana Jenkins
2023; Sheriff Curtis Landers 2025; Surv. John
Waffenschmidt; Treas. Jayne Welch 2023

Linn County

County Seat: Courthouse, 300 SW Fourth Ave., Albany 97321
Phone: 541-967-3825 (General); 541-967-3802 (Court Administrator)
Fax: 541-926-8226
Email: sdruckenmiller@co.linn.or.us
Web: http://www.co.linn.or.us
Established:
 Dec. 28, 1847
Elev. at Albany:
 210'
Area: 2,297 sq. mi.
Average Temp.:
 January 39.0°
 July 65.6°
Assessed Value:
 $11,190,869,227
Real Market Value: $18,853,415,069
(includes the value of non-taxed properties)
Annual Precipitation: 42.55"
Economy: Agriculture, forest products, rare metals, manufacturing and recreation
Points of Interest: Willamette and Santiam Rivers; Foster, Green Peter and Detroit Reservoirs; Cascade Range mountains with Mount Jefferson, Hoodoo Ski Bowl and the Pacific Crest Trail; covered bridges; Fair and Expo Center; Brownsville Museum, Albany historic districts

Linn County was created in 1847 and named for U.S. Senator Lewis F. Linn of Missouri, who was the author of the Donation Land Act which provided free land to settlers in the West. Linn County is in the center of the Willamette Valley, with the Willamette River as its western boundary and the crest of the Cascades as its eastern boundary. The climate and soil conditions provide one of Oregon's most diversified agriculture areas, allowing a wide variety of specialty crops and leading the nation in the production of common and perennial ryegrass. Linn County is also home to major producers of processed food, manufactured homes and motor homes, as well as the traditional logging and wood products industries.

Recreational opportunities are extensive and include hiking, climbing and skiing, picnicking and camping in county and state parks; boating, water skiing and fishing on lakes and rivers; petrified wood and agate beds; covered bridges and historic districts and events.
County Officials: Commissioners—John K. Lindsey (R) 2023, Roger Nyquist (R) 2025; Sherrie Sprenger (R) 2025; Dist. Atty. Douglas Marteeny 2025; Assess. Andy Stevens 2025; Clerk Steven Druckenmiller 2023; Judge Jessica K. Meyer 2027; Sheriff Jim Yon 2023; Surv. Thomas Casey 2025; Treas. Michelle Hawkins 2025; Co. Admin. Darrin L. Lane

Malheur County

County Seat: 251 B St. W, Vale 97918
Phone: 541-473-5151 (General); 541-473-5171 (Court Administrator)
Fax: 541-473-5523
Email: CountyClerk@malheurco.org
Web: https://www.malheurco.org
Established:
 Feb. 17, 1887
Elev. at Vale:
 2,243'
Area: 9,926 sq. mi.
Average Temp.:
 January 28.7°
 July 75.6°
Assessed Value:
 $2,307,309,311
Real Market Value: $4,053,946,100
(includes the value of non-taxed properties)
Annual Precipitation: 9.64"
Economy: Agriculture, livestock, food processing and recreation
Points of Interest: Oregon Trail, Keeney Pass, Owyhee Lake, Succor Creek State Park, Leslie Gulch Canyon, Jordan Craters, grave of trapper John Baptiste Charbonneau, Nyssa Agricultural Museum, Vale Oregon Trail Murals, Jordan Valley Basque Pelota Court, Four Rivers Cultural Center

Malheur County was created in 1887 from Baker County. Malheur County derives its name from the "Riviere au Malheur" or "Unfortunate River" (later changed to "Malheur River"), named by French trappers whose property and furs were stolen from their river encampment.

Malheur County is a place filled with fascinating history, diverse landscape and friendly people. The landscape is enchanting and provides for a wide variety of excellent recreation such as hunting, fishing, hiking, rock climbing, rock hounding, boating and water skiing. The county is 94 percent rangeland. Basques, primarily shepherds, settled in Jordan Valley in the 1890s. Irrigated fields in the county's northeast corner, known as Western Treasure Valley, are the center of intensive and diversified farming.
County Officials: County Court—Judge Dan Joyce (R) 2023, Donald Hodge (R) 2023, Ron Jacobs (R) 2025; Dist. Atty. David M. Goldthorpe 2023; Assess. Dave Ingram 2025; Clerk Gayle Trotter 2023; Justice of the Peace Margaret "Margie" Mahony 2025; Sheriff Brian E. Wolfe 2025; Surv. Tom Edwards; Treas. Jennifer Forsyth 2023; Co. Admin. and Chief Information Officer Lorinda DuBois

Marion County

County Seat: 100 High St. NE, Salem 97301
Phone: 503-588-5225 (General); 503-588-5105
(Court Administrator)
Fax: 503-373-4408
Email: recording@co.marion.or.us
Web: http://www.co.marion.or.us
Established:
July 5, 1843
Elev. at Salem:
154'

Area: 1,194 sq. mi.
Average Temp.:
January 39.3°
July 66.3°
Assessed Value:
$27,997,769,590
Real Market Value: $47,864,280,366
(includes the value of non-taxed properties)
Annual Precipitation: 40.35"
Economy: Government, agriculture, food processing, forest products, manufacturing, education and tourism
Points of Interest: State Capitol, Champoeg State Park, Silver Falls State Park, The Oregon Garden, Wheatland Ferry, Buena Vista Ferry, Detroit Dam and Santiam River, Breitenbush Hot Springs, Mount Angel Abbey, food processing plants, Willamette University, Chemeketa Community College, Willamette Heritage Center and Mission Mill Museum Village, Bush House, Deepwood House, Gilbert House Children's Museum

Marion County, then called Champooick, was created by the Provisional Government in 1843, sixteen years before Oregon gained statehood. In 1849, the name was changed to Marion in honor of General Francis Marion.

The county, located in the heart of the Willamette Valley, has the Willamette River as its western boundary and the Cascade Range on the east. Salem, the county seat, is one of the valley's oldest cities. Among its public buildings are the Marion County Courthouse, State Capitol, Capitol Mall buildings and Salem Civic Center. The county was presided over by the Marion County Court until January 1, 1963, when the court was abolished and replaced by a Board of Commissioners.

County Officials: Commissioners—Danielle Bethell 2025, Colm Willis 2023, Kevin Cameron 2023; Dist. Atty. Paige Clarkson 2023; Assess. Tom Rohlfing 2025; Clerk Bill Burgess 2025; Justice of the Peace Janice D. Zyryanoff 2025; Sheriff Joe Kast 2023; Surv. Kent Inman; Treas. Laurie Steele 2023; CFO Janice Fritz

Morrow County

County Seat: Courthouse, 100 S Court St., Heppner; PO Box 788, Heppner 97836
Phone: 541-676-5600 (General); 541-676-2529
(Court Administrator)
Fax: 541-676-5621
Email: bchilders@co.morrow.or.us
Web: https://www.co.morrow.or.us
Established:
Feb. 16, 1885
Elev. at Heppner:
1,955'
Area: 2,049 sq. mi.
Average Temp.:
January 33.1°
July 69.0°
Assessed Value:
$2,592,991,849
Real Market Value: $6,414,471,973
(includes the value of non-taxed properties)
Annual Precipitation: 12.5"
Economy: Agriculture, food processing, dairies, utilities, forest products, livestock and recreation
Points of Interest: Columbia River, Blue Mountains, Umatilla National Forest, Oregon Trail, Blue Mountain Scenic Byway, Morrow County Museum, Port of Morrow, Lewis and Clark Route

Morrow County, created from Umatilla County in 1885, is located east of the Cascades in north-central Oregon. It was named for J. L. Morrow, an early resident. Morrow County contains more than one million acres of gently rolling plains and broad plateaus. This rich agricultural land can be roughly divided into three occupational zones—increasing amounts of irrigation farming in the north, vast fields of wheat yielding to cattle ranches in the center, and timber products in the south. With the advent of center pivot irrigation technology, Morrow County became one of Oregon's fastest growing areas in terms of population, personal income, and agricultural and industrial development. The Port of Morrow, second largest in the state in terms of tonnage, serves as a gateway to the Pacific Northwest and Pacific Rim markets.

County Officials: Commissioners—Jim Doherty 2025, Melissa J. Lindsay 2023, Don Russell 2023; Dist. Atty. Justin Nelson 2023; Assess. Mike Gorman 2023; Clerk Bobbi Childers 2025; Justice of the Peace Glen G. Diehl 2027; Sheriff Kenneth Matlack 2025; Surv. Stephen Haddock; Treas. Jaylene Papineau 2025

Multnomah County

County Seat: 501 SE Hawthorne Blvd., Portland 97214

Phone: 503-823-4000 (General); 503-988-3957 (Court Administrator)

Web: https://multco.us

Established:
Dec. 22, 1854

Elev. at Portland:
77'

Area: 465 sq. mi.

Average Temp.:
January 38.9°
July 67.7°

Assessed Value:
$89,783,658,820

Real Market Value: $195,651,290,147 (includes the value of non-taxed properties)

Annual Precipitation: 37.39"

Economy: Manufacturing, transportation, wholesale and retail trade, and tourism

Points of Interest: Oregon History Center, Oregon Museum of Science and Industry, Oregon Zoo, Portland Art Museum, Washington Park, International Rose Test Gardens, Japanese Gardens, Columbia River Gorge, Multnomah Falls, Blue Lake Park, Oxbow Park, Pittock Mansion, Port of Portland, Memorial Coliseum and Rose Quarter, Oregon Convention Center, Moda Center Arena, Vista House

Lewis and Clark made note of "Multnomah," the tribal village on Sauvie Island, in 1805 and applied that name to all tribal people of the area. The name is derived from "nematlnomaq," probably meaning "downriver." Multnomah County was created from parts of Washington and Clackamas counties by the Territorial Legislature in 1854, five years before Oregon became a state, because citizens found it inconvenient to travel to Hillsboro to conduct county business.

The county is both the smallest in size and largest in population in Oregon. Over 50 percent of its people live in Portland, a busy metropolis dominated by rivers and greenery. The remaining area includes picturesque rural land, from pastoral farms on Sauvie Island to the rugged Columbia River Gorge and the western slopes of Mount Hood.

County Officials: Commissioners—Chair Deborah Kafoury 2023, Sharon Meieran 2025, Susheela Jayapal 2023, Lori Stegmann 2025, Jessica Vega Pederson 2025; Dist. Atty. Mike Schmidt 2025; Sheriff Mike Reese 2023; Auditor Jennifer McGuirk 2023; Assess. Michael Vaughn; Elections Director Tim Scott; Recorder Ellenmarie Murray; Surv. James Clayton; Attorney Jenny Madkour; Engineer Ian Cannon

Polk County

County Seat: Courthouse, 850 Main St., Dallas 97338

Phone: 503-623-8173 (General); 503-623-3154 (Court Administrator)

Fax: 503-623-0896

Email: unger.valerie@co.polk.or.us

Web: https://www.co.polk.or.us

Established:
Dec. 22, 1845

Elev. at Dallas: 325'

Area: 745 sq. mi.

Average Temp.:
January 39.1°
July 65.6°

Assessed Value:
$6,772,174,758

Real Market Value: $11,718,663,086 (includes the value of non-taxed properties)

Annual Precipitation: 51.66"

Economy: Agriculture, forest products, manufacturing, electronics and education

Points of Interest: Western Oregon University, covered bridges, historic courthouse, Brunk House, Baskett Slough Wildlife Refuge, mountain scenery, wineries, National Historic Trail, Confederated Tribes of Grand Ronde Headquarters, Spirit Mountain Casino

Polk County was created from the original Yamhill district in 1845 by the Provisional Legislature. It was named for then President James Knox Polk. The first county seat was at Cynthia Ann. City officials later changed its name to Dallas, after Vice-President George M. Dallas, and moved the community about a mile to improve its water supply.

The first courthouse was at Cynthia Ann. A second courthouse burned in 1898 and was replaced with the present building built with sandstone quarried three miles west of Dallas. A three-story office annex was completed in 1966. Polk County Human Services was consolidated in the newly acquired Academy Building in 1989.

Traveling back roads in Polk County will reveal many attractions, from covered bridges and pleasant parks to vineyards, wineries, and bed and breakfast lodgings spotting the surrounding hills. Many roads meander through beautiful fertile valleys from the Willamette River to the timbered foothills of the Coast Range. Polk County was the primary destination of early wagon trains which took the southern route to Oregon. Cities located in Polk County include Dallas, Independence, Monmouth, Falls City and portions of Salem and Willamina.

County Officials: Commissioners—Chair Craig Pope 2023, Mike Ainsworth 2023, Lyle R. Mordhorst 2025; Dist. Atty. Aaron Felton 2025; Assess. Valerie Patoine 2025; Clerk Valerie Unger 2025; Sheriff Mark A. Garton 2025; Surv. Eric Berry; Treas. Steve Milligan 2025; Co. Admin. Greg P. Hansen

Sherman County

County Seat: Courthouse, 500 Court St., Moro 97039
Phone: 541-565-3606 (Clerk); 541-565-3650 (Court Clerk)
Fax: 541-565-3771
Email: countyclerk@shermancounty.net
Web: https://www.co.sherman.or.us
Established:
Feb. 25, 1889
Elev. at Moro:
1,807'
Area: 831 sq. mi.
Average Temp.:
January 30.7°
July 67.9°

Assessed Value:
$488,867,911
Real Market Value: $1,673,217,979
(includes the value of non-taxed properties)
Annual Precipitation: 9.15"
Economy: Tourism, wind energy, wheat, barley and cattle
Points of Interest: Historic county courthouse, Sherman County Museum, Gordon Ridge, John Day Dam, Sherar's Grade, Deschutes State Park, LePage Park, Giles French Park, Sherman County Fairgrounds, Recreational Vehicle Park

Sherman County, created in 1889 from the northeast corner of Wasco County, was named for General William Tecumseh Sherman. It was separated from Wasco County as much for its unique geological setting as for the settlers' desire to have their own political process. The rolling hills are bordered by the deep canyons of the John Day River to the east, the Columbia River to the north, and the Deschutes River and Buck Hollow to the west and south.

The county was settled in the 1870s by stockmen. By 1881, the homesteaders arrived, permanently changing the area by plowing and fencing the land. Since then, the county has been a wheat-growing area with miles of waving grain on rolling hills of wind-blown glacial silt. The total absence of timber in the county exemplifies the true meaning of the "wide open spaces of the West." Its pastoral landscape has spectacular views of canyons and rivers with mountains silhouetted in the distance. Recreation abounds on the rivers, from the famous and scenic fly-fishing and whitewater rafting stream of the Deschutes to water-skiing, wind-surfing, boating, fishing and rafting on the John Day and Columbia Rivers. Sherman County is one of Oregon's leaders in soil and water conservation.

County Officials: County Court—Judge Joe Dabulskis 2025, Joan Bird 2025, Justin Miller 2023; Dist. Atty. Wade McLeod 2023; Assess. Ross Turney 2023; Clerk Kristi Brown 2025; Treas. Marnene Benson-Wood 2023; Justice of the Peace Ron McDermid 2027; Sheriff Brad Lohrey 2025; Surv. Daryl Ingebo

Tillamook County

County Seat: Courthouse, 201 Laurel Ave., Tillamook 97141
Phone: 503-842-2034 (General); 503-842-2596, ext. 124 (Court Administrator)
Fax: 503-842-2721
Email: toneil@co.tillamook.or.us
Web: http://www.co.tillamook.or.us
Established:
Dec. 15, 1853
Elev. at Tillamook:
22'
Area: 1,125 sq. mi.
Average Temp.:
January 42.2°
July 58.2°
Assessed Value:
$5,494,400,037
Real Market Value: $7,726,815,106
(includes the value of non-taxed properties)
Annual Precipitation: 90.90"
Economy: Agriculture, forest products, fishing and recreation
Points of Interest: Neah-Kah-Nie Mountain; Tillamook, Nehalem, Netarts and Nestucca bays; Oswald West State Park, Nehalem Bay State Park, Bob Straub State Park, Cape Lookout State Park; Pioneer Museum, Blue Heron Cheese Factory, Tillamook Cheese Factory, Naval Air Station Museum, Haystack Rock at Cape Kiwanda, Whalen Island State Park

Tillamook County was formed in 1853 from Yamhill and Clatsop counties. The name Tillamook comes from the Tillamook (or Killamook) Tribe.

Dairy farms dominate the county's fertile valley. It is the home of the world famous Tillamook Cheese Factory. The reforested 355,000-acre "Tillamook Burn" area continues to mature. Commercial thinning will become increasingly evident. With 75 miles of scenic coastline, four bays and nine rivers, Tillamook County offers the finest deep-sea and stream fishing, charter and dory boats, clamming, crabbing, beachcombing and hiking. Its forests also furnish excellent hunting.

County Officials: Commissioners—Chair David Yamamoto 2025, Bill Baertlein 2025, Mary Faith Bell 2023; Dist. Atty. William Porter 2023; Assess. Denise Vandecoevering 2025; Clerk Tassi O'Neil 2025; Justice of the Peace Ryan Connell 2025; Sheriff Josh Brown 2025; Surv. Michael Rice; Treas. Shawn Blanchard 2023

Umatilla County

County Seat: Courthouse, 216 SE Fourth St., Pendleton 97801
Phone: 541-276-7111 (General); 541-278-0341, Pendleton, 541-667-3020, Hermiston (Court Administrators)
Email: records@umatillacounty.net
Web: http://www.co.umatilla.or.us
Established:
  Sept. 27, 1862
Elev. at Pendleton:
  1,069'
Area: 3,231 sq. mi.
Average Temp.:
  January 31.9°
  July 73.6°
Assessed Value:
  $6,748,638,377
Real Market Value: $10,507,631,782
(includes the value of non-taxed properties)
Annual Precipitation: 12.97"
Economy: Agriculture, food processing, forest products, manufacturing, recreation, aggregate production and wind power generation
  Tourism is also increasingly important to Umatilla County where "Let-er-Buck" is heard by Pendleton Round-Up crowds.
Points of Interest: Pendleton Round-Up & Happy Canyon Indian Pageant & Wild West Show, Old Town Pendleton, Pendleton Woolen Mills, Pendleton Whisky Music Festival, Pendleton Bike Week, County Historical Society, Pendleton Underground, McNary Dam and Recreation Area, Echo Museum and Historic Area, Hat Rock, Battle Mountain and Emigrant Springs State Parks, Weston Historic District, Frazier Farmstead Museum in Milton-Freewater, North Fork Umatilla Wilderness Area, Tollgate-Spout Springs Recreation Area, Courthouse Clock Tower, Stateline Wind Project, Confederated Tribes of the Umatilla Indian Reservation's Tamastslikt Cultural Center and Wildhorse Casino
  Umatilla County traces its creation in 1862 to the regional gold rushes, which spawned the riverport of Umatilla City and brought stockraisers to the lush grasslands.
  Although Lewis and Clark and the Oregon Trail pioneers passed through Umatilla County, it did not bloom until the arrival of the railroad in 1881 and the development of dryland wheat farming.
  Water in the form of irrigation has been key to economic diversification and growth, most recently in the Hermiston area, where the desert now yields lush watermelons and other products.
County Officials: Commissioners—Chair John Shafer 2023, Dan Dorran 2025, George Murdock 2023; Dist. Atty. Daniel R. Primus 2025; Sheriff Terry Rowan 2025; Assess. Paul Chalmers; Rec. Mgr. Steve Churchill; Surv. David Krumbein; Financial Mgr. Robert Pahl; Admin. Serv. Director Dan Lonai

Union County

County Seat: Union County Commissioners, 1106 K Ave., La Grande 97850
Phone: 541-963-1001 (General); 541-962-9500, ext. 232 (Court Administrator)
Fax: 541-963-1079
Email: rchurch@union-county.org
Web: http://union-county.org
Established:
  Oct. 14, 1864
Elev. at La Grande:
  2,788'
Area: 2,038 sq. mi.
Average Temp.:
  January 30.9°
  July 70.4°
Assessed Value:
  $2,148,757,626
Real Market Value: $3,484,319,810
(includes the value of non-taxed properties)
Annual Precipitation: 18.79"
Economy: Agriculture, forest products, education and government
Points of Interest: Meacham and Tollgate winter sports areas, Grande Ronde Valley, Eastern Oregon University (La Grande)
  Union County was created in 1864 and named for the town of Union, which had been established two years before and named by its founders for patriotic reasons during the Civil War. The county comprised a part of the northern portion of Baker County. In 1899, Union County gave up its eastern portion to Wallowa County.
  The Grande Ronde Valley in Union County is nearly table flat and is covered with the rich silt of an old lake bed. Highly diversified, with a 160-day growing season and an annual rainfall of 20 inches, the valley boasts of never having had a general crop failure. The county's 1,092 farms average 473 acres a unit.
  Union County's front door opens to the rugged Wallowa Mountains. Its back door faces the Blue Mountains, which attract hikers, skiers and hunters.
County Officials: Commissioners—Chair Paul Anderes 2023, Donna Beverage 2025, Matt Scarfo 2023; Dist. Atty. Kelsie McDaniel 2023; Assess. Cody Vavra 2025; Clerk Robin Church 2025; Sheriff Cody Bowen 2025; Surv. Rick Robinson 2025; Treas. Donna Marshall 2025; Co. Admin. and Chief Info. Officer Shelley Burgess

Wallowa County

County Seat: Courthouse, 101 S River St., Enterprise 97828
Phone: 541-426-4543 ext. 15 (General); 541-426-4991 (Court Administrator)
Fax: 541-426-0582
Email: wcclerk@co.wallowa.or.us
Web: https://co.wallowa.or.us
Established:
Feb. 11, 1887
Elev. at Enterprise:
3,757'
Area: 3,153 sq. mi.
Average Temp.:
January 24.2°
July 63.0°
Assessed Value: $902,405,606
Real Market Value: $2,326,561,290
(includes the value of non-taxed properties)
Annual Precipitation: 13.08"
Economy: Agriculture, art, livestock, forest products and recreation
Points of Interest: Wallowa Lake; art galleries; Mount Howard gondola; Eagle Cap Wilderness; Hells Canyon National Recreation Area; Minam, Wallowa and Grande Ronde Rivers

This rather isolated area was claimed by the Chief Joseph band of the Nez Perce as its hunting and fishing grounds. The Nez Perce used the word "wallowa" to designate a tripod of poles used to support fish nets. In 1871, the first white settlers came to Wallowa County crossing the mountains in search of livestock feed in the Wallowa Valley. The area had been part of Union County since 1864, but it was carved from that county in 1887 by a legislative act.

Wallowa County is a land of rugged mountains, gentle valleys and deep canyons. Peaks in the Wallowa Mountains soar to almost 10,000 feet in elevation and the Snake River drops over 8,500 feet in elevation over its length. Hells Canyon, carved by the Snake, is the nation's deepest gorge averaging 5,500 feet from rim to river.

The scenery in the county is spectacular and serves as a magnet for tourists. Unrivaled opportunities for outdoor recreation create the county's reputation as a visitors' paradise. Permanent residents enjoy the same recreation opportunities, adding to a high quality of life supported by traditional farm and forest industries, as well as art and tourism.

County Officials: Commissioners—Chair Todd Nash 2025, John Hillock 2023, Susan Roberts 2025; Dist. Atty. Rebecca Frolander 2023; Assess. Randy Wortman 2025; Clerk Sandy Lathrop 2023; Sheriff Joel Fish 2025; Treas. Ginger Goebel-Burns 2023; Surv. Richard Shaver

Wasco County

County Seat: Courthouse, 511 Washington St., The Dalles 97058
Phone: 541-506-2500 (General); 541-506-2700 (Court Administrator)
Fax: 541-506-2531
Email: countyclerk@co.wasco.or.us
Web: https://www.co.wasco.or.us
Established:
Jan. 11, 1854
Elev. at The Dalles:
98'
Area: 2,396 sq. mi.
Average Temp.:
January 33.4°
July 73.1°
Assessed Value:
$2,631,462,669
Real Market Value: $6,721,122,853
(includes the value of non-taxed properties)
Annual Precipitation: 14.9"
Economy: Agriculture, forest products, manufacturing, electric power, aluminum and transportation
Points of Interest: Columbia and Deschutes Rivers, Fort Dalles Museum, Pulpit Rock, The Dalles Dam, Celilo Converter Station, Confederated Tribes of the Warm Springs Reservation, Mount Hood, Sorosis Park, original Wasco County Courthouse, St. Peter's Landmark, Columbia River Gorge Discovery Center

When the Territorial Legislature created Wasco County in 1854 from parts of Clackamas, Lane, Linn and Marion Counties, it embraced all of Oregon east of the Cascade Range, most of Idaho and parts of Montana and Wyoming. It was named for the Wasco, or Wascopam, Tribe.

Wasco's county seat is The Dalles. Now the trading hub of north-central Oregon, The Dalles gained earlier fame as the town at the end of the Oregon Trail. Thousands of years before that, humans scratched pictographs on rocks overlooking the Columbia River in this area. Later, tribes gathered for generations near Celilo Falls to trade and fish. The county's tribal heritage continues in evidence today.

County Officials: Commissioners—Scott Hege 2023, Steve Kramer 2025, Kathy Schwartz 2023; Dist. Atty. Matthew Ellis 2025; Assess. Jill Filla Amery 2025; Clerk Lisa Gambee 2025; Sheriff Lane Magill 2025; Surv. Brad Cross; Treas. Elijah Preston 2025

Washington County

County Seat: 155 N First Ave., Suite 300, Hillsboro 97124
Phone: 503-846-8611 (General); 503-846-8888 (Court Administrator)
Fax: 503-846-4545
Email: elections@co.washington.or.us
Web: https://www.co.washington.or.us
Established:
  July 5, 1843
Elev. at Hillsboro:
  196'
Area: 727 sq. mi.
Average Temp.:
  January 39.9°
  July 66.6°
Assessed Value:
  $71,273,364,154
Real Market Value: $131,743,445,322
(includes the value of non-taxed properties)
Annual Precipitation: 37.71"
Economy: Agriculture, horticulture, forest products, food processing, high tech, sports equipment and apparel
Points of Interest: Tualatin Valley orchards and vineyards, Pacific University, Wilson River and Sunset Highway, Hagg Lake, Old Scotch Church

The original four counties created by the Provisional Government of Oregon were Twality, Clackamas, Yamhill and Champoick. Twality was changed to Washington in honor of President George Washington by the Territorial Legislature on September 3, 1849. The actual organization of Washington County government followed several years later.

Now one of the state's fastest developing areas, the fertile Tualatin Valley was once filled with beaver and was a favorite hunting ground for Hudson's Bay Company trappers. The first white settlers arrived around 1840, lured by rich soil. Despite its rapid urbanization, the valley still contains prime agricultural land. Many small towns rich in history dot the area. Pacific University, founded as Tualatin Academy in 1849, is one of the oldest colleges in the West. Washington County operates under a home rule charter approved by voters in 1962. The Northwest's largest enclosed shopping center, Washington Square, is located south of Beaverton.
County Officials: Commissioners—Chair Kathryn Harrington 2023; Roy Rogers 2025, Nafisa Fai 2025, Pam Treece 2023; Jerry Willey 2023, Dist. Atty. Kevin Barton 2023; Justice of the Peace Dan Cross 2023; Sheriff Pat Garrett 2025; Auditor John Hutzler 2023; Assess./Clerk Margaret Garza; Surv. Scott Young; Co. Admin. Tanya Ange; CIOs Phillip Bransford & Julie McCloud

Wheeler County

County Seat: Courthouse, 701 Adams St., Fossil 97830
Phone: 541-763-2400 (General); 541-763-2541 (Court Administrator)
Fax: 541-763-2026
Email: bsnowpotter@co.wheeler.or.us
Web: http://www.wheelercountyoregon.com
Established:
  Feb. 17, 1899
Elev. at Fossil:
  2,654'
Area: 1,715 sq. mi.
Average Temp.:
  January 35°
  July 66°
Assessed Value:
  $156,134,996
Real Market Value: $781,425,311
(includes the value of non-taxed properties)
Annual Precipitation: 14.66"
Economy: Livestock and tourism
Points of Interest: Painted Hills, John Day Fossil Beds, John Day River

Wheeler County was formed by the Oregon Legislature in 1899 from parts of Grant, Gilliam and Crook counties and was named for Henry H. Wheeler, who operated the first mail stage line from The Dalles to Canyon City. The new county consisted of 1,656 square miles with an estimated 46 townships, a population of 1,600 and taxable property worth one million dollars.

Wheeler County is as rugged and uneven as any Oregon county, with the terrain varying widely from sagebrush, juniper and rim rock to stands of pine and fir. Portions of two national forests lie within its boundaries with forest lands covering nearly one-third of the county. The area is probably best known as one of the most outstanding depositories of prehistoric fossils on the North American continent.
County Officials: County Court—Judge Lynn Morley 2023; Clinton Dyer 2025, Rick Shaffer 2023; Dist. Atty. Gretchen M. Ladd 2025; Assess. Auralea Woods 2023; Clerk Brenda Snow Potter 2025; Justice of the Peace Robin Ordway 2027; Sheriff Mike Smith 2025; Surv. Jason L. Hatfield 2025; Treas. Sandra K. Speer 2023

Yamhill County

County Seat: Courthouse, 535 NE Fifth St., McMinnville 97128
Phone: 503-434-7501 (General); 503-434-7530 (Court Administrator)
Fax: 503-434-7553
Email: clerk@co.yamhill.or.us
Web: https://www.co.yamhill.or.us
Established:
July 5, 1843

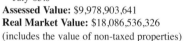

Elev. at McMinnville:
157'
Area: 718 sq. mi.
Average Temp.:
January 39.0°
July 65.0°
Assessed Value: $9,978,903,641
Real Market Value: $18,086,536,326
(includes the value of non-taxed properties)
Annual Precipitation: 43.6"
Economy: Agriculture, wine production, manufacturing, forest products, dental instruments, education, health care and social assistance
Points of Interest: Linfield College, George Fox University, Herbert Hoover House, Yamhill County Historical Museum, Wheatland Ferry, Captain Michael K. Smith Evergreen Aviation and Space Museum, Rogers Landing

Created in 1843, Yamhill County was one of Oregon's original four districts. Its current boundaries were established in 1860. The county was named after the Yamhelas, members of the Kalapuya Tribe, who lived along the Yamhill River in the western Willamette Valley.

Agriculture is still the county's primary industry. Nursery and greenhouse crops; fruit trees, nuts, wine grapes, berries, hay, silage, field and grass seeds are major agricultural products. Yamhill County ranks sixth among the counties in annual market value of its agricultural production. Yamhill County is also the heart of Oregon's wine industry. Over 80 wineries and 200 vineyards represent the largest concentration of wine growers an producers in any county in the state. One third of the county is covered with commercial timber. The mainstay of the western valley area is logging and timber products. With 276 manufacturers, Yamhill County produces everything from snack foods to rebar, timber products to plastic tubing and textiles to dental equipment.
County Officials: Commissioners—Casey Kulla 2023, Lindsay Berschauer 2025, Mary Starrett 2023; Dist. Atty. Bradley Berry 2025; Assess. Derrick Wharff 2025; Clerk Brian Van Bergen 2025; Sheriff Tim Svenson 2023; Treas. Kris Bledsoe 2025; Surveyor Bill Gille

REGIONAL GOVERNMENTS

Formed in 1984 under ORS Chapter 190, the Oregon Regional Councils Association (ORCA) promotes cooperation among levels of government.

The multi-jurisdictional councils are voluntary associations cooperating on issues and problems which cross city, county, and in some cases, state boundaries. The association provides a forum for exchanging and discussing common issues.

Central Oregon Intergovernmental Council

Contact: Tammy Baney, Executive Director
Address: 334 NE Hawthorne Ave., Bend 97701
Phone: 541-504-3306
Fax: 541-923-3416
Web: https://coic2.org

Lane Council of Governments

Contact: Brenda Wilson, Executive Director
Address: 859 Willamette St., Suite 500, Eugene 97401
Phone: 541-682-4283
Fax: 541-682-4099
Web: http://www.lcog.org

Mid-Willamette Valley Council of Governments

Contact: Renata Wakeley, Executive Director
Address: 100 High St. SE, Suite 200, Salem 97301
Phone: 503-588-6177
Web: http://www.mwvcog.org

Northwest Senior and Disability Services

Contact: Melinda Compton, Program Director; Tayna DeHart Operations Director
Address: 3410 Cherry Ave. NE, Salem 97303
Phone: 503-304-3400; Toll-free: 1-800-206-4799
Fax: 503-304-3434
Web: http://nwsds.org

Oregon Cascades West Council of Governments

Contact: Ryan Vogt, Executive Director
Address: 1400 Queen Ave. SE, Suite 201, Albany 97322
Phone: 541-924-8465
Fax: 541-967-6123
Web: http://www.ocwcog.org

Rogue Valley Council of Governments

Contact: Michael Cavallaro, Executive Director
Address: 155 N First St., PO Box 3275, Central Point 97502
Phone: 541-423-1335
Fax: 541-664-7927
Web: http://rvcog.org

METRO

Contact: Andy Shaw, Government Affairs Director
Address: Metro Regional Center, 600 NE Grand Ave., Portland 97232-2736
Phone: 503-797-1700
Fax: 503-797-1799
Web: https://www.oregonmetro.gov
Councilors: President Lynn Peterson 2022; Dist. 1 Shirley Craddick 2022; Dist. 2 Christine Lewis 2022; Dist. 3 Gerritt Rosenthal 2024; Dist. 4 Juan Carlos Gonzalez 2022; Dist. 5 Mary Nolan 2024; Dist. 6 Bob Stacey 2024; Auditor Brian Evans 2022

A hippopotamus at the Oregon Zoo in Portland. The zoo is operated by Metro. (Oregon State Archives scenic photo)

The council president and auditor are elected regionally. The remaining six councilors are
elected by district. All serve four-year terms. The auditor reviews Metro's operations.

Metro is a regional government responsible for managing issues that cross city and county lines and serving more than 1.6 million residents in the 24 cities and three counties in the Portland area. Metro's core responsibilities include management of the region's garbage, compost and recycling system; support of the economy through management of the Oregon Convention Center and Expo Center; preserving farm and forestland through regional planning and management of the region's urban growth boundary; management of a regional affordable housing and supportive housing program; preservation of our environment through management of more than 18,000 acres of parks and natural areas; and management of some of the state's top entertainment venues, including the Oregon Zoo and Portland's Centers for the Arts.

An elected seven-member council oversees Metro, and its day-to-day affairs are managed by a chief operating officer, who is appointed by the council.

The Portland region has been coming together to manage regional planning since the 1940s. In 1957, representatives from Clackamas, Multnomah and Washington Counties formed a Metropolitan Planning Commission to handle some research related to long-range planning. The Metropolitan Service District was formed in 1970, and voters gave it expanded powers in 1979.

In 1990, voters in the Portland region granted Metro home rule power. The current Metro charter and system of governance was approved in 2002.

PORT DISTRICTS OF OREGON

Port of Alsea, Established 1910
Address: 365 Port St., PO Box 1060, Waldport 97394
Phone: 541-563-3872
Web: https://portofalsea.com
Commissioners: Chair Rob Bishop, Chuck Pavlik, Buster Pankey, Jan Power, Joe Rohleder; Port Mgr. Roxie Cuellar. Meets third Thursday of the month.

Port of Arlington, Established 1933
Address: 100 Port Island Rd., PO Box 279, Arlington 97812
Phone: 541-454-2868
Web: https://www.portofarlington.com
Commissioners: President Ron Wilson; Steve Shaffer, Kevin Hunking, Dewey Kennedy, Rod McGuire; Port Mgr. Peter Mitchell. Meets second Tuesday of the month.

Port of Astoria, Established 1914
Address: 422 Gateway Ave., Suite 100, Astoria 97103
Phone: 503-741-3300
Fax: 503-741-3345
Web: https://www.portofastoria.com
Commissioners: President Dirk Rohne, James Campbell, Scott McClaine, Frank Spence, Robert Stevens; Exec. Dir. Will Isom. Meets first and third Tuesdays of the month.

Port of Bandon, Established 1913
Address: 390 First St. SW, PO Box 206, Bandon 97411
Phone: 541-347-3206
Fax: 541-347-4645
Web: http://www.portofbandon.com
Commissioners: President Reg Pullen, Wayne Butler, Rick Goche, Donny Goddard, Harv Schubothe; Port Mgr. Jeff Griffin; Harbor Master Shawn Winchell. Meets fourth Thursday of the month at 5:00 p.m.

Port of Brookings Harbor, Estab. 1956
Address: 16330 Lower Harbor Rd., PO Box 848, Brookings 97415
Phone: 541-469-2218
Fax: 541-359-3999
Web: https://www.portofbrookingsharbor.com

Commissioners: President Roy Davis, Sharon Hartung, Richard Heap, Kenneth Range, Joe Speir; Port Mgr. Gary Dehlinger. Meets third Tuesday of the month.

Port of Cascade Locks, Estab. 1937

Address: 427 Portage Rd., PO Box 307, Cascade Locks 97014
Phone: 541-374-8619
Fax: 541-374-8428
Web: http://portofcascadelocks.org
Commissioners: President Jess Groves, Dean Bump, Joeinne Caldwell, Brad Lorang, John Stipan; Port Mgr. Olga Kaganova. Meets first and third Thursdays of the month.

Port of Columbia County, Established 1941

Address: 100 E St., PO Box 190, Columbia City 97018
Phone: 503-397-2888
Fax: 503-397-6924
Web: www.portofcolumbiacounty.org
Commissioners: President Larry Ericksen, Chip Bubl, Chris Iverson, Robert Keyser, Nancy Ward; Exec. Dir. Douglas Hayes. Meets second Wednesday of the month.

International Port of Coos Bay, Established 1909

Address: 125 Central Ave., Suite. 300, PO Box 1215, Coos Bay 97420
Phone: 541-267-7678
Fax: 541-269-1475
Web: https://www.portofcoosbay.com
Commissioners: President David Kronsteiner, Eric Farm, Robert Garcia, Brianna Hanson, Vacant; CEO John Burns. Meets third Tuesday of the month.

Port of Garibaldi, Established 1910

Address: 402 S Seventh St., PO Box 10, Garibaldi 97118
Phone: 503-322-3292
Fax: 503-322-0029
Web: http://portofgaribaldi.org
Commissioners: President Valerie Folkema, Kelly Barnett, Robert Browning, Paul Daniels, John Luquette; Port Mgr. Michael Saindon. Meets second Wednesday of the month.

Port of Gold Beach, Established 1955

Address: 29891 Harbor Way, PO Box 1126, Gold Beach 97444
Phone: 541-247-6269
Fax: 541-247-6268
Web: http://portofgoldbeach.com
Commissioners: President Bill McNair, Hank Eckardt, Mike Luzmoor, Charles Riddle, Walter Scherbarth; Port Mgr. Andrew Wright. Meets third Thursday of the month.

Port of Hood River, Established 1933

Address: 1000 E Port Marina Dr., Hood River 97031
Phone: 541-386-1645
Web: https://portofhoodriver.com
Commissioners: President John Everitt, Kristi Chapman, David Meriwether, Ben Sheppard, Hoby Streich; Exec. Dir. Michael McElwee. Meets first and third Tuesdays of the month at 5:00 p.m.

Port of Morrow, Established 1958

Address: 2 Marine Dr., PO Box 200, Boardman 97818
Phone: 541-481-7678
Fax: 541-481-2679
Web: http://www.portofmorrow.com
Commissioners: President Rick Stokoe, Jerry Healy, John Murray, Marv Padberg, Joe Taylor; Gen. Mgr. Ryan Neal. Meets second Wednesday of the month.

Port of Nehalem, Established 1909

Address: 36060 6th St., PO Box 476, Nehalem 97131-0476
Phone: 503-368-7212
Fax: 503-368-7234
Web: https://portofnehalem.org
Commissioners: President Steve Huber, Dave Devault, Cory Hua, Janice Laviolette, Darrell Winegar; Office Manager Gene Dieken. Meets fourth Wednesday of the month, third Wednesday in November and December.

Port of Newport, Established 1910

Address: 600 SE Bay Blvd., Newport 97365
Phone: 541-265-7758
Fax: 541-265-4235
Web: http://www.portofnewport.com
Commissioners: President Jim Burke, Walter Chuck, Jeff Lackey, Kelley Retherford, Gil Sylvia; Interim Gen. Mgr Teri Dresler. Meets fourth Tuesday of the month.

Port of Port Orford, Established 1919

Address: 300 Dock Rd., PO Box 490, Port Orford 97465
Phone: 541-332-7121
Web: https://portofportorford.org
Commissioners: President Aaron Ashdown, David Bassett, Tom Calvanese, Leila Thompson, Brett Webb; Port Mgr. Pat Cox. Meets third Tuesday of the month.

International Port of Portland, Established 1891

Address: 7200 NE Airport Wy., Portland 97208; PO Box 3529, Portland 97218
Phone: 503-415-6000; 1-800-547-8411
Web: http://www.portofportland.com
Commissioners: President Alice Cuprill-Comas, Michael Alexander, Sean O'Hollaren, Katherine Lam, Robert L. Levy, Patricia McDonald, Meg

Niemi, Linda Pearce, Tom Tsuruta, Gary Young; Exec. Dir. Curtis Robinhold. Meets second Wednesday of the month.

The Swan Island Industrial Park on the Willamette River is managed by the Port of Portland. (Oregon State Archives scenic photo)

Port of Siuslaw, Established 1909
Address: 100 Harbor St., Florence 97439
Phone: 541-997-3426
Fax: 541-997-9407
Web: http://portofsiuslaw.com
Commissioners: President Terry Duman, Mike Buckwald, Bill Meyer, Robert Ward, Craig Zolezzi; Port Mgr. David Huntington. Meets third Wednesday of the month.

Port of The Dalles, Established 1933
Address: 3636 Klindt Dr., The Dalles 97058
Phone: 541-298-4148
Web: https://www.portofthedalles.com
Commissioners: President Greg Weast, Staci Coburn, Mike Courtney, David Griffith, Robert Wallace; Exec. Dir. Andrea Klaas. Meets second Wednesday of the month.

Port of Tillamook Bay, Estab. 1953
Address: 4000 Blimp Blvd., Suite 100, Tillamook 97141
Phone: 503-842-2413
Fax: 503-842-3680
Web: https://potb.org
Commissioners: President Jack Mulder, Sierra Lauder, Matt Mumford, Chris Sween, Jim Young; General Mgr. Michele Bradley. Meets the first Tuesday after the 15th of each month.

Port of Toledo, Established 1910
Address: 496 NE Hwy. 20, Unit #1, PO Box 428 Toledo 97391-9720
Phone: 541-336-5207
Web: https://www.portoftoledo.org
Commissioners: President Chuck Gerttula, Zack Dahl, Rick Graff, Michael Kriz, Penny Ryerson; Port Mgr. Bud Shoemake. Meets third Tuesday of the month.

Port of Umatilla, Established 1940
Address: 500 Willamette Ave., PO Box 879, Umatilla 97882
Phone: 541-922-3224
Fax: 541-922-5609
Web: https://portofumatilla.org
Commissioners: President Jerry Baker, Bob Blanc, Jerry Imsland, Jerry Simpson, Jeff Snell; Gen. Mgr. Kim Puzey. Meets Tuesday after first Wednesday of the month.

Port of Umpqua, Established 1913
Address: 1877 Winchester Ave., PO Box 388, Reedsport 97467
Phone: 541-271-2232
Fax: 541-271-2747
Web: http://portofumpqua.net
Commissioners: President Keith Tymchuk, Lee Bridge, Carey Jones, Barry Nelson, Deanna Schafer; Port Mgr. Charmaine Vitek. Meets third Wednesday of the month.

SPECIAL SERVICE DISTRICTS

Contact: Frank Stratton, Executive Director
Address: Special Districts Association of Oregon, PO Box 12613, Salem 97309-0613
Phone: 503-371-8667; Toll-free: 1-800-285-5461
Fax: 503-371-4781
Web: https://www.sdao.com/

ORS 198.010 and 198.335 authorize 28 types of districts: water control, irrigation, ports, regional air quality control authorities, fire, hospital, mass transit, sanitary districts and authorities, people's utility, domestic water supply districts and authorities, cemetery, park and recreation, metropolitan service, special road, road assessment, highway lighting, health, vector control, water improvement, weather modification, geothermal heating, transportation, county service, chemical control, weed control, emergency communications, diking, and soil and water conservation districts.

Special Districts are financed through property taxes, fees for services, or a combination thereof. Most special districts are directed by a governing body elected by the voters.

Formed in 1979, the Special Districts Association of Oregon (SDAO) provides support services to member districts throughout the state in the areas of research and technical assistance, legislative representation, training programs, insurance services, information and reference materials, financing services, and employee benefits programs.

STUDENT ESSAY CONTEST WINNER
Jessie M. Honeyman Memorial State Park

Aidan Lin
Brenda Jensen's 4th Grade Class
Ashbrook Independent School, Corvallis

This drawing by Aidan Lin shows people playing on the sand dunes and Cleawox Lake at Jessie M. Honeyman Memorial State Park.

I woke up to some pitter pattering. My eyes opened to a rising sun. I got out of my blue sleeping bag and looked out of our tent. My eyes were greeted by the beauty of the droplets of rain on the grass. We arrived at Honeyman State Park yesterday night for a camping weekend. I was already having an extraordinary time! I learned about the lake's inhabitants at the visitor's center and we made smores over a campfire. Today was going to be even better. We were going to the lake.

As we walked through the luscious green trails, a massive sand dune appeared. It was like a mountain of sand. At its edge, you could see a sparkling lake with hundreds of trees on the other side. I sprinted down, hopped onto my hands and knees, and started building a sand castle. When I went to get wet sand, I saw something squiggly in the corner of my eye. It was a salamander! And there wasn't just one, there were tons!! I started to dig a watery hole by the water, and filled it with salamanders. This was by far the most fun I had at the park.

After a day of playing in the sand, paddle boarding, and sand boarding, we went back to our campsite. We were leaving early the next day. As I packed up my things, I hoped we would come back again. Honeyman was by far, my favorite park I have ever visited.

Elections and Records

The "Oregon System"—procedures for initiative, referendum and recall—gained Oregon national recognition for the degree of citizen involvement in the processes of self-government. Most recently, vote by mail and the Oregon Motor Voter processes have drawn national attention to Oregon. This detailed history of elections in Oregon illustrates the tangible results of participation in our government.

VOTING AND VOTER REGISTRATION

Source: Office of the Secretary of State, Elections Division
Address: 255 Capitol St. NE, Suite 501, Salem 97310
Phone: 503-986-1518
Web: www.oregonvotes.gov

Elections in Oregon

All regular elections in Oregon are held on one of four days each year, except in cases of emergency. The election days are the second Tuesday in March, the third Tuesday in May, the third Tuesday in September and the first Tuesday after the first Monday in November. Elections are conducted exclusively by mail. Voters who are registered as of the 21st day before an election are mailed a ballot to vote and return by election day.

The use of vote by mail was first approved on a limited basis by the Legislature in 1981 and was made a permanent feature of some elections in 1987. In 1998, Oregon voters amended state law to require that the primary and general elections in May and November of even-numbered years also be conducted through vote by mail. Beginning in 2000, primary and general elections have been conducted by mail. In 2007, the Legislature provided that all elections be conducted by mail. In 2019, the Legislature approved funding for postage paid envelopes to be provided for returning ballots starting in 2020.

Major political parties use the primary election to nominate candidates to run for partisan office in the general election. Minor political parties nominate candidates to run for partisan office in the general election according to party rule, and those candidates do not appear on the primary election ballot. Partisan offices include U.S. President, U.S. Senator, U.S. Representative, Governor, Secretary of State, State Treasurer, Attorney General, State Senator and State Representative.

Oregon's primary is closed, meaning only registered voters of a major political party can vote for candidates of the same party. At the primary election, voters who are not registered in one of the major political parties would receive a ballot containing nonpartisan contests, such as judicial elections, which all registered voters may vote on.

At the general election, voters will receive a ballot containing both partisan and nonpartisan offices and can vote for any candidate even if they are not of the same party. Most statewide ballot measures are on the general election ballot.

Registering to Vote

Every Oregonian who is at least 16 years old, a U.S. citizen and an Oregon resident can register to vote. To participate in an election a voter must be registered at least 21 days before the election. Persons registered to vote in other states may not transfer their voter registration to Oregon.

There are three ways to register to vote in Oregon, Oregon Motor Voter automatic voter registration, online voter registration and paper registration.

The Oregon Motor Voter (OMV) registration law took effect on January 1, 2016, making Oregon the first state in the nation to implement automatic voter registration. Automatic registration is available to those who apply for an original, renewal or replacement driver's license, permit or identification card and provide evidence of citizenship at a Driver and Motor Vehicle Division (DMV) office.

The OMV registration process takes approximately three weeks until a voter's registration is effective. If an election will occur in the two months following the DMV interaction, one of the other methods of registering to vote should be used to ensure the voter will be eligible to vote.

Paper voter registration forms can also be mailed or hand-delivered to a county election office, or a voter can complete the form electronically at oregonvotes.gov. Forms are located in many public buildings, in every county elections office and in many state agencies including the Office of the Secretary of State, Elections Division.

Registration Deadlines

A completed registration form must be postmarked or delivered to a county elections office or voter registration agency (e.g., DMV) no later than 21 days before the election. Electronic registrations must be completed no later than 11:59 p.m. 21 days before the election. Oregon residents who are not U.S. citizens by the deadline to register to vote, but who will be citizens by election day, should contact their county elections office for information about how to register to vote.

Persons who become residents of Oregon after the deadline to register for a U.S. presidential election may be eligible to vote for U.S. president and vice-president. Contact your county elections office for more information.

Maintaining a Current Voter Registration

Registered voters should update their registration if their home address or mailing address changes, their name or signature changes, if they want to change or select a political party or will be away from home on election day.

A registered voter can provide the new information online at www.oregonvotes.gov or by completing and returning a voter registration card to a county elections office or voter registration agency (e.g., DMV).

With the exception of changes to a voter's political party affiliation, updates can be made at any time including as late as election day in order to vote in that election. Political party changes, which determine the type of ballot a voter receives for the primary election, must be made no later than 21 days before the election.

Voting Absentee

Absentee ballots are mailed to military and other out-of-state voters in advance of the regular mailing of ballots. Voters should contact their local elections office to obtain an absentee ballot if they will be away from home on election day.

Voters' Pamphlets

For each primary and general election and for most special elections, the Elections Division produces and distributes to every household, a pamphlet containing information about candidates and measures that will appear on the ballot at the election. Many counties also produce pamphlets that contain information about local candidates and measures.

2022 FILING DEADLINES

Primary Election: The candidate filing period for the May 17, 2022, primary election begins on September 10, 2021, and ends on March 8, 2022. The deadline for filing *Voters' Pamphlet* material with the Elections Division is no sooner than January 17, 2022, and no later than March 20, 2022.

General Election: The candidate filing period for the November 8, 2022, general election begins on June 1, 2022, and ends on August 20, 2022. The deadline for filing *Voters' Pamphlet* material with the Elections Division is not sooner than July 11, 2022, and no later than August 30, 2022.

RECENT ELECTION HISTORY

2020 Primary Election

Election Date: May 19, 2020
Source: Abstracts of Votes, available from the Office of the Secretary of State, Elections Division, 255 Capitol St. NE, Suite 501, Salem 97310
Web: www.oregonvotes.gov
Key: *Nominated; **Elected

United States President

Democrat	Total
Biden, Joseph R.*	408,315
Gabbard, Tulsi	10,717
Sanders, Bernie	127,345
Warren, Elizabeth	59,355
Miscellaneous	12,979
Republican	
Trump, Donald J.*	361,010
Miscellaneous	24,247

United States Senator

Democrat	Total
Merkley, Jeff*	564,878
Miscellaneous	7,386
Republican	
Perkins, Jo Rae*	178,004
Romero Jr., Paul J	109,783
Schwartz, Robert	40,196
Verbeek, John	29,382
Miscellaneous	4,250

United States Representative

1st Congressional District

Democrat	Total
Barajas, Ricky	2,948
Bonamici, Suzanne*	100,733
Briones, Heidi	8,260
Siebe, Amanda	8,055
Miscellaneous	523
Republican	
Christensen, Christopher C.*	27,417
Murray, Army (Armidia)	20,509
Miscellaneous	1,162

2nd Congressional District

Democrat	Total
Heuertz, Nick (Nik) L.	22,685
Holm, John P.	5,908
Howard, Jack	6,047

Spenser, Alex*	23,482
Vaughn, Chris	13,351
Miscellaneous	1,734
Republican	
Atkinson, Jason A.	23,274
Bentz, Cliff*	37,488
Buehler, Knute C.	26,405
Campbell, David R.	418
Carey, Glenn	283
Crumpacker, Jimmy	21,507
Fager, Travis A.	4,265
Livingston, Justin	1,350
Medenbach, Kenneth W.	267
Roberts, Mark R.	1,336
Smith, Jeff	2,539
Miscellaneous	450

3rd Congressional District

Democrat	Total
Barnett, Charles Rand	953
Blumenauer, Earl*	140,812
Davis, Matthew S.	1,101
Lee, Albert	29,311
Wilcox, Dane	1,966
Miscellaneous	714
Republican	
Harbour, Joanna*	21,114
Harrison, Tom	7,751
Hecker, Frank	4,147
Miscellaneous	612

4th Congressional District

Democrat	Total
Canning, Doyle Elizabeth	17,701
DeFazio, Peter*	96,077
Miscellaneous	974
Republican	
Ijih, Nelson	10,325
Skarlatos, Alek*	70,599
Miscellaneous	780

5th Congressional District

Democrat	Total
Gamba, Mark F.	24,327
Reynolds, Blair G.	7,910
Schrader, Kurt*	73,060
Miscellaneous	841
Republican	
Dinkel, G. Shane	15,626
Nations, Joey	13,534
Roman, Angela	6,155
Ryan Courser, Amy*	41,417
Miscellaneous	1,003

Secretary of State

Democrat	Total
Fagan, Shemia*	209,682
Hass, Mark D.	205,230
McLeod-Skinner	159,430
Miscellaneous	4,395

Republican	
Stauffer, Dave W.	48,839
Thatcher, Kim*	312,296
Miscellaneous	3,625

State Treasurer

Democrat	Total
Read, Tobias*	464,429
Miscellaneous	5,956
Republican	
Gudman, Jeff*	305,589
Miscellaneous	3,223

Attorney General

Democrat	Total
Rosenblum, Ellen*	483,273
Miscellaneous	4,661
Republican	
Cross, Michael*	279,909
Miscellaneous	9,537

Judge of the Supreme Court

Nonpartisan	Total

Position 1

Balmer, Thomas A.**	727,421
Pounds, Van	295,887
Miscellaneous	3,638

Position 7

Walters, Martha**	828,329
Miscellaneous	10,625

Judge of the Court of Appeals

Nonpartisan	Total

Position 1

Mooney, Josephine H.**	806,796
Miscellaneous	10,680

Position 11

DeVore, Joel**	572,427
Krohn, Kyle L.	415,922
Miscellaneous	3,363

Position 12

Lagesen, Erin C.**	804,231
Miscellaneous	8,595

Position 13

Tookey, Doug**	793,533
Miscellaneous	9,836

Judge of the Circuit Court

Nonpartisan	Total

1st District—Position 1

Mejia, Lorenzo A.**	44,532
Miscellaneous	288

1st District—Position 2

Hoppe, David**	43,328
Miscellaneous	305

1st District—Position 3

Ravassipour, Kelly W.**	45,822
Miscellaneous	238

1st District—Position 6

Barnack, Timothy**	43,516
Miscellaneous	341

1st District—Position 8

Charter, Joe**	35,226
Greif, Lisa C.	26,123
Miscellaneous	86

1st District—Position 10

Kochlacs, Charles G.**	44,253
Miscellaneous	249

2nd District—Position 2

Carlson, Charles D.**	65,073
Miscellaneous	1,003

2nd District—Position 3

Cascagnette, Bradley A.**	65,025
Miscellaneous	925

2nd District—Position 4

Zennache', Charles M.**	65,830
Miscellaneous	927

2nd District—Position 15

Rigmaiden, Clara L.**	65,499
Miscellaneous	923

3rd District—Position 2

Prall, Tracy A.**	52,189
Miscellaneous	582

3rd District—Position 3

Pellegrini, Cheryl**	51,878
Miscellaneous	593

3rd District—Position 14

Tripp, Susan M.**	51,972
Miscellaneous	684

3rd District—Position 15

Perez, Manuel**	51,409
Miscellaneous	670

4th District—Position 1

Troy, Francis**	152,095
Miscellaneous	1,672

4th District—Position 2

Waller, Nan G.**	162,577
Miscellaneous	1,464

4th District—Position 5

Marshall, Christopher J.**	153,929
Miscellaneous	1,820

4th District—Position 11

Franco Lucero, Angela M.**	159,338
Miscellaneous	1,566

4th District—Position 12

Brown, Adrian L.*	67,169
Ghandour, Rima*	47,747
Herranz, Monica	12,162
Montalbano, Sonia	39,565
Schlosser, John E.	15,572
Warren Jr., Ernest	23,623
Miscellaneous	673

4th District—Position 13

Long, Morgan Wren**	156,794
Miscellaneous	1,366

4th District—Position 14

Holmes Hehn, Amy**	152,037
Miscellaneous	1,552

4th District—Position 18

Ryan, Tom**	150,837
Miscellaneous	1,568

4th District—Position 19

Greenlick, Michael A.**	150,799
Miscellaneous	1,584

4th District—Position 21

Bushong, Stephen K.**	153,939
Miscellaneous	1,415

4th District—Position 33

Loy, Michael S.**	149,799
Miscellaneous	1,561

4th District—Position 34

Allen, Beth**	151,552
Miscellaneous	1,461

4th District—Position 36

Moawad, Heidi**	155,129
Miscellaneous	1,390

4th District—Position 38

Baggio, Amy M.**	150,980
Miscellaneous	1,445

5th District—Position 6

Steele, Kathie F.**	77,361
Miscellaneous	869

5th District—Position 8

Karabeika, Heather L.**	76,882
Miscellaneous	838

7th District—Position 3

Ostrye, Karen**	12,024
Miscellaneous	143

11th District—Position 5

Miller, Randy**	43,379
Miscellaneous	315

11th District—Position 7

Emerson, Alison**	43,709
Miscellaneous	287

15th District—Position 6

Beaman, Cynthia L.**	18,138
Miscellaneous	240

16th District—Position 1

Simmons, Ann Marie**	21,412
Miscellaneous	398

17th District—Position 1

Bachart, Sheryl M.**	12,118
Baldwin, Russell L.	4,957
Miscellaneous	28

18th District—Position 1

Peterson, Beau V.**	9,390
Miscellaneous	115

19th District—Position 1

Callahan, Cathleen B.**	12,335
Miscellaneous	290

19th District—Position 2

Grove, Ted E.**	12,933
Miscellaneous	329

19th District—Position 3

Clarke, Michael T.*	7,009
Grant, Jenefer S.*	6,872
Huffman, James D.	2,729
Miscellaneous	62

20th District—Position 2

Guptill, Rebecca D.**	108,173
Miscellaneous	1,232

20th District—Position 5

Burke, Steven Charles	19,750
Kroll, Edward A.*	35,669
Lemarr, Kelly D.*	59,236
Ridehalgh, Ron	13,390
Miscellaneous	590

20th District—Position 7

Erwin, Andrew R.**	103,094
Miscellaneous	1,509

20th District—Position 8

Menchaca, Ricardo J.**	106,570
Miscellaneous	1,219

20th District—Position 12

Roberts, Beth L.**	104,135
Miscellaneous	1,340

21st District—Position 1

Williams, Locke A.**	19,520
Miscellaneous	221

21st District—Position 2

Donohue, Matthew**	19,262
Miscellaneous	201

22nd District—Position 2

McLane Mike, **	10,595
Miscellaneous	108

23rd District—Position 2

Delsman, David**	23,796
Miscellaneous	394

24th District—Position 1

Carpenter, Jim*	1,970
Lamborn, John B.	1,223
Raschio, Rob*	2,814
Miscellaneous	16

25th District—Position 4

Wiles, Ladd J.**	19,423
Miscellaneous	268

26th District—Position 1

Vandenberg, David M.**	2,048
Miscellaneous	40

27th District—Position 2

Trevino, Mari G.**	6,914
Miscellaneous	80

2020 General Election

Election Date: November 3, 2020

Source: *Abstracts of Votes,* available from the Office of the Secretary of State, Elections Division, 255 Capitol St. NE, Suite 501, Salem 97310

Web: www.oregonvotes.gov

Key: *Elected

C = Constitution Party
D = Democratic Party
I = Independent Party
L = Libertarian Party
NAV = Nonaffiliated
PG = Pacific Green Party
P = Progressive Party
R = Republican Party
WF = Working Families Party

United States President

	Total
Biden, Joseph R.—D*	1,340,383
Hawkins, Howie—PG	11,831
Hunter, Dario—P	4,988
Jorgensen, Jo—L	41,582
Trump, Donald J.—R	958,448
Miscellaneous	17,089

United States Senator

	Total
Dye, Gary—L	42,747
Merkley, Jeff—D*	1,321,047
Perkins, Jo Rae—R	912,814
Taher, Ibrahim A.—PG	42,239
Miscellaneous	2,402

United States Representative

1st Congressional District

	Total
Bonamici, Suzanne—D*	297,071
Christensen, Christopher C. —R	161,928
Miscellaneous	900

2nd Congressional District

	Total
Bentz, Cliff—R*	273,835
Spenser, Alex—D	168,881
Werch, Robert—L	14,094
Miscellaneous	623

3rd Congressional District

	Total
Blumenauer, Earl—D*	343,574
DiBlasi, Alex C.—PG	8,872
Harbour, Joanna—R	110,570
Solomon, Josh—L	6,869
Miscellaneous	621

4th Congressional District

	Total
DeFazio, Peter—D*	240,950
Hoffay, Daniel—PG	10,118
Skarlatos, Alek—R	216,081
Miscellaneous	556

5th Congressional District

	Total
Rix, Matthew James—L	12,640
Ryan Courser, Amy—R	204,372
Schrader, Kurt—D*	234,863
Miscellaneous	771

Secretary of State

	Total
Fagan, Shemia—D*	1,146,370
Markley, Kyle—L	62,985
Paravicini, Nathalie—PG	82,211
Thatcher, Kim—R	984,597
Miscellaneous	2,340

State Treasurer

	Total
Gudman, Jeff—R	936,916
Henry, Chris—I	99,870
Marsh, Michael P.—C	51,894
Read, Tobias—D*	1,166,703
Miscellaneous	2,072

Attorney General

	Total
Cross, Michael—R	934,357
Hedbor, Lars D. H.—L	52,087
Rosenblum, Ellen—D*	1,264,716
Miscellaneous	8,490

Judge of the Supreme Court

Nonpartisan

Position 4

	Total
Garrett, Christopher L.*	1,366,654
Miscellaneous	38,206

Judge of the Court of Appeals

Nonpartisan

Position 9

	Total
Kamins, Jacqueline S.*	1,354,230
Miscellaneous	33,333

Judge of the Circuit Court

Nonpartisan

2nd District—Position 6

	Total
Kapoor, Amit*	115,134
Miscellaneous	2,901

2nd District—Position 10

Shugar, Kamala*	119,002
Miscellaneous	2,796

4th District—Position 12

Brown, Adrian L.*	199,784
Ghandour, Rima	146,718
Miscellaneous	3,956

4th District—Position 26

Alexander, Steffan*	264,796
Miscellaneous	6,530

8th District—Position 1

Shirtcliff, Matt*	7,245
Miscellaneous	177

11th District—Position 4

Sykora, Alycia N.*	72,000
Miscellaneous	1,248

13th District—Position 2

Edgeworth Kersey, Alycia*	13,676
Guest, Joshua C.	1,490
Lam, Bonnie A.	4,893
Ratliff, Nathan	12,218
Miscellaneous	76

14th District—Position 1

Thorpe, Amanda	19,347
Thueson, Brandon S.*	19,819
Miscellaneous	242

14th District—Position 4

Hayward, Jason D.	14,331
McGlaughlin, Sarah E.*	25,978
Miscellaneous	197

17th District—Position 2

Benjamin, Amanda	12,738
Buckley, Marcia*	12,888
Miscellaneous	99

19th District—Position 3

Clarke, Michael T.*	14,091
Grant, Jenefer S.	13,408
Miscellaneous	152

20th District—Position 5

Lemarr, Kelly D.*	192,504
Miscellaneous	3,709

20th District—Position 10

Thompson, Brandon M.*	187,296
Miscellaneous	3,801

21st District—Position 3

Demarest, Joan E.*	33,064
Miscellaneous	586

23rd District—Position 4

Kane, Brendan J.*	41,909
Miscellaneous	980

24th District—Position 1

Carpenter, Jim	1,475
Raschio, Rob*	5,106
Miscellaneous	1,551

Voter Participation 1990–2020

*Presidential election year

Primary Election

Year	Registered Voters	Voted	Percent
1990	1,437,462	660,990	46.0
1992*	1,543,353	758,459	49.1
1994	1,730,562	661,717	38.2
1996*	1,851,499	698,990	37.8
1998	1,906,677	665,340	34.9
2000*	1,808,080	927,351	51.3
2002	1,839,072	858,524	46.6
2004*	1,862,919	864,833	46.4
2006	1,965,939	758,393	38.6
2008*	2,008,957	1,170,526	58.3
2010	2,033,951	846,515	41.6
2012*	2,021,263	787,847	38.9
2014	2,113,430	758,604	35.9
2016*	2,281,555	1,231,843	54.0
2018	2,660,183	908,166	34.1
2020*	2,845,634	1,310,919	46.1

General Election

Year	Registered Voters	Voted	Percent
1990	1,476,500	1,133,125	76.7
1992*	1,775,416	1,498,959	84.4
1994	1,832,774	1,254,265	68.4
1996*	1,962,155	1,399,180	71.3
1998	1,965,981	1,160,400	59.0
2000*	1,954,006	1,559,215	79.8
2002	1,872,615	1,293,756	69.1
2004*	2,141,243	1,851,593	86.5
2006	1,976,669	1,399,650	70.8
2008*	2,153,914	1,845,251	85.7
2010	2,068,798	1,487,210	71.9
2012*	2,199,360	1,820,507	82.8
2014	2,174,763	1,541,782	70.9
2016*	2,561,657	2,056,310	80.3
2018	2,748,232	1,914,923	69.7
2020*	2,944,588	2,413,890	82.0

Voter Registration by County—November 3, 2020

County	Democrat	Republican	*Nonaffiliated	**Other	Total
Baker	2,064	5,900	3,733	826	12,523
Benton	26,877	13,010	16,906	3,746	60,539
Clackamas	106,247	87,034	93,473	21,356	308,110
Clatsop	10,339	7,442	10,123	2,051	29,955
Columbia	12,315	11,412	13,687	2,772	40,186
Coos	12,245	15,536	16,614	3,284	47,679
Crook	3,414	8,599	5,907	1,298	19,218
Curry	4,571	6,233	6,464	1,394	18,662
Deschutes	47,299	45,735	46,027	11,614	150,675
Douglas	17,310	33,209	27,267	5,760	83,546
Gilliam	267	619	418	89	1,393
Grant	900	2,741	1,532	337	5,510
Harney	865	2,769	1,516	333	5,483
Hood River	6,404	3,142	5,221	947	15,714
Jackson	47,188	50,916	51,680	11,378	161,162
Jefferson	3,440	5,531	5,956	1,149	16,076
Josephine	15,055	25,001	23,802	4,972	68,830
Klamath	8,717	19,946	17,136	3,227	49,026
Lake	701	2,796	1,606	313	5,416
Lane	107,846	63,366	83,990	18,852	274,054
Lincoln	13,549	8,701	13,578	2,598	38,426
Linn	22,798	32,691	31,878	6,591	93,958
Malheur	2,482	6,397	7,081	769	16,729
Marion	63,478	62,971	74,284	13,522	214,255
Morrow	1,210	2,457	2,648	438	6,753
Multnomah	301,880	64,647	169,755	35,101	571,383
Polk	17,923	19,538	19,234	4,029	60,724
Sherman	265	700	379	87	1,431
Tillamook	6,515	6,058	6,764	1,369	20,706
Umatilla	8,892	15,538	18,863	3,008	46,301
Union	3,776	8,315	5,694	1,266	19,051
Wallowa	1,243	2,797	1,550	342	5,932
Wasco	5,310	5,069	6,525	1,265	18,169
Washington	146,727	82,730	129,972	22,903	382,332
Wheeler	215	555	256	71	1,097
Yamhill	20,792	23,489	24,085	5,218	73,584
Totals	**1,051,119**	**753,590**	**945,604**	**194,275**	**2,944,588**

*A "nonaffiliated" voter is one who has chosen not to be a member of any political party and has indicated this on his or her voter registration card.

**"Other" includes all voters registered with minor political parties.

OREGON ELECTION HISTORY

Voter Registration for General Elections 1990–2020

Year	Democrat	Republican	*Other	Total
1990	692,100	570,933	213,467	1,476,500
1992	792,551	642,206	340,659	1,775,416
1994	786,990	665,956	379,828	1,832,774
1996	805,286	714,548	442,321	1,962,155
1998	791,970	704,593	469,418	1,965,981
2000	769,195	699,179	485,632	1,954,006
2002	729,460	680,444	462,711	1,872,615
2004	829,193	761,715	550,335	2,141,243
2006	767,562	706,365	502,742	1,976,669
2008	929,741	695,677	528,496	2,153,914
2010	863,322	664,123	541,353	2,068,798

Year	Democrat	Republican	*Other	Total
2012	872,361	684,858	642,141	2,199,360
2014	825,701	653,048	696,014	2,174,763

Year	Democrat	Republican	Independent	*Other	Total
2016	981,153	717,497	117,389	745,618	2,561,657
2018	976,908	705,833	124,187	941,304	2,748,232

Year	Democrat	Republican	*Other	Total
2020	1,051,119	753,590	1,139,879	2,944,588

*"Other" includes all voters registered with minor political parties and nonaffiliated voters.

Votes Cast in Oregon for United States President 1860–2020

Key: *Elected; **Received highest vote in Oregon but lost election nationwide

Year	Candidate	Party	Votes
1860	John Bell	Constitutional Union	212
	John C. Breckenridge	Democrat	5,074
	Stephen Douglas	Douglas Democrat	4,131
	Abraham Lincoln*	Republican	5,344
1864	Abraham Lincoln*	Republican	9,888
	George McClellan	Democrat	8,457
1868	U.S. Grant*	Republican	10,961
	Horatio Seymour**	Democrat	11,125
1872	U.S. Grant*	Republican	11,818
	Horace Greeley	Democrat-Liberal Republicans	7,742
	Charles O'Connor	National Labor Reformers	587
1876	Peter Cooper	Greenback	510
	Rutherford B. Hayes*	Republican	15,214
	Samuel Tilden	Democrat	14,157
1880	James A. Garfield*	Republican	20,619
	Winfield Hancock	Democrat	19,955
	James B. Weaver	Greenback Labor	249
1884	James G. Blaine**	Republican	26,860
	General B.F. Butler	Greenback Labor (Workingman)	726
	Grover Cleveland*	Democrat	24,604
	John P. St. John	Prohibition	492
1888	Grover Cleveland	Democrat	26,522
	Robert H. Cowdrey	United Labor	363
	Clinton B. Fisk	Prohibition	1,677
	Benjamin Harrison*	Republican	33,291
1892	John Bidwell	Prohibition	2,281
	Grover Cleveland*	Democrat	14,243
	Benjamin Harrison**	Republican	35,002
	James B. Weaver[1]	Populist	26,965
1896	William J. Bryan	Democrat, People's Party and Silver Republican	46,739
	Joshua Levering	Prohibition	919
	William McKinley*	Republican	48,779
	John M. Palmer	National (Gold) Democrat	977
1900	Wharton Barker	Regular People's	275
	William J. Bryan	Democrat People's	33,385
	Eugene V. Debs	Social-Democrats	1,494
	William McKinley*	Republican	46,526
	John G. Woolley	Prohibition	2,536
1904	Eugene V. Debs	Socialist	7,619
	Alton Parker	Democrat	17,327
	Theodore Roosevelt*	Republican	60,455
	Silas C. Swallow	Prohibition	3,806
	Thomas E. Watson	People's	753

Year	Candidate	Party	Votes
1908	William J. Bryan	Democrat	38,049
	Eugene W. Chafin	Prohibition	2,682
	Eugene V. Debs	Socialist	7,339
	Thomas L. Hisgen	Independence	289
	William H. Taft*	Republican	62,530
1912	Eugene W. Chafin	Prohibition	4,360
	Eugene V. Debs	Socialist	13,343
	Theodore Roosevelt	Progressive	37,600
	William H. Taft	Republican	34,673
	Woodrow Wilson*	Democrat	47,064
1916	Allan L. Benson	Socialist	9,711
	J. Frank Hanley	Prohibition	4,729
	Charles Evans Hughes**	Republican	126,813
	John M. Parker[2]	Progressive	310
	Woodrow Wilson*	Democrat	120,087
1920	James M. Cox	Democrat	80,019
	William W. Cox	Industrial Labor	1,515
	Eugene V. Debs	Socialist	9,801
	Warren G. Harding*	Republican	143,592
	Aaron S. Watkins	Prohibition	3,595
1924	Calvin Coolidge*	Republican	142,579
	John W. Davis	Democrat	67,589
	Frank T. Johns	Socialist Labor	917
	Robert M. LaFollette	Independent	68,403
1928	William Z. Foster	Independent	1,094
	Herbert Hoover*	Republican	205,341
	Verne L. Reynolds	Socialist Labor	1,564
	Alfred E. Smith	Democrat	109,223
	Norman Thomas	Socialist Principles-Independent	2,720
1932	William Z. Foster	Communist	1,681
	Herbert Hoover	Republican	136,019
	Verne L. Reynolds	Socialist Labor	1,730
	Franklin D. Roosevelt*	Democrat	213,871
	Norman Thomas	Socialist	15,450
1936	John W. Aiken	Socialist Labor	500
	Alfred M. Landon	Republican	122,706
	William Lemke	Independent	21,831
	Franklin D. Roosevelt*	Democrat	266,733
	Norman Thomas	Independent	2,143
1940	John W. Aiken	Socialist Labor	2,487
	Franklin D. Roosevelt*	Democrat	258,415
	Wendell L. Willkie	Republican	219,555
1944	Thomas E. Dewey	Republican	225,365
	Franklin D. Roosevelt*	Democrat	248,635
	Norman Thomas	Independent	3,785
	Claude A. Watson	Independent	2,362
1948	Thomas E. Dewey**	Republican	260,904
	Norman Thomas	Independent	5,051
	Harry S. Truman*	Democrat	243,147
	Henry A. Wallace	Progressive	14,978
1952	Dwight D. Eisenhower*	Republican	420,815
	Vincent Hallinan	Independent	3,665
	Adlai Stevenson	Democrat	270,579
1956	Dwight D. Eisenhower*	Republican	406,393
	Adlai Stevenson	Democrat	329,204
1960	John F. Kennedy*	Democrat	367,402
	Richard M. Nixon**	Republican	408,060
1964	Barry M. Goldwater	Republican	282,779
	Lyndon B. Johnson*	Democrat	501,017
1968	Hubert H. Humphrey	Democrat	358,866

Year	Candidate	Party	Votes
	Richard M. Nixon*	Republican	408,433
	George C. Wallace	Independent	49,683
1972	George S. McGovern	Democrat	392,760
	Richard M. Nixon*	Republican	486,686
	John G. Schmitz	Independent	46,211
1976	Jimmy Carter*	Democrat	490,407
	Gerald Ford**	Republican	492,120
	Eugene J. McCarthy	Independent	40,207
1980	John Anderson	Independent	112,389
	Jimmy Carter	Democrat	456,890
	Ed Clark	Libertarian	25,838
	Barry Commoner	Independent	13,642
	Ronald Reagan*	Republican	571,044
1984	Walter F. Mondale	Democrat	536,479
	Ronald Reagan*	Republican	685,700
1988	George Bush*	Republican	560,126
	Michael S. Dukakis**	Democrat	616,206
	Lenora B. Fulani	Independent	6,487
	Ron Paul	Libertarian	14,811
1992	George Bush	Republican	475,757
	Bill Clinton*	Democrat	621,314
	Lenora Fulani	New Alliance Party	3,030
	Andre Marrou	Libertarian	4,277
	Ross Perot	Independent Initiative Party of Oregon	354,091
1996	Harry Browne	Libertarian	8,903
	Bill Clinton*	Democrat	649,641
	Bob Dole	Republican	538,152
	John Hagelin	Natural Law	2,798
	Mary Cal Hollis	Socialist	1,922
	Ralph Nader	Pacific	49,415
	Ross Perot	Reform	121,221
	Howard Phillips	U.S. Taxpayers	3,379
2000	Harry Browne	Libertarian	7,447
	Patrick J. Buchanan	Independent	7,063
	George W. Bush*	Republican	713,577
	Al Gore**	Democrat	720,342
	John Hagelin	Reform	2,574
	Ralph Nader	Pacific Green	77,357
	Howard Phillips	Constitution	2,189
2004	Michael Badnarik	Libertarian	7,260
	George W. Bush*	Republican	866,831
	David Cobb	Pacific Green	5,315
	John F. Kerry**	Democrat	943,163
	Michael Anthony Peroutka	Constitution	5,257
2008	Baldwin, Chuck	Constitution	7,693
	Barr, Bob	Libertarian	7,635
	McCain, John	Republican	738,475
	McKinney, Cynthia	Pacific Green	4,543
	Nader, Ralph	Peace	18,614
	Obama, Barack*	Democrat	1,037,291
2012	Anderson, Ross C. (Rocky)	Progressive	3,384
	Christensen, Will	Constitution	4,432
	Johnson, Gary	Libertarian	24,089
	Obama, Barack*	Democrat	970,488
	Romney, Mitt	Republican	754,175
	Stein, Jill	Pacific Green	19,427
2016	Clinton, Hillary**	Democrat	1,002,106
	Johnson, Gary	Libertarian	94,231
	Stein, Jill	Pacific Green	50,002
	Trump, Donald J.*	Republican	782,403

Year	Candidate	Party	Votes
2020	Biden, Joseph R.*	Democrat	1,340,383
	Hawkins, Howie	Pacific Green	11,831
	Hunter, Dario	Progressive	4,988
	Jorgensen, Jo	Libertarian	41,582
	Trump, Donald J	Republican	958,448

[1]One Weaver elector was endorsed by the Democrats and elected as a Fusionist, receiving 35,811 votes.

[2]Vice-presidential candidate

Initiative, Referendum and Recall

In 1902, Oregon voters overwhelmingly approved a legislatively referred ballot measure that created Oregon's initiative and referendum process. In 1904, voters enacted the direct primary and in 1908, Oregon's Constitution was amended to allow for recall of public officials. These were the culmination of efforts by the Direct Legislation League, a group of political activists that progressive leader William S. U'Ren founded in 1898.

This system of empowering the people to propose new laws or change the Constitution of Oregon through a general election ballot measure became nationally known as "the Oregon System."

Initiative: Petition process that allows registered voters to propose amendments to the Oregon Constitution or changes to the Oregon Revised Statutes (ORS).

Referendum: Petition process that allows registered voters to adopt or reject any nonemergency Act or portion of a nonemergency Act passed by the Legislature.

Referral: Process that allows the Legislature to place on the ballot for voters' approval, any bill it passes. Any amendment to the Oregon Constitution proposed by the Legislature must be placed on the ballot for voters to approve or reject.

Since 1902, the people have passed 130 of the 375 initiative measures placed on the ballot and 24 of the 66 referenda on the ballot. During the same period, the Legislature has referred 434 measures to the people, of which 253 have passed.

Both houses of the Legislature must vote to refer a statute or constitutional amendment for popular vote. Such referrals cannot be vetoed by the governor.

To place an initiative or referendum on the ballot, supporters must obtain a specified number of signatures from registered voters. The number required is determined by a fixed percentage of the votes cast for all candidates for governor at the last general election where the governor was elected to a full term. In the 2018 General Election, 1,866,997 votes were cast for governor. Therefore, referendum petitions require 4 percent, or 74,680 signatures; initiative petitions for statutory enactments require 6 percent, or 112,020 signatures; and initiative petitions for constitutional amendments require 8 percent, or 149,360 signatures.

The original constitutional amendment, passed in 1902, provided that a fixed percentage of the votes cast for justice of the Supreme Court would determine the number of signatures required to place an initiative or referendum on the ballot. Both a statutory enactment and a constitutional amendment required 8 percent of the votes cast, while a referendum required 5 percent of the votes cast. In 1954, the people amended the Oregon Constitution to increase the required number of signatures to 10 percent for a constitutional amendment. In 1968, a vote of the people established the current requirements.

Prior to 1954, measures on the ballot were not numbered. They are listed below in order of appearance on the ballot. The 2001 Legislature amended state law to require that ballot measure numbers not repeat in any subsequent election. Numbers assigned for each election begin with the next number after the last number assigned in the previous election.

Key: *Adopted; L = Referred by the Legislature; I = Submitted by initiative petition; R = Referendum by petition; (Also see footnotes on p. 272)

Election Date/Measure Number/Ballot Title	Yes	No
June 2, 1902		
1. Limits Uses Initiative and Referendum—L[1]	*62,024	5,668
June 6, 1904		
1. Office of State Printer—L[1]	*45,334	14,031
2. Direct Primary Nominating Convention Law—I[2]	*56,205	16,354
3. Local Option Liquor Law—I[2]	*43,316	40,198
June 4, 1906		
1. Shall act appropriating money maintaining Insane Asylum, Penitentiary, Deaf-Mute, Blind School, University, Agricultural College, and Normal Schools be approved—R	*43,918	26,758

Election Date/Measure Number/Ballot Title	Yes	No
2. Equal Suffrage Constitutional Amendment—I[1]	36,902	47,075
3. Amendment to local option law giving anti-prohibitionists and prohibitionists equal privileges—I[2]	35,297	45,144
4. Law to abolish tolls on the Mount Hood and Barlow Road and providing for its ownership by the State—I[2]	31,525	44,527
5. Constitutional amendment providing method of amending constitution and applying the referendum to all laws affecting constitutional conventions and amendments—I[1]	*47,661	18,751
6. Constitutional amendment giving cities and towns exclusive power to enact and amend their charters—I[1]	*52,567	19,852
7. Constitutional amendment to allow the state printing, binding, and Printers' compensation to be regulated by law at any time—I[1]	*63,749	9,571
8. Constitutional amendment for the initiative and referendum on local, special and municipal laws and parts of laws—I[1]	*47,678	16,735
9. Bill for a law prohibiting free passes and discrimination by railroad companies and other public service corporations—I[2]	*57,281	16,779
10. An act requiring sleeping car companies, refrigerator car companies and oil companies to pay an annual license upon gross earnings—I[2]	*69,635	6,441
11. An act requiring express companies, telegraph companies and telephone companies to pay an annual license upon gross earnings—I[2]	*70,872	6,360

June 1, 1908

	Yes	No
1. To Increase Compensation of Legislators from $120 to $400 Per Session—L[1]	19,691	68,892
2. Permitting Location of State Institutions at Places Other than the State Capitol—L[1]	*41,975	40,868
3. Reorganization System of Courts and Increasing the Number of Supreme Judges from Three to Five—L[1]	30,243	50,591
4. Changing Date of General Elections from June to November—L[1]	*65,728	18,590
5. Giving Sheriffs Control of County Prisoners—R	*60,443	30,033
6. Requiring Railroads to Give Public Officials Free Passes—R	28,856	59,406
7. Appropriating $100,000 for Building Armories—R	33,507	54,848
8. Increasing Annual Appropriation for University of Oregon from $47,500 to $125,000—R	*44,115	40,535
9. Equal Suffrage—I[1]	36,858	58,670
10. Fishery Law Proposed by Fishwheel Operators—I[2]	*46,582	40,720
11. Giving Cities Control of Liquor Selling, Poolrooms, Theaters, etc., subject to local option law—I[1]	39,442	52,346
12. Modified Form of Single Tax Amendment—I[1]	32,066	60,871
13. Recall Power on Public Officials—I[1]	*58,381	31,002
14. Instructing Legislature to Vote for People's Choice for United States Senator—I[2]	*69,668	21,162
15. Authorizing Proportional Representation Law—I[1]	*48,868	34,128
16. Corrupt Practices Act Governing Elections—I[2]	*54,042	31,301
17. Fishery Law Proposed by Gillnet Operators—I[2]	*56,130	30,280
18. Requiring Indictment To Be By Grand Jury—I[1]	*52,214	28,487
19. Creating Hood River County—I[2]	*43,948	26,778

November 8, 1910

	Yes	No
1. Permitting Female Taxpayers to Vote—I[1]	35,270	59,065
2. Establishing Branch Insane Asylum in Eastern Oregon—L[2]	*50,134	41,504
3. Calling Convention to Revise State Constitution—L[2]	23,143	59,974
4. Providing Separate Districts for Election of Each State Senator and Representative—L[1]	24,000	54,252
5. Repealing Requirements That All Taxes Shall Be Equal and Uniform—L[1]	37,619	40,172
6. Permitting Organized Districts to Vote Bonds for Construction of Railroads by Such Districts—L[1]	32,884	46,070
7. Authorizing Collection of State and County Taxes on Separate Classes of Property—L[1]	31,629	41,692

Elections and Records

Election Date/Measure Number/Ballot Title	Yes	No
8. Requiring Baker County to Pay $1,000 a Year to Circuit Judge in Addition to His State Salary—R	13,161	71,503
9. Creating Nesmith County From Parts of Lane and Douglas—I²	22,866	60,951
10. To Establish a State Normal School at Monmouth—I²	*50,191	40,044
11. Creating Otis County From Parts of Harney, Malheur and Grant—I²	17,426	62,016
12. Annexing Part of Clackamas County to Multnomah—I²	16,250	69,002
13. Creating Williams County From Parts of Lane and Douglas—I²	14,508	64,090
14. Permitting People of Each County to Regulate Taxation for County Purposes and Abolishing Poll Taxes—I¹	*44,171	42,127
15. Giving Cities and Towns Exclusive Power to Regulate Liquor Traffic Within Their Limits—I¹	*53,321	50,779
16. For Protection of Laborers in Hazardous Employment, Fixing Employers' Liability, etc.—I²	*56,258	33,943
17. Creating Orchard County From Part of Umatilla—I²	15,664	62,712
18. Creating Clark County From Part of Grant—I²	15,613	61,704
19. To Establish State Normal School at Weston—I²	40,898	46,201
20. To Annex Part of Washington County to Multnomah—I²	14,047	68,221
21. To Establish State Normal School at Ashland—I²	38,473	48,655
22. Prohibiting Liquor Traffic—I¹	43,540	61,221
23. Prohibiting the Sale of Liquors and Regulating Shipments of Same, and Providing for Search for Liquor—I²	42,651	63,564
24. Creating Board to Draft Employers' Liability Law for Submission to Legislature—I²	32,224	51,719
25. Prohibiting Taking of Fish in Rogue River Except With Hook and Line—I²	*49,712	33,397
26. Creating Deschutes County Out of Part of Crook—I²	17,592	60,486
27. Bill for General Law Under Which New Counties May Be Created or Boundaries Changed—I²	37,129	42,327
28. Permitting Counties to Vote Bonds for Permanent Road Improvement—I¹	*51,275	32,906
29. Permitting Voters in Direct Primaries to Express Choice for President and Vice President, to Select Delegates to National Convention and Nominate Candidates for Presidential Electors—I²	*43,353	41,624
30. Creating Board of People's Inspectors of Government, Providing for Reports of Board in Official State Gazette to be Mailed to All Registered Voters Bi-monthly—I²	29,955	52,538
31. Extending Initiative and Referendum, Making Term of Members of Legislature Six Years, Increasing Salaries, Requiring Proportional Representation in Legislature, Election of President of Senate and Speaker of House Outside of Members, etc.—I¹	37,031	44,366
32. Permitting Three-Fourths Verdict in Civil Cases—I¹	*44,538	39,399

November 5, 1912

	Yes	No
1. Equal Suffrage Amendment—I¹	*61,265	57,104
2. Creating Office of Lieutenant Governor—L¹	50,562	61,644
3. Divorce of Local and State Taxation—L¹	51,582	56,671
4. Permitting Different Tax Rates on Classes of Property—L¹	52,045	54,483
5. Repeal of County Tax Option—L¹	*63,881	47,150
6. Majority Rule on Constitutional Amendments—L¹	32,934	70,325
7. Double Liability on Bank Stockholders—L¹	*82,981	21,738
8. Statewide Public Utilities Regulation—R	*65,985	40,956
9. Creating Cascade County—I²	26,463	71,239
10. Millage Tax for University and Agricultural College—I²	48,701	57,279
11. Majority Rule on Initiated Laws—I¹	35,721	68,861
12. County Bond and Road Construction Act—Grange Bill—I²	49,699	56,713
13. Creating State Highway Department—Grange Bill—I²	23,872	83,846
14. Changing Date State Printer Bill Becomes Effective—I²	34,793	69,542
15. Creating Office of Hotel Inspector—I²	16,910	91,995
16. Eight-hour Day on Public Works—I²	*64,508	48,078
17. Blue Sky Law—I²	48,765	57,293
18. Relating to Employment of State Prisoners—I²	*73,800	37,492

Election Date/Measure Number/Ballot Title	Yes	No
19. Relating to Employment of County and City Prisoners—I²	*71,367	37,731
20. State Road Bonding Act—I²	30,897	75,590
21. Limiting State Road Indebtedness—I¹	*59,452	43,447
22. County Bonding Act—I²	43,611	60,210
23. Limiting County Road Indebtedness—I¹	*57,258	43,858
24. Providing Method for Consolidating Cities and Creating New Counties—I²	40,199	56,992
25. Income Tax Amendment—I¹	52,702	52,948
26. Tax Exemption on Household Effects—I²	*60,357	51,826
27. Tax Exemption on Moneys and Credits—I²	42,491	66,540
28. Revising Inheritance Tax Laws—I²	38,609	63,839
29. Freight Rates Act—I²	*58,306	45,534
30. County Road Bonding Act—I¹	38,568	63,481
31. Abolishing Senate; Proxy Voting; U'Ren Constitution—I¹	31,020	71,183
32. Statewide Single Tax with Graduated Tax Provision—I¹	31,534	82,015
33. Abolishing Capital Punishment—I²	41,951	64,578
34. Prohibits Boycotts and Pickets—I²	49,826	60,560
35. Prohibits Use of Public Streets, Parks and Grounds in Cities over 5,000 Without Permit—I²	48,987	62,532
36. Appropriation for University of Oregon—R	29,437	78,985
37. Appropriation for University of Oregon—R	27,310	79,376
November 4, 1913 (Special Referendum Election)		
1. State University Building Repair Fund—R	*56,659	40,600
2. University of Oregon New Building Appropriation—R	*53,569	43,014
3. Sterilization Act—R	41,767	53,319
4. County Attorney Act—R	*54,179	38,159
5. Workmen's Compensation Act—R	*67,814	28,608
November 3, 1914		
1. Requiring Voters to be Citizens of the United States—L¹	*164,879	39,847
2. Creating Office of Lieutenant Governor—L¹	52,040	143,804
3. Permitting Certain City and County Boundaries to be Made Identical, and Governments Consolidated—L¹	77,392	103,194
4. Permitting State to Create an Indebtedness Not to Exceed Two Percent of Assessed Valuation for Irrigation and Power Projects and Development of Untilled Lands—L¹	49,759	135,550
5. Omitting Requirement that "All Taxation Shall Be Equal And Uniform"—L¹	59,206	116,490
6. Changing Existing Rule of Uniformity and Equality of Taxation—Authorizing Classification of Property for Taxation Purposes—L¹	52,362	122,704
7. To Establish State Normal School at Ashland—L²	84,041	109,643
8. Enabling Incorporated Municipalities to Surrender Charters and To Be Merged in Adjoining City or Town—L¹	*96,116	77,671
9. To Establish State Normal School at Weston—L²	87,450	105,345
10. Providing Compensation for Members of Legislature at Five Dollars Per Day—L¹	41,087	146,278
11. Universal Constitutional Eight Hour Day Amendment—I¹	49,360	167,888
12. Eight-hour Day and Room-Ventilation Law for Female Workers—I²	88,480	120,296
13. Nonpartisan Judiciary Bill Prohibiting Party Nominations for Judicial Officers—I²	74,323	107,263
14. $1,500 Tax Exemption Amendment—I¹	65,495	136,193
15. Public Docks and Water Frontage Amendment—I¹	67,128	114,564
16. Municipal Wharves and Docks Bill—I²	67,110	111,113
17. Prohibition Constitutional Amendment—I¹	*136,842	100,362
18. Abolishing Death Penalty—I¹	*100,552	100,395
19. Specific Personal Graduated Extra-tax Amendment of Article IX, Oregon Constitution—I¹	59,186	124,943
20. Consolidating Corporation and Insurance Departments—I²	55,469	120,154
21. Dentistry Bill—I²	92,722	110,404
22. County Officers Term Amendment—I¹	82,841	107,039
23. A Tax Code Commission Bill—I²	34,436	143,468

Election Date/Measure Number/Ballot Title	Yes	No
24. Abolishing Desert Land Board and Reorganizing Certain State Offices—I^2	32,701	143,366
25. Proportional Representation Amendment to Oregon Constitution—I^1	39,740	137,116
26. State Senate Constitutional Amendment—I^1	62,376	123,429
27. Department of Industry and Public Works Amendment—I^1	57,859	126,201
28. Primary Delegate Election Bill—I^2	25,058	153,638
29. Equal Assessment and Taxation and $300 Exemption Amendment—$I^1$	43,280	140,507
November 7, 1916		
1. Single Item Veto Amendment—L^1	*141,773	53,207
2. Ship Tax Exemption Amendment—L^1	*119,652	65,410
3. Negro and Mulatto Suffrage Amendment—L^1	100,027	100,701
4. Full Rental Value Land Tax and Homemakers' Loan Fund Amendment—I^1	43,390	154,980
5. For Pendleton Normal School and Ratifying Location Certain State Institutions—I^1	96,829	109,523
6. Anti-compulsory Vaccination Bill—I^2	99,745	100,119
7. Bill Repealing and Abolishing the Sunday Closing Law—I^2	*125,836	93,076
8. Permitting Manufacture and Regulating Sale 4 Percent Malt Liquors—I^1	85,973	140,599
9. Prohibition Amendment Forbidding Importation of Intoxicating Liquors for Beverage Purposes—I^1	*114,932	109,671
10. Rural Credits Amendment—I^1	*107,488	83,887
11. State-wide Tax and Indebtedness Limitation Amendment—I^1	*99,536	84,031
June 4, 1917 (Special Election)		
1. Authorizing Ports to Create Limited Indebtedness to Encourage Water Transportation—L^1	*67,445	54,864
2. Limiting Number of Bills Introduced and Increasing Pay of Legislators—L^1	22,276	103,238
3. Declaration Against Implied Repeal of Constitutional Provisions by Amendments Thereto—L^1	37,187	72,445
4. Uniform Tax Classification Amendment—L^1	*62,118	53,245
5. Requiring Election City, Town and State Officers at Same Time—L^1	*83,630	42,296
6. Four Hundred Thousand Dollar Tax Levy for a New Penitentiary—L^2	46,666	86,165
7. Six Million Dollar State Road Bond Issue and Highway Bill—L^2	*77,316	63,803
November 5, 1918		
1. Establishing and Maintaining Southern and Eastern Oregon Normal Schools—L^1	49,935	66,070
2. Establishing Dependent, Delinquent and Defective Children's Home, Appropriating Money Therefor—L^2	43,441	65,299
3. Prohibiting Seine and Setnet Fishing in Rogue River and Tributaries—R	45,511	50,227
4. Closing the Willamette River to Commercial Fishing South of Oswego—R	*55,555	40,908
5. Delinquent Tax Notice Bill—I^2	*66,652	41,594
6. Fixing Compensation for Publication of Legal Notice—I^2	*50,073	41,816
7. Authorizing Increase in Amount of Levy of State Taxes for Year 1919 (submitted by state tax commission under chapter 150, Laws 1917)	41,364	56,974
June 3, 1919 (Special Election)		
1. Six Percent County Indebtedness for Permanent Roads Amendment—L^1	*49,728	33,561
2. Industrial and Reconstruction Hospital Amendment—L^1	38,204	40,707
3. State Bond Payment of Irrigation and Drainage District Bond Interest—L^1	*43,010	35,948
4. Five Million Dollar Reconstruction Bonding Amendment—L^1	39,130	40,580
5. Lieutenant Governor Constitutional Amendment—L^1	32,653	46,861
6. The Roosevelt Coast Military Highway Bill—L^2	*56,966	29,159
7. Reconstruction Bonding Bill—L^2	37,294	42,792
8. Soldiers', Sailors' and Marines' Educational Financial Aid Bill—L^2	*49,158	33,513
9. Market Roads Tax Bill—L^2	*53,191	28,039
May 21, 1920 (Special Election)		
1. Extending Eminent Domain Over Roads and Ways—L^1	*100,256	35,655
2. Limitation of 4 Percent State Indebtedness for Permanent Roads—L^1	*93,392	46,084

Election Date/Measure Number/Ballot Title	Yes	No
3. Restoring Capital Punishment—L[1]	*81,756	64,589
4. Crook and Curry Counties Bonding Amendment—L[1]	*72,378	36,699
5. Successor to Governor—L[1]	*78,241	56,946
6. Higher Educational Tax Act—L[2]	*102,722	46,577
7. Soldiers', Sailors' and Marines' Educational Aid Revenue Bill—L[2]	*91,294	50,482
8. State Elementary School Fund Tax—L[2]	*110,263	39,593
9. Blind School Tax Measure—L[2]	*115,337	30,739

November 2, 1920

	Yes	No
1. Compulsory Voting and Registration Amendment—L[1]	61,258	131,603
2. Constitutional Amendment Regulating Legislative Sessions and the Payment of Legislators—L[1]	80,342	85,524
3. Oleomargarine Bills—R	67,101	119,126
4. Single Tax Constitutional Amendment—I[1]	37,283	147,426
5. Fixing Term of Certain County Officers—I[1]	*97,854	80,983
6. Port of Portland Dock Commission Consolidation—I[2]	80,493	84,830
7. Anti-compulsory Vaccination Amendment—I[1]	63,018	127,570
8. Constitutional Amendment Fixing Legal Rate of Interest in Oregon—I[1]	28,976	158,673
9. Roosevelt Bird Refuge—I[2]	78,961	107,383
10. Divided Legislative Session Constitutional Amendment—I[1]	57,791	101,179
11. State Market Commission Act—I[2]	51,605	119,464

June 7, 1921 (Special Election)

	Yes	No
1. Legislative Regulation and Compensation Amendment—L[1]	42,924	72,596
2. World War Veterans' State Aid Fund, Constitutional Amendment—L[1]	*88,219	37,866
3. Emergency Clause Veto Constitutional Amendment—L[1]	*62,621	45,537
4. Hygiene Marriage Examination and License Bill—L[2]	56,858	65,793
5. Women Jurors and Revised Jury Law—L[2]	*59,882	59,265

November 7, 1922

	Yes	No
1. Amendment Permitting Linn County Tax Levy to Pay Outstanding Warrants—L	*89,177	57,049
2. Amendment Permitting Linn and Benton Counties to Pay Outstanding Warrants—L[1]	*86,547	53,844
3. Single Tax Amendment—I[1]	39,231	132,021
4. 1925 Exposition Tax Amendment—I[1]	82,837	95,587
5. Income Tax Amendment—I[2]	54,803	112,197
6. Compulsory Education Bill—I[2]	*115,506	103,685

November 6, 1923 (Special Election)

	Yes	No
1. Income Tax Act—L[2]	*58,647	58,131

November 4, 1924

	Yes	No
1. Voters' Literacy Amendment—L[1]	*184,031	48,645
2. Public Use and Welfare Amendment—L[1]	*134,071	65,133
3. Bonus Amendment—L[1]	*131,199	92,446
4. Oleomargarine Condensed Milk Bill—R	91,597	157,324
5. Naturopath Bill—I[2]	75,159	122,839
6. Workmen's Compulsory Compensation Law for Hazardous Occupations—I[1]	73,270	151,862
7. Income Tax Repeal—I[2]	*123,799	111,055

November 2, 1926

	Yes	No
1. Klamath County Bonding Amendment—L[1]	*81,954	68,128
2. Six Percent Limitation Amendment—L[1]	54,624	99,125
3. Repeal of Free Negro and Mulatto Section of the Constitution—L[1]	*108,332	64,954
4. Amendment Prohibiting Inheritance and Income Taxes—L[1]	59,442	121,973
5. The Seaside Normal School Act—L[2]	47,878	124,811
6. The Eastern Oregon State Normal School Act—L[2]	*101,327	80,084
7. The Recall Amendment—L[1]	*100,324	61,307
8 Curry County Bonding or Tax Levy Amendment—L[1]	*78,823	61,472
9. Amendment Relating to Elections to Fill Vacancies in Public Offices—L[1]	*100,397	54,474
10. Klamath and Clackamas County Bonding Amendment—L[1]	*75,229	61,718
11. The Eastern Oregon Tuberculosis Hospital Act—L[2]	*131,296	48,490
12. Cigarette and Tobacco Tax Bill—R	62,254	123,208

Election Date/Measure Number/Ballot Title	Yes	No
13. Motor Bus and Truck Bill—R	*99,746	78,685
14. Act Appropriating Ten Percent of Self-sustaining Boards' Receipts—R	46,389	97,460
15. Income Tax Bill With Property Tax Offset—I²	50,199	122,512
16. Bus and Truck Operating License Bill—I²	76,164	94,533
17. Fish Wheel, Trap, Seine and Gillnet Bill—I²	*102,119	73,086
18. Income Tax Bill—I²	83,991	93,997
19. Oregon Water and Power Board Development Measure—I¹	35,313	147,092
20. Amendment Fixing Salaries of County Officers of Umatilla County—L²	1,988	2,646
21. To Provide Salaries for Certain Officials of Clackamas County—L²	2,826	6,199

June 28, 1927 (Special Election)

	Yes	No
1. Repeal of Negro, Chinaman and Mulatto Suffrage Section of Constitution—L¹	*69,373	41,887
2. Portland School District Tax Levy Amendment—L¹	46,784	55,817
3. Criminal Information Amendment—L¹	*64,956	38,774
4. Legislators' Pay Amendment—L¹	28,380	81,215
5. Voters' Registration Amendment—L¹	*55,802	49,682
6. State and County Officers, Salary Amendment—L¹	46,999	61,838
7. City and County Consolidation Amendment—L¹	41,309	57,613
8. Veterans' Memorial and Armory Amendment—L¹	25,180	80,476
9. State Tax Limitation Amendment—L¹	19,393	84,697
10. Income Tax Bill—L²	48,745	67,039
11. Property Assessment and Taxation Enforcement Bill—L²	31,957	70,871
12. Nestucca Bay Fish Closing Bill—R	*53,684	47,552

November 6, 1928

	Yes	No
1. Five Cent Gasoline Tax Bill—I¹	71,824	198,798
2. Bill for Reduction of Motor Vehicle License Fees—I¹	98,248	174,219
3. Income Tax Bill—I²	118,696	132,961
4. Limiting Power of Legislature Over Laws Approved by the People—I¹	108,230	124,200
5. Deschutes River Water and Fish Bill—I²	78,317	157,398
6. Rogue River Water and Fish Bill—I²	79,028	156,009
7. Umpqua River Water and Fish Bill—I²	76,108	154,345
8. McKenzie River Water and Fish Bill—I²	77,974	153,418

November 4, 1930

	Yes	No
1. Repeal of State Payment of Irrigation and Drainage District Interest—L¹	*96,061	74,892
2. State Cabinet Form of Government Constitutional Amendment—L¹	51,248	135,412
3. Bonus Loan Constitutional Amendment—L¹	92,602	101,785
4. Motor Vehicle License Tax Constitutional Amendment—L¹	71,557	115,480
5. Motor Vehicle License Tax Constitutional Amendment—L¹	63,683	111,441
6. Constitutional Amendment for Filling Vacancies in the Legislature—L¹	*85,836	76,455
7. Legislators' Compensation Constitutional Amendment—L¹	70,937	108,070
8. Two Additional Circuit Judges Bill—R	39,770	137,549
9. Income Tax Bill—R	*105,189	95,207
10. Anti-cigarette Constitutional Amendment—I¹	54,231	156,265
11. Rogue River Fishing Constitutional Amendment—I¹	96,596	99,490
12. Lieutenant Governor Constitutional Amendment—I¹	92,707	95,277
13. People's Water and Power Utility Districts Constitutional Amendment—I¹	*117,776	84,778

November 8, 1932

	Yes	No
1. Taxpayer Voting Qualification Amendment—L¹	*189,321	124,160
2. Amendment Authorizing Criminal Trials Without Juries by Consent of Accused—L¹	*191,042	111,872
3. Six Percent Tax Limitation Amendment—L¹	*149,833	121,852
4. Oleomargarine Tax Bill—R	131,273	200,496
5. Bill Prohibiting Commercial Fishing on the Rogue River—R	127,445	180,527
6. Higher Education Appropriation Bill—R	58,076	237,218
7. Bill to Repeal State Prohibition Law of Oregon—I²	*206,619	138,775
8. The Freight Truck and Bus Bill—I²	151,790	180,609
9. Bill Moving University, Normal and Law Schools, Establishing Junior Colleges—I²	47,275	292,486

Election Date/Measure Number/Ballot Title	Yes	No
10. Tax and Debt Control Constitutional Amendment—I[1]	99,171	162,552
11. Tax Supervising and Conservation Bill—I[2]	117,940	154,206
12. Personal Income Tax Law Amendment—I[2]	144,502	162,468
13. State Water Power and Hydroelectric Constitutional Amendment—I[1]	*168,937	130,494
July 21, 1933 (Special Election)		
1. An Amendment to the Constitution of the United States of America—L[0]	*136,713	72,854
2. Soldiers and Sailors Bonus Limitation Amendment—L[1]	*113,267	75,476
3. County Manager Form of Government Constitutional Amendment—L[1]	66,425	117,148
4. Prosecution by Information and Grand Jury Modification Amendment—L[1]	67,192	110,755
5. Debt and Taxation Limitations for Municipal Corporations Constitutional Amendment—L[1]	82,996	91,671
6. State Power Fund Bonds—L[2]	73,756	106,153
7. Sales Tax Bill—L[2]	45,603	167,512
8. Repeal of Oregon Prohibition Constitutional Amendment—L[1]	*143,044	72,745
9. Oleomargarine Tax Bill—R	66,880	144,542
May 18, 1934 (Special Election)		
1. County Indebtedness and Funding Bond Constitutional Amendment—L[1]	83,424	96,629
2. Criminal Trial Without Jury and Non-unanimous Verdict Constitutional Amendment—L[1]	*117,446	83,430
3. Bill Authorizing a State Tuberculosis Hospital in Multnomah County—L[2]	*104,459	98,815
4. Bill Authorizing a State Insane Hospital in Multnomah County—L[2]	92,575	108,816
5. School Relief Sales Tax Bill—R	64,677	156,182
November 6, 1934		
1. Grange Power Bill—R	124,518	139,283
2. Limitations of Taxes on Taxable Property Constitutional Amendment—I[1]	100,565	161,644
3. Healing Arts Constitutional Amendment—I[1]	70,626	191,836
January 31, 1936 (Special Election)		
1. Bill Changing Primary Elections to September With Other Resulting Changes—L[2]	61,270	155,922
2. Compensation of Members of the Legislature Constitutional Amendment—L[1]	28,661	184,332
3. Sales Tax Bill—L[2]	32,106	187,319
4. Bill Authorizing Student Activity Fees in State Higher Educational Institutions—R	50,971	163,191
November 3, 1936		
1. Bill Amending Old Age Assistance Act of 1935—R	174,293	179,236
2. Amendment Forbidding Prevention or Regulation of Certain Advertising If Truthful—I[1]	100,141	222,897
3. Tax Limitation Constitutional Amendment for School Districts Having 100,000 Population—I[1]	112,546	203,693
4. Noncompulsory Military Training Bill—I[2]	131,917	214,246
5. Amendment Limiting and Reducing Permissible Taxes on Tangible Property—I[1]	79,604	241,042
6. State Power Bill—I[2]	131,489	208,179
7. State Hydroelectric Temporary Administrative Board Constitutional Amendment—I[1]	100,356	208,741
8. State Bank Bill—I[2]	82,869	250,777
November 8, 1938		
1. Governor's 20-day Bill Consideration Amendment—L[1]	*233,384	93,752
2. Amendment Repealing the Double Liability of Stockholders in Banking Corporations—L[1]	133,525	165,797
3. Legislators Compensation Constitutional Amendments—L[1]	149,356	169,131
4. Bill Requiring Marriage License Applicants Medically Examined; Physically and Mentally—L[2]	*277,099	66,484
5. Slot Machines Seizure by Sheriffs and Destruction on Court Order—R	*204,561	126,580
6. Prohibiting Slot Machines, Pin-ball, Dart and Other Similar Games—R	*197,912	129,043

Elections and Records

Election Date/Measure Number/Ballot Title	Yes	No
7. Townsend Plan Bill—I[3]	*183,781	149,711
8. Citizens' Retirement Annuity Bill; Levying Transactions Tax to Provide Fund—I[2]	112,172	219,557
9. Bill Regulating Picketing and Boycotting by Labor Groups and Organizations—I[2]	*197,771	148,460
10. Water Purification and Prevention of Pollution Bill—I[2]	*247,685	75,295
11. Bill Regulating Sale of Alcoholic Liquor for Beverage Purposes—I[2]	118,282	222,221
12. Constitutional Amendment Legalizing Certain Lotteries and Other Forms of Gambling—I[1]	141,792	180,329
November 5, 1940		
1. Amendment Removing Office Time Limit of State Secretary and Treasurer—L[1]	163,942	213,797
2. Amendment Making Three Years' Average People's Voted Levies, Tax Base—L[1]	129,699	183,488
3. Amendment Repealing the Double Liability of Stockholders of State Banks—L[1]	157,891	191,290
4. Legislators' Compensation Constitutional Amendment—L[1]	186,830	188,031
5. Bill Changing the Primary Nominating Elections from May to September—R	156,421	221,203
6. Bill to Further Regulate Sale and Use of Alcoholic Liquor—R	158,004	235,128
7. Bill Repealing Present Liquor Law; Authorizing Private Sale, Licensed, Taxed—I[2]	90,681	309,183
8. Amendment Legalizing Certain Gambling and Gaming Devices and Certain Lotteries—I[1]	150,157	258,010
9. Bill to Repeal the Oregon Milk Control Law—I[2]	201,983	213,838
November 3, 1942		
1. Legislators' Compensation Constitutional Amendment—L[1]	*129,318	109,898
2. Rural Credits Loan Fund Repeal Amendment—L[1]	*101,425	88,857
3. Amendment Specifying Exclusive Uses of Gasoline and Motor Vehicle Taxes—L[1]	*125,990	86,332
4. Amendment Authorizing Regulation by Law of Voting Privilege Forfeiture—L[1]	101,508	103,404
5. Cigarette Tax Bill—R	110,643	127,366
6. Bill Restricting and Prohibiting Net Fishing Coastal Streams and Bays—R	97,212	137,177
7. Bill Distributing Surplus Funds to School Districts, Reducing Taxes Therein—I[2]	*136,321	92,623
November 7, 1944		
1. Amendment To Provide Alternative Means for Securing Bank Deposits—L[1]	*228,744	115,745
2. Amendment Authorizing Change to Managerial Form of County Government—L[1]	*175,716	154,504
3. Amendment Authorizing "Oregon War Veterans' Fund," Providing Tax Therefor—L[1]	*190,520	178,581
4. Amendment to Authorize Legislative Regulation of Voting Privilege Forfeiture—L[1]	*183,855	156,219
5. Bill Providing Educational Aid to Certain Veterans World War II—L[2]	*238,350	135,317
6. Bill Imposing Tax on Retail Sales of Tangible Personal Property—L[2]	96,697	269,276
7. Burke Bill; Only State Selling Liquor over 14 Hundredths Alcohol—R	*228,853	180,158
8. Constitutional Amendment Increasing State Tax Fund for Public School Support—I[1]	177,153	186,976
9. Constitutional Amendment Providing Monthly Annuities From a Gross Income Tax—I[1]	180,691	219,981
June 22, 1945 (Special Election)		
1. Bill Authorizing Tax Levy for State Building Fund—L[2]	*78,269	49,565
2. Bill Authorizing Cigarette Tax to Support Public Schools—L[2]	60,321	67,542

Election Date/Measure Number/Ballot Title	Yes	No
November 5, 1946		
1. Constitutional Amendment Providing for Succession to Office of Governor—L[1]	*221,547	70,322
2. Bill Authorizing Tax for Construction and Equipment of State Armories—L[2]	75,693	219,006
3. Bill Establishing Rural School Districts and School Boards—L[2]	*155,733	134,673
4. Bill Authorizing Chinamen to Hold Real Estate and Mining Claims—L[1]	*161,865	133,111
5. Amendment Permitting Legislative Bills to be Read by Title Only—L[1]	*145,248	113,279
6. Constitutional Amendment Increasing Number of Senators to Thirty-one—L[1]	88,717	185,247
7. Bill Regulating Fishing in Coastal Streams and Inland Waters—R	*196,195	101,398
8. To Create State Old-age and Disability Pension Fund—I[2]	86,374	244,960
9. To Create Basic School Support Fund by Annual Tax Levy—I[2]	*157,904	151,765
October 7, 1947 (Special Election)		
1. Bill Taxing Retail Sales for School, Welfare and Governmental Purposes—L[2]	67,514	180,333
2. Cigarette Tax Bill—R	103,794	140,876
November 2, 1948		
1. Constitutional Six Percent Tax Limitation Amendment—L[1]	150,032	268,155
2. Constitutional Amendment Authorizing Indebtedness for State Forestation—L[1]	*211,912	209,317
3. Bill Authorizing State Boys' Camp Near Timber, Oregon—L[2]	*227,638	219,196
4. Bill Amending Licensing and Acquisition Provisions for Hydroelectric Commission Act—R	173,004	242,100
5. Constitutional Amendment Fixing Qualifications of Voters in School Elections—I[1]	*284,776	164,025
6. Oregon Old Age Pension Act—I[2]	*313,212	172,531
7. Bill Increasing Personal Income Tax Exemptions—I[2]	*405,842	63,373
8. Oregon Liquor Dispensing Licensing Act—I[2]	210,108	273,621
9. World War II Veterans' Bonus Amendment—I[1]	198,283	265,805
10. Prohibiting Salmon Fishing in Columbia River With Fixed Appliances—I[2]	*273,140	184,834
11. Question of Authorizing Additional State Tax, to be Offset by Income Tax Funds—R	143,856	256,167
November 7, 1950		
1. Constitutional Amendment Fixing Legislators' Annual Compensation—L[1]	*243,518	205,361
2. Constitutional Amendment Lending State Tax Credit for Higher Education Buildings—L[1]	*256,895	192,573
3. Constitutional Amendment Augmenting "Oregon War Veterans' Fund"—L[1]	*268,171	183,724
4. Increasing Basic School Support Fund by Annual Tax Levy—L[2]	*234,394	231,856
5. Needy Aged Persons Public Assistance Act—R	*310,143	158,939
6. Providing Uniform Standard Time in Oregon—R	*277,633	195,319
7. World War II Veterans' Compensation Fund—I[1]	*239,553	216,958
8. Constitutional Amendment for Legislative Representation Reapportionment—I[1]	190,992	215,302
9. Making Sale of Promotively Advertised Alcoholic Beverage Unlawful—I[2]	113,524	378,732
November 4, 1952		
1. Amendment Making Superintendent of Public Instruction Appointive—L[1]	282,882	326,199
2. World War Veterans' State Aid Sinking Fund Repeal—L[1]	*454,898	147,128
3. Act Authorizing Domiciliary State Hospital for Aged Mentally Ill—L[2]	*480,479	153,402
4. Amendment Legal Voters of Taxing Unit Establish Tax Base—L[1]	*355,136	210,373
5. Amendment to Augment Oregon War Veterans' Fund—L[1]	*465,605	132,363
6. Amendment Creating Legislative Assembly Emergency Committee—L[1]	*364,539	194,492
7. Amendment Fixing Elective Terms of State Senators and Representatives—L[1]	*483,356	103,357

Election Date/Measure Number/Ballot Title	Yes	No
8. Amendatory Act Title Subject Amendment—L[1]	*315,071	191,087
9. Act Limiting State Property Tax—L[2]	*318,948	272,145
10. Motor Carrier Highway Transportation Tax Act—R	*409,588	230,241
11. School District Reorganization Act—R	295,700	301,974
12. Cigarette Stamp Tax Revenue Act—R	233,226	413,137
13. Establishing United States Standard Time in Oregon—I[2]	*399,981	256,981
14. Constitutional Amendment Prohibiting Lotteries, Bookmaking, Pari-mutuel Betting on Animal Racing—I[1]	230,097	411,884
15. Constitutional Amendment Authorizing Alcoholic Liquor Sale by Individual Glass—I[1]	*369,127	285,446
16. Constitutional Amendment Providing Equitable Taxing Method for Use of Highways—I[1]	135,468	484,730
17. Milk Production and Marketing Act Bill—I[2]	313,629	337,750
18. Constitutional Legislative Senator and Representative Apportionment Enforcement Amendment—I[1]	*357,550	194,292

November 2, 1954

	Yes	No
1. Salaries of State Legislators—L[1]	216,545	296,008
2. Subdividing Counties for Electing State Legislators—L[1]	*268,337	208,077
3. Mental Hospital In or Near Portland—L[2]	*397,625	128,685
4. Constitutional Amendments—How Proposed by People—L[1]	*251,078	230,770
5. State Property Tax—L[1]	208,419	264,569
6. Establishing Daylight Saving Time—I[2]	252,305	300,007
7. Prohibiting Certain Fishing in Coastal Streams—I[2]	232,775	278,805
8. Repealing Milk Control Law—I[2]	*293,745	247,591

November 6, 1956

	Yes	No
1. State Tax Laws—Immediate Effect Authorized—L[1]	175,932	487,550
2. Authorizing State Acceptance of Certain Gifts—L[1]	*498,633	153,033
3. Salaries of Certain State Officers—L[1]	*390,338	263,155
4. Qualifications for County Coroner and Surveyor—L[1]	*455,485	182,550
5. Salaries of State Legislators—L[1]	320,741	338,365
6. Cigarette Tax—R	280,055	414,613
7. Prohibiting Certain Fishing in Coastal Streams—I[2]	*401,882	259,309

November 4, 1958

	Yes	No
1. Fixing State Boundaries—L[1]	*399,396	114,318
2. Increasing Funds for War Veterans' Loans—L[1]	232,246	318,685
3. Salaries of State Legislators—L[1]	236,000	316,437
4. Capital Punishment Bill—L[1]	264,434	276,487
5. Financing Urban Redevelopment Projects—L[1]	221,330	268,716
6. Modifying County Debt Limitation—L[1]	*252,347	224,426
7. Special Grand Jury Bill—L[1]	*357,792	136,745
8. Authorizes Different Use of State Institution—L[1]	*303,282	193,177
9. Temporary Appointment and Assignment of Judges—L[1]	*373,466	125,898
10. State Power Development—L[1]	218,662	291,210
11. County Home Rule Amendment—L[1]	*311,516	157,023
12. Authorizing Discontinuing Certain State Tuberculosis Hospitals—L[1]	*319,790	195,945
13. Persons Eligible to Serve in Legislature—I[1]	*320,751	201,700

May 20, 1960

	Yes	No
1. Salaries of State Legislators—L[1]	250,456	281,542

November 8, 1960

	Yes	No
1. Fixing Commencement of Legislators' Term—L[1]	*579,022	92,187
2. Daylight Saving Time—L[2]	357,499	393,652
3. Financing Urban Redevelopment Projects—L[1]	*335,792	312,187
4. Permitting Prosecution by Information or Indictment—L[1]	306,190	340,197
5. Authorizing Legislature to Propose Revised Constitution—L[1]	*358,367	289,895
6. State Bonds for Higher Education Facilities—L[1]	*467,557	233,759
7. Voter Qualification Amendment—L[1]	508,108	183,977
8. Authorizing Bonds for State Building Program—L[1]	232,250	433,515
9. Compulsory Retirement for Judges—L[1]	*578,471	123,283
10. Elective Offices: When to Become Vacant—L[1]	*486,019	169,865

Election Date/Measure Number/Ballot Title	Yes	No
11. Financing Improvements in Home Rule Counties—L[1]	*399,210	222,736
12. Continuity of Government in Enemy Attack—L[1]	*578,266	88,995
13. War Veterans' Bonding and Loan Amendment—L[1]	*415,931	266,630
14. Personal Income Tax Bill—R	115,610	570,025
15. Billboard Control Measure—I[2]	261,735	475,290
May 18, 1962		
1. Six Percent Limitation Amendment—L[1]	141,728	262,140
2. Salaries of State Legislators—L[1]	*241,171	178,749
November 6, 1962		
1. Reorganize State Militia—L[1]	*312,680	234,440
2. Forest Rehabilitation Debt Limit Amendment—L[1]	*323,799	199,174
3. Permanent Road Debt Limit Amendment—L[1]	*319,956	200,236
4. Power Development Debt Limit Amendment—L[1]	*298,255	208,755
5. State Courts Creation and Jurisdiction—L[1]	*307,855	193,487
6. Daylight Saving Time—L[2]	*388,154	229,661
7. Constitutional Six Percent Limitation Amendment—L[1]	*270,637	219,509
8. Legislative Apportionment Constitutional Amendment—I[1]	197,322	325,182
9. Repeals School District Reorganization Law—I[2]	206,540	320,917
October 15, 1963 (Special Election)		
1. Personal and Corporation Income Tax Bill—R	103,737	362,845
May 15, 1964		
1. Authorizing Bonds for Education Building Program—L[1]	*327,220	252,372
November 3, 1964		
1. Capital Punishment Bill—L[1]	*455,654	302,105
2. Leasing Property for State Use—L[1]	*477,031	238,241
3. Amending State Workmen's Compensation Law—I[2]	205,182	549,414
4. Prohibiting Commercial Fishing for Salmon, Steelhead—I[2]	221,797	534,731
May 24, 1966		
1. Cigarette Tax Bill—L[2]	*310,743	181,957
2. Superintendent of Public Instruction Constitutional Amendment—L[1]	197,096	267,319
November 8, 1966		
1. Public Transportation System Employes Constitutional Amendment—L[1]	*468,103	123,964
2. State Bonds for Educational Facilities—L[1]	237,282	332,983
May 28, 1968		
1. Common School Fund Constitutional Amendment—L[1]	*372,915	226,191
2. Constitutional Amendment Changing Initiative — Referendum Requirements—L[1]	*321,731	244,750
3. Higher Education and Community College Bonds—L[1]	*353,383	261,014
November 5, 1968		
1. Constitutional Amendment Broadening Veterans Loan Eligibility—L[1]	*651,250	96,065
2. Constitutional Amendment for Removal of Judges—L[1]	*690,989	56,973
3. Empowering Legislature to Extend Ocean Boundaries—L[1]	*588,166	143,768
4. Constitutional Amendment Broadening County Debt Limitation—L[1]	331,617	348,866
5. Government Consolidation City-County Over 300,000—L[1]	*393,789	278,483
6. Bond Issue to Acquire Ocean Beaches—I[1]	315,175	464,140
7. Constitutional Amendment Changing Property Tax Limitation—I[1]	276,451	503,443
June 3, 1969 (Special Election)		
1. Property Tax Relief and Sales Tax—L[1]	65,077	504,274
May 26, 1970		
1. Capital Construction Bonds for State Government—L[1]	190,257	300,126
2. Repeals "White Foreigner" Section of Constitution—L[1]	*326,374	168,464
3. Revised Constitution for Oregon—L[1]	182,074	322,682
4. Pollution Control Bonds—L[1]	*292,234	213,835
5. Lowers Oregon Voting Age to 19—L[1]	202,018	336,527
6. Local School Property Tax Equalization Measure—L[1]	180,602	323,189
November 3, 1970		
1. Constitutional Amendment Concerning Convening of Legislature—L[1]	261,428	340,104
2. Automatic Adoption, Federal Income Tax Amendments—L[1]	*342,138	269,467

Election Date/Measure Number/Ballot Title	Yes	No
3. Constitutional Amendment Concerning County Debt Limitation—L[1]	283,659	294,186
4. Investing Funds Donated to Higher Education—L[1]	*332,188	268,588
5. Veterans' Loan Amendment—L[1]	*481,031	133,564
6. Limits Term of Defeated Incumbents—L[1]	*436,897	158,409
7. Constitutional Amendment Authorizing Education Bonds—L[1]	269,372	318,651
8. Allows Penal Institutions Anywhere in Oregon—L[1]	*352,771	260,100
9. Scenic Waterways Bill—I[2]	*406,315	214,243
10. New Property Tax Bases for Schools—I[1]	223,735	405,437
11. Restricts Governmental Powers Over Rural Property—I[1]	272,765	342,503

January 18, 1972 (Special Election)

	Yes	No
1. Increases Cigarette Tax—R	*245,717	236,937

May 23, 1972

	Yes	No
1. Eliminates Literacy Requirement; Lowers Voting Age—L[1]	327,231	349,746
2. Repeals Requirement for Decennial State Census—L[1]	*420,568	206,436
3. Allows Legislators to Call Special Sessions—L[1]	241,371	391,698
4. Capital Construction Bonds for State Government—L[1]	232,391	364,323
5. Irrigation and Water Development Bonds—L[1]	233,175	374,295
6. Enabling County-City Vehicle Registration Tax—R	120,027	491,551

November 7, 1972

	Yes	No
1. Eliminates Location Requirements for State Institutions—L[1]	*594,080	232,948
2. Qualifications for Sheriff Set By Legislature—L[1]	*572,619	281,720
3. Amends County Purchase and Lease Limitations—L[1]	329,669	462,932
4. Changes State Constitution Provision Regarding Religion—L[1]	336,382	519,196
5. Minimum Jury Size of Six Members—L[1]	*591,191	265,636
6. Broadens Eligibility for Veterans' Loans—L[1]	*736,802	133,139
7. Repeals Governor's Retirement Act—I[2]	*571,959	292,561
8. Changes Succession to Office of Governor—I[1]	*697,297	151,174
9. Prohibits Property Tax for School Operations—I[1]	342,885	558,136

May 1, 1973 (Special Election)

	Yes	No
1. Property Tax Limitation; School Tax Revision—L[2]	253,682	358,219

May 28, 1974

	Yes	No
1. Income, Corporate Tax, School Support Increase—L[2]	136,851	410,733
2. Highway Fund Use for Mass Transit—L[1]	190,899	369,038
3. New School District Tax Base Limitation—L[1]	166,363	371,897
4. Authorizes Bonds for Water Development Fund—L[1]	198,563	328,221
5. Increases Veterans' Loan Bonding Authority—L[1]	*381,559	164,953
6. Permits Legislature to Call Special Session—L[1]	246,525	298,373

November 5, 1974

	Yes	No
1. Liquor Licenses for Public Passenger Carriers—L[1]	353,357	384,521
2. Opens All Legislative Deliberations to Public—L[1]	*546,255	165,778
3. Revises Constitutional Requirements for Grand Juries—L[1]	*437,557	246,902
4. Governor Vacancy Successor Age Requirement Eliminated—L[1]	*381,593	331,756
5. The measure designated as Number 5 by the 1973 Legislature was moved to the May 28, 1974 primary election by the 1974 special session. On the advice of the Attorney General, this measure number was left blank.		
6. Permits Establishing Qualifications for County Assessors—L[1]	*552,737	146,364
7. Tax Base Includes Revenue Sharing Money—L[1]	322,023	329,858
8. Revises School District Election Voting Requirements—L[1]	337,565	378,071
9. Permits State Employes to be Legislators—L[1]	218,846	476,547
10. Revises Oregon Voter Qualification Requirements—L[1]	*362,731	355,506
11. Right to Jury in Civil Cases—L[1]	*480,631	216,853
12. Community Development Fund Bonds—L[1]	277,723	376,747
13. Obscenity and Sexual Conduct Bill—R	*393,743	352,958
14. Public Officials' Financial Ethics and Reporting. This measure was also referred to all 36 counties, with 30 voting yes and 6 voting no; and all cities with governing bodies, with 153 voting yes and 90 voting no.—L[2]	*498,002	177,946
15. Prohibits Purchase or Sale of Steelhead—I[2]	*458,417	274,182

Election Date/Measure Number/Ballot Title	Yes	No
May 25, 1976		
1. Expands Veterans' Home-Farm Loan Eligibility — L[1]	*549,553	158,997
2. Discipline of Judges — L[1]	*639,977	59,774
3. Housing Bonds — L[1]	*315,588	362,414
4. Authorizes Vehicle Tax Mass Transit Use — L[1]	170,331	531,219
November 2, 1976		
1. Validates Inadvertently Superseded Statutory Amendments — L[1]	*607,325	247,843
2. Allows Changing City, County Election Days — L[1]	376,489	536,967
3. Lowers Minimum Age for Legislative Service — L[1]	285,777	679,517
4. Repeals Emergency Succession Provision — L[1]	*507,308	368,646
5. Permits Legislature to Call Special Session — L[1]	*549,126	377,354
6. Allows Charitable, Fraternal, Religious Organizations Bingo — L[1]	*682,252	281,696
7. Partial Public Funding of Election Campaigns — L[2]	263,738	659,327
8. Increases Motor Fuel, Ton-Mile Taxes — R	465,143	505,124
9. Regulates Nuclear Power Plant Construction Approval — I[2]	423,008	584,845
10. Repeals Land Use Planning Coordination Statutes — I[2]	402,608	536,502
11. Prohibits Adding Fluorides to Water Systems — I[2]	419,567	555,981
12. Repeals Intergovernmental Cooperation, Planning District Statutes — I[2]	333,933	525,868
May 17, 1977 (Special Election)		
1. School Operating Levy Measure — L[1]	112,570	252,061
2. Authorizes Additional Veterans' Fund Uses — L[1]	*200,270	158,436
3. Increases Veterans' Loan Bonding Authority — L[1]	*250,783	106,953
November 8, 1977 (Special Election)		
1. Water Development Loan Fund Created — L[1]	*124,484	118,953
2. Development of Nonnuclear Energy Resources — L[1]	105,219	137,693
May 23, 1978		
1. Home Rule County Initiative-Referendum Requirements — L[1]	*306,506	156,623
2. Open Meetings Rules for Legislature — L[1]	*435,338	80,176
3. Housing for Low Income Elderly — L[1]	*291,778	250,810
4. Domestic Water Fund Created — L[1]	148,822	351,843
5. Highway Repair Priority, Gas Tax Increase — L[2]	190,301	365,170
6. Reorganizes Metropolitan Service District, Abolishes CRAG — L[2,4]	*110,600	91,090
November 7, 1978		
1. Appellate Judge Selection, Running on Record — L[1]	358,504	449,132
2. Authorizes Senate Confirmation of Governor's Appointments — L[1]	*468,458	349,604
3. Vehicle and Fee Increase Referendum — R	208,722	673,802
4. Shortens Formation Procedures for People's Utility Districts — I[2]	375,587	471,027
5. Authorizes, Regulates Practice of Denture Technology — I[2]	*704,480	201,463
6. Limitations on Ad Valorem Property Taxes — I[1]	424,029	453,741
7. Prohibits State Expenditures, Programs or Services for Abortion — I[1]	431,577	461,542
8. Requires Death Penalty for Murder under Specified Conditions — I[2]	*573,707	318,610
9. Limitations on Public Utility Rate Base — I[2]	*589,361	267,132
10. Land Use Planning, Zoning Constitutional Amendment — I[1]	334,523	515,138
11. Reduces Property Tax Payable by Homeowner and Renter — L[1]	383,532	467,765
12. Support of Constitutional Amendment (Federal) Requires Balance Budget — L[5]	*641,862	134,758
May 20, 1980		
1. Constitutional Amendment Limits Uses of Gasoline and Highway User Taxes — L[1]	*451,695	257,230
2. Amends Liquor by the Drink Constitutional Provision — L[1]	325,030	384,346
3. State Bonds for Small Scale Local Energy Project Loan Fund — L[1]	*394,466	278,125
4. Veterans' Home and Farm Loan Eligibility Changes — L[1]	*574,148	130,452
5. Continues Tax Reduction Program — L[2]	*636,565	64,979
6. Definition of Multifamily Low Income Elderly Housing — L[1]	*536,002	138,675
November 4, 1980		
1. Repeal of Constitutional Provision Requiring Elected Superintendent of Public Instruction — L[1]	291,142	820,892
2. Guarantees Mentally Handicapped Voting Rights, Unless Adjudged Incompetent to Vote — L[1]	*678,573	455,020

Election Date/Measure Number/Ballot Title	Yes	No
3. Dedicates Oil, Natural Gas Taxes to Common School Fund—L[1]	*594,520	500,586
4. Increases Gas Tax from Seven to Nine Cents per Gallon—L[2]	298,421	849,745
5. Forbids Use, Sale of Snare, Leghold Traps for Most Purposes—I[2]	425,890	728,173
6. Constitutional Real Property Tax Limit Preserving 85% Districts' 1977 Revenue—I[1]	416,029	711,617
7. Nuclear Plant Licensing Requires Voter Approval, Waste Disposal Facility Existence—I[2]	*608,412	535,049
8. State Bonds for Fund to Finance Correctional Facilities—L[1]	523,955	551,383
May 18, 1982		
1. Use of State Bond Proceeds to Finance Municipal Water Projects—L[1]	*333,656	267,137
2. Multifamily Housing for Elderly and Disabled Persons—L[1]	*389,820	229,049
3. State Bonds for Fund to Finance Corrections Facilities—L[1]	281,548	333,476
4. Raises Taxes on Commercial Vehicles, Motor Vehicles Fuels for Roads—L[2]	308,574	323,268
5. Governor to Appoint Chief Justice of Oregon Supreme Court—L[2]	159,811	453,415
November 2, 1982		
1. Increases Tax Base When New Property Construction Increases District's Value—L[1]	219,034	768,150
2. Lengthens Governor's Time for Postsession Veto or Approval of Bills—L[1]	385,672	604,864
3. Constitutional Real Property Tax Limit Preserving 85% Districts' 1979 Revenue—I[1]	504,836	515,626
4. Permits Self-Service Dispensing of Motor Vehicle Fuel at Retail—I[2]	440,824	597,970
5. People of Oregon Urge Mutual Freeze on Nuclear Weapons Development—I[3]	*623,089	387,907
6. Ends State's Land Use Planning Powers, Retains Local Planning—I[2]	461,271	565,056
May 15, 1984		
1. State May Borrow and Lend Money for Public Works Projects—L[1]	332,175	365,571
2. Increases Fees for Licensing and Registration of Motor Vehicles—L[2]	234,060	487,457
November 6, 1984		
1. Changes Minimum Requirements for Recall of Public Officers—L[1]	*664,464	470,139
2. Constitutional Real Property Tax Limit—I[1]	599,424	616,252
3. Creates Citizens' Utility Board to Represent Interests of Utility Consumers—I[2]	*637,968	556,826
4. Constitutional Amendment Establishes State Lottery, Commission; Profits for Economic Development—I[1]	*794,441	412,341
5. Statutory Provisions for State Operated Lottery if Constitutionally Authorized—I[2]	*786,933	399,231
6. Exempts Death Sentences from Constitutional Guarantees Against Cruel, Vindictive Punishments—I[1]	*653,009	521,687
7. Requires by Statute Death or Mandatory Imprisonment for Aggravated Murder—I[2]	*893,818	295,988
8. Revises Numerous Criminal Laws Concerning Police Powers, Trials, Evidence, Sentencing—I[2]	552,410	597,964
9. Adds Requirements for Disposing Wastes Containing Naturally Occurring Radioactive Isotopes—I[2]	*655,973	524,214
September 17, 1985 (Special Election)		
1. Amends Constitution. Approves Limited 5% Sales Tax for Local Education—L[1]	189,733	664,365
May 20, 1986		
1. Constitutional Amendment: Bans Income Tax on Social Security Benefits—L[1]	*534,476	118,766
2. Constitutional Amendment: Effect on Merger of Taxing Units on Tax Base—L[1]	*333,277	230,886
3. Constitutional Amendment: Verification of Signatures on Initiative and Referendum Petitions—L[1]	*460,148	132,101
4. Requires Special Election for U.S. Senator Vacancy, Removes Constitutional Provision—L[1]	*343,005	269,305

Election Date/Measure Number/Ballot Title	Yes	No
5. Constitutional Amendment: $96 Million Bonds for State-County Prison Buildings—L[1]	300,674	330,429
November 4, 1986		
1. Deletes Constitutional Requirement that Secretary of State Live in Salem—L[1]	*771,959	265,999
2. Constitutional Amendment Revising Legislative District Reapportionment Procedures After Federal Census—L[1]	*637,410	291,355
3. Constitutional Amendment Allows Charitable, Fraternal, Religious Organizations to Conduct Raffles—L[1]	*736,739	302,957
4. Replaces Public Utility Commissioner with Three Member Public Utility Commission—L[2]	*724,577	297,973
5. Legalizes Private Possession and Growing of Marijuana for Personal Use—I[2]	279,479	781,922
6. Constitutional Amendment Prohibits State Funding Abortions. Exception: Prevent Mother's Death—I[1]	477,920	580,163
7. Constitutional 5% Sales Tax, Funds Schools, Reduces Property Tax—I[1]	234,804	816,369
8. Prohibits Mandatory Local Measured Telephone Service Except Mobile Phone Service—I[2]	*802,099	201,918
9. Amends Constitution. Limits Property Tax Rates and Assessed Value Increases—I[1]	449,548	584,396
10. Revises Many Criminal Laws Concerning Victims' Rights, Evidence, Sentencing, Parole—I[2]	*774,766	251,509
11. Homeowner's, Renter's Property Tax Relief Program; Sales Tax Limitation Measure—I[1]	381,727	639,034
12. State Income Tax Changes, Increased Revenue to Property Tax Relief—I[2]	299,551	720,034
13. Constitutional Amendment: Twenty Day Pre-election Voter Registration Cutoff—I[1]	*693,460	343,450
14. Prohibits Nuclear Power Plant Operation Until Permanent Waste Site Licensed—I[2]	375,241	674,641
15. Supersedes "Radioactive Waste" Definition; Changes Energy Facility Payment Procedure—I[2]	424,099	558,741
16. Phases Out Nuclear Weapons Manufactured With Tax Credits, Civil Penalty—I[2]	400,119	590,971
May 19, 1987 (Special Election)		
1. State Role In Selection of High-Level Nuclear Waste Repository Site—L[2]	*299,581	100,854
2. Continues Existing Levies To Prevent School Closures: Tax Base Elections—L[1]	*223,417	178,839
May 17, 1988		
1. Authorizes Water Development Fund Loans for Fish Protection, Watershed Restoration—L[1]	*485,629	191,008
2. Protective Headgear for Motorcycle Operators and Passengers and Moped Riders—L[2]	*486,401	224,655
November 8, 1988		
1. Extends Governor's Veto Deadline After Legislature Adjourns; Requires Prior Announcement—L[1]	*615,012	520,939
2. Common School Fund Investments; Using Income for State Lands Management—L[1]	*621,894	510,694
3. Requires the Use of Safety Belts—L[2]	528,324	684,747
4. Requires Full Sentences Without Parole, Probation for Certain Repeat Felonies—I[2]	*947,805	252,985
5. Finances Intercollegiate Athletic Fund by Increasing Malt Beverage, Cigarette Taxes—I[2]	449,797	759,360
6. Indoor Clean Air Law Revisions Banning Public Smoking—I[2]	430,147	737,779
7. Oregon Scenic Waterway System—I[2]	*663,604	516,998
8. Revokes Ban on Sexual Orientation Discrimination in State Executive Branch—I[2]	*626,751	561,355

Election Date/Measure Number/Ballot Title	Yes	No
May 16, 1989 (Special Election)		
1. Establishes New Tax Base Limits on Schools—L[1]	183,818	263,283
June 27, 1989 (Special Election)		
1. Removes Constitutional Limitation on Use of Property Forfeited To State—L[1]	*340,506	141,649
2. Prohibits Selling/Exporting Timber from State Lands Unless Oregon Processed—L[1]	*446,151	48,558
May 15, 1990		
1. Permits Using Local Vehicle Taxes for Transit if Voters Approve—L[1]	294,099	324,458
2. Amends Constitution; Allows Pollution Control Bond Use for Related Activities—L[1]	*352,922	248,123
3. Amends State Constitution; Requires Annual Legislative Sessions of Limited Duration—L[1]	294,664	299,831
4. Amends Laws on Organization of International Port of Coos Bay—L[2]	4,234	4,745
5A. Advisory Vote: Changing the School Finance System—L[5]	*462,090	140,747
5B. Advisory Vote: Income Tax Increase Reducing Homeowner School Property Taxes—L[5]	177,964	408,842
5C. Advisory Vote: Income Tax Increase Eliminating Homeowner School Property Taxes—L[5]	128,642	449,725
5D. Advisory Vote: Sales Tax Reducing School Property Taxes—L[5]	202,367	385,820
5E. Advisory Vote: Sales Tax Eliminating School Property Taxes—L[5]	222,611	374,466
November 6, 1990		
1. Grants Metropolitan Service District Electors Right to Home Rule—L[1]	*510,947	491,170
2. Constitutional Amendment Allows Merged School Districts to Combine Tax Bases—L[1]	*680,463	354,288
3. Repeals Tax Exemption, Grants Additional Benefit Payments for PERS Retirees—R	406,372	617,586
4. Prohibits Trojan Operation Until Nuclear Waste, Cost, Earthquake Standards Met—I[2]	446,795	660,992
5. State Constitutional Limit on Property Taxes for Schools, Government Operations—I[1]	*574,833	522,022
6. Product Packaging Must Meet Recycling Standards or Receive Hardship Waiver—I[2]	467,418	636,804
7. Six-County Work in Lieu of Welfare Benefits Pilot Program—I[2]	*624,744	452,853
8. Amends Oregon Constitution to Prohibit Abortion With Three Exceptions—I[1]	355,963	747,599
9. Requires the Use of Safety Belts—I[2]	*598,460	512,872
10. Doctor Must Give Parent Notice Before Minor's Abortion—I[2]	530,851	577,806
11. School Choice System, Tax Credit for Education Outside Public Schools—I[1]	351,977	741,863
May 19, 1992		
1. Amends Constitution: Future Fuel Taxes May Go to Police—L[1]	244,173	451,715
November 3, 1992		
1. Bonds May be Issued for State Parks—L[1]	653,062	786,017
2. Future Fuel Taxes May Go to Parks—L[1]	399,259	1,039,322
3. Limits Terms for Legislature, Statewide Offices, Congressional Offices—I[1]	*1,003,706	439,694
4. Bans Operation of Triple Truck-Trailer Combinations on Oregon Highways—I[2]	567,467	896,778
5. Closes Trojan Until Nuclear Waste, Cost, Earthquake, Health Conditions Met—I[2]	585,051	874,636
6. Bans Trojan Power Operation Unless Earthquake, Waste Storage Conditions Met—I[2]	619,329	830,850
7. Raises Tax Limit on Certain Property; Residential Renters' Tax Relief—I[1]	362,621	1,077,206
8. Restricts Lower Columbia Fish Harvests to Most Selective Means Available—I[2]	576,633	828,096
9. Government Cannot Facilitate, Must Discourage Homosexuality, Other "Behaviors"—I[1]	638,527	828,290

Election Date/Measure Number/Ballot Title	Yes	No
June 29, 1993 (Special Election)		
1. Allows Voter Approval of Urban Renewal Bond Repayment Outside Limit—L[1]	180,070	482,714
November 9, 1993 (Special Election)		
1. Should We Pass A 5% Sales Tax for Public Schools with these Restrictions?—L[1]	240,991	721,930
May 17, 1994		
2. Allows New Motor Vehicle Fuel Revenues for Dedicated Purposes—L[1]	158,028	446,665
November 8, 1994		
3. Amends Constitution: Changes Deadline for Filling Vacancies at General Election—L[1]	*776,197	382,126
4. Amends Constitution: Creates Vacancy if State Legislator Convicted of Felony—L[1]	*1,055,111	145,499
5. Amends Constitution: Bars New or Increased Taxes without Voter Approval—I[1]	543,302	671,025
6. Amends Constitution: Candidates May Use Only Contributions from District Residents—I[1]	*628,180	555,019
7. Amends Constitution: Guarantees Equal Protection: Lists Prohibited Grounds of Discrimination—I[1]	512,980	671,021
8. Amends Constitution: Public Employees Pay Part of Salary for Pension—I[1]	*611,760	610,776
9. Adopts Contribution and Spending Limits, Other Campaign Finance Law Changes—I[2]	*851,014	324,224
10. Amends Constitution: Legislature Cannot Reduce Voter-Approved Sentence Without 2/3 Vote—I[1]	*763,507	415,678
11. Mandatory Sentences for Listed Felonies; Covers Persons 15 and Up—I[2]	*788,695	412,816
12. Repeals Prevailing Rate Wage Requirement for Workers on Public Works—I[2]	450,553	731,146
13. Amends Constitution: Governments Cannot Approve, Create Classifications Based on, Homosexuality—I[1]	592,746	630,628
14. Amends Chemical Process Mining Laws: Adds Requirements, Prohibitions, Standards, Fees—I[1]	500,005	679,936
15. Amends Constitution: State Must Maintain Funding for Schools, Community Colleges—I[1]	438,018	760,853
16. Allows Terminally Ill Adults to Obtain Prescription for Lethal Drugs—I[2]	*627,980	596,018
17. Amends Constitution: Requires State Prison Inmates to Work Full Time—I[1]	*859,896	350,541
18. Bans Hunting Bears with Bait, Hunting Bears, Cougars with Dogs—I[2]	*629,527	586,026
19. Amends Constitution: No Free Speech Protection for Obscenity, Child Pornography—I[1]	549,754	652,139
20. Amends Constitution: "Equal Tax" on Trade Replaces Current Taxes—I[1]	284,195	898,416
May 16, 1995 (Special Election)		
21. Dedication of Lottery Funds to Education—L[1]	*671,027	99,728
22. Inhabitancy in State Legislative Districts—L[1]	*709,931	45,311
May 21, 1996		
23. Amends Constitution: Increases Minimum Value in Controversy Required to Obtain Jury Trial—L[1]	*466,580	177,218
24. Amends Constitution: Initiative Petition Signatures Must Be Collected From Each Congressional District—L[1]	279,399	360,592
25. Amends Constitution: Requires 3/5 Majority in Legislature to Pass Revenue-Raising Bills—L[1]	*349,918	289,930
November 5, 1996		
26. Amends Constitution: Changes the Principles that Govern Laws for Punishment of Crime—L[1]	*878,677	440,283
27. Amends Constitution: Grants Legislature New Power Over Both New, Existing Administrative Rules—L[1]	349,050	938,819

Election Date/Measure Number/Ballot Title	Yes	No
28. Amends Constitution: Repeals Certain Residency Requirements for State Veterans' Loans—L[1]	*708,341	593,136
29. Amends Constitution: Governor's Appointees Must Vacate Office If Successor Not Timely Confirmed—L[1]	335,057	958,947
30. Amends Constitution: State Must Pay Local Governments Costs of State-Mandated Programs—L[1]	*731,127	566,168
31. Amends Constitution: Obscenity May Receive No Greater Protection Than Under Federal Constitution—L[1]	630,980	706,974
32. Authorizes Bonds for Portland Region Light Rail, Transportation Projects Elsewhere—R[2]	622,764	704,970
33. Amends Constitution: Limits Legislative Change to Statutes Passed by Voters—I[1]	638,824	652,811
34. Wildlife Management Exclusive to Commission; Repeals 1994 Bear/Cougar Initiative—I[2]	570,803	762,979
35. Restricts Bases for Providers to Receive Pay for Health Care—I[2]	441,108	807,987
36. Increases Minimum Hourly Wage to $6.50 Over Three Years—I[2]	*769,725	584,303
37. Broadens Types of Beverage Containers Requiring Deposit and Refund Value—I[2]	540,645	818,336
38. Prohibits Livestock in Certain Polluted Waters or on Adjacent Lands—I[2]	479,921	852,661
39. Amends Constitution: Government, Private Entities Cannot Discriminate Among Health Care Provider Categories—I[1]	569,037	726,824
40. Amends Constitution: Gives Crime Victims Rights, Expands Admissible Evidence, Limits Pretrial Release—I[1]	*778,574	544,301
41. Amends Constitution: States How Public Employee Earnings Must Be Expressed—I[1]	446,115	838,088
42. Amends Constitution: Requires Testing of Public School Students; Public Report—I[1]	460,553	857,878
43. Amends Collective Bargaining Law for Public Safety Employees—I[2]	547,131	707,586
44. Increases, Adds Cigarette and Tobacco Taxes; Changes Tax Revenue Distribution—I[2]	*759,048	598,543
45. Amends Constitution: Raises Public Employees' Normal Retirement Age; Reduces Benefits—I[1]	458,238	866,461
46. Amends Constitution: Counts Non-Voters As "No" Votes on Tax Measures—I[1]	158,555	1,180,148
47. Amends Constitution: Reduces and Limits Property Taxes; Limits Local Revenues, Replacement Fees—I[1]	*704,554	642,613
48. Amends Constitution: Instructs State, Federal Legislators to Vote for Congressional Term Limits—I[1,3]	624,771	671,095
May 20, 1997 (Special Election)		
49. Amends Constitution: Restricts Inmate Lawsuits; Allows Interstate Shipment of Prison Made Products—L[1]	*699,813	70,940
50. Amends Constitution: Limits Assessed Value of Property for Tax Purposes; Limits Property Tax Rates—L[1]	*429,943	341,781
November 4, 1997 (Special Election)		
51. Repeals Law Allowing Terminally Ill Adults To Obtain Lethal Prescription—L[2]	445,830	666,275
52. Authorizes State Lottery Bond Program To Finance Public School Projects—L[2]	*805,742	293,425
May 19, 1998		
53. Amends Constitution: Eliminates Voter Turnout Requirement For Passing Certain Property Tax Measures—L[1]	303,539	319,871
November 3, 1998		
54. Amends Constitution: Authorizes State To Guarantee Bonded Indebtedness Of Certain Education Districts—L[1]	*569,982	474,727
55. Amends Constitution: Permits State To Guarantee Earnings On Prepaid Tuition Trust Fund—L[1]	456,464	579,251
56. Expands Notice To Landowners Regarding Changes To Land Use Laws—L[2]	*874,547	212,737

Election Date/Measure Number/Ballot Title	Yes	No
57. Makes Possession Of Limited Amount Of Marijuana Class C Misdemeanor—R[2]	371,967	736,968
58. Requires Issuing Copy Of Original Oregon Birth Certificate to Adoptees—I[2]	*621,832	462,084
59. Amends Constitution: Prohibits Using Public Resources To Collect Money For Political Purposes—I[1]	539,757	561,952
60. Requires Vote By Mail In Biennial Primary, General Elections—I[2]	*757,204	334,021
61. Vote Not Tallied By Court Order		
62. Amends Constitution: Requires Campaign Finance Disclosures; Regulates Signature Gathering; Guarantees Contribution Methods—I[1]	*721,448	347,112
63. Amends Constitution: Measures Proposing Supermajority Voting Requirements Require Same Supermajority For Passage—I[1]	*566,064	457,762
64. Prohibits Many Present Timber Harvest Practices, Imposes More Restrictive Regulations—I[2]	215,491	897,535
65. Amends Constitution: Creates Process For Requiring Legislature To Review Administrative Rules—I[1]	483,811	533,948
66. Amends Constitution: Dedicates Some Lottery Funding To Parks, Beaches; Habitat, Watershed Protection—I[1]	*742,038	362,247
67. Allows Medical Use Of Marijuana Within Limits; Establishes Permit System—I[2]	*611,190	508,263

November 2, 1999 (Special Election)

	Yes	No
68. Amends Constitution: Allows Protecting Business, Certain Government Programs From Prison Work Programs—L[1]	*406,526	289,407
69. Amends Constitution: Grants Victims Constitutional Rights In Criminal Prosecutions, Juvenile Court Delinquency Proceedings—L[1]	*406,393	292,419
70. Amends Constitution: Gives Public, Through Prosecutor, Right To Demand Jury Trial In Criminal Cases—L[1]	289,783	407,429
71. Amends Constitution: Limits Pretrial Release Of Accused Person To Protect Victims, Public—L[1]	*404,404	292,696
72. Amends Constitution: Allows Murder Conviction By 11 To 1 Jury Verdict—L[1]	316,351	382,685
73. Amends Constitution: Limits Immunity From Criminal Prosecution Of Person Ordered To Testify About His Or Her Conduct—L[1]	320,160	369,843
74. Amends Constitution: Requires Terms Of Imprisonment Announced In Court Be Fully Served, With Exceptions—L[1]	*368,899	325,078
75. Amends Constitution: Persons Convicted Of Certain Crimes Cannot Serve On Grand Juries, Criminal Trial Juries—L[1]	*399,671	292,445
76. Amends Constitution: Requires Light, Heavy Motor Vehicle Classes Proportionately Share Highway Costs—L[1]	*372,613	314,351

May 16, 2000

	Yes	No
77. Amends Constitution: Makes Certain Local Taxing Districts' Temporary Property Tax Authority Permanent—L[1]	336,253	432,541
78. Amends Constitution: Lengthens Period For Verifying Signatures On Initiative And Referendum Petitions—L[1]	*528,129	327,440
79. Amends Constitution: Increases Signatures Required To Place Initiative Amending Constitution On Ballot—L[1]	356,912	505,081
80. Amends Constitution: Authorizes Using Fuel Tax, Vehicle Fees For Increasing Highway Policing—L[1]	310,640	559,941
81. Amends Constitution: Allows Legislature To Limit Recovery Of Damages In Civil Actions—L[1]	219,009	650,348
82. Repeals Truck Weight-Mile Tax; Establishes And Increases Fuel Taxes—R[2]	109,741	767,329

November 7, 2000

	Yes	No
83. Amends Constitution: Authorizes New Standards, Priorities For Veterans' Loans; Expands Qualified Recipients—L[1]	*1,084,870	365,203
84. Amends Constitution: State Must Continue Paying Local Governments For State-Mandated Programs—L[1]	*1,211,384	222,723
85. Amends Constitution: Modifies Population, Minimum Area Requirements For Formation Of New Counties—L[1]	634,307	767,366

Election Date/Measure Number/Ballot Title	Yes	No
86. Amends Constitution: Requires Refunding General Fund Revenues Exceeding State Estimates To Taxpayers—L[1]	*898,793	550,304
87. Amends Constitution: Allows Regulation Of Location Of Sexually Oriented Businesses Through Zoning—L[1]	694,410	771,901
88. Increases Maximum Deductible In Oregon For Federal Income Taxes Paid—L[2]	*739,270	724,097
89. Dedicates Tobacco Settlement Proceeds To Specified Health, Housing, Transportation Programs—L[2]	622,814	828,117
90. Authorizes Rates Giving Utilities Return On Investments In Retired Property—R[2]	158,810	1,208,545
91. Amends Constitution: Makes Federal Income Taxes Fully Deductible On Oregon Tax Returns—I[1]	661,342	814,885
92. Amends Constitution: Prohibits Payroll Deductions For Political Purposes Without Specific Written Authorization—I[1]	656,250	815,338
93. Amends Constitution: Voters Must Approve Most Taxes, Fees; Requires Certain Approval Percentage—I[1]	581,186	865,091
94. Repeals Mandatory Minimum Sentences For Certain Felonies, Requires Resentencing—I[2]	387,068	1,073,275
95. Amends Constitution: Student Learning Determines Teacher Pay; Qualifications, Not Seniority, Determine Retention—I[1]	514,926	962,250
96. Amends Constitution: Prohibits Making Initiative Process Harder, Except Through Initiative; Applies Retroactively—I[1]	527,613	866,588
97. Bans Body-Gripping Animal Traps, Some Poisons; Restricts Fur Commerce—I[2]	606,939	867,219
98. Amends Constitution: Prohibits Using Public Resources For Political Purposes; Limits Payroll Deductions—I[1]	678,024	776,489
99. Amends Constitution: Creates Commission Ensuring Quality Home Care Services For Elderly, Disabled—I[1]	*911,217	539,414
1. Amends Constitution: Legislature Must Fund School Quality Goals Adequately; Report; Establish Grants—I[1]	*940,223	477,461
2. Amends Constitution: Creates Process For Requiring Legislature To Review Administrative Rules—I[1]	605,575	779,190
3. Amends Constitution: Requires Conviction Before Forfeiture; Restricts Proceeds Usage; Requires Reporting, Penalty—I[1]	*952,792	465,081
4. Dedicates Tobacco-Settlement Proceeds; Earnings Fund Low-Income Health Care—I[2]	650,850	789,543
5. Expands Circumstances Requiring Background Checks Before Transfer Of Firearm—I[2]	*921,926	569,996
6. Provides Public Funding To Candidates Who Limit Spending, Private Contributions—I[2]	586,910	838,011
7. The Secretary of State has been enjoined from canvassing the votes for this measure—I[1]		
8. Amends Constitution: Limits State Appropriations To Percentage Of State's Prior Personal Income—I[1]	608,090	789,699
9. Prohibits Public School Instruction Encouraging, Promoting, Sanctioning Homosexual, Bisexual Behaviors—I[2]	702,572	788,691
May 21, 2002		
10. Amends Constitution: Allows Public Universities to Receive Equity in Private Companies as Compensation for Publicly Created Technology—L[1]	*608,640	177,004
11. Amends Constitution: Authorizes Less Expensive General Obligation Bond financing for OHSU Medical Research and other Capital Costs—L[1]	*589,869	190,226
12. Removed from Ballot		
13. Amends Constitution: Authorizes Using Education Fund Principal in Specified Circumstances; Transfers $220 Million to School Fund—L[1]	376,605	411,923
September 17, 2002 (Special Election, see Note below)		
19. Amends Constitution: Authorizes Using Education Stability Fund Principal in Specified Circumstances; Transfers $150 Million to State School Fund; Creates School Capital Matching Subaccount in Stability Fund—L[1]	*496,815	306,440
20. Increases Cigarette Tax; Uses Revenue for Health Plan, Other Programs—L[2]	*522,613	289,119

Election Date/Measure Number/Ballot Title	Yes	No
November 5, 2002		
14. Amends Constitution: Removes Historical Racial References in Obsolete Sections of Constitution—L[1]	*867,901	352,027
15. Amends Constitution: Authorizes State to Issue General Obligation Bonds for Seismic Rehabilitation of Public Education Buildings—L[1]	*671,640	535,638
16. Amends Constitution: Authorizes State to Issue General Obligation Bonds for Seismic Rehabilitation of Emergency Services Buildings—L[1]	*669,451	530,587
17. Amends Constitution: Reduces Minimum Age Requirement to Serve as State Legislator from 21 Years to 18 Years—L[1]	341,717	910,331
18. Amends Constitution: Allows Certain Tax Districts to Establish Permanent Property Tax Rates and Divide into Tax Zones—L[1]	450,444	704,116
Note: An early Special Election was held for Measures 19 and 20 (see above)		
21. Amends Constitution: Revises Procedure for Filling Judicial Vacancies, Electing Judges; Allows Vote for "None of the Above"—I[1]	526,450	668,256
22. Amends Constitution: Requires Supreme Court Judges and Court of Appeals Judges to be Elected by District—I[1]	595,936	610,063
23. Creates Health Care Finance Plan for Medically Necessary Services; Creates Additional Income, Payroll Taxes—I[2]	265,310	969,537
24. Allows Licensed Denturists to Install Partial Dentures; Authorizes Cooperative Dentist-Denturist Business Ventures—I[2]	*907,979	286,492
25. Increases Minimum Wage to $6.90 in 2003; Increases for Inflation in Future Years—I[2]	*645,016	611,658
26. Amends Constitution: Prohibits Payment, Receipt of Payment Based on the Number of Initiative, Referendum Petition Signatures Obtained—I[1]	*921,606	301,415
27. Requires Labeling of Genetically-Engineered Foods Sold or Distributed in or from Oregon—I[2]	371,851	886,806
January 28, 2003 (Special Election)		
28. Temporarily Increases Income Tax Rates—L[2]	575,846	676,312
September 16, 2003 (Special Election)		
29. Amends Constitution: Authorizes State of Oregon to Incur General Obligation Debt for Savings on Pension Liabilities—L[1]	*360,209	291,778
February 3, 2004 (Special Election)		
30. Enacts Temporary Personal Income Tax Surcharge; Increases, Changes Corporate, Other Taxes; Avoids Specific Budget Cuts—R[2]	481,315	691,462
November 2, 2004		
31. Amends Constitution: Authorizes Law Permitting Postponement of Election for Particular Public Office When Nominee for Office Dies—L[1]	*1,122,852	588,502
32. Amends Constitution: Deletes Reference to Mobile Homes from Provision Dealing with Taxes and Fees on Motor Vehicles—L[1]	*1,048,090	661,576
33. Amends Medical Marijuana Act: Requires Marijuana Dispensaries for Supplying Patients/Caregivers; Raises Patients' Possession Limit—I[2]	764,015	1,021,814
34. Requires Balancing Timber Production, Resource Conservation/Preservation in Managing State Forests; Specifically Addresses Two Forests—I[2]	659,467	1,060,496
35. Amends Constitution: Limits Noneconomic Damages (Defined) Recoverable for Patient Injuries Caused by Healthcare Provider's Negligence or Recklessness—I[1]	869,054	896,857
36. Amends Constitution: Only Marriage Between One Man and One Woman Is Valid or Legally Recognized as Marriage—I[1]	*1,028,546	787,556
37. Governments Must Pay Owners, or Forgo Enforcement, when Certain Land Use Restrictions Reduce Property Value—I[2]	*1,054,589	685,079
38. Abolishes SAIF; State Must Reinsure, Satisfy SAIF's Obligations; Dedicates Proceeds, Potential Surplus to Public Purposes—I[2]	670,935	1,037,722
November 7, 2006		
39. Prohibits Public Body from Condemning Private Real Property If Intends to Convey to Private Party—I[2]	*881,820	431,844
40. Amends Constitution: Requires Oregon Supreme Court Judges and Court of Appeals Judges To Be Elected by District—I[1]	576,153	749,404
41. Allows Income Tax Deduction Equal to Federal Exemptions Deduction to Substitute for State Exemption Credit—I[2]	483,443	818,452

Election Date/Measure Number/Ballot Title	Yes	No
42. Prohibits Insurance Companies from Using Credit Score or "Credit Worthiness" in Calculating Rates or Premiums—I^2	479,935	876,075
43. Requires 48-Hour Notice to Unemancipated Minor's Parent Before Providing Abortion; Authorizes Lawsuits, Physician Discipline—I^2	616,876	746,606
44. Allows Any Oregon Resident Without Prescription Drug Coverage to Participate in Oregon Prescription Drug Program—I^2	*1,049,594	296,649
45. Amends Constitution: Limits State Legislators: Six Years as Representative, Eight Years as Senator, Fourteen Years in Legislature—I^1	555,016	788,895
46. Amends Constitution: Allows Laws Regulating Election Contributions, Expenditures Adopted by Initiative or 3/4 of Both Legislative Houses—I^1	520,342	770,251
47. Revises Campaign Finance Laws: Limits or Prohibits Contributions and Expenditures; Adds Disclosure, New Reporting Requirements—I^2	*694,918	615,256
48. Amends Constitution: Limits Biennial Percentage Increase in State Spending to Percentage Increase in State Population, Plus Inflation—I^1	379,971	923,629

November 6, 2007 (Special Election)

	Yes	No
49. Modifies Measure 37: Clarifies Right to Build Homes; Limits Large Developments; Protects Farms, Forests, Groundwater—L^2	*718,023	437,351
50. Amends Constitution: Dedicates Funds to Provide Health Care for Children, Fund Tobacco Prevention, Through Increased Tobacco Tax—L^1	472,063	686,470

May 20, 2008

	Yes	No
51. Amends Constitution: Enables Crime Victims to Enforce Existing Constitutional Rights in Prosecutions, Delinquency Proceedings; Authorizes Implementing Legislation—L^1	*744,195	249,143
52. Amends Constitution: Enables Crime Victims to Enforce Existing Constitutional Rights in Prosecutions, Delinquency Proceedings; Authorizes Implementing Legislation—L^1	*738,092	247,738
53. Amends Constitution: Modifies Provisions Governing Civil Forfeitures Related to Crimes; Permits Use of Proceeds by Law Enforcement—L^1	*490,158	489,477

November 4, 2008

	Yes	No
54. Amends Constitution: Standardizes Voting Eligibility for School Board Elections with Other State and Local Elections—L^1	*1,194,173	450,979
55. Amends Constitution: Changes Operative Date of Redistricting Plans; Allows Affected Legislators to Finish Term in Original District—L^1	*1,251,478	364,993
56. Amends Constitution: Provides that May and November Property Tax Elections are Decided by Majority of Voters Voting—L^1	*959,118	735,500
57. Increases Sentences for Drug Trafficking, Theft Against Elderly and Specified Repeat Property and Identity Theft Crimes; Requires Addiction Treatment for Certain Offenders—L^2	*1,058,955	665,942
58. Prohibits Teaching Public School Student in Language Other Than English for More Than Two Years—I^2	756,903	977,696
59. Creates an Unlimited Deduction for Federal Income Taxes on Individual Taxpayers' Oregon Income-Tax Returns—I^2	615,894	1,084,422
60. Teacher "Classroom Performance," Not Seniority, Determines Pay Raises; "Most Qualified" Teachers Retained, Regardless of Seniority—I^2	673,296	1,070,682
61. Creates Mandatory Minimum Prison Sentences for Certain Theft, Identity Theft, Forgery, Drug, and Burglary Crimes—I^2	848,901	887,165
62. Amends Constitution: Allocates 15% of Lottery Proceeds to Public Safety Fund for Crime Prevention, Investigation, Prosecution—I^2	674,428	1,035,756
63. Exempts Specified Property Owners From Building Permit Requirements for Improvements Valued At/Under 35,000 Dollars—I^2	784,376	928,721
64. Penalizes Person, Entity for Using Funds Collected with "Public Resource" (Defined) for "Political Purpose"—I^2	835,563	854,327
65. Changes General Election Nomination Processes for Major/Minor Party, Independent Candidates for Most Partisan Offices—I^2	553,640	1,070,580

January 26, 2010 (Special Election)

	Yes	No
66. Raises tax on household income at and above $250,000 (and $125,000 for individual filers). Reduces income taxes on unemployment benefits in 2009. Provides funds currently budgeted for education, health care, public safety, other services—R^2	*692,687	583,707

Election Date/Measure Number/Ballot Title	Yes	No
67. Raises $10 corporate minimum tax, business minimum tax, corporate profits tax. Provides funds currently budgeted for education, health care, public safety, other services—R[2]	*682,720	591,188
May 18, 2010		
68. Revises Constitution: Allows State To Issue Bonds To Match Voter Approved School District Bonds For School Capital Costs—L[1]	*498,073	267,052
69. Amends Constitution: Continues And Modernizes Authority For Lowest Cost Borrowing For Community Colleges And Public Universities—L[1]	*546,649	216,157
November 2, 2010		
70. Amends Constitution: Expands availability of home ownership loans for Oregon veterans through Oregon War Veterans' Fund—L[1]	*1,180,933	217,679
71. Amends Constitution: Requires legislature to meet annually; limits length of legislative sessions; provides exceptions—L[1]	*919,040	435,776
72. Amends Constitution: Authorizes exception to $50,000 state borrowing limit for state's real and personal property projects—L[1]	*774,582	536,204
73. Requires increased minimum sentences for certain repeated sex crimes, incarceration for repeated driving under influence—I[2]	*802,388	608,317
74. Establishes medical marijuana supply system and assistance and research programs; allows limited selling of marijuana—I[2]	627,016	791,186
75. Authorizes Multnomah County casino; casino to contribute monthly revenue percentage to state for specified purposes—I[2]	448,162	959,342
76. Amends Constitution: Continues lottery funding for parks, beaches, wildlife habitat, watershed protection beyond 2014; modifies funding process—I[1]	*972,825	432,552
November 6, 2012		
77. Amends Constitution: Governor may declare "catastrophic disaster" (defined); requires legislative session; authorizes suspending specified constitutional spending restrictions—L[1]	*957,646	673,468
78. Amends Constitution: Changes constitutional language describing governmental system of separation of powers; makes grammatical and spelling changes—L[1]	*1,165,963	458,509
79. Amends Constitution: Prohibits real estate transfer taxes, fees, other assessments, except those operative on December 31, 2009—I[1]	*976,587	679,710
80. Allows personal marijuana, hemp cultivation/use without license; commission to regulate commercial marijuana cultivation/sale—I[2]	810,538	923,071
81. Prohibits commercial non-tribal fishing with gillnets in Oregon "inland waters," allows use of seine nets—I[2]	567,996	1,072,614
82. Amends Constitution: Authorizes establishment of privately-owned casinos; mandates percentage of revenues payable to dedicated state fund—I[1]	485,240	1,226,331
83. Authorizes privately-owned Wood Village casino; mandates percentage of revenues payable to dedicated state fund—I[2]	500,123	1,207,508
84. Phases out existing inheritance taxes on large estates, and all taxes on intra-family property transfers—I[2]	776,143	912,541
85. Amends Constitution: Allocates corporate income/excise tax "kicker" refund to additionally fund K through 12 public education—I[1]	*1,007,122	672,586
November 4, 2014		
86. Amends Constitution: Requires creation of fund for Oregonians pursuing post-secondary education, authorizes state indebtedness to finance fund—L[1]	614,439	821,596
87. Amends Constitution: Permits employment of state judges by National Guard (military service) and state public universities (teaching)—L[1]	*817,709	600,015
88. Provides Oregon resident "driver card" without requiring proof of legal presence in the United States—R[2]	506,751	983,576
89. Amends Constitution: State/political subdivision shall not deny or abridge equality of rights on account of sex—I[1]	*925,892	514,907
90. Changes general election nomination processes: provides for single primary ballot listing candidates; top two advance—I[2]	459,629	987,050
91. Allows possession, manufacture, sale of marijuana by/to adults, subject to state licensing, regulation, taxation—I[2]	*847,865	663,346

Elections and Records

Election Date/Measure Number/Ballot Title	Yes	No
92. Requires food manufacturers, retailers to label "genetically engineered" foods as such; state, citizens may enforce—I²	752,737	753,574
May 17, 2016		
93. Majority yes vote disincorporates City of Damascus; property to Clackamas County, net assets to taxpayers—L⁶	*2,834	1,400
November 8, 2016		
94. Amends Constitution: Eliminates mandatory retirement age for state judges—L¹	699,689	1,194,167
95. Amends Constitution: Allows investments in equities by public universities to reduce financial risk and increase investments to benefit students—L¹	*1,301,183	546,919
96. Amends Constitution: Dedicates 1.5% of state lottery net proceeds to funding support services for Oregon veterans—L¹	*1,611,367	312,526
97. Increases corporate minimum tax when sales exceed $25 million; funds education, healthcare, senior services—I²	808,310	1,164,658
98. Requires state funding for dropout-prevention, career and college readiness programs in Oregon high schools—I²	*1,260,163	650,347
99. Creates "Outdoor School Education Fund," continuously funded through Lottery, to provide outdoor school programs statewide—I²	*1,287,095	630,735
100. Prohibits purchase or sale of parts or products from certain wildlife species; exceptions; civil penalties—I²	*1,306,213	574,631
January 23, 2018 (Special Election)		
101 Approves temporary assessments to fund health care for low-income individuals and families, and to stabilize health insurance premiums. Temporary assessments on insurance companies, some hospitals, and other providers of insurance or health care coverage. Insurers may not increase rates on health insurance premiums by more than 1.5 percent as a result of these assessments—R²	*657,117	408,387
November 6, 2018		
102 Amends Constitution: Allows local bonds for financing affordable housing with nongovernmental entities. Requires voter approval, annual audits—L¹	*1,037,922	786,225
103 Amends Constitution: Prohibits taxes/fees based on transactions for "groceries" (defined) enacted or amended after September 2017—I¹	791,687	1,062,752
104 Amends Constitution: Expands (beyond taxes) application of requirement that three-fifths legislative majority approve bills raising revenue—I¹	631,211	1,182,023
105 Repeals law limiting use of state/local law enforcement resources to enforce federal immigration laws—I²	675,389	1,172,774
106 Amends Constitution: Prohibits spending "public funds" (defined) directly/indirectly for "abortion" (defined); exceptions; reduces abortion access—I¹	658,793	1,195,718
November 3, 2020		
107 Amends Constitution: Allows laws limiting political campaign contributions and expenditures, requiring disclosure of political campaign contributions and expenditures, and requiring political campaign advertisements to identify who paid for them—L¹	*1,763,276	488,413
108 Increases cigarette and cigar taxes. Establishes tax on e-cigarettes and nicotine vaping devices. Funds health programs.—L²	*1,535,866	779,311
109 Allows manufacture, delivery, administration of psilocybin at supervised, licensed facilities; imposes two-year development period—I²	*1,270,057	1,008,199
110 Provides statewide addiction/recovery services; marijuana taxes partially finance; reclassifies possession/penalties for specified drugs—I²	*1,333,268	947,313

⁰Repeal of federal prohibition amendment
¹Constitutional amendment
²Statutory enactment
³Required communication to federal officials on behalf of people of Oregon

[4]Tri-county measure voted on in Clackamas, Multnomah and Washington Counties
[5]Advisory vote for legislators' information
[6]Voted on in Clackamas County

Earliest Authorities in Oregon

Pacific Fur Company*
Fort Astoria

Name	Term of Service	By What Authority/Remarks
McDougall, Duncan	Mar. 22, 1811–Feb. 15, 1812 Aug. 4, 1812–Aug. 20, 1813 Aug. 26, 1813–Oct. 16, 1813	Acting agent and partner; served in absence of Wilson Price Hunt by agreement with partners
Hunt, Wilson Price	Feb. 15, 1812–Aug. 4, 1812 Aug. 20, 1813–Aug. 26, 1813	Agent and partner by Articles of Agreement, June 23, 1810, Article 21

*Sold to John George McTavish and John Stuart, partners of the North West Company, Oct. 16, 1813; sale confirmed by Wilson Price Hunt, agent, March 10, 1814

North West Company
Headquarters, Columbia District, Fort George (Astoria)

Name	Term of Service	By What Authority/Remarks
McTavish, John George	Oct. 16, 1813–Dec. 1, 1813	Acting governor and partner
McDonald, John (of Garth)	Dec. 1, 1813–Apr. 4, 1814	Governor and partner, Alexander Henry, trader
McTavish, Donald	Apr. 23, 1814–May 22, 1814	Governor and partner; with Alexander Henry, drowned in the Columbia River
Keith, James	May 22, 1814–June 7, 1816	Acting governor and partner

Chief of the Coast	Term of Service	Chief of the Interior
Keith, James	June 7, 1816–Mar. 21, 1821	McKenzie, Donald

Hudson's Bay Company*
Headquarters, Columbia District, Fort George (Astoria) 1821–1825; Fort Vancouver, 1825–1846

Chief Factor	Term of Service	Junior Chief Factor
McMillan, James	Spring, 1821–Fall, 1821	Cameron, John Dougald
Cameron, John Dougald	Fall, 1821–Spring, 1824	Kennedy, Alexander
Kennedy, Alexander	Spring, 1824–Mar. 18, 1825	McLoughlin, John
McLoughlin, John	Mar. 18, 1825–May 31, 1845	None appointed

*Appointments in 1821 by agreement with North West Company; and 1822–1825 by council of Northern Department, Sir George Simpson, Governor

Oregon (Walamet) Mission of the Methodist Episcopal Church
Mission Bottom 1834–1841; Chemeketa (Salem) 1841–1847

Name	Term of Service	Position
Lee, Jason	Oct. 6, 1834–Mar. 26, 1838	Appointed superintendent upon recommendation of the Board of Managers of the Missionary Society
Leslie, David	Mar. 26, 1838–May 27, 1840	Acting superintendent in absence of Lee
Lee, Jason	May 27, 1840–Dec. 25, 1843	Superintendent
Leslie, David	Dec. 25, 1843–June 1, 1844	Acting superintendent in absence of Lee
Gary, George	June 1, 1844–July 18, 1847	Appointed superintendent; instructed to dissolve the mission properties

Provisional Government Executive Committee

Name	Term of Service	By What Authority/Remarks
Hill, David; Beers, Alanson; Gale, Joseph	July 5, 1843–May 25, 1844	Elected by meeting of inhabitants of

Name/Political Party	Term of Service	By What Authority/Remarks
		the Oregon Territory
Stewart, P.G.; Russell Osborn; Bailey, W.J.	May 25, 1844–July 14, 1845	By vote of the people

Governors of Oregon

Under Provisional Government

Name	Term of Service	By What Authority/Remarks
Abernethy, George	July 14, 1845–Mar. 3, 1849	By people at 1845 general election; reelected 1848

Under Territorial Government

Name/Political Party[1]	Term of Service	By What Authority/Remarks
Lane, Joseph—D	Mar. 3, 1849–June 18, 1850	Appointed by President Polk; resigned
Prichette, Kintzing—D	June 18, 1850–Aug. 18, 1850	Acting governor, was secretary
Gaines, John P.—W	Aug. 18, 1850–May 16, 1853	Appointed by President Taylor
Lane, Joseph—D	May 16, 1853–May 19, 1853	Appointed by President Pierce; resigned
Curry, George L.—D	May 19, 1853–Dec. 2, 1853	Acting governor, was secretary
Davis, John W.—D	Dec. 2, 1853–Aug. 1, 1854	Appointed by President Pierce; resigned
Curry, George L.—D	Aug. 1, 1854–Mar. 3, 1859	Acting governor, was secretary; appointed by President Pierce, Nov. 1, 1854

Under State Government

Whiteaker, John—D	Mar. 3, 1859–Sept. 10, 1862	Elected 1858
Gibbs, A.C.—R	Sept. 10, 1862–Sept. 12, 1866	Elected 1862
Woods, George L.—R	Sept. 12, 1866–Sept. 14, 1870	Elected 1866
Grover, LaFayette—D	Sept. 14, 1870–Feb. 1, 1877	Elected 1870; reelected 1874; resigned
Chadwick, Stephen F.—D	Feb. 1, 1877–Sept. 11, 1878	Was secretary of state
Thayer, W.W.—D	Sept. 11, 1878–Sept. 13, 1882	Elected 1878
Moody, Z.F.—R	Sept. 13, 1882–Jan. 12, 1887	Elected 1882
Pennoyer, Sylvester—DP	Jan. 12, 1887–Jan. 14, 1895	Elected 1886; reelected 1890
Lord, William Paine—R	Jan. 14, 1895–Jan. 9, 1899	Elected 1894
Geer, T.T.—R	Jan. 9, 1899–Jan. 14, 1903	Elected 1898
Chamberlain, George E.—D	Jan. 15, 1903–Feb. 28, 1909	Elected 1902; reelected 1906; resigned
Benson, Frank W.—R	Mar. 1, 1909–June 17, 1910	Was secretary of state; resigned
Bowerman, Jay[2]—R	June 17, 1910–Jan. 8, 1911	Was president of Senate
West, Oswald—D	Jan. 11, 1911–Jan. 12, 1915	Elected 1910
Withycombe, James—R	Jan. 12, 1915–Mar. 3, 1919	Elected 1914; reelected 1918; died in office
Olcott, Ben W.—R	Mar. 3, 1919–Jan. 8, 1923	Was secretary of state
Pierce, Walter M.—D	Jan. 8, 1923–Jan. 10, 1927	Elected 1922
Patterson, I.L.—R	Jan. 10, 1927–Dec. 21, 1929	Elected 1926; died in office
Norblad, A.W.[3]—R	Dec. 22, 1929–Jan. 12, 1931	Was president of Senate
Meier, Julius L.—I	Jan. 12, 1931–Jan. 14, 1935	Elected 1930
Martin, Charles H.—D	Jan. 14, 1935–Jan. 9, 1939	Elected 1934
Sprague, Charles A.—R	Jan. 9, 1939–Jan. 11, 1943	Elected 1938
Snell, Earl—R	Jan. 11, 1943–Oct. 28, 1947	Elected 1942; reelected 1946; died in office
Hall, John H.[4]—R	Oct. 30, 1947–Jan. 10, 1949	Was speaker of House
McKay, Douglas—R	Jan. 10, 1949–Dec. 27, 1952	Elected 1948; reelected 1950; resigned
Patterson, Paul L.—R	Dec. 27, 1952–Jan. 31, 1956	Was president of Senate; elected 1954; died in office
Smith, Elmo—R	Feb. 1, 1956–Jan. 14, 1957	Was president of Senate
Holmes, Robert D.—D	Jan. 14, 1957–Jan. 12, 1959	Elected 1956
Hatfield, Mark O.—R	Jan. 12, 1959–Jan. 9, 1967	Elected 1958; reelected 1962

Name/Political Party[1]	Term of Service	By What Authority/Remarks
McCall, Tom—R	Jan. 9, 1967–Jan 13, 1975	Elected 1966; reelected 1970
Straub, Robert W.—D	Jan. 13, 1975–Jan. 8, 1979	Elected 1974
Atiyeh, Victor G.—R	Jan. 8, 1979–Jan. 12, 1987	Elected 1978; reelected 1982
Goldschmidt, Neil—D	Jan. 12, 1987–Jan. 14, 1991	Elected 1986
Roberts, Barbara—D	Jan. 14, 1991–Jan. 9, 1995	Elected 1990
Kitzhaber, John—D	Jan. 9, 1995–Jan. 13, 2003	Elected 1994; reelected 1998
Kulongoski, Theodore R.—D	Jan. 13, 2003–Jan. 10, 2011	Elected 2002; reelected 2006
Kitzhaber, John—D	Jan. 10, 2011–Feb. 18, 2015	Elected 2010; reelected 2014; resigned
Brown, Kate[5]—D	Feb. 18, 2015–	Succeeded Kitzhaber; elected 2016; reelected 2018

[1]D = Democrat; R = Republican; DP = Democrat People's; I = Independent; W = Whig

[2]Jay Bowerman became governor when Frank Benson, who was serving as both governor and secretary of state, became incapacitated. Benson resigned as governor but continued as secretary of state until his death.

[3]In 1920, the Constitution was changed to allow the president of the Senate to succeed as governor.

[4]A plane crash on October 28, 1947, killed Governor Earl Snell, Secretary of State Robert S. Farrell, Jr., President of the Senate Marshall E. Cornett and the pilot, Cliff Hogue. John H. Hall, Speaker of the House and next in line of succession, automatically became governor. Earl Newbry was appointed by John H. Hall to the position of secretary of state.

[5]Kate Brown was serving as secretary of state when John Kitzhaber vacated the office of governor. The Oregon Constitution requires that the secretary of state is next in line to fill the vacancy. In 2016, Brown was elected to serve the remaining two years of Kitzhaber's term.

Secretaries of State of Oregon

Under Provisional Government

Name/Political Party	Term of Service	By What Authority/Remarks
LeBreton, George W.	Feb. 18, 1841–Mar. 4, 1844	Elected by meeting of inhabitants of the Willamette Valley to office of clerk of courts and public recorder, thus served as first secretary; reelected 1843; died in office
Johnson, Overton	Mar. 4, 1844–May 25, 1844	Appointed clerk and recorder
Long, Dr. John E.	May 25, 1844–June 21, 1846	Elected clerk and recorder by people at first 1844 general election; reelected 1845 general election; reelected 1845 by Legislature; drowned
Prigg, Frederick	June 26, 1846–Sept. 16, 1848	Appointed secretary to succeed Long; elected 1846 by Legislature; resigned
Holderness, Samuel M.	Sept. 19, 1848–Mar. 10, 1849	Appointed to succeed Prigg; elected 1848 by Legislature

Under Territorial Government

Magruder, Theophilus	Mar. 10, 1849–Apr. 9, 1849	Elected by Legislature
Prichette, Kintzing—D	Apr. 9, 1849–Sept. 18, 1850	Appointed by President Polk
Hamilton, Gen. E.D.—W	Sept. 18, 1850–May 14, 1853	Appointed by President Taylor
Curry, George L.—D	May 14, 1853–Jan. 27, 1855	Appointed by President Pierce
Harding, Benjamin—D	Jan. 27, 1855–Mar. 3, 1859	Appointed by President Pierce

Under State Government

Heath, Lucien—D	Mar. 3, 1859–Sept. 8, 1862	Elected 1858
May, Samuel E.—R	Sept. 8, 1862–Sept. 10, 1870	Elected 1862; reelected 1866
Chadwick, Stephen F.[1]—D	Sept. 10, 1870–Sept. 2, 1878	Elected 1870; reelected 1874
Earhart, R.P.—R	Sept. 2, 1878–Jan. 10, 1887	Elected 1878; reelected 1882
McBride, George W.—R	Jan. 10, 1887–Jan. 14, 1895	Elected 1886; reelected 1890
Kincaid, Harrison R.—R	Jan. 14, 1895–Jan. 9, 1899	Elected 1894

Name/Political Party	Term of Service	By What Authority/Remarks
Dunbar, Frank I.—R	Jan. 9, 1899–Jan. 14, 1907	Elected 1898; reelected 1902
Benson, Frank W.[2]—R	Jan. 15, 1907–Apr. 14, 1911	Elected 1906; reelected 1910; died in office
Olcott, Ben W.[3]—R	Apr. 17, 1911–May 28, 1920	Appointed by Governor West; elected 1912; reelected 1916; resigned
Kozer, Sam A.—R	May 28, 1920–Sept. 24, 1928	Appointed by Governor Olcott; elected 1920; reelected 1924; resigned
Hoss, Hal E.—R	Sept. 24, 1928–Feb. 6, 1934	Appointed by Governor Patterson; elected 1928; reelected 1932; died in office
Stadelman, P.J.—R	Feb. 9, 1934–Jan. 7, 1935	Appointed by Governor Meier
Snell, Earl—R	Jan. 7, 1935–Jan. 4, 1943	Elected 1934; reelected 1938
Farrell, Robert S., Jr.—R	Jan. 4, 1943–Oct. 28, 1947	Elected 1942; reelected 1946; died in office
Newbry, Earl T.—R	Nov. 3, 1947–Jan. 7, 1957	Appointed by Governor Hall; elected 1948; reelected 1952
Hatfield, Mark O.—R	Jan. 7, 1957–Jan. 12, 1959	Elected 1956; resigned
Appling, Howell, Jr.—R	Jan. 12, 1959–Jan. 4, 1965	Appointed by Governor Hatfield; elected 1960
McCall, Tom—R	Jan. 4, 1965–Jan. 9, 1967	Elected 1964; resigned
Myers, Clay—R	Jan. 9, 1967–Jan. 3, 1977	Appointed by Governor McCall; elected 1968; reelected 1972
Paulus, Norma—R	Jan. 3, 1977–Jan. 7, 1985	Elected 1976; reelected 1980
Roberts, Barbara—D	Jan. 7, 1985–Jan. 14, 1991	Elected 1984; reelected 1988; resigned
Keisling, Phil—D	Jan. 14, 1991–Nov. 8, 1999	Appointed by Governor Roberts; elected 1992; reelected 1996; resigned
Bradbury, Bill—D	Nov. 8, 1999–Jan. 5, 2009	Appointed by Governor Kitzhaber; elected 2000; reelected 2004
Brown, Kate[4]—D	Jan. 5, 2009–Feb. 17, 2015	Elected 2008; reelected 2012; succeeded Governor Kitzhaber
Atkins, Jeanne P.—D	Mar. 11, 2015–Jan. 2, 2017	Appointed by Governor Brown
Richardson, Dennis—R	Jan. 2, 2017–Feb. 26, 2019	Elected 2016; died in office
Bev Clarno[5]—R	March 31, 2019–Jan. 2, 2021	Appointed by Governor Brown
Shemia Fagan—D	January 4, 2021–	Elected 2020

[1]When Stephen Chadwick succeeded L. F. Grover as governor in 1877, he did not resign as secretary of state. He signed documents and proclamations twice—as governor and as secretary of state—until September 1878.

[2]Frank Benson served as both secretary of state and governor. See Footnote 2 under Governors of Oregon.

[3]When James Withycombe died in office on March 3, 1919, Ben W. Olcott succeeded him as governor. However, Governor Olcott did not resign or appoint a new secretary of state until May 28, 1920.

[4]When Governor John Kitzhaber resigned during office, Secretary of State Kate Brown became governor according to the order of succession required by the Oregon Constitution.

[5]When Dennis Richardson died in office on Feb. 26, 2019, his deputy Leslie Cummings served as acting secretary until Governor Kate Brown appointed Bev Clarno.

Treasurers of Oregon

Under Provisional Government

Name/Political Party	Term of Service	By What Authority/Remarks
Gray, W.H.	Mar. 1, 1843–July 5, 1843	Elected by meeting of citizens of the Willamette Valley

Name/Political Party	Term of Service	By What Authority/Remarks
Willson, W.H.	July 5, 1843–May 14, 1844	Elected by meeting of the inhabitants of the Willamette settlements
Foster, Phillip	July 2, 1844–July 7, 1845	Elected by people at first 1844 general election
Ermatinger, Francis	July 7, 1845–Mar. 3, 1846	Elected by people at 1845 general election; reelected 1845 by Legislature; resigned
Couch, John H.	Mar. 4, 1846–Sept. 27, 1847	Appointed to succeed Ermatinger; elected by Legislature 1846; resigned
Kilbourn, William K.	Oct. 11, 1847–Sept. 28, 1849	Appointed to succeed Couch; elected by Legislature 1849

Under Territorial Government

Taylor, James	Sept. 28, 1849–Feb. 8, 1851	Elected by Legislature
Rice, L.A.	Feb. 8, 1851–Sept. 22, 1851	Elected by Legislature; resigned
Buck, William W.	Sept. 27, 1851–Dec. 16, 1851	Appointed to succeed Rice
Boon, John D.—D	Dec. 16, 1851–Mar. 1, 1855	Elected by Legislature
Lane, Nat H.—D	Mar. 1, 1855–Jan. 10, 1856	Elected by Legislature
Boon, John D.—D	Jan. 10, 1856–Mar. 3, 1859	Elected by Legislature

Under State Government

Boon, John D.—D	Mar. 3, 1859–Sept. 8, 1862	Elected 1858
Cooke, E.N.—R	Sept. 8, 1862–Sept. 12, 1870	Elected 1862; reelected 1866
Fleischner, L.—D	Sept. 12, 1870–Sept. 14, 1874	Elected 1870
Brown, A.H.—D	Sept. 14, 1874–Sept. 9, 1878	Elected 1874
Hirsch, E.—R	Sept. 9, 1878–Jan. 10, 1887	Elected 1878; reelected 1882
Webb, G.W.—D	Jan. 10, 1887–Jan. 12, 1891	Elected 1886
Metschan, Phil—R	Jan. 12, 1891–Jan. 9, 1899	Elected 1890; reelected 1894
Moore, Charles S.—R	Jan. 9, 1899–Jan. 14, 1907	Elected 1898; reelected 1902
Steel, George A.—R	Jan. 15, 1907–Jan. 3, 1911	Elected 1906
Kay, Thomas B.—R	Jan. 4, 1911–Jan. 6, 1919	Elected 1910; reelected 1914
Hoff, O.P.—R	Jan. 6, 1919–Mar. 18, 1924	Elected 1918; reelected 1922; died in office
Myers, Jefferson—D	Mar. 18, 1924–Jan. 4, 1925	Appointed by Governor Pierce
Kay, Thomas B.—R	Jan. 4, 1925–April 29, 1931	Elected 1924; reelected 1928; died in office
Holman, Rufus C.—R	May 1, 1931–Dec. 27, 1938	Appointed by Governor Meier; elected 1932; reelected 1936; resigned
Pearson, Walter E.—D	Dec. 27, 1938–Jan. 6, 1941	Appointed by Governor Martin
Scott, Leslie M.—R	Jan. 6, 1941–Jan. 3, 1949	Elected 1940; reelected 1944
Pearson, Walter J.—D	Jan. 3, 1949–Jan. 5, 1953	Elected 1948
Unander, Sig—R	Jan. 5, 1953–Dec. 31, 1959	Elected 1952; reelected 1956; resigned
Belton, Howard C.—R	Jan. 4, 1960–Jan. 4, 1965	Appointed by Governor Hatfield; elected 1960
Straub, Robert—D	Jan. 4, 1965–Jan. 1, 1973	Elected 1964; reelected 1968
Redden, James A.—D	Jan. 1, 1973–Jan. 3, 1977	Elected 1972
Myers, Clay—R	Jan. 3, 1977–Apr. 1, 1984	Elected 1976; reelected 1980; resigned
Rutherford, Bill—R	Apr. 1, 1984–July 9, 1987	Appointed by Governor Atiyeh; elected 1984; resigned
Meeker, Tony—R	July 9, 1987–Jan. 4, 1993	Appointed by Governor Goldschmidt; elected 1988
Hill, Jim—D	Jan. 4, 1993–Jan. 1, 2001	Elected 1992; reelected 1996
Edwards, Randall—D	Jan. 1, 2001–Jan. 5, 2009	Elected 2000; reelected 2004
Westlund, Ben—D	Jan. 5, 2009–Mar. 7, 2010	Elected 2008; died in office
Ted Wheeler—D	Mar. 11, 2010–Jan. 2, 2017	Appointed by Governor Kulongoski; elected 2010; reelected 2012
Read, Tobias—D	Jan. 2, 2017–	Elected 2016; reelected 2020

Oregon Supreme Court Justices[1]

Under Provisional Government

Name	Term of Service	By What Authority/Remarks
Babcock, Dr. Ira L.	Feb. 18, 1841–May 1, 1843	Supreme judge with probate powers elected at meeting of inhabitants of the Willamette Valley
Wilson, W.E.	No record of service	Supreme judge with probate powers; elected at meeting of inhabitants of the Willamette Settlements, May 2, 1843
Russell, Osborn	Oct. 2, 1843–May 14, 1844	Supreme judge and probate judge; appointed by the Executive Committee
Babcock, Dr. Ira L.	June 27, 1844–Nov. 11, 1844	Presiding judge, Circuit Court; elected at first general election May 1844; resigned
Nesmith, James W.	Dec. 25, 1844–Aug. 9, 1845	Presiding judge, Circuit Court; appointed by Executive Committee; elected by people 1845
Ford, Nathaniel	Declined service	Supreme judge; elected by Legislature Aug. 9, 1845; declined to serve
Burnett, Peter H.	Sept. 6, 1845–Dec. 29, 1846	Supreme judge; elected by Legislature; declined appointment to Supreme Court 1848
Thornton, J. Quinn	Feb. 20, 1847–Nov. 9, 1847	Supreme judge; appointed by Governor Abernethy; resigned
Lancaster, Columbia	Nov. 30, 1847–Apr. 9, 1849	Supreme judge; appointed by Governor Abernethy
Lovejoy, A.L.	No record of service	Supreme judge; elected by Legislature Feb. 16, 1849

Under Territorial[2] and State Government[3]

Name	Term of Service	By What Authority/Remarks
Bryant, William P.	1848–1850	Appointed 1848; resigned 1850; chief justice 1848–1850
Pratt, Orville C.	1848–1852	Appointed 1848; term ended 1852
Nelson, Thomas	1850–1853	Appointed 1850 to succeed Bryant; term ended 1853; chief justice 1850–1853
Strong, William	1850–1853	Appointed 1850 to succeed Burnett; term ended 1853
Williams, George H.	1853–1858	Appointed 1853, 1857; resigned 1858; chief justice 1853–1858
Olney, Cyrus	1853–1858	Appointed 1853, 1857; resigned 1858
Deady, Matthew P.	1853–1859	Appointed 1853, 1857; elected 1858; resigned 1859
McFadden, Obadiah B.	1853–1854	Appointed 1853; term ended 1854
Boise, Reuben P.	1858–1870, 1876–1880	Appointed 1858 to succeed Olney; elected 1859; reelected 1864; term ended 1870; elected 1876; term ended 1878; appointed 1878; term ended 1880; chief justice 1862–1864, 1867–1870
Wait, Aaron E.	1859–1862	Elected 1858; resigned May 1, 1862; chief justice 1859–1862
Stratton, Riley E.	1859–1866	Elected 1858, 1864; died Dec. 26, 1866
Prim, Paine Page	1859–1880	Appointed 1859 to succeed Deady; elected 1860; reelected 1866, 1872; term ended 1878; appointed 1878; term ended 1880; chief justice 1864–1866, 1870–1872, 1876–1878
Page, William W.	1862	Appointed May 1862 to succeed Wait; term ended Sept. 1862
Shattuck, Erasmus D.	1862–1867, 1874–1878	Elected 1862; resigned Dec. 1867; elected 1874; term ended 1878; chief justice 1866–1867
Wilson, Joseph G.	1862–1870	New appointment Oct. 17, 1862; elected 1864; resigned May 1870
Skinner, Alonzo A.	1866–1867	Appointed 1866 to succeed Stratton; term ended 1867

Name	Term of Service	By What Authority/Remarks
Upton, William W.	1867–1874	Appointed Dec. 1867 to succeed Shattuck; elected 1868; term ended 1874; chief justice 1872–1874
Kelsay, John	1868–1870	Elected 1868 to succeed Stratton; term ended 1870
Whitten, Benoni	1870	Appointed May 1870 to succeed Wilson; term ended Sept. 1870
McArthur, Lewis L.	1870–1878	Elected 1870; reelected 1876; term ended 1878
Thayer, Andrew J.	1870–1873	Elected 1870; died Apr. 26, 1873
Bonham, Benjamin F.	1870–1876	Elected 1870; term ended 1876; chief justice 1874–1876
Moser, Lafayette F.	1873–1874	Appointed May 1873 to succeed A.J. Thayer; term ended 1874
Burnett, John	1874–1876	Elected 1874; term ended 1876
Watson, James F.	1876–1878	Elected 1876; term ended 1878
Kelly, James K.	1878–1880	Appointed 1878; term ended 1880; chief justice 1878–1880
Lord, William P.	1880–1894	Elected 1880; reelected 1882, 1888; term ended 1894; chief justice 1880–1882, 1886–1888, 1892–1894
Watson, Edward B.	1880–1884	Elected 1880; term ended 1884; chief justice 1882–1884
Waldo, John B.	1880–1886	Elected 1880; term ended 1886; chief justice 1884–1886
Thayer, William W.	1884–1890	Elected 1884; term ended 1890; chief justice 1888–1890
Strahan, Reuben S.	1886–1892	Elected 1886; term ended 1892; chief justice 1890–1892
Bean, Robert S.	1890–1909	Elected 1890; reelected 1896, 1902, 1908; resigned May 1, 1909; chief justice 1894–1896, 1900–1902, 1905–1909
Moore, Frank A.	1892–1918	Elected 1892; reelected 1898, 1904, 1910, 1916; died Sept. 25, 1918; chief justice 1896–1898, 1902–1905, 1909–1911, 1915–1917
Wolverton, Charles E.	1894–1905	Elected 1894, 1900; resigned Dec. 4, 1905; chief justice 1898–1900, 1905
Hailey, Thomas G.	1905–1907	Appointed Dec. 5, 1905 to succeed Wolverton; term ended Jan. 15, 1907
Eakin, Robert	1907–1917	Elected 1906, 1912; resigned Jan. 8, 1917; chief justice 1911–1913
King, William R.	1909–1911	Appointed Feb. 12, 1909; term ended Jan. 1, 1911
Slater, Woodson T.	1909–1911	Appointed Feb. 12, 1909; term ended Jan. 1, 1911
McBride, Thomas A.	1909–1930	Appointed May 1, 1909 to succeed Robert S. Bean; elected 1914; reelected 1920, 1926; died Sept. 9, 1930; chief justice 1913–1915, 1917–1921, 1923–1927
Bean, Henry J.	1911–1941	Elected 1910; reelected 1914, 1920, 1926, 1932, 1938; died May 8, 1941; chief justice 1931–1933, 1937–1939
Burnett, George H.	1911–1927	Elected 1910; reelected 1916, 1922; died Sept. 10, 1927; chief justice 1921–1923, 1927
McNary, Charles L.	1913–1915	Appointed June 3, 1913; term ended Jan. 4, 1915
Ramsey, William M.	1913–1915	Appointed June 3, 1913; term ended Jan. 4, 1915
Benson, Henry L.	1915–1921	Elected 1914; reelected 1920; died Oct. 16, 1921
Harris, Lawrence T.	1915–1924	Elected 1914; reelected 1920; resigned Jan. 15, 1924
McCamant, Wallace	1917–1918	Appointed Jan. 8, 1917 to succeed Eakin; resigned June 4, 1918
Johns, Charles A.	1918–1921	Appointed June 4, 1918 to succeed McCamant; elected 1918; resigned Oct. 7, 1921
Olson, Conrad P.	1918–1919	Appointed Sept. 27, 1918 to succeed Moore; term ended Jan. 7, 1919
Bennett, Alfred S.	1919–1920	Elected 1918; resigned Oct. 5, 1920

Name	Term of Service	By What Authority/Remarks
Brown, George M.	1920–1933	Appointed Oct. 14, 1920 to succeed Bennett; elected 1920; reelected 1926; term ended 1933
McCourt, John	1921–1924	Appointed Oct. 8, 1921 to succeed Johns; elected 1922; died Sept. 12, 1924
Rand, John L.	1921–1942	Appointed Oct. 18, 1921 to succeed Benson; elected 1922; reelected 1928, 1934, 1940; died Nov. 19, 1942; chief justice 1927–1929, 1933–1935, 1939–1941
Coshow, Oliver P.	1924–1931	Appointed Jan. 15, 1924 to succeed Harris; elected 1924; term ended 1931; chief justice 1929–1931
Pipes, Martin L.	1924	Appointed Sept. 1924 to succeed McCourt; term ended Dec. 31, 1924
Belt, Harry H.	1925–1950	Elected 1924; reelected 1930, 1936, 1942, 1948; died Aug. 6, 1950; chief justice 1945–1947
Rossman, George	1927–1965	Appointed Sept. 13, 1927 to succeed George H. Burnett; elected 1928; reelected 1934, 1940, 1946, 1952, 1958; term ended 1965; chief justice 1947–1949
Kelly, Percy R.	1930–1949	Appointed Sept. 24, 1930 to succeed McBride; elected 1930; reelected 1936, 1942, 1948; died June 14, 1949; chief justice 1941–1943
Campbell, James U.	1931–1937	Elected 1930; reelected 1936; died July 16, 1937; chief justice 1935–1937
Bailey, John O.	1933–1950	Elected 1932; reelected 1938, 1944; resigned Nov. 15, 1950; chief justice 1943–1945
Lusk, Hall S.	1937–1960	Appointed July 22, 1937 to succeed Campbell; elected 1938; reelected 1944, 1950, 1956; resigned Mar. 15, 1960; 1961–1968 recalled to temporary active service 1961 through 1968; chief justice 1949–1951
Brand, James T.	1941–1958	Appointed May 14, 1941 to succeed Henry J. Bean; elected 1942; reelected 1948, 1954; resigned June 30, 1958; chief justice 1951–1953
Hay, Arthur D.	1942–1952	Appointed Nov. 28, 1942 to succeed Rand; elected 1944; reelected 1950; died Dec. 19, 1952
Page, E.M.	1949–1950	Appointed July 8, 1949 to succeed Percy R. Kelly; resigned Jan. 18, 1950
Latourette, Earl C.	1950–1956	Appointed Jan. 19, 1950 to succeed E.M. Page; elected 1950; died Aug. 18, 1956; chief justice 1953–1955
Warner, Harold J.	1950–1963	Appointed Sept. 5, 1950 to succeed Belt; elected 1950; reelected 1956; term ended 1963; chief justice 1955–1957
Tooze, Walter L.	1950–1956	Appointed Nov. 16, 1950 to succeed Bailey; elected 1950; reelected 1956; died Dec. 21, 1956
Perry, William C.	1952–1970	Appointed Dec. 26, 1952 to succeed Hay; elected 1954; reelected 1960, 1966; resigned June 1, 1970; chief justice 1957–1959, 1967–1970
McAllister, William M.	1956–1976	Appointed Aug. 24, 1956 to succeed Latourette; elected 1956; reelected 1962, 1968, 1974; resigned Dec. 31, 1976; chief justice 1959–1967
Kester, Randall B.	1957–1958	Appointed Jan. 3, 1957 to succeed Tooze; resigned Mar. 1, 1958
Sloan, Gordon	1958–1970	Appointed Mar. 1, 1958 to succeed Kester; elected 1958; reelected 1964; resigned Oct. 1, 1970
O'Connell, Kenneth J.	1958–1977	Appointed July 1, 1958 to succeed Brand; elected 1958; reelected 1964, 1970; term ended 1977; chief justice 1970–1976
Goodwin, Alfred T.	1960–1969	Appointed Mar. 18, 1960 to succeed Lusk; elected 1960; reelected 1966; resigned Dec. 19, 1969
Denecke, Arno H.	1963–1982	Elected 1962; reelected 1968, 1974, 1980; resigned June 30, 1982; chief justice 1976–1982

Name	Term of Service	By What Authority/Remarks
Holman, Ralph M.	1965–1980	Elected 1964; reelected 1970, 1976; resigned Jan. 20, 1980
Tongue, Thomas H.	1969–1982	Appointed Dec. 29, 1969 to succeed Goodwin; elected 1970; reelected 1976; resigned Feb. 7, 1982
Howell, Edward H.	1970–1980	Appointed June 1, 1970 to succeed Perry; elected 1970; reelected 1976; resigned Nov. 30, 1980
Bryson, Dean F.	1970–1979	Elected 1970; appointed Oct. 23, 1970 (before elective term began) to succeed Sloan; reelected 1976; resigned April 1, 1979
Lent, Berkeley	1977–1988	Elected 1976; reelected 1982; resigned Sept. 30, 1988; chief justice 1982–1983
Linde, Hans	1977–1990	Appointed Jan. 3, 1977 to succeed McAllister; elected 1978; reelected 1984; resigned Jan. 31, 1990
Peterson, Edwin J.	1979–1993	Appointed May 15, 1979 to succeed Bryson; elected 1980; reelected 1986, 1992; resigned Dec. 31, 1993; chief justice 1983–1991
Tanzer, Jacob	1980–1982	Appointed Jan. 21, 1980 to succeed Holman; elected 1980; resigned Dec. 31, 1982
Campbell, J.R.	1980–1988	Appointed Dec. 1, 1980 to succeed Howell; elected 1982; resigned Dec. 31, 1988
Roberts, Betty	1982–1986	Appointed Feb. 8, 1982 to succeed Tongue; elected 1982; resigned Feb. 7, 1986
Carson, Wallace P., Jr.	1982–2006	Appointed July 14, 1982 to succeed Denecke; elected 1982; reelected 1988, 1994, 2000; chief justice 1991–2005; resigned Dec. 31, 2006
Jones, Robert E.	1983–1990	Appointed Dec. 16, 1982 to succeed Tanzer; elected 1984; resigned April 30, 1990
Gillette, W. Michael	1986–2011	Appointed Feb. 10, 1986 to succeed Roberts; elected 1986; reelected 1992, 1998, 2004
Van Hoomissen, George	1988–2001	Elected May 17, 1988 to succeed Lent; reelected 1994; resigned Dec. 31, 2000
Fadeley, Edward N.	1988–1998	Elected Nov. 8, 1988 to succeed Campbell; reelected 1994; resigned Jan. 31, 1998
Unis, Richard	1990–1996	Appointed Feb. 1, 1990 to succeed Linde; elected 1990; resigned June 30, 1996
Graber, Susan P.[4]	1990–1998	Appointed May 2, 1990 and Jan. 7, 1991 to succeed Jones; elected 1992; resigned April 1, 1998
Durham, Robert D.	1994–2013	Appointed Jan. 4, 1994 to succeed Peterson; elected 1994; reelected 2000, 2006
Kulongoski, Ted	1997–2001	Elected May, 1996; resigned June 14, 2001
Leeson, Susan M.	1998–2003	Appointed Feb. 26, 1998 to succeed Fadeley; elected 1998; resigned Jan. 31, 2003
Riggs, R. William	1998–2006	Appointed Sept. 8, 1998 to succeed Graber; elected 1998; reelected 2004, resigned Sept. 30, 2006
De Muniz, Paul J.	2001–2013	Elected Nov. 7, 2000 to succeed Van Hoomissen; reelected 2006; chief justice 2006–2012
Balmer, Thomas A.	2001–	Appointed Sept. 20, 2001 to succeed Kulongoski; elected 2002; reelected 2008, 2014; chief justice 2012–2018; reelected 2020
Kistler, Rives	2003–2018	Appointed Aug. 15, 2003 to succeed Leeson; elected 2004; reelected 2010, 2016; retired Dec. 31, 2018
Walters, Martha Lee	2006–	Appointed Oct. 1, 2006 to succeed Riggs; elected 2008; reelected 2014, 2020; chief justice 2018 to date
Linder, Virginia L.	2007–2015	Elected Nov. 7, 2006 to succeed Carson; reelected 2012; retired Dec. 31, 2015
Landau, Jack L.	2011–2017	Elected 2010 to succeed Gillette; reelected 2016; retired Dec. 31, 2017
Brewer, Dave	2013–2017	Elected 2012 to succeed De Muniz; retired June 30, 2017
Baldwin, Richard C.	2013–2017	Elected 2012 to succeed Durham; retired March 31, 2017

Name	Term of Service	By What Authority/Remarks
Nakamoto, Lynn	2016–	Appointed Jan. 1, 2016 to succeed Linder; elected 2016
Duncan, Rebecca	2017–	Appointed July 6, 2017 to succeed Brewer; elected 2018
Flynn, Meagan A.	2017–	Appointed April 4, 2017 to succeed Baldwin; elected 2018
Nelson, Adrienne C.	2018–	Appointed Jan. 2, 2018 to succeed Landau; elected 2018
Garrett, Chris	2019–	Appointed Jan. 2, 2019 to succeed Kistler; elected 2020

[1]Unless otherwise noted, justices took office in the year in which elected until 1905. Since then, terms have started on the first Monday in January and continued until the first Monday six years hence or until a successor has been sworn in, if later.

[2]Appointments under territorial government were made by the president of the United States.

[3]From 1859 to 1862, there were four Supreme Court justices. In 1862, a fifth justice was added. The justices at that time also rode circuit. In 1878, the Supreme Court and Circuit Court were separated; the Supreme Court then had three justices. In 1910, the number increased to five. The final increase to the present seven occurred in 1913.

[4]When Justice Jones resigned, he had already filed to run for another term and his name appeared on the ballot at the 1990 primary election. Because he was elected for another term, which began January 7, 1991, he had to resign from his new term, and Justice Graber was appointed again at that time.

Judges of the Oregon Court of Appeals

The Oregon Court of Appeals was established July 1, 1969 with five members, expanded to six members October 5, 1973 and to ten members September 1, 1977.

Name	Term of Service	By What Authority/Remarks
Langtry, Virgil	1969–1976	Appointed July 1, 1969; elected 1970; resigned Sept. 15, 1976
Foley, Robert H.	1969–1976	Appointed July 1, 1969; elected 1970; resigned Aug. 16, 1976
Schwab, Herbert M.	1969–1980	Appointed July 1, 1969; elected 1970; reelected 1976; resigned Dec. 31, 1980; chief judge 1969–1980
Fort, William S.	1969–1977	Appointed July 1, 1969; elected 1970; term ended 1977
Branchfield, Edward	1969–1971	Appointed July 1, 1969; term ended 1971
Thornton, Robert Y.	1971–1983	Elected 1970; reelected 1976; term ended 1983
Tanzer, Jacob	1973–1975, 1976–1980	Appointed to new seat Oct. 5, 1973; term ended Jan. 6, 1975; elected 1976; appointed Aug. 16, 1976 (before elective term began) to succeed Foley; resigned Jan. 21, 1980
Lee, Jason	1975–1980	Elected 1974; died Feb. 19, 1980
Johnson, Lee	1977–1978	Elected 1976; resigned Dec. 18, 1978
Richardson, William L.	1976–1997	Elected 1976; appointed Oct. 15, 1976 (before elective term began) to succeed Langtry; reelected 1982, 1988, 1994; chief judge 1993–1997; resigned June 30, 1997
Buttler, John H.	1977–1992	Appointed to new seat Sept. 1, 1977; elected 1978; reelected 1984, 1990; resigned Dec. 31, 1992
Joseph, George M.	1977–1992	Appointed to new seat Sept. 1, 1977; elected 1978; reelected 1984, 1990; resigned Dec. 31, 1992; chief judge 1981–1992
Gillette, W. Michael	1977–1986	Appointed to new seat Sept. 1, 1977; elected 1978; reelected 1984; resigned Feb. 10, 1986
Roberts, Betty	1977–1982	Appointed to new seat Sept. 1, 1977; elected 1978; resigned Feb. 8, 1982
Campbell, J.R.	1979–1980	Appointed Mar. 19, 1979 to succeed Johnson; elected 1980; resigned Nov. 30, 1980
Warden, John C.	1980–1988	Appointed Feb. 19, 1980 to succeed Tanzer; term ended Jan. 5, 1981; appointed Jan. 6, 1981 to

Name	Term of Service	By What Authority/Remarks
		succeed Schwab; elected 1982; resigned Dec. 30, 1988
Warren, Edward H.	1980–1999	Appointed Mar. 10, 1980 to succeed Lee; elected 1980; reelected 1986, 1992, 1998; resigned 1999
Van Hoomissen, George A.	1981–1988	Elected 1980; reelected 1986; resigned Sept. 30, 1988
Young, Thomas F.	1981–1988	Appointed Jan. 5, 1981 to succeed Campbell; elected 1982; died Jan. 3, 1988
Rossman, Kurt C.	1982–1994	Appointed Mar. 2, 1982 to succeed Roberts; elected 1982; reelected 1988; resigned Dec. 31, 1994
Newman, Jonathan	1983–1991	Elected 1982; reelected 1988; resigned Aug. 31, 1991
Deits, Mary J.	1986–2004	Appointed Feb. 28, 1986 to succeed Gillette; elected 1986; reelected 1992, 1998; chief judge 1997–2004; resigned Oct. 31, 2004
Riggs, R. William	1988–1998	Appointed Oct. 24, 1988 to fill Van Hoomissen position; elected 1988 to succeed Warden; reelected 1994; resigned Sept. 8, 1998
Graber, Susan P.	1988–1990	Appointed Feb. 11, 1988 to succeed Young; elected 1988; resigned May 2, 1990
Edmonds, Walter I., Jr.	1989–2009	Appointed Jan. 1, 1989 to succeed Van Hoomissen; elected 1990; reelected 1996, 2002, 2008; retired Dec. 31, 2009
De Muniz, Paul J.	1990–2000	Appointed May 11, 1990 to succeed Graber; elected 1990; reelected 1996; resigned Dec. 29, 2000
Durham, Robert D.	1991–1994	Appointed Nov. 14, 1991 to succeed Newman; elected 1992; resigned Jan. 4, 1994
Landau, Jack L.	1993–2011	Appointed Dec. 15, 1992 to succeed Joseph; elected 1994; reelected 2000, 2006; resigned Jan. 3, 2011
Leeson, Susan M.	1993–1998	Appointed Dec. 15, 1992 to succeed Buttler; elected 1994; resigned Feb. 26, 1998
Haselton, Rick T.	1994–2015	Appointed Mar. 4, 1994 to succeed Durham; elected 1994; reelected 2000, 2006, 2012; chief judge 2012–2015; retired Dec. 31, 2015
Armstrong, Rex	1995–	Elected 1994; reelected 2000, 2006, 2012, 2018
Linder, Virginia L.	1997–2007	Appointed Sept. 24, 1997 to succeed Richardson; elected 1998; reelected 2004; resigned Jan. 2, 2007
Wollheim, Robert D.	1998–2014	Appointed Feb. 27, 1998 to succeed Leeson; elected 1998; reelected 2004, 2010; retired Oct. 31, 2014
Brewer, Dave	1999–2012	Appointed Jan. 14, 1999 to succeed Warren; elected 2000; reelected 2006; chief judge 2004–2012
Kistler, Rives	1999–2003	Appointed Jan. 14, 1999 to succeed Riggs; elected 2000; resigned Aug. 14, 2003
Schuman, David	2001–2014	Appointed March 19, 2001 to succeed De Muniz; elected 2002; reelected 2008; retired Jan. 31, 2014
Ortega, Darleen	2003–	Appointed Oct. 13, 2003 to succeed Kistler; elected 2004; reelected 2010, 2016
Rosenblum, Ellen F.	2007–2011	Elected 2006; retired May 1, 2011
Sercombe, Timothy	2007–2017	Appointed March 26, 2007 to succeed Linder; elected 2008; reelected 2014; retired July 1, 2017
Duncan, Rebecca	2010–2017	Appointed Jan. 7, 2010 to succeed Edmonds; elected 2010; reelected 2016; resigned 2017
Nakamoto, Lynn	2011–2015	Appointed Dec. 7, 2010 to succeed Landau; elected 2012; resigned Dec. 31, 2015
Hadlock, Erika	2011–2019	Appointed July 7, 2011 to succeed Rosenblum; elected 2012; chief judge 2016–2017; reelected 2018; retired Oct. 31, 2019
Egan, James C.	2013–	Elected 2012; reelected 2018; chief judge 2018 to date

Name	Term of Service	By What Authority/Remarks
DeVore, Joel	2013–	Appointed Oct. 17, 2013; elected 2014; reelected 2020
Lagesen, Erin C.	2013–	Appointed Oct. 17, 2013; elected 2014; reelected 2020
Tookey, Douglas L.	2013–	Appointed Oct. 17, 2013; elected 2014; reelected 2020
Garrett, Chris	2014–2018	Appointed Dec. 24, 2013 to succeed Schuman; elected 2014; resigned Jan. 1, 2019
Flynn, Meagan A.	2014–2017	Appointed Sept. 25, 2014 to succeed Wollheim; elected 2016; resigned April 3, 2017
DeHoog, Roger J.	2016–	Appointed Dec. 7, 2015 to succeed Nakamoto; elected 2016
Shorr, Scott A.	2016–	Appointed Dec. 7, 2015 to succeed Haselton; elected 2016
James, Bronson D.	2017–	Appointed July 17, 2017 to succeed Duncan; elected 2018
Aoyagi, Robyn Ridler	2017–	Appointed July 17, 2017 to succeed Sercombe; elected 2018
Powers, Steven R.	2017–	Appointed July 20, 2017 to succeed Flynn; elected 2018
Mooney, Josephine H.	2019–	Appointed June 3, 2019 to succeed Garrett; elected 2020
Kamins, Jacqueline S.	2020–	Appointed February 10, 2020 to succeed Hadlock; elected 2020

Judges of the Oregon Tax Court

The Oregon Tax Court was established January 1, 1962.

Name	Term of Service	By What Authority/Remarks
Gunnar, Peter M.	1962–1965	Appointed by Governor Hatfield Jan. 1, 1962; elected 1962; resigned Feb. 18, 1965
Howell, Edward H.	1965–1970	Appointed by Governor Hatfield Feb. 19, 1965; elected 1966; resigned May 31, 1970
Roberts, Carlisle B.	1970–1983	Appointed by Governor McCall June 1, 1970; elected 1970; reelected 1976; term ended 1983
Stewart, Samuel B.	1983–1985	Elected 1982; died Feb. 25, 1985
Byers, Carl N.	1985–2001	Appointed by Governor Atiyeh Mar. 6, 1985; elected 1986; reelected 1992, 1998; retired 2001
Breithaupt, Henry C.	2001–2017	Appointed by Governor Kitzhaber June 29, 2001 to succeed Byers; elected 2002; reelected 2008, 2014; retired Dec. 31, 2017
Manicke, Robert	2018–	Appointed by Governor Brown Jan 1, 2018 to succeed Breithaupt; elected 2018

Attorneys General of Oregon

Name/Political Party	Term of Service	By What Authority/Remarks
Chamberlain, George E.—D	May 20, 1891–Jan. 14, 1895	Appointed by Governor Pennoyer; elected June 1892
Idleman, Cicero M.—R	Jan. 14, 1895–Jan. 9, 1899	Elected 1894
Blackburn, D.R.N.—R	Jan. 9, 1899–Jan. 12, 1903	Elected 1898
Crawford, Andrew M.—R	Jan. 13, 1903–Jan. 3, 1915	Elected 1902; reelected 1906, 1910
Brown, George M.—R	Jan. 4, 1915–Oct. 14, 1920	Elected 1914; reelected 1918; resigned
Van Winkle, Isaac H.—R	Oct. 14, 1920–Dec. 14, 1943	Appointed by Governor Olcott; elected 1920; reelected 1924, 1928, 1932, 1936, 1940; died in office
Neuner, George—R	Dec. 21, 1943–Jan. 5, 1953	Appointed by Governor Snell; elected 1944; reelected 1948
Thornton, Robert Y.—D	Jan. 5, 1953–May 20, 1969	Elected 1952; reelected 1956, 1960, 1964

Name/Political Party	Term of Service	By What Authority/Remarks
Johnson, Lee—R	May 20, 1969–Jan. 3, 1977	Elected 1968; reelected 1972
Redden, James—D	Jan. 3, 1977–Mar. 24, 1980	Elected 1976
Brown, James M.—D	Mar. 24, 1980–Jan. 4, 1981	Appointed by Governor Atiyeh
Frohnmayer, David B.—R	Jan. 5, 1981–Dec. 31, 1991	Elected 1980; reelected 1984, 1988; resigned 1991
Crookham, Charles S.—R	Jan. 2, 1992–Jan. 3, 1993	Appointed by Governor Roberts
Kulongoski, Ted—D	Jan. 4, 1993–Jan. 4, 1997	Elected 1992
Myers, Hardy—D	Jan. 6, 1997–Jan. 5, 2009	Elected 1996; reelected 2000, 2004
Kroger, John R.—D	Jan. 5, 2009–June 29, 2012	Elected 2008; resigned 2012
Rosenblum, Ellen—D	June 29, 2012–	Appointed by Governor Kitzhaber; elected 2012; reelected 2016, 2020

Commissioners of the Bureau of Labor and Industries[1]

Name/Political Party	Term of Service	By What Authority/Remarks
Hoff, O.P.—R	June 2, 1903–Jan. 6, 1919	Appointed by Governor Chamberlain; elected 1906; reelected 1910, 1914
Gram, C.H.—R	Jan. 6, 1919–Jan. 4, 1943	Elected 1918; reelected 1922, 1926, 1930, 1934, 1938
Kimsey, W.E.—R	Jan. 4, 1943–Jan. 3, 1955	Elected 1942; reelected 1946, 1950
Nilsen, Norman O.—D	Jan. 3, 1955–Jan. 6, 1975	Elected 1954; reelected 1958, 1962, 1966, 1970
Stevenson, Bill—D	Jan. 6, 1975–Jan. 1, 1979	Elected 1974
Roberts, Mary Wendy—D.	Jan. 1, 1979–Jan 2, 1995	Elected 1978; reelected 1982, 1986, 1990
Roberts, Jack—R	Jan. 2, 1995–Jan. 6, 2003	Elected 1994; reelected 1998
Gardner, Dan[2]	Jan. 6, 2003–April 7, 2008	Elected 2002; reelected 2006; resigned 2008
Avakian, Brad[3]	Apr. 8, 2008–Jan. 6, 2019	Appointed by Governor Kulongoski; elected 2008; reelected 2012, 2014
Hoyle, Val	Jan. 7, 2019	Elected 2018

[1]This position, originally called Labor Commissioner, was changed to Commissioner of the Bureau of Labor Statistics and Inspector of Factories and Workshops in 1918. In 1930, the name changed to Commissioner of the Bureau of Labor. The 1979 Legislature changed the name to Commissioner of the Bureau of Labor and Industries.

[2]The 1995 Legislature made this position nonpartisan, and the 1998 election was the first for this position after the change.

[3]Due to the appointment and election of Brad Avakian in 2008, the 2009 Legislature's House Bill 2095 provided that the Commissioner of the Bureau of Labor and Industries position be placed on the 2012 ballot for a two-year term. This restored the position to its regular election schedule in 2014.

Superintendents of Public Instruction[1]

Name/Political Party	Term of Service	By What Authority/Remarks
Simpson, Sylvester C.—D	Jan. 29, 1873–Sept. 14, 1874	Appointed by Governor Grover
Rowland, L.L.—R	Sept. 14, 1874–Sept. 9, 1878	Elected 1874
Powell, J.L.—R	Sept. 9, 1878–Sept. 11, 1882	Elected 1878
McElroy, E.B.—R	Sept. 11, 1882–Jan. 14, 1895	Elected 1882; reelected 1886, 1890
Irwin, G.M.—R	Jan. 14, 1895–Jan. 9, 1899	Elected 1894
Ackerman, J.H.—R	Jan. 9, 1899–Jan. 3, 1911	Elected 1898; reelected 1902, 1906
Alderman, L.R.—R	Jan. 4, 1911–Jan. 28, 1913	Elected 1910; resigned
Churchill, J.A.—R	July 1, 1913–June 1, 1926	Appointed by Governor West; elected 1914; reelected 1918, 1922; resigned
Turner, R.R.—D	June 1, 1926–Jan. 3, 1927	Appointed by Governor Pierce
Howard, Charles A.—R	Jan. 3, 1927–Sept. 1, 1937	Elected 1926; reelected 1930, 1934; resigned
Putnam, Rex—D	Sept. 1, 1937–Jan. 31, 1961	Appointed by Governor Martin; elected 1938; reelected 1942, 1946, 1950, 1954, 1958; resigned

Name/Political Party	Term of Service	By What Authority/Remarks
Minear, Leon P.	Feb. 1, 1961–Mar. 31, 1968	Appointed by Governor Hatfield; elected 1966; resigned
Fasold, Jesse V.	Apr. 8, 1968–June 30, 1968	Appointed by Governor McCall; resigned
Parnell, Dale	July 1, 1968–Mar. 31, 1974	Appointed by Governor McCall; elected 1968; reelected 1970; resigned
Fasold, Jesse V.	Apr. 1, 1974–Jan. 6, 1975	Appointed by Governor McCall
Duncan, Verne A.	Jan. 6, 1975–Nov. 15, 1989	Elected 1974; reelected 1978, 1982, 1986; resigned 1989
Erickson, John	Dec. 18, 1989–Sept. 30, 1990	Appointed by Governor Goldschmidt; resigned
Paulus, Norma	Oct. 1, 1990–Jan. 4, 1999	Elected 1990; appointed by Governor Goldschmidt (before elective term began); reelected 1994
Bunn, Stan	Jan. 4, 1999–Jan. 6, 2003	Elected 1998
Castillo, Susan[2]	Jan. 6, 2003–June 29, 2012	Elected 2002; reelected 2006, 2010; resigned 2012

[1]From 1942 to 1961, this office was filled by election on nonpartisan ballot. In 1961, the state Legislature passed a statute making the office appointive by the State Board of Education. The Supreme Court declared this unconstitutional in 1965, and a constitutional amendment to place the method of selection in the hands of the state Legislature was defeated in 1966. Another attempt to repeal the constitutional provision requiring election was defeated in 1980.

[2]In 2011, Senate Bill 552 created a new statutory provision naming the governor as Superintendent of Public Instruction. Susan Castillo served until her 2012 resignation as the last elected superintendent.

Presidents of the Senate

Session	Name/Political Party	City	County
1860	Elkins, Luther—D		Linn
1862	Bowlby, Wilson—R		Washington
1864	Mitchell, J.H.—R	Portland	Multnomah
1865[1]	Mitchell, J.H.—R	Portland	Multnomah
1866	Cornelius, T.R.—R		Washington
1868	Burch, B.F.—D		Polk
1870	Fay, James D.—D		Jackson
1872	Fay, James D.—D		Jackson
1874	Cochran, R.B.—D		Lane
1876	Whiteaker, John—D		Lane
1878	Whiteaker, John—D		Lane
1880	Hirsch, Sol—R	Portland	Multnomah
1882	McConnell, W.J.—R		Yamhill
1885[2]	Waldo, William—R	Salem	Marion
1887	Carson, John C.—R	Portland	Multnomah
1889	Simon, Joseph—R	Portland	Multnomah
1891	Simon, Joseph—R	Portland	Multnomah
1893	Fulton, C.W.—R	Astoria	Clatsop
1895	Simon, Joseph—R	Portland	Multnomah
1897	Simon, Joseph—R	Portland	Multnomah
1898[1]	Simon, Joseph—R	Portland	Multnomah
1899	Taylor, T.C.—R	Pendleton	Umatilla
1901	Fulton, C.W.—R	Astoria	Clatsop
1903[2]	Brownell, George C.—R	Oregon City	Clackamas
1905	Kuykendall, W.—R	Eugene	Lane
1907	Haines, E.W.—R	Forest Grove	Washington
1909[2]	Bowerman, Jay—R	Condon	Gilliam
1911	Selling, Ben—R	Portland	Multnomah
1913	Malarkey, Dan J.—R	Portland	Multnomah
1915	Thompson, W. Lair—R	Lakeview	Lake
1917	Moser, Gus C.—R	Portland	Multnomah
1919	Vinton, W.T.—R	McMinnville	Yamhill

2021–2022 Oregon Blue Book

Session	Name/Political Party	City	County
1920[1]	Vinton, W.T.—R	McMinnville	Yamhill
1921[2]	Ritner, Roy W.—R	Pendleton	Umatilla
1923	Upton, Jay—R	Prineville	Crook
1925	Moser, Gus C.—R	Portland	Multnomah
1927	Corbett, Henry L.—R	Portland	Multnomah
1929	Norblad, A.W.—R	Astoria	Clatsop
1931	Marks, Willard L.—R	Albany	Linn
1933[3]	Kiddle, Fred E.—R	Island City	Union
1935[2]	Corbett, Henry L.—R	Portland	Multnomah
1937	Franciscovich, F.M.—R	Astoria	Clatsop
1939	Duncan, Robert M.—R	Burns	Harney
1941	Walker, Dean H.—R	Independence	Polk
1943	Steiwer, W.H.—R	Fossil	Wheeler
1945	Belton, Howard C.—R	Canby	Clackamas
1947	Cornett, Marshall E.—R	Klamath Falls	Klamath
1949	Walsh, William E.—R	Coos Bay	Coos
1951	Patterson, Paul L.—R	Hillsboro	Washington
1953	Marsh, Eugene E.—R	McMinnville	Yamhill
1955	Smith, Elmo—R	John Day	Grant
1957[2]	Overhulse, Boyd R.—D	Madras	Jefferson
1959	Pearson, Walter J.—D	Portland	Multnomah
1961	Boivin, Harry D.—D	Klamath Falls	Klamath
1963[2]	Musa, Ben—D	The Dalles	Wasco
1965[2]	Boivin, Harry D.—D	Klamath Falls	Klamath
1967[2]	Potts, E.D.—D	Grants Pass	Josephine
1969	Potts, E.D.—D	Grants Pass	Josephine
1971[2]	Burns, John D.—D	Portland	Multnomah
1973	Boe, Jason—D	Reedsport	Douglas
1974[1]	Boe, Jason—D	Reedsport	Douglas
1975	Boe, Jason—D	Reedsport	Douglas
1977	Boe, Jason—D	Reedsport	Douglas
1978[1]	Boe, Jason—D	Reedsport	Douglas
1979	Boe, Jason—D	Reedsport	Douglas
1980[1]	Boe, Jason—D	Reedsport	Douglas
1981[4]	Heard, Fred W.—D	Klamath Falls	Klamath
1983[3]	Fadeley, Edward N.—D	Eugene	Lane
1985	Kitzhaber, M.D., John A.—D	Roseburg	Douglas
1987	Kitzhaber, M.D., John A.—D	Roseburg	Douglas
1989[2]	Kitzhaber, M.D., John A.—D	Roseburg	Douglas
1991	Kitzhaber, M.D., John A.—D	Roseburg	Douglas
1993	Bradbury, Bill—D	Bandon	Coos
1995[2]	Smith, Gordon H.—R	Pendleton	Umatilla
1997	Adams, Brady—R	Grants Pass	Josephine
1999	Adams, Brady—R	Grants Pass	Josephine
2001[5]	Derfler, Gene—R	Salem	Marion
2003	Courtney, Peter—D	Salem	Marion
2005	Courtney, Peter—D	Salem	Marion
2007	Courtney, Peter—D	Salem	Marion
2009	Courtney, Peter—D	Salem	Marion
2011	Courtney, Peter—D	Salem	Marion
2013	Courtney, Peter—D	Salem	Marion
2015	Courtney, Peter—D	Salem	Marion
2017	Courtney, Peter—D	Salem	Marion
2019	Courtney, Peter—D	Salem	Marion
2021	Courtney, Peter—D	Salem	Marion

[1]Special session

[2]Regular and special session

[3]Regular and two special sessions

[4]Regular and four special sessions

[5]Regular and five special sessions

Speakers of the House of Representatives

Session	Name/Political Party	City	County
1860	Harding, B.F.—D		Marion
1862	Palmer, Joel—R		Yamhill
1864	Moores, I.R.—R		Marion
1865[1]	Moores, I.R.—R		Marion
1866	Chenoweth, F.A.—R		Benton
1868	Whiteaker, John J.—D		Lane
1870	Hayden, Benjamin—D		Polk
1872	Mallory, Rufus—R		Marion
1874	Drain, J.C.—D		Douglas
1876	Weatherford, J.K.—D	Albany	Linn
1878	Thompson, J.M.—D		Lane
1880	Moody, Z.F.—R	The Dalles	Wasco
1882	McBride, George W.—R		Columbia
1885[2]	Keady, W.P.—R	Corvallis	Benton
1887	Gregg, J.T.—R	Salem	Marion
1889	Smith, E.L.—R	Hood River	Hood River
1891	Geer, T.T.—R	Macleay	Marion
1893	Keady, W.P.—R	Portland	Multnomah
1895	Moores, C.B.—R	Salem	Marion
1897[4]	House failed to organize		
1898[1]	Carter, E.V.—R	Ashland	Jackson
1899	Carter, E.V.—R	Ashland	Jackson
1901	Reeder, L.B.—R	Pendleton	Umatilla
1903[2]	Harris, L.T.—R	Eugene	Lane
1905	Mills, A.L.—R	Portland	Multnomah
1907	Davey, Frank—R	Salem	Marion
1909[2]	McArthur, C.N.—R	Portland	Multnomah
1911	Rusk, John P.—R	Joseph	Wallowa
1913	McArthur, C.N.—R	Portland	Multnomah
1915	Selling, Ben—R	Portland	Multnomah
1917	Stanfield, R.N.—R	Stanfield	Umatilla
1919	Jones, Seymour—R	Salem	Marion
1920[1]	Jones, Seymour—R	Salem	Marion
1921[2]	Bean, Louis E.—R	Eugene	Lane
1923	Kubli, K.K.—R	Portland	Multnomah
1925	Burdick, Denton G.—R	Redmond	Deschutes
1927	Carkin, John H.—R	Medford	Jackson
1929	Hamilton, R.S.—R	Bend	Deschutes
1931	Lonergan, Frank J.—R	Portland	Multnomah
1933[3]	Snell, Earl W.—R	Arlington	Gilliam
1935	Cooter, John E.—D	Toledo	Lincoln
1935[1]	Latourette, Howard—D	Portland	Multnomah
1937	Boivin, Harry D.—D	Klamath Falls	Klamath
1939	Fatland, Ernest R.—R	Condon	Gilliam
1941	Farrell, Robert S., Jr.—R	Portland	Multnomah
1943	McAllister, William M.—R	Medford	Jackson
1945	Marsh, Eugene E.—R	McMinnville	Yamhill
1947	Hall, John H.—R	Portland	Multnomah
1949	Van Dyke, Frank J.—R	Medford	Jackson
1951	Steelhammer, John F.—R	Salem	Marion
1953	Wilhelm, Rudie, Jr.—R	Portland	Multnomah
1955	Geary, Edward A.—R	Klamath Falls	Klamath
1957[2]	Dooley, Pat—D	Portland	Multnomah
1959	Duncan, Robert B.—D	Medford	Jackson
1961	Duncan, Robert B.—D	Medford	Jackson
1963[2]	Barton, Clarence—D	Coquille	Coos
1965[2]	Montgomery, F.F.—R	Eugene	Lane
1967[2]	Montgomery, F.F.—R	Eugene	Lane
1969	Smith, Robert F.—R	Burns	Harney

Session	Name/Political Party	City	County
1971[2]	Smith, Robert F.—R	Burns	Harney
1973	Eymann, Richard O.—D	Springfield	Lane
1974[1]	Eymann, Richard O.—D	Springfield	Lane
1975	Lang, Philip D.—D	Portland	Multnomah
1977	Lang, Philip D.—D	Portland	Multnomah
1978[1]	Lang, Philip D.—D	Portland	Multnomah
1979	Myers, Hardy—D	Portland	Multnomah
1980[1]	Myers, Hardy—D	Portland	Multnomah
1981[5]	Myers, Hardy—D	Portland	Multnomah
1983[3]	Kerans, Grattan—D	Eugene	Lane
1985	Katz, Vera—D	Portland	Multnomah
1987	Katz, Vera—D	Portland	Multnomah
1989[2]	Katz, Vera—D	Portland	Multnomah
1991	Campbell, Larry—R	Eugene	Lane
1993	Campbell, Larry—R	Eugene	Lane
1995[2]	Clarno, Bev—R	Bend	Deschutes
1997	Lundquist, Lynn—R	Powell Butte	Deschutes
1999	Snodgrass, Lynn—R	Boring	Clackamas
2001[6]	Simmons, Mark—R	Elgin	Union
2003	Minnis, Karen—R	Wood Village	Multnomah
2005	Minnis, Karen—R	Wood Village	Multnomah
2007	Merkley, Jeff—D	Portland	Multnomah
2009	Hunt, Dave—D	Gladstone	Clackamas
2011	Hanna, Bruce (co-speaker)—R	Roseburg	Douglas, Lane
2011	Roblan, Arnie (co-speaker)—D	Coos Bay	Coos, Douglas, Lane
2013	Kotek, Tina—D	Portland	Multnomah
2015	Kotek, Tina—D	Portland	Multnomah
2017	Kotek, Tina—D	Portland	Multnomah
2019	Kotek, Tina—D	Portland	Multnomah
2021	Kotek, Tina—D	Portland	Multnomah

[1]Special session

[2]Regular and special session

[3]Regular and two special sessions

[4]E.J. Davis was elected speaker by less than a quorum. Subsequently, Henry L. Benson was elected speaker by less than a quorum. The Supreme Court revised an 1871 decision and ordered the secretary of state to audit claims and draw warrants for all claims which the Legislature, through its enactments, permitted and directed, either expressly or by implication.

[5]Regular and four special sessions

[6]Regular and five special sessions

U.S. Senators from Oregon

First Position[2]

Name/Political Party	Term of Service[1]	By What Authority/Remarks
Smith, Delazon[3]—D	Feb. 14–Mar. 3, 1859	Elected by Legislature 1858
Baker, Edward[4]—R	Dec. 5, 1860–Oct. 21, 1861	Elected by Legislature 1860; died in office
Stark, Benjamin—D	Oct. 29, 1861–Sept. 11, 1862	Appointed by Governor Whiteaker to succeed Baker
Harding, Benjamin F.—D	Sept. 11, 1862–1865	Elected by Legislature to succeed Baker
Williams, George H.—R	1865–1871	Elected by Legislature 1864
Kelly, James K.—D	1871–1877	Elected by Legislature 1870
Grover, LaFayette—D	1877–1883	Elected by Legislature 1876
Dolph, Joseph N.—R	1883–1895	Elected by Legislature 1882; reelected 1889
McBride, George W.—R	1895–1901	Elected by Legislature 1895
Mitchell, John H.—R	1901–1905	Elected by Legislature 1901; died in office Dec. 8, 1905

Name/Political Party	Term of Service[1]	By What Authority/Remarks
Gearin, John M.—D	Dec. 12, 1905–Jan. 23, 1907	Appointed by Governor Chamberlain to succeed Mitchell
Mulkey, Fred W.—R	Jan. 23–Mar. 2, 1907	Selected by general election 1906 for short term; elected by Legislature to serve remaining term of Mitchell and Gearin
Bourne, Jonathan, Jr.—R	1907–1913	Selected by general election 1906; elected by Legislature 1907
Lane, Harry—D	1913–May 23, 1917	Selected by general election 1912; elected by Legislature 1913; died in office
McNary, Charles L.—R	May 29, 1917–Nov. 5, 1918	Appointed by Governor Withycombe to succeed Lane
Mulkey, Fred W.—R	Nov. 5–Dec. 17, 1918	Elected 1918 for short term; resigned to permit reappointment of McNary
McNary, Charles L.—R	Dec. 17, 1918–Feb. 24, 1944	Appointed 1918 for unexpired short term; elected 1918; reelected 1924, 1930, 1936, 1942; died in office
Cordon, Guy—R	Mar. 4, 1944–1955	Appointed by Governor Snell to succeed McNary; elected 1944; reelected 1948
Neuberger, Richard L.—D	1955–Mar. 9, 1960	Elected 1954; died in office
Lusk, Hall S.—D	Mar. 16, 1960–Nov. 8, 1960	Appointed by Governor Hatfield to succeed Neuberger
Neuberger, Maurine—D	Nov. 8, 1960–1967	Elected 1960 for short and full terms
Hatfield, Mark O.—R	1967–1997	Elected 1966; reelected 1972, 1978, 1984, 1990
Smith, Gordon H.—R	1997–2009	Elected 1996; reelected 2002
Merkley, Jeff—D	2009–	Elected 2008; reelected 2014, 2020

Second Position[2]

Lane, Joseph—D	Feb. 14, 1859–1861	Elected by Legislature 1858
Nesmith, James W.—D	1861–1867	Elected by Legislature 1860
Corbett, Henry W.—R	1867–1873	Elected by Legislature 1866
Mitchell, John H.—R	1873–1879	Elected by Legislature 1872
Slater, James H.—D	1879–1885	Elected by Legislature 1878
Mitchell, John H.—R	1885–1897	Elected by Legislature 1885; reelected 1891
Corbett, Henry W.—R[5]	March, 1897	Appointed by Governor Lord, not seated
Simon, Joseph—R	Oct. 6, 1898–1903	Elected by Legislature to fill vacancy
Fulton, Charles W.—R	1903–1909	Elected by Legislature 1903
Chamberlain, George E.—D[6]	1909–1921	Selected by general election 1908; elected by Legislature; reelected by people 1914
Stanfield, Robert N.—R	1921–1927	Elected 1920
Steiwer, Frederick—R	1927–Feb. 1, 1938	Elected 1926; reelected 1932; resigned
Reames, Alfred Evan—D	Feb. 1–Nov. 9, 1938	Appointed by Governor Martin to succeed Steiwer
Barry, Alex G.—R	Nov. 9, 1938–1939	Elected 1938 for short term
Holman, Rufus C.—R	1939–1945	Elected 1938
Morse, Wayne[7]—D	1945–1969	Elected 1944; reelected 1950, 1956, 1962
Packwood, Robert—R	1969–1995	Elected 1968; reelected 1974, 1980, 1986, 1992; resigned 1995
Wyden, Ron[8]—D	1996–	Elected 1996; reelected 1998, 2004, 2010, 2016

[1]Unless otherwise noted, normal terms of office began on the fourth day of March and ended on the third day of March until 1933 when terms were changed to begin and end on the third day of January, unless a different date was set by Congress.

[2]Delazon Smith and Joseph Lane drew lots in 1859 for the short and long term senate seats. Smith won the short term of only 17 days expiring March 3, 1859 (designated first position). Lane won the long term expiring March 3, 1861 (designated second position).

[3]When the Legislature first met after statehood in May 1859, Smith was defeated for reelection, and no successor was named. Consequently, Oregon had only one U.S. senator from March 3, 1859 until Baker was elected October 1, 1860.

[4]Senator Edward Baker was killed in the Battle of Balls Bluff, Virginia while serving as a colonel in the Civil War, the only U.S. senator to serve in military action while a senator. His statue, cast of horatio stone and marble, stands 6 ft. 5 in. tall in the Capitol rotunda in Washington, D.C.

[5]When the Legislature failed to elect a successor to Mitchell, Governor Lord appointed Henry Corbett. After conflict, however, the U.S. Senate decided the governor did not have this authority and refused to seat Corbett. Therefore, Oregon was represented by only one U.S. senator from March 4, 1897 to October 6, 1898.

[6]Direct election of U.S. senators resulted from Oregon's ratification of Article XVII of the U.S. Constitution on January 23, 1913 (effective May 31, 1913). Oregon initiated a direct primary for selecting candidates in 1904.

[7]Wayne Morse was elected as a Republican in 1944 and reelected as a Republican in 1950. He changed to Independent in 1952, and to Democrat in 1955. He was reelected as a Democrat in 1956 and 1962.

[8]Elected to fill the unexpired term of Robert Packwood due to Senator Packwood's resignation. The elections, both primary and general, to fill Senator Packwood's seat were conducted by mail. The special primary and general elections were the first statewide vote-by-mail elections to fill a federal office in United States history.

U.S. Representatives from Oregon

Name/Political Party	Term of Service[1]	By What Authority/Remarks
Thurston, Samuel R.—D	June 6, 1849–Apr. 9, 1851	Territorial Delegate elected 1849; died at sea returning home from first session
Lane, Joseph—D	June 2, 1851–Feb. 14, 1859	Territorial Delegate elected 1851; reelected 1853, 1855, 1857
Grover, LaFayette—D	Feb. 15–Mar. 3, 1859	First Representative at large, elected 1858 for short term
Stout, Lansing—D	1859–1861	Elected 1858
Shiel, George K.—D	1861–1863	Elected 1860
McBride, John R.—R	1863–1865	Elected 1862
Henderson, J.H.D.—R	1865–1867	Elected 1864
Mallory, Rufus—R	1867–1869	Elected 1866
Smith, Joseph S.—D	1869–1871	Elected 1868
Slater, James H.—D	1871–1873	Elected 1870
Wilson, Joseph G.—R	1873	Elected 1872; died in July, 1873 before qualifying
Nesmith, James W.—D	1873–1875	Elected 1873
La Dow, George A.—D	1875	Elected 1874; died Mar. 4, 1875 before qualifying
Lane, Lafayette—D	Oct. 25, 1875–1877	Elected 1875
Williams, Richard—R	1877–1879	Elected 1876
Whiteaker, John—D	1879–1881	Elected 1878
George, Melvin C.—R	1881–1885	Elected 1880; reelected 1882
Hermann, Binger—R	1885–1893	Elected 1884; reelected 1886, 1888, 1890

1st District

Name/Political Party	Term of Service	By What Authority/Remarks
Hermann, Binger—R	1893–1897	Elected 1892; reelected 1894
Tongue, Thomas H.—R	1897–Jan. 11, 1903	Elected 1896; reelected 1898, 1900, 1902; died in office
Hermann, Binger—R	June 1, 1903–1907	Elected 1903 to succeed Tongue; reelected 1904

Name/Political Party	Term of Service[1]	By What Authority/Remarks
Hawley, Willis C.—R	1907–1933	Elected 1906; reelected 1908, 1910, 1912, 1914, 1916, 1918, 1920, 1922, 1924, 1926, 1928, 1930
Mott, James W.—R	1933–Nov. 12, 1945	Elected 1932; reelected 1934, 1936, 1938, 1940, 1942, 1944; died in office
Norblad, A. Walter, Jr.—R	Jan. 11, 1946–Sept. 20, 1964	Elected 1945 to succeed Mott; reelected 1946, 1948, 1950, 1952, 1954, 1956, 1958, 1960, 1962; died in office
Wyatt, Wendell—R	Nov. 3, 1964–1975	Elected 1964 to succeed Norblad; reelected 1966, 1968, 1970, 1972
AuCoin, Les—D	1975–1993	Elected 1974; reelected 1976, 1978, 1980, 1982, 1984, 1986, 1988, 1990
Furse, Elizabeth—D	1993–1999	Elected 1992; reelected 1994, 1996
Wu, David—D	1999–2011	Elected 1998; reelected 2000, 2002, 2004, 2006, 2008, 2010; resigned 2011
Bonamici, Suzanne—D[2]	2012–	Elected 2012; reelected 2012, 2014, 2016, 2018, 2020

2nd District

Ellis, William R.—R	1893–1899	Elected 1892; reelected 1894, 1896
Moody, Malcolm A.—R	1899–1903	Elected 1898; reelected 1900
Williamson, John N.—R	1903–1907	Elected 1902; reelected 1904
Ellis, William R.—R	1907–1911	Elected 1906; reelected 1908
Lafferty, Abraham W.—R.	1911–1913	Elected 1910
Sinnott, N.J.—R	1913–May 31, 1928	Elected 1912; reelected 1914, 1916, 1918, 1920, 1922, 1924, 1926; resigned
Butler, Robert R.—R	Nov. 6, 1928–Jan. 7, 1933	Elected 1928 to succeed Sinnott; reelected 1930; died in office
Pierce, Walter M.—D	1933–1943	Elected 1932; reelected 1934, 1936, 1938, 1940
Stockman, Lowell—R	1943–1953	Elected 1942; reelected 1944, 1946, 1948, 1950
Coon, Samuel H.—R	1953–1957	Elected 1952; reelected 1954
Ullman, Albert C.—D	1957–1981	Elected 1956; reelected 1958, 1960, 1962, 1964, 1966, 1968, 1970, 1972, 1974, 1976,1978
Smith, Denny—R	1981–1983	Elected 1980
Smith, Robert F.—R	1983–1995	Elected 1982; reelected 1984, 1986, 1988, 1990, 1992
Cooley, Wes—R	1995–1997	Elected 1994
Smith, Robert F.—R	1997–1999	Elected 1996
Walden, Greg—R	1999–2020	Elected 1998; reelected 2000, 2002, 2004, 2006, 2008, 2010, 2012, 2014, 2016, 2018
Bentz, Cliff—R	2021–	Elected 2020

3rd District

Lafferty, Abraham W.—R	1913–1915	Elected 1912
McArthur, Clifton N.—R	1915–1923	Elected 1914; reelected 1916, 1918, 1920
Watkins, Elton—D	1923–1925	Elected 1922
Crumpacker, Maurice E.—R	1925–July 25, 1927	Elected 1924; reelected 1926; died in office
Korell, Franklin F.—R	Oct. 18, 1927–1931	Elected 1927; reelected 1928
Martin, Charles H.—D	1931–1935	Elected 1930; reelected 1932
Ekwall, William A.—R	1935–1937	Elected 1934
Honeyman, Nan Wood—D	1937–1939	Elected 1936

Name/Political Party	Term of Service[1]	By What Authority/Remarks
Angell, Homer D.—R	1939–1955	Elected 1938; reelected 1940, 1942, 1944, 1946, 1948, 1950, 1952
Green, Edith S.—D	1955–1975	Elected 1954; reelected 1956, 1958, 1960, 1962, 1964, 1966, 1968, 1970, 1972
Duncan, Robert B.—D	1975–1981	Elected 1974; reelected 1976, 1978
Wyden, Ron—D	1981–1996	Elected 1980; reelected 1982, 1984, 1986, 1988, 1990, 1992, 1994
Blumenauer, Earl—D[3]	1996–	Elected 1996; reelected 1998, 2000, 2002, 2004, 2006, 2008, 2010, 2012, 2014, 2016, 2018, 2020

4th District

Ellsworth, Harris—R	1943–1957	Elected 1942; reelected 1944, 1946, 1948, 1950, 1952, 1954
Porter, Charles O.—D	1957–1961	Elected 1956; reelected 1958
Durno, Edwin R.—R	1961–1963	Elected 1960
Duncan, Robert B.—D	1963–1967	Elected 1962; reelected 1964
Dellenback, John—R	1967–1975	Elected 1966; reelected 1968, 1970, 1972
Weaver, James—D	1975–1987	Elected 1974; reelected 1976, 1978, 1980, 1982, 1984
DeFazio, Peter A.—D	1987–	Elected 1986; reelected 1988, 1990, 1992, 1994, 1996, 1998, 2000, 2002, 2004, 2006, 2008, 2010, 2012, 2014, 2016, 2018, 2020

5th District

Smith, Denny—R	1983–1991	Elected 1982; reelected 1984, 1986, 1988
Kopetski, Mike	1991–1995	Elected 1990; reelected 1992
Bunn, Jim—R	1995–1997	Elected 1994
Hooley, Darlene—D	1997–2009	Elected 1996; reelected 1998, 2000, 2002, 2004, 2006
Schrader, Kurt—D	2009–	Elected 2008, reelected 2010, 2012, 2014, 2016, 2018, 2020

[1]Unless otherwise noted, normal terms of office began on the fourth day of March and ended on the third day of March until 1933 when terms were changed to begin and end on the third day of January, unless a different date was set by Congress.

[2]Elected in the January 31, 2012, Special Election to finish the unexpired term of Representative David Wu.

[3]Elected in 1996 to finish the unexpired term of Representative Ron Wyden. Reelected to a full term at the November 5, 1996, General Election.

History

Historian Bob Reinhardt's essay introduces readers to the myriad ways that different people interacted with their environments to create this place we know as Oregon — from the Native people who made this land their home for thousands of years before Lewis and Clark, to the complex challenges rural and urban Oregonians alike will grapple with in the coming decades.

OREGON HISTORY

Oregon Environments, Oregon People: A History

Written by Bob H. Reinhardt, Ph.D.
Assistant Professor of History at Boise State University, where he works in the fields of environmental history and the history of the American West.

Oregonians have a long and complex relationship with the extraordinary environments and natural worlds in which they live. Take predators like coyotes and wolves, for example. In the oral traditions of many Oregon Native peoples, Coyote is a clever trickster whose adventures teach moral lessons that deserve respect and understanding. Wolves commanded respect from the British, French-Canadians, and Americans living in Oregon in the mid-19th century, too. Their fear of wolves brought them together along the banks of the Willamette River for the "Wolf Meetings" in 1843, to discuss how to eliminate predators (additionally, they created Oregon's first government). That anxiety faded in the following decades as Oregonians developed the ability to control wolves, which disappeared from the state by the 1940s. But when wolves returned to Oregon at the end of the 20th century, they once again warranted the respect of Oregonians: many rural residents regarded the animals as a continued dangerous threat to life and property, while city-dwellers often saw them as noble, wild creatures deserving protection.

These wolf stories provide a glimpse into many aspects of Oregon's history: the long presence of humans, the variety of communities that have made this place home, the combination of pragmatism and ideology that characterizes Oregon politics, the tension between the state's urban and rural populations and the spirit of cooperation and compromise that often brings Oregonians together. Through it all, a larger theme emerges: the changing relationship between Oregonians and nature. For millennia, Oregon's landscape demanded respect and adaptation from the people who lived here. That changed in the late 19th

century as Oregonians developed tools and methods to manipulate and to try to master their environments. Over time, many Oregonians came to question the destructive effects of such manipulation and instead developed an interest in the aesthetic, the recreational and even the inherent value of Oregon's landscape. Understanding Oregon's history requires understanding how Oregonians have related to their environments — and to each other.

Traditional stories of Native peoples told of the eruption of Mount Mazama, which created Crater Lake. (Oregon State Archives scenic photo)

Original Oregonians

Modern geology and archaeology hold that humans arrived in Oregon at least 14,000 years ago, after a centuries-long migration from Asia via the Bering Strait land bridge and sea-borne routes along the coast. But there are other origin stories, too. Oral traditions from the Klamath and Modoc Native peoples, for instance, speak of beings who dug tunnels under the earth, created the marshes and rivers, made the people, and caused the eruption of Mount Mazama and the creation of Crater Lake. The stories told by science and tradition both emphasize the importance of environmental change at a variety of scales: geological shifts producing the Cascade Mountains, the Missoula floods that raged through the Columbia Basin between 13,000 and 15,000 years ago, and volcanic eruptions like that of Mount Mazama around

7,000 years ago. Such forces and transformations produced evolving ecosystems that dozens of American Indian groups both adapted to and changed. To make sense of this diversity, historians and anthropologists often refer to three (occasionally four) culture areas in Oregon: the Great Basin; the Columbia Plateau; the Northwest Coast which also includes the "western interior" of the Willamette Valley; and Southern Oregon.

Northern Paiute peoples thrived in a range of Great Basin environments such as the Alvord Desert. (Oregon State Archives scenic photo)

To an outsider, the Great Basin might seem desolate and even barren. But the Northern Paiute peoples and their ancestors created life and opportunity in this home. Encompassing the southeast quarter of Oregon and stretching far beyond the state, the Great Basin includes Steens Mountain, the Alvord Desert, and Harney and Malheur lakes. Those who knew the landscape, manipulated and made sense of these environments not just to survive, but to thrive. That knowledge started with a deep understanding of the location and development of food and other resource production in different places at different times of the year. Northern Paiute peoples made "seasonal rounds" throughout the diverse landscapes of the Great Basin, migrating to places where they knew they would find resources. In the spring, women and children dug up and dried *tsuga* (biscuitroot), which they made into loaves; men speared and trapped salmon at the headwaters of the Malheur River. Summertime saw the Northern Paiute peoples travelling widely to the north and south in pursuit of deer, elk, groundhogs, and other game, as well as a variety of plants, such as huckleberries and chokecherries. The work continued into the fall, when the Wada'Tika band of Northern Paiutes along the shores of Malheur Lake harvested *waada* (seepweed), extracting the plant's nutritious seeds that were stored for the winter. As the days turned shorter and colder, the Northern Paiute peoples gathered at their winter encampments near lakes, living in homes they made of willow branches and tule plants. Along the eastern side of the Cascade mountains in southern Oregon, the Klamath peoples of the Klamath Basin cultivated the additional resources of that area, such as different kinds of fish and waterfowl. Through their knowledge, expertise

and the labor represented in their seasonal rounds and the homes they made, these peoples — including today's Burns Paiute Tribe, the Paiutes of the Confederated Tribes of Warm Springs, and the Yahooskin band of Paiutes of the Klamath — sustained complex and enriching lives in the Great Basin environment.

North of the Great Basin lies the Columbia Plateau, a region defined by the Columbia River's drainage system east of the Cascade Mountains into northeastern Oregon and beyond to Washington, Idaho, Montana, and British Columbia. The *Nimiipuu* (Nez Perce), Umatilla, Cayuse, and other peoples of the Plateau developed sophisticated seasonal rounds that ranged throughout the region's different ecological zones, each providing a variety of foods and other resources. Plateau peoples spent their winters in villages along the upper Columbia River and its tributaries, living in longhouses made of tule mats and consuming carefully-preserved food. They crafted baskets, digging implements, fishing spears and nets, weapons and other kinds of technologies. Those tools were put to good use in the spring, first with the gathering of *qém'es* (camas) and other plants, and then with the expert harvesting of spring *nacó'x* (salmon). Fishing continued into the summer with steelhead and sockeye salmon runs, along with harvests of *cemíitx* (huckleberries), *mi'ttip* (elderberry), and other fruits. The fall meant more plant harvests, supplemented by the hunting of mule deer and the taking of fall *nacó'x*, which was carefully dried and processed into nutritious and long-lasting pemmican.

These foods also served as valuable trade goods, contributing to a vast network of exchange that connected the Plateau people to other Native peoples throughout and beyond the Columbia River watershed. *Wyam* (Celilo Falls) on the Columbia River was the largest trading site in what would become Oregon. There, where the river's power and its huge salmon runs squeezed through narrow passages, Native peoples built communities — including Celilo Village, the oldest continuously-occupied site in Oregon — and cultures that merged traditions from the lower and upper Columbia. Wyam drew people not just for the harvesting of salmon, which became disoriented in the rapids, but also for the trade of an astonishing variety of goods from far-flung locales: whale oil and shells from the west, bison meat and robes from the east, obsidian and weapons from the south, skins and baskets from the north, and more. The diversity of goods available at Wyam and at other trading sites indicates the depth and breadth of the material abundance, societies and cultures created by Native peoples.

Some of those who gathered at Wyam came from the Northwest Coast, a cultural region stretching from Alaska to California and defined by mild climate, dense forests and wetness from rain, fog and rivers. In Oregon, Coastal Indian groups included the Clatsop, Tillamook, Siletz, Siuslaw, Coos and Chetco, each developing sophisticated adaptations to and manipulations of their environments. Coastal peoples moved far less frequently or widely compared to the peoples of the Columbia Plateau and Great Basin, instead drawing on and cultivating the rich resources of their local and remarkably diverse environments, including the Pacific Ocean, coastal estuaries, freshwater rivers, plains and mountain ranges. From *ghvs-t'utlh* (cedar), they crafted clothing, dugout canoes, and houses, and they lived in permanent and often large villages at the mouths of rivers. From those rivers, Coastal Indians drew many different kinds of fish, including *luuk'e* (salmon), which at times so filled the streams that a person could cross the water on their backs — or so it was said. Knowing and understanding the seasonal rhythms by which salmon came and went, Coastal Indians developed elaborate ceremonies of respect that had the effect of maintaining salmon populations, while allowing them to harvest enough so that each person living in the region ate on average one pound of salmon per day.

The Coast Range Mountains divided the homelands of Coastal Indian groups from the Native peoples of the Western Interior. (Oregon State Archives scenic photo)

East and south of the coastal mountain ranges and in the valleys of the Willamette, Umpqua and Rogue rivers, the Native peoples of the Western Interior created lives that in many ways merged those of Coastal, Great Basin and Plateau Indians. Salmon and other fish contributed to the diets of these peoples, including the Kalapuya and Upper Umpqua, but expert hunting of *amu'ki'* (deer) and *antká'* (elk) were also common sources of protein. Their seasonal rounds did not range as far as those of the Plateau and Great Basin peoples, but their knowledge of different environments and opportunities was just as sophisticated, particularly in their harvesting and processing of edible plants, including *dinibgwí' ampgwi'* (hazelnuts), many types of berries, and, most importantly, *dinidi "p* (camas). Western Interior Indians developed the knowledge to harvest the camas bulb and roast it in preparation for both storage as well as, in large amounts, trading; they, like other Native peoples, also regularly burned prairies and savannahs, which assisted in plant propagation. Fire also facilitated berry and acorn collection by creating open areas, assisted in the harvest of tarweed seeds in the fall, and developed fringe environments on the edges of prairies and

forests that attracted game for hunting. Those foods, carefully preserved, carried the peoples of the valleys through the cooler and wetter months of winter, when they returned to permanent villages, often close to lakes.

The original Oregonians participated in worlds of cycle and tradition, but also of change. Major disruptions, such as the eruption of Mount Mazama or earthquakes in the Pacific that produced enormous tidal waves, led to significant changes for Native peoples, including displacement. Less dramatic changes, such as the gradual cooling of the climate 4,000 years ago, also led to migration and further adaptation. Seasonal rounds took Native peoples to familiar grounds, but their travels changed for a variety of reasons: a particularly dry or wet season that delayed or accelerated root and edible plant production, for example, or the development and improvement of new tools and technologies such as weirs for harvesting fish. Native societies expanded, contracted and evolved in response to new goods, ideas and people incorporated through trade networks. These networks also brought horses, which arrived on the Columbia Plateau in the 1700s, leading to more mobility and significant social change among the Cayuse, Nimiipuu and Umatilla. These animals, reintroduced to North America by the Spanish, were one of the most significant manifestations of a new connection to Europe, from which trade goods, diseases, and eventually people soon would enter the worlds of the original people of Oregon.

Oregon and Imperial Ambition

The Europeans who came to Oregon beginning in the 1500s recognized in their own ways the power of the nonhuman world. They arrived by means of the Pacific Ocean, an immensely powerful force that regularly destroyed ships and stole lives. But thirst for knowledge, hunger for wealth and imperial ambitions drove Europeans and Euro-Americans to try to overcome and control the forces of nature. The Pacific Ocean offered not only danger, but also economic and political opportunities, especially if one could find a water route through North America that would facilitate global trade between Europe and Asia. Spain was the first European empire to send ships to Oregon: initially, in the mid-1500s, in purposeful pursuit of a water route through the continent; then, throughout the 1600s, by accident as galleons travelling the Pacific occasionally wrecked off the Oregon coast; and finally, in the mid-1700s, with a series of naval expeditions meant to establish Spain's claim to the entire Pacific Coast and defend its colonies, mines and other imperial interests in Mexico. Spain imagined competition from Russian fur traders in the north, who had by the late-1700s established extensive operations in Alaska. But Russia never posed a real threat to Spain's claims to the Pacific Northwest. The wealth of nature, both in the imagined water trade route through North

America and the real riches in animal pelts, drew a much more formidable opponent toward Oregon.

The English first came to the Pacific Northwest in search of the mythical Northwest Passage bridging the Pacific and Atlantic, but they returned because of the real and profitable pelts of sea otters, beavers and other fur-bearing animals. England's interest in the Pacific Northwest began in earnest with Captain James Cook, whose 1776–1780 voyage not only made landfall on the Oregon coast, but also established and publicized the enormous profits available in the sea otter fur trade. British traders soon were plying the Northwest coastline for ports, and trading with Native peoples, directly challenging Spain's claims to the entire Pacific coast. In 1790, Spain finally relinquished those claims, and British mariners and merchants asserted their dominance to explore and trade in the region. In another attempt to find a water passage through North America, the British admiralty sent Captain George Vancouver to the Pacific coast in 1792. Vancouver's ships carefully probed the coastline over the course of three years, creating detailed maps, gathering information on Native peoples and their environments, and establishing with certainty that no sea route through North America existed. The British still exploited fur-bearing animals for enormous profit, but doing so required crossing the continent by land and multiple rivers, such as the Columbia, which Vancouver's expedition traveled through and officially claimed for Great Britain.

Vancouver had a strong imperial claim to the Columbia River, but it was not the only such claim, and it would not be enough to hold the Oregon Country for Great Britain. The American sea captain Robert Gray first traveled to the Oregon coast in 1788, when he traded and fought with the Tillamook people at Tillamook Bay. He returned four years later, taking his ship *Columbia Rediviva* into the mouth of a great river that Vancouver had bypassed just two weeks earlier. Gray named the river after his ship, traded for a few hundred pelts, and left, neglecting to officially take possession of the river for the United States. It hardly mattered. News of Gray's voyages, as well as reports from Vancouver and other expeditions, traveled quickly, attracting dozens of American ships to the Pacific Northwest and challenging British claims to sovereignty and the wealth of the fur trade. Although these ships flew under different flags, Americans and Britons shared the view that Oregon's environments could be known and owned, and that they should extract wealth from those environments.

For the first two decades of the 19th century, British and American merchants and traders, with the support of their respective governments, competed over Oregon's wealth. Lewis and Clark's famous expedition of 1805–06 brought official agents of the United States into Oregon Country, seeking a navigable route to the Pacific, scientific knowledge, economic opportunities for trade with

Native peoples, and stronger claims to land that President Thomas Jefferson hoped might extend the American "empire of liberty." Four years later, the Boston entrepreneur John Jacob Astor sent two parties, one by land and one by sea, toward Oregon Country to found an ambitious global fur empire called the Pacific Fur Company. These parties established Fort Astoria in 1811, but it (and the Pacific Fur Company) only lasted until 1813, when the British North West Company bought Astor's fort and renamed it Fort George, incorporating it into their extensive network of fur trading posts in the Pacific Northwest. While American and British negotiators agreed in 1818 to jointly occupy Oregon, British fur traders established their dominance, particularly after the Hudson's Bay Company (HBC) acquired the North West Company in 1821. Under the leadership of Dr. John McLoughlin, from its new Columbia District headquarters at Fort Vancouver, the HBC vigorously pursued its vision for Oregon Country. While cultivating trade relationships with Native trappers west of the Cascades, the HBC urged trappers in the east to hunt beavers into extinction, hoping to create a "fur desert" that would discourage American traders and trappers.

This strategy failed to reckon with the power of another view of Oregon's environment: its potential for agriculture. While the fur trade offered short-term profits by extracting nature's wealth, many Euro-Americans looked to agriculture for long-term progress through cultivation and "improvement" of nature. The Lewis and Clark expedition recorded the remarkable diversity of Oregon's environments, particularly the farming opportunities in the Willamette Valley. The expedition's journals and other reports on Oregon suggested that Euro-American farmers could and should fulfill what they believed to be Oregon's true destiny as an agricultural paradise. Especially among Americans in the Midwest looking for a better life, Oregon became a place in which to live, thrive and make one's home. That view had been present even before Americans came to Oregon: some former fur trappers and HBC employees built farms and set down roots in the Willamette Valley, including the company's chief factor, McLoughlin, who claimed land for a home in what is now Oregon City. But McLoughlin and his fellow British citizens were increasingly joined — and soon were outnumbered by — Americans who saw in Oregon not just the possibility, but the inevitability of agricultural settlement under the U.S. flag.

Oregon Becomes American

The Americans' belief in the righteousness of managing nature through agriculture, coupled with a belief in the righteousness of Christianity, confronted the lifeways and worldviews of Native peoples in Oregon. While McLoughlin developed his claim in the area around Willamette Falls, American newspapers in 1833 circulated reports of a small group of Nimiipuu who came to St. Louis looking for Bibles and Christianity. For Americans steeped in the evangelical fervor of the Second Great Awakening, such reports confirmed their calling to spread the Gospel. The Methodists first answered the call in 1834, sending the preacher Jason Lee, his nephew Daniel, and three laymen, who established a mission on the Willamette River about 13 miles north of what is now Salem. Two years later, an ecumenical Protestant party led by Dr. Marcus Whitman and his wife, Narcissa, settled near the Blue Mountains of northeastern Oregon to evangelize among the Cayuse, Umatilla and Nimiipuu. Fathers Francois Blanchet and Modeste Demers arrived in Oregon in 1838, establishing Catholic missions first on the Cowlitz River and then among retired French-Canadian HBC employees and their families living at French Prairie, in what is now St. Paul. These missionaries brought not only Bibles and Christianity, but also farming tools and agricultural practices: the gospel of progress through management of nature.

These evangelizing efforts failed to convert Oregon's Native peoples to a new faith in great numbers, but the missions drastically changed life in Oregon. Protestant missionaries in particular critiqued Native belief systems and insisted on the superiority of White agricultural settlement rather than Native seasonal rounds. They also contributed to the spread of disease and death among Native peoples. Even prior to regular contact with White explorers, fur traders, sailors and farmers, Native peoples experienced the devastating effects of smallpox, measles and other Old World diseases. That devastation increased in the early 1830s, when a series of malaria epidemics decimated Chinookan and Kalapuyan societies along the lower Columbia River and in the Willamette Valley, killing perhaps 90 percent of the Native population. Missionaries and their families contributed to these epidemics both through their own biological presence, and by facilitating the immigration of more White families and the diseases they brought with them. Their reports and public presentations delivered back east trumpeted the agricultural potential of the Willamette Valley, where diseases had decimated Native populations, leaving behind the rich, open fields produced by Native burning practices. Those reports, along with other positive accounts from Oregon boosters like Hall Jackson Kelley and John Wyeth, drew more and more settlers to the Willamette Valley, which held an estimated 150 Americans in 1841. The next year, more than 100 Americans migrated to Oregon, and approximately 900 more came the year after that. By 1845 — just 11 years after Jason Lee arrived — the Willamette Valley was home to approximately 6,000 Euro-Americans and just 500 Kalapuyans. These emigrants to Oregon were part of a wave of mass migration that washed over the globe during the nineteenth century, when millions of settlers and workers from Europe and Asia descended on the American West, Australia, South Africa and elsewhere.

Thousands of Americans packed their possessions into covered wagons and traveled the Oregon Trail in the 1840s. (Oregon State Archives scenic photo)

The Americans who came over the Oregon Trail in the 1840s traveled relatively lightly but carried weighty hopes for the future and strong beliefs about religion, society and nature. They came from the newer states of the Midwest and the Upper South — Illinois, Indiana, Ohio, Kentucky and Missouri, especially. Most were Protestants, and they found in Oregon spiritual and material support from the missions that had shifted from saving Indian souls to encouraging White settlement. They traveled the Oregon Trail and settled in Oregon as patriarchal families, establishing extensive kin networks with distinct roles for women and men in family and work. These new Oregonians also had particularly strong ideas about racial hierarchies. Although very few held slaves, nearly all White Americans in Oregon believed that Blacks were inferior. White Oregonians also helped quicken the decline of Native populations. They poured into the Willamette Valley and took Kalapuyan land by "squatting," claiming land for homesteads by virtue of the advances of American civilization and agriculture, preceding any legal action by the United States government towards Native lands.

The new Oregonians brought with them plants, livestock, and agricultural techniques that remade the landscape in the image of the farms they had left behind back east. Americans tilled the land and built fences; they planted corn, wheat and vegetable gardens; they raised cattle, oxen and hogs. This resettlement of Oregon – for the country had once been the settled home of Native people – depended on the labor of Native peoples, hired to work fields that had been cleared by the burning practices of their parents, grandparents and ancestors. American resettlers concentrated on establishing subsistence farmsteads that would sustain their families and future generations. But the new Oregonians gradually cleared larger fields, built longer fences, and established sawmills, gristmills and granaries to prepare

History

their products for market; these processes accelerated and expanded as farming and transportation technologies improved over the 19th century. These new Oregonians found willing buyers, too, especially when the California Gold Rush increased demand for Oregon's wheat and wood. But even before 1849, American resettlers had remade the environment of the Willamette Valley with homesteads, vegetable gardens, tilled fields, fruit orchards and other signs of Euro-American cultivation and culture. In so doing, these new Oregonians acted out another aspect of their mid-19th century religious ideology: their understanding of the Biblical instruction to "have dominion" over nature. The changes they wrought transformed the environments upon which Native peoples had developed their seasonal rounds and other ways of thriving in their lands.

These White resettlers quickly turned to economic and political organization to reaffirm their view of nature and their ambitious claims to Oregon. They especially valued domesticated animals, which not only provided meat and milk, but also represented control over the wild nature that surrounded them. In 1837, a group of settlers formed the Willamette Cattle Company and sent a party led by former fur trapper Ewing Young to California to buy cattle. Young returned with more than 600 longhorns, which increased the availability of valuable livestock, transformed the valley's landscapes by eating native plants and enriched the company's investors, including Young. He died in 1841 without a will or any heirs, causing a minor legal emergency. To determine what to do with Young's cattle-based estate, White settlers elected a judge and three law enforcement officials. In short, cattle — more specifically, the value White settlers placed on them — gave birth to political organization in Oregon country.

A State Capitol mural of the 1843 "Wolf Meetings." (Oregon State Archives scenic photo)

Livestock also instigated the next big move toward government in 1843, during what would later be known as the "Wolf Meetings." During those meetings, Willamette Valley settlers not only created a tax-funded bounty system meant to destroy wolves, bears, and other predators preying on livestock, but also decided to found a Provisional Government. The Wolf Meetings alienated many British citizens living in Oregon, and nearly all Britons abandoned the meetings, rejecting what was a clearly an American-led effort to establish American-style government in anticipation of the official extension of American authority. Those settlers were soon overwhelmed by rapidly-increasing numbers of Americans, who expanded the role of the Provisional Government and called on the United States to assert more authority in Oregon. The Americans especially wanted to guarantee their extensive land claims: up to a full square mile of land under the Provisional Government's code of laws — which, of course, were not recognized by Great Britain, which still jointly occupied Oregon with the United States. The Oregon Treaty of 1846 provided some security by finally settling the boundary between U.S. and British claims at the 49th parallel. But Americans in Oregon wanted more: to become a U.S. territory, which would bring federal recognition of their land claims and, more importantly, federal intervention against Native peoples. It was their and the nation's "Manifest Destiny" — the popular mid-century explanation of and justification for what many White Americans believed was the natural, inevitable and righteous expansion of the United States to the Pacific Ocean.

A deadly conflict with the Cayuse people of the Columbia Plateau brought Americans in Oregon the territorial status, recognition and intervention they wanted. Since its founding in 1838, the Whitman Mission had produced more conflict than conversion: the Whitmans accused the Cayuse, Nimiipu, and Umatilla peoples of laziness and backwardness, while the Native peoples became frustrated with the missionaries' abusive evangelism and the ecological destruction caused by increasing numbers of American settlers and travelers. In 1847, the tension boiled over into war. A group of Cayuse and Umatilla, suspecting Marcus Whitman of causing a measles epidemic that killed more than 200 of their people, attacked the mission, killing a dozen Whites (including the Whitmans) and taking 53 hostages. They eventually released the hostages, but not before White settlers in the Willamette Valley sent a volunteer militia on raids against the Cayuse demanding federal action and protection. The federal government responded in 1848 by passing the Organic Act, which created Oregon Territory, and by sending the U.S. Army to assist the White vigilantes, who returned to Oregon with five of the Cayuses involved in the Whitman attack. On May 24, 1850, after a two-day trial and 75 minutes of deliberation, a jury of twelve White men convicted the five Cayuses of murder, and they were executed on June 3. That same year, the U.S. Congress passed the Oregon Donation Land Law, which legitimized existing land claims and allowed new White immigrant families arriving before Dec. 1, 1850 to claim up to 640 acres (later arrivals would get half as much land). Congress also authorized treaty commissioners to negotiate with Oregon tribes for their land, although that work did not commence until 1851, well after Congressional authorization of the distribution of Native lands. With official incorporation into the United States, the federal government's commitment to obtaining Native lands, and their own land claims secured, the new Oregonians could continue to pursue their hopes for a better future and their vision for Oregon's landscapes.

Creating an Exclusive Paradise

Other peoples and cultures would have to make way for that particular vision. In the 1850s and 1860s, U.S. Indian agents and treaty commissioners secured agreements with dozens of Native tribes and bands throughout Oregon, sometimes through honest negotiations, but often by means of dishonest or willfully ignorant negotiations. These forced treaties ceded enormous amounts of Native lands and confined Native peoples to marginal territories on reservations. Treaties that were regarded as insufficiently generous to White interests often went unratified or simply ignored until government officials secured harsher terms requiring the sacrifice of more Native land. In addition to establishing reservations, the U.S. government also built military posts throughout Oregon to keep Native peoples separated from the growing numbers of White settlers. Devastated by disease and displacement, many Native peoples were forced to move to reservations, where some adopted sedentary agriculture and accepted as a necessity poorly-paid wage labor, while attempting to preserve their families, societies and cultures as much as possible.

Other Native peoples refused to tolerate White aggression and the ecological havoc wrought by Whites and the invasive plants and animals that came with them. In the 1850s in southwestern Oregon, bands of Shasta, Tututni, and other Native groups attacked White settlers and miners, responding to years of raids and violence against Native peoples and the destruction of the plants and animals on which they depended. The ensuing Rogue River Wars lasted until 1856, when the U.S. Army forcibly removed Native peoples to far-off reservations on the western side of the coastal mountain range. In the Great Basin in the 1860s, Northern Paiute bands raided miners, ranchers and other overland travelers who strained the region's scarce resources. After a vigorous campaign by the U.S. Army in 1866–68, most Northern Paiute surrendered and moved to reservations, although some later joined the Bannock people of Idaho in their resistance to federal authority. Further south on the Oregon-California border, the Modoc War of 1872 pitted more than 1,000 U.S. soldiers against a few dozen Modoc warriors who could no longer tolerate the poor conditions at the Klamath Reservation. The Modocs held out for nearly six months before the U.S. Army finally chased them down,

executing some of the leaders and sending the rest to far-away Indian Territory in Oklahoma. On the Columbia Plateau, White travelers, settlers and miners continued to strain the environment on which the Cayuse, Umatilla and Nimiipuu depended, leading to a series of treaties, reservations and finally conflicts: the Yakima War of 1855–58, the Nez Perce War of 1877, and the Bannock War of 1878.

The Warm Springs River flows through the Warm Springs Indian Reservation. (Oregon State Archives scenic photo)

By the end of the 1880s, multiple methods of force — treaties, displacement to reservations and violence — had removed Native peoples from their homes throughout Oregon. The Nimiipuu were scattered to different places: the Warm Springs and Umatilla Indian Reservations in Oregon, Colville Indian Reservation in Washington and Nez Perce Indian Reservation in Idaho. Some Northern Paiutes remained in the Burns area, while others moved to the Warm Springs Reservation, joining Wascoes and other people from the Columbia Plateau; other Plateau peoples were forcibly moved to the Umatilla Indian Reservation. Other tribes also lived on these reservations, as well as at the Klamath, Grand Ronde, and Siletz Reservations. Still other Native peoples, together as small communities or families or individually, lived away from reservations in or close to towns and urban areas. Hundreds of Native children were forced to attend and live at the Chemawa Indian School, established in Forest Grove in 1880 and moved to its present location north of Salem in 1885. In such challenging situations and environments, Native peoples would continue to claim their place in Oregon's history, while their homelands became subject to the exclusive possession and control of White resettlers, prospectors and speculators.

The vision of civilization, agriculture, and progress embraced by White Oregonians also excluded other nonwhite peoples. From the earliest stages of American political organization in Oregon, White settlers took deliberate steps to keep out people of color. Even before Oregon became a U.S. territory, the Provisional Government enacted laws that banned both free and enslaved Blacks from

History (vertical margin text)

Oregon and threatened to whip those who stayed. The territorial government reinforced these exclusionary efforts by barring nonwhites from testifying in court, and the Oregon Donation Land Law of 1850 excluded Blacks from its generous provisions. At the critical moment of statehood in 1857, Whites once again attempted to keep out Blacks: voters rejected slavery, but by an even greater margin they also reaffirmed the exclusion of Blacks from Oregon. The Oregon constitution thereby became the first state constitution to explicitly exclude free Blacks. White Oregonians made it clear that other nonwhite peoples also were not welcome: the Donation Land Law excluded Hawaiians, who had worked and lived in Oregon since the early 1800s, and the state constitution barred Chinese people from voting. White Oregonians wanted a White state, and they got one: according to the 1860 census, they made up more than 90 percent of the state's 52,465 inhabitants, although that figure did not fully record the state's Native population.

The Civil War and its aftermath confirmed that Oregon's environments would be owned, cultivated and manipulated by Whites only. Oregon's Democratic, Whig, Know-Nothing and Republican party leaders shouted at each other about abstract issues such as property rights and self-determination, but like their White male constituents who approved the exclusionary Oregon constitution, they generally agreed that the state must exclude both slavery and free Blacks. While other parts of the United States violently divided over slavery, the Civil War most directly affected Oregon by temporarily restricting the federal government's negotiations and conflicts with Oregon's Native peoples. Watching the Civil War from a distance, White Oregonians generally approved of the Union's success, with isolated but notable expressions of Southern sympathy in Jacksonville and Eugene. But White Oregonians did not embrace the Civil War's greater meaning for rights and equality. Instead, Oregonians passed laws that banned interracial marriage and required nonwhites to pay extra taxes. In 1870, they rejected the 15th Amendment, which protected the right to vote for all men, regardless of "race, color, or previous condition of servitude." White American settlers jealously guarded their agricultural paradise in Oregon.

Expanding into New Environments

In the 1840s and 1850s, that agricultural paradise centered on the Willamette Valley, where the landscape most easily accommodated the immigrants' efforts to create market-oriented, subsistence-based family farms. But even before Oregon joined the United States in 1859, new challenges and opportunities drew recent arrivals out into Oregon's diverse environments. One challenge was finding land: thanks to the generous provisions of the Donation Land Law, early White immigrants had gobbled up most of the good free land in the Willamette Valley, so new immigrants either paid premiums for a farm

there or were pushed out to unclaimed, less-ideal land elsewhere. New opportunities in Oregon's environments also pulled immigrants to other parts of the state. Discoveries of gold drew not only prospectors hoping for a quick strike, but also miners, traders and settlers who tried to turn temporary gold boom towns into permanent settlements. As American settlers and the federal government increased their pressure on Native peoples, especially after the Civil War, more land opened up in different parts of the state for different kinds of work, including ranching and logging. No matter where they went or how they tried to make a living, these Oregonians, like those who settled in the Willamette Valley, brought with them both anxiety about the environments they confronted and a desire to turn those challenges into opportunities.

Even before the Willamette Valley filled up, some American settlers headed to southwestern Oregon to farm or find faster ways to profit off the land. In 1846, a party led by Jesse and Lindsay Applegate blazed a new trail to the Willamette Valley that passed through southern Oregon, and a few years later, the Applegate party families moved south and settled in the Umpqua River Valley. Other farmers followed them there and later moved into other river valleys in southwestern Oregon, including the Rogue River area. Miners and traders soon joined them, first on their way to and from the gold fields of California, and then to make their own claims after the discovery of gold in the Rogue River Valley in 1851. Prospectors spread throughout southwestern Oregon, sifting, digging and blasting for gold from the broad coastal beaches to the smallest tributaries of the Rogue and Umpqua rivers. Many of the miners stayed after the boom years, establishing their own small farmsteads or continuing to squeeze ever-smaller amounts of gold out the streams and hillsides. Among these miners were Chinese migrants, who worked creeks and streams throughout southwest Oregon, ran merchant businesses, and established communities, such as Jacksonville's Chinatown. Southwestern Oregon landscapes also offered another source of riches: ancient forests full of timber, ready to be cut, processed and shipped off to California markets. By 1870, the lure of timber, gold and soil had drawn 15 percent of Oregon's population to southwestern Oregon.

American immigrants initially avoided eastern Oregon, where the climate and landscape challenged their agricultural pursuits. But gold, free land and ranching opportunities soon pulled American speculators and settlers east of the Cascades. Methodist missionaries established a station at The Dalles in 1838, and soon emigrants on the Oregon Trail were stopping there to rest before continuing on to the Willamette Valley, occasionally by way of the Barlow Road around Mount Hood. Some American settlers stayed in The Dalles, and the town developed into a small but important trading link between the west and east sides of the Cascades, much as it had

The Dalles on the Columbia River became an important transportation center on the Oregon Trail, as this mural detail in The Dalles by Don Crook depicts. (Oregon State Archives scenic photo)

been for the Native peoples of the Columbia Plateau and western valleys. The White population of eastern Oregon remained very small — only 3 percent of the state's Whites lived there in 1860 — until the discovery of gold in 1861 in the John Day and Powder River valleys. As in southwestern Oregon, thousands of prospectors followed the rumors of gold, scouring the hillsides and streambeds and establishing dozens of short-lived mining towns. The rush also contributed to the economic growth of The Dalles, Umatilla Landing, La Grande and other trading and shipping sites on the Columbia River and the surrounding valleys. That growth was shaped by a growing Chinese population of miners, merchants, physicians and more, who built thriving communities in John Day, The Dalles, Baker City and elsewhere in northeastern Oregon.

To serve the appetites of those miners and communities, another form of resource extraction developed: raising and grazing cattle and sheep, which thrived on the semi-arid lands east of the Cascades. Recent Willamette Valley settlers and their children looking for open lands and new economic opportunities led these initial ranching efforts, which continued even after the gold booms went bust. In a few pockets of eastern Oregon, including Harney Basin, some subsistence farming families established homesteads and adapted their agricultural practices to the higher altitude and drier climate. But the landscapes east of the Cascades presented a few too many challenges to White settlers, and the area remained sparsely populated, with just 14 percent of the state's White population in 1870.

As White settlers spread throughout the state, they redefined, remade, and, to some degree, overcame Oregon's environments. Americans drew the territory and state of Oregon with straight eastern and southern boundaries that recognized political interests rather than ecological reality. As they claimed land through the Donation Land Law and successive legislation, White settlers imprinted on

the landscape a peculiar patchwork of square and rectangular homesteads. Farmers eliminated some predators and raised imported plants and livestock that pushed out existing flora and fauna. Miners rearranged streams and dug into hillsides, loggers cut down trees and ranchers grazed cattle and sheep on native grasslands. Despite such changes, the new Oregonians recognized some limits to their efforts to overcome nature. They relied on manual and animal labor and used relatively simple tools, limiting the extent and intensity of ecological transformations. They depended on and remained vulnerable to seasonal cycles, hoping for enough rain to grow crops, but not so much as to flood them out of home and farm. Even political boundaries and land claims bent to the realities of nature: the Pacific Ocean and Columbia River bounded the state to the west and north, and environmental obstacles, such as rivers and mountains, often defined the practical limits of where farmers could plant crops. In short, the first generation of new Oregonians accepted the power of nature. Many of their children would have a different view of their relationship to Oregon's environments.

Section II: Confidence in Control of Oregon's Environments

Connecting Oregon

Transportation improvements provided the key not only to overcoming nature, but to controlling it. Oregon's environments presented a variety of transportation challenges, from the sheer size of the state to natural obstacles like rivers, mountains and canyons. These obstacles hindered the movement of people, ideas, goods and investment capital, slowing efforts to develop Oregon's environments. Roads offered the first and generally least-effective measure for overcoming these challenges. Backed by investors and state charters guaranteeing a monopoly, private toll road companies transformed old trails and rough wagon paths into "improved" roads made of dirt tracks, planks and bridges. Some companies failed; the Portland & Valley Plank Road Company, for example, went bust within two years. Others thrived, especially when they received federal and state land grants to sell or lease, supposedly to help pay for what they called "military wagon roads." In reality, speculators took most of the profits from the land grants, which totaled nearly 2.5 million acres, and farmers, not soldiers, primarily used the roads. That, after all, was the point: to move people, ideas, goods and capital more quickly throughout the state and accelerate the transformation of Oregon's environments into profitable natural resources. But these connections were unreliable, difficult and slow, as bridges collapsed, planks decayed, and rain turned dirt paths into impassable mud pits. Oregonians seeking to get their products to market looked beyond wagon roads for their transportation solutions.

Oregon's waterways offered faster and easier transportation options, especially as they became better understood and even managed. By 1851, steam-powered ships traveled up and down the Willamette and Columbia rivers and cruised along the Oregon coastline, delivering wheat, wood and other products to internal and external markets, especially in San Francisco. But water transportation could be difficult, unreliable and dangerous. When European and American ships began plying the Columbia River in the early nineteenth century, they relied heavily on the expertise of Native guides to find their way around the river's bars and other hazards. Throughout the 1800s, the U.S. government invested heavily in the safety and navigability of the Oregon coastline, building lighthouses and lifesaving stations and producing reliable charts of anchorages and safe passages into the Coos Bay estuary, Tillamook Bay, and other ports and rivers. Meanwhile, exploration and first-hand experience on the Columbia and Willamette rivers provided important information for shippers: the location of sandbars and other hazards, the routes through the rivers' deepest and safest passages, and the times of year when water ran high and fast enough to allow transportation.

But knowledge of natural waterways was not enough. To increase the reliability and speed of water transportation, Oregonians changed waterways by deepening bars at harbor entrances, rerouting streams into straighter and faster canals, and using dynamite and specially-designed boats to remove snags and trees from rivers. There were significant limits, though: river transportation depended on rainfall and snowmelt to keep water levels high enough for boats and ships, major falls like those at Oregon City and The Dalles remained impassable, and eastern Oregon offered essentially no water transportation options. Waterways, like wagon

roads, could only move Oregonians so far and fast towards their goal of controlling nature.

Even as they built and maintained wagon roads and waterways, Oregonians eagerly anticipated the arrival of an even more powerful and transformative force: railroads. Railroads offered many promises to Oregonians eager to free themselves from the constraints of nature. While floods or low flow stopped water transportation on the Willamette River and other streams, and heavy rains washed out the Great Plank Road and other wagon roads, trains could run almost without regard to weather or season. Railroads could reach every corner of the state, including east of the Cascades where the lack of navigable waterways cut off farmers, ranchers, and other producers from markets. Most importantly, trains promised amazing speeds that seemed to smash through the natural barriers of time and distance. Within just a few years of statehood, railroads had spread through every region of Oregon: in 1862, the Oregon Steam Navigation Company built tracks along the Columbia River at the Cascades and Celilo Falls; the Oregon & California Railroad connected Portland to Eugene by 1871 and reached California in 1887; and in 1883, transcontinental train transportation came to Oregon via the Northern Pacific Railroad. As with wagon roads and water transportation, federal investment helped speed railroad construction: federal surveyors started exploring the best routes in the 1850s, and the federal government gave away millions of acres to railroad companies, including 3.7 million acres to the Oregon & California Railroad.

This Carleton Watkins photo shows a railroad train at Upper Cascades on the Columbia River in the 1860s. (Oregon State Archives photo)

By the end of the century, 1,850 miles of railroad track crisscrossed Oregon, utterly transforming the state's environments. This dramatic transformation was made possible by immigrants, first and most prominently from China, but also Greece, Italy, Japan and elsewhere. Construction crews built bridges across rivers and canyons and blasted away mountainsides to make room for railroad beds, ties and rails. Those wooden ties came by cutting and processing millions of trees from surrounding forests. Once built, the tracks allowed and encouraged Oregonians to accelerate environmental transformation: plant more wheat to send to distant markets, process more timber to transport on the railroads, and graze more cattle to herd towards rail shipping points. Trains carried not only the products of Oregon's environments, but also the increasingly efficient and expensive agricultural equipment, logging machinery, and other industrial tools used to transform nature. And, of course, the railroads carried people: old and new immigrants, including people of color, moving through and throughout the state in pursuit of a better life. Along with water transportation routes, which remained vitally important, railroads helped incorporate Oregon, connecting farmers, ranchers, miners and loggers to land, resources and markets.

Industrialization and Urbanization

Transportation revolutions in Oregon accelerated ongoing transformations of the state's environment. Oregon's farmers and ranchers expanded and intensified their tilling, planting, grazing and other productive efforts. West of the Cascades, plentiful water created a lush and fruitful environment, but it caused farmers plenty of problems, too. Abundant rain and overflowing streams soaked the soil and ruined crops, and farmers could not extend their fields into marshes, wetlands and commonly flooded areas. Although they could not control the water falling from the sky, farmers managed it once it hit the ground: they built protective dikes to restrain rivers and dug ditches and ran underground pipes to drain water from fields, creating more cultivable land planted with wheat and other crops for market. East of the Cascades on the Columbia Plateau, insufficient water meant fewer transportation options and the inability to grow the thirsty crops that thrived in the Willamette Valley. Railroads, financed and controlled by capitalists and managers in Eastern centers of capital, helped solve the first problem; farmers overcame the second by developing small-scale irrigation projects and by planting winter wheat, a hardier but still profitable crop. Farmers on the Columbia Plateau were soon growing more wheat than their competitors west of the Cascades. Southeastern Oregon was too remote and too dry for wheat, but cattle and sheep ranching grew and flourished on a massive scale. By 1900, more than 15,000 cattle and 400,000 sheep roamed Harney and Malheur counties. Again, railroads allowed and encouraged this expansion. The Central Pacific's shipping facility at Winnemucca, Nevada and the Union Pacific's tracks into eastern Oregon gave ranchers access to markets in San Francisco, Chicago and beyond.

As Oregon's fields and rangelands industrialized, so did its hillsides, forests, rivers and oceans. Equipped with new technology, often powered by steam, miners, loggers, fishers and manufacturers asserted more control over Oregon's environments and the wealth they contained. After the placer miners had taken all the "easy" gold from southern and eastern Oregon stream beds during the early mining booms, larger-scale operations took their place. Industrial miners, working for corporations overseen by external investors, dynamited their way into mountains and then used machines to crush and smelt precious mineral-bearing ore, or rechanneled streams and built high-pressure water cannons to wash away hillsides that were then sifted through for gold. Industrial technology and market forces increased timber production, too. Strong cross-cut saws replaced axes to fell trees, small railroads and "steam donkey" machines replaced real animals pulling logs out of forests, and steam-powered mills replaced water-powered mills to turn logs into marketable timber.

New technologies made logging and other industries more efficient in the years around 1900. (Oregon State Archives scenic photo)

Equipped with such technology, timber companies with headquarters in Minneapolis, San Francisco, the Puget Sound and elsewhere reached into previously inaccessible forests — stands of Douglas fir in the Nehalem Valley, for example, and Ponderosa pine in Klamath and Deschutes counties — and cut down as many trees as the market could handle. Oregon's rivers also became industrial sites for the harvesting and processing of salmon traveling to and from the Pacific Ocean. In the last quarter of the 1800s, fishers constructed a gauntlet of salmon harvesting technologies on the Columbia River: nets, traps, weirs, seines and fish wheels that took out hundreds of thousands of pounds of salmon. Oregon's salmon canning industry grew quickly, from 4,000 cases in 1866 to a high of 620,000 in 1884. The state took a variety of measures to conserve fish populations; for example, in 1898, the state legislature passed a law that regulated salmon fishing and encouraged salmon propagation through hatcheries and the removal of fish passage barriers. Such efforts sought to allay concerns about the potential exhaustion of natural resources that might result from the transformation of Oregon's rivers, forests, hillsides and fields.

The timber, ore, grains and fish coming out of Oregon's environments traveled on railroads and waterways towards Oregon's growing and increasingly diverse cities and towns. Portland quickly became Oregon's largest city and commercial hub, thanks to its location at the confluence of the

Willamette and Columbia rivers and its citizens' aggressive and successful efforts to attract railroads to the city. From a population of less than 3,000 in 1860, Portland grew into a metropolis of 90,426 by 1900. The state's financial power also centered on Portland, home to the state's first bank and its richest citizens. Other cities and towns developed along rivers and railroads during the 1800s, too, including Astoria (population 8,381 in 1900), Baker City (6,663), Pendleton (4,406), and Salem (4,258). In towns both big and small, Oregonians busily transformed the products of the state's environments. To serve markets near and far, a variety of manufacturing and processing industries developed, from flour and woolen mills to fish canneries and brick factories. Urban areas also offered many other commercial and retail services: printers, blacksmiths, bankers, launderers, bakers, carpenters, photographers and more, depending on the size and age of the town.

While power over these industries and enterprises rested in the hands of elites in Portland, San Francisco, New York, and other centers of capital, the actual transformation of environments came at the hands of old and new immigrants alike, drawn to natural resource extraction work in the countryside and commercial and manufacturing jobs in Oregon's cities. Oregonians of western European descent generally welcomed and quickly integrated other immigrants from the countries of their homeland, including the United Kingdom, Germany, and Scandinavian nations. Other immigrant groups remained more distinct and subject to exclusion. Groups of Chinese immigrants initially came to Oregon to work in and around mines and on railroads; later, they worked in fish canneries and in cities as launderers, gardeners, grocers and other service workers. Immigrants from Japan and southern and eastern Europe also arrived in the late 1800s, adding to the ethnic diversity of Oregon's towns, especially Portland. Portland was also home to most of Oregon's Black population, who worked for railroads and as domestic workers in hotels and the homes of the well-to-do. People of color and immigrants often faced severe discrimination; Chinese immigrants, for example, were forced to pay special taxes and were confronted by violent White rioters during the 1880s. These marginalized groups persevered through these challenges, and of the 413,536 inhabitants of Oregon counted by the 1900 census, 4.5 percent were listed as other than White, and 15.9 percent had been born outside of the United States. Transforming Oregon's environments, it turned out, required the hard work of people from all over the world.

Reforming Industrial Oregon

Some Oregonians worried about the effects of these transformations: the potential exhaustion of natural resources, the concentrated power of political and economic actors, community and social disruption, and more. They had a different vision for Oregon, and at the end of the 1800s and beginning of the 1900s, they tried to reform Oregon politics, government, society and environments. Many of these efforts originated among farmers and workers who experienced first-hand the transformation of Oregon's environments. Frustrated with high interest rates on bank loans, expensive shipping costs, and the low prices their crops got at market, farmers joined the Patrons of Husbandry — the Grange, established in 1873 — and local chapters of the Farmers' Alliance, an advocacy organization that appeared in Oregon in 1891. Laborers in Oregon's cities, forests, farms, mines and fisheries had their own frustrations, including low pay, poor and often dangerous working conditions, and long hours. Beginning in 1880, White workers organized into chapters of the Knights of Labor, a union that advocated for better pay and working conditions, and also supported legislation and violence directed against Chinese workers. Entrenched political and economic interests stymied these reform organizations, and so these farmers and workers stepped into Oregon politics with the formation of the People's Party, or Populists, in 1892 and the Union Party in 1899. The People's Party quickly fragmented and disintegrated, but enthusiasm for reform continued and grew. In the 1910s, reformers secured a series of transformative laws, including the initiative and referendum process, direct election of senators, and the recall of elected officials. This package of reforms became known as the Oregon System — a set of political tools that put more power directly in the hands of the electorate.

During the first two decades of the 1900s, activists used the Oregon System to implement a variety of reforms. Voters approved initiatives that taxed telephone, telegraph and railroad companies, prohibited railroads from bribing public officials with free passes and regulated shipping rates. Oregon established a minimum wage, workers' compensation, an eight-hour work day for public works projects, and maximum hours and other protections for women workers. Some reformers also tried to address broader social issues with anti-prostitution and gambling campaigns, and, most famously and controversially, the prohibition of alcohol by constitutional amendment in 1914. Women led the prohibition campaign and many other reform efforts that sought to improve their communities by encouraging safer, more sanitary and more healthy environments. Through the Woman's Christian Temperance Union, the Oregon Federation of Women's Clubs and other organizations, as well as individually, women reformers asserted a powerful role in public life. In contrast to the racism and nativism that sometimes paired with Progressive Era reform efforts, the movement for women's suffrage in Oregon relied on partnerships between White women and women of color in groups such as the Colored Women's Equal Suffrage Association. The struggle to secure the right of women to vote took decades, failing five times before finally succeeding by initiative in 1912, eight years before it passed nationally. Women's suffrage represented perhaps the most significant reform, while other ambitious and even radical efforts failed or quickly faded away. Despite long and intense efforts, advocates of the "single tax" — a 100 percent tax on the unearned value and profits on land — failed every time they went to the ballot. The Socialist Party of Oregon found limited but often enthusiastic support, especially in Portland and in southwestern Oregon; the citizens of Coquille, for example, elected a socialist mayor, although the party's statewide efforts had little success. Though not quite the radical transformation that some Oregonians wanted, reform efforts significantly changed Oregon society.

Oregon women march in the first national suffrage parade in Washington D.C. in 1913. (Courtesy of Library of Congress)

Oregonians also directed reform efforts towards the state's environments. Reformers believed that Oregon's forests, fisheries and other natural resources should be conserved and preserved for the public good, rather than exclusively possessed and exploited by private individuals and companies. The Oregon Land Fraud Trials (1904–1910) led to the prosecution of private speculators, government employees and elected officials who had abused homestead laws to illegally claim public land in Oregon and then sell it cheaply to timber and livestock companies. In 1911, the state legislature created the Oregon Board of Forestry and Department of Forestry, tasked with reducing forest fires, encouraging reforestation and enforcing other conservation measures. The federal government assisted reform efforts by setting aside land for preservation and conservation: it established Crater Lake National Park (1902) and Oregon Caves National Monument (1909), returned unsold Oregon & California Railroad land grants to the government (1914) and created millions of acres of national forest reserves. Reformers focused on Oregon's oceans and rivers, too, asserting open public access to the state's beaches (1913) and passing initiatives meant to conserve fish populations on the Rogue and Columbia rivers.

Even as they slowed or stopped some transformations of Oregon's environments, reformers encouraged other "improvements." These changes were particularly visible on the Columbia River, where the Army Corps of Engineers completed the Cascade Locks in 1896 and Celilo Locks and Canal in 1916 to improve navigation and shipping. Reclamation projects — draining swampy land or irrigating dry land to "reclaim" it for farming — had an even greater effect in southern Oregon. Beginning in 1905, the federal Bureau of Reclamation built a complex system of dams, ditches, canals and other mechanisms that created more than 200,000 acres of farmland in the Klamath Basin while damaging the basin's wetland ecosystems. The Klamath Irrigation Project and Columbia River locks and canals set the stage for even more ambitious reconfigurations of river systems later in the century. These developments, coupled with successful reform efforts, reinforced the view that Oregonians could and should control the state's environments.

World War I and Reactionary Oregon

World War I turned Oregonians away from reform and back to more intense environmental transformations for the purposes of economic growth and war production. Heightened European demand for wheat and wood led to increased production in the fields and forests of Oregon. Airplane manufacturers wanted the light and strong wood of Sitka spruce trees, which grew especially well in coastal environments, including on lands that the U.S. government had removed from the Siletz and Grand Ronde Indian Reservations and sold to timber companies. To supplement private timber company production, the federal government in 1917 established the United States Spruce Production Division, which sent more than 7,500 soldiers into Oregon coastal forests to cut down spruce trees for the war effort. The war also brought changes to the ports of Astoria, Coos Bay, Tillamook and elsewhere on Oregon's coast and the Columbia River, as the federal government's Emergency Fleet Corporation contracted with a dozen shipyards to build wooden and steel ships. The increased demand for wartime material led to a shortage of labor, which briefly empowered workers and their unions. Timber workers in the Industrial Workers of the World (IWW) went on strike in the summer of 1917, demanding shorter hours, more pay and better working and living conditions. Timber companies refused, and the federal government stepped in, creating the Loyal Legion of Loggers and Lumbermen (the 4-L), an industry-wide, timber company-friendly union that prohibited strikes, demanded loyalty pledges and instituted eight-hour days and better conditions. The 4-L undermined support for the IWW while government officials, politicians, law enforcement and vigilante groups attacked union members and officials. Workers suffered further with the end of the war in

1918: the international market for wood and wheat contracted, economic growth slowed and more workers competed for fewer jobs. The economic boom was over, but wartime production left behind logging equipment, shipyards, agricultural machinery and other tools and infrastructure that soon would transform Oregon's environments again.

The Ku Klux Klan grew in power in Oregon in the aftermath of World War I. (Courtesy of Library of Congress)

The immediate postwar period in Oregon brought a reaction against progressive reform and expanded efforts by some Oregonians to marginalize and exclude others. By 1920, the momentum for reform had slowed. In the 10 years following World War I, Oregonians voted on 89 ballot measures, compared to 147 measures in the decade before the war. Some of those initiatives, along with a variety of other laws and actions, sought to more closely define which peoples and cultures did and did not belong in Oregon. In 1922, voters approved the Compulsory School Bill, which required all students to attend public schools — a direct attack on Catholic schools and Oregon's Catholic communities. The next year, the state legislature passed discriminatory laws that banned religious garb in schools (another assault on Catholic culture) and allowed city governments to deny business licenses to Japanese immigrants. The state legislature also passed a law prohibiting "aliens ineligible for citizenship" — especially Japanese immigrants — from purchasing or leasing land, an act that denied such immigrants equal participation and ownership in the agricultural transformation of Oregon's environments. A variety of organized groups and civic associations supported these exclusionary efforts, including the American Legion and, most infamously, the Ku Klux Klan, which became a powerful political and social force in Oregon beginning in 1921. Some of this reactionary tide was pulled back — the Supreme Court ruled the Compulsory School Bill unconstitutional in 1924, and the Oregon Klan disintegrated by the end of the decade — but these exclusionary efforts left a hateful mark on the state's history.

Discrimination also took more violent forms. The laws directed against Japanese Oregonians stayed in effect, and Japanese communities faced repeated harassment and violence, such as a 1925 incident in which a mob expelled Japanese workers from Toledo. Black Oregonians faced similar discrimination, including legal segregation, "sundown laws" that threatened them with violence if they remained in certain towns after dark, and real estate practices that restricted where they could live. Native Oregonians, too, were further marginalized. Native peoples were ineligible for American citizenship until 1924; Native children were forced into boarding and day schools that prohibited Native languages and dress; and Native peoples were prohibited from leaving reservations, which in western Oregon dramatically shrank in the aftermath of the Dawes Allotment Act of 1887, which allocated some reservation lands for ownership by tribal members, but sold most of the land as "surplus" to the highest bidder.

These Oregonians resisted such marginalization. Native Oregonians survived and thrived: some retained title to their lands and integrated into mainstream Oregon society, while others found ways to preserve their culture. Other peoples also protected their families and cultures by sustaining independent ethnic communities, such as Portland's three different Chinatowns or the Japanese communities that prospered in Salem, Hood River and elsewhere. Black communities thrived with independent civic organizations, churches, and businesses, and they advocated for equality through such means as the Advocate newspaper and the Portland National Association for the Advancement of Colored People (NAACP) — the first NAACP chapter west of the Mississippi River. Oregonians also made two symbolic yet important political steps towards equality: in 1926, they repealed the section of the state constitution that excluded Blacks from Oregon, and in 1927, they overturned the state constitution's prohibition of Black and Chinese suffrage.

By the late 1920s, Oregon had transformed in ways that could seem contradictory. Reformers had created the Oregon System and passed hundreds of initiatives and laws that sought to improve state society and environments. But those efforts only went so far. Many Oregonians rejected not only radicalism and reform, but also ethnic groups and communities that some White, Protestant Oregonians believed too foreign, strange, or unassimilable. Oregon's landscapes bore the marks of this exclusion, such as the limits on Japanese ownership of land. Environmental conservation efforts also revealed other contradictory characteristics of these reforms. For example, Oregon established its first state park in 1922 and Oregon's senior U.S. senator, Charles McNary, co-sponsored a federal act in 1924 that encouraged forest fire protection and reforestation. But McNary's bill also avoided federal regulation of private harvesting practices, leaving timber companies in Oregon essentially free to cut as much as they wanted wherever they wanted. And the state park system had its origins in the State Highway Commission, whose central purpose was to build more, better, faster roads that cut through forests and farmlands. For Oregonians in the 1920s, these did not seem like contradictions, but rather evidence that they could and should reform, improve and control Oregon's social and natural environments.

Confidence Amidst the Crises of Depression and World War II

Oregonians' confidence in and enthusiasm for control of nature continued even as the world crashed into economic catastrophe and global conflict. The Great Depression was particularly obvious and severe in Oregon's cities, with massive unemployment in manufacturing and the service industries and the appearance of "Hoovervilles" in Portland's Sullivan Gulch and the "Hotel de Minto," a shelter for young unemployed men on the top floor of Salem's city hall. The Depression hit rural areas, too, as prices, production and employment crashed in Oregon's forests, mills, farms, fisheries and ranches. In Mill City, for example, the A.B. Hammond Timber Company mills quickly cut back the work week to 20 hours, then 10 hours, and finally shut down operations in 1935. Oregonians showed remarkable resilience and confidence in the face of this economic catastrophe. In rural areas, they turned to Oregon's rich environments, relying on subsistence farming, fishing, hunting, and gathering and creating bartering economies that supported their communities. In towns and cities, municipal governments, civic organizations and other groups provided food and relief work for the unemployed. But the depth and severity of the Depression overwhelmed such noble efforts.

At the urgent demand of many Oregonians, the federal government stepped in with the New Deal, which provided relief, assistance, and action. The government encouraged workers to join unions and provided assistance to farmers through the Soil Conservation Service and the Rural Electrification Administration. Some federal programs were directed at Native peoples. The Indian Reorganization Act of 1934 halted the allotment of reservation land, provided credit opportunities and funds for the purchase of additional lands, and provided a path towards federally-recognized self-government and economic development, like that followed by the Warm Springs tribes, which incorporated as the Confederated Tribes of the Warm Springs Reservation in 1937. Native Oregonians also participated in federal work programs including the Civilian Conservation Corps (CCC), the Works Progress Administration (WPA), the Public Works Administration (PWA); these and many other agencies provided paychecks and left a permanent mark on Oregon's society and landscape. The CCC built trails, fire lookouts, warming shelters and more in Oregon's forests; the WPA constructed Timberline Lodge on Mount Hood, hired artists and writers for cultural projects and created other employment opportunities; and the PWA built parks, schools, and government buildings, constructed bridges connecting Highway 101 on the coast and added other infrastructure throughout the state. Some of these federal projects radically changed Oregon's environments, especially Bonneville Dam, funded by the PWA and built by the Army Corps of Engineers between 1933 and 1938. Bonneville Dam created a 48-mile-long reservoir on the Columbia River, improved navigation, and generated electricity, but it also damaged salmon habitats. Water projects bloomed during the New Deal: the Bureau of Reclamation completed the Vale-Owyhee Project in the mid-1930s, creating more than 24,000 acres of irrigable farmland by the end of the decade, and federal studies of the Columbia River and its tributaries promised more river development for irrigation, hydropower, flood control and more. These studies, projects and programs represented an optimistic confidence that by transforming and controlling nature, Oregonians could overcome any obstacle, even the Great Depression.

The Isaac Lee Patterson Bridge over the Rogue River at Gold Beach is one of several coastal bridges built during the 1930s. (Oregon State Archives scenic photo)

The Depression was eclipsed by the even greater cataclysm of World War II, which ended the economic catastrophe and impacted Oregonians in a variety of ways. More than 2,800 Oregonians died and 5,000 were wounded in the line of duty, and six people died when a balloon bomb floated over the Pacific Ocean from Japan and exploded in Bly in May 1945. The U.S. military built training camps and facilities throughout the state, including Camp Adair north of Corvallis, Camp White near Medford and Camp Abbott (which later became the resort village of Sunriver). Oregonians rationed food and fuel, staffed lookouts to protect forest resources, bought war bonds, saved and recycled metal and rubber and mobilized into civilian defense and air patrol units. They also worked long hours producing war materiel in existing factories, like the Thomas Kay Woolen Mill in Salem that ran three shifts to make Army blankets, and in brand-new facilities, including the Kaiser shipyards in Portland, which produced 455 ships and employed tens of thousands of workers during the war.

The war presented both opportunities and challenges to women and minorities in Oregon. The Bracero program brought more than 15,000 Mexican contract laborers to Oregon to plant, weed and harvest crops. Although they generally received better wages than in Mexico, Bracero workers faced racism, poor working and living conditions, and broken promises that they would be paid when they returned home. Thousands of Blacks came to work in Portland, where they found discrimination and an acute housing crisis. These problems were only partially alleviated by the rapid construction of Vanport, which provided homes, schools, nurseries, and other services to 35,000 residents, 35 percent of whom were Black, and all of whom lived directly in the path of the Columbia River, which flooded and destroyed the city in 1948. Women also found work at the Kaiser shipyards, the Kay Woolen Mill, and other manufacturers supplying the war effort. Despite persistent sexual harassment and unequal treatment — at the end of the war, they were the first to be fired — women proved the value of their work to themselves and to others.

Oregonians of Japanese descent endured particularly tragic discrimination during World War II. Beginning in April 1942, Japanese Oregonians — both immigrants who were prohibited by federal law from American citizenship as well as their children, who were birthright citizens of the United States — were forcibly evacuated from their homes in Portland, Hood River and throughout western Oregon, crowded into unsanitary transfer facilities, and sent to concentration camps in California, Idaho and Tule Lake, just across the southern Oregon border in California. At the same time, hundreds of Japanese Oregonians enlisted and served in the armed forces. When the camps closed and the war ended in 1945, Japanese Oregonians found themselves unwelcomed in their former homes, and many decided they could not return. But almost 70 percent did go back, because they — like Latino and Latinas, Blacks, women and everyone who had helped Oregon prosper during the war — rightfully called Oregon home.

All Oregonians lived and worked in landscapes that had radically transformed in just a few decades. A single generation had seen wagon trails turned into railroads, animal power replaced by mechanized farm equipment, rivers dammed and rerouted, deserts irrigated, swamps drained, and astonishing quantities of lumber, food crops, livestock, fish and minerals produced from Oregon's environments. Forests, fields, rangelands and waterways had industrialized, and Oregon more generally urbanized: in 1870, more than 90 percent of Oregonians lived in rural areas, but by 1930, the numbers of urban and rural residents were about equal. Oregonians knew that such transformations could have negative effects, but they were confident they could minimize such consequences through reform and management. For example, in 1941, the state legislature passed the Oregon Forest Conservation Act, which required commercial logging operations to leave enough trees standing and/or plant new trees to maintain forest growth. Such efforts seemed to show Oregonians that not only could they overcome natural obstacles, but they could control and eliminate those obstacles. The end of economic depression and the war unleashed this confidence, and Oregonians found new and dramatic ways to assert control over nature. But such efforts, they soon learned, also had dramatic consequences.

Section III: Pursuing Growth and Sustainability

Postwar Boom

Although confident that they could and should control Oregon's environments, Oregonians also were anxious that the years after World War II might bring a return to the Great Depression or some other calamity. Just the opposite, it turned out: Oregon's population and economy, like the rest of the nation, boomed. In 1940, the federal census counted 1,089,684 people in Oregon; by 1960, 1,768,687 people called Oregon home. Between 1945 and 1965, Oregon's per capita income more than doubled and Oregonians cashed in their paychecks, war bonds and savings to buy cars, radios, refrigerators, washing machines, and, most importantly, houses. Real estate developers and home builders went on a construction spree, expanding cities, towns, and suburbs. Eugene, for instance, added 4,717 acres between 1950 and 1960, and Corvallis grew by more than 3,000 acres in that same decade. An increasingly dense network of roads and highways, including Interstate 5, connected these places and facilitated economic growth.

The smooth asphalt freeways and freshly-painted housing developments suggested that all Oregonians shared in and enthusiastically embraced this growth. But this appearance of consensus was forced upon some Native Oregonians through a process called tribal termination, by which the federal government sought to eliminate its trusteeship of Native lands and force the assimilation of Native peoples. Beginning in 1953, the U.S. Congress passed a series of laws that effectively ended federal recognition of tribal sovereignty and terminated the federal government's responsibility to oversee and protect the lands, resources and interests of the Klamath and all Native groups west of the Cascades (the Warm Springs and Umatilla Reservations successfully prevented termination). The laws brought disastrous results: reservation lands were sold off, private speculators swindled Natives out of their land and property, Natives lost all services (such as health and education) formerly provided by the federal government, tribal governments disbanded, and Native communities scattered. The problems with termination suggested tension and trouble under the surface of Oregon's postwar growth and confidence.

The Dalles Dam on the Columbia River is one of many projects intended to harness the power of Oregon rivers in the postwar era. (Oregon State Archives scenic photo)

Pursuing broader economic growth and inspired by new technologies, Oregonians expanded and intensified their efforts to master Oregon's rivers, fields and forests in the two decades after World War II. The U.S. Army Corps of Engineers, Bureau of Reclamation, and local utility companies built dozens of dams, from massive structures like the 260-foot-high concrete The Dalles Dam on the Columbia to smaller projects like the 78-foot-high earthen fill Keene Creek Dam on the Rogue River. Oregon's farmers, chambers of commerce and civic groups cheered these river development projects, which promised flood control, improved navigation, inexpensive electricity, pollution mitigation, recreational opportunities and irrigation. While irrigation allowed farmers to control the timing, quantity and distribution of water in their fields, new chemical herbicides helped them manage weeds, and powerful insecticides effectively eliminated — for a short time — grasshoppers and other pests. These technologies, along with field burning, fertilizers, new tractors and combines and other investments, produced impressive results: for example, between 1945 and 1965, Oregon yields of field crops (barley, corn, hay, hops, oats, peas, rye, sugar beets and wheat) increased by 65 percent and production grew by 50 percent. Oregon timber production also increased: from 6,046 million board-feet in 1945 to 9,394 million board-feet 20 years later. Chainsaws, diesel-powered tractors and trucks and improved mill technology and processes facilitated this leap in production, as independent loggers and timber companies large and small supplied local, national, and international lumber markets. While technology increased efficiency, increased production also required the labor of tens of thousands of workers in forests, fields and pastures. In 1959, the U.S. Census of Agriculture counted 16,332 hired farm workers in Oregon, more than half of whom worked as seasonal labor.

These efforts to master nature produced worrisome consequences for both Oregon's environments and its peoples. As the growth in timber production began to exhaust the supply of timber on private lands, logging shifted to federal Forest Service and Bureau of Land Management public lands. Old growth forests were to be "converted" into tree farms and accessed by thousands of miles of logging roads; a 1956 forestry report called for nearly 15,000 miles of new access roads in Oregon's national forests. Such practices produced unsightly landscapes, upset complex ancient forest ecosystems and damaged fish habitat in streams and rivers. On Oregon's rivers, dams blocked salmon migrating to and from the Pacific Ocean, and fish hatcheries, fish ladders and other technical solutions only partially mitigated the loss in salmon populations. Dams slowed and warmed rivers — another problem for salmon — and inundated some communities and fishing sites with water; the most infamous example is Celilo Falls, drowned by The Dalles Dam in 1957.

Changes in Oregon's agricultural landscapes revealed other problematic consequences — political and cultural, as well as environmental — from the transformations of the post-war period. While farm production and yields increased, the state's agricultural character underwent a fundamental shift: by 1970, only 5 percent of Oregonians were farmers, as more people moved to Oregon's towns and cities for work. This change was particularly obvious west of the Cascades and especially in the Willamette Valley, which lost 20 percent of its farmland to residential, commercial and industrial development between 1950 and 1965. Such development gobbled up farmland and other open spaces, overwhelmed sewer and water systems, and polluted Oregon's water and soil with sewage and industrial contaminants. Changes to farming also raised concerns in the 1960s about the efficacy and safety of pesticides, herbicides and other chemicals that had been used to increase agricultural production. Moreover, these shifts in Oregon's economic and demographic character revealed increasing concentration in the Willamette Valley not just of Oregon's population, but also political and economic power. Oregon's urban and rural environments were undergoing a remarkable transformation, and not always for the best.

The Oregon Story and Other Narratives

These problems attracted the attention of a growing number of Oregonians, including some in positions of power, who supported a series of innovative and landmark environmental protection initiatives. Pollution was a particularly visible problem on the Willamette River, where industrial pollutants, sewage, and other contaminants led to unsafe water quality, especially during drier months. During the 1960s and 1970s, the Oregon State Sanitary Authority and its successor, the Department of Environmental Quality (established in 1969),

History

strengthened and enforced efforts to limit pollution from Willamette River cities and industries, especially pulp and paper mills. By 1972, all municipalities and all but one pulp and paper mill met pollution treatment requirements. The state also sought to reduce other kinds of waste and encourage conservation: the "Bottle Bill" of 1971 established a deposit and return system for beverage containers; the "Bicycle Bill" (also 1971) required jurisdictions building roads, streets, or highways to also include facilities for bicycles and pedestrians; and state agencies, as well as some private businesses, implemented a variety of energy conservation measures.

Other environmental protection efforts of the time sought to preserve open spaces for public enjoyment and recreation. In 1967, the "Beach Bill" established that all of Oregon's beaches, from the water to the dunes, were open to the public and were not for private ownership and development, expanding and strengthening existing protections established in 1913. Six years later, Oregon established a groundbreaking statewide land-use planning system that required all cities and counties to create zoning ordinance and long-range land-use plans. These plans established urban growth boundaries to regulate sprawl and set goals in 19 areas, including energy conservation, preservation of agricultural and forest lands, and air, water and land resource quality. Taken together, these and other environmental protection initiatives represented what then-Governor Tom McCall called "The Oregon Story": a belief that Oregonians should take innovative action to improve the quality of life in their state.

A 1973 statewide land use planning system law aimed to regulate sprawl and protect farmland, such as in the Willamette Valley. (Oregon State Archives scenic photo)

Other Oregon Stories also were being written during the 1960s and 1970s, as minorities, women and other marginalized groups continued to assert their power and equality. The ongoing women's rights movement secured significant political victories, including the state legislature's vote to ratify the federal Equal Rights Amendment, the election of the first woman to statewide office (Norma Paulus, elected Secretary of State in 1977), and

state legislation that prohibited discrimination against women in employment and retirement, removed marital status or cohabitation as a defense against rape, and more. Blacks in Oregon had achieved important political victories in the two decades after World War II, including state laws prohibiting discrimination in housing, employment and public accommodations. That political work continued through the following decades, along with protests, community organization and activism in groups like the Black United Front. Such activism confronted school segregation, police brutality, and other persistent forms of discrimination, including issues of environmental justice. Black Oregonians resisted "urban renewal" projects that destroyed Black homes and businesses, and they fought back against disproportionate levels of pollution in Black communities – for example, the high loads of toxins in Portland's Columbia Slough, a waterway generally neglected by Oregon environmentalists focused on more "natural" rivers and streams.

Native Oregonians, too, fought back against discrimination and marginalization through activist groups, in tribal communities, and individually. East of the Cascades, the Warm Springs tribes developed successful timber operations and the Kah-Nee-Tah Resort, and the Burns Paiute Tribe secured federal recognition and reservation lands in 1972. Over the next two decades, the terminated tribes west of the Cascades successfully campaigned to restore federal recognition of tribal sovereignty: Siletz (1977), Cow Creek (1982), Grand Ronde (1983), Coos, Lower Umpqua, and Siuslaw (1984), Klamath (1986), and Coquille (1989). Latino communities in Oregon continued to grow, developing a variety of cultural, educational, and political organizations, including Pro Fiestas Mexicanas, the Valley Migrant League, and Colegio César Chávez. By 1980, 5.4 percent of Oregon's population was nonwhite, compared to 1.2 percent 40 years earlier. Through political activism, community organization and evolving cultural heritage, these communities contributed their own narratives to an increasingly diverse Oregon Story.

Much of that Oregon Story was being written in, by, and for the urban residents of the Willamette Valley, the center of the state's political and economic power. But the narrative looked different in rural parts of Oregon. While urban areas grew and diversified, the rural population of the state remained relatively homogenous: only 20 percent of the Oregon's nonwhite population in 1980 lived in rural areas. The Willamette Valley's enthusiasm for environmental protection certainly affected rural Oregon communities, but those communities expressed far less enthusiasm for such regulations. Timber production remained vitally important, providing not only jobs in the woods and in the mills, but also revenue from federal timber sales to pay for schools and other public services. Although Oregon passed a comprehensive Forest Practices Act in 1971 that sought to protect soil, air, water, and wildlife on both public and private land, the timber industry, state and federal regulatory agencies, and politicians alike continued to support the lucrative practice of clearcutting old growth forests. Land use planning found strong opposition in rural communities east of the Cascades and in southern Oregon. Voters in timber-dependent and ranching communities supported initiatives in 1976, 1978 and 1983 that would have rolled back Oregon's comprehensive land use planning laws, but they were outnumbered by Willamette Valley opponents to the initiatives. By the 1980s, rural and urban Oregonians often were deeply divided over the meaning of The Oregon Story.

The Gaps Widen

In the 1980s and 1990s, the divisions among Oregonians seemed to widen, including differences in perceptions and uses of Oregon's environments. The divisions became most obvious in fights over Oregon's old growth forests. An economic recession in the early 1980s, coupled with the introduction of labor-saving computerized technology, led to mill closures and layoffs; in 1982, forest work employed 20 percent fewer people than just 10 years before. Some of those jobs returned in the mid-1980s as the economy improved, demand for timber increased, and logging on federal lands, especially in old growth forests, jumped to record levels. This raised worries among some scientists and others concerned about the loss of wildlife and old growth forests. The controversy crystalized around the northern spotted owl, whose population serves as an indicator for the ecological health and complexity of the old growth forests where it lives. In 1990, the owl was listed as a threatened species under the 1973 Endangered Species Act, requiring action to protect the owl and its habitat. Four years later, the federal government adopted the Northwest Forest Plan, which significantly reduced logging on federal lands. The management plan contributed to ongoing job loss in the timber industry, where the workforce already was shrinking due to logging and milling technology.

Oregonians also saw more conflicts over dams, irrigation projects, and other river development schemes that negatively affected fish habitat. In the 1990s, a variety of salmon populations were designated as threatened or endangered, leading to more regulations on fishing, hydroelectric power generation, and irrigation, and affecting the management of the Columbia and other Oregon rivers. In the news media and often on the ground, it appeared that such measures pitted rural Oregonians, whose communities depended on farming, logging, and other forms of natural resource extraction, against urban Oregonians, who generally supported efforts to preserve the state's environments for wildlife and recreation.

Divisions among Oregonians became even more pronounced around other transformations in Oregon society. As it had throughout its history, Oregon

attracted new immigrants from different backgrounds, and the state's population continued to diversify, with 7 percent of Oregonians identifying as nonwhite in the 1990 census, compared to 5.4 percent 10 years before. Minorities in Oregon achieved important measures of progress in the 1980s and 1990s, from the election of the first Blacks to the state legislature and statewide offices to the establishment of Pineros y Campesinos Unidos del Noroeste (PCUN), a Latino forest- and farm-worker union. But minority populations continued to experience discrimination, marginalization, and even hatred. Racist skinhead groups developed in some Oregon communities, including Portland, where a skinhead murdered Ethiopian exchange student Mulugeta Seraw in 1988. Skinheads also murdered two Salem residents in an apartment firebombing in 1992: Hattie Mae Cohens, a 29-year-old Black lesbian, and Brian Mock, a 45-year-old gay man.

These murders occurred within the context of a conservative backlash against the gay and lesbian rights' movement, which had secured notable victories in the 1970s and 1980s, including limited anti-discrimination laws in Portland (1974), Eugene (1977), and at the state level (1987). Some Oregonians opposed such developments and presented voters with anti-gay rights ballot measures: in 1988, voters repealed the state's efforts to prohibit discrimination against gays in state employment, but in 1992, 1994 and 2000, Oregonians rejected ballot measures that sought to restrict civil rights protection based on sexual orientation and, more generally, discourage homosexuality. Most of the opposition to these initiatives came from urban areas, while more voters in rural Oregon supported them and passed local anti-gay rights ordinances. The state legislature and court system overturned these city and county measures — another example, some rural Oregonians said, of the increasing cultural and political chasm between the urban Willamette Valley and the rest of the state.

Oregonians also divided over public spending, taxes, and economic differences more generally in the 1980s and 1990s. Following a national trend that started in the late 1970s and continued into the 1980s, a fiscally-conservative anti-tax movement developed in Oregon that focused especially on cutting property taxes. Such taxes supported schools, social services and state programs directed at the conservation of Oregon's environments, but many Oregonians regarded their contribution as too onerous, especially in Portland, where property values and taxes had increased rapidly in the 1980s. By 1989, Oregon property taxes were the 7th highest per capita in the United States. In 1990, voters approved Measure 5, an initiative that constitutionally limited property taxes; seven years later, voters approved Measure 50, which capped annual increases on property taxes. Together, these initiatives decreased how much of their personal income Oregonians paid to state and local taxes (from 12.1 percent in 1989 to 10.5 percent in 1999) and shifted the burden for paying for schools from local property taxes to the state general fund, which relied more and more on income taxes. Oregon voters also overwhelmingly defeated sales tax initiatives in 1985, 1986 and 1993, leaving the state dependent on income taxes to fund education, environmental conservation and preservation programs, and other government functions.

Those taxes came from vastly different income levels that largely fell along an urban/rural divide. The historic concentration of wealth in the Willamette Valley was well established by 1970, when the Portland area had the highest median income level, while the seven counties with the lowest levels were located outside the Valley. That division remained firmly in place 30 years later: Washington, Clackamas and Yamhill counties had the three highest median income levels, while Wheeler, Lake and Curry counties had the three lowest. At the end of the 20th century, it seemed that Oregon's people were as divided in economic, political and cultural issues as they were in their perceptions and uses of Oregon's environments.

Bridges and Divides

Those differences in income levels reflected deeper changes to Oregon's economy, which increasingly shifted away from logging, farming, ranching and other ways of working directly in Oregon's environments. By the end of the 20th century, the technology industry was booming in Washington County and a few other spots in the state, collectively called the "Silicon Forest." Some of these companies were homegrown, such as Electro Scientific Industries and Tektronix in the Portland area and Entek International in Lebanon. But Oregon's technology sector really took off with the arrival of out-of-state businesses, including Hewlett-Packard and Intel in 1976 to Corvallis and Portland, respectively. The Silicon Forest grew as other companies such as Japan's Fujitsu and Epson arrived in Oregon and smaller companies spun off from Intel, Tektronix and other established businesses. By 2005, nearly 20 percent of Oregon's economy came from the technology sector. Reflecting the shift from environmental extraction to environmental recreation, a thriving sportswear industry also developed in Oregon, building on the legacy of Jantzen (established 1916), Columbia (1937) and Nike (1984), as well as Germany-based Adidas. These companies maintained corporate offices and design departments (but not manufacturing facilities) in the Portland area. The Great Recession of 2008 slowed this economic growth — unemployment almost hit 12 percent in April 2009 — but the economic transformations continued, as many other technology, service and consumer-oriented businesses moved to the state and especially to Portland, which grew in national and international popularity as a fashionable place to work, live and play.

The large Nike campus in Beaverton anchors Oregon's thriving sportswear industry in the Portland area. (Oregon State Archives scenic photo)

In many ways, Oregon's environments made such growth possible: cheap and abundant water and electricity attracted technology firms, and Oregon's reputation as a mecca for outdoor recreation drew many other businesses and workers. Building on this reputation as a "Pacific Wonderland" — a license plate slogan originally used in 1959 and reissued in 2010 — Oregon's tourism industry grew dramatically at the end of the 20th and beginning of the 21st century. In 2003, the state legislature created the Oregon Tourism Commission, also known as Travel Oregon, to advertise the state to the nation and world: from adventure-based activities such as mountain biking and windsurfing to more easily accessible car camping at state parks and motorized boating on reservoirs created by river development projects. Other tourist attractions included Oregon's flourishing wine and craft beer industries, whale-watching and other activities at the Oregon Coast, and shopping, including the Woodburn Premium Outlets, which became a top tourist destination. The growth of tourism represented not only a significant shift in Oregon's economy, but also in the way that Oregonians perceived and interacted with their environments.

The tourism industry included the state's casinos, all owned by Oregon tribes — which, like other minorities and women, continued to assert their power and equality in the state's economy, politics and society. Following the passage of the federal Indian Gaming Regulatory Act in 1988, all nine federally-recognized tribes in Oregon built casinos, beginning with Seven Feathers Hotel and Casino Resort, owned by the Cow Creek Band of Umpqua Tribe of Indians. While paling in comparison to the revenue generated by the state-run Oregon Lottery system, these casinos not only brought tourists and their dollars to the state, but also created employment for local economies, provided funds for charitable work, contributed funds for road and highway improvements and generated revenue and services, including health and educational programs. Such transformations contributed to ongoing efforts to preserve and cultivate Native culture, society, and governance, and the 2010 census counted more than 53,000 American Indians and Alaska Natives in Oregon.

Other minority populations in Oregon also grew: nonwhites accounted for 12 percent of Oregon's population in 2010, nearly double the percentage of just 20 years before. With a population of more than 450,000 in 2010, Latinx made up the largest minority population in Oregon and played an increasingly important role in state culture and politics. In 1997, Susan Castillo became the first Latina to serve in the state legislature; five years later, she became Oregon superintendent of schools, the first Latina elected to a statewide office. Castillo joined other Oregon women winning important elected offices: Barbara Roberts served as governor from 1991–95, Ellen Rosenblum became the state's first female attorney general in 2002, and in 2015, Kate Brown became the state's second female governor and the first openly bisexual governor in the nation. Brown's ascendancy to the governorship represented in some ways the success of the gay and lesbian rights movement. In 2004, Oregon voters approved Measure 36, which defined marriage as a union between man and woman. But in 2007, the state legislature passed bills permitting same-sex couples to adopt children and prohibiting discrimination based on sexual orientation and gender identity. Measure 36 was reversed in 2015, when the U.S. Supreme Court ruled that bans on same-sex marriage were unconstitutional. Despite this victory for lesbian, gay, bisexual, transgender and queer and/or questioning (LGBTQ) people, minorities and women continued to face discrimination and prejudice in 21st century Oregon. The forces of gentrification in increasingly hip and expensive Portland, as well as neighborhoods in other Oregon cities, priced many Blacks out of their homes, and a vigorous effort in 2020 for racial justice during the Black Lives Matter movement met with a more vigorous police and federal law enforcement response, as well as disdain from some rural residents who imagined lawlessness and anarchy in Oregon's largest city.

While the state's demographics changed, Oregonians continued to grapple with the fundamental question of how they ought to interact with Oregon's environments. Even with the growth of technology, tourism and other newer sectors of Oregon's economy, many Oregonians still made their living working directly with Oregon's fields and forests. In 2015, nearly 35,000 Oregon farms and ranches occupied about 16 million acres and produced more than $5 billion in agricultural products, from the cattle, hay and wheat often grown east of the Cascades to the more specialized products of western Oregon, including filberts, hops, grass seed, landscaping plants, berries, grapes for wine and much more. Although timber production did not reach the historic high levels of the 1960s and 1970s, logging continued and even stabilized to some degree, averaging 4,250 million board-feet between 2000 and 2015, with a notable drop to 2,748 million board-feet in 2009 during the Great Recession. At the same time, the push to preserve and protect Oregon's environments also continued, driven by the state's reputation as environmentally-friendly, urban Oregonians' desire to recreate in non-urban settings, and, for some people, a deeper sense of the intrinsic value of nature. These different ways of interacting with Oregon's environments produced plenty of tension at the beginning of the 21st century. A particularly heated conflict erupted in the Klamath Basin in 2001, when the Bureau of Reclamation shut off Klamath project irrigation water in an effort to save endangered Coho salmon and two species of sucker fish valued by the Klamath Tribes. This led to a series of public and dangerous confrontations between farmers, federal officials, environmentalists, and tribal members. But the confrontations eventually gave way to conversations and, by 2010, an agreement not only to share the Klamath River's water, but also to remove four older dams to help restore fish habitat. Although the potential for conflict remained, much of the heat of the confrontation dissipated as Oregonians from diverse backgrounds tried to reconcile their different views of Oregon's environments.

The Potential for Conflict and Pragmatic Compromise

At the dawn of the 21st century, wolves returned to Oregon, sparking conversations that revealed both change and continuity in the complex relationships between Oregon's peoples and Oregon's environments. When settlers gathered at the Wolf Meetings of 1843, they created a proto-government to issue bounties on wolves and other predators, a century-long effort that eliminated grey wolves from Oregon by the mid-1940s. When wolves reappeared in northeastern Oregon in 1999, 25 years after being listed as an endangered species, they inspired a different set of responses. Oregon environmentalists rejoiced in the wolves' return, embracing the animals as a symbol of wildness and pointing to the role played by predators in the landscapes of northeastern Oregon — concepts that would have been totally foreign to the settlers who gathered at the Wolf Meetings of 1843. In contrast, cattle ranchers saw wolves as predators that destroyed valuable livestock, echoing the arguments of the Wolf Meetings. But by the 21st century, there were no serious suggestions to exterminate wolves. Instead, the Oregon Fish and Wildlife Commission created the Oregon Wolf Conservation and Management Plan (adopted in 2005; revised in 2010; updated in 2019) with the objective of both protecting livestock and recovering a "self-sustaining population" of grey wolves. Town hall meetings, legislative and court hearings, and other public fora about the wolf plan generated plenty of controversy and conflict, particularly when the Commission removed wolves from the state's endangered species list in 2016. Nevertheless, both environmentalists and ranchers insisted on the need for cooperation as they discussed new approaches to the 150-year-old question of wolves and their place in Oregon.

A sign near Elgin reflects concerns of ranchers about livestock destroyed by wolves. (Oregon State Archives scenic photo)

Such conversations and openness to cooperation will be crucial as Oregonians continue to face complex challenges in the 21st century. Economic, social, and cultural differences between rural and urban communities will continue to divide Oregonians on a variety of political issues, from tax policy, public services, and racial justice to land use planning and environmental regulations. Demographic changes will accelerate, producing even more diverse communities that will enrich the state and challenge Oregon's legacy of homogeneity. Climate change will produce unprecedented environmental transformations in every corner of the state, including rising sea levels, decreased snowpack, unpredictable precipitation, intense droughts and storms, more wildfires and floods, and a host of other dangers. These challenges surely will prompt conflict, as Oregonians confront their different and evolving ways of interacting with their environments. But such challenges will also prompt conversations that may lead to pragmatic compromise and cooperation — an important and defining characteristic of the history of Oregon's people and environments.

Further Reading

This brief survey cannot adequately address the many people, events, themes and analytical approaches that make up Oregon's history. Readers are encouraged to explore the books and websites listed below, which represent only a sampling of recent scholarship that has inspired this essay and which continues to expand and deepen as Oregon's history evolves.

Barber, Katrine. *Death of Celilo Falls*. Seattle: University of Washington Press, 2005.

Beckham, Stephen Dow. *Oregon Indians: Voices from Two Centuries*. Corvallis: Oregon State University Press, 2006.

Berg, Laura, ed. *The First Oregonians*. Portland: Oregon Council for the Humanities, 2007.

Boag, Peter. *Same-Sex Affairs: Constructing and Controlling Homosexuality in the Pacific Northwest.* Berkeley: University of California Press, 2003.

Cox, Thomas. *The Other Oregon: People, Environment, and History East of the Cascades.* Corvallis: Oregon State University Press, 2019.

Eisenberg, Ellen. *Embracing a Western Identity: Jewish Oregonians, 1849-1950.* Corvallis: Oregon State University Press, 2015.

Gamboa, Erasmo and Carolyn M. Buan, eds. Nosotros: *The Hispanic People of Oregon: Essays and Recollections*. Portland: Oregon Council for the Humanities, 1995.

Jensen, Kimberly. *Oregon's Doctor to the World: Esther Pohl Lovejoy and a Life in Activism.* Seattle: University of Washington Press, 2012.

Jetté, Melinda Marie. *At the Hearth of the Crossed Races: A French-Indian Community in Nineteenth-Century Oregon*, 1812-1859. Corvallis: Oregon State University Press, 2015.

"Oregon Women's History Consortium." http://www.oregonwomenshistory.org/.

Peterson del Mar, David. *Oregon's Promise: An Interpretive History*. Corvallis: Oregon State University Press, 2003.

Robbins, William G. *Landscapes of Conflict: The Oregon Story, 1940-2000*. Seattle: University of Washington Press, 2004.

– – –. Oregon: *This Storied Land*. Portland: Oregon Historical Society Press, 2005.

Robbins, William G. Landscapes of Promise: The Oregon Story, 1800-1940. Seattle: University of Washington Press, 1999.

Tamura, Linda. *The Hood River Issei: An Oral History of Japanese Settlers in Oregon's Hood River Valley*. Urbana: University of Illinois Press, 1993.

Taylor, Joseph E. *Persistent Callings: Seasons of Work and Identity on the Oregon Coast*. Corvallis: Oregon State University Press, 2019.

"The Oregon Encyclopedia." https://oregonencyclopedia.org/.

Whaley, Gray H. *Oregon and the Collapse of Illahee: U.S. Empire and the Transformation of an Indigenous World, 1792-1859*. Chapel Hill: University of North Carolina Press, 2010.

ACT OF CONGRESS ADMITTING OREGON INTO THE UNION

Preamble

Whereas the people of Oregon have framed, ratified and adopted a constitution of state government which is republican in form, and in conformity with the Constitution of the United States and have applied for admission into the Union on an equal footing with the other states; therefore —

1. Admission of State—Boundaries

That Oregon be, and she is hereby, received into the Union on an equal footing with the other states in all respects whatever, with the following boundaries: In order that the boundaries of the state may be known and established, it is hereby ordained and declared that the State of Oregon shall be bounded as follows, to wit: Beginning one marine league at sea, due west from the point where the forty-second parallel of north latitude intersects the same, thence northerly, at the same distance from the line of the coast lying west and opposite the state, including all islands within the jurisdiction of the United States, to a point due west and opposite the middle of the north ship channel of the Columbia River; thence easterly, to and up the middle channel of said river, and, where it is divided by islands, up the middle and widest channel thereof, to a point near Fort Walla Walla, where the forty-sixth parallel of north latitude crosses said river, thence east, on said parallel, to the middle of the main channel of the Shoshone or Snake River; thence up the middle of the main channel of said river, to the mouth of the Owyhee River; thence due south, to the parallel of latitude forty-two degrees north; thence west, along said parallel, to the place of beginning, including jurisdiction in civil and criminal cases upon the Columbia River and Snake River, concurrently with states and territories of which those rivers form a boundary in common with this state.

2. Concurrent Jurisdiction on Columbia & Other Rivers—Navigable Waters to be Common Highways

The said State of Oregon shall have concurrent jurisdiction on the Columbia and all other rivers and waters bordering on the said State of Oregon, so far as the same shall form a common boundary to said state, and any other state or states now or hereafter to be formed or bounded by the same; and said rivers and waters, and all the navigable waters of said state, shall be common highways and forever free, as well as to the inhabitants of said state as to all other citizens of the United States, without any tax, duty & impost, or toll thereof.

3. Representation in Congress

Until the next census and apportionment of representatives, the State of Oregon shall be entitled to one representative in the Congress of the United States.

4. Propositions Submitted to People of State

The following propositions be and the same are hereby offered to the said people of Oregon for their free acceptance or rejection, which, if accepted, shall be obligatory on the United States and upon the said State of Oregon, to wit:

School Lands

First, that sections numbered sixteen and thirty-six in every township of public lands in said state, and where either of said sections, or any part thereof, has been sold or otherwise disposed of, other lands equivalent thereto, and as contiguous as may be, shall be granted to said state for the use of schools.

University Lands

Second, the seventy-two sections of land shall be set apart and reserved for the use and support of a state university, to be selected by the Governor of said state, subject to the approval of the Commissioner of the General Land Office, and to be appropriated and applied in such manner as the legislature of said state may prescribe for the purpose aforesaid, but for no other purpose.

Lands For Public Buildings

Third, that ten entire sections of land, to be selected by the Governor of said state, in legal subdivisions, shall be granted to said state for the purpose of completing the public buildings, or for the erection of others at the seat of government, under the direction of the legislature thereof.

Salt Springs & Contiguous Lands

Fourth, that all salt springs within said state, not exceeding twelve in number, with six sections of land adjoining, or as contiguous as may be to each, shall be granted to said state for its use, the same to be selected by the Governor thereof within one year after the admission of said state, and when so selected, to be used or disposed of on such terms, conditions and regulations as the legislature shall direct; provided, that no salt spring or land, the right whereof is now vested in any individual or individuals, or which may be hereafter confirmed or adjudged to any individual or individuals, shall by this article be granted to said state.

Percentage on Land Sales

Fifth, that 5 per centum of the net proceeds of sales of all public lands lying within said state which shall be sold by Congress after the admission of said state into the Union, after deducting all the expenses incident to the same, shall be paid to said state, for the purpose of making public roads and internal improvements, as the legislature shall direct; provided, that the foregoing propositions, hereinbefore offered, are on the condition that the people of Oregon shall provide by an ordinance, irrevocable without the consent of the United States, that said state shall never interfere with the primary disposal of the soil within the same by the United States, or with any regulations Congress may find necessary for securing the title in said soil to bona fide purchasers thereof; and that in no case shall nonresident proprietors be taxed higher than residents.

Conditions on Which Propositions Are Offered

Sixth, and that the state shall never tax the lands or the property of the United States in said state; provided, however, that in case any of the lands herein granted to the State of Oregon have heretofore been confirmed to the Territory of Oregon for the purposes specified in this act, the amount so confirmed shall be deducted from the quantity specified in this act.

5. Residue of Territory

Until Congress shall otherwise direct, the residue of the Territory of Oregon shall be and is hereby incorporated into and made a part of the Territory of Washington.

Approved February 14, 1859. Proposition of Congress accepted by the Legislative Assembly of the State of Oregon on June 3, 1859.

100 YEARS OF OREGON'S STATE PARKS

Written by Kristine Deacon

The Oregon State Parks system celebrates its centennial in 2022, a century after Oregon Trail pioneer Sarah Helmick donated land for the first state park (**Sarah Helmick State Park**, near Monmouth). In 1913, the Oregon State Legislature created the Oregon State Highway Commission, taking the first step toward creating state parks. In 1947, the Commission created a state parks unit, which in 1963 the legislature authorized to "obtain and develop scenic and historical places." In 1989, the legislature created the Oregon Parks and Recreation Department, and in 1998, voters decided that 7.5 percent of Oregon Lottery revenue would be dedicated to state parks. Today OPRD hosts 42 million visitors a year.

The centennial of Helmick's gift is a time to celebrate the parks' many one-of-a-kind stories. The stories range from the profound, like the beach bills that preserved Oregon's coast for public use, to the wacky, like daredevil Al Faussett's 1928 boat trip over a 184-foot waterfall at Silver Falls State Park. Sublime, silly, significant – the state parks' stories are the stories of Oregon.

OPRD's mission is "to provide and protect outstanding natural, scenic, cultural, historic and recreational sites for the enjoyment and education of present and future generations." Oregon's scenic wonders and cultural artifacts, its history and its places to play are inseparable. For example, at **Oswald West State Park**, hikers can climb forest cliffs, admire seals sunning on the beach, and,sometimes, discover clumps of beeswax from a shipwrecked Spanish galleon that explored the Pacific Northwest in the 1700s. Scenery, recreation, history — the parks present them all.

OPRD divides the parks into 8 districts: Portland/Columbia Gorge, Central Oregon, Eastern Oregon, Southern Oregon, Willamette Valley and the south, central and north coasts.

Portland/Columbia Gorge:

In 1850, President Millard Fillmore appointed John B. Preston to be the Oregon Territory's first surveyor general and tasked him with creating detailed maps of the region. The next year, Preston set a cedar stake in what is now **Willamette Stone State Heritage Site** in Portland's west hills. This spot, where the Willamette meridian and the Willamette baseline cross, is the origin point for all maps and surveys of the Pacific Northwest. In 1988, the federal Department of the Interior memorialized the spot with a steel marker and a brass plaque.

"There was a lot of pot smoking and skinny dipping, but nobody was killed." That's how Governor Tom McCall summed up Vortex 1, Oregon's version of the Woodstock music festival. In the summer of 1970, Vietnam War protests were growing increasingly violent, and President Richard Nixon announced plans to attend the national American Legion convention in Portland. Anti-war activists planned to disrupt Nixon's visit. The FBI predicted rioting. One small peace activist group, The Family, offered up a free solution, that with the Governor's office's sponsorship, they could put on a rock festival during Nixon's visit. McCall's office agreed, and green-lighted a week-long festival at **Milo McIver State Park,** 30 miles southeast of Portland. Approximately 50,000 people partied along the Clackamas River, without incident. The Oregon National Guard patrolled the park with a light touch. Nixon cancelled his visit, and there were no anti-war riots. McCall later said, "It was the damnedest confrontation you'll ever see."

Also in the 1960s, Oregon turned its attention to the 187-mile Willamette River, which runs north from the Cascade Range east of Springfield into the Columbia River. For decades, industries and municipalities clustered along the Willamette River's ports dumped sewage, industrial waste, and other pollutants into the river. Trains started running through the valley in 1871, followed by roads and eventually the I-5 interstate highway, and by 1960, the Willamette River was neglected, abused and badly polluted. The **Willamette River Greenway**, a water trail strongly championed by governors Bob Straub and Tom McCall, was created to restore and protect the river. Oregon state parks, working with cities and counties bordering the river, bought, traded, rented and accepted gifts of land to create the greenway, which includes docks for boats, local and state parks and campgrounds. State parks river rangers patrol the river with boats, surveying and repairing properties.

"The $100,000 Outhouse" was the inelegant nickname for a majestic rest stop overlooking the Columbia River Highway. The highway, considered a technological jewel when construction began in 1913, winds up and around Crown Point, a cliff overlooking the Columbia Gorge. Engineers chose Crown Point as the site for Vista House, a three-floor, octagonal building under a dome roof with public restrooms. Queen Marie of Romania visited Vista House on November 4, 1926. As she and her lady-in-waiting privately used the basement rest-room, a crowd of press and dignitaries waited in the corridor when an Oregonian photographer called out, "Listen for it, folks! A royal flush!" The build-ing, now a museum, is a popular observation point in the **Crown Point State Scenic Corridor**.

Vista House, with spectacular views of the Columbia River Gorge, has outlasted its early critics. (Oregon State Archives scenic photo)

Heading east, **White River Falls State Park** near Maupin is all about water; its 90-foot waterfall feeds into a now-deserted hydropower plant. The plant channeled the waterfall into a turbine-filled powerhouse which, from 1910 to 1960, provided electrical power to Wasco and Sherman counties. Originally built in 1902, the facility provided power for the Wasco Warehouse Milling Company's flour mills in The Dalles. The company built a small grist mill near the falls, along with four company houses for workers. The massive rock-and-concrete structure, the turbines and remnants of the grist mill are still there.

A message scratched into a rock wall inside of the Mosier Twin Tunnels, east of Hood River on the **Historic Columbia River Highway State Trail,** tells the story of early automobile-era transportation. The trail is three individual paved paths along parts of the historic Columbia River Highway, the first road to connect Portland with The Dalles. Today, hikers and bicyclists can travel though the Mosier Twin Tunnels, where a blizzard trapped 10 cars full of travelers on November 19, 1921. The next day the travelers, except for Charlie Sadilek and E.B. Martin, hiked through the snow to Mosier, where they stayed until a barge could take them and their cars to Portland. Sadilek, who was headed for Portland after hunting for geese, and Martin didn't want to leave their cars, so they stayed in the tunnel for 8 days, living on Sadilek's geese, Martin's apples and the other travelers' whiskey. The hardy pair etched "Snowbound, Nov.

19 to 27 – 1921, Chas. J. Sadilek, E.B. Martin" before being rescued and headed to Portland.

Central Oregon:

Oregon's State Parks, like all of Oregon, sit on the homelands of Native peoples, and many of the parks invite visitors to appreciate and learn about how different Native peoples thrived in diverse landscapes. **Fort Rock State Natural Area,** an ancient volcanic crater, sprawls in the high desert of south central Oregon. From a distance it looks like a military fort. Ancestors of the Klamath and Northern Paiute people used this site, leaving behind sandals made of sagebrush bark; some of those sandals date to almost 11,000 years old, mak-ing them the oldest footwear in the world.

Another example of the long presence and deep complexity of Native cultures can be seen at **The Cove Palisades State Park**, near Madras. The Crooked River Petroglyph, an 80-ton sandstone boulder, is covered with intricate symbols and drawings, etched into the rock by unknown tribes. When the Round Butte Dam was completed in 1965 creating Lake Billy Chinook reservoir, it looked like the reservoir's water would submerge the petroglyph. Instead, park staff moved the boulder to higher ground, where its message endures and waits to be decoded.

Eastern Oregon:

Travelers crossing the Oregon Trail in oxen-drawn wagons in the 1800s were happy to stop at the site of **Emigrant Springs State Heritage Area** near Meacham. They were able to refresh their dwindling water supplies and finally relax under shade trees. The focal point of the park is an Oregon Trail memorial, which President Warren G. Harding dedicated on July 3, 1923. Thousands of people crammed into the park to see the president. Members of the Cayuse, Umatilla and Walla Walla tribes marched in the Meacham parade, and the Cayuse tribe adopted President Harding and first lady Florence Harding.

Iwetemlaykin State Heritage Site near Joseph, Oregon, is part of the ancestral homeland of the Nez Perce Tribe and is sacred land to the Confederated Tribes of the Colville Reservation and the Confederated Tribes of the Umatilla Indian Reservation.

After years of fighting and negotiations, the federal government sent troops, led by General O.O. Howard, to eject members of the Nimi'ipuu or Nez Perce tribes, from the Wallowa Valley in the northeastern corner of Oregon in 1887. Heinmot Tooyalakekt, widely known as Chief Joseph, led his band of approximately 750 Nez Perce men, women and children on a daring escape. For more than three months, the Nez Perce evaded the army, only to surrender less than 40 miles from the Canada border on October 5, 1887.

Farther south, **Lake Owyhee State Park** sits below Owyhee Dam, which was the tallest dam in the world from its completion in 1932 until 1934. Lake Owyhee is named for three Hawaiian fur trappers who disappeared in 1811 while exploring the region; "Owyhee" is a phonetic spelling of "Hawaii." The dam workers' residential housing was turned into a Civilian Conservation Corps camp during the Great Depression. In 1942, the federal government turned the camp into a detention center for Japanese-Americans, interned in wartime concentration camps in Idaho and Colorado. The detainees were sent to the area with their families to harvest crops. The area surrounding Lake Owyhee State Park was the center of a thriving community of Basque immigrants from the 1880s to the 1940s. Most Basque immigrants to Oregon initially herded sheep or worked in the cattle industry until after World War II, when many families moved to Oregon cities.

The historic Frenchglen Hotel continues to welcome visitors to its remote southeast Oregon location. (Oregon State Archives scenic photo)

In the southeastern Oregon high desert, the **Frenchglen Hotel State Heritage Site** and the **Pete French Round Barn State Heritage Site** are reminders of the period in Oregon's history when Euro-American cowboys and Mexican vaqueros ran the cattle industry, and homesteaders fought, killed and died for water rights.

Pete French, working in California for his future father-in-law, Hugh Glenn, drove a herd of cattle to southeastern Oregon in 1872. Assisted by vaqueros from California, French built an empire around Harney Lake and Malheur Lake. His properties included a large, round, wood barn – actually, a roofed paddock – where cowboys could train horses in the winter. In the process of dominating Harney County, French alienated many of his neighbors, including Ed Oliver. Oliver lived in a homestead on the bank of Malheur Lake, land that French claimed. After many lawsuits, Oliver shot and killed French the day after Christmas, 1897. Today, the Round Barn is open to visitors.

The Frenchglen Hotel, 35 miles south of the barn, is named for both Pete French and Hugh Glenn. The hotel was built in 1924 in dirt so hard that workers used dynamite to create holes so that they could plant trees to shade the two-story hotel. Park visitors can rent rooms and dine there in the summer.

North of the Frenchglen Hotel, **Kam Wah Chung State Heritage Site**, a small stone building, housed a Chinese grocery store, health clinic, temple, and social club for Chinese immigrants from about 1870 to 1948. In 1880, more than 2,000 Chinese immigrants lived in Grant County, drawn by gold mines and railroad jobs. Partners Lung On, an entrepreneur, and physician Ing "Doc" Hay lived and worked in the John Day building, which was also a boarding house for Chinese miners. The building, still stuffed with medicine containers, red-tasseled chandeliers, clothes, furniture, and games, is much as it was when Hay died in 1948. Its collection of artifacts and archives is one of the most complete records in the United States of Chinese herbal medicine and the pioneer life and culture of Chinese immigrants.

Nearby, the **Sumpter Valley Dredge State Heritage Site** in Sumpter bears witness to the end of Oregon's gold rush. When hard rock gold mining in the region became less profitable, miners turned to digging up rivers to get gold. From 1935 to 1954, the dredge, a three-level wood boat, chewed its way through the Powder River, scooping up rocks and sand. Massive iron buckets moved the riverbed into the dredge, where, using water and sluices, workers separated gold from the rocks, then dumped the rocks back into the river. The overwhelming environmental damage the process caused is still visible today.

Southern Oregon:

On the west side of the Cascade Range, the **Wolf Creek Inn State Heritage Site** is a counterpart to the Frenchglen Hotel. Built around 1883, it served travelers and stagecoach passengers passing through the Rogue River Valley. Today, it still rents hotel rooms and serves meals to visitors. Author Jack London stayed at the inn in 1911 while finishing his fifteenth novel, *Valley of the Moon*. Rumor has it that movie star Clark Gable hid out there when he needed a break from Hollywood. Nestled into the densely forested mountains north of Grants Pass, the hotel and restaurant retain the feel of a bygone era. The first floor lobby includes separate men's and women's parlors and a dining room. A ballroom takes up much of the second floor, and the attic once provided budget bunk lodging. In the late 1880s, cowboys who couldn't afford a room could sleep in the attic for 10 cents a night. They often would jam their spurs into the wooden rafters, to anchor themselves in place; their spur marks are still visible.

"Kids, come on down from that wheel skidder right now!" Visitors hearing that were most likely visiting **Collier Memorial State Park**, an outdoor museum of logging equipment. North of Chiloquin, the park offers camping spaces and freshwater fishing, and displays the biggest collection of historic logging equipment in the state. The outdoor and indoor museums contain artifacts from the first days of logging to modern day, showing the evolution from axes and oxen to timber tug boats and trains. Its collection of chain saws is a perennial crowd pleaser. Visitors can admire the antique equipment displayed outside.

Willamette Valley:

Erratic Rock State Park near McMinnville bears witness to some of the geologic forces that shaped Oregon's landscape. During the Ice Age, icebergs floated down the Columbia River, flooding the Willamette Valley. One of those floods swept up a forty-ton boulder from the northern Rocky Mountains, and deposited it in that spot. Sitting in solitary splendor, the rock is a testament to the awesome power of climate change.

Not far from Erratic Rock, **Fort Yamhill State Heritage Area** recalls a time of major social change – the United States' wars against indigenous peoples. The first people known to live in the area were of the Yamhelas Indian Tribe, part of the Kalapooian family. By 1856, thousands of Native Americans in the Willamette Valley had died of diseases introduced by white settlers, and that year, Congress forced 27 tribes – about 2,000 people – into the Grand Ronde Agency Coastal Reservation. That March, the U.S. Army began building Fort Yamhill to protect and control Indians on the reservation, and to be a buffer between the Indians and white settlers. The army dispatched young Lieutenant Philip Sheridan to oversee construction of the fort; Sheridan served there until leaving to lead U.S. Army troops in the Civil War.

The fort included a sentry box, barracks, a hospital, general store, blacksmith shop and a block house.

The army abandoned the fort in 1866. Its block house was moved to the Valley Junction area where it was used as a jail, and later moved about 30 miles east to Dayton. The building that had housed the officers' quarters was also moved but has been returned to its original site. Archaeologists have uncovered the sandstone foundations of most of the fort's buildings, providing a clear picture of the layout of a pre-Civil War military base.

In the 1840s, Euro-American emigrants gathered at what is now **Champoeg State Heritage Center** near Newberg to create Oregon's first formal government. On May 2, 1843, they voted, 52-50, to form a provisional government and to petition the federal government for support. Today, several buildings, including the Historic Butteville Store and a museum, give visitors a feel for the early pioneers' lives. A stone obelisk lists the names of the 52 men who voted to create a provisional government.

Oregon's largest state park, **Silver Falls State Park**, near Salem, is on land that was originally inhabited by Kalapooian Indians, whom the federal government forced to move to the Grand Ronde Agency Coastal Reservation in 1856. Loggers then heavily harvested the forested land, and wildfires further damaged the watershed. The area became a state park in 1933, during the Great Depression. The federal government created a Civilian Conservation Corps camp at the park, where workers planted trees, cleared trails and built a lodge. Federal Arts Project workers handcrafted myrtlewood furniture for the lodge, still in use today.

Lower South Falls is one of many dramatic waterfalls along the Trail of Ten Falls at Silver Falls State Park. (Oregon State Archives scenic photo)

Looking at the ten waterfalls at the park, few people would think, "I'd like to ride a tiny canvas boat over the biggest waterfall, with no helmet," but exhibitionist Al Faussett thought it was a dandy idea. Faussett, bored with being a logger, had made a major mid-life career change and became a professional daredevil, specializing in plunging over waterfalls. Thousands of spectators came to the South Falls to watch him take the plunge on July 1, 1928. He ended up in the hospital but survived his trip over the South Falls in a 12-foot boat stuffed with rubber inner tubes.

The twenty-one acres surrounding the Oregon State Capitol in Salem have been a state park since 2006. Park rangers guide tours of **Oregon State Capitol State Park**, which consist of Willson Park to the west of the building and Capitol Park, to the east. The first capitol burned in 1855. When the second capitol burned in 1935, clean-up crews simply pushed the destroyed building's stone columns into nearby Mill Creek. Today, fragments of columns are displayed on the grounds of the third capitol, built in 1936.

The grounds display fountains, carvings, and other art. These works narrate a story of Oregon's past that omits the history of Native and non-white peoples in favor of a simplified Euro-American-centric history: art includes copies of the bronze statues which represent Oregon in Congress' National Statuary Hall, in Washington, D.C.; Methodist minister Jason Lee's statue clutches a Bible and a petition to Congress; and fur trader John McLoughlin's image holds a beaver top hat, a nod to the state's beaver trade. Thirty-six stone plaques, one for each of Oregon's counties, list the county seats. The landscaping includes the Moon Tree, a Douglas Fir grown from a seed taken to the moon and back on Apollo 14 in 1971.

Farther down the Willamette Valley, halfway between Albany and Eugene, **Thompson's Mills State Heritage Site** opened for business the year before Oregon became a state and operated until 2004. German immigrants Martin and Sophia Thompson bought the mill in 1891, and three generations of the Thompson family operated the enterprise. The mill building grew, rather haphazardly, as the family adapted the business to changing times, expanding from milling flour for local farmers to buying wheat and selling flour throughout the state, and eventually switching to producing animal feed. The mill operated on power generated from its private hydropower plant on the Calapooia River, which is channeled through a concrete tunnel under the main building. In its final years of commercial operation, the mill, having difficulty making a profit from animal feed, instead sold the power it generated to a local utility. The twenty-acre park includes the six-floor mill building, World-War I-era silos, the millkeeper's 1906 Queen Anne family home and outbuildings.

South, central and north coasts:

Oregon's 363-mile coast is dotted with lighthouses, shipwrecks and maritime history. In 1913, Oregon Governor Oswald West and the Oregon legislature designated all of the coast's "wet sand" areas a state highway, which means they belonged to the public, not individuals. In 1967, Governor Tom McCall and the legislature expanded public ownership of the coast to include areas from the low tide mark to sixteen vertical feet above it.

The coast lighthouses represent a past when most goods, explorers, and soldiers – including, in 1852, young army captain, and future United States president, Ulysses S. Grant – came to Oregon by ships – or were destroyed trying. The oldest lighthouse, at **Cape Blanco State Park**, stands in tribute to working mothers everywhere. Mabel Bretherton, widowed mother of three children under the age of 10, became Oregon's first female lighthouse keeper there in 1903. Head up the coast to **Umpqua Lighthouse State Park** and check out its lighthouse; head north again to **Heceta Head Lighthouse State Scenic Viewpoint** and watch out for a sense of déjà vu. The U.S. Lighthouse Board built Heceta Head in 1892, and then to save money,

used the same architectural plans to build the Umpqua River Lighthouse two years later.

Just north of Florence sits Oregon's most macabre picnic spot, **Darlingtonia State Natural Site**. The only Oregon state park property dedicated to preserving a single plant species, the bog is filled with Darlingtonia californica, also known as "the cobra lily." The carnivorous beauty uses its sweet nectar to lure insects into its bright yellow flowers … then eats them. A wooden boardwalk winds its way through thickets of the three-foot tall plants. United States botanist John Torrey named the plant for his botany professor William Darlington, who died before he saw his namesake plant.

The fortified Base End Station is one of numerous historic buildings at Fort Stevens State Park. (Oregon State Archives scenic photo)

At Oregon's northern tip, **Fort Stevens State Park** preserves 84 years of military history. When built at the end of the Civil War, the fort had a moat and drawbridge to protect it from attackers. Fort Stevens was an active military installation until 1947; during World War II, 2,500 men were stationed there. On June 21, 1942, a Japanese submarine fired 17 shells at the coastal fort, making Fort Stevens the only military base in the lower 48 states to be attacked during World War II. The Japanese bombs didn't kill anyone and caused very little damage. Today, visitors can check out the park's military history museum, walk on its concrete gun batteries and take a guided underground tour of its bunkers.

October 25, 1906, was a blustery day when the British cargo ship Peter Iredale approached the mouth of the Columbia River, just south of Fort Stevens. The four-masted British ship was coming in empty to Portland from Acapulco through a dark, thick mist, a rising tide and strong westerly winds. It ran aground on the Clatsop Spit and got stuck in the sand. Captain H. Lawrence ordered the crew to abandon ship. A lifeboat rescued all 27 sailors and two stowaways, but the ship was well and truly stuck, and all attempts to haul it back out to sea failed. The Peter Iredale remains mired on the beach, where visitors can climb on what is left of the wreck.

A century after Sarah Helmick donated land for a state park, the Oregon Parks and Recreation Department's role has expanded. Rangers at Thompson's Mills show children how to turn grain into flour. River rangers patrol waterways by boat, while at **Wallowa Lake State Park** near Joseph, rangers lead tours on snowshoes. The **Depoe Bay Whale Watching Center** broadcasts live video streams of migrating gray whales, so Oregonians anywhere in the state can watch whales' seasonal travels. At the **Rough and Ready Botanical Wayside** in the Siskiyou Mountains, protected rare, delicate plants thrive in delicate soil. And at **Smith Rock State Park** near Redmond, rock climbers from around the world gather to scale its pinnacles and spires. As it provides and protects the state's natural, scenic, cultural, historic and recreational sites, Oregon state parks enters its second century involved in every aspect of Oregon.

Kristine Deacon is a graduate of the University of Oregon School of Journalism and was a journalist at the Bend Bulletin and the Statesman-Journal, in Salem, before becoming a Pacific Northwest historian.

CHRONOLOGICAL HISTORY OF OREGON

Oregon's history contains many more significant dates than space will permit, but this list may prove helpful to those embarking on a study of the state.

Oregon Country 1543–1847

1543—Bartolome Ferrelo sails north as far as the southwest coast of Oregon

1565—Manila Galleon trade route opens across North Pacific

1579—Sir Francis Drake allegedly visits Oregon

1603—Martin d-Aguilar sails along the Pacific Coast, sighting and naming Cape Blanco and reaching Coos Bay and possibly sighting the Columbia River

1707—*San Francisco Xavier* probably wrecks at Nehalem

1738—Pierre Gaultier de la Verendrye leads first expedition into Oregon

1765—First use of word "Ouragon" in Maj. Robert Rogers' petition to explore American West

1774—Spanish explorer Capt. Juan Perez sails to Northwest Coast

1775—Capt. Bruno Heceta sees mouth of Columbia River and names it Rio San Roque

1775–1780—First smallpox outbreak among Oregon's indigenous people

1778—Capt. James Cook makes landfall at Cape Foulweather and discovers fur wealth of Northwest Coast

1788—Capt. Robert Gray trades with tribes in Tillamook Bay; Markus Lopius, Black African traveling with Gray, probably killed at Tillamook

1792—Capt. Robert Gray enters and names the Columbia River; Capt. George Vancouver expedition charts Columbia estuary; Lt. William E. Broughton names Mount Hood after British naval officer Alexander Arthur Hood

1801–1802—Second smallpox outbreak among Oregon's Tribes

1803—Louisiana Purchase extends United States to Rocky Mountains

1804—President Thomas Jefferson dispatches Lewis and Clark Expedition

1805—Lewis and Clark Expedition explores lower Snake and Columbia Rivers and establishes Fort Clatsop

1806—Lewis and Clark Expedition returns to the United States

1811—John Jacob Astor's Pacific Fur Company establishes Fort Astoria

1812—Overland Astorians discover South Pass in Wyoming, later route of Oregon Trail

1813—North West Company, a British enterprise, purchases Fort Astoria and names it Fort George

1814—First white woman to arrive in Oregon County, Jane Barnes, arrives at Fort George on North West Company's ship; First domestic livestock imported by sea from California

1817—William Cullen Bryant refers to "Oregon" in poem "Thanatopsis"

1818—North West Company establishes Fort Nez Perce; James Biddle and John Prevost assert United States interests in Oregon; United States and Great Britain agree to "joint occupancy" of Oregon

1819—Adams-Onis Treaty cedes Spain's discovery rights north of 42 degrees to the U.S.

1821—Hudson's Bay Company subsumes North West Company

1824—U.S. and Russia agree to 50 degrees latitude as southern boundary of Russian interests; Dr. John McLoughlin begins long tenure as Chief Factor for Hudson's Bay Company

1825—Workmen build Fort Vancouver on Columbia River

1827—First sawmill begins cutting lumber near Fort Vancouver

1828—Jedediah Smith's party travels overland from California; First grist mill starts making flour at Fort Vancouver

1829—Dr. John McLoughlin establishes claim at Willamette Falls, later Oregon City

1830—Fever pandemic begins calamitous death toll of tribes

1832—Newspapers report four Indians from Pacific Northwest in St. Louis seeking missionaries; Capt. B. L. E. Bonneville arrives overland to trap and trade for furs on Columbia Plateau; Hudson's Bay Company establishes Fort Umpqua at Elkton

1833—First school opens at Fort Vancouver; First lumber exports by Hudson's Bay Company to China

1834—Jason Lee's party establishes Methodist Mission near Wheatland

1836—First steamship *Beaver* begins service for Hudson's Bay Company on the Columbia River; Lt. William Slacum mounts reconnaissance of western Oregon; Whitman-Spalding mission party arrives overland via Oregon Trail; Washington Irving publishes *Astoria*

1838—Willamette Cattle Company drives livestock overland from California; Priests Blanchet and Demers arrive overland from Canada and celebrate first Catholic mass in the Pacific Northwest

1839—Catholics establish mission at St. Paul; First printing press in the Northwest brought to Lapwai (now Idaho) from Honolulu and used to print a Nez Perce primer, the first book produced in the Pacific Northwest

1841—Ewing Young's death leads to public meetings; First Catholic boys' school founded at Saint Paul; First ship, *Star of Oregon,* built by settlers

1842—Methodist missionaries found the Oregon Institute in Salem, a predecessor to Willamette University; First brick building, a house, erected by George Gay in Polk County

1843—First large migration of over 900 immigrants arrives via Oregon Trail; Lt. John C. Fremont mounts reconnaissance of Oregon Trail; "Wolf Meetings" lead to Provisional Government; Oregonians submit petition to Senate seeking U.S. jurisdiction

1844—First town plat surveyed at Oregon City; First Catholic girls' school founded at Saint Paul; Acts to prohibit slavery and exclude blacks and mulattoes from Oregon Territory were passed and the "Lash Law" enacted requiring Blacks – "be they free or slave – be whipped twice a year until he or she shall quit the territory"

1845—Meek Cutoff opens as alleged short cut to Oregon Trail; Estimated 3,000 overland immigrants arrive; Oregonians petition Congress for federal services; First Provisional governor, George Abernethy, elected; Francis Pettygrove and A. L. Lovejoy name Portland and commence plat of city

1846—Barlow Road opens as toll route; Applegate Trail, alternative to Oregon Trail, opens; Oregon Treaty affirms U.S. sovereignty to Pacific Northwest; First newspaper on the west coast, *Oregon Spectator,* founded in Oregon City

1847—First Indian war, the Cayuse War begins at Waiilatpu (also known as the Witman Massacre); First postmaster, John Shively, named at Astoria; First English book, a *Blue Back Speller,* printed in Oregon City

Oregon Territory 1848–1858

1848—Joseph Meek carries petition east seeking federal "patronage"; Organic Act creates Oregon Territory; James Marshall discovers gold in California; First U.S. Customs Service office opens in Astoria

1849—First territorial governor, Joseph Lane, assumes duties; First Mounted Riflemen of U.S. Army arrive overland; First "Beaver" gold coins minted in Oregon City

1850—Congress passes Oregon Donation Land Act; First capital punishment—five Cayuse are hanged in Oregon City; Investors start printing *The Oregonian* in Portland

1851—First General Land Office opens in Oregon City; Willamette Valley Treaty Commission negotiates treaties; Teamsters discover gold in Rogue River Valley; Anson Dart convenes Tansy Point Treaty Council at mouth of Columbia River; First U.S. Army post, Fort Orford, built at Port Orford; U.S. Coast Survey begins charting shoreline; First Chinese immigrant, Mr. Sung Sung establishes the Sung boarding house and restaurant on Portland's Second Avenue

1852—U.S. Army establishes Fort Dalles on Oregon Trail; Congress names Salem capital of Oregon Territory

1853—Territorial legislature adopts Oregon law code; U.S. Army establishes Fort Lane in Rogue River Valley; Territorial legislature publishes *Oregon Archives*; Congress funds Scottsburg-Myrtle Creek Wagon Road; Cow Creek and Rogue River Tribes negotiate treaties with U.S.; Oregon Institute becomes Willamette University; Congress carves Washington Territory out of Oregon Territory; First coal exports begin on southwest Oregon coast; The Typographical Society, Oregon's first labor union is organized

1854—Volunteers massacre Coquille Indians; Legislature prohibits sale of ardent spirits, arms and ammunition to tribes; Legislature bars testimony of "Negroes, mulattoes, and Indians, or persons one half or more of Indian blood" in proceedings involving a white person

1855—Umatilla, Nez Perce, Warm Springs and Walla Walla tribes sign treaties reserving land and rights to food resources; Rogue River Indian War and Yakima Indian War begin; President James Buchanan creates Siletz Reservation; Territorial Capitol burns in Salem

1856—U.S. Army establishes Forts Umpqua, Hoskins and Yamhill; President James Buchanan creates Grand Ronde Reservation; U.S. Army orders closure of settlement east of Cascades because of warfare with tribes

1857—Constitutional Convention meets in Salem; Draft constitution bans slavery and bars African-Americans from residency and decides that voting will be for white male citizens only; Aaron Meier and Emil Frank found Meier & Frank Department Store

1858—First election selects state officials

State of Oregon 1859–Present

1859—Congress grants Oregon statehood on February 14, becoming only state admitted to Union with exclusion laws in their constitution; First bank established by Ladd & Tilton in Portland; First elected governor of state, John Whiteaker, inaugurated

1860—Oregon Steam Navigation Company begins service; First daily stage operates between Portland and Sacramento

1861—First Oregon State Fair held at Oregon City

1862—Congress passes Homestead Act; First Oregon Cavalry raises six companies; Gold Rush begins in Blue Mountains; First portage railroad completed at Cascades; Laws passed banning interracial marriages and requiring Blacks, Chinese, Hawaiians (Kanakas) and Mulattos to pay annual $5 tax – those not able to pay required to perform road maintenance

1863—U.S. Army establishes Fort Klamath

1864—Treaty creates Klamath Reservation; Telegraph line connects Portland-Sacramento; Popular vote approves Salem as state capital

1865—Long Tom Rebellion confirms pro-southern sympathies

1866—First lighthouse, Cape Arago, illuminates light signal; Married Women's Property Act protects women's rights

1867—U.S. Army establishes Fort Harney; first Chinese temple or "Joss House" was built at corner of Portland's Oak St. and SW 2nd Ave.

1868—Oregon State Agricultural College opens (later becomes Oregon State University)

Numerous grange building, such as this one east of Prineville, were constructed in Oregon in the decades after 1873. (Oregon State Archives scenic photo)

1869—Direct export of wheat to Europe begins

1870—First woman suffrage organizations form in Albany and Salem; Despite failing in Oregon election, U.S. Constitution adds 15th Amendment, granting African-American men the right to vote

1871—Susan B. Anthony and Abigail Scott Duniway advocate women's rights in Pacific Northwest; Duniway launches women's rights newspaper *The New Northwest*

1872—Oregon & California Railroad completes line to Roseburg; Modoc Indian War begins

1873—Oregon Patrons of Husbandry (Grange) forms chapters; Modoc tribesmen face trial and execution at Fort Klamath; Oregon Pioneer Association forms; Great fire destroys much of downtown Portland; Oregon State Equal Suffrage Association formed

1875—First U.S. Life-Saving Service station opens near Coos Bay

1876—University of Oregon opens; Robert D. Hume builds salmon cannery on Rogue River

1877—Nez Perce Indian War involves Chief Joseph's band; Congress passes Desert Land Act

1878—High schools authorized for districts with 1,000 students; Bannock-Paiute Indian War sweeps into southeastern Oregon; Some women gain right to vote in school elections

1879—BIA Indian Training School opens in Forest Grove, third boarding school of its type, designed to assimilate tribal children into white culture and teach vocational skills

1880—Great Gale snow and wind storm devastates parts of Oregon and Washington; O. R. & N. Company begins railroad through Gorge; first person/woman of Japanese ancestry settles in Oregon, near Gresham

1882—Normal schools open in Monmouth, Ashland and Drain to train teachers

1883—O. R. & N. Company railroad reaches Umatilla, providing transcontinental links

1884—Oregon Short Line railroad extends to Huntington

1885—Mary Leonard first female lawyer in Oregon; Bureau of Indian Affairs moves Forest Grove boarding school to Salem, later renamed Chemawa Indian School

1886—Oregon Supreme Court admits Oregon's first female lawyer, Mary Gysin Leonard, to the state bar; Chief Joseph's Nez Perce band locates on Colville Reservation

1887—Locals rob and massacre 34 Chinese gold miners at Deep Creek in Hells Canyon; General Allotment Act assaults tribal lands on reservations; Cranberry harvests begin; First state to make Labor Day a holiday

1888—First Agricultural Experiment Station opens at Corvallis

1890—Congress passes Oregon Indian Depredation Claims Act; Chinese Consolidated Benevolent Association founded

1891—Congress passes Forest Reserve Act

1892—Congress authorizes Columbia River Lightship No. 50

1894—Mazama Club forms to promote outdoor adventure

1896—Workmen complete Cascade Locks

1897—Holdup of 1897 blocks state legislature

1898—Oregon Historical Society receives charter

1900—Workmen complete Yamhill River Locks

1902—Crater Lake National Park opens; Congress passes Federal Reclamation Act; Voters amend Constitution for Initiative and Referendum, allowing citizens to propose new laws and constitutional amendments

1903—Heppner Flood kills 225 people; First *Voters' Pamphlet* published

1904—Direct primary law passes; First African-American, George Hardin, named officer in Portland Police Bureau

1905—Lewis and Clark Centennial Exposition commemorates the 100th anniversary of the Lewis and Clark Expedition; Klamath Irrigation Project begins; Oregon land fraud trials pursue wrongdoers

1906—City home rule law approved, allowing extensive city lawmaking authority; Indictment by grand jury law approved; Taxes begin on telephone, telegraph and railroads; First meeting of Association of Oregon Counties

1907—President Theodore Roosevelt creates "Midnight Reserves," setting aside millions of acres of national forests

1908—Constitution amended for Recall provision; First woman, Lola Baldwin, named head of Women's Division, Portland Police

1909—State's Central Fish Hatchery opens at Bonneville; Oregon Caves National Monument created; Pendleton Round-Up begins; Congress passes Enlarged Homestead Act; Carolyn B. Shelton served as acting governor when Governor Chamberlain resigned to be sworn in as U.S. Senator. She served in this capacity for 48 hours, becoming Oregon's first female governor

1910—Three-fourths verdict in civil cases approved; Employers' Liability Act approved

1911—Columbia River Gorge Highway construction begins; First U.S. primary elections held in Oregon; Oregon Trunk Railroad completes line to Bend

1912—Women's suffrage approved; Prohibition of private convict labor approved; Eight-hour day on public works approved; First U.S. minimum wage law approved

Construction of the Historic Columbia River Highway began in 1911. The highway was dedicated in 1916. (Oregon State Archives scenic photo)

1913—Presidential preference primary law approved; Governor Oswald West declares beaches open to public

1914—Death penalty abolished; Prohibition approved; Eight-hour day approved for women; Congress revests O & C Railroad land grant; Marian B. Towne elected as first woman to serve in Oregon's House of Representatives; Legislature requires publication of *Oregon Blue Book*

1915—Kathryn Clarke wins Douglas County special election to serve as first woman in the Oregon Senate

1916—Workmen complete Celilo Locks and Canal; Congress passes Stock-Raising Homestead Act

1917—U.S. Army Spruce Production Division begins logging

1918—Influenza pandemic kills hundreds; Emergency Fleet Corporation contracts for ships; Oregonians enlist to serve in World War I

1919—First state gasoline tax in U.S. authorized to fund highways

1920—Death penalty reinstated; Oregon League of Women Voters founded

1921—Ku Klux Klan organizes chapters; Hurricane hits Oregon and Washington; ballot measure allowing women to serve as jurors passes

1922—First state park opened by Oregon Highway Commission south of Monmouth, named for Sarah Helmick; Compulsory School Act approved, outlawing private and parochial schools and requiring children aged 8 to 18 to attend public school; First African-American woman, Beatrice Cannady, graduates from Lewis & Clark Law School; Japanese-American Citizens' League founded

1923—Alien Land Law approved, preventing first generation Japanese-Americans from owning or leasing land; Alien Business Restriction Law approved, denying business licenses to first generation Japanese-Americans; Prohibition of sectarian garb in schools approved

1924—Compulsory School Act held unconstitutional; Congress extends citizenship to Native Americans; Mary Jane Spurlin first female judge in Oregon; Clarke-McNary Act aids federal-state forest fire protection

1925—State parks and waysides authorized; League of Oregon Cities founded

1926—Fishwheels abolished; Astor Column completed; Exclusion of African-Americans clause removed from Constitution

1927—State Constitution amended to remove voting restrictions against African and Chinese Americans

1929—State Park Commission created

1930—Vale Irrigation Project begins water delivery; First Oregon woman judge, Mary Jane Spurlin, appointed to Multnomah County District Court

1933—Tillamook Burn destroys 350,000 acres of old growth timber; Civilian Conservation Corps and Works Projects Administration start projects

1934—First grazing district under Taylor Grazing Act forms at Bonanza

1935—Congress authorizes Bonneville Dam; Fire destroys State Capitol

1936—Bandon Fire destroys town, 11 residents die; Work completed on five major bridges on Highway 101; First Oregon woman Nan Wood Honeyman elected to U.S. House of Representatives

1937—President Franklin D. Roosevelt dedicates Timberline Lodge and Bonneville Dam; Gas chamber built at Oregon State Penitentiary for capital punishment; Oregon Shakespeare Festival forms in Ashland; Congress creates Bonneville Power Administration; Bankhead-Jones Act authorizes buyout of homesteaders

1938—544 Report approved for Willamette River flood control; Bonneville Dam completed

1939—Second Tillamook Burn destroys 310,000 forest acres; State capitol completed in Salem

1941—Oregonians enlist to serve in World War II

1942—Executive Order 9066 authorizes removal of Japanese-Americans to internment camps; Japanese submarine shells Fort Stevens; Siskiyou National Forest firebombed by Japanese; U.S. Army builds Camp Adair and Camp Abbot; U.S. Navy builds Tillamook and Tongue Point Naval Air Stations; Vanport founded to house wartime workers

1945—Six Oregonians die in explosion of Japanese incendiary balloon near Bly; Third Tillamook Burn destroys 125,000 forest acres; Supplement to 1923 Alien Land Law passes

1946—Portland State University (PSU) founded; Rural School Law encourages consolidation of districts

1947—Plane crash kills Governor Snell, Secretary of State Farrell, and others

1948—Columbia River Flood destroys Vanport; Vollum and Murdock found Tektronix

1949—State Department of Forestry begins replanting Tillamook Burn; Fair Labor Practices Commission established; State Supreme Court invalidates 1923 and 1945 Alien Land acts; First woman, Dorothy McCullough Lee, elected Portland mayor

1951—Law prohibiting interracial marriges repealed; Fourth Tillamook Burn destroys 130,000 forest acres

1952—Constitution amended to provide for equal representation in state legislature

1953—Public Accommodations Law prohibits racial discrimination by businesses

1954—Congress terminates Western Oregon tribes; Supreme Court upholds *Brown v. Board of Education of Topeka*, abolishing segregated schools

1956—Congress authorizes Interstate freeway system; Congress terminates Klamath Tribe

1957—Oregon Fair Housing Act passes

1959—Oregon ratifies 15th Amendment to the U.S. Constitution, granting African-American men the right to vote, 89 years after its adoption

1960—Congress passes Multiple Use-Sustained Yield Act for management of national forests; Mercedes Deiz first African American female lawyer in Oregon; First female U.S. Senator from Oregon, Maurine Neuberger, elected

1962—Columbus Day Storm causes major damage in Western Oregon; Oregon State University football player, Terry Baker, (QB) becomes state's first Heisman Trophy winner

1964—Death penalty abolished; National Civil Rights Act outlaws unequal voter registation requirements and racial segregation in schools, the workplace and public places

1965—Congress passes Voting Rights Act, prohibiting qualifications or prerequisites to voting

1966—Workmen complete Astoria-Megler Bridge spanning Columbia River estuary; I-5 affords non-stop driving through Oregon

1967—Beach Bill approved, ensuring public access to all of Oregon's coastal beaches; Racial tensions escalate into riots in Portland

1969—Federal District Court in *Sohappy v. Smith* affirms tribal treaty fishing rights in Columbia River

1971—Bottle Bill approved; Congress confirms Burns Paiute Reservation

1973—Statewide major land use planning legislation approved; Public Meetings Law approved; Public Records Law for access approved; Tillamook State Forest created; Congress approves Endangered Species Act; Oregon ratifies U.S. Equal Rights Amendment

1974—Congress creates John Day Fossil Beds National Monument; Oregon Health Sciences

History

University forms out of mergers; Governor Tom McCall sets odd/even gasoline refueling days

1975—Congress creates Hells Canyon National Recreation Area

1976—First woman, Norma Paulus, elected secretary of state; Trojan, Oregon's first nuclear power plant built near Saint Helens

The TriMet MAX light rail system began service in the Portland metropolitan area in 1986. (Oregon State Archives scenic photo)

1977—Oregon first state to ban aerosol sprays by law; Congress restores Confederated Tribes of Siletz; First woman Betty Roberts appointed to Oregon Court of Appeals

1978—Death penalty reinstated

1979—Federal District Court in *Kimball v. Callahan* affirms Klamath tribal hunting and fishing rights within former reservation; Portland-area voters create "Metro," the first elective metropolitan council in the U.S.

1980—Congress creates new Siletz Reservation; Mount Saint Helens eruption disrupts ship traffic on Columbia River

1981—Bhagwan Shree Rajneesh establishes Rajneeshpuram near Antelope

1982—Congress restores Cow Creek Band of Umpqua Tribe; First woman, Betty Roberts, appointed justice of Oregon Supreme Court

1983—Congress restores Confederated Tribes of Grand Ronde

1984—Congress restores Confederated Tribes of Coos, Lower Umpqua and Siuslaw; First Oregon lottery ratified by voters; First African-American woman, Margaret Carter, elected to state legislature

1985—Bhagwan Shree Rajneesh deported and fined $400,000; First woman, Vera Katz, selected speaker of Oregon House

1986—Congress restores Klamath Tribe; Metropolitan Area Express (MAX) begins light-rail service in Portland

1988—Congress creates Grand Ronde Reservation; Congress approves Civil Liberties Act paying

$20,000 to each surviving interned Japanese-American; Ballot Measure 8 bans discrimination based on sexual orientation

1989—Congress restores Coquille Tribe; African exchange student, Mulugeta Seraw, killed by racist skinheads in Portland

1990—Ballot Measure 5 limits property taxes to support schools and government; U.S. Department of Fish and Wildlife lists Northern Spotted Owl as endangered

1991—First woman, Barbara Roberts, elected governor

1992—First African-American, James A. Hill, Jr., elected to statewide office as state treasurer; First gaming compact for casinos signed with Cow Creek and Umpqua Tribes

1993—First statewide vote-by-mail election held in U.S.

1994—First Death With Dignity Act approved, permitting doctor-assisted suicide

1995—Beverly Clarno becomes first woman to serve as speaker of the Oregon's House of Representatives

1996—First vote-by-mail election for federal office held

1999—*New Carissa,* freighter runs aground near Coos Bay; U.S. Department of Fish and Wildlife lists several salmon species from Columbia and Willamette Rivers as endangered

2002—Susan Castillo, first Hispanic woman elected to statewide office as school superintendent; Forest fires leave nearly 100,000 acres burned; Measure requiring removal of racist language from state Constitution passes

2003—Oregon begins ten-year plan to fix deteriorating bridges

2004—Trojan, Oregon's only nuclear power plant, decommissioned; L. L. Stub Stewart State Park opens, Oregon's first new state park campground in more than 30 years

2005—Oregon State Quarter released with design featuring Crater Lake

2006—Trojan, Oregon's decommissioned nuclear power plant, imploded

2007—Oregon's constitution 150 years old; Sandy River's Marmot Dam, built in 1912, removed; Oregon Equality Act passes

2008—*New Carissa,* freighter that ran aground on Coos Bay beach in 1999, dismantled and removed

2009—Oregon celebrates its sesquicentennial on February 14, 2009; Oregon unemployment rate tops 12% amid recession

2010—Governor's panel predicts 10 years of state budget deficits

2012—Oregon legislature begins annual sessions with the even-numbered years having a month-long session in February

2013—Klamath Tribes' senior water rights in Upper Klamath Basin reaffirmed by courts; Drought and lightning produced most expensive wildfire season on record, leave over 100,000 acres burned; Josephine County's last sawmill closes for lack of logs

2014—U.S. District court strikes down same-sex marriage ban; Voters approve recreational marijuana use; Equal Rights for Women in Oregon Constitution; University of Oregon football quarterback Marcus Mariota, wins the Heisman Trophy

2015—Governor John Kitzhaber resigns Feb. 18, 2015 and Secretary of State Kate Brown becomes governor according to the order of succession required by the Oregon Constitution; Minoru Yasui, Hood River Attorney, posthumously awarded the Presidential Medal of Freedom in recognition of his challenge of a military curfew placed on Japanese-Americans during World War II and for his lifetime of civil rights work.

2016—Armed militants seize and occupy the headquarters of Harney County's Malheur National Wildlife Refuge for 41 days.

2017—Total solar eclipse crosses Oregon on August 21, 2017. Visible across the U.S., Oregon cities in the path of totality include Lincoln City, Newport, Salem, Albany, Madras, John Day, Baker City and Ontario. After public funding campaign, Oregon's 158 year old Constitution is professionally restored and put on permanent display

2018—Oregonian Colin O'Brady first to traverse Antarctica solo and unaided

2020—Governor Brown invokes the Emergency Conflagration Act as fires threaten structures in Clackamas, Douglas, Jackson, Josephine, Klamath, Lake, Lane, Marion and Washington Counties; Boardman, Oregon's only coal-fired power plant, closes after 40 years in operation; A Washington County man was Oregon's first diagnosed COVID-19 case on February 28, 2020; A Multnomah County man was Oregon's first reported COVID-19 death on March 14, 2020; On December 16, 2020 Oregon gave its first COVID-19 vaccines to health care workers in three Portland hospitals and one Ontario hospital; when the *2021-2022 Blue Book* went to press, Oregon had recorded 129,109 cases, and its 1,708th death due to COVID-19

STUDENT ESSAY CONTEST WINNER

Fort Stevens State Park

Lucas Hurd
Mrs. O'Leary's 5th Grade Class
Buff Elementary School, Madras

This drawing by Lucas Hurd shows one of the military structures at Fort Stevens State Park at the mouth of the Columbia River.

Note: The text is displayed as written.

The state park I am writting about is Fort Stevens. Today Fort Stevens is calm but it was once booming with excitement. Fort Stevens is realy cool because it is right between the Columbia and the coast. Another reason it is amazing is becase it is a retired military base.

Fort Stevens is amazing because it right between the coast and Columbia. You can drive on the beach once a year. You can fish on the Columbia. Fort Stevens even has a camp ground for camping spots.

Fort Stevens astoshing because it is a retired military base. Fort Stevens was used in the Civil War, World War I and World War II. Fort Stevens even has army truck and fort tours. Fort Stevens even has a museum. You can go climb on all the forts.

I picked Fort Stevens. Fort Stevens is tremendous. Because it is right between the coast and Columbia. I was also an active military base. Can you imagine what Fort Stevens was like when it was active?

CONSTITUTION OF OREGON
2019 EDITION

The Oregon Constitution was framed by a convention of 60 delegates chosen by the people. The convention met on the third Monday in August 1857 and adjourned on September 18 of the same year. On November 9, 1857, the Constitution was approved by vote of the people of the Oregon Territory. The Act of Congress admitting Oregon into the Union was approved February 14, 1859, and on that date the Constitution went into effect.

The Constitution is here published as it is in effect following the approval of amendments and revisions on November 6, 2018. The text of the original signed copy of the Constitution filed in the office of the Secretary of State is retained unless it has been repealed or superseded by amendment or revision. Where the original text has been amended or revised or where a new provision has been added to the original Constitution, the source of the amendment, revision or addition is indicated in the source note immediately following the text of the amended, revised or new section. Notations also have been made setting out the history of repealed sections.

Unless otherwise specifically noted, the leadlines for the sections have been supplied by the Office of the Legislative Counsel.

PREAMBLE

We the people of the State of Oregon to the end that Justice be established, order maintained, and liberty perpetuated, do ordain this Constitution. —

ARTICLE I
BILL OF RIGHTS

Section 1. Natural rights inherent in people. We declare that all men, when they form a social compact are equal in right: that all power is inherent in the people, and all free governments are founded on their authority, and instituted for their peace, safety, and happiness; and they have at all times a right to alter, reform, or abolish the government in such manner as they may think proper.—

Section 2. Freedom of worship. All men shall be secure in the Natural right, to worship Almighty God according to the dictates of their own consciences.—

Section 3. Freedom of religious opinion. No law shall in any case whatever control the free exercise, and enjoyment of religeous [sic] opinions, or interfere with the rights of conscience.—

Section 4. No religious qualification for office. No religious test shall be required as a qualification for any office of trust or profit.—

Section 5. No money to be appropriated for religion. No money shall be drawn from the Treasury for the benefit of any religeous [sic], or theological institution, nor shall any money be appropriated for the payment of any religeous [sic] services in either house of the Legislative Assembly.—

Section 6. No religious test for witnesses or jurors. No person shall be rendered incompetent as a witness, or juror in consequence of his opinions on matters of religeon [sic]; nor be questioned in any Court of Justice touching his religeous [sic] belief to affect the weight of his testimony.—

Section 7. Manner of administering oath or affirmation. The mode of administering an oath, or affirmation shall be such as may be most consistent with, and binding upon the conscience of the person to whom such oath or affirmation may be administered.—

Section 8. Freedom of speech and press. No law shall be passed restraining the free expression of opinion, or restricting the right to speak, write, or print freely on any subject whatever; but every person shall be responsible for the abuse of this right.—

Section 9. Unreasonable searches or seizures. No law shall violate the right of the people to be secure in their persons, houses, papers, and effects, against unreasonable search, or seizure; and no warrant shall issue but upon probable cause, supported by oath, or affirmation, and particularly describing the place to be searched, and the person or thing to be seized.—

Section 10. Administration of justice. No court shall be secret, but justice shall be administered, openly and without purchase, completely and without delay, and every man shall have remedy by due course of law for injury done him in his person, property, or reputation.—

Section 11. Rights of Accused in Criminal Prosecution. In all criminal prosecutions, the accused shall have the right to public trial by an impartial jury in the county in which the offense shall have been committed; to be heard by himself and counsel; to demand the nature and cause of the accusation against him, and to have a copy thereof; to meet the witnesses face to face, and to have compulsory process for obtaining witnesses in his favor; provided, however, that any accused person, in other than capital cases, and with the consent of the trial judge, may elect to waive trial by jury and consent to be tried by the judge of the court alone, such election to be in writing; provided, however, that in the circuit court ten members of the jury may render a verdict of guilty or not guilty, save and except a verdict of guilty of first degree murder, which shall be found only by a unanimous verdict, and not otherwise; provided further, that the existing laws and constitutional provisions relative to criminal prosecutions shall be continued and remain in effect as to all prosecutions for crimes committed before the taking effect of this amendment. [Constitution of 1859; Amendment proposed by S.J.R. 4, 1931, and adopted by the people Nov. 8, 1932; Amendment proposed by S.J.R. 4, 1931 (2d s.s.), and adopted by the people May 18, 1934]

Note: The leadline to section 11 was a part of the measure submitted to the people by S.J.R. 4, 1931.

Section 12. Double jeopardy; compulsory self-incrimination. No person shall be put in jeopardy twice for the same offence [sic], nor be compelled in any criminal prosecution to testify against himself.—

Section 13. Treatment of arrested or confined persons. No person arrested, or confined in jail, shall be treated with unnecessary rigor.—

Section 14. Bailable offenses. Offences [sic], except murder, and treason, shall be bailable by sufficient sureties.

Murder or treason, shall not be bailable, when the proof is evident, or the presumption strong.—

Section 15. Foundation principles of criminal law. Laws for the punishment of crime shall be founded on these principles: protection of society, personal responsibility, accountability for one's actions and reformation. [Constitution of 1859; Amendment proposed by S.J.R. 32, 1995, and adopted by the people Nov. 5, 1996]

Section 16. Excessive bail and fines; cruel and unusual punishments; power of jury in criminal case. Excessive bail shall not be required, nor excessive fines imposed. Cruel and unusual punishments shall not be inflicted, but all penalties shall be proportioned to the offense.—In all criminal cases whatever, the jury shall have the right to determine the law, and the facts under the direction of the Court as to the law, and the right of new trial, as in civil cases.

Section 17. Jury trial in civil cases. In all civil cases the right of Trial by Jury shall remain inviolate.—

Section 18. Private property or services taken for public use. Private property shall not be taken for public use, nor the particular services of any man be demanded, without just compensation; nor except in the case of the state, without such compensation first assessed and tendered; provided, that the use of all roads, ways and waterways necessary to promote the transportation of the raw products of mine or farm or forest or water for beneficial use or drainage is necessary to the development and welfare of the state and is declared a public use. [Constitution of 1859; Amendment proposed by S.J.R. 17, 1919, and adopted by the people May 21, 1920; Amendment proposed by S.J.R. 8, 1923, and adopted by the people Nov. 4, 1924]

Section 19. Imprisonment for debt. There shall be no imprisonment for debt, except in case of fraud or absconding debtors.—

Section 20. Equality of privileges and immunities of citizens. No law shall be passed granting to any citizen or class of citizens privileges, or immunities, which, upon the same terms, shall not equally belong to all citizens.—

Section 21. Ex-post facto laws; laws impairing contracts; laws depending on authorization in order to take effect; laws submitted to electors. No ex-post facto law, or law impairing the obligation of contracts shall ever be passed, nor shall any law be passed, the taking effect of which shall be made to depend upon any authority, except as provided in this Constitution; provided, that laws locating the Capitol of the State, locating County Seats, and submitting town, and corporate acts, and other local, and Special laws may take effect, or not, upon a vote of the electors interested.—

Section 22. Suspension of operation of laws. The operation of the laws shall never be suspended, except by the Authority of the Legislative Assembly.

Section 23. Habeas corpus. The privilege of the writ of habeas corpus shall not be suspended unless in case of rebellion, or invasion the public safety require it.—

Section 24. Treason. Treason against the State shall consist only in levying war against it, or adhering to its enemies, giving them aid or comfort.—No person shall be convicted of treason unless on the testimony of two witnesses to the same overt act, or confession in open Court.—

Section 25. Corruption of blood or forfeiture of estate. No conviction shall work corruption of blood, or forfeiture of estate.—

Section 26. Assemblages of people; instruction of representatives; application to legislature. No law shall be passed restraining any of the inhabitants of the State from assembling together in a peaceable manner to consult for their common good; nor from instructing their Representatives; nor from applying to the Legislature for redress of greviances [sic].—

Section 27. Right to bear arms; military subordinate to civil power. The people shall have the right to bear arms for the defence [sic] of themselves, and the State, but the Military shall be kept in strict subordination to the civil power[.]

Section 28. Quartering soldiers. No soldier shall, in time of peace, be quartered in any house, without the consent of the owner, nor in time of war, except in the manner prescribed by law.

Section 29. Titles of nobility; hereditary distinctions. No law shall be passed granting any title of Nobility, or conferring hereditary distinctions.—

Section 30. Emigration. No law shall be passed prohibiting emigration from the State.—

Section 31. Rights of aliens; immigration to state. [Constitution of 1859; repeal proposed by H.J.R. 16, 1969, and adopted by the people May 26, 1970]

Section 32. Taxes and duties; uniformity of taxation. No tax or duty shall be imposed without the consent of the people or their representatives in the Legislative Assembly; and all taxation shall be uniform on the same class of subjects within the territorial limits of the authority levying the tax. [Constitution of 1859; Amendment proposed by H.J.R. 16, 1917, and adopted by the people June 4, 1917]

Section 33. Enumeration of rights not exclusive. This enumeration of rights, and privileges shall not be construed to impair or deny others retained by the people.—

Section 34. Slavery or involuntary servitude. There shall be neither slavery, nor involuntary servitude in the State, otherwise than as a punishment for crime, whereof the party shall have been duly convicted.— [Added to Bill of Rights as unnumbered section by vote of the people at time of adoption of the Oregon Constitution in accordance with section 4 of Article XVIII thereof]

Section 35. Restrictions on rights of certain persons. [Added to Bill of Rights as unnumbered section by vote of the people at time of adoption of the Oregon Constitution in accordance with Section 4 of Article XVIII thereof; Repeal proposed by H.J.R. 8, 1925, and adopted by the people Nov. 2, 1926]

Section 36. Liquor prohibition. [Created through initiative petition filed July 1, 1914, and adopted by the people Nov. 3, 1914; Repeal proposed by initiative petition filed March 20, 1933, and adopted by the people July 21, 1933]

Section 36. Capital punishment abolished. [Created through initiative petition filed July 2, 1914, and adopted by the people Nov. 3, 1914; Repeal proposed by S.J.R. 8, 1920 (s.s.), and adopted by the people May 21, 1920, as Const. Art. I, §38]

Note: At the general election in 1914 two sections, each designated as section 36, were created and added to the Constitution by separate initiative petitions. One of these sections was the prohibition section and the other abolished capital punishment.

Section 36a. Prohibition of importation of liquors. [Created through initiative petition filed July 6, 1916, and adopted by the people Nov. 7, 1916; Repeal proposed by initiative petition filed March 20, 1933, and adopted by the people July 21, 1933]

Section 37. Penalty for murder in first degree. [Created through S.J.R. 8, 1920, and adopted by the people May 21, 1920; Repeal proposed by S.J.R. 3, 1963, and adopted by the people Nov. 3, 1964]

Section 38. Laws abrogated by amendment abolishing death penalty revived. [Created through S.J.R. 8, 1920, and adopted by the people May 21, 1920; Repeal proposed by S.J.R. 3, 1963, and adopted by the people Nov. 3, 1964]

Section 39. Sale of liquor by individual glass. The State shall have power to license private clubs, fraternal organizations, veterans' organizations, railroad corporations operating interstate trains and commercial establishments where food is cooked and served, for the purpose of selling alcoholic liquor by the individual glass at retail, for consumption on the premises, including mixed drinks and cocktails, compounded or mixed on the premises only. The Legislative Assembly shall provide in such detail as it shall deem advisable for carrying out and administering the provisions of this amendment and shall provide adequate safeguards to carry out the original intent and purpose of the Oregon Liquor Control Act, including the promotion of temperance in the use and consumption of alcoholic beverages, encourage the use and consumption of lighter beverages and aid in the establishment of Oregon industry. This power is subject to the following:

(1) The provisions of this amendment shall take effect and be in operation sixty (60) days after the approval and adoption by the people of Oregon; provided, however, the right of a local option election exists in the counties and in any incorporated city or town containing a population of at least five hundred (500). The Legislative Assembly shall prescribe a means and a procedure by which the voters of any county or incorporated city or town as limited above in any county, may through a local option election determine whether to prohibit or permit such power, and such procedure shall specifically include that whenever fifteen per cent (15%) of the registered voters of any county in the state or of any incorporated city or town as limited above, in any county in the state, shall file a petition requesting an election in this matter, the question shall be voted upon at the next regular November biennial election, provided said petition is filed not less than sixty (60) days before the day of election.

(2) Legislation relating to this matter shall operate uniformly throughout the state and all individuals shall be treated equally; and all provisions shall be liberally construed for the accomplishment of these purposes. [Created through initiative petition filed July 2, 1952, and adopted by the people Nov. 4, 1952]

Section 40. Penalty for aggravated murder. Notwithstanding sections 15 and 16 of this Article, the penalty for aggravated murder as defined by law shall be death upon unanimous affirmative jury findings as provided by law and otherwise shall be life imprisonment with minimum sentence as provided by law. [Created through initiative petition filed July 6, 1983, and adopted by the people Nov. 6, 1984]

Section 41. Work and training for corrections institution inmates; work programs; limitations; duties of corrections director. (1) Whereas the people of the state of Oregon find and declare that inmates who are confined in corrections institutions should work as hard as the taxpayers who provide for their upkeep; and whereas the people also find and declare that inmates confined within corrections institutions must be fully engaged in productive activity if they are to successfully re-enter society with practical skills and a viable work ethic; now, therefore, the people declare:

(2) All inmates of state corrections institutions shall be actively engaged full-time in work or on-the-job training. The work or on-the-job training programs shall be established and overseen by the corrections director, who shall ensure that such programs are cost-effective and are designed to develop inmate motivation, work capabilities and cooperation. Such programs may include boot camp prison programs. Education may be provided to inmates as part of work or on-the-job training so long as each inmate is engaged at least half-time in hands-on training or work activity.

(3) Each inmate shall begin full-time work or on-the-job training immediately upon admission to a corrections institution, allowing for a short time for administrative intake and processing. The specific quantity of hours per day to be spent in work or on-the-job training shall be determined by the corrections director, but the overall time spent in work or training shall be full-time. However, no inmate has a legally enforceable right to a job or to otherwise participate in work, on-the-job training or educational programs or to compensation for work or labor performed while an inmate of any state, county or city corrections facility or institution. The corrections director may reduce or exempt participation in work or training programs by those inmates deemed by corrections officials as physically or mentally disabled, or as too dangerous to society to engage in such programs.

(4) There shall be sufficient work and training programs to ensure that every eligible inmate is productively involved in one or more programs. Where an inmate is drug and alcohol addicted so as to prevent the inmate from effectively participating in work or training programs, corrections officials shall provide appropriate drug or alcohol treatment.

(5) The intent of the people is that taxpayer-supported institutions and programs shall be free to benefit from inmate work. Prison work programs shall be designed and carried out so as to achieve savings in government operations, so as to achieve a net profit in private sector activities or so as to benefit the community.

(6) The provisions of this section are mandatory for all state corrections institutions. The provisions of this section are permissive for county or city corrections facilities. No law, ordinance or charter shall prevent or restrict a county or city governing body from implementing all or part of the provisions of this section. Compensation, if any, shall be determined and established by the governing body of the county or city which chooses to engage in prison work programs, and the governing body may choose to adopt any power or exemption allowed in this section.

(7) The corrections director shall contact public and private enterprises in this state and seek proposals to use inmate work. The corrections director may: (a) install and equip plants in any state corrections institution, or any other location, for the employment or training of any of the inmates therein; or (b) purchase, acquire, install, maintain and operate materials, machinery and appliances necessary to the conduct and operation of such plants. The corrections director shall use every effort to enter into contracts or agreements with private business concerns or government agencies to accomplish the production or marketing of products or services produced or performed by inmates. The corrections director may carry out the director's powers and duties under this section by delegation to others.

(8) Compensation, if any, for inmates who engage in prison work programs shall be determined and established by the corrections director. Such compensation shall not be subject to existing public or private sector minimum or prevailing wage laws, except where required to comply with federal law. Inmate compensation from enterprises entering into agreements with the state shall be exempt from unemployment compensation taxes to the extent allowed under federal law. Inmate injury or disease attributable to any inmate work shall be covered by a corrections system inmate injury fund rather than the workers compensation law. Except as otherwise required by federal law to permit transportation in interstate commerce of goods, wares or merchandise manufactured, produced or mined, wholly or in part by inmates or except as otherwise required by state law, any compensation earned through prison work programs shall only be used for the following purposes: (a) reimbursement for all or a portion of the costs

of the inmate's rehabilitation, housing, health care, and living costs; (b) restitution or compensation to the victims of the particular inmate's crime; (c) restitution or compensation to the victims of crime generally through a fund designed for that purpose; (d) financial support for immediate family of the inmate outside the corrections institution; and (e) payment of fines, court costs, and applicable taxes.

(9) All income generated from prison work programs shall be kept separate from general fund accounts and shall only be used for implementing, maintaining and developing prison work programs. Prison industry work programs shall be exempt from statutory competitive bid and purchase requirements. Expenditures for prison work programs shall be exempt from the legislative appropriations process to the extent the programs rely on income sources other than state taxes and fees. Where state taxes or fees are the source of capital or operating expenditures, the appropriations shall be made by the legislative assembly. The state programs shall be run in a businesslike fashion and shall be subject to regulation by the corrections director. Expenditures from income generated by state prison work programs must be approved by the corrections director. Agreements with private enterprise as to state prison work programs must be approved by the corrections director. The corrections director shall make all state records available for public scrutiny and the records shall be subject to audit by the Secretary of State.

(10) Prison work products or services shall be available to any public agency and to any private enterprise of any state, any nation or any American Indian or Alaskan Native tribe without restriction imposed by any state or local law, ordinance or regulation as to competition with other public or private sector enterprises. The products and services of corrections work programs shall be provided on such terms as are set by the corrections director. To the extent determined possible by the corrections director, the corrections director shall avoid establishing or expanding for-profit prison work programs that produce goods or services offered for sale in the private sector if the establishment or expansion would displace or significantly reduce preexisting private enterprise. To the extent determined possible by the corrections director, the corrections director shall avoid establishing or expanding prison work programs if the establishment or expansion would displace or significantly reduce government or nonprofit programs that employ persons with developmental disabilities. However, the decision to establish, maintain, expand, reduce or terminate any prison work program remains in the sole discretion of the corrections director.

(11) Inmate work shall be used as much as possible to help operate the corrections institutions themselves, to support other government operations and to support community charitable organizations. This work includes, but is not limited to, institutional food production; maintenance and repair of buildings, grounds, and equipment; office support services, including printing; prison clothing production and maintenance; prison medical services; training other inmates; agricultural and forestry work, especially in parks and public forest lands; and environmental clean-up projects. Every state agency shall cooperate with the corrections director in establishing inmate work programs.

(12) As used throughout this section, unless the context requires otherwise: "full-time" means the equivalent of at least forty hours per seven day week, specifically including time spent by inmates as required by the Department of Corrections, while the inmate is participating in work or on-the-job training, to provide for the safety and security of the public, correctional staff and inmates; "corrections director" means the person in charge of the state corrections system.

(13) This section is self-implementing and supersedes all existing inconsistent statutes. This section shall become effective April 1, 1995. If any part of this section or its application to any person or circumstance is held to be invalid for any reason, then the remaining parts or applications to any persons or circumstances shall not be affected but shall remain in full force and effect. [Created through initiative petition filed Jan. 12, 1994, and adopted by the people Nov. 8, 1994; Amendment proposed by H.J.R. 2, 1997, and adopted by the people May 20, 1997; Amendment proposed by H.J.R. 82, 1999, and adopted by the people Nov. 2, 1999]

Note: Added to Article I as unnumbered section by initiative petition (Measure No. 17, 1994) adopted by the people Nov. 8, 1994.

Note: An initiative petition (Measure No. 40, 1996) proposed adding a new section relating to crime victims' rights to the Oregon Constitution. That section, appearing as section 42 of Article I in previous editions of this Constitution, was declared void for not being enacted in compliance with section 1, Article XVII of this Constitution. See Armatta v. Kitzhaber, 327 Or. 250, 959 P.2d 49 (1998).

Section 42. Rights of victim in criminal prosecutions and juvenile court delinquency proceedings. (1) To preserve and protect the right of crime victims to justice, to ensure crime victims a meaningful role in the criminal and juvenile justice systems, to accord crime victims due dignity and respect and to ensure that criminal and juvenile court delinquency proceedings are conducted to seek the truth as to the defendant's innocence or guilt, and also to ensure that a fair balance is struck between the rights of crime victims and the rights of criminal defendants in the course and conduct of criminal and juvenile court delinquency proceedings, the following rights are hereby granted to victims in all prosecutions for crimes and in juvenile court delinquency proceedings:

(a) The right to be present at and, upon specific request, to be informed in advance of any critical stage of the proceedings held in open court when the defendant will be present, and to be heard at the pretrial release hearing and the sentencing or juvenile court delinquency disposition;

(b) The right, upon request, to obtain information about the conviction, sentence, imprisonment, criminal history and future release from physical custody of the criminal defendant or convicted criminal and equivalent information regarding the alleged youth offender or youth offender;

(c) The right to refuse an interview, deposition or other discovery request by the criminal defendant or other person acting on behalf of the criminal defendant provided, however, that nothing in this paragraph shall restrict any other constitutional right of the defendant to discovery against the state;

(d) The right to receive prompt restitution from the convicted criminal who caused the victim's loss or injury;

(e) The right to have a copy of a transcript of any court proceeding in open court, if one is otherwise prepared;

(f) The right to be consulted, upon request, regarding plea negotiations involving any violent felony; and

(g) The right to be informed of these rights as soon as practicable.

(2) This section applies to all criminal and juvenile court delinquency proceedings pending or commenced on or after the effective date of this section. Nothing in this section reduces a criminal defendant's rights under the Constitution of the United States. Except as otherwise specifically provided, this section supersedes any conflicting section of this Constitution. Nothing in this section is intended to create any cause of action for compensation or damages nor may this section be used to invalidate an accusatory instrument, conviction or adjudication or otherwise terminate any criminal or juvenile delinquency

Constitution

proceedings at any point after the case is commenced or on appeal. Except as otherwise provided in subsections (3) and (4) of this section, nothing in this section may be used to invalidate a ruling of a court or to suspend any criminal or juvenile delinquency proceedings at any point after the case is commenced.

(3)(a) Every victim described in paragraph (c) of subsection (6) of this section shall have remedy by due course of law for violation of a right established in this section.

(b) A victim may assert a claim for a right established in this section in a pending case, by a mandamus proceeding if no case is pending or as otherwise provided by law.

(c) The Legislative Assembly may provide by law for further effectuation of the provisions of this subsection, including authorization for expedited and interlocutory consideration of claims for relief and the establishment of reasonable limitations on the time allowed for bringing such claims.

(d) No claim for a right established in this section shall suspend a criminal or juvenile delinquency proceeding if such a suspension would violate a right of a criminal defendant guaranteed by this Constitution or the Constitution of the United States.

(4) Upon the victim's request, the prosecuting attorney, in the attorney's discretion, may assert and enforce a right established in this section.

(5) Upon the filing by the prosecuting attorney of an affidavit setting forth cause, a court shall suspend the rights established in this section in any case involving organized crime or victims who are minors.

(6) As used in this section:

(a) "Convicted criminal" includes a youth offender in juvenile court delinquency proceedings.

(b) "Criminal defendant" includes an alleged youth offender in juvenile court delinquency proceedings.

(c) "Victim" means any person determined by the prosecuting attorney or the court to have suffered direct financial, psychological or physical harm as a result of a crime and, in the case of a victim who is a minor, the legal guardian of the minor.

(d) "Violent felony" means a felony in which there was actual or threatened serious physical injury to a victim or a felony sexual offense.

(7) In the event that no person has been determined to be a victim of the crime, the people of Oregon, represented by the prosecuting attorney, are considered to be the victims. In no event is it intended that the criminal defendant be considered the victim. [Created through H.J.R. 87, 1999, and adopted by the people Nov. 2, 1999; Amendment proposed by H.J.R. 49, 2007, and adopted by the people May 20, 2008]

Note: The effective date of House Joint Resolutions 87, 89, 90 and 94, compiled as sections 42, 43, 44 and 45, Article I, is Dec. 2, 1999.

Note: Sections 42, 43, 44 and 45, were added to Article I as unnumbered sections by the amendments proposed by House Joint Resolutions 87, 89, 90 and 94, 1999, and adopted by the people Nov. 2, 1999.

Section 43. Rights of victim and public to protection from accused person during criminal proceedings; denial of pretrial release. (1) To ensure that a fair balance is struck between the rights of crime victims and the rights of criminal defendants in the course and conduct of criminal proceedings, the following rights are hereby granted to victims in all prosecutions for crimes:

(a) The right to be reasonably protected from the criminal defendant or the convicted criminal throughout the criminal justice process and from the alleged youth offender or youth offender throughout the juvenile delinquency proceedings.

(b) The right to have decisions by the court regarding the pretrial release of a criminal defendant based upon the principle of reasonable protection of the victim and the public, as well as the likelihood that the criminal defendant will appear for trial. Murder, aggravated murder and treason shall not be bailable when the proof is evident or the presumption strong that the person is guilty. Other violent felonies shall not be bailable when a court has determined there is probable cause to believe the criminal defendant committed the crime, and the court finds, by clear and convincing evidence, that there is danger of physical injury or sexual victimization to the victim or members of the public by the criminal defendant while on release.

(2) This section applies to proceedings pending or commenced on or after the effective date of this section. Nothing in this section abridges any right of the criminal defendant guaranteed by the Constitution of the United States, including the rights to be represented by counsel, have counsel appointed if indigent, testify, present witnesses, cross-examine witnesses or present information at the release hearing. Nothing in this section creates any cause of action for compensation or damages nor may this section be used to invalidate an accusatory instrument, conviction or adjudication or otherwise terminate any criminal or juvenile delinquency proceeding at any point after the case is commenced or on appeal. Except as otherwise provided in paragraph (b) of subsection (4) of this section and in subsection (5) of this section, nothing in this section may be used to invalidate a ruling of a court or to suspend any criminal or juvenile delinquency proceedings at any point after the case is commenced. Except as otherwise specifically provided, this section supersedes any conflicting section of this Constitution.

(3) As used in this section:

(a) "Victim" means any person determined by the prosecuting attorney or the court to have suffered direct financial, psychological or physical harm as a result of a crime and, in the case of a victim who is a minor, the legal guardian of the minor.

(b) "Violent felony" means a felony in which there was actual or threatened serious physical injury to a victim or a felony sexual offense.

(4)(a) The prosecuting attorney is the party authorized to assert the rights of the public established by this section.

(b) Upon the victim's request, the prosecuting attorney, in the attorney's discretion, may assert and enforce a right established in this section.

(5)(a) Every victim described in paragraph (a) of subsection (3) of this section shall have remedy by due course of law for violation of a right established in this section.

(b) A victim may assert a claim for a right established in this section in a pending case, by a mandamus proceeding if no case is pending or as otherwise provided by law.

(c) The Legislative Assembly may provide by law for further effectuation of the provisions of this subsection, including authorization for expedited and interlocutory consideration of claims for relief and the establishment of reasonable limitations on the time allowed for bringing such claims.

(d) No claim for a right established in this section shall suspend a criminal or juvenile delinquency proceeding if such a suspension would violate a right of a criminal defendant or alleged youth offender guaranteed by this Constitution or the Constitution of the United States.

(6) In the event that no person has been determined to be a victim of the crime, the people of Oregon, represented by the prosecuting attorney, are considered to be the victims. In no event is it intended that the criminal defendant be considered the victim. [Created through H.J.R. 90, 1999,

and adopted by the people Nov. 2, 1999; Amendment proposed by H.J.R. 50, 2007, and adopted by the people May 20, 2008]

Note: See notes under section 42 of this Article.

Section 44. Term of imprisonment imposed by court to be fully served; exceptions. (1)(a) A term of imprisonment imposed by a judge in open court may not be set aside or otherwise not carried out, except as authorized by the sentencing court or through the subsequent exercise of:

(A) The power of the Governor to grant reprieves, commutations and pardons; or

(B) Judicial authority to grant appellate or post-conviction relief.

(b) No law shall limit a court's authority to sentence a criminal defendant consecutively for crimes against different victims.

(2) This section applies to all offenses committed on or after the effective date of this section. Nothing in this section reduces a criminal defendant's rights under the Constitution of the United States. Except as otherwise specifically provided, this section supersedes any conflicting section of this Constitution. Nothing in this section creates any cause of action for compensation or damages nor may this section be used to invalidate an accusatory instrument, ruling of a court, conviction or adjudication or otherwise suspend or terminate any criminal or juvenile delinquency proceedings at any point after the case is commenced or on appeal.

(3) As used in this section, "victim" means any person determined by the prosecuting attorney to have suffered direct financial, psychological or physical harm as a result of a crime and, in the case of a victim who is a minor, the legal guardian of the minor. In the event no person has been determined to be a victim of the crime, the people of Oregon, represented by the prosecuting attorney, are considered to be the victims. In no event is it intended that the criminal defendant be considered the victim. [Created through H.J.R. 94, 1999, and adopted by the people Nov. 2, 1999]

Note: See notes under section 42 of this Article.

Section 45. Person convicted of certain crimes not eligible to serve as juror on grand jury or trial jury in criminal case. (1) In all grand juries and in all prosecutions for crimes tried to a jury, the jury shall be composed of persons who have not been convicted:

(a) Of a felony or served a felony sentence within the 15 years immediately preceding the date the persons are required to report for jury duty; or

(b) Of a misdemeanor involving violence or dishonesty or served a sentence for a misdemeanor involving violence or dishonesty within the five years immediately preceding the date the persons are required to report for jury duty.

(2) This section applies to all criminal proceedings pending or commenced on or after the effective date of this section, except a criminal proceeding in which a jury has been impaneled and sworn on the effective date of this section. Nothing in this section reduces a criminal defendant's rights under the Constitution of the United States. Except as otherwise specifically provided, this section supersedes any conflicting section of this Constitution. Nothing in this section is intended to create any cause of action for compensation or damages nor may this section be used to disqualify a jury, invalidate an accusatory instrument, ruling of a court, conviction or adjudication or otherwise suspend or terminate any criminal proceeding at any point after a jury is impaneled and sworn or on appeal. [Created through H.J.R. 89, 1999, and adopted by the people Nov. 2, 1999]

Note: See notes under section 42 of this Article.

Section 46. Prohibition on denial or abridgment of rights on account of sex. (1) Equality of rights under the law shall not be denied or abridged by the State of Oregon or by any political subdivision in this state on account of sex.

(2) The Legislative Assembly shall have the power to enforce, by appropriate legislation, the provisions of this section.

(3) Nothing in this section shall diminish a right otherwise available to persons under section 20 of this Article or any other provision of this Constitution. [Created through initiative petition filed Oct. 24, 2013, and adopted by the people Nov. 4, 2014]

ARTICLE II
SUFFRAGE AND ELECTIONS

Section 1. Elections free. All elections shall be free and equal.—

Section 2. Qualifications of electors. (1) Every citizen of the United States is entitled to vote in all elections not otherwise provided for by this Constitution if such citizen:

(a) Is 18 years of age or older;

(b) Has resided in this state during the six months immediately preceding the election, except that provision may be made by law to permit a person who has resided in this state less than 30 days immediately preceding the election, but who is otherwise qualified under this subsection, to vote in the election for candidates for nomination or election for President or Vice President of the United States or elector of President and Vice President of the United States; and

(c) Is registered not less than 20 calendar days immediately preceding any election in the manner provided by law.

(2) Provision may be made by law to require that persons who vote upon questions of levying special taxes or issuing public bonds shall be taxpayers. [Constitution of 1859; Amendment proposed by initiative petition filed Dec. 20, 1910, and adopted by the people Nov. 5, 1912; Amendment proposed by S.J.R. 6, 1913, and adopted by the people Nov. 3, 1914; Amendment proposed by S.J.R. 6, 1923, and adopted by the people Nov. 4, 1924; Amendment proposed by H.J.R. 7, 1927, and adopted by the people June 28, 1927; Amendment proposed by H.J.R. 5, 1931, and adopted by the people Nov. 8, 1932; Amendment proposed by H.J.R. 26, 1959, and adopted by the people Nov. 8, 1960; Amendment proposed by H.J.R. 41, 1973, and adopted by the people Nov.

5, 1974; Amendment proposed by initiative petition filed July 20, 1986, and adopted by the people Nov. 4, 1986; Amendment proposed by H.J.R. 4, 2007, and adopted by the people Nov. 4, 2008]

Note: The leadline to section 2 was a part of the measure submitted to the people by initiative petition (Measure No. 13, 1986) and adopted by the people Nov. 4, 1986.

Section 3. Rights of certain electors. A person suffering from a mental handicap is entitled to the full rights of an elector, if otherwise qualified, unless the person has been adjudicated incompetent to vote as provided by law. The privilege of an elector, upon conviction of any crime which is punishable by imprisonment in the penitentiary, shall be forfeited, unless otherwise provided by law. [Constitution of 1859; Amendment proposed by S.J.R. 9, 1943, and adopted by the people Nov. 7, 1944; Amendment proposed by S.J.R. 26, 1979, and adopted by the people Nov. 4, 1980]

Section 4. Residence. For the purpose of voting, no person shall be deemed to have gained, or lost a residence, by reason of his presence, or absence while employed in the service of the United States, or of this State; nor while engaged in the navigation of the waters of this State, or of the United States, or of the high seas; nor while a student of any Seminary of Learning; nor while kept at any alms house, or other assylum [sic], at public expence [sic]; nor while confined in any public prison.—

Section 5. Soldiers, seamen and marines; residence; right to vote. No soldier, seaman, or marine in the Army, or Navy of the United States, or of their allies, shall be deemed to have acquired a residence in the state, in consequence of having been stationed within the same; nor shall any such soldier, seaman, or marine have the right to vote.—

Section 6. Right of suffrage for certain persons. [Constitution of 1859; Repeal proposed by H.J.R. 4, 1927, and adopted by the people June 28, 1927]

Section 7. Bribery at elections. Every person shall be disqualified from holding office, during the term for which he may have been elected, who shall have given, or offered a bribe, threat, or reward to procure his election.—

Section 8. Regulation of elections. The Legislative Assembly shall enact laws to support the privilege of free suffrage, prescribing the manner of regulating, and conducting elections, and prohibiting under adequate penalties, all undue influence therein, from power, bribery, tumult, and other improper conduct.—

Section 9. Penalty for dueling. Every person who shall give, or accept a challenge to fight a duel, or who shall knowingly carry to another person such challenge, or who shall agree to go out of the State to fight a duel, shall be ineligible to any office of trust, or profit.—

Section 10. Lucrative offices; holding other offices forbidden. No person holding a lucrative office, or appointment under the United States, or under this State, shall be eligible to a seat in the Legislative Assembly; nor shall any person hold more than one lucrative office at the same time, except as in this Constitution [sic] expressly permitted; Provided, that Officers in the Militia, to which there is attached no annual salary, and the Office of Post Master, where the compensation does not exceed One Hundred Dollars per annum, shall not be deemed lucrative.—

Section 11. When collector or holder of public moneys ineligible to office. No person who may hereafter be a collector, or holder of public moneys, shall be eligible to any office of trust or profit, until he shall have accounted for, and paid over according to law, all sums for which he may be liable.—

Section 12. Temporary appointments to office. In all cases, in which it is provided that an office shall not be filled by the same person, more than a certain number of years continuously, an appointment pro tempore shall not be reckoned a part of that term.—

Section 13. Privileges of electors. In all cases, except treason, felony, and breach of the peace, electors shall be free from arrest in going to elections, during their attendance there, and in returning from the same; and no elector shall be obliged to do duty in the Militia on any day of election, except in time of war, or public danger.—

Section 14. Time of holding elections and assuming duties of office. The regular general biennial election in Oregon for the year A. D. 1910 and thereafter shall be held on the first Tuesday after the first Monday in November. All officers except the Governor, elected for a six year term in 1904 or for a four year term in 1906 or for a two year term in 1908 shall continue to hold their respective offices until the first Monday in January, 1911; and all officers, except the Governor elected at any regular general biennial election after the adoption of this amendment shall assume the duties of their respective offices on the first Monday in January following such election. All laws pertaining to the nomination of candidates, registration of voters and all other things incident to the holding of the regular biennial election shall be enforced and be effected the same number of days before the first Tuesday after the first Monday in November that they have heretofore been before the first Monday in June biennially, except as may hereafter be provided by law. [Constitution of 1859; Amendment proposed by H.J.R. 7, 1907, and adopted by the people June 1, 1908]

Section 14a. Time of holding elections in incorporated cities and towns. Incorporated cities and towns shall hold their nominating and regular elections for their several elective officers at the same time that the primary and general biennial elections for State and county officers are held, and the election precincts and officers shall be the same for all elections held at the same time. All provisions of the charters and ordinances of incorporated cities and towns pertaining to the holding of elections shall continue in full force and effect except so far as they relate to the time of holding such elections. Every officer who, at the time of the adoption of this amendment, is the duly qualified incumbent of an elective office of an incorporated city or town shall hold his office for the term for which he was elected and until his successor is elected and qualified. The Legislature, and cities and towns, shall enact such supplementary legislation as may be necessary to carry the provisions of this amendment into effect. [Created through H.J.R. 22, 1917, and adopted by the people June 4, 1917]

Section 15. Method of voting in legislature. In all elections by the Legislative Assembly, or by either branch thereof, votes shall be given openly or viva voce, and not by ballot, forever; and in all elections by the people, votes shall be given openly, or viva voce, until the Legislative Assembly shall otherwise direct.—

Section 16. Election by plurality; proportional representation. In all elections authorized by this constitution until otherwise provided by law, the person or persons receiving the highest number of votes shall be declared elected, but provision may be made by law for elections by equal proportional representation of all the voters for every office which is filled by the election of two or more persons whose official duties, rights and powers are equal and concurrent. Every qualified elector resident in his precinct and registered as may be required by law, may vote for one person under the title for each office. Provision may be made by law for the voter's direct or indirect expression of his first, second or additional choices among the candidates for any office. For an office which is filled by the election of one person it may be required by law that the person elected shall be the final choice of a majority of the electors voting for candidates for that office. These principles may be applied by law to nominations by political parties and organizations. [Constitution of 1859; Amendment proposed by initiative petition filed Jan. 29, 1908, and adopted by the people June 1, 1908]

Section 17. Place of voting. All qualified electors shall vote in the election precinct in the County where they may reside, for County Officers, and in any County in the State for State Officers, or in any County of a Congressional District in which such electors may reside, for Members of Congress.—

Section 18. Recall; meaning of words "the legislative assembly shall provide." (1) Every public officer in Oregon is subject, as herein provided, to recall by the electors of the state or of the electoral district from which the public officer is elected.

(2) Fifteen per cent, but not more, of the number of electors who voted for Governor in the officer's electoral district at the most recent election at which a candidate for Governor was elected to a full term, may be required to file their petition demanding the officer's recall by the people.

(3) They shall set forth in the petition the reasons for the demand.

(4) If the public officer offers to resign, the resignation shall be accepted and take effect on the day it is offered, and the vacancy shall be filled as may be provided by law. If the public officer does not resign within five days after the petition is filed, a special election shall be ordered to be held within 35 days in the electoral district to determine whether the people will recall the officer.

(5) On the ballot at the election shall be printed in not more than 200 words the reasons for demanding the recall of the officer as set forth in the recall petition, and, in not more than 200 words, the officer's justification of the officer's course in office. The officer shall continue to perform the duties of office until the result of the special election is officially declared. If an officer is recalled from any public office the vacancy shall be filled immediately in the manner provided by law for filling a vacancy in that office arising from any other cause.

(6) The recall petition shall be filed with the officer with whom a petition for nomination to such office should be filed, and the same officer shall order the special election when it is required. No such petition shall be circulated against any officer until the officer has actually held the office six months, save and except that it may be filed against a senator or representative in the legislative assembly at any time after five days from the beginning of the first session after the election of the senator or representative.

(7) After one such petition and special election, no further recall petition shall be filed against the same officer during the term for which the officer was elected unless such further petitioners first pay into the public treasury which has paid such special election expenses, the whole amount of its expenses for the preceding special election.

(8) Such additional legislation as may aid the operation of this section shall be provided by the legislative assembly, including provision for payment by the public treasury of the reasonable special election campaign expenses of such officer. But the words, "the legislative assembly shall provide," or any similar or equivalent words in this constitution or any amendment thereto, shall not be construed to grant to the legislative assembly any exclusive power of lawmaking nor in any way to limit the initiative and referendum powers reserved by the people. [Created through initiative petition filed Jan. 29, 1908, and adopted by the people June 1, 1908; Amendment proposed by S.J.R. 16, 1925, and

adopted by the people Nov. 2, 1926; Amendment proposed by H.J.R. 1, 1983, and adopted by the people Nov. 6, 1984]

Note: "Recall." constituted the leadline to section 18 and was a part of the measure submitted to the people by S.J.R. 16, 1925.

Note: An initiative petition (Measure No. 3, 1992) proposed adding new sections relating to term limits to the Oregon Constitution. Those sections, appearing as sections 19, 20 and 21 of Article II in previous editions of this Constitution, were declared void for not being enacted in compliance with section 1, Article XVII of this Constitution. See Lehman v. Bradbury, 333 Or. 231, 37 P.3d 989 (2002).

Section 22. Political campaign contribution limitations. Section (1) For purposes of campaigning for an elected public office, a candidate may use or direct only contributions which originate from individuals who at the time of their donation were residents of the electoral district of the public office sought by the candidate, unless the contribution consists of volunteer time, information provided to the candidate, or funding provided by federal, state, or local government for purposes of campaigning for an elected public office.

Section (2) Where more than ten percent (10%) of a candidate's total campaign funding is in violation of Section (1), and0 the candidate is subsequently elected, the elected official shall forfeit the office and shall not hold a subsequent elected public office for a period equal to twice the tenure of the office sought. Where more than ten percent (10%) of a candidate's total campaign funding is in violation of Section (1) and the candidate is not elected, the unelected candidate shall not hold a subsequent elected public office for a period equal to twice the tenure of the office sought.

Section (3) A qualified donor (an individual who is a resident within the electoral district of the office sought by the candidate) shall not contribute to a candidate's campaign any restricted contributions of Section (1) received from an unqualified donor for the purpose of contributing to a candidate's campaign for elected public office. An unqualified donor (an entity which is not an individual and who is not a resident of the electoral district of the office sought by the candidate) shall not give any restricted contributions of Section (1) to a qualified donor for the purpose of contributing to a candidate's campaign for elected public office.

Section (4) A violation of Section (3) shall be an unclassified felony. [Created through initiative petition filed Jan. 25, 1993, and adopted by the people Nov. 8, 1994]

Note: An initiative petition (Measure No. 6, 1994) adopted by the people Nov. 8, 1994, proposed a constitutional amendment as an unnumbered section. Section 22 sections (1), (2), (3) and (4) were designated in the proposed amendment as "SECTION 1.," "SECTION 2." "SECTION 3." and "SECTION 4.," respectively.

Section 23. Approval by more than majority required for certain measures submitted to people. (1) Any measure that includes any proposed requirement for more than a majority of votes cast by the electorate to approve any change in law or government action shall become effective only if approved by at least the same percentage of voters specified in the proposed voting requirement.

(2) For the purposes of this section, "measure" includes all initiatives and all measures referred to the voters by the Legislative Assembly.

(3) The requirements of this section apply to all measures presented to the voters at the November 3, 1998 election and thereafter.

(4) The purpose of this section is to prevent greater-than-majority voting requirements from being imposed by only a majority of the voters. [Created through initiative petition filed Jan. 15, 1998, and adopted by the people Nov. 3, 1998]

Constitution

Section 24. Death of candidate prior to election. When any vacancy occurs in the nomination of a candidate for elective public office in this state, and the vacancy is due to the death of the candidate, the Legislative Assembly may provide by law that:

(1) The regularly scheduled election for that public office may be postponed;

(2) The public office may be filled at a subsequent election; and

(3) Votes cast for candidates for the public office at the regularly scheduled election may not be considered. [Created through S.J.R. 19, 2003, and adopted by the people Nov. 2, 2004]

ARTICLE III
DISTRIBUTION OF POWERS

Sec. 1. Separation of powers
2. Budgetary control over executive and administrative officers and agencies
3. Joint legislative committee to allocate emergency fund appropriations and to authorize expenditures beyond budgetary limits
4. Senate, confirmation of executive appointments

Section 1. Separation of powers. The powers of the Government shall be divided into three separate branches, the Legislative, the Executive, including the administrative, and the Judicial; and no person charged with official duties under one of these branches, shall exercise any of the functions of another, except as in this Constitution expressly provided. [Constitution of 1859; Amendment proposed by H.J.R. 44, 2011, and adopted by the people Nov. 6, 2012]

Section 2. Budgetary control over executive and administrative officers and agencies. The Legislative Assembly shall have power to establish an agency to exercise budgetary control over all executive and administrative state officers, departments, boards, commissions and agencies of the State Government. [Created through S.J.R. 24, 1951, and adopted by the people Nov. 4, 1952]

Note: Section 2 was designated as "Sec. 1" by S.J.R. 24, 1951, and adopted by the people Nov. 4, 1952.

Section 3. Joint legislative committee to allocate emergency fund appropriations and to authorize expenditures beyond budgetary limits. (1) The Legislative Assembly is authorized to establish by law a joint committee composed of members of both houses of the Legislative Assembly, the membership to be as fixed by law, which committee may exercise, during the interim between sessions of the Legislative Assembly, such of the following powers as may be conferred upon it by law:

(a) Where an emergency exists, to allocate to any state agency, out of any emergency fund that may be appropriated to the committee for that purpose, additional funds beyond the amount appropriated to the agency by the Legislative Assembly, or funds to carry on an activity required by law for which an appropriation was not made.

(b) Where an emergency exists, to authorize any state agency to expend, from funds dedicated or continuously appropriated for the uses and purposes of the agency, sums in excess of the amount of the budget of the agency as approved in accordance with law.

(c) In the case of a new activity coming into existence at such a time as to preclude the possibility of submitting a budget to the Legislative Assembly for approval, to approve, or revise and approve, a budget of the money appropriated for such new activity.

(d) Where an emergency exists, to revise or amend the budgets of state agencies to the extent of authorizing transfers between expenditure classifications within the budget of an agency.

(2) The Legislative Assembly shall prescribe by law what shall constitute an emergency for the purposes of this section.

(3) As used in this section, "state agency" means any elected or appointed officer, board, commission, department, institution, branch or other agency of the state government.

(4) The term of members of the joint committee established pursuant to this section shall run from the adjournment of one odd-numbered year regular session to the organization of the next odd-numbered year regular session. No member of a committee shall cease to be such member solely by reason of the expiration of his term of office as a member of the Legislative Assembly. [Created through S.J.R. 24, 1951, and adopted by the people Nov. 4, 1952; Amendment proposed by S.J.R. 41, 2010, and adopted by the people Nov. 2, 2010]

Note: Section 3 was designated as "Sec. 2" by S.J.R. 24, 1951, and adopted by the people Nov. 4, 1952.

Section 4. Senate confirmation of executive appointments. (1) The Legislative Assembly in the manner provided by law may require that all appointments and reappointments to state public office made by the Governor shall be subject to confirmation by the Senate.

(2) The appointee shall not be eligible to serve until confirmed in the manner required by law and if not confirmed in that manner, shall not be eligible to serve in the public office.

(3) In addition to appointive offices, the provisions of this section shall apply to any state elective office when the Governor is authorized by law or this Constitution to fill any vacancy therein, except the office of judge of any court, United States Senator or Representative and a district, county or precinct office. [Created through S.J.R. 20, 1977, and adopted by the people Nov. 7, 1978]

ARTICLE IV
LEGISLATIVE BRANCH

Section 1. Legislative power; initiative and referendum. (1) The legislative power of the state, except for the initiative and referendum powers reserved to the people, is vested in a Legislative Assembly, consisting of a Senate and a House of Representatives.

(2)(a) The people reserve to themselves the initiative power, which is to propose laws and amendments to the Constitution and enact or reject them at an election independently of the Legislative Assembly.

(b) An initiative law may be proposed only by a petition signed by a number of qualified voters equal to six percent of the total number of votes cast for all candidates for Governor at the election at which a Governor was elected for a term of four years next preceding the filing of the petition.

(c) An initiative amendment to the Constitution may be proposed only by a petition signed by a number of qualified voters equal to eight percent of the total number of votes cast for all candidates for Governor at the election at which a Governor was elected for a term of four years next preceding the filing of the petition.

(d) An initiative petition shall include the full text of the proposed law or amendment to the Constitution. A proposed law or amendment to the Constitution shall embrace one subject only and matters properly connected therewith.

(e) An initiative petition shall be filed not less than four months before the election at which the proposed law or amendment to the Constitution is to be voted upon.

(3)(a) The people reserve to themselves the referendum power, which is to approve or reject at an election any Act, or part thereof, of the Legislative Assembly that does not become effective earlier than 90 days after the end of the session at which the Act is passed.

(b) A referendum on an Act or part thereof may be ordered by a petition signed by a number of qualified voters equal to four percent of the total number of votes cast for all candidates for Governor at the election at which a Governor was elected for a term of four years next preceding the filing of the petition. A referendum petition shall be filed not more than 90 days after the end of the session at which the Act is passed.

(c) A referendum on an Act may be ordered by the Legislative Assembly by law. Notwithstanding section 15b, Article V of this Constitution, bills ordering a referendum and bills on which a referendum is ordered are not subject to veto by the Governor.

(4)(a) Petitions or orders for the initiative or referendum shall be filed with the Secretary of State. The Legislative Assembly shall provide by law for the manner in which the Secretary of State shall determine whether a petition contains the required number of signatures of qualified voters. The Secretary of State shall complete the verification process within the 30-day period after the last day on which the petition may be filed as provided in paragraph (e) of subsection (2) or paragraph (b) of subsection (3) of this section.

(b) Initiative and referendum measures shall be submitted to the people as provided in this section and by law not inconsistent therewith.

(c) All elections on initiative and referendum measures shall be held at the regular general elections, unless otherwise ordered by the Legislative Assembly.

(d) Notwithstanding section 1, Article XVII of this Constitution, an initiative or referendum measure becomes effective 30 days after the day on which it is enacted or approved by a majority of the votes cast thereon. A referendum ordered by petition on a part of an Act does not delay the remainder of the Act from becoming effective.

(5) The initiative and referendum powers reserved to the people by subsections (2) and (3) of this section are further reserved to the qualified voters of each municipality and district as to all local, special and municipal legislation of every character in or for their municipality or district. The manner of exercising those powers shall be provided by general laws, but cities may provide the manner of exercising those powers as to their municipal legislation. In a city, not more than 15 percent of the qualified voters may be required to propose legislation by the initiative, and not more than 10 percent of the qualified voters may be required to order a referendum on legislation. [Created through H.J.R. 16, 1967, and adopted by the people May 28, 1968 (this section adopted in lieu of former sections 1 and 1a of this Article); Amendment proposed by H.J.R. 27, 1985, and adopted by the people May 20, 1986; Amendment proposed by S.J.R. 3, 1999, and adopted by the people May 16, 2000]

Note: An initiative petition (Measure No. 62, 1998) proposed adding new sections and a subsection relating to political campaigns to the Oregon Constitution. Those sections, appearing as sections 24 to 32 of Article II and sections 1 (6), 1b and 1c of Article IV in previous editions of this Constitution, were declared void for not being enacted in compliance with section 1, Article XVII of this Constitution. See Swett v. Bradbury, 333 Or. 597, 43 P.3d 1094 (2002).

Section 1. Legislative authority vested in assembly; initiative and referendum; style of bills. [Constitution of 1859; Amendment proposed by H.J.R. 1, 1901, and adopted by the people June 2, 1902; Amendment proposed by S.J.R. 6, 1953, and adopted by the people Nov. 2, 1954; Repeal proposed by H.J.R. 16, 1967, and adopted by the people May 28, 1968 (present section 1 of this Article adopted in lieu of this section)]

Section 1a. Initiative and referendum on parts of laws and on local, special and municipal laws. [Created through initiative petition filed Feb. 3, 1906, and adopted by the people June 4, 1906; Repeal proposed by H.J.R. 16, 1967, and adopted by the people May 28, 1968 (present section 1 of this Article adopted in lieu of this section)]

Note: Section 1b as submitted to the people was preceded by the following:

To protect the integrity of initiative and referendum petitions, the People of Oregon add the following provisions to the Constitution of the State of Oregon:

Section 1b. Payment for signatures. It shall be unlawful to pay or receive money or other thing of value based on the number of signatures obtained on an initiative or referendum petition. Nothing herein prohibits payment for signature gathering which is not based, either directly or indirectly, on the number of signatures obtained. [Created through initiative petition filed Nov. 7, 2001, and adopted by the people Nov. 5, 2002]

Note: Added as unnumbered section to the Constitution but not to any Article therein by initiative petition (Measure No. 26, 2002) adopted by the people Nov. 5, 2002.

Section 1d. Effective date of amendment to section 1, Article IV, by S.J.R. 3, 1999. [Created through S.J.R. 3, 1999, and adopted by the people May 16, 2000; Repealed Dec. 31, 2002, as specified in text of section adopted by the people May 16, 2000]

Section 2. Number of Senators and Representatives. The Senate shall consist of sixteen, and the House of Representatives of thirty four members, which number shall not be increased until the year Eighteen Hundred and Sixty, after which time the Legislative Assembly may increase the number of Senators and Representatives, always keeping as near as may be the same ratio as to the number of Senators, and Representatives: Provided that the Senate shall never exceed thirty and the House of Representatives sixty members.—

Section 3. How Senators and Representatives chosen; filling vacancies; qualifications. (1) The senators and representatives shall be chosen by the electors of the respective counties or districts or subdistricts within a county or district into which the state may from time to time be divided by law.

(2)(a) If a vacancy occurs in the office of senator or representative from any county or district or subdistrict, the vacancy shall be filled as may be provided by law.

(b) Except as provided in paragraph (c) of this subsection, a person who is appointed to fill a vacancy in the office of senator or representative must be an inhabitant of the district the person is appointed to represent for at least one year next preceding the date of the appointment.

(c) For purposes of an appointment occurring during the period beginning on January 1 of the year a reapportionment becomes operative under section 6 of this Article, the person must have been an inhabitant of the district for one year next preceding the date of the appointment or from January 1 of the year the reapportionment becomes operative to the date of the appointment, whichever is less. [Constitution of 1859; Amendment proposed by S.J.R. 20, 1929, and adopted by the people Nov. 4, 1930; Amendment proposed by H.J.R. 20, 1953, and adopted by the people Nov. 2, 1954; Amendment proposed by S.J.R. 14, 1995, and adopted by the people May 16, 1995; Amendment proposed by H.J.R. 31, 2007, and adopted by the people Nov. 4, 2008]

Section 3a. Applicability of qualifications for appointment to legislative vacancy. [Section 3a was designated section 1b, which was created by S.J.R. 14, 1995, and adopted by the people May 16, 1995; Repealed Dec. 31, 1999, as specified in text of section adopted by the people May 16, 1995]

Section 4. Term of office of legislators; classification of Senators. (1) The Senators shall be elected for the term of four years, and Representatives for the term of two years. The term of each Senator and Representative shall commence on the second Monday in January following his election, and shall continue for the full period of four years or two years, as the case may be, unless a different commencing day for such terms shall have been appointed by law.

(2) The Senators shall continue to be divided into two classes, in accordance with the division by lot provided for under the former provisions of this Constitution, so that one-half, as nearly as possible, of the number of Senators shall be elected biennially.

(3) Any Senator or Representative whose term, under the former provisions of this section, would have expired on the first Monday in January 1961, shall continue in office until the second Monday in January 1961. [Constitution of 1859; Amendment proposed by S.J.R. 23, 1951, and adopted by the people Nov. 4, 1952; Amendment proposed by S.J.R. 28, 1959, and adopted by the people Nov. 8, 1960]

Section 5. Census. [Constitution of 1859; Repeal proposed by H.J.R. 16, 1971, and adopted by the people May 23, 1972]

Section 6. Apportionment of Senators and Representatives. [Constitution of 1859; Amendment proposed by initiative petition filed July 3, 1952, and adopted by the people Nov. 4, 1952; Repeal proposed by H.J.R. 6, 1985, and adopted by the people Nov. 4, 1986 (present section 6 of this Article adopted in lieu of this section)]

Section 6. Apportionment of Senators and Representatives; operative date. (1) At the odd-numbered year regular session of the Legislative Assembly next following an enumeration of the inhabitants by the United States Government, the number of Senators and Representatives shall be fixed by law and apportioned among legislative districts according to population. A senatorial district shall consist of two representative districts. Any Senator whose term continues through the next odd-numbered year regular legislative session after the operative date of the reapportionment shall be specifically assigned to a senatorial district. The ratio of Senators and Representatives, respectively, to population shall be determined by dividing the total population of the state by the number of Senators and by the number of Representatives. A reapportionment by the Legislative Assembly becomes operative as described in subsection (6) of this section.

(2) This subsection governs judicial review and correction of a reapportionment enacted by the Legislative Assembly.

(a) Original jurisdiction is vested in the Supreme Court, upon the petition of any elector of the state filed with the Supreme Court on or before August 1 of the year in which the Legislative Assembly enacts a reapportionment, to review any reapportionment so enacted.

(b) If the Supreme Court determines that the reapportionment thus reviewed complies with subsection (1) of this section and all law applicable thereto, it shall dismiss the petition by written opinion on or before September 1 of the same year and the reapportionment becomes operative as described in subsection (6) of this section.

(c) If the Supreme Court determines that the reapportionment does not comply with subsection (1) of this section and all law applicable thereto, the reapportionment shall be void. In its written opinion, the Supreme Court shall specify with particularity wherein the reapportionment fails to comply. The opinion shall further direct the Secretary of State to draft a reapportionment of the Senators and Representatives in accordance with the provisions of subsection (1) of this section and all law applicable thereto. The Supreme Court shall file its order with the Secretary of State on or before September 15. The Secretary of State shall conduct a hearing on the reapportionment at which the public may submit evidence, views and argument. The Secretary of State shall cause a transcription of the hearing to be prepared which, with the evidence, shall become part of the record. The Secretary of State shall file the corrected reapportionment with the Supreme Court on or before November 1 of the same year.

(d) On or before November 15, the Supreme Court shall review the corrected reapportionment to assure its compliance with subsection (1) of this section and all law applicable thereto and may further correct the reapportionment if the court considers correction to be necessary.

(e) The corrected reapportionment becomes operative as described in subsection (6) of this section.

(3) This subsection governs enactment, judicial review and correction of a reapportionment if the Legislative Assembly fails to enact any reapportionment by July 1 of the year of the odd-numbered year regular session of the Legislative Assembly next following an enumeration of the inhabitants by the United States Government.

(a) The Secretary of State shall make a reapportionment of the Senators and Representatives in accordance with the provisions of subsection (1) of this section and all law applicable thereto. The Secretary of State shall conduct a hearing on the reapportionment at which the public may submit evidence, views and argument. The Secretary of State shall cause a transcription of the hearing to be prepared which, with the evidence, shall become part of the record. The reapportionment so made shall be filed with the Supreme Court by August 15 of the same year. The reapportionment becomes operative as described in subsection (6) of this section.

(b) Original jurisdiction is vested in the Supreme Court upon the petition of any elector of the state filed with the Supreme Court on or before September 15 of the same year to review any reapportionment and the record made by the Secretary of State.

(c) If the Supreme Court determines that the reapportionment thus reviewed complies with subsection (1) of this section and all law applicable thereto, it shall dismiss the petition by written opinion on or before October 15 of the same year and the reapportionment becomes operative as described in subsection (6) of this section.

(d) If the Supreme Court determines that the reapportionment does not comply with subsection (1) of this section and all law applicable thereto, the reapportionment shall be void. The Supreme Court shall return the reapportionment by November 1 to the Secretary of State accompanied by a written opinion specifying with particularity wherein the reapportionment fails to comply. The opinion shall further direct the Secretary of State to correct the reapportionment in those particulars, and in no others, and file the corrected reapportionment with the Supreme Court on or before December 1 of the same year.

(e) On or before December 15, the Supreme Court shall review the corrected reapportionment to assure its compliance with subsection (1) of this section and all law applicable thereto and may further correct the reapportionment if the court considers correction to be necessary.

(f) The reapportionment becomes operative as described in subsection (6) of this section.

(4) Any reapportionment that becomes operative as provided in this section is a law of the state except for purposes of initiative and referendum.

(5) Notwithstanding section 18, Article II of this Constitution, after the convening of the next odd-numbered year regular legislative session following the reapportionment, a Senator whose term continues through that legislative session is subject to recall by the electors of the district to which the Senator is assigned and not by the electors of the district existing before the latest reapportionment. The number of signatures required on the recall petition is 15 percent of the total votes cast for all candidates for Governor at the most recent election at which a candidate for Governor was elected to a full term in the two representative districts comprising the senatorial district to which the Senator was assigned.

(6)(a) Except as provided in paragraph (b) of this subsection, a reapportionment made under this section becomes operative on the second Monday in January of the next odd-numbered year after the applicable deadline for making a final reapportionment under this section.

(b) For purposes of electing Senators and Representatives to the next term of office that commences after the applicable deadline for making a final reapportionment under this section, a reapportionment made under this section becomes operative on January 1 of the calendar year next following the applicable deadline for making a final reapportionment under this section. [Created through H.J.R. 6, 1985, and adopted by the people Nov. 4, 1986 (this section adopted in lieu of former section 6 of this Article); Amendment proposed by H.J.R. 31, 2007, and adopted by the people Nov. 4, 2008; Amendment proposed by S.J.R. 41, 2010, and adopted by the people Nov. 2, 2010]

Section 7. Senatorial districts; senatorial and representative subdistricts. A senatorial district, when more than one county shall constitute the same, shall be composed of contiguous counties, and no county shall be divided in creating such senatorial districts. Senatorial or representative districts comprising not more than one county may be divided into subdistricts from time to time by law. Subdistricts shall be composed of contiguous territory within the district; and the ratios to population of senators or representatives, as the case may be, elected from the subdistricts, shall be substantially equal within the district. [Constitution of 1859; Amendment proposed by H.J.R. 20, 1953, and adopted by the people Nov. 2, 1954]

Section 8. Qualification of Senators and Representatives; effect of felony conviction. (1)(a) Except as provided in paragraph (b) of this subsection, a person may not be a Senator or Representative if the person at the time of election:

(A) Is not a citizen of the United States; and

(B) Has not been for one year next preceding the election an inhabitant of the district from which the Senator or Representative may be chosen.

(b) For purposes of the general election next following the applicable deadline for making a final apportionment under section 6 of this Article, the person must have been an inhabitant of the district from January 1 of the year following the applicable deadline for making the final reapportionment to the date of the election.

(2) Senators and Representatives shall be at least twenty one years of age.

(3) A person may not be a Senator or Representative if the person has been convicted of a felony during:

(a) The term of office of the person as a Senator or Representative; or

(b) The period beginning on the date of the election at which the person was elected to the office of Senator or Representative and ending on the first day of the term of office to which the person was elected.

(4) A person is not eligible to be elected as a Senator or Representative if that person has been convicted of a felony and has not completed the sentence received for the conviction prior to the date that person would take office if elected. As used in this subsection, "sentence received for the conviction" includes a term of imprisonment, any period of probation or post-prison supervision and payment of a monetary obligation imposed as all or part of a sentence.

(5) Notwithstanding sections 11 and 15, Article IV of this Constitution:

(a) The office of a Senator or Representative convicted of a felony during the term to which the Senator or Representative was elected or appointed shall become vacant on the date the Senator or Representative is convicted.

(b) A person elected to the office of Senator or Representative and convicted of a felony during the period beginning on the date of the election and ending on the first day of the term of office to which the person was elected shall be ineligible to take office and the office shall become vacant on the first day of the next term of office.

(6) Subject to subsection (4) of this section, a person who is ineligible to be a Senator or Representative under subsection (3) of this section may:

(a) Be a Senator or Representative after the expiration of the term of office during which the person is ineligible; and

(b) Be a candidate for the office of Senator or Representative prior to the expiration of the term of office during which the person is ineligible.

(7)(a) Except as provided in paragraph (b) of this subsection, a person may not be a Senator or Representative if the person at all times during the term of office of the person as a Senator or Representative is not an inhabitant of the district from which the Senator or Representative may be chosen or which the Senator or Representative has been appointed to represent. A person does not lose status as an inhabitant of a district if the person is absent from the district for purposes of business of the Legislative Assembly.

(b) Following the applicable deadline for making a final apportionment under section 6 of this Article, until the expiration of the term of office of the person, a person may be an inhabitant of any district. [Constitution of 1859; Amendment proposed by H.J.R. 6, 1985, and adopted by the people Nov. 4, 1986; Amendment proposed by S.J.R. 33, 1993, and adopted by the people Nov. 8, 1994; Amendment proposed by S.J.R. 14, 1995, and adopted by the people May 16, 1995; Amendment proposed by H.J.R. 31, 2007, and adopted by the people Nov. 4, 2008]

Section 8a. Applicability of qualification for legislative office. [Created by S.J.R. 14, 1995, and adopted by the people May 16, 1995; Repealed Dec. 31, 1999, as specified in text of section adopted by the people May 16, 1995]

Section 9. Legislators free from arrest and not subject to civil process in certain cases; words uttered in debate. Senators and Representatives in all cases, except for treason, felony, or breaches of the peace, shall be privileged from arrest during the session of the Legislative Assembly, and in going to and returning from the same; and shall not be subject to any civil process during the session of the Legislative Assembly, nor during the fifteen days next before the commencement thereof: Nor shall a member for words uttered in debate in either house, be questioned in any other place.—

Section 10. Annual regular sessions of the Legislative Assembly; organizational session; extension of regular sessions. (1) The Legislative Assembly shall hold annual sessions at the Capitol of the State. Each session must begin on the day designated by law as the first day of the session. Except as provided in subsection (3) of this section:

(a) A session beginning in an odd-numbered year may not exceed 160 calendar days in duration; and

(b) A session beginning in an even-numbered year may not exceed 35 calendar days in duration.

(2) The Legislative Assembly may hold an organizational session that is not subject to the limits of subsection (1) of this section for the purposes of introducing measures and performing the duties and effecting the organization described in sections 11 and 12 of this Article. The Legislative Assembly may not undertake final consideration of a measure or reconsideration of a measure following a gubernatorial veto when convened in an organizational session.

(3) A regular session, as described in subsection (1) of this section, may be extended for a period of five calendar days by the affirmative vote of two-thirds of the members of each house. A session may be extended more than once. An extension must begin on the first calendar day after the

end of the immediately preceding session or extension except that if the first calendar day is a Sunday, the extension may begin on the next Monday. [Constitution of 1859; Amendment proposed by S.J.R. 41, 2010, and adopted by the people Nov. 2, 2010]

Section 10a. Emergency sessions of the Legislative Assembly. In the event of an emergency the Legislative Assembly shall be convened by the presiding officers of both Houses at the Capitol of the State at times other than required by section 10 of this Article upon the written request of the majority of the members of each House to commence within five days after receipt of the minimum requisite number of requests. [Created through H.J.R. 28, 1975, and adopted by the people Nov. 2, 1976]

Section 11. Legislative officers; rules of proceedings; adjournments. Each house when assembled, shall choose its own officers, judge of the election, qualifications, and returns of its own members; determine its own rules of proceeding, and sit upon its own adjournments; but neither house shall without the concurrence of the other, adjourn for more than three days, nor to any other place than that in which it may be sitting.—

Section 12. Quorum; failure to effect organization. Two thirds of each house shall constitute a quorum to do business, but a smaller number may meet; adjourn from day to day, and compel the attendance of absent members. A quorum being in attendance, if either house fail to effect an organization within the first five days thereafter, the members of the house so failing shall be entitled to no compensation from the end of the said five days until an organization shall have been effected.—

Section 13. Journal; when yeas and nays to be entered. Each house shall keep a journal of its proceedings.—The yeas and nays on any question, shall at the request of any two members, be entered, together with the names of the members demanding the same, on the journal; provided that on a motion to adjourn it shall require one tenth of the members present to order the yeas, and nays.

Section 14. Deliberations to be open; rules to implement requirement. The deliberations of each house, of committees of each house or joint committees and of committees of the whole, shall be open. Each house shall adopt rules to implement the requirement of this section and the houses jointly shall adopt rules to implement the requirements of this section in any joint activity that the two houses may undertake. [Constitution of 1859; Amendment proposed by S.J.R. 36, 1973, and adopted by the people Nov. 5, 1974; Amendment proposed by H.J.R. 29, 1977, and adopted by the people May 23, 1978]

Section 15. Punishment and expulsion of members. Either house may punish its members for disorderly behavior, and may with the concurrence of two thirds, expel a member; but not a second time for the same cause.—

Section 16. Punishment of nonmembers. Either house, during its session, may punish by imprisonment, any person, not a member, who shall have been guilty of disrespect to the house by disorderly or contemptious [sic] behavior in its presence, but such imprisonment shall not at any time, exceed twenty [sic] twenty four hours.—

Section 17. General powers of Legislative Assembly. Each house shall have all powers necessary for a chamber of the Legislative Branch, of a free, and independent State. [Constitution of 1859; Amendment proposed by H.J.R. 44, 2011, and adopted by the people Nov. 6, 2012]

Section 18. Where bills to originate. Bills may originate in either house, but may be amended, or rejected in the other; except that bills for raising revenue shall originate in the House of Representatives.—

Section 19. Reading of bills; vote on final passage. Every bill shall be read by title only on three several days, in each house, unless in case of emergency two-thirds of the house where such bill may be pending shall, by a vote of yeas and nays, deem it expedient to dispense with this rule; provided, however, on its final passage such bill shall be read section by section unless such requirement be suspended by a vote of two-thirds of the house where such bill may be pending, and the vote on the final passage of every bill or joint resolution shall be taken by yeas and nays. [Constitution of 1859; Amendment proposed by S.J.R. 15, 1945, and adopted by the people Nov. 5, 1946]

Section 20. Subject and title of Act. Every Act shall embrace but one subject, and matters properly connected therewith, which subject shall be expressed in the title. But if any subject shall be embraced in an Act which shall not be expressed in the title, such Act shall be void only as to so much thereof as shall not be expressed in the title.

This section shall not be construed to prevent the inclusion in an amendatory Act, under a proper title, of matters otherwise germane to the same general subject, although the title or titles of the original Act or Acts may not have been sufficiently broad to have permitted such matter to have been so included in such original Act or Acts, or any of them. [Constitution of 1859; Amendment proposed by S.J.R. 41, 1951, and adopted by the people Nov. 4, 1952]

Section 21. Acts to be plainly worded. Every act, and joint resolution shall be plainly worded, avoiding as far as practicable the use of technical terms.—

Section 22. Mode of revision and amendment. No act shall ever be revised, or amended by mere reference to its title, but the act revised, or section amended shall be set forth, and published at full length. However, if, at any session of the Legislative Assembly, there are enacted two or more acts amending the same section, each of the acts shall be given effect to the extent that the amendments do not conflict in purpose. If the amendments conflict in purpose, the act last signed by the Governor shall control. [Constitution of 1859; Amendment proposed by S.J.R. 28, 1975, and adopted by the people Nov. 2, 1976]

Section 23. Certain local and special laws prohibited. The Legislative Assembly, shall not pass special or local laws, in any of the following enumerated cases, that is to say:—

Regulating the jurisdiction, and duties of justices of the peace, and of constables;

For the punishment of Crimes, and Misdemeanors;

Regulating the practice in Courts of Justice;

Providing for changing the venue in civil, and Criminal cases;

Granting divorces;

Changing the names of persons;

For laying, opening, and working on highways, and for the election, or appointment of supervisors;

Vacating roads, Town plats, Streets, Alleys, and Public squares;

Summoning and empanneling [sic] grand, and petit jurors;

For the assessment and collection of Taxes, for State, County, Township, or road purposes;

Providing for supporting Common schools, and for the preservation of school funds;

In relation to interest on money;

Providing for opening, and conducting the elections of State, County, and Township officers, and designating the places of voting;

Providing for the sale of real estate, belonging to minors, or other persons laboring under legal disabilities, by executors, administrators, guardians, or trustees.—

Section 24. Suit against state. Provision may be made by general law, for bringing suit against the State, as to all liabilities originating after, or existing at the time of the adoption of this Constitution; but no special act authorizing [sic] such suit to be brought, or making compensation to any person claiming damages against the State, shall ever be passed.—

Section 25. Majority necessary to pass bills and resolutions; special requirements for bills raising revenue; signatures of presiding officers required. (1) Except as otherwise provided in subsection (2) of this section, a majority of all the members elected to each House shall be necessary to pass every bill or Joint resolution.

(2) Three-fifths of all members elected to each House shall be necessary to pass bills for raising revenue.

(3) All bills, and Joint resolutions passed, shall be signed by the presiding officers of the respective houses. [Constitution of 1859; Amendment proposed by H.J.R. 14, 1995, and adopted by the people May 21, 1996]

Section 26. Protest by member. Any member of either house, shall have the right to protest, and have his protest, with his reasons for dissent, entered on the journal.—

Section 27. All statutes public laws; exceptions. Every Statute shall be a public law, unless otherwise declared in the Statute itself.—

Section 28. When Act takes effect. No act shall take effect, until ninety days from the end of the session at which the same shall have been passed, except in case of emergency; which emergency shall be declared in the preamble, or in the body of the law.

Section 29. Compensation of members. The members of the Legislative Assembly shall receive for their services a salary to be established and paid in the same manner as the salaries of other elected state officers and employes. [Constitution of 1859; Amendment proposed by S.J.R. 3, 1941, and adopted by the people Nov. 3, 1942; Amendment proposed by H.J.R. 5, 1949, and adopted by the people Nov. 7, 1950; Amendment proposed by H.J.R. 8, 1961, and adopted by the people May 18, 1962]

Section 30. Members not eligible to other offices. No Senator or Representative shall, during the time for which he may have been elected, be eligible to any office the election to which is vested in the Legislative Assembly; nor shall be appointed to any civil office of profit which shall have been created, or the emoluments of which shall have been increased during such term; but this latter provision shall not be construed to apply to any officer elective by the people.—

Section 31. Oath of members. The members of the Legislative Assembly shall before they enter on the duties of their respective offices, take and subscribe the following oath or affirmation;—I do solemnly swear (or affirm as the case may be) that I will support the Constitution of the United States, and the Constitution of the State of Oregon, and that I will faithfully discharge the duties of Senator (or Representative as the case may be) according to the best of my Ability, And such oath may be administered by the Govenor [sic], Secretary of State, or a judge of the Supreme Court.—

Section 32. Income tax defined by federal law; review of tax laws required. Notwithstanding any other provision of this Constitution, the Legislative Assembly, in any law imposing a tax or taxes on, in respect to or measured by income, may define the income on, in respect to or by which such tax or taxes are imposed or measured, by reference to any provision of the laws of the United States as the same may be or become effective at any time or from time to time, and may prescribe exceptions or modifications to any such provisions. At each regular session the Legislative Assembly shall, and at any special session may, provide for a review of the Oregon laws imposing a tax upon or measured by income, but no such laws shall be amended or repealed except by a legislative Act. [Created through H.J.R. 3, 1969, and adopted by the people Nov. 3, 1970]

Section 33. Reduction of criminal sentences approved by initiative or referendum process. Notwithstanding the provisions of section 25 of this Article, a two-thirds vote of all the members elected to each house shall be necessary to pass a bill that reduces a criminal sentence approved by the people under section 1 of this Article. [Created through initiative petition filed Nov. 16, 1993, and adopted by the people Nov. 8, 1994]

ARTICLE V
EXECUTIVE BRANCH

Sec. 1. Governor as chief executive; term of office; period of eligibility
2. Qualifications of Governor
3. Who not eligible
4. Election of Governor
5. Greatest number of votes decisive; election by legislature in case of tie
6. Contested elections
7. Term of office
8a. Vacancy in office of Governor
9. Governor as commander in chief of state military forces
10. Governor to see laws executed
11. Recommendations to legislature
12. Governor may convene legislature
13. Transaction of governmental business
14. Reprieves, commutations and pardons; remission of fines and forfeitures
15a. Single item and emergency clause veto
15b. Legislative enactments; approval by Governor; notice of intention to disapprove; disapproval and reconsideration by legislature; failure of Governor to return bill
16. Governor to Fill Vacancies by Appointment
17. Governor to issue writs of election to fill vacancies in legislature
18. Commissions

Section 1. Governor as chief executive; term of office; period of eligibility. The cheif [sic] executive power of the State, shall be vested in a Governor, who shall hold his office for the term of four years; and no person shall be eligible to such office more than Eight, in any period of twelve years.—

Section 2. Qualifications of Governor. No person except a citizen of the United States, shall be eligible to the Office of Governor, nor shall any person be eligible to that office who shall not have attained the age of thirty years, and who shall not have been three years next preceding his election, a resident within this State. The minimum age requirement of this section does not apply to a person who succeeds to the office of Governor under section 8a of this Article. [Constitution of 1859; Amendment proposed by H.J.R. 52, 1973, and adopted by the people Nov. 5, 1974]

Section 3. Who not eligible. No member of Congress, or person holding any office under the United States, or under this State, or under any other power, shall fill the Office of Governor, except as may be otherwise provided in this Constitution.—

Section 4. Election of Governor. The Governor shall be elected by the qualified Electors of the State at the times, and places of choosing members of the Legislative Assembly; and the returns of every Election for Governor, shall be sealed up, and transmitted to the Secretary of State; directed to the Speaker of the House of Representatives, who shall open, and publish them in the presence of both houses of the Legislative Assembly.—

Section 5. Greatest number of votes decisive; election by legislature in case of tie. The person having the highest number of votes for Governor, shall be elected; but in case two or more persons shall have an equal and the highest number of votes for Governor, the two houses of the Legislative Assembly at the next regular session thereof, shall forthwith by joint vote, proceed to elect one of the said persons Governor.—

Section 6. Contested elections. Contested Elections for Governor shall be determined by the Legislative Assembly in such manner as may be prescribed by law.—

Section 7. Term of office. The official term of the Governor shall be four years; and shall commence at such times as may be prescribed by this constitution, or prescribed by law.—

Section 8. Vacancy in office of Governor. [Constitution of 1859; Amendment proposed by S.J.R. 10, 1920 (s.s.), and adopted by the people May 21, 1920; Amendment proposed by S.J.R. 8, 1945, and adopted by the people Nov. 5, 1946; Repeal proposed by initiative petition filed July 7, 1972, and adopted by the people Nov. 7, 1972 (present section 8a of this Article adopted in lieu of this section)]

Section 8a. Vacancy in office of Governor. In case of the removal from office of the Governor, or of his death, resignation, or disability to discharge the duties of his office as prescribed by law, the Secretary of State; or if there be none, or in case of his removal from office, death, resignation, or disability to discharge the duties of his office as prescribed by law, then the State Treasurer; or if there be none, or in case of his removal from office, death, resignation, or disability to discharge the duties of his office as prescribed by law, then the President of the Senate; or if there be none, or in case of his removal from office, death, resignation, or disability to discharge the duties of his office as prescribed by law, then the Speaker of the House of Representatives, shall become Governor until the disability be removed, or a Governor be elected at the next general biennial election. The Governor elected to fill the vacancy shall hold office for the unexpired term of the outgoing Governor. The Secretary of State or the State Treasurer shall appoint a person to fill his office until the election of a Governor, at which time the office so filled by appointment shall be filled by election; or, in the event of a disability of the Governor, to be Acting Secretary of State or Acting State Treasurer until the disability be removed. The person so appointed shall not be eligible to succeed to the office of Governor by automatic succession under this section during the term of his appointment. [Created through initiative petition filed July 7, 1972, and adopted by the people Nov. 7, 1972 (this section adopted in lieu of former section 8 of this Article)]

Section 9. Governor as commander in chief of state military forces. The Governor shall be commander in cheif [sic] of the military, and naval forces of this State, and may call out such forces to execute the laws, to suppress insurection [sic], or to repel invasion.

Section 10. Governor to see laws executed. He shall take care that the Laws be faithfully executed.—

Section 11. Recommendations to legislature. He shall from time to time give to the Legislative Assembly information touching the condition of the State, and reccomend [sic] such measures as he shall judge to be expedient[.]

Section 12. Governor may convene legislature. He may on extraordinary occasions convene the Legislative Assembly by proclamation, and shall state to both houses when assembled, the purpose for which they shall have been convened.—

Section 13. Transaction of governmental business. He shall transact all necessary business with the officers of government, and may require information in writing from the offices of the Administrative, and Military Departments upon any subject relating to the duties of their respective offices.—

Section 14. Reprieves, commutations and pardons; remission of fines and forfeitures. He shall have power to grant reprieves, commutations, and pardons, after conviction, for all offences [sic] except treason, subject to such regulations as may be provided by law. Upon conviction for treason he shall have power to suspend the execution of the sentence until the case shall be reported to the Legislative Assembly, at its next meeting, when the Legislative Assembly shall either grant a pardon, commute the sentence, direct the execution of the sentence, or grant a farther [sic] reprieve.—

He shall have power to remit fines, and forfeitures, under such regulations as may be prescribed by law; and shall report to the Legislative Assembly at its next meeting each case of reprieve, commutation, or pardon granted, and the reasons for granting the same; and also the names of all persons in whose favor remission of fines, and forfeitures shall have been made, and the several amounts remitted[.]

Section 15. [This section of the Constitution of 1859 is redesignated as section 15b by the amendment proposed by S.J.R. 12, 1915, and adopted by the people Nov. 7, 1916]

Section 15a. Single item and emergency clause veto. The Governor shall have power to veto single items in appropriation bills, and any provision in new bills declaring an emergency, without thereby affecting any other provision of such bill. [Created through S.J.R. 12, 1915, and adopted by the people Nov. 7, 1916; Amendment proposed by S.J.R. 13, 1921, and adopted by the people June 7, 1921]

Section 15b. Legislative enactments; approval by Governor; notice of intention to disapprove; disapproval and reconsideration by legislature; failure of Governor to return bill. (1) Every bill which shall have passed the Legislative Assembly shall, before it becomes a law, be presented to the Governor; if the Governor approve, the Governor shall sign it; but if not, the Governor shall return it with written objections to that house in which it shall have originated, which house shall enter the objections at large upon the journal and proceed to reconsider it.

(2) If, after such reconsideration, two-thirds of the members present shall agree to pass the bill, it shall be sent, together with the objections, to the other house, by which it shall likewise be reconsidered, and, if approved by two-thirds of the members present, it shall become a law. But in all such cases, the votes of both houses shall be determined by yeas and nays, and the names of the members voting for or against the bill shall be entered on the journal of each house respectively.

(3) If any bill shall not be returned by the Governor within five days (Saturdays and Sundays excepted) after it shall have been presented to the Governor, it shall be a law without signature, unless the general adjournment shall prevent its return, in which case it shall be a law, unless the Governor within thirty days next after the adjournment (Saturdays and Sundays excepted) shall file such bill, with written objections thereto, in the office of the Secretary of State, who shall lay the same before the Legislative Assembly at its next session in like manner as if it had been returned by the Governor.

(4) Before filing a bill after adjournment with written objections, the Governor must announce publicly the possible intention to do so at least five days before filing the bill with written objections. However, nothing in this subsection requires the Governor to file any bill with objections because of the announcement. [Created through S.J.R. 12, 1915, and adopted by the people Nov. 7, 1916;

Amendment proposed by H.J.R. 9, 1937, and adopted by the people Nov. 8, 1938; Amendment proposed by S.J.R. 4, 1987, and adopted by the people Nov. 8, 1988]

Note: See note at section 15, Article V.

Section 16. Governor to Fill Vacancies by Appointment. When during a recess of the legislative assembly a vacancy occurs in any office, the appointment to which is vested in the legislative assembly, or when at any time a vacancy occurs in any other state office, or in the office of judge of any court, the governor shall fill such vacancy by appointment, which shall expire when a successor has been elected and qualified. When any vacancy occurs in any elective office of the state or of any district or county thereof, the vacancy shall be filled at the next general election, provided such vacancy occurs more than sixty-one (61) days prior to such general election. [Constitution of 1859; Amendment proposed by H.J.R. 5, 1925, and adopted by the people Nov. 2, 1926; Amendment proposed by H.J.R. 30, 1985, and adopted by the people May 20, 1986; Amendment proposed by S.J.R. 4, 1993, and adopted by the people Nov. 8, 1994]

Note: The leadline to section 16 was a part of the measure submitted to the people by H.J.R. 5, 1925.

Section 17. Governor to issue writs of election to fill vacancies in legislature. He shall issue writs of Election to fill such vacancies as may have occured [sic] in the Legislative Assembly.

Section 18. Commissions. All commissions shall issue in the name of the State; shall be signed by the Govenor [sic], sealed with the seal of the State, and attested by the Secretary of State.—

ARTICLE VI
ADMINISTRATIVE DEPARTMENT

Sec. 1. Election of Secretary and Treasurer of state; terms of office; period of eligibility
2. Duties of Secretary of State
3. Seal of state
4. Powers and duties of Treasurer
5. Offices and records of executive officers
6. County Officers
7. Other officers
8. County officers' qualifications; location of offices of county and city officers; duties of such officers
9. Vacancies of county, township, precinct and city offices
10. County home rule under county charter

Section 1. Election of Secretary and Treasurer of state; terms of office; period of eligibility. There shall be elected by the qualified electors of the State, at the times and places of choosing Members of the Legislative Assembly, a Secretary, and Treasurer of State, who shall severally hold their offices for the term of four years; but no person shall be eligible to either of said offices more than Eight in any period of Twelve years.—

Section 2. Duties of Secretary of State. The Secretary of State shall keep a fair record of the official acts of the Legislative Assembly, and Executive Branch; and shall when required lay the same, and all matters relative thereto before either chamber of the Legislative Assembly. The Secretary of State shall be by virtue of holding the office, Auditor of Public Accounts, and shall perform such other duties as shall be assigned to the Secretary of State by law. [Constitution of 1859; Amendment proposed by H.J.R. 44, 2011, and adopted by the people Nov. 6, 2012]

Section 3. Seal of state. There shall be a seal of State, kept by the Secretary of State for official purposes, which shall be called "The seal of the State of Oregon".—

Section 4. Powers and duties of Treasurer. The powers, and duties of the Treasurer of State shall be such as may be prescribed by law.—

Section 5. Offices and records of executive officers. The Governor, Secretary of State, and Treasurer of State shall severally keep the public records, books and papers at the seat of government in any manner relating to their respective offices. [Constitution of 1859; Amendment proposed by S.J.R. 13, 1985, and adopted by the people Nov. 4, 1986]

Section 6. County Officers: There shall be elected in each county by the qualified electors thereof at the time of holding general elections, a county clerk, treasurer and sheriff who shall severally hold their offices for the term of four years. [Constitution of 1859; Amendment proposed by initiative petition filed June 9, 1920, and adopted by the people Nov. 2, 1920; Amendment proposed by H.J.R. 7, 1955, and adopted by the people Nov. 6, 1956]

Note: The leadline to section 6 was a part of the measure proposed by initiative petition filed June 9, 1920, and adopted by the people Nov. 2, 1920.

Section 7. Other officers. Such other county, township, precinct, and City officers as may be necessary, shall be elected, or appointed in such manner as may be prescribed by law.—

Section 8. County officers' qualifications; location of offices of county and city officers; duties of such officers. Every county officer shall be an elector of the county, and the county assessor, county sheriff, county coroner and county surveyor shall possess such other qualifications as may be prescribed by law. All county and city officers shall keep their respective offices at such places therein, and perform such duties, as may be prescribed by law. [Constitution of 1859; Amendment proposed by H.J.R. 7, 1955, and adopted by the people Nov. 6, 1956; Amendment proposed by H.J.R. 42, 1971, and adopted by the people Nov. 7, 1972; Amendment proposed by H.J.R. 22, 1973, and adopted by the people Nov. 5, 1974]

Section 9. Vacancies in county, township, precinct and city offices. Vacancies in County, Township, precinct and City offices shall be filled in such manner as may be prescribed by law.—

Section 9a. County manager form of government. [Created through H.J.R. 3, 1943, and adopted by the people Nov. 7, 1944; Repeal proposed by H.J.R. 22, 1957, and adopted by the people Nov. 4, 1958]

Section 10. County home rule under county charter. The Legislative Assembly shall provide by law a method whereby the legal voters of any county, by majority vote of such voters voting thereon at any legally called election, may adopt, amend, revise or repeal a county charter. A county charter may provide for the exercise by the county of authority over matters of county concern. Local improvements shall be financed only by taxes, assessments or charges imposed on benefited property, unless otherwise provided by law or charter. A county charter shall prescribe the organization of the county government and shall provide directly, or by its authority, for the number, election or appointment, qualifications, tenure, compensation, powers and duties of such officers as the county deems necessary. Such officers shall among them exercise all the powers and perform all the duties, as distributed by the county charter or by its authority, now or hereafter, by the Constitution or laws of this state, granted to or imposed upon any county officer. Except as expressly provided by general law, a county charter shall not affect the selection, tenure, compensation, powers or duties prescribed by law for judges in their judicial capacity, for justices of the peace or for district attorneys. The initiative and referendum powers reserved to the people by this Constitution hereby are further reserved to the legal voters of every county relative to the adoption, amendment, revision or repeal of a county charter and to legislation passed by counties which have adopted such a charter; and no county shall require that referendum petitions be filed less than 90 days after the provisions of the charter or the legislation proposed for referral is adopted by the county governing body. To be circulated, referendum or initiative petitions shall set forth in full the charter or legislative provisions proposed for adoption or referral. Referendum petitions shall not be required to include a ballot title to be circulated. In a county a number of signatures of qualified voters equal to but not greater than four percent of the total number of all votes cast in the county for all candidates for Governor at the election at which a Governor was elected for a term of four years next preceding the filing of the petition shall be required for a petition to order a referendum on county legislation or a part thereof. A number of signatures equal to but not greater than six percent of the total number of votes cast in the county for all candidates for Governor at the election at which a Governor was elected for a term of four years next preceding the filing of the petition shall be required for a petition to propose an initiative ordinance. A number of signatures equal to but not greater than eight percent of the total number of votes cast in the county for all candidates for Governor at the election at which a Governor was elected for a term of four years next preceding the filing of the petition shall be required for a petition to propose a charter amendment. [Created through H.J.R. 22, 1957, and adopted by the people Nov. 4, 1958; Amendment proposed by S.J.R. 48, 1959, and adopted by the people Nov. 8, 1960; Amendment proposed by H.J.R. 21, 1977, and adopted by the people May 23, 1978]

ARTICLE VII (Amended)
THE JUDICIAL BRANCH

Sec. 1. Courts; election of judges; term of office; compensation

1a. Retirement of judges; recall to temporary active service

2. Amendment's effect on courts, jurisdiction and judicial system; Supreme Court's original jurisdiction

2a. Temporary appointment and assignment of judges

2b. Inferior courts may be affected in certain respects by special or local laws

3. Jury trial; re-examination of issues by appellate court; record on appeal to Supreme Court; affirmance notwithstanding error; determination of case by Supreme Court

4. Supreme Court; terms; statements of decisions of court

5. Juries; indictment; information; verdict in civil cases

6. Incompetency or malfeasance of public officer

7. Oath of office of Judges of Supreme Court

8. Removal, suspension or censure of judges

9. Juries of less than 12 jurors

Section 1. Courts; election of judges; term of office; compensation. The judicial power of the state shall be vested in one supreme court and in such other courts as may from time to time be created by law. The judges of the supreme and other courts shall be elected by the legal voters of the state or of their respective districts for a term of six years, and shall receive such compensation as may be provided by law, which compensation shall not be diminished during the term for which they are elected. [Created through initiative petition filed July 7, 1910, and adopted by the people Nov. 8, 1910]

Section 1a. Retirement of judges; recall to temporary active service. Notwithstanding the provisions of section 1, Article VII (Amended) of this Constitution, a judge of any court shall retire from judicial office at the end of the calendar year in which he attains the age of 75 years. The Legislative Assembly or the people may by law:

(1) Fix a lesser age for mandatory retirement not earlier than the end of the calendar year in which the judge attains the age of 70 years;

(2) Provide for recalling retired judges to temporary active service on the court from which they are retired; and

(3) Authorize or require the retirement of judges for physical or mental disability or any other cause rendering judges incapable of performing their judicial duties.

This section shall not affect the term to which any judge shall have been elected or appointed prior to or at the time of approval and ratification of this section. [Created through S.J.R. 3, 1959, and adopted by the people Nov. 8, 1960]

Section 2. Amendment's effect on courts, jurisdiction and judicial system; Supreme Court's original jurisdiction. The courts, jurisdiction, and judicial system of Oregon, except so far as expressly changed by this amendment, shall remain as at present constituted until otherwise provided by law. But the supreme court may, in its own discretion, take original jurisdiction in mandamus, quo warranto and habeas corpus proceedings. [Created through initiative petition filed July 7, 1910, and adopted by the people Nov. 8, 1910]

Section 2a. Temporary appointment and assignment of judges. The Legislative Assembly or the people may by law empower the Supreme Court to:

(1) Appoint retired judges of the Supreme Court or judges of courts inferior to the Supreme Court as temporary members of the Supreme Court.

(2) Appoint members of the bar as judges pro tempore of courts inferior to the Supreme Court.

(3) Assign judges of courts inferior to the Supreme Court to serve temporarily outside the district for which they were elected.

A judge or member of the bar so appointed or assigned shall while serving have all the judicial powers and duties of a regularly elected judge of the court to which he is assigned or appointed. [Created through S.J.R. 30, 1957, and adopted by the people Nov. 4, 1958]

Section 2b. Inferior courts may be affected in certain respects by special or local laws. Notwithstanding the provisions of section 23, Article IV of this Constitution, laws creating courts inferior to the Supreme Court or prescribing and defining the jurisdiction of such courts or the manner in which such jurisdiction may be exercised, may be made applicable:

(1) To all judicial districts or other subdivisions of this state; or

(2) To designated classes of judicial districts or other subdivisions; or

(3) To particular judicial districts or other subdivisions. [Created through S.J.R. 34, 1961, and adopted by the people Nov. 6, 1962]

Section 3. Jury trial; re-examination of issues by appellate court; record on appeal to Supreme Court; affirmance notwithstanding error; determination of case by Supreme Court. In actions at law, where the value in controversy shall exceed $750, the right of trial by jury shall be preserved, and no fact tried by a jury shall be otherwise re-examined in any court of this state, unless the court can affirmatively say there is no evidence to support the verdict. Until otherwise provided by law, upon appeal of any case to the supreme court, either party may have attached to the bill of exceptions the whole testimony, the instructions of the court to the jury, and any other matter material to the decision of the appeal. If the supreme court shall be of opinion, after consideration of all the matters thus submitted, that the judgment of the court appealed from was such as should have been rendered in the case, such judgment shall be affirmed, notwithstanding any error committed during the trial; or if, in any respect, the judgment appealed from should be changed, and the supreme court shall be of opinion that it can determine what judgment should have been entered in the court below, it shall direct such judgment to be entered in the same manner and with like effect as decrees are now entered in equity cases on appeal to the supreme court. Provided, that nothing in this section shall be construed to authorize the supreme court to find the defendant in a criminal case guilty of an offense for which a greater penalty is provided than that of which the accused was convicted in the lower court. [Created through initiative petition filed July 7, 1910, and adopted by the people Nov. 8, 1910; Amendment proposed by H.J.R. 71, 1973, and adopted by the people Nov. 5, 1974; Amendment proposed by H.J.R. 47, 1995, and adopted by the people May 21, 1996]

Section 4. Supreme Court; terms; statements of decisions of court. The terms of the supreme court shall be appointed by law; but there shall be one term at the seat of government annually. At the close of each term the judges shall file with the secretary of state concise written statements of the decisions made at that term. [Created through initiative petition filed July 7, 1910, and adopted by the people Nov. 8, 1910]

Section 5. Juries; indictment; information. [Created through initiative petition filed July 7, 1910, and adopted by the people Nov. 8, 1910; Amendment proposed by S.J.R. 23, 1957, and adopted by the people Nov. 4, 1958; Repeal proposed by S.J.R. 1, 1973, and adopted by the people Nov. 5, 1974 (present section 5 of this Article adopted in lieu of this section)]

Section 5. Juries; indictment; information; verdict in civil cases. (1) The Legislative Assembly shall provide by law for:

(a) Selecting juries and qualifications of jurors;

(b) Drawing and summoning grand jurors from the regular jury list at any time, separate from the panel of petit jurors;

(c) Empaneling more than one grand jury in a county; and

(d) The sitting of a grand jury during vacation as well as session of the court.

(2) A grand jury shall consist of seven jurors chosen by lot from the whole number of jurors in attendance at the court, five of whom must concur to find an indictment.

(3) Except as provided in subsections (4) and (5) of this section, a person shall be charged in a circuit court with the commission of any crime punishable as a felony only on indictment by a grand jury.

(4) The district attorney may charge a person on an information filed in circuit court of a crime punishable as a felony if the person appears before the judge of the circuit court and knowingly waives indictment.

(5) The district attorney may charge a person on an information filed in circuit court if, after a preliminary hearing before a magistrate, the person has been held to answer upon a showing of probable cause that a crime punishable as a felony has been committed and that the person has committed it, or if the person knowingly waives preliminary hearing.

(6) An information shall be substantially in the form provided by law for an indictment. The district attorney may file an amended indictment or information whenever, by ruling of the court, an indictment or information is held to be defective in form.

(7) In civil cases three-fourths of the jury may render a verdict. [Created through S.J.R. 1, 1973, and adopted by the

people Nov. 5, 1974 (this section adopted in lieu of former section 5 of this Article)]

Section 6. Incompetency or malfeasance of public officer. Public officers shall not be impeached; but incompetency, corruption, malfeasance or delinquency in office may be tried in the same manner as criminal offenses, and judgment may be given of dismissal from office, and such further punishment as may have been prescribed by law. [Created through initiative petition filed July 7, 1910, and adopted by the people Nov. 8, 1910]

Section 7. Oath of office of Judges of Supreme Court. Every judge of the supreme court, before entering upon the duties of his office, shall take and subscribe, and transmit to the secretary of state, the following oath:

"I, _____, do solemnly swear (or affirm) that I will support the constitution of the United States, and the constitution of the State of Oregon, and that I will faithfully and impartially discharge the duties of a judge of the supreme court of this state, according to the best of my ability, and that I will not accept any other office, except judicial offices, during the term for which I have been elected." [Created through initiative petition filed July 7, 1910, and adopted by the people Nov. 8, 1910]

Section 8. Removal, suspension or censure of judges. (1) In the manner provided by law, and notwithstanding section 1 of this Article, a judge of any court may be removed or suspended from his judicial office by the Supreme Court, or censured by the Supreme Court, for:

(a) Conviction in a court of this or any other state, or of the United States, of a crime punishable as a felony or a crime involving moral turpitude; or

(b) Wilful misconduct in a judicial office where such misconduct bears a demonstrable relationship to the effective performance of judicial duties; or

(c) Wilful or persistent failure to perform judicial duties; or

(d) Generally incompetent performance of judicial duties; or

(e) Wilful violation of any rule of judicial conduct as shall be established by the Supreme Court; or

(f) Habitual drunkenness or illegal use of narcotic or dangerous drugs.

(2) Notwithstanding section 6 of this Article, the methods provided in this section, section 1a of this Article and in section 18, Article II of this Constitution, are the exclusive methods of the removal, suspension, or censure of a judge. [Created through S.J.R. 9, 1967, and adopted by the people Nov. 5, 1968; Amendment proposed by S.J.R. 48, 1975, and adopted by the people May 25, 1976]

Section 9. Juries of less than 12 jurors. Provision may be made by law for juries consisting of less than 12 but not less than six jurors. [Created through S.J.R. 17, 1971, and adopted by the people Nov. 7, 1972]

ARTICLE VII (Original)
THE JUDICIAL BRANCH

Note: Original Article VII, compiled below, has been supplanted in part by amended Article VII and in part by statutes enacted by the Legislative Assembly. The provisions of original Article VII relating to courts, jurisdiction and the judicial system, by the terms of section 2 of amended Article VII, are given the status of a statute and are subject to change by statutes enacted by the Legislative Assembly, except so far as changed by amended Article VII.

Section 1. Courts in which judicial power vested. The Judicial power of the State shall be vested in a Suprume [sic] Court, Circuits [sic] Courts, and County Courts, which shall be Courts of Record having general jurisdiction, to be defined, limited, and regulated by law in accordance with this Constitution.— Justices of the Peace may also be invested with limited Judicial powers, and Municipal Courts may be created to administer the regulations of incorporated towns, and cities. —

Section 2. Supreme Court. The Supreme Court shall consist of Four Justices to be chosen in districts by the electors thereof, who shall be citizens of the United States, and who shall have resided in the State at least three years next preceding their election, and after their election to reside in their respective districts: The number of Justices, the Districts may be increased, but shall never exceed seven; and the boundaries of districts may be changed, but no Change of Districts, shall have the effect to remove a Judge from office, or require him to change his residence without his consent. [Constitution of 1859; Amendment proposed by S.J.R. 7, 2001, and adopted by the people Nov. 5, 2002]

Section 3. Terms of office of Judges. The Judges first chosen under this Constitution shall allot among themselves, their terms of office, so that the term of one of them shall expire in Two years, one in Four years, and Two in Six years, and thereafter, one or more shall be chosen every Two years to serve for the term of Six years. —

Section 4. Vacancy. Every vacancy in the office of Judge of the Supreme Court shall be filled by election for the remainder of the vacant term, unless it would expire at the next election, and until so filled, or when it would so expire, the Governor shall fill the vacancy by appointment. —

Section 5. Chief Justice. The Judge who has the shortest term to serve, or the oldest of several having such shortest term, and not holding by appointment shall be the Chief [sic] Justice. —

Section 6. Jurisdiction. The Supreme Court shall have jurisdiction only to revise the final decisions of the Circuit Courts, and every cause shall be tried, and every decision shall be made by those Judges only, or a majority of them, who did not try the cause, or make the decision in the Circuit Court. —

Section 7. Term of Supreme Court; statements of decisions of court. The terms of the Supreme Court shall be appointed by Law; but there shall be one term at the seat of Government annually: —

And at the close of each term the Judges shall file with the Secretary of State, Concise written Statements of the decisions made at that term. —

Note: Section 7 is in substance the same as section 4 of amended Article VII.

Section 8. Circuit court. The Circuits [sic] Courts shall be held twice at least in each year in each County organized for judicial purposes, by one of the Justices of the Supreme Court at times to be appointed by law; and at such other times as may be appointed by the Judges severally in pursuance of law. —

Section 9. Jurisdiction of circuit courts. All judicial power, authority, and jurisdiction not vested by this Constitution, or by laws consistent therewith, exclusively in some other Court shall belong to the Circuit Courts, and they shall have appellate jurisdiction, and supervisory control over the County Courts, and all other inferior Courts, Officers, and tribunals. —

Section 10. Supreme and circuit judges; election in classes. The Legislative Assembly, may provide for the election of Supreme, and Circuit Judges, in distinct classes, one of which classes shall consist of three Justices of the Supreme Court, who shall not perform Circuit duty, and the other class shall consist of the necessary number of Circuit Judges, who shall hold full terms without allotment, and who shall take the same oath as the Supreme Judges. [Constitution of 1859; Amendment proposed by S.J.R. 7, 2001, and adopted by the people Nov. 5, 2002]

Section 11. County judges and terms of county courts. There shall be elected in each County for the term of Four years a County Judge, who shall hold the County Court at times to be regulated by law. —

Section 12. Jurisdiction of county courts; county commissioners. The County Court shall have the jurisdiction pertaining to Probate Courts, and boards of County Commissioners, and such other powers, and duties, and such civil Jurisdiction, not exceeding the amount or value of five hundred dollars, and such criminal jurisdiction not extending to death or imprisonment in the penitentiary, as may be prescribed by law. — But the Legislative Assembly may provide for the election of Two Commissioners to sit with the County Judge whilst transacting County business, in any, or all of the Counties, or may provide a seperate [sic] board for transacting such business. —

Section 13. Writs granted by county judge; habeas corpus proceedings. The County Judge may grant preliminary injuctions [sic], and such other writs as the Legislative Assembly may authorize him to grant, returnable to the Circuit Court, or otherwise as may be provided by law; and may hear, and decide questions arising upon habeas corpus; provided such decision be not against the authority, or proceedings of a Court, or Judge of equal, or higher jurisdiction. —

Section 14. Expenses of court in certain counties. The Counties having less than ten thousand inhabitants, shall be reimbursed wholly or in part for the salary, and expenses of the County Court by fees, percentage, & other equitable taxation, of the business done in said Court & in the office of the County Clerk. [Constitution of 1859; Amendment proposed by S.J.R. 7, 2001, and adopted by the people Nov. 5, 2002]

Section 15. County clerk; recorder. A County Clerk shall be elected in each County for the term of Two years, who shall keep all the public records, books, and papers of the County; record conveyances, and perform the duties of Clerk of the Circuit, and County Courts, and such other duties as may be prescribed by law: — But whenever the number of voters in any County shall exceed Twelve Hundred, the Legislative Assembly may authorize the election of one person as Clerk of the Circuit Court, one person as Clerk of the County Court, and one person Recorder of conveyances. —

Section 16. Sheriff. A sheriff shall be elected in each County for the term of Two years, who shall be the minis-

terial officer of the Circuit, and County Courts, and shall perform such other duties as may be prescribed by law.—

Section 17. Prosecuting attorneys. There shall be elected by districts comprised of one, or more counties, a sufficient number of prosecuting Attorneys, who shall be the law officers of the State, and of the counties within their respective districts, and shall perform such duties pertaining to the administration of Law, and general police as the Legislative Assembly may direct. —

Section 18. Verdict by Three-fourths Jury in Civil Cases; Jurors; Grand Jurors; Indictment May Be Amended, When. [Constitution of 1859; Amendment proposed by initiative petition filed Jan. 30, 1908, and adopted by the people June 1, 1908; Amendment proposed by H.J.R. 14, 1927, and adopted by the people June 28, 1927; Repeal proposed by S.J.R. 23, 1957, and adopted by the people Nov. 4, 1958]

Section 19. Official delinquencies. Public Officers shall not be impeached, but incompetency, corruption, malfeasance, or delinquency in office may be tried in the same manner as criminal offences [sic], and judgment may be given of dismissal from Office, and such further punishment as may have been prescribed by law. —

Note: Section 19 is the same as section 6 of amended Article VII.

Section 20. Removal of Judges of Supreme Court and prosecuting attorneys from office. The Govenor [sic] may remove from Office a Judge of the Supreme Court, or Prosecuting Attorney upon the Joint resolution of the Legislative Assembly, in which Two Thirds of the members elected to each house shall concur, for incompetency, Corruption, malfeasance, or delinquency in office, or other sufficient cause stated in such resolution. —

Section 21. Oath of office of Supreme Court Judges. Every judge of the Supreme Court before entering upon the duties of his office shall take, subscribe, and transmit to the Secretary of State the following oath. — I _____ do solemnly swear (or affirm) that I will support the Constitution of the United States, and the constitution of the State of Oregon, and that I will faithfully, and impartially discharge the duties of a Judge of the Supreme, and Circuits [sic] Courts of said State according to the best of my ability, and that I will not accept any other office, except Judicial offices during the term for which I have been elected. —

ARTICLE VIII
EDUCATION AND SCHOOL LANDS

Section 1. Superintendent of Public Instruction. The Governor shall be superintendent of public instruction, and his powers, and duties in that capacity shall be such as may be prescribed by law; but after the term of five years from the adoption of this Constitution, it shall be competent for the Legislative Assembly to provide by law for the election of a superintendent, to provide for his compensation, and prescribe his powers and duties.—

Section 2. Common School Fund. (1) The sources of the Common School Fund are:

(a) The proceeds of all lands granted to this state for educational purposes, except the lands granted to aid in the establishment of institutions of higher education under the

Acts of February 14, 1859 (11 Stat. 383) and July 2, 1862 (12 Stat. 503).

(b) All the moneys and clear proceeds of all property which may accrue to the state by escheat.

(c) The proceeds of all gifts, devises and bequests, made by any person to the state for common school purposes.

(d) The proceeds of all property granted to the state, when the purposes of such grant shall not be stated.

(e) The proceeds of the five hundred thousand acres of land to which this state is entitled under the Act of September 4, 1841 (5 Stat. 455).

(f) The five percent of the net proceeds of the sales of public lands to which this state became entitled on her admission into the union.

(g) After providing for the cost of administration and any refunds or credits authorized by law, the proceeds from any tax or excise levied on, with respect to or measured by the extraction, production, storage, use, sale, distribution or receipt of oil or natural gas and the proceeds from any tax or excise levied on the ownership of oil or natural gas. However, the rate of such taxes shall not be greater than six percent of the market value of all oil and natural gas produced or salvaged from the earth or waters of this state as and when owned or produced. This paragraph does not include proceeds from any tax or excise as described in section 3, Article IX of this Constitution.

(2) All revenues derived from the sources mentioned in subsection (1) of this section shall become a part of the Common School Fund. The State Land Board may expend moneys in the Common School Fund to carry out its powers and duties under subsection (2) of section 5 of this Article. Unexpended moneys in the Common School Fund shall be invested as the Legislative Assembly shall provide by law and shall not be subject to the limitations of section 6, Article XI of this Constitution. The State Land Board may apply, as it considers appropriate, income derived from the investment of the Common School Fund to the operating expenses of the State Land Board in exercising its powers and duties under subsection (2) of section 5 of this Article. The remainder of the income derived from the investment of the Common School Fund shall be applied to the support of primary and secondary education as prescribed by law. [Constitution of 1859; Amendment proposed by H.J.R. 7, 1967, and adopted by the people May 28, 1968; Amendment proposed by H.J.R. 6, 1979, and adopted by the people Nov. 4, 1980; Amendment to subsection (2) proposed by S.J.R. 1, 1987, and adopted by the people Nov. 8, 1988; Amendment to paragraph (b) of subsection (1) proposed by H.J.R. 3, 1989, and adopted by the people June 27, 1989]

Section 3. System of common schools. The Legislative Assembly shall provide by law for the establishment of a uniform, and general system of Common schools.

Section 4. Distribution of school fund income. Provision shall be made by law for the distribution of the income of the common school fund among the several Counties of this state in proportion to the number of children resident therein between the ages, four and twenty years.—

Section 5. State Land Board; land management. (1) The Governor, Secretary of State and State Treasurer shall constitute a State Land Board for the disposition and management of lands described in section 2 of this Article, and other lands owned by this state that are placed under their jurisdiction by law. Their powers and duties shall be prescribed by law.

(2) The board shall manage lands under its jurisdiction with the object of obtaining the greatest benefit for the people of this state, consistent with the conservation of this resource under sound techniques of land management.

[Constitution of 1859; Amendment proposed by H.J.R. 7, 1967, and adopted by the people May 28, 1968]

Section 6. Qualifications of electors at school elections. [Created through initiative petition filed June 25, 1948, and adopted by the people Nov. 2, 1948; Repeal proposed by H.J.R. 4, 2007, and adopted by the people Nov. 4, 2008]

Note: The leadline to section 6 was a part of the measure proposed by initiative petition filed June 25, 1948, and adopted by the people Nov. 2, 1948.

Section 7. Prohibition of sale of state timber unless timber processed in Oregon. (1) Notwithstanding subsection (2) of section 5 of this Article, the State Land Board shall not authorize the sale or export of timber from lands described in section 2 of this Article unless such timber will be processed in Oregon. The limitation on sale or export in this subsection shall not apply to species, grades or quantities of timber which may be found by the State Land Board to be surplus to domestic needs.

(2) Notwithstanding any prior agreements or other provisions of law or this Constitution, the Legislative Assembly shall not authorize the sale or export of timber from state lands other than those described in section 2 of this Article unless such timber will be processed in Oregon. The limitation on sale or export in this subsection shall not apply to species, grades or quantities of timber which may be found by the State Forester to be surplus to domestic needs.

(3) This section first becomes operative when federal law is enacted allowing this state to exercise such authority or when a court or the Attorney General of this state determines that such authority lawfully may be exercised. [Created through S.J.R. 8, 1989, and adopted by the people June 27, 1989]

Section 8. Adequate and Equitable Funding. (1) The Legislative Assembly shall appropriate in each biennium a sum of money sufficient to ensure that the state's system of public education meets quality goals established by law, and publish a report that either demonstrates the appropriation is sufficient, or identifies the reasons for the insufficiency, its extent, and its impact on the ability of the state's system of public education to meet those goals.

(2) Consistent with such legal obligation as it may have to maintain substantial equity in state funding, the Legislative Assembly shall establish a system of Equalization Grants to eligible districts for each year in which the voters of such districts approve local option taxes as described in Article XI, section 11 (4)(a)(B) of this Constitution. The amount of such Grants and eligibility criteria shall be determined by the Legislative Assembly. [Created through initiative petition filed Oct. 22, 1999, and adopted by the people Nov. 7, 2000]

Note: Added to Article VIII as unnumbered section by initiative petition (Measure No. 1, 2000) adopted by the people Nov. 7, 2000.

Note: The leadline to section 8 was a part of the measure submitted to the people by Measure No. 1, 2000.

ARTICLE IX
FINANCE

Section 1. Assessment and taxation; uniform rules; uniformity of operation of laws. The Legislative Assembly shall, and the people through the initiative may, provide by law uniform rules of assessment and taxation. All taxes shall be levied and collected under general laws operating uniformly throughout the State. [Constitution of 1859; Amendment proposed by H.J.R. 16, 1917, and adopted by the people June 4, 1917]

Section 1a. Poll or head tax; declaration of emergency in tax laws. No poll or head tax shall be levied or collected in Oregon. The Legislative Assembly shall not declare an emergency in any act regulating taxation or exemption. [Created through initiative petition filed June 23, 1910, and adopted by the people Nov. 8, 1910; Amendment proposed by S.J.R. 10, 1911, and adopted by the people Nov. 5, 1912]

Section 1b. Ships exempt from taxation until 1935. All ships and vessels of fifty tons or more capacity engaged in either passenger or freight coasting or foreign trade, whose home ports of registration are in the State of Oregon, shall be and are hereby exempted from all taxes of every kind whatsoever, excepting taxes for State purposes, until the first day of January, 1935. [Created through S.J.R. 18, 1915, and adopted by the people Nov. 7, 1916]

Section 1c. Financing redevelopment and urban renewal projects. The Legislative Assembly may provide that the ad valorem taxes levied by any taxing unit, in which is located all or part of an area included in a redevelopment or urban renewal project, may be divided so that the taxes levied against any increase in the assessed value, as defined by law, of property in such area obtaining after the effective date of the ordinance or resolution approving the redevelopment or urban renewal plan for such area, shall be used to pay any indebtedness incurred for the redevelopment or urban renewal project. The legislature may enact such laws as may be necessary to carry out the purposes of this section. [Created through S.J.R. 32, 1959, and adopted by the people Nov. 8, 1960; Amendment proposed by H.J.R. 85, 1997, and adopted by the people May 20, 1997]

Section 2. Legislature to provide revenue to pay current state expenses and interest. The Legislative Assembly shall provide for raising revenue sufficiently to defray the expenses of the State for each fiscal year, and also a sufficient sum to pay the interest on the State debt, if there be any.—

Section 3. Laws imposing taxes; gasoline and motor vehicle taxes. [Constitution of 1859; Amendment proposed by S.J.R. 11, 1941, and adopted by the people Nov. 3, 1942;

Repeal proposed by S.J.R. 7, 1979, and adopted by the people May 20, 1980]

Section 3. Tax imposed only by law; statement of purpose. No tax shall be levied except in accordance with law. Every law imposing a tax shall state distinctly the purpose to which the revenue shall be applied. [Created through S.J.R. 7, 1979, and adopted by the people May 20, 1980 (this section and section 3a adopted in lieu of former section 3 of this Article)]

Section 3a. Use of revenue from taxes on motor vehicle use and fuel; legislative review of allocation of taxes between vehicle classes. (1) Except as provided in subsection (2) of this section, revenue from the following shall be used exclusively for the construction, reconstruction, improvement, repair, maintenance, operation and use of public highways, roads, streets and roadside rest areas in this state:

(a) Any tax levied on, with respect to, or measured by the storage, withdrawal, use, sale, distribution, importation or receipt of motor vehicle fuel or any other product used for the propulsion of motor vehicles; and

(b) Any tax or excise levied on the ownership, operation or use of motor vehicles.

(2) Revenues described in subsection (1) of this section:

(a) May also be used for the cost of administration and any refunds or credits authorized by law.

(b) May also be used for the retirement of bonds for which such revenues have been pledged.

(c) If from levies under paragraph (b) of subsection (1) of this section on campers, motor homes, travel trailers, snowmobiles, or like vehicles, may also be used for the acquisition, development, maintenance or care of parks or recreation areas.

(d) If from levies under paragraph (b) of subsection (1) of this section on vehicles used or held out for use for commercial purposes, may also be used for enforcement of commercial vehicle weight, size, load, conformation and equipment regulation.

(3) Revenues described in subsection (1) of this section that are generated by taxes or excises imposed by the state shall be generated in a manner that ensures that the share of revenues paid for the use of light vehicles, including cars, and the share of revenues paid for the use of heavy vehicles, including trucks, is fair and proportionate to the costs incurred for the highway system because of each class of vehicle. The Legislative Assembly shall provide for a biennial review and, if necessary, adjustment, of revenue sources to ensure fairness and proportionality. [Created through S.J.R. 7, 1979, and adopted by the people May 20, 1980 (this section and section 3 adopted in lieu of former section 3 of this Article); Amendment proposed by S.J.R. 44, 1999, and adopted by the people Nov. 2, 1999; Amendment proposed by S.J.R. 14, 2003, and adopted by the people Nov. 2, 2004]

Section 3b. Rate of levy on oil or natural gas; exception. Any tax or excise levied on, with respect to or measured by the extraction, production, storage, use, sale, distribution or receipt of oil or natural gas, or the ownership thereof, shall not be levied at a rate that is greater than six percent of the market value of all oil and natural gas produced or salvaged from the earth or waters of this state as and when owned or produced. This section does not apply to any tax or excise the proceeds of which are dedicated as described in sections 3 and 3a of this Article. [Created through H.J.R. 6, 1979, and adopted by the people Nov. 4, 1980]

Note: Section 3b was designated as "Section 3a" by H.J.R. 6, 1979, and adopted by the people Nov. 4, 1980.

Section 4. Appropriation necessary for withdrawal from treasury. No money shall be drawn from the treasury, but in pursuance of appropriations made by law.—

Section 5. Publication of accounts. An accurate statement of the receipts, and expenditures of the public money shall be published with the laws of each odd-numbered year regular session of the Legislative Assembly. [Constitution of 1859; Amendment proposed by S.J.R. 41, 2010, and adopted by the people Nov. 2, 2010]

Section 6. Deficiency of funds; tax levy to pay. Whenever the expenses, of any fiscal year, shall exceed the income, the Legislative Assembly shall provide for levying a tax, for the ensuing fiscal year, sufficient, with other sources of income, to pay the deficiency, as well as the estimated expense of the ensuing fiscal year.—

Section 7. Appropriation laws not to contain provisions on other subjects. Laws making appropriations, for the salaries of public officers, and other current expenses of the State, shall contain provisions upon no other subject.—

Section 8. Stationery for use of state. All stationary [sic] required for the use of the State shall be furnished by the lowest responsible bidder, under such regulations as may be prescribed by law. But no State Officer, or member of the Legislative Assembly shall be interested in any bid, or contract for furnishing such stationery.—

Section 9. Taxation of certain benefits prohibited. Benefits payable under the federal old age and survivors insurance program or benefits under section 3(a), 4(a) or 4(f) of the federal Railroad Retirement Act of 1974, as amended, or their successors, shall not be considered income for the purposes of any tax levied by the state or by a local government in this state. Such benefits shall not be used in computing the tax liability of any person under any such tax. Nothing in this section is intended to affect any benefits to which the beneficiary would otherwise be entitled. This section applies to tax periods beginning on or after January 1, 1986. [Created through H.J.R. 26, 1985, and adopted by the people May 20, 1986]

Section 10. Retirement plan contributions by governmental employees. (1) Notwithstanding any existing State or Federal laws, an employee of the State of Oregon or any political subdivision of the state who is a member of a retirement system or plan established by law, charter or ordinance, or who will receive a retirement benefit from a system or plan offered by the state or a political subdivision of the state, must contribute to the system or plan an amount equal to six percent of their salary or gross wage.

(2) On and after January 1, 1995, the state and political subdivisions of the state shall not thereafter contract or otherwise agree to make any payment or contribution to a retirement system or plan that would have the effect of relieving an employee, regardless of when that employee was employed, of the obligation imposed by subsection (1) of this section.

(3) On and after January 1, 1995, the state and political subdivisions of the state shall not thereafter contract or otherwise agree to increase any salary, benefit or other compensation payable to an employee for the purpose of offsetting or compensating an employee for the obligation imposed by subsection (1) of this section. [Created through initiative petition filed May 10, 1993, and adopted by the people Nov. 8, 1994]

Section 11. Retirement plan rate of return contract guarantee prohibited. (1) Neither the state nor any political subdivision of the state shall contract to guarantee any rate of interest or return on the funds in a retirement system or plan established by law, charter or ordinance for the benefit of an employee of the state or a political subdivi-

sion of the state. [Created through initiative petition filed May 10, 1993, and adopted by the people Nov. 8, 1994]

Section 12. Retirement not to be increased by unused sick leave. (1) Notwithstanding any existing Federal or State law, the retirement benefits of an employee of the state or any political subdivision of the state retiring on or after January 1, 1995, shall not in any way be increased as a result of or due to unused sick leave. [Created through initiative petition filed May 10, 1993, and adopted by the people Nov. 8, 1994]

Section 13. Retirement plan restriction severability. If any part of Sections 10, 11 or 12 of this Article is held to be unconstitutional under the Federal or State Constitution, the remaining parts shall not be affected and shall remain in full force and effect. [Created through initiative petition filed May 10, 1993, and adopted by the people Nov. 8, 1994]

Section 14. Revenue estimate; retention of excess corporate tax revenue in General Fund for public education funding; return of other excess revenue to taxpayers; legislative increase in estimate. (1) As soon as is practicable after adjournment sine die of an odd-numbered year regular session of the Legislative Assembly, the Governor shall cause an estimate to be prepared of revenues that will be received by the General Fund for the biennium beginning July 1. The estimated revenues from corporate income and excise taxes shall be separately stated from the estimated revenues from other General Fund sources.

(2) As soon as is practicable after the end of the biennium, the Governor shall cause actual collections of revenues received by the General Fund for that biennium to be determined. The revenues received from corporate income and excise taxes shall be determined separately from the revenues received from other General Fund sources.

(3) If the revenues received by the General Fund from corporate income and excise taxes during the biennium exceed the amount estimated to be received from corporate income and excise taxes for the biennium, by two percent or more, the total amount of the excess shall be retained in the General Fund and used to provide additional funding for public education, kindergarten through twelfth grade.

(4) If the revenues received from General Fund revenue sources, exclusive of those described in subsection (3) of this section, during the biennium exceed the amount estimated to be received from such sources for the biennium, by two percent or more, the total amount of the excess shall be returned to personal income taxpayers.

(5) The Legislative Assembly may enact laws:

(a) Establishing a tax credit, refund payment or other mechanism by which the excess revenues are returned to taxpayers, and establishing administrative procedures connected therewith.

(b) Allowing the excess revenues to be reduced by administrative costs associated with returning the excess revenues.

(c) Permitting a taxpayer's share of the excess revenues not to be returned to the taxpayer if the taxpayer's share is less than a de minimis amount identified by the Legislative Assembly.

(d) Permitting a taxpayer's share of excess revenues to be offset by any liability of the taxpayer for which the state is authorized to undertake collection efforts.

(6)(a) Prior to the close of a biennium for which an estimate described in subsection (1) of this section has been made, the Legislative Assembly, by a two-thirds majority vote of all members elected to each House, may enact legislation declaring an emergency and increasing the amount of the estimate prepared pursuant to subsection (1) of this section.

(b) The prohibition against declaring an emergency in an act regulating taxation or exemption in section 1a, Article IX of this Constitution, does not apply to legislation enacted pursuant to this subsection.

(7) This section does not apply:

(a) If, for a biennium or any portion of a biennium, a state tax is not imposed on or measured by the income of individuals.

(b) To revenues derived from any minimum tax imposed on corporations for the privilege of carrying on or doing business in this state that is imposed as a fixed amount and that is nonapportioned (except for changes of accounting periods).

(c) To biennia beginning before July 1, 2001. [Created through H.J.R. 17, 1999, and adopted by the people Nov. 7, 2000; Amendment proposed by S.J.R. 41, 2010, and adopted by the people Nov. 2, 2010; Amendment proposed by initiative petition filed Dec. 7, 2011, and adopted by the people Nov. 6, 2012]

Section 15. Prohibition on tax, fee or other assessment upon transfer of interest in real property; exception. The state, a city, county, district or other political subdivision or municipal corporation of this state shall not impose, by ordinance or other law, a tax, fee or other assessment upon the transfer of any interest in real property, or measured by the consideration paid or received upon the transfer of any interest in real property. This section does not apply to any tax, fee or other assessment in effect and operative on December 31, 2009. [Created through initiative petition filed March 4, 2010, and adopted by the people Nov. 6, 2012]

Note: Added to Article IX as unnumbered section by initiative petition (Measure No. 79, 2012) adopted by the people Nov. 6, 2012.

ARTICLE X
THE MILITIA

Sec. 1. State militia
  2. Persons exempt
  3. Officers

Section 1. State militia. The Legislative Assembly shall provide by law for the organization, maintenance and discipline of a state militia for the defense and protection of the State. [Constitution of 1859; Amendment proposed by H.J.R. 5, 1961, and adopted by the people Nov. 6, 1962]

Section 2. Persons exempt. Persons whose religious tenets, or conscientious scruples forbid them to bear arms shall not be compelled to do so. [Constitution of 1859; Amendment proposed by H.J.R. 5, 1961, and adopted by the people Nov. 6, 1962]

Section 3. Officers. The Governor, in his capacity as Commander-in-Chief of the military forces of the State, shall appoint and commission an Adjutant General. All other officers of the militia of the State shall be appointed and commissioned by the Governor upon the recommendation of the Adjutant General. [Constitution of 1859; Amendment proposed by H.J.R. 5, 1961, and adopted by the people Nov. 6, 1962]

Section 4. Staff officers; commissions. [Constitution of 1859; Repeal proposed by H.J.R. 5, 1961, and adopted by the people Nov. 6, 1962]

Section 5. Legislature to make regulations for militia. [Constitution of 1859; Repeal proposed by H.J.R. 5, 1961, and adopted by the people Nov. 6, 1962]

Section 6. Continuity of government in event of enemy attack. [Created through H.J.R. 9, 1959, and adopted by the people Nov. 8, 1960; Repeal proposed by H.J.R. 24, 1975, and adopted by the people Nov. 2, 1976]

ARTICLE X-A
CATASTROPHIC DISASTERS

Sec. 1. Definitions; declaration of catastrophic disaster; convening of Legislative Assembly
  2. Additional powers of Governor; use of General Fund moneys and lottery funds
  3. Procedural requirements for Legislative Assembly
  4. Additional powers of Legislative Assembly
  5. Participation in session of Legislative Assembly by electronic or other means
  6. Termination of operation of this Article; extension by Legislative Assembly; transition provisions; limitation on power of Governor to invoke this Article

Section 1. Definitions; declaration of catastrophic disaster; convening of Legislative Assembly. (1) As used in this Article, "catastrophic disaster" means a natural or human-caused event that:

(a) Results in extraordinary levels of death, injury, property damage or disruption of daily life in this state; and

(b) Severely affects the population, infrastructure, environment, economy or government functioning of this state.

(2) As used in this Article, "catastrophic disaster" includes, but is not limited to, any of the following events if the event meets the criteria listed in subsection (1) of this section:

(a) Act of terrorism.

(b) Earthquake.

(c) Flood.

(d) Public health emergency.

(e) Tsunami.

(f) Volcanic eruption.

(g) War.

(3) The Governor may invoke the provisions of this Article if the Governor finds and declares that a catastrophic disaster has occurred. A finding required by this subsection shall specify the nature of the catastrophic disaster.

(4) At the time the Governor invokes the provisions of this Article under subsection (3) of this section, the Governor shall issue a proclamation convening the Legislative Assembly under section 12, Article V of this Constitution, unless:

(a) The Legislative Assembly is in session at the time the catastrophic disaster is declared; or

(b) The Legislative Assembly is scheduled to convene in regular session within 30 days after the date the catastrophic disaster is declared.

(5) If the Governor declares that a catastrophic disaster has occurred, the Governor shall manage the immediate response to the disaster. The actions of the Legislative Assembly under sections 3 and 4 of this Article are limited to actions necessary to implement the Governor's immediate response to the disaster and to actions necessary to aid recovery from the disaster. [Created through H.J.R. 7, 2011, and adopted by the people Nov. 6, 2012]

Section 2. Additional powers of Governor; use of General Fund moneys and lottery funds. (1) If the Governor declares that a catastrophic disaster has occurred, the Governor may:

(a) Use moneys appropriated from the General Fund to executive agencies for the current biennium to respond to the catastrophic disaster, regardless of the legislatively expressed purpose of the appropriation at the time the appropriation was made.

(b) Use lottery funds allocated to executive agencies for the current biennium to respond to the catastrophic disaster, regardless of the legislatively expressed purpose of the allocation at the time the allocation was made. The Governor may not reallocate lottery funds under this paragraph for purposes not authorized by section 4, Article XV of this Constitution.

(2) The authority granted to the Governor by this section terminates upon the taking effect of a law enacted after the declaration of a catastrophic disaster that specifies purposes for which appropriated General Fund moneys or allocated lottery funds may be used, or upon the date on which the provisions of sections 1 to 5 of this Article cease to be operative as provided in section 6 of this Article, whichever is sooner. [Created through H.J.R. 7, 2011, and adopted by the people Nov. 6, 2012]

Section 3. Procedural requirements for Legislative Assembly. If the Governor declares that a catastrophic disaster has occurred:

(1) Notwithstanding sections 10 and 10a, Article IV of this Constitution, the Legislative Assembly may convene in a place other than the Capitol of the State if the Governor or the Legislative Assembly determines that the Capitol is inaccessible.

(2) Notwithstanding section 12, Article IV of this Constitution, during any period of time when members of the Legislative Assembly are unable to compel the attendance of two-thirds of the members of each house because the catastrophic disaster has made it impossible to locate members or impossible for them to attend, two-thirds of the members of each house who are able to attend shall constitute a quorum to do business.

(3) In a session of the Legislative Assembly that is called because of the catastrophic disaster or that was imminent or ongoing at the time the catastrophic disaster was declared, the number of members of each house that constitutes a quorum under subsection (2) of this section may suspend the rule regarding reading of bills under the same circumstances and in the same manner that two-thirds of the members may suspend the rule under section 19, Article IV of this Constitution.

(4) Notwithstanding section 25, Article IV of this Constitution, during any period of time when members of the Legislative Assembly are unable to compel the attendance of two-thirds of the members of each house because the catastrophic disaster has made it impossible to locate members or impossible for them to attend, three-fifths of the members of each house who are able to attend a session described in subsection (3) of this section shall be necessary to pass every bill or joint resolution.

(5) Notwithstanding section 1a, Article IX of this Constitution, the Legislative Assembly may declare an emergency in any bill regulating taxation or exemption, including but not limited to any bill that decreases or suspends taxes or postpones the due date of taxes, if the Legislative Assembly determines that the enactment of the bill is necessary to provide an adequate response to the catastrophic disaster. [Created through H.J.R. 7, 2011, and adopted by the people Nov. 6, 2012]

Section 4. Additional powers of Legislative Assembly. (1) If the Governor declares that a catastrophic disaster has occurred:

(a) The Legislative Assembly may enact laws authorizing the use of revenue described in section 3a, Article IX of this Constitution, for purposes other than those described in that section.

(b) The Legislative Assembly may, by a vote of the number of members of each house that constitutes a quorum under subsection (2) of section 3 of this Article, appropriate moneys that would otherwise be returned to taxpayers under section 14, Article IX of this Constitution, to state agencies for the purpose of responding to the catastrophic disaster.

(c) Notwithstanding section 7, Article XI of this Constitution, the Legislative Assembly may lend the credit

of the state or create debts or liabilities in an amount the Legislative Assembly considers necessary to provide an adequate response to the catastrophic disaster.

(d) The provisions of section 15, Article XI of this Constitution, do not apply to any law that is approved by three-fifths of the members of each house who are able to attend a session described in subsection (3) of section 3 of this Article.

(e) The Legislative Assembly may take action described in subsection (6) of section 15, Article XI of this Constitution, upon approval by three-fifths of the members of each house who are able to attend a session described in subsection (3) of section 3 of this Article.

(f) Notwithstanding section 4, Article XV of this Constitution, the Legislative Assembly may allocate proceeds from the State Lottery for any purpose and in any ratio the Legislative Assembly determines necessary to provide an adequate response to the catastrophic disaster.

(2) Nothing in this section overrides or otherwise affects the provisions of section 15b, Article V of this Constitution. [Created through H.J.R. 7, 2011, and adopted by the people Nov. 6, 2012]

Section 5. Participation in session of Legislative Assembly by electronic or other means. For purposes of sections 3 and 4 of this Article, a member of the Legislative Assembly who cannot be physically present at a session convened under section 1 of this Article shall be considered in attendance if the member is able to participate in the session through electronic or other means that enable the member to hear or read the proceedings as the proceedings are occurring and enable others to hear or read the member's votes or other contributions as the votes or other contributions are occurring. [Created through H.J.R. 7, 2011, and adopted by the people Nov. 6, 2012]

Section 6. Termination of operation of this Article; extension by Legislative Assembly; transition provisions; limitation on power of Governor to invoke this Article. (1) Except as provided in subsection (2) of this section, the provisions of sections 1 to 5 of this Article, once invoked, shall cease to be operative not later than 30 days following the date the Governor invoked the provisions of sections 1 to 5 of this Article, or on an earlier date recommended by the Governor and determined by the Legislative Assembly. The Governor may not recommend a date under this subsection unless the Governor finds and declares that the immediate response to the catastrophic disaster has ended.

(2) Prior to expiration of the 30-day limit established in subsection (1) of this section, the Legislative Assembly may extend the operation of sections 1 to 5 of this Article beyond the 30-day limit upon the approval of three-fifths of the members of each house who are able to attend a session described in subsection (3) of section 3 of this Article.

(3) The determination by the Legislative Assembly required by subsection (1) of this section or an extension described in subsection (2) of this section shall take the form of a bill. A bill that extends the operation of sections 1 to 5 of this Article shall establish a date upon which the provisions of sections 1 to 5 of this Article shall cease to be operative. A bill described in this subsection shall be presented to the Governor for action in accordance with section 15b, Article V of this Constitution.

(4) A bill described in subsection (3) of this section may include any provisions the Legislative Assembly considers necessary to provide an orderly transition to compliance with the requirements of this Constitution that have been overridden under this Article because of the Governor's declaration of a catastrophic disaster.

(5) The Governor may not invoke the provisions of sections 1 to 5 of this Article more than one time with respect

to the same catastrophic disaster. A determination under subsection (1) of this section or an extension described in subsection (2) of this section that establishes a date upon which the provisions of sections 1 to 5 of this Article shall cease to be operative does not prevent invoking the provisions of sections 1 to 5 of this Article in response to a new declaration by the Governor that a different catastrophic disaster has occurred. [Created through H.J.R. 7, 2011, and adopted by the people Nov. 6, 2012]

ARTICLE XI
CORPORATIONS AND INTERNAL IMPROVEMENTS

Section 1. Prohibition of state banks. The Legislative Assembly shall not have the power to establish, or incorporate any bank or banking company, or monied [sic] institution whatever; nor shall any bank company, or institution [sic] exist in the State, with the privilege of making, issuing, or putting in circulation, any bill, check, certificate, prommisory [sic] note, or other paper, or the paper of any bank company, or person, to circulate as money. —

Note: The semicolon appearing in the signed Constitution after the word "whatever" in section 1 was not in the original draft reported to and adopted by the convention and is not part of the Constitution. State v. H.S. & L.A., 8 Or. 396, 401 (1880).

Section 2. Formation of corporations; municipal charters; intoxicating liquor regulation. Corporations may be formed under general laws, but shall not be created by the Legislative Assembly by special laws. The Legislative Assembly shall not enact, amend or repeal any charter or act of incorporation for any municipality, city or town. The legal voters of every city and town are hereby granted power to enact and amend their municipal charter, subject to the Constitution and criminal laws of the State of Oregon, and the exclusive power to license, regulate, control, or to suppress or prohibit, the sale of intoxicating liquors therein is vested in such municipality; but such municipality shall within its limits be subject to the provisions of the local option law of the State of Oregon. [Constitution of 1859; Amendment proposed by initiative petition filed Dec.13, 1905, and adopted by the people June 4, 1906; Amendment proposed by initiative petition filed June 23, 1910, and adopted by the people Nov. 8, 1910]

Section 2a. Merger of adjoining municipalities; county-city consolidation. (1) The Legislative Assembly, or the people by the Initiative, may enact a general law providing a method whereby an incorporated city or town or municipal corporation may surrender its charter and be merged into an adjoining city or town, provided a majority of the electors of each of the incorporated cities or towns or municipal corporations affected authorize the surrender or merger, as the case may be.

(2) In all counties having a city therein containing over 300,000 inhabitants, the county and city government thereof may be consolidated in such manner as may be provided by law with one set of officers. The consolidated county and city may be incorporated under general laws providing for incorporation for municipal purposes. The provisions of this Constitution applicable to cities, and also those applicable to counties, so far as not inconsistent or prohibited to cities, shall be applicable to such consolidated government. [Created through H.J.R. 10, 1913, and adopted by the people Nov. 3, 1914; Amendment proposed by S.J.R. 29, 1967, and adopted by the people Nov. 5, 1968]

Section 3. Liability of stockholders. The stockholders of all corporations and joint stock companies shall be liable for the indebtedness of said corporation to the amount of their stock subscribed and unpaid and no more, excepting that the stockholders of corporations or joint stock companies conducting the business of banking shall be individually liable equally and ratably and not one for another, for the benefit of the depositors of said bank, to the amount of their stock, at the par value thereof, in addition to the par value of such shares, unless such banking corporation shall have provided security through membership in the federal deposit insurance corporation or other instrumentality of the United States or otherwise for the benefit of the depositors of said bank equivalent in amount to such double liability of said stockholders. [Constitution of 1859; Amendment proposed by S.J.R. 13, 1911, and adopted by the people Nov. 5, 1912; Amendment proposed by H.J.R. 2, 1943, and adopted by the people Nov. 7, 1944]

Section 4. Compensation for property taken by corporation. No person's property shall be taken by any corporation under authority of law, without compensation being first made, or secured in such manner as may be prescribed by law. —

Section 5. Restriction of municipal powers in Acts of incorporation. Acts of the Legislative Assembly, incorporating towns, and cities, shall restrict their powers of taxation, borrowing money, contracting debts, and loaning their credit. —

Section 6. State not to be stockholder in company; exceptions. (1) Except as provided in subsection (3) of this section, the state shall not subscribe to, or be interested in the stock of any company, association or corporation. However, as provided by law the state may hold and dispose of stock, including stock already received, that is donated or bequeathed; and may invest, in the stock of any company, association or corporation, any funds or moneys that:

(a) Are donated or bequeathed for higher education purposes;

(b) Are the proceeds from the disposition of stock that is donated or bequeathed for higher education purposes, including stock already received; or

(c) Are dividends paid with respect to stock that is donated or bequeathed for higher education purposes, including stock already received.

(2) Notwithstanding the limits contained in subsection (1) of this section, the state may hold and dispose of stock:

(a) Received in exchange for technology created in whole or in part by a public institution of post-secondary education; or

(b) Received prior to December 5, 2002, as a state asset invested in the creation or development of technology or resources within Oregon.

(3) Subsections (1) and (2) of this section do not apply to public universities. [Constitution of 1859; Amendment proposed by H.J.R. 11, 1955, and adopted by the people Nov. 6, 1956; Amendment proposed by H.J.R. 27, 1969, and adopted by the people Nov. 3, 1970; Amendment proposed by S.J.R. 17, 2001, and adopted by the people May 21, 2002; Amendment proposed by H.J.R. 203, 2016, and adopted by the people Nov. 8, 2016]

Note: H.J.R. 203, 2016, adopted by the people Nov. 8, 2016, did not properly indicate that the initial "the" should be printed lowercase.

Section 7. Credit of State Not to Be Loaned; Limitation Upon Power of Contracting Debts. The Legislative Assembly shall not lend the credit of the state nor in any manner create any debt or liabilities which shall singly or in the aggregate with previous debts or liabilities exceed the sum of fifty thousand dollars, except in case of war or to repel invasion or suppress insurrection or to build and maintain permanent roads; and the Legislative Assembly shall not lend the credit of the state nor in any manner create any debts or liabilities to build and maintain permanent roads which shall singly or in the aggregate with previous debts or liabilities incurred for that purpose exceed one percent of the true cash value of all the property of the state taxed on an ad valorem basis; and every contract of indebtedness entered into or assumed by or on behalf of the state in violation of the provisions of this section shall be void and of no effect. This section does not apply to any agreement entered into pursuant to law by the state or any agency thereof for the lease of real property to the state or agency for any period not exceeding 20 years and for a public purpose. [Constitution of 1859; Amendment proposed by initiative petition filed July 2, 1912, and adopted by the people Nov. 5, 1912; Amendment proposed by H.J.R. 11, 1920, and adopted by the people May 21, 1920; Amendment proposed by S.J.R. 4, 1961, and adopted by the people Nov. 6, 1962; Amendment proposed by S.J.R. 19, 1963, and adopted by the people Nov. 3, 1964]

Note: The leadline to section 7 was a part of the measure submitted to the people by H.J.R. 11, 1920 (s.s.).

Section 8. State not to assume debts of counties, towns or other corporations. The State shall never assume the debts of any county, town, or other corporation whatever, unless such debts, shall have been created to repel invasion, suppress insurrection, or defend the State in war. —

Section 9. Limitations on powers of county or city to assist corporations. (1) No county, city, town or other municipal corporation, by vote of its citizens, or otherwise, shall become a stockholder in any joint company, corporation or association, whatever, or raise money for, or loan its credit to, or in aid of, any such company, corporation or association.

(2) Notwithstanding subsection (1) of this section, any municipal corporation designated as a port under any general or special law of the state of Oregon may be empowered by statute to raise money and expend the same in the form of a bonus to aid in establishing water transportation lines between such port and any other domestic or foreign port or ports, and to aid in establishing water transportation lines on the interior rivers of this state, or on the rivers between Washington and Oregon, or on the rivers of Washington and Idaho reached by navigation from Oregon's rivers. Any debts of a municipality to raise money created for the aforesaid purpose shall be incurred only on approval of a majority of those voting on the question, and shall not, either singly or in the aggregate, with previous debts and liabilities incurred for that purpose, exceed one percent of the assessed valuation of all property in the municipality.

(3) The prohibitions and limitations set forth in subsection (1) of this section do not apply to the use by a county, city, town or other municipal corporation of bonded indebtedness that is payable from ad valorem taxes not subject to limitation under section 11 or 11b of this Article to finance capital costs of affordable housing, but only if:

(a) The bonded indebtedness is approved by the majority of voters voting on the measure authorizing the bonded indebtedness at an election that meets the requirements of subsection (8) of section 11 of this Article, as modified by section 11k of this Article;

(b) The measure authorizing the bonded indebtedness describes "affordable housing" for purposes of the measure;

(c) The jurisdiction authorizing the bonded indebtedness provides for annual audits of and public reporting on the expenditure of proceeds of the bonded indebtedness; and

(d) The principal amount of the jurisdiction's bonded indebtedness outstanding for such purpose does not exceed one-half of one percent of the real market value of all property in the jurisdiction. [Constitution of 1859; Amendment proposed by S.J.R. 13, 1917, and adopted by the people June 4, 1917; Amendment proposed by H.J.R. 201, 2018, and adopted by the people Nov. 6, 2018]

Section 10. County debt limitation. No county shall create any debt or liabilities which shall singly or in the aggregate, with previous debts or liabilities, exceed the sum of $5,000; provided, however, counties may incur bonded indebtedness in excess of such $5,000 limitation to carry out purposes authorized by statute, such bonded indebtedness not to exceed limits fixed by statute. [Constitution of 1859; Amendment proposed by initiative petition filed July 7, 1910, and adopted by the people Nov. 8, 1910; Amendment proposed by initiative petition filed July 2, 1912, and adopted by the people Nov. 5, 1912; Amendment proposed by S.J.R. 11, 1919, and adopted by the people June 3, 1919; Amendment proposed by H.J.R. 7, 1920 (s.s.), and adopted by the people May 21, 1920; Amendment proposed by S.J.R. 1, 1921 (s.s.), and adopted by the people Nov. 7, 1922; Amendment proposed by S.J.R. 5, 1921 (s.s.), and adopted by the people Nov. 7, 1922; Amendment proposed by H.J.R. 3, 1925, and adopted by the people Nov. 2, 1926; Amendment proposed by S.J.R. 18, 1925, and adopted by the people Nov. 2, 1926; Amendment proposed by H.J.R. 19, 1925, and adopted by the people Nov. 2, 1926; Amendment proposed by H.J.R. 21, 1957, and adopted by the people Nov. 4, 1958]

Section 11. Tax and indebtedness limitation. [Created through initiative petition filed July 6, 1916, and adopted by the people Nov. 7, 1916; Amendment proposed by H.J.R. 9, 1931, and adopted by the people Nov. 8, 1932; Amendment proposed by H.J.R. 9, 1951, and adopted by the people Nov. 4, 1952; Repeal proposed by S.J.R. 33, 1961, and adopted by the people Nov. 6, 1962 (second section 11 of this Article adopted in lieu of this section)]

Section 11. Tax base limitation. [Created through S.J.R. 33, 1961, and adopted by the people Nov. 6, 1962 (this section adopted in lieu of first section 11 of this Article); Amendment proposed by H.J.R. 28, 1985, and adopted by the people May

20, 1986; Repeal proposed by H.J.R. 85, 1997, and adopted by the people May 20, 1997 (present section 11 of this Article adopted in lieu of this section and sections 11a, 11f, 11g, 11h, 11i and 11j of this Article)]

Section 11. Property tax limitations on assessed value and rate of tax; exceptions. (1)(a) For the tax year beginning July 1, 1997, each unit of property in this state shall have a maximum assessed value for ad valorem property tax purposes that does not exceed the property's real market value for the tax year beginning July 1, 1995, reduced by 10 percent.

(b) For tax years beginning after July 1, 1997, the property's maximum assessed value shall not increase by more than three percent from the previous tax year.

(c) Notwithstanding paragraph (a) or (b) of this subsection, property shall be valued at the ratio of average maximum assessed value to average real market value of property located in the area in which the property is located that is within the same property class, if on or after July 1, 1995:

(A) The property is new property or new improvements to property;

(B) The property is partitioned or subdivided;

(C) The property is rezoned and used consistently with the rezoning;

(D) The property is first taken into account as omitted property;

(E) The property becomes disqualified from exemption, partial exemption or special assessment; or

(F) A lot line adjustment is made with respect to the property, except that the total assessed value of all property affected by a lot line adjustment shall not exceed the total maximum assessed value of the affected property under paragraph (a) or (b) of this subsection.

(d) Property shall be valued under paragraph (c) of this subsection only for the first tax year in which the changes described in paragraph (c) of this subsection are taken into account following the effective date of this section. For each tax year thereafter, the limits described in paragraph (b) of this subsection apply.

(e) The Legislative Assembly shall enact laws that establish property classes and areas sufficient to make a determination under paragraph (c) of this subsection.

(f) Each property's assessed value shall not exceed the property's real market value.

(g) There shall not be a reappraisal of the real market value used in the tax year beginning July 1, 1995, for purposes of determining the property's maximum assessed value under paragraph (a) of this subsection.

(2) The maximum assessed value of property that is assessed under a partial exemption or special assessment law shall be determined by applying the percentage reduction of paragraph (a) and the limit of paragraph (b) of subsection (1) of this section, or if newly eligible for partial exemption or special assessment, using a ratio developed in a manner consistent with paragraph (c) of subsection (1) of this section to the property's partially exempt or specially assessed value in the manner provided by law. After disqualification from partial exemption or special assessment, any additional taxes authorized by law may be imposed, but in the aggregate may not exceed the amount that would have been imposed under this section had the property not been partially exempt or specially assessed for the years for which the additional taxes are being collected.

(3)(a)(A) The Legislative Assembly shall enact laws to reduce the amount of ad valorem property taxes imposed by local taxing districts in this state so that the total of all ad valorem property taxes imposed in this state for the tax year beginning July 1, 1997, is reduced by 17 percent from the total of all ad valorem property taxes that would have been imposed under repealed sections 11 and 11a of this Article (1995 Edition) and section 11b of this Article but not taking into account Ballot Measure 47 (1996), for the tax year beginning July 1, 1997.

(B) The ad valorem property taxes to be reduced under subparagraph (A) of this paragraph are those taxes that would have been imposed under repealed sections 11 or 11a of this Article (1995 Edition) or section 11b of this Article, as modified by subsection (11) of this section, other than taxes described in subsection (4), (5), (6) or (7) of this section, taxes imposed to pay bonded indebtedness described in section 11b of this Article, as modified by paragraph (d) of subsection (11) of this section, or taxes described in section 1c, Article IX of this Constitution.

(C) It shall be the policy of this state to distribute the reductions caused by this paragraph so as to reflect:

(i) The lesser of ad valorem property taxes imposed for the tax year beginning July 1, 1995, reduced by 10 percent, or ad valorem property taxes imposed for the tax year beginning July 1, 1994;

(ii) Growth in new value under subparagraph (A), (B), (C), (D) or (E) of paragraph (c) of subsection (1) of this section, as added to the assessment and tax rolls for the tax year beginning July 1, 1996, or July 1, 1997 (or, if applicable, for the tax year beginning July 1, 1995); and

(iii) Ad valorem property taxes authorized by voters to be imposed in tax years beginning on or after July 1, 1996, and imposed according to that authority for the tax year beginning July 1, 1997.

(D) It shall be the policy of this state and the local taxing districts of this state to prioritize public safety and public education in responding to the reductions caused by this paragraph while minimizing the loss of decision-making control of local taxing districts.

(E) If the total value for the tax year beginning July 1, 1997, of additions of value described in subparagraph (A), (B), (C), (D) or (E) of paragraph (c) of subsection (1) of this section that are added to the assessment and tax rolls for the tax year beginning July 1, 1996, or July 1, 1997, exceeds four percent of the total assessed value of property statewide for the tax year beginning July 1, 1997 (before taking into account the additions of value described in subparagraph (A), (B), (C), (D) or (E) of paragraph (c) of subsection (1) of this section), then any ad valorem property taxes attributable to the excess above four percent shall reduce the dollar amount of the reduction described in subparagraph (A) of this paragraph.

(b) For the tax year beginning July 1, 1997, the ad valorem property taxes that were reduced under paragraph (a) of this subsection shall be imposed on the assessed value of property in a local taxing district as provided by law, and the rate of the ad valorem property taxes imposed under this paragraph shall be the local taxing district's permanent limit on the rate of ad valorem property taxes imposed by the district for tax years beginning after July 1, 1997, except as provided in subsection (5) of this section.

(c)(A) A local taxing district that has not previously imposed ad valorem property taxes and that seeks to impose ad valorem property taxes shall establish a limit on the rate of ad valorem property tax to be imposed by the district. The rate limit established under this subparagraph shall be approved by a majority of voters voting on the question. The rate limit approved under this subparagraph shall serve as the district's permanent rate limit under paragraph (b) of this subsection.

(B) The voter participation requirements described in subsection (8) of this section apply to an election under this paragraph.

(d) If two or more local taxing districts seek to consolidate or merge, the limit on the rate of ad valorem property tax to be imposed by the consolidated or merged district shall be the rate that would produce the same tax revenue as the local taxing districts would have cumulatively produced in the year of consolidation or merger, if the consolidation or merger had not occurred.

(e)(A) If a local taxing district divides, the limit on the rate of ad valorem property tax to be imposed by each local taxing district after division shall be the same as the local taxing district's rate limit under paragraph (b) of this subsection prior to division.

(B) Notwithstanding subparagraph (A) of this paragraph, the limit determined under this paragraph shall not be greater than the rate that would have produced the same amount of ad valorem property tax revenue in the year of division, had the division not occurred.

(f) Rates of ad valorem property tax established under this subsection may be carried to a number of decimal places provided by law and rounded as provided by law.

(g) Urban renewal levies described in this subsection shall be imposed as provided in subsections (15) and (16) of this section and may not be imposed under this subsection.

(h) Ad valorem property taxes described in this subsection shall be subject to the limitations described in section 11b of this Article, as modified by subsection (11) of this section.

(4)(a)(A) A local taxing district other than a school district may impose a local option ad valorem property tax that exceeds the limitations imposed under this section by submitting the question of the levy to voters in the local taxing district and obtaining the approval of a majority of the voters voting on the question.

(B) The Legislative Assembly may enact laws permitting a school district to impose a local option ad valorem property tax as otherwise provided under this subsection.

(b) A levy imposed pursuant to legislation enacted under this subsection may be imposed for no more than five years, except that a levy for a capital project may be imposed for no more than the lesser of the expected useful life of the capital project or 10 years.

(c) The voter participation requirements described in subsection (8) of this section apply to an election held under this subsection.

(5)(a) Any portion of a local taxing district levy shall not be subject to reduction and limitation under paragraphs (a) and (b) of subsection (3) of this section if that portion of the levy is used to repay:

(A) Principal and interest for any bond issued before December 5, 1996, and secured by a pledge or explicit commitment of ad valorem property taxes or a covenant to levy or collect ad valorem property taxes;

(B) Principal and interest for any other formal, written borrowing of moneys executed before December 5, 1996, for which ad valorem property tax revenues have been pledged or explicitly committed, or that are secured by a covenant to levy or collect ad valorem property taxes;

(C) Principal and interest for any bond issued to refund an obligation described in subparagraph (A) or (B) of this paragraph; or

(D) Local government pension and disability plan obligations that commit ad valorem property taxes and to ad valorem property taxes imposed to fulfill those obligations.

(b)(A) A levy described in this subsection shall be imposed on assessed value as otherwise provided by law in an amount sufficient to repay the debt described in this subsection. Ad valorem property taxes may not be imposed under this subsection that repay the debt at an earlier date

or on a different schedule than established in the agreement creating the debt.

(B) A levy described in this subsection shall be subject to the limitations imposed under section 11b of this Article, as modified by subsection (11) of this section.

(c)(A) As used in this subsection, "local government pension and disability plan obligations that commit ad valorem property taxes" is limited to contractual obligations for which the levy of ad valorem property taxes has been committed by a local government charter provision that was in effect on December 5, 1996, and, if in effect on December 5, 1996, as amended thereafter.

(B) The rates of ad valorem property taxes described in this paragraph may be adjusted so that the maximum allowable rate is capable of raising the revenue that the levy would have been authorized to raise if applied to property valued at real market value.

(C) Notwithstanding subparagraph (B) of this paragraph, ad valorem property taxes described in this paragraph shall be taken into account for purposes of the limitations in section 11b of this Article, as modified by subsection (11) of this section.

(D) If any proposed amendment to a charter described in subparagraph (A) of this paragraph permits the ad valorem property tax levy for local government pension and disability plan obligations to be increased, the amendment must be approved by voters in an election. The voter participation requirements described in subsection (8) of this section apply to an election under this subparagraph. No amendment to any charter described in this paragraph may cause ad valorem property taxes to exceed the limitations of section 11b of this Article, as amended by subsection (11) of this section.

(d) If the levy described in this subsection was a tax base or other permanent continuing levy, other than a levy imposed for the purpose described in subparagraph (D) of paragraph (a) of this subsection, prior to the effective date of this section, for the tax year following the repayment of debt described in this subsection the local taxing district's rate of ad valorem property tax established under paragraph (b) of subsection (3) of this section shall be increased to the rate that would have been in effect had the levy not been excepted from the reduction described in subsection (3) of this section. No adjustment shall be made to the rate of ad valorem property tax of local taxing districts other than the district imposing a levy under this subsection.

(e) If this subsection would apply to a levy described in paragraph (d) of this subsection, the local taxing district imposing the levy may elect out of the provisions of this subsection. The levy of a local taxing district making the election shall be included in the reduction and ad valorem property tax rate determination described in subsection (3) of this section.

(6)(a) The ad valorem property tax of a local taxing district, other than a city, county or school district, that is used to support a hospital facility shall not be subject to the reduction described in paragraph (a) of subsection (3) of this section. The entire ad valorem property tax imposed under this subsection for the tax year beginning July 1, 1997, shall be the local taxing district's permanent limit on the rate of ad valorem property taxes imposed by the district under paragraph (b) of subsection (3) of this section.

(b) Ad valorem property taxes described in this subsection shall be subject to the limitations imposed under section 11b of this Article, as modified by subsection (11) of this section.

(7) Notwithstanding any other existing or former provision of this Constitution, the following are validated, ratified, approved and confirmed:

(a) Any levy of ad valorem property taxes approved by a majority of voters voting on the question in an election held before December 5, 1996, if the election met the voter participation requirements described in subsection (8) of this section and the ad valorem property taxes were first imposed for the tax year beginning July 1, 1996, or July 1, 1997. A levy described in this paragraph shall not be subject to reduction under paragraph (a) of subsection (3) of this section but shall be taken into account in determining the local taxing district's permanent rate of ad valorem property tax under paragraph (b) of subsection (3) this section. This paragraph does not apply to levies described in subsection (5) of this section or to levies to pay bonded indebtedness described in section 11b of this Article, as modified by subsection (11) of this section.

(b) Any serial or one-year levy to replace an existing serial or one-year levy approved by a majority of the voters voting on the question at an election held after December 4, 1996, and to be first imposed for the tax year beginning July 1, 1997, if the rate or the amount of the levy approved is not greater than the rate or the amount of the levy replaced.

(c) Any levy of ad valorem property taxes approved by a majority of voters voting on the question in an election held on or after December 5, 1996, and before the effective date of this section if the election met the voter participation requirements described in subsection (8) of this section and the ad valorem property taxes were first imposed for the tax year beginning July 1, 1997. A levy described in this paragraph shall be treated as a local option ad valorem property tax under subsection (4) of this section. This paragraph does not apply to levies described in subsection (5) of this section or to levies to pay bonded indebtedness described in section 11b of this Article, as modified by subsection (11) of this section.

(8) An election described in subsection (3), (4), (5)(c)(D), (7)(a) or (c) or (11) of this section shall authorize the matter upon which the election is being held only if:

(a) At least 50 percent of registered voters eligible to vote in the election cast a ballot; or

(b) The election is a general election in an even-numbered year.

(9) The Legislative Assembly shall replace, from the state's General Fund, revenue lost by the public school system because of the limitations of this section. The amount of the replacement revenue shall not be less than the total replaced in fiscal year 1997-1998.

(10)(a) As used in this section:

(A) "Improvements" includes new construction, reconstruction, major additions, remodeling, renovation and rehabilitation, including installation, but does not include minor construction or ongoing maintenance and repair.

(B) "Ad valorem property tax" does not include taxes imposed to pay principal and interest on bonded indebtedness described in paragraph (d) of subsection (11) of this section.

(b) In calculating the addition to value for new property and improvements, the amount added shall be net of the value of retired property.

(11) For purposes of this section and for purposes of implementing the limits in section 11b of this Article in tax years beginning on or after July 1, 1997:

(a)(A) The real market value of property shall be the amount in cash that could reasonably be expected to be paid by an informed buyer to an informed seller, each acting without compulsion in an arm's length transaction occurring as of the assessment date for the tax year, as established by law.

(B) The Legislative Assembly shall enact laws to adjust the real market value of property to reflect a substantial casualty loss of value after the assessment date.

(b) The $5 (public school system) and $10 (other government) limits on property taxes per $1,000 of real market value described in subsection (1) of section 11b of this Article shall be determined on the basis of property taxes imposed in each geographic area taxed by the same local taxing districts.

(c)(A) All property taxes described in this section are subject to the limits described in paragraph (b) of this subsection, except for taxes described in paragraph (d) of this subsection.

(B) If property taxes exceed the limitations imposed under either category of local taxing district under paragraph (b) of this subsection:

(i) Any local option ad valorem property taxes imposed under this subsection shall be proportionally reduced by those local taxing districts within the category that is imposing local option ad valorem property taxes; and

(ii) After local option ad valorem property taxes have been eliminated, all other ad valorem property taxes shall be proportionally reduced by those taxing districts within the category, until the limits are no longer exceeded.

(C) The percentages used to make the proportional reductions under subparagraph (B) of this paragraph shall be calculated separately for each category.

(d) Bonded indebtedness, the taxes of which are not subject to limitation under this section or section 11b of this Article, consists of:

(A) Bonded indebtedness authorized by a provision of this Constitution;

(B) Bonded indebtedness issued on or before November 6, 1990; or

(C) Bonded indebtedness:

(i) Incurred for capital construction or capital improvements; and

(ii)(I) If issued after November 6, 1990, and approved prior to December 5, 1996, the issuance of which has been approved by a majority of voters voting on the question; or

(II) If approved by voters after December 5, 1996, the issuance of which has been approved by a majority of voters voting on the question in an election that is in compliance with the voter participation requirements in subsection (8) of this section.

(12) Bonded indebtedness described in subsection (11) of this section includes bonded indebtedness issued to refund bonded indebtedness described in subsection (11) of this section.

(13) As used in subsection (11) of this section, with respect to bonded indebtedness issued on or after December 5, 1996, "capital construction" and "capital improvements":

(a) Include public safety and law enforcement vehicles with a projected useful life of five years or more; and

(b) Do not include:

(A) Maintenance and repairs, the need for which could reasonably be anticipated.

(B) Supplies and equipment that are not intrinsic to the structure.

(14) Ad valorem property taxes imposed to pay principal and interest on bonded indebtedness described in section 11b of this Article, as modified by subsection (11) of this section, shall be imposed on the assessed value of the property determined under this section or, in the case of specially assessed property, as otherwise provided by law or as limited by this section, whichever is applicable.

(15) If ad valorem property taxes are divided as provided in section 1c, Article IX of this Constitution, in order to

Constitution

fund a redevelopment or urban renewal project, then notwithstanding subsection (1) of this section, the ad valorem property taxes levied against the increase shall be used exclusively to pay any indebtedness incurred for the redevelopment or urban renewal project.

(16) The Legislative Assembly shall enact laws that allow collection of ad valorem property taxes sufficient to pay, when due, indebtedness incurred to carry out urban renewal plans existing on December 5, 1996. These collections shall cease when the indebtedness is paid. Unless excepted from limitation under section 11b of this Article, as modified by subsection (11) of this section, nothing in this subsection shall be construed to remove ad valorem property taxes levied against the increase from the dollar limits in paragraph (b) of subsection (11) of this section.

(17)(a) If, in an election on November 5, 1996, voters approved a new tax base for a local taxing district under repealed section 11 of this Article (1995 Edition) that was not to go into effect until the tax year beginning July 1, 1998, the local taxing district's permanent rate limit under subsection (3) of this section shall be recalculated for the tax year beginning on July 1, 1998, to reflect:

(A) Ad valorem property taxes that would have been imposed had repealed section 11 of this Article (1995 Edition) remained in effect; and

(B) Any other permanent continuing levies that would have been imposed under repealed section 11 of this Article (1995 Edition), as reduced by subsection (3) of this section.

(b) The rate limit determined under this subsection shall be the local taxing district's permanent rate limit for tax years beginning on or after July 1, 1999.

(18) Section 32, Article I, and section 1, Article IX of this Constitution, shall not apply to this section.

(19)(a) The Legislative Assembly shall by statute limit the ability of local taxing districts to impose new or additional fees, taxes, assessments or other charges for the purpose of using the proceeds as alternative sources of funding to make up for ad valorem property tax revenue reductions caused by the initial implementation of this section, unless the new or additional fee, tax, assessment or other charge is approved by voters.

(b) This subsection shall not apply to new or additional fees, taxes, assessments or other charges for a government product or service that a person:

(A) May legally obtain from a source other than government; and

(B) Is reasonably able to obtain from a source other than government.

(c) As used in this subsection, "new or additional fees, taxes, assessments or other charges" does not include moneys received by a local taxing district as:

(A) Rent or lease payments;

(B) Interest, dividends, royalties or other investment earnings;

(C) Fines, penalties and unitary assessments;

(D) Amounts charged to and paid by another unit of government for products, services or property; or

(E) Payments derived from a contract entered into by the local taxing district as a proprietary function of the local taxing district.

(d) This subsection does not apply to a local taxing district that derived less than 10 percent of the local taxing district's operating revenues from ad valorem property taxes, other than ad valorem property taxes imposed to pay bonded indebtedness, during the fiscal year ending June 30, 1996.

(e) An election under this subsection need not comply with the voter participation requirements described in subsection (8) of this section.

(20) If any provision of this section is determined to be unconstitutional or otherwise invalid, the remaining provisions shall continue in full force and effect. [Created through H.J.R. 85, 1997, and adopted by the people May 20, 1997 (this section adopted in lieu of former sections 11, 11a, 11f, 11g, 11h, 11i and 11j of this Article)]

Note: The effective date of House Joint Resolution 85, 1997, is June 19, 1997.

Section 11a. School district tax levy. [Created through S.J.R. 3, 1987, and adopted by the people May 19, 1987; Repeal proposed by H.J.R. 85, 1997, and adopted by the people May 20, 1997 (present section 11 adopted in lieu of this section and sections 11, 11f, 11g, 11h, 11i and 11j of this Article)]

Section 11b. Property tax categories; limitation on categories; exceptions. (1) During and after the fiscal year 1991-92, taxes imposed upon any property shall be separated into two categories: One which dedicates revenues raised specifically to fund the public school system and one which dedicates revenues raised to fund government operations other than the public school system. The taxes in each category shall be limited as set forth in the table which follows and these limits shall apply whether the taxes imposed on property are calculated on the basis of the value of that property or on some other basis:

MAXIMUM ALLOWABLE TAXES

For Each $1000.00 of Property's Real Market Value

Fiscal Year	School System	Other than Schools
1991-1992	$15.00	$10.00
1992-1993	$12.50	$10.00
1993-1994	$10.00	$10.00
1994-1995	$ 7.50	$10.00
1995-1996	$ 5.00	$10.00
and thereafter		

Property tax revenues are deemed to be dedicated to funding the public school system if the revenues are to be used exclusively for educational services, including support services, provided by some unit of government, at any level from pre-kindergarten through post-graduate training.

(2) The following definitions shall apply to this section:

(a) "Real market value" is the minimum amount in cash which could reasonably be expected by an informed seller acting without compulsion, from an informed buyer acting without compulsion, in an "arms-length" transaction during the period for which the property is taxed.

(b) A "tax" is any charge imposed by a governmental unit upon property or upon a property owner as a direct consequence of ownership of that property except incurred charges and assessments for local improvements.

(c) "Incurred charges" include and are specifically limited to those charges by government which can be controlled or avoided by the property owner.

(i) because the charges are based on the quantity of the goods or services used and the owner has direct control over the quantity; or

(ii) because the goods or services are provided only on the specific request of the property owner; or

(iii) because the goods or services are provided by the governmental unit only after the individual property owner has failed to meet routine obligations of ownership and such action is deemed necessary to enforce regulations pertaining to health or safety. Incurred charges shall not exceed the actual costs of providing the goods or services.

(d) A "local improvement" is a capital construction project undertaken by a governmental unit

(i) which provides a special benefit only to specific properties or rectifies a problem caused by specific properties, and

(ii) the costs of which are assessed against those properties in a single assessment upon the completion of the project, and

(iii) for which the payment of the assessment plus appropriate interest may be spread over a period of at least ten years. The total of all assessments for a local improvement shall not exceed the actual costs incurred by the governmental unit in designing, constructing and financing the project.

(3) The limitations of subsection (1) of this section apply to all taxes imposed on property or property ownership except

(a) Taxes imposed to pay the principal and interest on bonded indebtedness authorized by a specific provision of this Constitution.

(b) Taxes imposed to pay the principal and interest on bonded indebtedness incurred or to be incurred for capital construction or improvements, provided the bonds are offered as general obligations of the issuing governmental unit and provided further that either the bonds were issued not later than November 6, 1990, or the question of the issuance of the specific bonds has been approved by the electors of the issuing governmental unit.

(4) In the event that taxes authorized by any provision of this Constitution to be imposed upon any property should exceed the limitation imposed on either category of taxing units defined in subsection (1) of this section, then, notwithstanding any other provision of this Constitution, the taxes imposed upon such property by the taxing units in that category shall be reduced evenly by the percentage necessary to meet the limitation for that category. The percentages used to reduce the taxes imposed shall be calculated separately for each category and may vary from property to property within the same taxing unit. The limitation imposed by this section shall not affect the tax base of a taxing unit.

(5) The Legislative Assembly shall replace from the State's general fund any revenue lost by the public school system because of the limitations of this section. The Legislative Assembly is authorized, however, to adopt laws which would limit the total of such replacement revenue plus the taxes imposed within the limitations of this section in any year to the corresponding total for the previous year plus 6 percent. This subsection applies only during fiscal years 1991-92 through 1995-96, inclusive. [Created through initiative petition filed May 8, 1990, and adopted by the people Nov. 6, 1990]

Section 11c. Limits in addition to other tax limits. The limits in section 11b of this Article are in addition to any limits imposed on individual taxing units by this Constitution. [Created through initiative petition filed May 8, 1990, and adopted by the people Nov. 6, 1990]

Section 11d. Effect of section 11b on exemptions and assessments. Nothing in sections 11b to 11e of this Article is intended to require or to prohibit the amendment of any current statute which partially or totally exempts certain classes of property or which prescribes special rules for assessing certain classes of property, unless such amendment is required or prohibited by the implementation of the limitations imposed by section 11b of this Article. [Created through initiative petition filed May 8, 1990, and adopted by the people Nov. 6, 1990]

Section 11e. Severability of sections 11b, 11c and 11d. If any portion, clause or phrase of sections 11b to 11e of this Article is for any reason held to be invalid or unconstitutional by a court of competent jurisdiction, the remaining portions, clauses and phrases shall not be affected but shall remain in full force and effect. [Created through initiative petition filed May 8, 1990, and adopted by the people Nov. 6, 1990]

Section 11f. School district tax levy following merger. [Created through H.J.R. 14, 1989, and adopted by the people Nov. 6, 1990; Repeal proposed by H.J.R. 85, 1997, and adopted by the people May 20, 1997 (present section 11 adopted in lieu of this section and sections 11, 11a, 11g, 11h, 11i and 11j of this Article)]

Note: Section 11f was designated as "Section 11b" by H.J.R. 14, 1989, and adopted by the people Nov. 6, 1990.

Section 11g. Tax increase limitation; exceptions. [Created through initiative petition filed Dec. 8, 1995, and adopted by the people Nov. 5, 1996; Repeal proposed by H.J.R. 85, 1997, and adopted by the people May 20, 1997 (present section 11 adopted in lieu of this section and sections 11, 11a, 11f, 11h, 11i and 11j of this Article)]

Section 11h. Voluntary contributions for support of schools or other public entities. [Created through initiative petition filed Dec. 8, 1995, and adopted by the people Nov. 5, 1996; Repeal proposed by H.J.R. 85, 1997, and adopted by the people May 20, 1997 (present section 11 adopted in lieu of this section and sections 11, 11a, 11f, 11g, 11i and 11j of this Article)]

Section 11i. Legislation to implement limitation and contribution provisions. [Created through initiative petition filed Dec. 8, 1995, and adopted by the people Nov. 5, 1996; Repeal proposed by H.J.R. 85, 1997, and adopted by the people May 20, 1997 (present section 11 adopted in lieu of this section and sections 11, 11a, 11f, 11g, 11h and 11j of this Article)]

Section 11j. Severability of sections 11g, 11h and 11i. [Created through initiative petition filed Dec. 8, 1995, and adopted by the people Nov. 5, 1996; Repeal proposed by H.J.R. 85, 1997, and adopted by the people May 20, 1997 (present section 11 adopted in lieu of this section and sections 11, 11a, 11f, 11g, 11h and 11i of this Article)]

Section 11k. Limitation on applicability of section 11 (8) voting requirements to elections on measures held in May or November of any year. Notwithstanding subsection (8) of section 11 of this Article, subsection (8) of section 11 of this Article does not apply to any measure voted on in an election held in May or November of any year. [Created through H.J.R. 15, 2007, and adopted by the people Nov. 4, 2008]

Section 11L. Limitation on applicability of sections 11 and 11b on bonded indebtedness to finance capital costs. (1) The limitations of sections 11 and 11b of this Article do not apply to bonded indebtedness incurred by local taxing districts if the bonded indebtedness was incurred on or after January 1, 2011, to finance capital costs as defined in subsection (5) of this section.

(2) Bonded indebtedness described in subsection (1) of this section includes bonded indebtedness issued to refund bonded indebtedness described in subsection (1) of this section.

(3) Notwithstanding subsection (1) of this section, subsection (8) of section 11 of this Article, as limited by section 11k of this Article, applies to measures that authorize bonded indebtedness described in subsection (1) of this section.

(4) The weighted average life of bonded indebtedness incurred on or after January 1, 2011, to finance capital costs may not exceed the weighted average life of the capital costs that financed with that indebtedness.

(5)(a) As used in this section, "capital costs" means costs of land and of other assets having a useful life of more than one year, including costs associated with acquisition, construction, improvement, remodeling, furnishing, equipping, maintenance or repair.

(b) "Capital costs" does not include costs of routine maintenance or supplies. [Created through H.J.R. 13, 2009, and adopted by the people May 18, 2010]

Section 12. People's utility districts. Peoples' [sic] Utility Districts may be created of territory, contiguous or otherwise, within one or more counties, and may consist of an incorporated municipality, or municipalities, with or without unincorporated territory, for the purpose of supplying water for domestic and municipal purposes; for the development of water power and/or electric energy; and for the distribution, disposal and sale of water, water power and electric energy. Such districts shall be managed by boards of directors, consisting of five members, who shall be residents of such districts. Such districts shall have power:

(a) To call and hold elections within their respective districts.

(b) To levy taxes upon the taxable property of such districts.

(c) To issue, sell and assume evidences of indebtedness.

(d) To enter into contracts.

(e) To exercise the power of eminent domain.

(f) To acquire and hold real and other property necessary or incident to the business of such districts.

(g) To acquire, develop, and/or otherwise provide for a supply of water, water power and electric energy.

Such districts may sell, distribute and/or otherwise dispose of water, water power and electric energy within or without the territory of such districts. The legislative assembly shall and the people may provide any legislation, that may be necessary, in addition to existing laws, to carry out the provisions of this section. [Created through initiative petition filed July 3, 1930, and adopted by the people Nov. 4, 1930]

Section 13. Interests of employes when operation of transportation system assumed by public body. Notwithstanding the provisions of section 20, Article I, section 10, Article VI, and sections 2 and 9, Article XI, of this Constitution, when any city, county, political subdivision, public agency or municipal corporation assumes responsibility for the operation of a public transportation system, the city, county, political subdivision, public agency or municipal corporation shall make fair and equitable arrangements to protect the interests of employes and retired employes affected. Such protective arrangements may include, without being limited to, such provisions as may be necessary for the preservation of rights, privileges and benefits (including continuation of pension rights and payment of benefits) under existing collective bargaining agreements, or otherwise. [Created through H.J.R. 13, 1965, and adopted by the people Nov. 8, 1966]

Section 14. Metropolitan service district charter. (1) The Legislative Assembly shall provide by law a method whereby the legal electors of any metropolitan service district organized under the laws of this state, by majority vote of such electors voting thereon at any legally called election, may adopt, amend, revise or repeal a district charter.

(2) A district charter shall prescribe the organization of the district government and shall provide directly, or by its authority, for the number, election or appointment, qualifications, tenure, compensation, powers and duties of such officers as the district considers necessary. Such officers shall among them exercise all the powers and perform all the duties, as granted to, imposed upon or distributed among district officers by the Constitution or laws of this state, by the district charter or by its authority.

(3) A district charter may provide for the exercise by ordinance of powers granted to the district by the Constitution or laws of this state.

(4) A metropolitan service district shall have jurisdiction over matters of metropolitan concern as set forth in the charter of the district.

(5) The initiative and referendum powers reserved to the people by this Constitution hereby are further reserved to the legal electors of a metropolitan service district relative to the adoption, amendment, revision or repeal of a district charter and district legislation enacted thereunder. Such powers shall be exercised in the manner provided for county measures under section 10, Article VI of this Constitution. [Created by S.J.R. 2, 1989, and adopted by the people Nov. 6, 1990]

Section 15. Funding of programs imposed upon local governments; exceptions. (1) Except as provided in subsection (7) of this section, when the Legislative Assembly or any state agency requires any local government to establish a new program or provide an increased level of service for an existing program, the State of Oregon shall appropriate and allocate to the local government moneys sufficient to pay the ongoing, usual and reasonable costs of performing the mandated service or activity.

(2) As used in this section:

(a) "Enterprise activity" means a program under which a local government sells products or services in competition with a nongovernment entity.

(b) "Local government" means a city, county, municipal corporation or municipal utility operated by a board or commission.

(c) "Program" means a program or project imposed by enactment of the Legislative Assembly or by rule or order of a state agency under which a local government must provide administrative, financial, social, health or other specified services to persons, government agencies or to the public generally.

(d) "Usual and reasonable costs" means those costs incurred by the affected local governments for a specific program using generally accepted methods of service delivery and administrative practice.

(3) A local government is not required to comply with any state law or administrative rule or order enacted or adopted after January 1, 1997, that requires the expenditure of money by the local government for a new program or increased level of service for an existing program until the state appropriates and allocates to the local government reimbursement for any costs incurred to carry out the law, rule or order and unless the Legislative Assembly provides, by appropriation, reimbursement in each succeeding year for such costs. However, a local government may refuse to comply with a state law or administrative rule or order under this subsection only if the amount appropriated and allocated to the local government by the Legislative Assembly for a program in a fiscal year:

(a) Is less than 95 percent of the usual and reasonable costs incurred by the local government in conducting the program at the same level of service in the preceding fiscal year; or

(b) Requires the local government to spend for the program, in addition to the amount appropriated and allocated by the Legislative Assembly, an amount that exceeds one-hundredth of one percent of the annual budget adopted by the governing body of the local government for that fiscal year.

(4) When a local government determines that a program is a program for which moneys are required to be appropriated and allocated under subsection (1) of this section, if the local government expended moneys to conduct the program and was not reimbursed under this section for the usual and reasonable costs of the program, the local government may submit the issue of reimbursement to nonbinding arbitration by a panel of three arbitrators. The

panel shall consist of one representative from the Oregon Department of Administrative Services, the League of Oregon Cities and the Association of Oregon Counties. The panel shall determine whether the costs incurred by the local government are required to be reimbursed under this section and the amount of reimbursement. The decision of the arbitration panel is not binding upon the parties and may not be enforced by any court in this state.

(5) In any legal proceeding or arbitration proceeding under this section, the local government shall bear the burden of proving by a preponderance of the evidence that moneys appropriated by the Legislative Assembly are not sufficient to reimburse the local government for the usual and reasonable costs of a program.

(6) Except upon approval by three-fifths of the membership of each house of the Legislative Assembly, the Legislative Assembly shall not enact, amend or repeal any law if the anticipated effect of the action is to reduce the amount of state revenues derived from a specific state tax and distributed to local governments as an aggregate during the distribution period for such revenues immediately preceding January 1, 1997.

(7) This section shall not apply to:

(a) Any law that is approved by three-fifths of the membership of each house of the Legislative Assembly.

(b) Any costs resulting from a law creating or changing the definition of a crime or a law establishing sentences for conviction of a crime.

(c) An existing program as enacted by legislation prior to January 1, 1997, except for legislation withdrawing state funds for programs required prior to January 1, 1997, unless the program is made optional.

(d) A new program or an increased level of program services established pursuant to action of the Federal Government so long as the program or increased level of program services imposes costs on local governments that are no greater than the usual and reasonable costs to local governments resulting from compliance with the minimum program standards required under federal law or regulations.

(e) Any requirement imposed by the judicial branch of government.

(f) Legislation enacted or approved by electors in this state under the initiative and referendum powers reserved to the people under section 1, Article IV of this Constitution.

(g) Programs that are intended to inform citizens about the activities of local governments.

(8) When a local government is not required under subsection (3) of this section to comply with a state law or administrative rule or order relating to an enterprise activity, if a nongovernment entity competes with the local government by selling products or services that are similar to the products and services sold under the enterprise activity, the nongovernment entity is not required to comply with the state law or administrative rule or order relating to that enterprise activity.

(9) Nothing in this section shall give rise to a claim by a private person against the State of Oregon based on the establishment of a new program or an increased level of service for an existing program without sufficient appropriation and allocation of funds to pay the ongoing, usual and reasonable costs of performing the mandated service or activity.

(10) Subsection (4) of this section does not apply to a local government when the local government is voluntarily providing a program four years after the effective date of the enactment, rule or order that imposed the program.

(11) In lieu of appropriating and allocating funds under this section, the Legislative Assembly may identify and direct the imposition of a fee or charge to be used by a local government to recover the actual cost of the program. [Created through H.J.R. 2, 1995, and adopted by the people Nov. 5, 1996]

Section 15a. Subsequent vote for reaffirmation of section 15. [Created through H.J.R. 2, 1995, and adopted by the people Nov. 5, 1996; Repeal proposed by S.J.R. 39, 1999, and adopted by the people Nov. 7, 2000]

ARTICLE XI-A
RURAL CREDITS

[Created through initiative petition filed July 6, 1916, and adopted by the people Nov. 7, 1916; Repeal proposed by S.J.R. 1, 1941, and adopted by the people Nov. 3, 1942]

ARTICLE XI-A
FARM AND HOME LOANS TO VETERANS

Sec. 1.   State empowered to make farm and home loans to veterans; standards and priorities for loans
   2.   Bonds
   3.   Eligibility to receive loans
   4.   Tax levy
   5.   Repeal of conflicting constitutional provisions
   6.   Refunding bonds

Section 1. State empowered to make farm and home loans to veterans; standards and priorities for loans. (1) Notwithstanding the limits contained in section 7, Article XI of this Constitution, the credit of the State of Oregon may be loaned and indebtedness incurred in an amount not to exceed eight percent of the true cash value of all the property in the state, for the purpose of creating a fund, to be known as the "Oregon War Veterans' Fund," to be advanced for the acquisition of farms and homes for the benefit of male and female residents of the State of Oregon who served in the Armed Forces of the United States. Secured repayment thereof shall be and is a prerequisite to the advancement of money from such fund, except that moneys in the Oregon War Veterans' Fund may also be appropriated to the Director of Veterans' Affairs to be expended, without security, for the following purposes:

(a) Aiding veterans' organizations in connection with their programs of service to veterans;

(b) Training service officers appointed by the counties to give aid as provided by law to veterans and their dependents;

(c) Aiding the counties in connection with programs of service to veterans;

(d) The duties of the Director of Veterans' Affairs as conservator of the estates of beneficiaries of the United States Veterans' Administration; and

(e) The duties of the Director of Veterans' Affairs in providing services to veterans, their dependents and survivors.

(2) The Director of Veterans' Affairs may establish standards and priorities with respect to the granting of loans from the Oregon War Veterans' Fund that, as determined by the director, best accomplish the purposes and promote the financial sustainability of the Oregon War Veterans' Fund, including, but not limited to, standards and priorities necessary to maintain the tax-exempt status of earnings from bonds issued under authority of this section and section 2 of this Article. [Created through H.J.R. 7, 1943, and adopted by the people Nov. 7, 1944; Amendment proposed by H.J.R. 1, 1949, and adopted by the people Nov. 7, 1950; Amendment proposed by H.J.R. 14, 1951, and adopted by the people Nov. 4, 1952; Amendment proposed by S.J.R. 14, 1959, and adopted by the people Nov. 8, 1960; Amendment proposed by H.J.R. 9, 1967, and adopted by the people Nov. 5,

1968; Amendment proposed by H.J.R. 33, 1969, and adopted by the people Nov. 3, 1970; Amendment proposed by H.J.R. 12, 1973, and adopted by the people May 28, 1974; Amendment proposed by H.J.R. 10, 1977, and adopted by the people May 17, 1977; Amendment proposed by S.J.R. 53, 1977, and adopted by the people May 17, 1977; Amendment proposed by S.J.R. 2, 1999, and adopted by the people Nov. 7, 2000; Amendment proposed by H.J.R. 7, 2009, and adopted by the people Nov. 2, 2010]

Section 2. Bonds. Bonds of the state of Oregon containing a direct promise on behalf of the state to pay the face value thereof, with the interest therein provided for, may be issued to an amount authorized by section 1 hereof for the purpose of creating said "Oregon War Veterans' Fund." Said bonds shall be a direct obligation of the state and shall be in such form and shall run for such periods of time and bear such rates of interest as provided by statute. [Created through H.J.R. 7, 1943, and adopted by the people Nov. 7, 1944; Amendment proposed by H.J.R. 1, 1949, and adopted by the people Nov. 7, 1950]

Section 3. Eligibility to receive loans. No person shall receive money from the Oregon War Veterans' Fund except the following:

(1) A person who:

(a) Resides in the State of Oregon at the time of applying for a loan from the fund;

(b) Is a veteran, as that term is defined by Oregon law;

(c) Served under honorable conditions on active duty in the Armed Forces of the United States; and

(d) Satisfies the requirements applicable to the funding source for the loan from the Oregon War Veterans' Fund.

(2)(a) The spouse of a person who is qualified to receive a loan under subsection (1) of this section but who has either been missing in action or a prisoner of war while on active duty in the Armed Forces of the United States even though the status of missing or being a prisoner occurred prior to completion of a minimum length of service or the person never resided in this state, provided the spouse resides in this state at the time of application for the loan.

(b) The surviving spouse of a person who was qualified to receive a loan under subsection (1) of this section but who died while on active duty in the Armed Forces of the United States even though the death occurred prior to completion of a minimum length of service or the person never resided in this state, provided the surviving spouse resides in this state at the time of application for the loan.

(c) The eligibility of a surviving spouse under this subsection shall terminate on the spouse's remarriage.

(3) As used in this section, "active duty" does not include attendance at a school under military orders, except schooling incident to an active enlistment or a regular tour of duty, or normal military training as a reserve officer or member of an organized reserve or National Guard unit. [Created through H.J.R. 7, 1943, and adopted by the people Nov. 7, 1944; Amendment proposed by H.J.R. 1, 1949, and adopted by the people Nov. 7, 1950; Amendment proposed by H.J.R. 14, 1951, and adopted by the people Nov. 4, 1952; Amendment proposed by S.J.R. 14, 1959, and adopted by the people Nov. 8, 1960; Amendment proposed by H.J.R. 9, 1967, and adopted by the people Nov. 5, 1968; Amendment proposed by S.J.R. 23, 1971, and adopted by the people Nov. 7, 1972; Amendment proposed by H.J.R. 23, 1975, and adopted by the people May 25, 1976; Amendment proposed by H.J.R. 23, 1979, and adopted by the people May 20, 1980; Amendment proposed by S.J.R. 3, 1995, and adopted by the people Nov. 5, 1996; Amendment proposed by S.J.R. 2, 1999, and adopted by the people Nov. 7, 2000; Amendment proposed by H.J.R. 7, 2009, and adopted by the people Nov. 2, 2010]

Section 4. Tax levy. There shall be levied each year, at the same time and in the same manner that other taxes are levied, a tax upon all property in the state of Oregon not exempt from taxation, not to exceed two (2) mills on each dollar valuation, to provide for the payment of principal and interest of the bonds authorized to be issued by this article. The two (2) mills additional tax herein provided for hereby is specifically authorized and said tax levy hereby authorized shall be in addition to all other taxes which may be levied according to law. [Created through H.J.R. 7, 1943, and adopted by the people Nov. 7, 1944; Amendment proposed by H.J.R. 85, 1997, and adopted by the people May 20, 1997]

Section 5. Repeal of conflicting constitutional provisions. The provisions of the constitution in conflict with this amendment hereby are repealed so far as they conflict herewith. [Created through H.J.R. 7, 1943, and adopted by the people Nov. 7, 1944]

Section 6. Refunding bonds. Refunding bonds may be issued and sold to refund any bonds issued under authority of sections 1 and 2 of this article. There may be issued and outstanding at any one time bonds aggregating the amount authorized by section 1 hereof, but at no time shall the total of all bonds outstanding, including refunding bonds, exceed the amount so authorized. [Created through H.J.R. 7, 1943, and adopted by the people Nov. 7, 1944]

ARTICLE XI-B
STATE PAYMENT OF IRRIGATION AND DRAINAGE DISTRICT INTEREST

[Created through H.J.R. 32, 1919, and adopted by the people June 3, 1919; Repeal proposed by H.J.R. 1, 1929, and adopted by the people Nov. 4, 1930]

ARTICLE XI-C
WORLD WAR VETERANS' STATE AID SINKING FUND

[Created through H.J.R. 12, 1921, and adopted by the people June 7, 1921; Amendment proposed by H.J.R. 7, 1923, and adopted by the people Nov. 4, 1924; Repeal proposed by S.J.R. 12, 1951, and adopted by the people Nov. 4, 1952]

ARTICLE XI-D
STATE POWER DEVELOPMENT

Sec. 1.　State's rights, title and interest to water and water-power sites to be held in perpetuity
2.　State's powers enumerated
3.　Legislation to effectuate article
4.　Construction of article

Section 1. State's rights, title and interest to water and water-power sites to be held in perpetuity. The rights, title and interest in and to all water for the development of water power and to water power sites, which the state of Oregon now owns or may hereafter acquire, shall be held by it in perpetuity. [Created through initiative petition filed July 7, 1932, and adopted by the people Nov. 8, 1932]

Section 2. State's powers enumerated. The state of Oregon is authorized and empowered:

(1) To control and/or develop the water power within the state;

(2) To lease water and water power sites for the development of water power;

(3) To control, use, transmit, distribute, sell and/or dispose of electric energy;

(4) To develop, separately or in conjunction with the United States, or in conjunction with the political subdivisions of this state, any water power within the state, and to

acquire, construct, maintain and/or operate hydroelectric power plants, transmission and distribution lines;(

(5) To develop, separately or in conjunction with the United States, with any state or states, or political subdivisions thereof, or with any political subdivision of this state, any water power in any interstate stream and to acquire, construct, maintain and/or operate hydroelectric power plants, transmission and distribution lines;

(6) To contract with the United States, with any state or states, or political subdivisions thereof, or with any political subdivision of this state, for the purchase or acquisition of water, water power and/or electric energy for use, transmission, distribution, sale and/or disposal thereof;

(7) To fix rates and charges for the use of water in the development of water power and for the sale and/or disposal of water power and/or electric energy;

(8) To loan the credit of the state, and to incur indebtedness to an amount not exceeding one and one-half percent of the true cash value of all the property in the state taxed on an ad valorem basis, for the purpose of providing funds with which to carry out the provisions of this article, notwithstanding any limitations elsewhere contained in this constitution;

(9) To do any and all things necessary or convenient to carry out the provisions of this article. [Created through initiative petition filed July 7, 1932, and adopted by the people Nov. 8, 1932; Amendment proposed by S.J.R. 6, 1961, and adopted by the people Nov. 6, 1962]

Section 3. Legislation to effectuate article. The legislative assembly shall, and the people may, provide any legislation that may be necessary in addition to existing laws, to carry out the provisions of this article; Provided, that any board or commission created, or empowered to administer the laws enacted to carry out the purposes of this article shall consist of three members and be elected without party affiliation or designation. [Created through initiative petition filed July 7, 1932, and adopted by the people Nov. 8, 1932]

Section 4. Construction of article. Nothing in this article shall be construed to affect in any way the laws, and the administration thereof, now existing or hereafter enacted, relating to the appropriation and use of water for beneficial purposes, other than for the development of water power. [Created through initiative petition filed July 7, 1932, and adopted by the people Nov. 8, 1932]

ARTICLE XI-E
STATE REFORESTATION

Section 1. State empowered to lend credit for forest rehabilitation and reforestation; bonds; taxation. The credit of the state may be loaned and indebtedness incurred in an amount which shall not exceed at any one time 3/16 of 1 percent of the true cash value of all the property in the state taxed on an ad valorem basis, to provide funds for forest rehabilitation and reforestation and for the acquisition, management, and development of lands for such purposes. So long as any such indebtedness shall remain outstanding, the funds derived from the sale, exchange, or use of said lands, and from the disposal of products therefrom, shall be applied only in the liquidation of such indebtedness. Bonds or other obligations issued pursuant hereto may be renewed or refunded. An ad valorem tax shall be levied annually upon all the property in the state of Oregon taxed on an ad valorem basis, in sufficient amount to provide for the payment of such indebtedness and the interest thereon. The legislative assembly may provide other revenues to supplement or replace the said tax levies. The legislature shall enact legislation to carry out the provisions hereof. This amendment shall supersede all constitutional provi-

sions in conflict herewith. [Created through H.J.R. 24, 1947, and adopted by the people Nov. 2, 1948; Amendment proposed by S.J.R. 7, 1961, and adopted by the people Nov. 6, 1962; Amendment proposed by H.J.R. 85, 1997, and adopted by the people May 20, 1997]

ARTICLE XI-F(1)
HIGHER EDUCATION BUILDING PROJECTS

Sec. 1. State empowered to lend credit for higher education building projects
2. Limitation on authorization to incur indebtedness
3. Sources of revenue
4. Bonds
5. Legislation to effectuate Article

Section 1. State empowered to lend credit for higher education building projects. The credit of the state may be loaned and indebtedness incurred in an amount which shall not exceed at any one time three-fourths of one percent of the true cash value of all the taxable property in the state, as determined by law to provide funds with which to acquire, construct, improve, repair, equip and furnish buildings, structures, land and other projects, or parts thereof, that the legislative assembly determines will benefit higher education institutions or activities. [Created through H.J.R. 26, 1949, and adopted by the people Nov. 7, 1950; Amendment proposed by H.J.R. 12, 1959, and adopted by the people Nov. 8, 1960; Amendment proposed by H.J.R. 101, 2010, and adopted by the people May 18, 2010]

Section 2. Limitation on authorization to incur indebtedness. Indebtedness shall not be incurred to finance projects described in section 1 of this Article unless the constructing authority conservatively estimates that the constructing authority will have sufficient revenues to pay the indebtedness and operate the projects financed with the proceeds of the indebtedness. For purposes of this section, "revenues" includes all funds available to the constructing authority except amounts appropriated by the legislative assembly from the General Fund. [Created through H.J.R. 26, 1949, and adopted by the people Nov. 7, 1950; Amendment proposed by H.J.R. 101, 2010, and adopted by the people May 18, 2010]

Section 3. Sources of revenue. Ad valorem taxes shall be levied annually upon all the taxable property in the state of Oregon in sufficient amount, with the aforesaid revenues, to provide for the payment of such indebtedness and the interest thereon. The legislative assembly may provide other revenues to supplement or replace such tax levies. [Created through H.J.R. 26, 1949, and adopted by the people Nov. 7, 1950; Amendment proposed by H.J.R. 101, 2010, and adopted by the people May 18, 2010]

Section 4. Bonds. Bonds issued pursuant to this article shall be the direct general obligations of the state, and be in such form, run for such periods of time, and bear such rates of interest, as shall be provided by statute. Such bonds may be refunded with bonds of like obligation. Unless provided by statute, no bonds shall be issued pursuant to this article for the construction of buildings or other structures for higher education until after all of the aforesaid outstanding revenue bonds shall have been redeemed or refunded. [Created through H.J.R. 26, 1949, and adopted by the people Nov. 7, 1950]

Section 5. Legislation to effectuate Article. The legislative assembly shall enact legislation to carry out the provisions hereof. This article shall supersede all conflicting constitutional provisions. [Created through H.J.R. 26, 1949, and adopted by the people Nov. 7, 1950]

ARTICLE XI-F(2)
VETERANS' BONUS

Sec. 1. State empowered to lend credit to pay veterans' bonus; issuance of bonds
2. Definitions
3. Amount of bonus
4. Survivors of certain deceased veterans entitled to maximum amount
5. Certain persons not eligible
6. Order of distribution among survivors
7. Bonus not saleable or assignable; bonus free from creditors' claims and state taxes
8. Administration of Article; rules and regulations
9. Applications
10. Furnishing forms; printing, office supplies and equipment; employes; payment of expenses

Section 1. State empowered to lend credit to pay veterans' bonus; issuance of bonds. Notwithstanding the limitations contained in Section 7 of Article XI of the constitution, the credit of the State of Oregon may be loaned and indebtedness incurred to an amount not exceeding 5 percent of the assessed valuation of all the property in the state, for the purpose of creating a fund to be paid to residents of the State of Oregon who served in the armed forces of the United States between September 16, 1940, and June 30, 1946, and were honorably discharged from such service, which fund shall be known as the "World War II Veterans' Compensation Fund."

Bonds of the State of Oregon, containing a direct promise on behalf of the state to pay the face value thereof with the interest thereon provided for may be issued to an amount authorized in Section 1 hereof for the purpose of creating said World War II Veterans' Compensation Fund. Refunding bonds may be issued and sold to refund any bonds issued under authority of Section 1 hereof. There may be issued and outstanding at any one time bonds aggregating the amount authorized by Section 1, but at no time shall the total of all bonds outstanding, including refunding bonds, exceed the amount so authorized. Said bonds shall be a direct obligation of the State and shall be in such form and shall run for such periods of time and bear such rates of interest as shall be provided by statute. No person shall be eligible to receive money from said fund except the veterans as defined in Section 3 of this act [sic]. The legislature shall and the people may provide any additional legislation that may be necessary, in addition to existing laws, to carry out the provisions of this section. [Created through initiative petition filed June 30, 1950, and adopted by the people Nov. 7, 1950]

Section 2. Definitions. The following words, terms, and phrases, as used in this act [sic] shall have the following meaning unless the text otherwise requires:

(1) "Domestic service" means service within the continental limits of the United States, excluding Alaska, Hawaii, Canal Zone and Puerto Rico.

(2) "Foreign Service" means service in all other places, including sea duty.

(3) "Husband" means the unremarried husband, and "wife" means the unremarried wife.

(4) "Child or Children" means child or children of issue, child or children by adoption or child or children to whom the deceased person has stood in loco parentis for one year or more immediately preceding his death.

(5) "Parent or Parents" means natural parent or parents; parent or parents by adoption; or, person or persons, including stepparent or stepparents, who have stood in loco parentis to the deceased person for a period of one year or more immediately prior to entrance into the armed service of the United States.

(6) "Veterans" means any person who shall have served in active duty in the armed forces of the United States at any time between September 16, 1940, and June 30, 1946, both dates inclusive, and who, at the time of commencing such service, was and had been a bona fide resident of the State of Oregon for at least one year immediately preceding the commencement of such service, and who shall have been separated from such service under honorable conditions, or who is still in such service, or who has been retired. [Created through initiative petition filed June 30, 1950, and adopted by the people Nov. 7, 1950]

Section 3. Amount of bonus. Every veteran who was in such service for a period of at least 90 days shall be entitled to receive compensation at the rate of Ten Dollars ($10.00) for each full month during which such veteran was in active domestic service and Fifteen Dollars ($15.00) for each full month during which such veteran was in active foreign service within said period of time. Any veteran who was serving on active duty in the armed forces between September 16, 1940, and June 30, 1946, whose services were terminated by reason of service-connected disabilities, and who, upon filing a claim for disabilities with the United States Veterans' Administration within three months after separation from the armed service, was rated not less than 50% disabled as a result of such claim, shall be deemed to have served sufficient time to entitle him or her to the maximum payment under this act [sic] and shall be so entitled. The maximum amount of compensation payable under this act [sic] shall be six hundred dollars ($600.00) and no such compensation shall be paid to any veteran who shall have received from another state a bonus or compensation because of such military service. [Created through initiative petition filed June 30, 1950, and adopted by the people Nov. 7, 1950]

Section 4. Survivors of certain deceased veterans entitled to maximum amount. The survivor or survivors, of the deceased veteran whose death was caused or contributed to by a service-connected disease or disability incurred in service under conditions other than dishonorable, shall be entitled, in the order of survivorship provided in this act [sic], to receive the maximum amount of said compensation irrespective of the amount such deceased would have been entitled to receive if living. [Created through initiative petition filed June 30, 1950, and adopted by the people Nov. 7, 1950]

Section 5. Certain persons not eligible. No compensation shall be paid under this act [sic] to any veteran who, during the period of service refused on conscientious, political or other grounds to subject himself to full military discipline and unqualified service, or to any veteran for any periods of time spent under penal confinement during the period of active duty, or for service in the merchant marine: Provided, however, that for the purposes of this act [sic], active service in the chaplain corps, or medical corps shall be deemed unqualified service under full military discipline. [Created through initiative petition filed June 30, 1950, and adopted by the people Nov. 7, 1950]

Section 6. Order of distribution among survivors. The survivor or survivors of any deceased veteran who would have been entitled to compensation under this act [sic], other than those mentioned in Section 4 of this act [sic], shall be entitled to receive the same amount of compensation as said deceased veteran would have received, if living, which shall be distributed as follows:

(1) To the husband or wife, as the case may be, the whole amount.

(2) If there be no husband or wife, to the child or children, equally; and

(3) If there be no husband or wife or child or children, to the parent or parents, equally. [Created through initiative petition filed June 30, 1950, and adopted by the people Nov. 7, 1950]

Section 7. Bonus not saleable or assignable; bonus free from creditors' claims and state taxes. No sale or assignment of any right or claim to compensation under this act [sic] shall be valid, no claims of creditors shall be enforcible against rights or claims to or payments of such compensation, and such compensation shall be exempt from all taxes imposed by the laws of this state. [Created through initiative petition filed June 30, 1950, and adopted by the people Nov. 7, 1950]

Section 8. Administration of article; rules and regulations. The director of Veterans' Affairs, State of Oregon, referred to herein as the "director" hereby is authorized and empowered, and it shall be his duty, to administer the provisions of this act [sic], and with the approval of the veterans advisory committee may make such rules and regulations as are deemed necessary to accomplish the purpose hereof. [Created through initiative petition filed June 30, 1950, and adopted by the people Nov. 7, 1950]

Section 9. Applications. All applications for certificates under this act [sic] shall be made within two years from the effective date hereof and upon forms to be supplied by the director. Said applications shall be duly verified by the claimant before a notary public or other person authorized to take acknowledgments, and shall set forth applicant's name, residence at the time of entry into the service, date and place of enlistment, induction or entry upon active federal service, beginning and ending dates of foreign service, date of discharge, retirement or release from active federal service, statement of time lost by reason of penal confinement during the period of active duty; together with the applicant's original discharge, or certificate in lieu of lost discharge, or certificate of service, or if the applicant has not been released at the time of application, a statement by competent military authority that the applicant during the period for which compensation is claimed did not refuse to subject himself to full military discipline and unqualified service, and that the applicant has not been separated from service under circumstances other than honorable. The director may require such further information to be included in such application as deemed necessary to enable him to determine the eligibility of the applicant. Such applications, together with satisfactory evidence of honorable service, shall be filed with the director. The director shall make such reasonable requirements for applicants as may be necessary to prevent fraud or the payment of compensation to persons not entitled thereto. [Created through initiative petition filed June 30, 1950, and adopted by the people Nov. 7, 1950]

Section 10. Furnishing forms; printing, office supplies and equipment; employes; payment of expenses. The director shall furnish free of charge, upon request, the necessary forms upon which applications may be made and may authorize the county clerks, Veterans organizations and other organizations, and notaries public willing to assist veterans without charge, to act for him in receiving application under this act [sic], and shall furnish such clerks, organizations and notaries public, with the proper forms for such purpose. The director hereby is authorized and directed with the approval of the veterans' advisory committee, to procure such printing, office supplies and equipment and to employ such persons as may be necessary in order to properly carry out the provisions of this act [sic], and all expense incurred by him in the administration thereof shall be paid out of the World War II Veterans' Compensation Fund, in the manner provided by law for payment of claims from other state funds. [Created through initiative petition filed June 30, 1950, and adopted by the people Nov. 7, 1950]

ARTICLE XI-G
HIGHER EDUCATION INSTITUTIONS AND ACTIVITIES; COMMUNITY COLLEGES

Sec. 1. State empowered to lend credit for financing higher education institutions and activities, and community colleges
2. Bonds
3. Sources of revenue

Section 1. State empowered to lend credit for financing higher education institutions and activities, and community colleges. (1) Notwithstanding the limitations contained in section 7, Article XI of this Constitution, and in addition to other exceptions from the limitations of such section, the credit of the state may be loaned and indebtedness incurred in an amount not to exceed at any time three-fourths of one percent of the true cash value of all taxable property in the state, as determined by law.

(2) Proceeds from any loan authorized or indebtedness incurred under this section shall be used to provide funds with which to acquire, construct, improve, repair, equip and furnish buildings, structures, land and other projects, or parts thereof, that the Legislative Assembly determines will benefit higher education institutions or activities or community colleges authorized by law to receive state aid.

(3) The amount of any indebtedness incurred under this section in any biennium shall be matched by an amount that is at least equal to the amount of the indebtedness. The matching amount must be used for the same or similar purposes as the proceeds of the indebtedness and may consist of moneys appropriated from the General Fund or any other moneys available to the constructing authority for such purposes. However, the matching amount may not consist of proceeds of indebtedness incurred by the state under any other Article of this Constitution. Any matching amount appropriated from the General Fund to meet the requirements of this subsection must be specifically designated therefor by the Legislative Assembly.

(4) Nothing in this section prevents the financing of projects, or parts thereof, by a combination of the moneys available under this section, under Article XI-F(1) of this Constitution, and from other lawful sources. [Created through H.J.R. 8, 1963 (s.s.), and adopted by the people May 15, 1964; Amendment proposed by H.J.R. 2, 1967 (s.s.), and adopted by the people May 28, 1968; Amendment proposed by H.J.R. 101, 2010, and adopted by the people May 18, 2010]

Section 2. Bonds. Bonds issued pursuant to this Article shall be the direct general obligations of the state and shall be in such form, run for such periods of time, and bear such rates of interest as the Legislative Assembly provides. Such bonds may be refunded with bonds of like obligation. [Created through H.J.R. 8, 1963 (s.s.), and adopted by the people May 15, 1964]

Section 3. Sources of revenue. Ad valorem taxes shall be levied annually upon the taxable property within the State of Oregon in sufficient amount to provide for the prompt payment of bonds issued pursuant to this Article and the interest thereon. The Legislative Assembly may provide other revenues to supplement or replace, in whole or in part, such tax levies. [Created through H.J.R. 8, 1963 (s.s.), and adopted by the people May 15, 1964]

ARTICLE XI-H
POLLUTION CONTROL

Sec. 1. State empowered to lend credit for financing pollution control facilities or related activities
2. Only facilities 70 percent self-supporting and self-liquidating authorized; exceptions
3. Authority of public bodies to receive funds

Section 1. State empowered to lend credit for financing pollution control facilities or related activities. In the manner provided by law and notwithstanding the limitations contained in sections 7 and 8, Article XI, of this Constitution, the credit of the State of Oregon may be loaned and indebtedness incurred in an amount not to exceed, at any one time, one percent of the true cash value of all taxable property in the state:

(1) To provide funds to be advanced, by contract, grant, loan or otherwise, to any municipal corporation, city, county or agency of the State of Oregon, or combinations thereof, for the purpose of planning, acquisition, construction, alteration or improvement of facilities for or activities related to, the collection, treatment, dilution and disposal of all forms of waste in or upon the air, water and lands of this state; and

(2) To provide funds for the acquisition, by purchase, loan or otherwise, of bonds, notes or other obligations of any municipal corporation, city, county or agency of the State of Oregon, or combinations thereof, issued or made for the purposes of subsection (1) of this section. [Created through H.J.R. 14, 1969, and adopted by the people May 26, 1970; Amendment proposed by S.J.R. 41, 1989, and adopted by the people May 22, 1990]

Section 2. Only facilities 70 percent self-supporting and self-liquidating authorized; exceptions. The facilities for which funds are advanced and for which bonds, notes or other obligations are issued or made and acquired pursuant to this Article shall be only such facilities as conservatively appear to the agency designated by law to make the determination to be not less than 70 percent self-supporting and self-liquidating from revenues, gifts, grants from the Federal Government, user charges, assessments and other fees. This section shall not apply to any activities for which funds are advanced and shall not apply to facilities for the collection, treatment, dilution, removal and disposal of hazardous substances. [Created through H.J.R. 14, 1969, and adopted by the people May 26, 1970; Amendment proposed by S.J.R. 41, 1989, and adopted by the people May 22, 1990]

Section 3. Authority of public bodies to receive funds. Notwithstanding the limitations contained in section 10, Article XI of this Constitution, municipal corporations, cities, counties, and agencies of the State of Oregon, or combinations thereof, may receive funds referred to in section 1 of this Article, by contract, grant, loan or otherwise and may also receive such funds through disposition to the state, by sale, loan or otherwise, of bonds, notes or other obligations issued or made for the purposes set forth in section 1 of this Article. [Created through H.J.R. 14, 1969, and adopted by the people May 26, 1970]

Section 4. Sources of revenue. Ad valorem taxes shall be levied annually upon all taxable property within the State of Oregon in sufficient amount to provide, together with the revenues, gifts, grants from the Federal Government, user charges, assessments and other fees referred to in section 2 of this Article for the payment of indebtedness incurred by the state and the interest thereon. The Legislative Assembly may provide other revenues to supplement or replace such tax levies. [Created through H.J.R. 14, 1969, and adopted by the people May 26, 1970]

Section 5. Bonds. Bonds issued pursuant to section 1 of this Article shall be the direct obligations of the state and shall be in such form, run for such periods of time, and bear such rates of interest, as shall be provided by law. Such bonds may be refunded with bonds of like obligation. [Created through H.J.R. 14, 1969, and adopted by the people May 26, 1970]

Section 6. Legislation to effectuate Article. The Legislative Assembly shall enact legislation to carry out the provisions of this Article. This Article shall supersede all conflicting constitutional provisions and shall supersede any conflicting provision of a county or city charter or act of incorporation. [Created through H.J.R. 14, 1969, and adopted by the people May 26, 1970]

ARTICLE XI-I(1)
WATER DEVELOPMENT PROJECTS

Section 1. State empowered to lend credit to establish Water Development Fund; eligibility; use. Notwithstanding the limits contained in sections 7 and 8, Article XI of this Constitution, the credit of the State of Oregon may be loaned and indebtedness incurred in an amount not to exceed one and one-half percent of the true cash value of all the property in the state for the purpose of creating a fund to be known as the Water Development Fund. The fund shall be used to provide financing for loans for residents of this state for construction of water development projects for irrigation, drainage, fish protection, watershed restoration and municipal uses and for the acquisition of easements and rights of way for water development projects authorized by law. Secured repayment thereof shall be and is a prerequisite to the advancement of money from such fund. As used in this section, "resident" includes both natural persons and any corporation or cooperative, either for profit or nonprofit, whose principal income is from farming in Oregon or municipal or quasi-municipal or other body subject to the laws of the State of Oregon. Not less than 50 percent of the potential amount available from the fund will be reserved for irrigation and drainage projects. For municipal use, only municipalities and communities with populations less than 30,000 are eligible for loans from the fund. [Created through S.J.R. 1, 1977, and adopted by the people Nov. 8, 1977; Amendment proposed by S.J.R. 6, 1981, and adopted by the people May 18, 1982; Amendment proposed by H.J.R. 45, 1987, and adopted by the people May 17, 1988]

Section 2. Bonds. Bonds of the State of Oregon containing a direct promise on behalf of the state to pay the face value thereof, with the interest therein provided for, may be issued to an amount authorized by section 1 of this Article for the purpose of creating such fund. The bonds shall be a direct obligation of the state and shall be in such form and shall run for such periods of time and bear such rates of interest as provided by statute. [Created through S.J.R. 1, 1977, and adopted by the people Nov. 8, 1977]

Section 3. Refunding bonds. Refunding bonds may be issued and sold to refund any bonds issued under authority of sections 1 and 2 of this Article. There may be issued and outstanding at any time bonds aggregating the amount authorized by section 1 of this Article but at no time shall the total of all bonds outstanding, including refunding bonds, exceed the amount so authorized. [Created through S.J.R. 1, 1977, and adopted by the people Nov. 8, 1977]

Section 4. Sources of revenue. Ad valorem taxes shall be levied annually upon all the taxable property in the State of Oregon in sufficient amount to provide for the payment of principal and interest of the bonds issued pursuant to this Article. The Legislative Assembly may provide other revenues to supplement or replace, in whole or in part, such tax levies. [Created through S.J.R. 1, 1977, and adopted by the people Nov. 8, 1977]

Section 5. Legislation to effectuate Article. The Legislative Assembly shall enact legislation to carry out the provisions of this Article. This Article supersedes any conflicting provision of a county or city charter or act of incorporation. [Created through S.J.R. 1, 1977, and adopted by the people Nov. 8, 1977]

ARTICLE XI-I(2)
MULTIFAMILY HOUSING FOR ELDERLY AND DISABLED

Section 1. State empowered to lend credit for multifamily housing for elderly and disabled persons. In the manner provided by law and notwithstanding the limitations contained in section 7, Article XI of this Constitution, the credit of the State of Oregon may be loaned and indebtedness incurred in an amount not to exceed, at any one time, one-half of one percent of the true cash value of all taxable property in the state to provide funds to be advanced, by contract, grant, loan or otherwise, for the purpose of providing additional financing for multifamily housing for the elderly and for disabled persons. Multifamily housing means a structure or facility designed to contain more than one living unit. Additional financing may be provided to the elderly to purchase ownership interest in the structure or facility. [Created through H.J.R. 61, 1977, and adopted by the people May 23, 1978; Amendment proposed by S.J.R. 34, 1979, and adopted by the people May 20, 1980; Amendment proposed by H.J.R. 1, 1981, and adopted by the people May 18, 1982]

Section 2. Sources of revenue. The bonds shall be payable from contract or loan proceeds; bond reserves; other funds available for these purposes; and, if necessary, state ad valorem taxes. [Created through H.J.R. 61, 1977, and adopted by the people May 23, 1978]

Section 3. Bonds. Bonds issued pursuant to section 1 of this Article shall be the direct obligations of the state and shall be in such form, run for such periods of time and bear such rates of interest as shall be provided by law. The bonds may be refunded with bonds of like obligation. [Created through H.J.R. 61, 1977, and adopted by the people May 23, 1978]

Section 4. Legislation to effectuate Article. The Legislative Assembly shall enact legislation to carry out the provisions of this Article. This Article shall supersede all conflicting constitutional provisions. [Created through H.J.R. 61, 1977, and adopted by the people May 23, 1978]

ARTICLE XI-J
SMALL SCALE LOCAL ENERGY LOANS

Section 1. State empowered to loan credit for small scale local energy loans; eligibility; use. Notwithstanding the limits contained in sections 7 and 8, Article XI of this Constitution, the credit of the State of Oregon may be loaned and indebtedness incurred in an amount not to exceed one-half of one percent of the true cash value of all the property in the state for the purpose of creating a fund to be known as the Small Scale Local Energy Project Loan Fund. The fund shall be used to provide financing for the development of small scale local energy projects. Secured repayment thereof shall be and is a prerequisite to the advancement of money from such fund. [Created through S.J.R. 24, 1979, and adopted by the people May 20, 1980]

Section 2. Bonds. Bonds of the State of Oregon containing a direct promise on behalf of the state to pay the face value thereof, with the interest therein provided for, may be issued to an amount authorized by section 1 of this Article for the purpose of creating such fund. The bonds shall be a direct obligation of the state and shall be in such form and shall run for such periods of time and bear such rates of interest as provided by statute. [Created through S.J.R. 24, 1979, and adopted by the people May 20, 1980]

Section 3. Refunding bonds. Refunding bonds may be issued and sold to refund any bonds issued under authority of sections 1 and 2 of this Article. There may be issued and outstanding at any time bonds aggregating the amount authorized by section 1 of this Article but at no time shall the total of all bonds outstanding including refunding bonds, exceed the amount so authorized. [Created through S.J.R. 24, 1979, and adopted by the people May 20, 1980]

Section 4. Sources of revenue. Ad valorem taxes shall be levied annually upon all the taxable property in the State of Oregon in sufficient amount to provide for the payment of principal and interest of the bonds issued pursuant to this Article. The Legislative Assembly may provide other revenues to supplement or replace, in whole or in part, such tax levies. [Created through S.J.R. 24, 1979, and adopted by the people May 20, 1980]

Section 5. Legislation to effectuate Article. The Legislative Assembly shall enact legislation to carry out the provisions of this Article. This Article supersedes any conflicting provision of a county or city charter or act of incorporation. [Created through S.J.R. 24, 1979, and adopted by the people May 20, 1980]

ARTICLE XI-K
GUARANTEE OF BONDED INDEBTEDNESS OF EDUCATION DISTRICTS

Section 1. State empowered to guarantee bonded indebtedness of education districts. To secure lower interest costs on the general obligation bonds of school districts, education service districts and community college districts, the State of Oregon may guarantee the general obligation bonded indebtedness of those districts as provided in sections 2 to 6 of this Article and laws enacted pursuant to this Article. [Created through H.J.R. 71, 1997, and adopted by the people Nov. 3, 1998]

Section 2. State empowered to lend credit for state guarantee of bonded indebtedness of education districts. In the manner provided by law and notwithstanding the limitations contained in sections 7 and 8, Article XI of this Constitution, the credit of the State of Oregon may be loaned and indebtedness incurred, in an amount not to exceed, at any one time, one-half of one percent of the true cash value of all taxable property in the state, to provide funds as necessary to satisfy the state guaranty of the bonded general obligation indebtedness of school districts, education service districts and community college districts that qualify, under procedures that shall be established by law, to issue general obligation bonds that are guaranteed by the full faith and credit of this state. The state may

Constitution

guarantee the general obligation debt of qualified school districts, education service districts and community college districts and may guarantee general obligation bonded indebtedness incurred to refund the school district, education service district or community college district general obligation bonded indebtedness. [Created through H.J.R. 71, 1997, and adopted by the people Nov. 3, 1998]

Section 3. Repayment by education districts. The Legislative Assembly may provide that reimbursement to the state shall be obtained from, but shall not be limited to, moneys that otherwise would be used for the support of the educational programs of the school district, the education service district or the community college district that incurred the bonded indebtedness with respect to which any payment under the state's guaranty is made. [Created through H.J.R. 71, 1997, and adopted by the people Nov. 3, 1998]

Section 4. Sources of revenue. The State of Oregon may issue bonds if and as necessary to provide funding to satisfy the state's guaranty obligations undertaken pursuant to this Article. In addition, notwithstanding anything to the contrary in Article VIII of this Constitution, the state may borrow available moneys from the Common School Fund if such borrowing is reasonably necessary to satisfy the state's guaranty obligations undertaken pursuant to this Article. The State of Oregon also may issue bonds if and as necessary to provide funding to repay the borrowed moneys, and any interest thereon, to the Common School Fund. The bonds may be payable from any moneys reimbursed to the state under section 3 of this Article, from any moneys recoverable from the school district, the education service district or the community college district that incurred the bonded indebtedness with respect to which any payment under the state's guaranty is made, any other funds available for these purposes and, if necessary, from state ad valorem taxes. [Created through H.J.R. 71, 1997, and adopted by the people Nov. 3, 1998]

Section 5. Bonds. Bonds of the state issued pursuant to this Article shall be the direct obligations of the state and shall be in such form, run for such periods of time and bear such rates of interest as shall be provided by law. The bonds may be refunded with bonds of like obligation. [Created through H.J.R. 71, 1997, and adopted by the people Nov. 3, 1998]

Section 6. Legislation to effectuate Article. The Legislative Assembly shall enact legislation to carry out the provisions of this Article, including provisions that authorize the state's recovery, from any school district, education service district or community college district that incurred the bonded indebtedness with respect to which any payment under the state's guaranty is made, any amounts necessary to make the state whole. This Article shall supersede all conflicting constitutional provisions and shall supersede any conflicting provision of any law, ordinance or charter pertaining to any school district, education service district or community college district. [Created through H.J.R. 71, 1997, and adopted by the people Nov. 3, 1998]

ARTICLE XI-L
OREGON HEALTH AND SCIENCE UNIVERSITY

Section 1. State empowered to lend credit for financing capital costs of Oregon Health and Science University; bonds. (1) In the manner provided by law and notwithstanding the limitations contained in section 7, Article XI of this Constitution, the credit of the State of Oregon may be loaned and indebtedness incurred, in an aggregate outstanding principal amount not to exceed, at any one time, one-half of one percent of the real market value of all property in the state, to provide funds to finance capital costs of Oregon Health and Science University. Bonds issued under this section may not be paid from ad valorem property taxes.

(2) Any indebtedness incurred under this section shall be in the form of general obligation bonds of the State of Oregon containing a direct promise on behalf of the State of Oregon to pay the principal, premium, if any, and interest on such bonds, in an aggregate outstanding principal amount not to exceed the amount authorized in subsection (1) of this section. The bonds shall be the direct obligation of the State of Oregon and shall be in such form, run for such period of time, have such terms and bear such rates of interest as may be provided by statute. The full faith and credit and taxing power of the State of Oregon shall be pledged to the payment of the principal, premium, if any, and interest on such bonds provided, however, that the ad valorem taxing power of the State of Oregon may not be pledged to the payment of such bonds.

(3) The proceeds from bonds issued under this section shall be used to finance capital costs of Oregon Health and Science University and costs of issuing bonds pursuant to this Article. Bonds issued under this section to finance capital costs of Oregon Health and Science University shall be issued in an aggregate principal amount that produces net proceeds for the university in an amount that does not exceed $200 million.

(4) The proceeds from bonds issued under this section may not be used to finance operating costs of Oregon Health and Science University.

(5) As used in this Article, "bonds" means bonds, notes or other financial obligations of the State of Oregon issued under this section. [Created through H.J.R. 19, 2001, and adopted by the people May 21, 2002]

Section 2. Sources of repayment. The principal, premium, if any, interest and any other amounts payable with respect to bonds issued under section 1 of this Article shall be repaid as determined by the Legislative Assembly from the following sources:

(1) Amounts appropriated for such purpose by the Legislative Assembly from the General Fund, including any taxes levied to pay the bonds other than ad valorem property taxes;

(2) Amounts allocated for such purpose by the Legislative Assembly from the proceeds of the State Lottery or from the Master Settlement Agreement entered into on November 23, 1998, by the State of Oregon and leading United States tobacco product manufacturers; and

(3) Amounts appropriated or allocated for such purpose by the Legislative Assembly from other sources of revenue. [Created through H.J.R. 19, 2001, and adopted by the people May 21, 2002]

Section 3. Refunding bonds. Bonds issued under section 1 of this Article may be refunded with bonds of like obligation. [Created through H.J.R. 19, 2001, and adopted by the people May 21, 2002]

Section 4. Legislation to effectuate Article. The Legislative Assembly may enact legislation to carry out the provisions of this Article. [Created through H.J.R. 19, 2001, and adopted by the people May 21, 2002]

Section 5. Relationship to conflicting provisions of Constitution. This Article shall supersede all conflicting provisions of this constitution. [Created through H.J.R. 19, 2001, and adopted by the people May 21, 2002]

ARTICLE XI-M
SEISMIC REHABILITATION OF PUBLIC EDUCATION BUILDINGS

Sec. 1.   State empowered to lend credit for seismic rehabilitation of public education buildings; bonds
2.   Sources of repayment
3.   Refunding bonds
4.   Legislation to effectuate Article
5.   Relationship to conflicting provisions of Constitution

Note: Article XI-M was designated as "Article XI-L" by S.J.R. 21, 2001, and adopted by the people Nov. 5, 2002.

Section 1. State empowered to lend credit for seismic rehabilitation of public education buildings; bonds. (1) In the manner provided by law and notwithstanding the limitations contained in section 7, Article XI of this Constitution, the credit of the State of Oregon may be loaned and indebtedness incurred, in an aggregate outstanding principal amount not to exceed, at any one time, one-fifth of one percent of the real market value of all property in the state, to provide funds for the planning and implementation of seismic rehabilitation of public education buildings, including surveying and conducting engineering evaluations of the need for seismic rehabilitation.

(2) Any indebtedness incurred under this section must be in the form of general obligation bonds of the State of Oregon containing a direct promise on behalf of the State of Oregon to pay the principal, premium, if any, interest and other amounts payable with respect to the bonds, in an aggregate outstanding principal amount not to exceed the amount authorized in subsection (1) of this section. The bonds are the direct obligation of the State of Oregon and must be in a form, run for a period of time, have terms and bear rates of interest as may be provided by statute. The full faith and credit and taxing power of the State of Oregon must be pledged to the payment of the principal, premium, if any, and interest on the general obligation bonds; however, the ad valorem taxing power of the State of Oregon may not be pledged to the payment of the bonds issued under this section.

(3) As used in this section, "public education building" means a building owned by the State Board of Higher Education, a school district, an education service district, a community college district or a community college service district. [Created through S.J.R. 21, 2001, and adopted by the people Nov. 5, 2002]

Section 2. Sources of repayment. The principal, premium, if any, interest and other amounts payable with respect to the general obligation bonds issued under section 1 of this Article must be repaid as determined by the Legislative Assembly from the following sources:

(1) Amounts appropriated for the purpose by the Legislative Assembly from the General Fund, including taxes, other than ad valorem property taxes, levied to pay the bonds;

(2) Amounts allocated for the purpose by the Legislative Assembly from the proceeds of the State Lottery or from the Master Settlement Agreement entered into on November 23, 1998, by the State of Oregon and leading United States tobacco product manufacturers; and

(3) Amounts appropriated or allocated for the purpose by the Legislative Assembly from other sources of revenue. [Created through S.J.R. 21, 2001, and adopted by the people Nov. 5, 2002]

Section 3. Refunding bonds. General obligation bonds issued under section 1 of this Article may be refunded with bonds of like obligation. [Created through S.J.R. 21, 2001, and adopted by the people Nov. 5, 2002]

Section 4. Legislation to effectuate Article. The Legislative Assembly may enact legislation to carry out the provisions of this Article. [Created through S.J.R. 21, 2001, and adopted by the people Nov. 5, 2002]

Section 5. Relationship to conflicting provisions of Constitution. This Article supersedes conflicting provisions of this Constitution. [Created through S.J.R. 21, 2001, and adopted by the people Nov. 5, 2002]

ARTICLE XI-N
SEISMIC REHABILITATION OF EMERGENCY SERVICES BUILDINGS

Sec. 1.   State empowered to lend credit for seismic rehabilitation of emergency services buildings; bonds
2.   Sources of repayment
3.   Refunding bonds
4.   Legislation to effectuate Article
5.   Relationship to conflicting provisions of Constitution

Note: Article XI-N was designated as "Article XI-L" by S.J.R. 22, 2001, and adopted by the people Nov. 5, 2002.

Section 1. State empowered to lend credit for seismic rehabilitation of emergency services buildings; bonds. (1) In the manner provided by law and notwithstanding the limitations contained in section 7, Article XI of this Constitution, the credit of the State of Oregon may be loaned and indebtedness incurred, in an aggregate outstanding principal amount not to exceed, at any one time, one-fifth of one percent of the real market value of all property in the state, to provide funds for the planning and implementation of seismic rehabilitation of emergency services buildings, including surveying and conducting engineering evaluations of the need for seismic rehabilitation.

(2) Any indebtedness incurred under this section must be in the form of general obligation bonds of the State of Oregon containing a direct promise on behalf of the State of Oregon to pay the principal, premium, if any, interest and other amounts payable with respect to the bonds, in an aggregate outstanding principal amount not to exceed the amount authorized in subsection (1) of this section. The bonds are the direct obligation of the State of Oregon and must be in a form, run for a period of time, have terms and bear rates of interest as may be provided by statute. The full faith and credit and taxing power of the State of Oregon must be pledged to the payment of the principal, premium, if any, and interest on the general obligation bonds; however, the ad valorem taxing power of the State of Oregon may not be pledged to the payment of the bonds issued under this section.

(3) As used in this section:

(a) "Acute inpatient care facility" means a licensed hospital with an organized medical staff, with permanent facilities that include inpatient beds, and with comprehensive medical services, including physician services and continuous nursing services under the supervision of registered nurses, to provide diagnosis and medical or surgical treatment primarily for but not limited to acutely ill patients and accident victims. "Acute inpatient care facility" includes the Oregon Health and Science University.

(b) "Emergency services building" means a public building used for fire protection services, a hospital building that contains an acute inpatient care facility, a police station, a sheriff's office or a similar facility used by a state, county, district or municipal law enforcement agency. [Created through S.J.R. 22, 2001, and adopted by the people Nov. 5, 2002]

Section 2. Sources of repayment. The principal, premium, if any, interest and other amounts payable with respect to the general obligation bonds issued under section 1 of this Article must be repaid as determined by the Legislative Assembly from the following sources:

Constitution

(1) Amounts appropriated for the purpose by the Legislative Assembly from the General Fund, including taxes, other than ad valorem property taxes, levied to pay the bonds;

(2) Amounts allocated for the purpose by the Legislative Assembly from the proceeds of the State Lottery or from the Master Settlement Agreement entered into on November 23, 1998, by the State of Oregon and leading United States tobacco product manufacturers; and

(3) Amounts appropriated or allocated for the purpose by the Legislative Assembly from other sources of revenue. [Created through S.J.R. 22, 2001, and adopted by the people Nov. 5, 2002]

Section 3. Refunding bonds. General obligation bonds issued under section 1 of this Article may be refunded with bonds of like obligation. [Created through S.J.R. 22, 2001, and adopted by the people Nov. 5, 2002]

Section 4. Legislation to effectuate Article. The Legislative Assembly may enact legislation to carry out the provisions of this Article. [Created through S.J.R. 22, 2001, and adopted by the people Nov. 5, 2002]

Section 5. Relationship to conflicting provisions of Constitution. This Article supersedes conflicting provisions of this Constitution. [Created through S.J.R. 22, 2001, and adopted by the people Nov. 5, 2002]

ARTICLE XI-O
PENSION LIABILITIES

Sec. 1.   State empowered to lend credit for pension liabilities
2.   Refunding obligations
3.   Legislation to effectuate Article
4.   Relationship to conflicting provisions of Constitution

Section 1. State empowered to lend credit for pension liabilities. (1) In the manner provided by law and notwithstanding the limitations contained in section 7, Article XI of this Constitution, the credit of the State of Oregon may be loaned and indebtedness incurred to finance the State of Oregon's pension liabilities. Indebtedness authorized by this section also may be used to pay costs of issuing or incurring indebtedness under this section.

(2) Indebtedness incurred under this section is a general obligation of the State of Oregon and must contain a direct promise on behalf of the State of Oregon to pay the principal, premium, if any, and interest on that indebtedness. The State of Oregon shall pledge its full faith and credit and taxing power to pay that indebtedness; however, the ad valorem taxing power of the State of Oregon may not be pledged to pay that indebtedness. The amount of indebtedness authorized by this section and outstanding at any time may not exceed one percent of the real market value of all property in the state. [Created through H.J.R. 18, 2003, and adopted by the people Sept. 16, 2003]

Section 2. Refunding obligations. Indebtedness incurred under section 1 of this Article may be refunded with like obligations. [Created through H.J.R. 18, 2003, and adopted by the people Sept. 16, 2003]

Section 3. Legislation to effectuate Article. The Legislative Assembly may enact legislation to carry out the provisions of this Article. [Created through H.J.R. 18, 2003, and adopted by the people Sept. 16, 2003]

Section 4. Relationship to conflicting provisions of Constitution. This Article supersedes all conflicting provisions of this Constitution. [Created through H.J.R. 18, 2003, and adopted by the people Sept. 16, 2003]

ARTICLE XI-P
SCHOOL DISTRICT CAPITAL COSTS

Sec. 1.   State empowered to lend credit for grants or loans to school districts to finance capital costs; general obligation bond proceeds as matching funds
2.   Sources of repayment
3.   Refunding bonds
4.   School capital matching fund
5.   "Capital costs" defined
6.   Legislation to effectuate Article
7.   Relationship to conflicting provision of Constitution

Section 1. State empowered to lend credit for grants or loans to school districts to finance capital costs; general obligation bond proceeds as matching funds. (1) In the manner provided by law and notwithstanding the limitations contained in section 7, Article XI of this Constitution, the State of Oregon may loan its credit and incur indebtedness, in an aggregate outstanding principal amount not to exceed, at any one time, one-half of one percent of the real market value of the real property in this state, to provide funds to be advanced by grant or loan to school districts to finance the capital costs of the school districts. Bonds issued under this section may not be paid from ad valorem property taxes.

(2) Indebtedness incurred under this section must be in the form of general obligation bonds of the State of Oregon containing a direct promise to pay the principal, interest and premium, if any, of the bonds in an aggregate outstanding principal amount not to exceed the amount authorized in subsection (1) of this section. The bonds are the direct obligation of the State of Oregon and must be in such form, run for such periods of time, have such terms and bear such rates of interest as may be provided by statute. The State of Oregon shall pledge its full faith and credit and taxing power to the payment of the principal, interest and premium, if any, of the bonds. However, the State of Oregon may not pledge its ad valorem taxing power to the payment of the bonds.

(3) The proceeds from bonds issued under this section may be used only to provide matching funds to finance the capital costs of school districts that have received voter approval for local general obligation bonds and to provide for the costs of issuing bonds and the payment of debt service.

(4) The proceeds from bonds issued under this section may not be used to finance the operating costs of school districts. [Created through H.J.R. 13, 2009, and adopted by the people May 18, 2010]

Section 2. Sources of repayment. The principal, interest and premium, if any, of the bonds issued under section 1 of this Article must be repaid as determined by the Legislative Assembly from the following sources:

(1) Amounts appropriated for repayment by the Legislative Assembly from the General Fund, including taxes levied to pay the bonds except ad valorem property taxes;

(2) Amounts appropriated or allocated for repayment by the Legislative Assembly from other sources of revenue; or

(3) Any other available moneys. [Created through H.J.R. 13, 2009, and adopted by the people May 18, 2010]

Section 3. Refunding bonds. Bonds issued under section 1 of this Article may be refunded with bonds of like obligation. [Created through H.J.R. 13, 2009, and adopted by the people May 18, 2010]

Section 4. School capital matching fund. (1) There is created a school capital matching fund. Moneys in the fund may be invested and the earnings shall be retained in the fund or expended as provided by the Legislative Assembly.

(2) The Legislative Assembly may by law appropriate, allocate or transfer moneys or revenue to the school capital matching fund.

(3) The Legislative Assembly may appropriate, allocate or transfer moneys in the school capital matching fund and earnings on moneys in the fund for the purposes of providing:

(a) State matching funds to school districts to finance capital costs; and

(b) Payment of debt service for general obligation bonds issued pursuant to this Article. [Created through H.J.R. 13, 2009, and adopted by the people May 18, 2010]

Section 5. "Capital costs" defined. As used in this Article, "capital costs" means costs of land and of other assets having a useful life of more than one year, including costs associated with acquisition, construction, improvement, remodeling, furnishing, equipping, maintenance or repair. [Created through H.J.R. 13, 2009, and adopted by the people May 18, 2010]

Section 6. Legislation to effectuate Article. The Legislative Assembly may enact legislation to carry out the provisions of this Article. [Created through H.J.R. 13, 2009, and adopted by the people May 18, 2010]

Section 7. Relationship to conflicting provision of Constitution. This Article supersedes any conflicting provision of this Constitution. [Created through H.J.R. 13, 2009, and adopted by the people May 18, 2010]

ARTICLE XI-Q
REAL OR PERSONAL PROPERTY OWNED OR OPERATED BY STATE

Sec. 1. State empowered to lend credit for real or personal property to be owned or operated by state; refinancing authority
2. Limit on indebtedness; general obligation of state
3. Legislation to effectuate Article
4. Relationship to conflicting provisions of Constitution

Note: Article XI-Q was designated as "Article XI-P" by S.J.R. 48, 2010, and adopted by the people Nov. 2, 2010.

Section 1. State empowered to lend credit for real or personal property to be owned or operated by state; refinancing authority. (1) In the manner provided by law and notwithstanding the limitations contained in section 7, Article XI of this Constitution, the credit of the State of Oregon may be loaned and indebtedness incurred to finance the costs of:

(a) Acquiring, constructing, remodeling, repairing, equipping or furnishing real or personal property that is or will be owned or operated by the State of Oregon, including, without limitation, facilities and systems;

(b) Infrastructure related to the real or personal property; or

(c) Indebtedness incurred under this subsection.

(2) In the manner provided by law and notwithstanding the limitations contained in section 7, Article XI of this Constitution, the credit of the State of Oregon may be loaned and indebtedness incurred to refinance:

(a) Indebtedness incurred under subsection (1) of this section.

(b) Borrowings issued before the effective date of this Article to finance or refinance costs described in subsection (1) of this section. [Created through S.J.R. 48, 2010, and adopted by the people Nov. 2, 2010]

Note: The effective date of Senate Joint Resolution 48, 2010, is Dec. 2, 2010.

Section 2. Limit on indebtedness; general obligation of state. (1) Indebtedness may not be incurred under section 1 of this Article if the indebtedness would cause the total principal amount of indebtedness incurred under sec-

tion 1 of this Article and outstanding to exceed one percent of the real market value of the property in this state.

(2) Indebtedness incurred under section 1 of this Article is a general obligation of the State of Oregon and must contain a direct promise on behalf of the State of Oregon to pay the principal, premium, if any, and interest on the obligation. The full faith and credit and taxing power of the State of Oregon must be pledged to payment of the indebtedness. However, the State of Oregon may not pledge or levy an ad valorem tax to pay the indebtedness. [Created through S.J.R. 48, 2010, and adopted by the people Nov. 2, 2010]

Section 3. Legislation to effectuate Article. The Legislative Assembly may enact legislation to carry out the provisions of this Article. [Created through S.J.R. 48, 2010, and adopted by the people Nov. 2, 2010]

Section 4. Relationship to conflicting provisions of Constitution. This Article supersedes conflicting provisions of this Constitution. [Created through S.J.R. 48, 2010, and adopted by the people Nov. 2, 2010]

ARTICLE XII
STATE PRINTING

Section 1. State printing; State Printer. Laws may be enacted providing for the state printing and binding, and for the election or appointment of a state printer, who shall have had not less than ten years' experience in the art of printing. The state printer shall receive such compensation as may from time to time be provided by law. Until such laws shall be enacted the state printer shall be elected, and the printing done as heretofore provided by this constitution and the general laws. [Constitution of 1859; Amendment proposed by S.J.R. 1, 1901, and adopted by the people June 6, 1904; Amendment proposed by initiative petition filed Feb. 3, 1906, and adopted by the people June 4, 1906]

ARTICLE XIII
SALARIES

Section 1. Salaries or other compensation of state officers. [Constitution of 1859; Repeal proposed by S.J.R. 12, 1955, and adopted by the people Nov. 6, 1956]

ARTICLE XIV
SEAT OF GOVERNMENT

Sec. 1. Seat of government
2. Erection of state house prior to 1865

Section 1. Seat of government. [Constitution of 1859; Repeal proposed by S.J.R. 41, 1957, and adopted by the people Nov. 4, 1958 (present section 1 and former 1958 section 3 of this Article adopted in lieu of this section and former original section 3 of this Article)]

Section 1. Seat of government. The permanent seat of government for the state shall be Marion County. [Created through S.J.R. 41, 1957, and adopted by the people Nov. 4, 1958 (this section and former 1958 section 3 of this Article adopted in lieu of former original sections 1 and 3 of this Article)]

Section 2. Erection of state house prior to 1865. No tax shall be levied, or money of the State expended, or debt contracted for the erection of a State House prior to the year eighteen hundred and sixty five. —

Section 3. Limitation on removal of seat of government; location of state institutions. [Constitution of 1859; Amendment proposed by S.J.R. 1, 1907, and adopted by the people June 1, 1908; Repeal proposed by S.J.R. 41, 1957, and adopted by the people Nov. 4, 1958 (present section 1 and former 1958 section 3 of this Article adopted in lieu of this section and former section 1 of this Article)]

Section 3. Location and use of state institutions. [Created through S.J.R. 41, 1957, and adopted by the people Nov. 4, 1958 (this section, designated as "Section 2" by S.J.R. 41, 1957, and present section 1 of this Article adopted in lieu of former original sections 1 and 3 of this Article); Repeal proposed by S.J.R. 9, 1971, and adopted by the people Nov. 7, 1972]

ARTICLE XV
MISCELLANEOUS

Section 1. Officers to hold office until successors elected; exceptions; effect on defeated incumbent. (1) All officers, except members of the Legislative Assembly and incumbents who seek reelection and are defeated, shall hold their offices until their successors are elected, and qualified.

(2) If an incumbent seeks reelection and is defeated, he shall hold office only until the end of his term; and if an election contest is pending in the courts regarding that office when the term of such an incumbent ends and a successor to the office has not been elected or if elected, has not qualified because of such election contest, the person appointed to fill the vacancy thus created shall serve only until the contest and any appeal is finally determined notwithstanding any other provision of this constitution. [Constitution of 1859; Amendment proposed by H.J.R. 51, 1969, and adopted by the people Nov. 3, 1970]

Section 2. Tenure of office; how fixed; maximum tenure. When the duration of any office is not provided for by this Constitution, it may be declared by law; and if not so declared, such office shall be held during the pleasure of the authority making the appointment. But the Legislative Assembly shall not create any office, the tenure of which shall be longer than four years.

Section 3. Oaths of office. Every person elected or appointed to any office under this Constitution, shall, before entering on the duties thereof, take an oath or affirmation to support the Constitution of the United States, and of this State, and also an oath of office.—

Note: The amendments to sections 4, 4a, 4b and 4c and the repeal of section 4d by Measure No. 76, 2010, as submitted to the people was preceded by a preamble that reads as follows:

PREAMBLE: The people of the State of Oregon find that renewing the current dedication in the Oregon Constitution of fifteen percent of lottery revenues to parks, water quality and fish and wildlife habitats will provide lasting social, economic, environmental and public health benefits. The people of the State of Oregon also find that renewal of the Parks and Natural Resources Fund will support voluntary efforts to:

(1) Protect and restore water quality, watersheds and habitats for native fish and wildlife that provide a healthy environment for current and future generations of Oregonians;

(2) Maintain and expand public parks, natural areas and recreation areas to meet the diverse needs of a growing population and to provide opportunities for [sic] to experience nature and enjoy outdoor recreation activities close to home and in the many special places throughout Oregon;

(3) Provide jobs and economic opportunities improving the health of our forests, prairies, lakes, streams, wetlands, rivers, and parks, including efforts to halt the spread of invasive species;

(4) Strengthen the audit and reporting requirements, identify desired outcomes and specify allowable uses of the fund in order to provide more strategic, accountable and efficient uses of the Parks and Natural Resources Fund; and

(5) Enhance the ability of public land managers, private organizations, individuals and businesses to work together in local, regional and statewide partnerships to expand recreation opportunities, improve water quality and conserve fish and wildlife habitat.

Section 4. Regulation of lotteries; state lottery; use of net proceeds from state lottery. (1) Except as provided in subsections (2), (3), (4), (8) and (9) of this section, lotteries and the sale of lottery tickets, for any purpose whatever, are prohibited, and the Legislative Assembly shall prevent the same by penal laws.

(2) The Legislative Assembly may provide for the establishment, operation, and regulation of raffles and the lottery commonly known as bingo or lotto by charitable, fraternal, or religious organizations. As used in this section, charitable, fraternal or religious organization means such organizations or foundations as defined by law because of their charitable, fraternal, or religious purposes. The regulations shall define eligible organizations or foundations, and may prescribe the frequency of raffles, bingo or lotto, set a maximum monetary limit for prizes and require a statement of the odds on winning a prize. The Legislative Assembly shall vest the regulatory authority in any appropriate state agency.

(3) There is hereby created the State Lottery Commission which shall establish and operate a State Lottery. All proceeds from the State Lottery, including interest, but excluding costs of administration and payment of prizes, shall be used for any of the following purposes: creating jobs, furthering economic development, financing public education in Oregon or restoring and protecting Oregon's parks, beaches, watersheds and native fish and wildlife.

(4)(a) The State Lottery Commission shall be comprised of five members appointed by the Governor and confirmed by the Senate who shall serve at the pleasure of the Governor. At least one of the Commissioners shall have a minimum of five years experience in law enforcement and at least one of the Commissioners shall be a certified public accountant. The Commission is empowered to promulgate rules related to the procedures of the Commission and the operation of the State Lottery. Such rules and any statutes enacted to further implement this article shall insure the integrity, security, honesty, and fairness of the Lottery. The Commission shall have such additional powers and duties as may be provided by law.

(b) The Governor shall appoint a Director subject to confirmation by the Senate who shall serve at the pleasure of the Governor. The Director shall be qualified by training and experience to direct the operations of a state-operated lottery. The Director shall be responsible for managing the affairs of the Commission. The Director may appoint and prescribe the duties of no more than four Assistant Directors as the Director deems necessary. One of the Assistant Directors shall be responsible for a security division to assure security, integrity, honesty, and fairness in the operations and administration of the State Lottery. To fulfill these responsibilities, the Assistant Director for security shall be qualified by training and experience, including at least five years of law enforcement experience, and knowledge and experience in computer security.

(c) The Director shall implement and operate a State Lottery pursuant to the rules, and under the guidance, of the Commission. The State Lottery may operate any game procedure authorized by the commission, except parimutuel racing, social games, and the games commonly known in Oregon as bingo or lotto, whereby prizes are distributed using any existing or future methods among adult persons who have paid for tickets or shares in that game; provided that, in lottery games utilizing computer terminals or other devices, no coins or currency shall ever be dispensed directly to players from such computer terminals or devices.

(d) There is hereby created within the General Fund the Oregon State Lottery Fund which is continuously appropriated for the purpose of administering and operating the Commission and the State Lottery. The State Lottery shall operate as a self-supporting revenue-raising agency of state government and no appropriations, loans, or other transfers of state funds shall be made to it. The State Lottery shall pay all prizes and all of its expenses out of the revenues it receives from the sale of tickets or shares to the public and turnover the net proceeds therefrom to a fund to be established by the Legislative Assembly from which the Legislative Assembly shall make appropriations for the benefit of any of the following public purposes: creating jobs, furthering economic development, financing public education in Oregon or restoring and protecting Oregon's parks, beaches, watersheds and native fish and wildlife. Effective July 1, 1997, 15% of the net proceeds from the State Lottery shall be deposited, from the fund created by the Legislative Assembly under this paragraph, in an education stability fund. Effective July 1, 2003, 18% of the net proceeds from the State Lottery shall be deposited, from the fund created by the Legislative Assembly under this paragraph, in an education stability fund. Earnings on moneys in the education stability fund shall be retained in the fund or expended for the public purpose of financing public education in Oregon as provided by law. Except as provided in subsection (6) of this section, moneys in the education stability fund shall be invested as provided by law and shall not be subject to the limitations of section 6, Article XI of this Constitution. The Legislative Assembly may appropriate other moneys or revenue to the education stability fund. The Legislative Assembly shall appropriate amounts sufficient to pay lottery bonds before appropriating the net proceeds from the State Lottery for any other purpose. At least 84% of the total annual revenues from the sale of all lottery tickets or shares shall be returned to the public in the form of prizes and net revenues benefiting the public purpose.

(5) Notwithstanding paragraph (d) of subsection (4) of this section, the amount in the education stability fund created under paragraph (d) of subsection (4) of this section may not exceed an amount that is equal to five percent of the amount that was accrued as revenues in the state's General Fund during the prior biennium. If the amount in the education stability fund exceeds five percent of the amount that was accrued as revenues in the state's General Fund during the prior biennium:

(a) Additional net proceeds from the State Lottery may not be deposited in the education stability fund until the amount in the education stability fund is reduced to less than five percent of the amount that was accrued as revenues in the state's General Fund during the prior biennium; and

(b) Fifteen percent of the net proceeds from the State Lottery shall be deposited into the school capital matching fund created under section 4, Article XI-P of this Constitution.

(6) The Legislative Assembly may by law appropriate, allocate or transfer any portion of the principal of the education stability fund created under paragraph (d) of subsection (4) of this section for expenditure on public education if:

(a) The proposed appropriation, allocation or transfer is approved by three-fifths of the members serving in each house of the Legislative Assembly and the Legislative Assembly finds one of the following:

(A) That the last quarterly economic and revenue forecast for a biennium indicates that moneys available to the state's General Fund for the next biennium will be at least three percent less than appropriations from the state's General Fund for the current biennium;

(B) That there has been a decline for two or more consecutive quarters in the last 12 months in seasonally adjusted nonfarm payroll employment; or

(C) That a quarterly economic and revenue forecast projects that revenues in the state's General Fund in the current biennium will be at least two percent below what the revenues were projected to be in the revenue forecast on which the legislatively adopted budget for the current biennium was based; or

(b) The proposed appropriation, allocation or transfer is approved by three-fifths of the members serving in each house of the Legislative Assembly and the Governor declares an emergency.

(7) The Legislative Assembly may by law prescribe the procedures to be used and identify the persons required to make the forecasts described in subsection (6) of this section.

(8) Effective July 1, 1999, 15% of the net proceeds from the State Lottery shall be deposited in a parks and natural resources fund created by the Legislative Assembly. Of the moneys in the parks and natural resources fund, 50% shall be deposited in a parks subaccount and distributed for the public purposes of financing the protection, repair, operation, and creation of state, regional and local public parks, ocean shore and public beach access areas, historic sites and recreation areas, and 50% shall be deposited in a natural resources subaccount and distributed for the public purposes of financing the restoration and protection of native fish and wildlife, watersheds and water quality in Oregon. The Legislative Assembly shall not limit expenditures from the parks and natural resources fund, or from the parks or natural resources subaccounts. The Legislative Assembly may appropriate other moneys or revenue to the parks and natural resources fund.

(9) Only one State Lottery operation shall be permitted in the State.

(10) The Legislative Assembly has no power to authorize, and shall prohibit, casinos from operation in the State of Oregon. [Constitution of 1859; Amendment proposed by H.J.R. 14, 1975, and adopted by the people Nov. 2, 1976; Amendment proposed by initiative petition filed April 3, 1984, and adopted by the people Nov. 6, 1984 (paragraph designations in subsection (4) were not included in the petition);

Amendment proposed by H.J.R. 20, 1985, and adopted by the people Nov. 4, 1986; Amendment proposed by H.J.R. 15, 1995, and adopted by the people May 16, 1995; Amendment proposed by initiative petition filed March 11, 1998, and adopted by the people Nov. 3, 1998; Amendment proposed by H.J.R. 80, 2002 (3rd s.s.), and adopted by the people Sept. 17, 2002; Revision proposed by H.J.R. 13, 2009, and adopted by the people May 18, 2010; Amendment proposed by initiative petition filed Dec. 22, 2009, and adopted by the people Nov. 2, 2010]

Note: The amendments to section 4, as adopted by the people in Measure No. 66, 1998, incorrectly set forth the text of section 4 as it existed at the time the measure was submitted to the people. The text of the measure, as approved by the voters, was printed here.

Note: The amendments to section 4, as adopted by the people in Measure No. 76, 2010, at the Nov. 2010 general election did not set forth the text of section 4 as it was revised by the people in Measure No. 68, 2010 (H.J.R. 13, 2009), at the May 2010 primary election. The text of section 4, as revised by Measure No. 68, 2010, and amended by Measure No. 76, 2010, is printed here.

Section 4a. Use of net proceeds from state lottery for parks and recreation areas. (1) In each biennium the Legislative Assembly shall appropriate all of the moneys in the parks subaccount of the parks and natural resources fund established under section 4 of this Article for the uses allowed in subsection (2) of this section, and to achieve all of the following:

(a) Provide additional public parks, natural areas or outdoor recreational areas to meet the needs of current and future residents of the State of Oregon;

(b) Protect natural, cultural, historic and outdoor recreational resources of state or regional significance;

(c) Manage public parks, natural areas and outdoor recreation areas to ensure their long-term ecological health and provide for the enjoyment of current and future residents of the State of Oregon; and

(d) Provide diverse and equitable opportunities for residents of the State of Oregon to experience nature and participate in outdoor recreational activities in state, regional, local or neighborhood public parks and recreation areas.

(2) The moneys in the parks subaccount shall be used only to:

(a) Maintain, construct, improve, develop, manage and operate state parks, ocean shores, public beach access areas, historic sites, natural areas and outdoor and recreation areas;

(b) Acquire real property, or interests therein, that has significant natural, scenic, cultural, historic or recreational values, for the creation or operation of state parks, ocean shores, public beach access areas, outdoor recreation areas and historic sites; and

(c) Provide grants to regional or local government entities to acquire property for public parks, natural areas or outdoor recreation areas, or to develop or improve public parks, natural areas or outdoor recreation areas.

(3) In each biennium the Legislative Assembly shall appropriate no less than twelve percent of the moneys in the parks subaccount for local and regional grants as authorized under paragraph (c) of subsection (2) of this section. However, if in any biennium the amount of net proceeds deposited in the parks and natural resources fund created under section 4 of this Article increases by more than fifty percent above the amount deposited in the 2009-2011 biennium, the Legislative Assembly shall appropriate no less than twenty-four percent of the moneys in the parks subaccount for local and regional grants as authorized under paragraph (c) of subsection (2) of this section. The grants shall be administered by a single state agency. The costs of the state agency in administering the grants shall not be paid out of the portion of the moneys in the parks

subaccount appropriated for local and regional grants. [Created through initiative petition filed March 11, 1998, and adopted by the people Nov. 3, 1998; Amendment proposed by initiative petition filed Dec. 22, 2009, and adopted by the people Nov. 2, 2010]

Section 4b. Use of net proceeds from state lottery for fish and wildlife, watershed and habitat protection. (1) In each biennium the Legislative Assembly shall appropriate all of the moneys in the natural resources subaccount of the parks and natural resources fund established under section 4 of this Article for the uses allowed in subsections (2) and (3) of this section, and to accomplish all of the following:

(a) Protect and improve water quality in Oregon's rivers, lakes, and streams by restoring natural watershed functions or stream flows;

(b) Secure long-term protection for lands and waters that provide significant habitats for native fish and wildlife;

(c) Restore and maintain habitats needed to sustain healthy and resilient populations of native fish and wildlife;

(d) Maintain the diversity of Oregon's plants, animals and ecosystems;

(e) Involve people in voluntary actions to protect, restore and maintain the ecological health of Oregon's lands and waters; and

(f) Remedy the conditions that limit the health of fish and wildlife, habitats and watershed functions in greatest need of conservation.

(2) In each biennium the Legislative Assembly shall appropriate no less than sixty-five percent of the moneys in the natural resources subaccount to one state agency, and that agency shall distribute those moneys as grants to entities other than state or federal agencies for projects that achieve the outcomes specified in subsection (1) of this section. However, if in any biennium the amount of net proceeds deposited in the parks and natural resources fund created under section 4 of this Article increases by more than fifty percent above the amount deposited in the 2009-2011 biennium, the Legislative Assembly shall appropriate no less than seventy percent of the moneys in the natural resources subaccount to one state agency, and that agency shall distribute those moneys as grants to entities other than state or federal agencies for projects that achieve the outcomes specified in subsection (1) of this section. In addition, these moneys shall be used only to:

(a) Acquire from willing owners interests in land or water that will protect or restore native fish or wildlife habitats, which interests may include but are not limited to fee interests, conservation easements or leases;

(b) Carry out projects to protect or restore native fish or wildlife habitats;

(c) Carry out projects to protect or restore natural watershed functions to improve water quality or stream flows; and

(d) Carry out resource assessment, planning, design and engineering, technical assistance, monitoring and outreach activities necessary for projects funded under paragraphs (a) through (c) of this subsection.

(3) In each biennium the Legislative Assembly shall appropriate that portion of the natural resources subaccount not appropriated under subsection (2) of this section to support all of the following activities:

(a) Develop, implement or update state conservation strategies or plans to protect or restore native fish or wildlife habitats or to protect or restore natural watershed functions to improve water quality or stream flows;

(b) Develop, implement or update regional or local strategies or plans that are consistent with the state strategies or plans described in paragraph (a) of this subsection;

(c) Develop, implement or update state strategies or plans to prevent, detect, control or eradicate invasive species that threaten native fish or wildlife habitats or that impair water quality;

(d) Support local delivery of programs or projects, including watershed education activities, that protect or restore native fish or wildlife habitats or watersheds;

(e) Pay the state agency costs of administering subsection (2) of this section, which costs shall not be paid out of the moneys available for grants under subsection (2) of this section; and

(f) Enforce fish and wildlife and habitat protection laws and regulations. [Created through initiative petition filed March 11, 1998, and adopted by the people Nov. 3, 1998; Amendment proposed by initiative petition filed Dec. 22, 2009, and adopted by the people Nov. 2, 2010]

Section 4c. Audit of agency receiving certain net proceeds from state lottery. The Secretary of State shall regularly audit any state agency that receives moneys from the parks and natural resources fund established under section 4 of this Article to address the financial integrity, compliance with applicable laws, efficiency and effectiveness of the use of the moneys. The costs of the audit shall be paid from the parks and natural resources fund. However, such costs may not be paid from the portions of such fund, or the subaccounts of the fund, that are dedicated to grants. The audit shall be submitted to the Legislative Assembly as part of a biennial report to the Legislative Assembly. In addition, each agency that receives moneys from the parks and natural resources fund shall submit a biennial performance report [sic] the Legislature [sic] Assembly that describes the measurable biennial and cumulative results of activities and programs financed by the fund. [Created through initiative petition filed March 11, 1998, and adopted by the people Nov. 3, 1998; Amendment proposed by initiative petition filed Dec. 22, 2009, and adopted by the people Nov. 2, 2010]

Note: Added as section 4c to the Constitution but not to any Article therein by initiative petition (Measure No. 66, 1998) adopted by the people Nov. 3, 1998.

Section 4d. Subsequent vote for reaffirmation of sections 4a, 4b and 4c and amendment to section 4. [Created through initiative petition filed March 11, 1998, and adopted by the people Nov. 3, 1998; Repeal proposed by initiative petition filed Dec. 22, 2009, and adopted by the people Nov. 2, 2010]

Section 4e. Transfer of moneys in school capital matching subaccount to school capital matching fund created under section 4, Article XI-P. [Created through H.J.R. 13, 2009, and adopted by the people May 18, 2010; Repealed Jan. 2, 2011, as specified in text of section adopted by the people May 18, 2010]

Section 4f. Percentage of lottery revenues to be expended for benefit of veterans. (1) Effective July 1, 2017, 1.5 percent of the net proceeds from the State Lottery shall be deposited, from the fund created by the Legislative Assembly under paragraph (d) of subsection (4) of section 4 of this Article, in a veterans' services fund created by the Legislative Assembly. The Legislative Assembly may appropriate other moneys or revenue to the veterans' services fund.

(2) The moneys in the veterans' services fund may be used only to provide services for the benefit of veterans. Such services may include, without limitation:

(a) Assistance for veterans with reintegration, employment, education benefits and tuition, housing, physical and mental health care and addiction treatment programs;

(b) Assistance for veterans, spouses of veterans or dependents of veterans in accessing state and federal benefits; and

(c) Funding services provided by county veterans' service officers, campus veterans' service officers or nonprofit or tribal veterans' service officers.

(3) As used in this section, "veteran" means a resident of the State of Oregon who served in the Armed Forces of the United States. [Created through H.J.R. 202, 2016, and adopted by the people Nov. 8, 2016]

Section 5. Property of married women not subject to debts of husband; registration of separate property. The property and pecuniary rights of every married woman, at the time of marriage or afterwards, acquired by gift, devise, or inheritance shall not be subject to the debts, or contracts of the husband; and laws shall be passed providing for the registration of the wife's seperate [sic] property.

Section 5a. Policy regarding marriage. It is the policy of Oregon, and its political subdivisions, that only a marriage between one man and one woman shall be valid or legally recognized as a marriage. [Created through initiative petition filed March 2, 2004, and adopted by the people Nov. 2, 2004]

Note: Added as unnumbered section to the Constitution but not to any Article therein by initiative petition (Measure No. 36, 2004) adopted by the people Nov. 2, 2004.

Section 6. Minimum area and population of counties. No county shall be reduced to an area of less than four hundred square miles; nor shall any new county be established in this State containing a less area, nor unless such new county shall contain a population of at least twelve hundred inhabitants.

Section 7. Officers not to receive fees from or represent claimants against state. No State officers, or members of the Legislative Assembly, shall directly or indirectly receive a fee, or be engaged as counsel, agent, or Attorney in the prosecution of any claim against this State.—

Section 8. Certain persons not to hold real estate or mining claims; working mining claims. [Constitution of 1859; Repeal proposed by S.J.R. 14, 1945, and adopted by the people Nov. 5, 1946]

Section 8. Persons eligible to serve in legislature; employment of judges by Oregon National Guard or public university. Notwithstanding the provisions of section 1, Article III, and section 10, Article II of this Constitution:

(1) A person employed by any board or commission established by law to supervise and coordinate the activities of Oregon's institutions of post-secondary education, a person employed by a public university as defined by law or a member or employee of any school board is eligible to serve as a member of the Legislative Assembly, and membership in the Legislative Assembly does not prevent the person from being employed by any board or commission established by law to supervise and coordinate the activities of Oregon's post-secondary institutions of education or by a public university as defined by law, or from being a member or employee of a school board.

(2) A person serving as a judge of any court of this state may be employed by the Oregon National Guard for the purpose of performing military service or may be employed by any public university as defined by law for the purpose of teaching, and the employment does not prevent the person from serving as a judge. [Created through initiative petition filed June 13, 1958, and adopted by the people Nov. 4, 1958; Amendment proposed by S.J.R. 203, 2014, and adopted by the people Nov. 4, 2014]

Constitution

Section 8a. [Created through S.J.R. 203, 2014, and adopted by the people Nov. 4, 2014; Section not compiled because of its temporary nature]

Section 9. When elective office becomes vacant. The Legislative Assembly may provide that any elective public office becomes vacant, under such conditions or circumstances as the Legislative Assembly may specify, whenever a person holding the office is elected to another public office more than 90 days prior to the expiration of the term of the office he is holding. For the purposes of this section, a person elected is considered to be elected as of the date the election is held. [Created through S.J.R. 41, 1959, and adopted by the people Nov. 8, 1960]

Section 10. The Oregon Property Protection Act of 2000. (1) This section may be known and shall be cited as the "Oregon Property Protection Act of 2000."

(2) Statement of principles. The People, in the exercise of the power reserved to them under the Constitution of the State of Oregon, declare that:

(a) A basic tenet of a democratic society is that a person is presumed innocent and should not be punished until proven guilty;

(b) The property of a person generally should not be forfeited in a forfeiture proceeding by government unless and until that person is convicted of a crime involving the property;

(c) The value of property forfeited should be proportional to the specific conduct for which the owner of the property has been convicted; and

(d) Proceeds from forfeited property should be used for treatment of drug abuse unless otherwise specified by law for another purpose.

(3) Forfeitures prohibited without conviction. Except as provided in this section, a judgment of forfeiture of property in a civil forfeiture proceeding by the State or any of its political subdivisions may not be entered until and unless the person claiming the property is convicted of a crime in Oregon or another jurisdiction and the property:

(a) Constitutes proceeds of the crime for which the claimant has been convicted;

(b) Was instrumental in committing or facilitating the crime for which the claimant has been convicted;

(c) Constitutes proceeds of one or more other crimes similar to the crime for which the claimant was convicted; or

(d) Was instrumental in committing or facilitating one or more other crimes similar to the crime for which the claimant was convicted.

(4) Forfeiture based on similar crimes. Property may be forfeited under paragraph (c) or (d) of subsection (3) of this section only if the claimant is notified in writing of the other crime or crimes claimed to be similar to the crime for which the claimant was convicted. The notice must be given at the time the claimant is given notice of the seizure of the property for forfeiture, and the claimant must have an opportunity to challenge the seizure and forfeiture of the property.

(5) Forfeiture without conviction of claimant. The property of a claimant who has not been convicted of a crime may be forfeited in a civil forfeiture proceeding only if the claimant consents to the forfeiture of the property or the forfeiting agency proves the property constitutes proceeds or an instrumentality of crime committed by another person as described in subsection (3) of this section and:

(a) The claimant took the property with the intent to defeat forfeiture of the property;

(b) The claimant knew or should have known that the property constituted proceeds or an instrumentality of criminal conduct; or

(c) The claimant acquiesced in the criminal conduct. A person shall be considered to have acquiesced in criminal conduct if the person knew of the criminal conduct and failed to take reasonable action under the circumstances to terminate the criminal conduct or prevent use of the property to commit or facilitate the criminal conduct.

(6) Standard of proof. (a) Except as provided in paragraph (b) of this subsection, if the property to be forfeited in a civil forfeiture action is personal property, the forfeiting agency must prove the elements specified in subsection (3) or (5) of this section by a preponderance of the evidence. If the property to be forfeited in a civil forfeiture action is real property, the forfeiting agency must prove the elements specified in subsection (3) or (5) of this section by clear and convincing evidence.

(b) If a forfeiting agency establishes in a forfeiture proceeding that cash, weapons or negotiable instruments were found in close proximity to controlled substances or to instrumentalities of criminal conduct, the burden is on any person claiming the cash, weapons or negotiable instruments to prove by a preponderance of the evidence that the cash, weapons or negotiable instruments are not proceeds of criminal conduct or an instrumentality of criminal conduct.

(7) Value of property forfeited. The value of the property forfeited under the provisions of this section may not be excessive and shall be substantially proportional to the specific conduct for which the owner of the property has been convicted. For purposes of this section, "property" means any interest in anything of value, including the whole of any lot or tract of land and tangible and intangible personal property, including currency, instruments or securities or any other kind of privilege, interest, claim or right whether due or to become due. Nothing in this section shall prohibit a person from voluntarily giving a judgment of forfeiture.

(8) Financial institutions. In a civil forfeiture proceeding, if a financial institution claiming an interest in the property demonstrates that it holds an interest, the financial institution's interest is not subject to forfeiture.

(9) Exception for unclaimed property and contraband. Notwithstanding the provisions of subsection (3) of this section, if, following notice to all persons known to have an interest or who may have an interest, no person claims an interest in the seized property or if the property is contraband, a judgment of forfeiture may be allowed and entered without a criminal conviction. For purposes of this subsection, "contraband" means personal property, articles or things, including but not limited to controlled substances or drug paraphernalia, that a person is prohibited by Oregon statute or local ordinance from producing, obtaining or possessing.

(10) Exception for forfeiture of animals. This section does not apply to the forfeiture of animals that have been abused, neglected or abandoned.

(11) Law enforcement seizures unaffected. Nothing in this section shall be construed to affect the temporary seizure of property for evidentiary, forfeiture, or protective purposes, or to alter the power of the Governor to remit fines or forfeitures under Article V, Section 14, of this Constitution.

(12) Disposition of property to drug treatment. Any sale of forfeited property shall be conducted in a commercially reasonable manner. Property forfeited in a civil forfeiture proceeding shall be distributed or applied in the following order:

(a) To the satisfaction of any foreclosed liens, security interests and contracts in the order of their priority;

(b) To the State or any of its political subdivisions for actual and reasonable expenses related to the costs of the forfeiture proceeding, including attorney fees, storage, maintenance, management, and disposition of the property incurred in connection with the sale of any forfeited property; and

(c) To the State or any of its political subdivisions to be used exclusively for drug treatment, unless another disposition is specially provided by law.

(13) Restrictions on State transfers. Neither the State of Oregon, its political subdivisions, nor any forfeiting agency shall transfer forfeiture proceedings to the federal government unless a state court has affirmatively found that:

(a) The activity giving rise to the forfeiture is interstate in nature and sufficiently complex to justify the transfer;

(b) The seized property may only be forfeited under federal law; or

(c) Pursuing forfeiture under state law would unduly burden the state forfeiting agencies.

(14) Penalty for violations. Any person acting under color of law, official title or position who takes any action intending to conceal, transfer, withhold, retain, divert or otherwise prevent any moneys, conveyances, real property, or any things of value forfeited under the law of this State or the United States from being applied, deposited or used in accordance with the requirements of this section shall be subject to a civil penalty in an amount treble the value of the forfeited property concealed, transferred, withheld, retained or diverted. Nothing in this subsection shall be construed to impair judicial immunity if otherwise applicable.

(15) Reporting requirement. All forfeiting agencies shall report the nature and disposition of all property seized for forfeiture or forfeited to a State asset forfeiture oversight committee that is independent of any forfeiting agency. The asset forfeiture oversight committee shall generate and make available to the public an annual report of the information collected. The asset forfeiture oversight committee shall also make recommendations to ensure that asset forfeiture proceedings are handled in a manner that is fair to innocent property owners and interest holders.

(16) Severability. If any part of this section or its application to any person or circumstance is held to be invalid for any reason, then the remaining parts or applications to any persons or circumstances shall not be affected but shall remain in full force and effect. [Created through initiative petition filed Jan. 5, 2000, and adopted by the people Nov. 7, 2000; Amendment proposed by S.J.R. 18, 2007, and adopted by the people May 20, 2008]

Note: The leadlines to section 10 and subsections (2), (3), (9) and (11) to (16) of section 10 were a part of the measure submitted by initiative petition (Measure No. 3, 2000) adopted by the people Nov. 7, 2000. The leadlines to subsections (4) to (8) and (10) of section 10 were a part of S.J.R. 18, 2007, which was adopted by the people May 20, 2008.

Note: The text of section 11 (sections 1 to 3, Measure No. 99, 2000) as submitted to the people was preceded by a preamble that reads as follows:

WHEREAS, thousands of Oregon seniors and persons with disabilities live independently in their own homes, which they prefer and is less costly than institutional care (i.e. nursing homes), because over 10,000 home care workers, (also known as client employed providers), paid by the State of Oregon provide in-home support services;

WHEREAS, home care workers provide services that range from housekeeping, shopping, meal preparation, money management and personal care to medical care and treatment, but receive little, if any, training in those areas resulting in a detrimental impact on quality of care;

WHEREAS, the quality of care provided to seniors and people with disabilities is diminished when there is a lack of stability in the workforce which is the result of home care workers receiving low wages, minimal training and benefits;

WHEREAS, both home care workers and clients receiving home care services would benefit from creating an entity which has the authority to provide, and is held accountable for the quality of services provided in Oregon's in-home system of long-term care.

Section 11. Home Care Commission. (1) Ensuring High Quality Home Care Services: Creation and Duties of the Quality Home Care Commission. (a) The Home Care Commission is created as an independent public commission consisting of nine members appointed by the Governor.

(b) The duties and functions of the Home Care Commission include, but are not limited to:

(A) Ensuring that high quality, comprehensive home care services are provided to the elderly and people with disabilities who receive personal care services in their homes by home care workers hired directly by the client and financed by payments from the State or by payments from a county or other public agency which receives money for that purpose from the State;

(B) Providing routine, emergency and respite referrals of qualified home care providers to the elderly and people with disabilities who receive personal care services by home care workers hired directly by the client and financed in whole or in part by the State, or by payment from a county or other public agency which receives money for that purpose from the State;

(C) Provide training opportunities for home care workers, seniors and people with disabilities as consumers of personal care services;

(D) Establish qualifications for home care workers;

(E) Establish and maintain a registry of qualified home care workers;

(F) Cooperate with area agencies on aging and disability services and other local agencies to provide the services described and set forth in this section.

(2) Home Care Commission Operation/Selection. (a) The Home Care Commission shall be comprised of nine members. Five members of the Commission shall be current or former consumers of home care services for the elderly or people with disabilities. One member shall be a representative of the Oregon Disabilities Commission, (or a successor entity, for as long as a comparable entity exists). One member shall be a representative of the Governor's Commission on Senior Services, (or a successor entity, for as long as a comparable entity exists). One member shall be a representative of the Oregon Association of Area Agencies on Aging and Disabilities, (or a successor entity, for as long as a comparable entity exists). One member shall be a representative of the Senior and Disabled Services Division, (or a successor entity, for as long as a comparable entity exists).

(b) The term of office of each member is three years, subject to confirmation by the Senate. If there is a vacancy for any cause, the Governor shall make an appointment to become immediately effective for the unexpired term. A member is eligible for reappointment and may serve no more than three consecutive terms. In making appointments to the Commission, the Governor may take into consideration any nominations or recommendations made by the representative groups or agencies.

(3) Other Provisions — Legal Duties and Responsibilities of the Commission. (a) The Home Care Commission shall, in its own name, for the purpose of carrying into effect and promoting its functions, have authority to contract, lease, acquire, hold, own, encumber, insure, sell, replace, deal in and with and dispose of real and personal property.

(b) When conducting any activities in this Section or in subsection (1) of this section, and in making decisions relating to those activities, the Home Care Commission shall first consider the effect of its activities and its decisions on improving the quality of service delivery and ensuring adequate hours of service are provided to clients who are served by home care workers.

(c) Clients of home care services retain their right to select the providers of their choice, including family members.

(d) Employees of the Commission are not employees of the State of Oregon for any purpose.

(e) Notwithstanding the provisions in paragraph (d) of this subsection, the State of Oregon shall be held responsible for unemployment insurance payments for home care workers.

(f) For purposes of collective bargaining, the Commission shall be the employer of record of home care workers hired directly by the client and paid by the State, or by a county or other public agency which receives money for that purpose from the State. Home care workers have the right to form, join and participate in the activities of labor organizations of their own choosing for the purpose of representation and collective bargaining with the Commission on matters concerning employment relations. These rights shall be exercised in accordance with the rights granted to public employees with mediation and interest arbitration as the method of concluding the collective bargaining process. Home care workers shall not have the right to strike.

(g) The Commission may adopt rules to carry out its functions. [Created through initiative petition filed Nov. 10, 1999, and adopted by the people Nov. 7, 2000]

Note: The leadlines to subsections (1), (2) and (3) of section 11, except the periods in subsections (2) and (3), were a part of the measure submitted to the people by initiative petition (Measure No. 99, 2000) and adopted by the people Nov. 7, 2000.

Note: Section 11 was submitted to the voters as sections 1, 2 and 3 and added to the Constitution but not to any Article therein by Measure No. 99, 2000.

Note: In Measure No. 99, 2000, subsection (1)(a) and (b)(A) to (F) were designated as section 1 (A) and (B)(1) to (6); subsection (2)(a) and (b) as section 2 (A) and (B); and subsection (3)(a) to (g) as section 3 (A) to (G). The reference to subsection (1) of this section was a reference to Section 1 above, and the reference to paragraph (d) of this subsection was a reference to subsection (D) of this section.

Note: In Measure No. 99, 2000, the period in subsection (1)(b)(F) appeared as a semicolon, and there was no period in subsection (3)(e).

ARTICLE XVI
BOUNDARIES

Section 1. State boundaries. The State of Oregon shall be bounded as provided by section 1 of the Act of Congress of February 1859, admitting the State of Oregon into the Union of the United States, until:

(1) Such boundaries are modified by appropriate interstate compact or compacts heretofore or hereafter approved by the Congress of the United States; or

(2) The Legislative Assembly by law extends the boundaries or jurisdiction of this state an additional distance seaward under authority of a law heretofore or hereafter enacted by the Congress of the United States. [Constitution of 1859; Amendment proposed by S.J.R. 4, 1957, and adopted by the people Nov. 4, 1958; Amendment proposed by H.J.R. 24, 1967, and adopted by the people Nov. 5, 1968]

ARTICLE XVII
AMENDMENTS AND REVISIONS

Sec. 1. Method of amending Constitution
2. Method of revising Constitution

Section 1. Method of amending Constitution. Any amendment or amendments to this Constitution may be proposed in either branch of the legislative assembly, and if the same shall be agreed to by a majority of all the members elected to each of the two houses, such proposed amendment or amendments shall, with the yeas and nays thereon, be entered in their journals and referred by the secretary of state to the people for their approval or rejection, at the next regular general election, except when the legislative assembly shall order a special election for that purpose. If a majority of the electors voting on any such amendment shall vote in favor thereof, it shall thereby become a part of this Constitution. The votes for and against such amendment, or amendments, severally, whether proposed by the legislative assembly or by initiative petition, shall be canvassed by the secretary of state in the presence of the governor, and if it shall appear to the governor that the majority of the votes cast at said election on said amendment, or amendments, severally, are cast in favor thereof, it shall be his duty forthwith after such canvass, by his proclamation, to declare the said amendment, or amendments, severally, having received said majority of votes to have been adopted by the people of Oregon as part of the Constitution thereof, and the same shall be in effect as a part of the Constitution from the date of such proclamation. When two or more amendments shall be submitted in the manner aforesaid to the voters of this state at the same election, they shall be so submitted that each amendment shall be voted on separately. No convention shall be called to amend or propose amendments to this Constitution, or to propose a new Constitution, unless the law providing for such convention shall first be approved by the people on a referendum vote at a regular general election. This article shall not be construed to impair the right of the people to amend this Constitution by vote upon an initiative petition therefor. [Created through initiative petition filed Feb. 3, 1906, and adopted by the people June 4, 1906]

Note: The above section replaces sections 1 and 2 of Article XVII of the original Constitution.

Section 2. Method of revising Constitution. (1) In addition to the power to amend this Constitution granted by section 1, Article IV, and section 1 of this Article, a revision of all or part of this Constitution may be proposed in either house of the Legislative Assembly and, if the proposed revision is agreed to by at least two-thirds of all the members of each house, the proposed revision shall, with the yeas and nays thereon, be entered in their journals and referred by the Secretary of State to the people for their approval or rejection, notwithstanding section 1, Article IV of this Constitution, at the next regular state-wide primary election, except when the Legislative Assembly orders a special election for that purpose. A proposed revision may deal with more than one subject and shall be voted upon as one question. The votes for and against the proposed revision shall be canvassed by the Secretary of State in the presence of the Governor and, if it appears to the Governor that the majority of the votes cast in the election on the proposed revision are in favor of the proposed revision, he shall, promptly following the canvass, declare, by his proclamation, that the proposed revision has received a majority of votes and has been adopted by the people as the Constitution of the State of Oregon or as a part of the Constitution of the State of Oregon, as the case may be. The revision shall be in effect as the Constitution or as a part of this Constitution from the date of such proclamation.

(2) Subject to subsection (3) of this section, an amendment proposed to the Constitution under section 1, Article IV, or under section 1 of this Article may be submitted to the people in the form of alternative provisions so that one provision will become a part of the Constitution if a proposed revision is adopted by the people and the other provision will become a part of the Constitution if a proposed revision is rejected by the people. A proposed amendment submitted in the form of alternative provisions as authorized by this subsection shall be voted upon as one question.

(3) Subsection (2) of this section applies only when:

(a) The Legislative Assembly proposes and refers to the people a revision under subsection (1) of this section; and

(b) An amendment is proposed under section 1, Article IV, or under section 1 of this Article; and

(c) The proposed amendment will be submitted to the people at an election held during the period between the adjournment of the legislative session at which the proposed revision is referred to the people and the next regular legislative session. [Created through H.J.R. 5, 1959, and adopted by the people Nov. 8, 1960]

ARTICLE XVIII
SCHEDULE

Section 1. Election to accept or reject Constitution. For the purpose of taking the vote of the electors of the State, for the acceptance or rejection of this Constitution, an election shall be held on the second Monday of November, in the year 1857, to be conducted according to existing laws regulating the election of Delegates in Congress, so far as applicable, except as herein otherwise provided.

Section 2. Questions submitted to voters. Each elector who offers to vote upon this Constitution, shall be asked by the judges of election this question:

Do you vote for the Constitution? Yes, or No.

And also this question:

Do you vote for Slavery in Oregon? Yes, or No.

And in the poll books shall be columns headed respectively.

"Constitution, Yes."   "Constitution, No"

"Slavery, Yes."   "Slavery, No".

And the names of the electors shall be entered in the poll books, together with their answers to the said questions, under their appropriate heads. The abstracts of the votes transmitted to the Secretary of the Territory, shall be publicly opened, and canvassed by the Governor and Secretary, or by either of them in the absence of the other; and the Governor, or in his absence the Secretary, shall forthwith issue his proclamation, and publish the same in the several newspapers printed in this State, declaring the result of the said election upon each of said questions. [Constitution of 1859; Amendment proposed by S.J.R. 7, 2001, and adopted by the people Nov. 5, 2002]

Section 3. Majority of votes required to accept or reject Constitution. If a majority of all the votes given for, and against the Constitution, shall be given for the Constitution, then this Constitution shall be deemed to be approved, and accepted by the electors of the State, and shall take effect accordingly; and if a majority of such votes shall be given against the Constitution, then this Constitution shall be deemed to be rejected by the electors of the State, and shall be void.—

Section 4. Vote on certain sections of Constitution. If this Constitution shall be accepted by the electors, and a majority of all the votes given for, and against slavery, shall be given for slavery, then the following section shall be added to the Bill of Rights, and shall be part of this Constitution:

"Sec. ___ "Persons lawfully held as slaves in any State, Territory, or District of the United States, under the laws thereof, may be brought into this State, and such Slaves, and their descendants may be held as slaves within this State, and shall not be emancipated without the consent of their owners."

And if a majority of such votes shall be given against slavery, then the foregoing section shall not, but the following sections shall be added to the Bill of Rights, and shall be a part of this Constitution.

"Sec. ___ There shall be neither slavery, nor involuntary servitude in the State, otherwise than as a punishment for crime, whereof the party shall have been duly convicted." [Constitution of 1859; Amendment proposed by S.J.R. 7, 2001, and adopted by the people Nov. 5, 2002]

Note: See sections 34 and 35 of Article I, Oregon Constitution.

Section 5. Apportionment of Senators and Representatives. Until an enumeration of the inhabitants of the State shall be made, and the senators and representatives apportioned as directed in the Constitution, the County of Marion shall have two senators, and four representatives.

Linn two senators, and four representatives.

Lane two senators, and three representatives.

Clackamas and Wasco, one senator jointly, and Clackamas three representatives, and Wasco one representative.

Yamhill one senator, and two representatives.

Polk one senator, and two representatives.

Benton one senator, and two representatives.

Multnomah, one senator, and two representatives.

Washington, Columbia, Clatsop, and Tillamook one senator jointly, and Washington one representative, and Washington and Columbia one representative jointly, and Clatsop and Tillamook one representative jointly.

Douglas, one senator, and two representatives.

Jackson one senator, and three representatives.

Josephine one senator, and one representative.

Umpqua, Coos and Curry, one senator jointly, and Umpqua one representative, and Coos and Curry one representative jointly. [Constitution of 1859; Amendment proposed by S.J.R. 7, 2001, and adopted by the people Nov. 5, 2002]

Section 6. Election under Constitution; organization of state. If this Constitution shall be ratified, an election shall be held on the first Monday of June 1858, for the election of members of the Legislative Assembly, a Representative in Congress, and State and County officers, and the Legislative Assembly shall convene at the Capital on the first Monday of July 1858, and proceed to elect two senators in Congress, and make such further provision as may be necessary to the complete organization of a State government.—

Section 7. Former laws continued in force. All laws in force in the Territory of Oregon when this Constitution takes effect, and consistent therewith, shall continue in force until altered, or repealed.—

Section 8. Officers to continue in office. All officers of the Territory of Oregon, or under its laws, when this Constitution takes effect, shall continue in office, until superseded by the State authorities.—

Section 9. Crimes against territory. Crimes and misdemeanors committed against the Territory of Oregon shall be punished by the State, as they might have been punished by the Territory, if the change of government had not been made.—

Section 10. Saving existing rights and liabilities. All property and rights of the Territory, and of the several counties, subdivisions, and political bodies corporate, of, or in the Territory, including fines, penalties, forfeitures, debts and claims, of whatsoever nature, and recognizances, obligations, and undertakings to, or for the use of the Territory, or any county, political corporation, office, or otherwise, to or for the public, shall inure to the State, or remain to the county, local division, corporation, officer, or public, as if the change of government had not been made. And private rights shall not be affected by such change.—

Section 11. Judicial districts. Until otherwise provided by law, the judicial districts of the State, shall be constituted as follows: The counties of Jackson, Josephine, and Douglas, shall constitute the first district. The counties of Umpqua, Coos, Curry, Lane, and Benton, shall constitute the second district.—The counties of Linn, Marion, Polk, Yamhill and Washington, shall constitute the third district.—The counties of Clackamas, Multnomah, Wasco, Columbia, Clatsop, and Tillamook, shall constitute the fourth district—and the County of Tillamook shall be attached to the county of Clatsop for judicial purposes.—

Index

Archives Division (Secretary of State), 13
Army Corps of Engineers' projects, 301, 303, 305
Army National Guard, Oregon, 64–65
Arts, 147–148
    major arts organizations, 147–148
    Oregon Arts Commission, 147
Asian and Pacific Islander Affairs, Commission on, 26
Asians. *See* Minorities
Asset management (Department of Administrative Services), 25
Assisted living facilities (Office of the Long-Term Care Ombudsman), 61
Astor, John Jacob, 292
Athletic Trainers, Board of (Health Licensing Office), 49
Attorney General, 18–20
    list of, by date, 278–279
Attorneys
    admission to practice, 83, 105
    Board of Bar Examiners, 105
    discipline of, 83
    Oregon State Bar, 105
Audiology, State Board of Examiners for Speech-Language Pathology and, 74
Auditing. *See* Accounting and auditing
Aurora Colony Historical Society, 150
Autism, 50
Autopsies (Medical Examiner Division), 70
Auto registration, 77
Aviation Department, 30

B

Background checks (Department of State Police), 70
Bail (Oregon Bill of Rights), 326, 327
Baker Heritage Museum, 150
Ballot initiatives. *See* Initiative, referendum and recall
Ballot measures. *See headings starting with "Measure"*
Banks and banking
    Constitution of Oregon, 351
    Financial Regulation Division (Department of Consumer and Business Services), 33
Barbers, 50
Bar Examiners, Board of, 105
"Beach Bill" (1967), 306
Beaches. *See* Coastline
Beauticians, 50
"Beaver State," 1
Beef Council (Department of Agriculture), 29
Beer
    craft breweries, 2
    hops production, 3
    Liquor Control Commission, 61
    Oregon Hop Commission (Department of Agriculture), 29

Behavior Analysis Regulatory Board (Health Licensing Office), 49–50
Benefits counseling (Department of Veterans' Affairs), 80
Benton County Historical Society & Museum, 150
Bentz, Cliff (U.S. Representative), 170
Beverage, state (milk), 1
Bicycle and Pedestrian Advisory Committee (Department of Transportation), 79
"Bicycle Bill" (1971), 306
Bill of Rights (Constitution of Oregon), 326–331
Bingo, 19
Birds. *See also headings starting with "Wildlife"*
    hunting regulation, 44–45
    state raptor, 2
    state songbird, 2
Birth
    Board of Direct Entry Midwifery (Health Licensing Office), 50
    statistics, 2
Black Affairs, Commission on, 26–27
Blackberry Commission, Oregon Raspberry and (Department of Agriculture), 29
Black Lives Matter movement, 309
Black Pioneers, Oregon, 151–152
Blind persons
    Commission for the Blind, 30–31
    Talking Book and Braille Services, 61
Blueberry Commission (Department of Agriculture), 29
Blue Mountain Community College, 141
Blue Mountains, 4–5
Blumenauer, Earl (U.S. Representative), 170
Board of Accountancy, 23–24
Board of Advanced Estheticians, 50
Board of Agriculture, 27, 28
Board of Architect Examiners, 30
Board of Bar Examiners, 105
Board of Boiler Rules, 32
Board of Chiropractic Examiners, 31
Board of Cosmetology (Health Licensing Office), 50
Board of Dentistry, 38
Board of Denture Technology (Health Licensing Office), 50
Board of Direct Entry Midwifery (Health Licensing Office), 50
Board of Education, 38–39, 139–140
Board of Electrologists and Body Art Practitioners (Health Licensing Office), 50
Board of Examiners for Engineering and Land Surveying, 42–43
Board of Examiners for Speech-Language Pathology and Audiology, 74
Board of Forestry, 46
Board of Geologist Examiners, 47–48
Board of Licensed Dietitians (Health Licensing Office), 50
Board of Licensed Professional Counselors and Therapists, 63

Community Colleges and Workforce Development Office, 52
Constitution of Oregon, 363
529 College Savings Network, 15
funding for state university system, 142, 363
independent colleges and universities, 144–145
legislators serving in supervisory capacity in, 373
Office of Degree Authorization, 52
Office of Student Access and Completion (OSAC), 53
Oregon College Savings Plan, 16
Oregon Opportunity Grants, 53
Oregon Promise Grants, 53
Oregon University System (OUS), 142–143
private postsecondary programs, 52
public universities, 142–143
tuition aid. *See* Educational assistance
Western Interstate Commission for Higher Education, 144
Collier Memorial State Park, 315
Columbia Gorge Community College, 141
Columbia Gorge Discovery Center, 152
Columbia River, 290, 292, 298, 305
Columbia River Correctional Institution, 37
Columbia River Gorge Commission, 31
Columbia River Maritime Museum, 150
Command Group (Military Department), 64
Commerce and Compliance Division (CCD; Department of Transportation), 78
Commercial livestock feeds (Animal Health Program), 28
Commissioner of Labor and Industries. *See* Labor and Industries Commissioner
Commissioner's Office and Program Services Division (Bureau of Labor and Industries), 17
Commission for the Blind, 30–31
Commission for Women, 27
Commission on Asian and Pacific Islander Affairs, 26
Commission on Black Affairs, 26–27
Commission on Hispanic Affairs, 27
Commission on Judicial Fitness and Disability, 106
Committee for Family Forestlands (State Forestry Department), 46
Commodities, agricultural commodity commissions, 28–30
Common School Fund, 15, 75, 345–346
Communications Office (Department of Corrections), 36
Communications Section (Department of Transportation), 78
Community colleges, 52, 140–142
Constitution of Oregon, 363
Community Colleges and Workforce Development Office, 52
Community Corrections (Department of Corrections), 36

Community Services Division (Department of Land Conservation and Development), 58–59
Compensation. *See* Wages
Confederated Tribes of Coos, Lower Umpqua, and Siuslaw, 174
Confederated Tribes of Grand Ronde Community, 176, 221
Confederated Tribes of Siletz Indians, 177, 218
Confederated Tribes of Umatilla Indian Reservation, 173, 177, 223
Confederated Tribes of Warm Springs Reservation, 173, 178, 216, 224
Conflict of interest
Constitution of Oregon, 373
Government Ethics Commission, 48
public officials (Constitution of Oregon), 332
Congress, U.S.
Representatives, U.S., 1, 170–171, 285–287, 377
Senators, U.S., 283–285
Conservation. *See* Environment; Natural resources; Wildlife
Constituent Services Office (Governor's Office), 12
Constitution of Oregon, 325–378
African Americans and, 296, 302
Bill of Rights, 326–331
convention and history of framework, 377
election to accept or reject, 377
Construction Contractors Board, 31–32
Construction industry. *See* Building regulation
Construction Industry Energy Board (Department of Consumer and Business Services), 33
Consular Corps, 178–179
Consumer and Business Services, Department of (DCBS), 32–35
Consumer protection, 19
agricultural products, 28
Department of Consumer and Business Services, 32–35
Weights and Measures Program, 28
Contractors. *See specific type*
Cook, James (Captain), 292
Coos, Lower Umpqua and Siuslaw, Confederated Tribes of, 174
Coos History Museum & Maritime Collection, 150
Coquille Indian Tribe, 175
Corban University, 144
Coronavirus. *See* COVID-19 pandemic
Coroners (Constitution of Oregon), 342
Corporate excise tax, 137, 160, 348
Corporate income tax, 137, 160
Corporation Division (Secretary of State), 13–14
Correctional institutions, 37. *See also* Prisons and prisoners
juveniles. *See* Juvenile delinquency and corrections
Correctional Services Division (Department of Corrections), 36
Corrections, Department of, 35–37

Index

investigations to determine cause of (Medical Examiner Division), 70

statistics, 2

Death penalty (Bill of Rights of Oregon), 327

Debt Management Division (State Treasury), 15

Debtors (Bill of Rights of Oregon), 327

Debt Policy Advisory Commission, Debt Management Division (State Treasury), 15

Deer Ridge Correctional Institution, 37

DeFazio, Peter (U.S. Representative), 171

Degree Authorization, Office of (Academic Policy and Authorization Office), 52

Delinquency. *See* Juvenile delinquency and corrections

Delivery and Operations Division (Department of Transportation), 77

Democratic Party, 172

Demographic trends
 aging population, effect of, 158
 Economic Analysis Office (Department of Administrative Services), 25

Dentistry, Oregon Board of, 38

Denture Technology, Board of (Health Licensing Office), 50

Department of Administrative Services, 24–26

Department of Agriculture, 27–30

Department of Aviation, 30

Department of Consumer and Business Services (DCBS), 32–35

Department of Corrections, 35–37

Department of Education, 38–40, 140. *See also* Schools

Department of Energy, 42

Department of Environmental Quality (DEQ), 43–44

Department of Fish and Wildlife (ODFW), 44–45

Department of Forestry, 45–47

Department of Geology and Mineral Industries, 48

Department of Human Services (DHS), 55–58

Department of Land Conservation and Development (DLCD), 58–59

Department of Public Safety Standards and Training (DPSST), 71–72

Department of Revenue, 73–74

Department of State Lands, 75

Department of State Police, 69–71

Department of Transportation (ODOT), 76–79

Department of Veterans' Affairs, 79–80

Depoe Bay Whale Watching Center, 317

Deputy Director, Housing and Community Services Department, 54

DEQ (Department of Environmental Quality), 43–44

Deschutes County Historical Society and Museum, 151

Developmental disabilities. *See also* Mental health
 Council on Developmental Disabilities, 58
 Developmental Disabilities Programs (Department of Human Services), 57–58

DHS (Department of Human Services), 55–58

Dietitians, Board of Licensed (Health Licensing Office), 50

Disabled persons. *See also* Developmental disabilities
 Aging and People with Disabilities Programs (Department of Human Services), 56–57
 Council on Developmental Disabilities (Department of Human Services), 58
 Deaf and Hard of Hearing Services Program, 56
 Disabilities Commission, Oregon, 56–57
 Home Care Commission, 375–376
 housing for, 365
 Northwest Senior and Disability Services, 226
 Oregon ABLE (Achieving a Better Life Experience) Savings Plan, 16
 Residential Service Protection Fund (Public Utility Commission), 72–73
 Vocational Rehabilitation Program, 41

Disasters
 Constitution of Oregon, 349–351
 Department of Geology and Mineral Industries, 48
 earthquakes, 367–368
 forest fires, 46

Discrimination. *See also* Minorities
 Bill of Rights, Oregon, 326
 Civil Rights Division (Bureau of Labor and Industries), 17
 equal employment opportunity, 17
 Equity and Inclusion Office (Health Authority), 49
 history of, 293, 295–296, 300, 302, 306, 307
 housing discrimination, 17
 Legislative Equity Office, 115
 sex discrimination prohibited (Bill of Rights, Oregon), 331
 Social Equity Office (Department of Transportation), 78

Diseases. *See also* COVID-19 pandemic
 animal, 28
 occupational, 34
 plant, 28

District Attorneys (Justice Department), 21–23

District Courts. *See* Circuit Courts

Diversity. *See* Discrimination

Divorce statistics, 2

DLCD (Department of Land Conservation and Development), 58–59

DNA identification (Department of State Police), 69

Domestic Violence Survivors, Temporary Assistance for, 58

Donation Land Act (1850), 294, 296, 297

Double jeopardy (Oregon Bill of Rights), 326

Double majority vote to increase property tax rate, 138

Environmental Health Registration Board (Health Licensing Office), 50

Environmental Quality Commission, 43

Environmental Quality Department (DEQ), 43–44

EOU (Eastern Oregon University), 143

Equity. *See* Discrimination

Equity and Inclusion Office (Health Authority), 49

Equity Office (Legislative Assembly), 115

Erratic Rock State Park, 315

Escrow agents (Real Estate Agency), 73

Estuarine reserves and sanctuaries (South Slough National Estuarine Research Reserve), 75

Ethics in government. *See also* Conflict of interest
Government Ethics Commission, 48

Evergreen Aviation & Space Museum, 152–153

Examiners for professional licensing. *See specific profession*

Executive branch of government, 11–82. *See also* Governor
Constitution of Oregon, 340–341

Executive Division (State Treasury), 15

Exports. *See* International trade

Exposition Center and State Fair, 74

Ex post facto laws (Oregon Bill of Rights), 327

Extradition, 12

F

Facilities Authority, Oregon (State Treasury), 15

Fagan, Shemia (Secretary of State), 12–13

Fair, State, 2, 74–75

Fair Dismissal Appeals Board (Department of Education), 39

Fallen Firefighters Memorial, 72

Fallen Law Enforcement Officers Memorial, 72

Families
counselors (Oregon Board of Licensed Professional Counselors and Therapists), 63
Family Services Review Commission (Department of Human Services), 58
medical and paid family leave, 41–42
paternity order enforcement, 19

Family Forestlands, Committee for (State Forestry Department), 46

Farms. *See* Agriculture

Federal government, 169–172. *See also* Congress, U.S.
contact information in Oregon, 172
funds from, 135
presidential elections (voting history 1860–2020), 239–242

Fertilizer (Pesticides Program), 28

Fescue
Fine Fescue Commission (Department of Agriculture), 29
Tall Fescue Commission (Department of Agriculture), 29

Festivals and local celebrations
Happy Canyon Indian Pageant and Wild West Show, 6

Oregon Shakespeare Festival, 147
State Fair, 2, 74–75

Field Services Division (Water Resources Department), 81

Film and Video Office, 44

Finance, government. *See* Government finance

Finance Division (State Treasury), 15

Financial Fraud/Consumer Protection Section (Justice Department), 19

Financial Regulation Division (Department of Consumer and Business Services), 33

Fingerprints (Department of State Police), 69

Fire
Emergency Fire Cost Committee (State Forestry Department), 46
Fallen Firefighters Memorial, 72
Fire Marshal, State (Department of State Police), 70–71
forest fires (State Forestry Department), 46

Fish and fishing. *See also specific type of fish (e.g., Salmon)*
Albacore Commission (Department of Agriculture), 29
hatcheries, 5, 44–45
Restoration and Enhancement Board (Department of Fish and Wildlife), 44–45
Salmon Commission (Department of Agriculture), 29
state fish, 2
Trawl Commission (Department of Agriculture), 29–30

Fish and Wildlife Commission (Department of Fish and Wildlife), 44, 309

Fish and Wildlife Department (ODFW), 44–45

Fish and Wildlife Division (Department of State Police), 70

Fish Division (Department of Fish and Wildlife), 44

529 College Savings Network, 15. *See also* Oregon College Savings Plan

Five Oaks Museum, 151

Flag, state, 2

Floods. *See also* Disasters
Department of Geology and Mineral Industries, 48

Flower, state, 2–3

Food and food safety
Food and Animal Health Programs (Department of Agriculture), 28
Laboratory Services (Department of Agriculture), 28

Forecasting, economic, 25

Foreign trade. *See* International trade

Forensic Science and Pathology Bureau (Department of State Police), 70

Forest Conservation Act (1941), 304

Forest fires, 302

Forest fires, Emergency Fire Cost Committee (State Forestry Department), 46

Forest Practices Act (1971), 306–307

Senate confirmation of appointments by, 112, 334

vacancy in office of, 340

veto of legislation, 11, 111, 341

Governor's Advocacy Office (Department of Human Services), 55–56

Governor's Commission on Senior Services (Department of Human Services), 56

Governor's Council of Economic Advisors (Department of Administrative Services), 25

Grand jury, 343

disqualification from service (Oregon Bill of Rights), 331

Grand Ronde Community, Confederated Tribes of, 176, 221

Grange, 300

Grant County Historical Museum, 151

Grants. *See also* Educational assistance

Department of Land Conservation and Development, Grants Advisory Committee, 59

Housing and Community Services Department, 54

Watershed Enhancement Board (OWEB), 82

Grape (state flower), 2–3

Grassland, national, 5

Grass seeds. *See* Seeds

Gray, Captain Robert, 292

Great Depression, 303

Great Recession, 159, 308, 309

Gresham Historical Society, 151

Ground water. *See headings starting with "Water"*

Groundwater Advisory Committee (Water Resources Department), 81–82

H

Habeas corpus, 327, 343

Hairdressers, 50

Hair removal, 50

Hairy triton (state seashell), 7

Hallie Ford Museum of Art, 148

Handicapped persons. *See* Disabled persons

Hanford Cleanup Board (Department of Energy), 42

Happy Canyon Indian Pageant and Wild West Show, 6

Hard of hearing persons. *See* Deaf and hard of hearing persons

Harney County Historical Society, 151

Harris Beach State Park (student essay by Ivy Elseth), 156

Hatcheries, fish, 5, 44–45

Hazelnut (state nut), 6

Hazelnut Commission (Department of Agriculture), 29

Health Authority, 48–52

Health care. *See also* Medical assistance

best practices, 68

Board of Naturopathic Medicine, 65

coordinated care organizations (CCOs), 49, 51

COVID-19 pandemic impacts, 159

Department of Corrections, 36

Department of Human Services, 55–58

Equity and Inclusion Office, 49

Health Care Interpreter program, 49

Health Insurance Marketplace (Department of Consumer and Business Services), 33

Health Licensing Office (Health Authority), 49

Health Policy and Analytics Division (Health Authority), 50–51

Hospital, Oregon State (Health Authority), 51

Long Term Care Administrators Board (Health Licensing Office), 50

Occupational Safety and Health Division (Department of Consumer and Business Services), 34

Oregon Health and Science University (OHSU), 366

Oregon Health & Science University (OHSU), 143–144

Oregon Health Policy Board, 49

Oregon State Hospital (Health Authority), 51

Paid Family and Medical Leave Insurance Division (Employment Department), 41–42

Patient Safety Commission, 68

Public Health Advisory Board (Health Authority), 51

Public Health Division (Health Authority), 51

Senior Health Insurance Benefits Assistance (Department of Consumer and Business Services), 35

State Board of Nursing, 65–66

Traditional Health Worker program, 49

Tribal Affairs Division (Health Authority), 51–52

Health, Housing, Educational and Cultural Facilities Authority (HHECFA). *See now* Oregon Facilities Authority

Health Insurance Marketplace, Oregon (Department of Consumer and Business Services), 33

Health Licensing Office (Health Policy and Research Office), 49

Health Policy and Analytics Division (Health Authority), 50–51

Health Policy Board (Health Authority), 49

Health Systems Division (Health Authority), 51

Hearing Aids, Advisory Council on (Health Licensing Office), 50

Heating fuel. *See* Energy

HECC (Higher Education Coordinating Commission), 52–54, 140

Heceta Head Lighthouse State Scenic Viewpoint, 316

Hell's Canyon (deepest gorge), 3

Heritage organizations, 148–152

Oregon Heritage Commission (State Parks and Recreation Department), 67

Heritage Station Museum, 152
The High Desert Museum, 153
Higher education. *See* Colleges and universities
Higher Education Coordinating Commission (HECC), 52–54, 140
High schools. *See* Schools
High-tech industries, 157–158, 159, 308
Highways and roads, 3
    Commerce and Compliance Division (Department of Transportation), 78
    Delivery and Operations Division (Department of Transportation), 77
    development, 297–298
    Highway Cost Allocation Study, 25
    Patrol Services Division (Department of State Police), 70
Hispanic Affairs, Commission on, 27
Hispanics and Latinx, 304, 307, 309. *See also* Minorities
Historical Records Advisory Board, Archives Division (Secretary of State), 13
Historical Society, 149
Historic Cemeteries, Commission on, 67
Historic Columbia River Highway State Trail, 313
Historic landmarks, national, 5–6
Historic markers (Travel Information Council), 79
Historic preservation (State Parks and Recreation Department)
    Oregon Heritage Commission, 67
    State Advisory Committee on Historic Preservation, 67
    State Historic Preservation Office, 66–67
History, 289–324
    agriculture, 293–294, 296–297, 305, 309
    British settlement, 292
    cattle and sheep business, 294, 297, 299, 309
    chronological history by year, 317–323
    Civil War, 296
    Depression era, 303
    discrimination, 293, 295–296, 300, 302, 306, 307
    earliest authorities governing state, 267–268
    economy, 299–300, 301, 307–308
    environmental concerns, 289, 301, 305–306, 309
    evangelical movement and missionaries, 293
    first natives, 289–291
    fur trade, 292
    geologic formation of Oregon, 289
    gold mining, 296–297, 299
    Great Recession, 308
    Indian wars, 295
    industrialization and urbanization, 299–300, 304
    minorities, 295–296, 298, 300, 304, 306, 307
    "The Oregon Story," 306–307
    Oregon System, 300–301, 302
    organizations, 148–152
    populist movement, 300–301
    post-WWII development, 304–305
    potential for conflict and pragmatic compromise, 309–310
    progressivism, 300–301
    Provisional Government, 295–296
    railroads, 298–299
    salmon fishing, 290–291, 299
    settlement of state, 293–295
    settlements, spread of, 296–297
    slavery, 295–296
    social and economic division, 307–308
    social reform and activism, 300–301
    statehood, 295, 310–312, 319
    technology sector development, 308
    territorial status, 294, 318–319
    timber industry, 299, 301, 302, 303
    tourism, 308
    transportation systems, 297–299
    World War I, 301
    World War II, 303–304, 316
History Museum of Hood River County, 151
HMSC (Hatfield Marine Science Center), 154
Holidays, legal, 4
Home Care Commission, 375–376
Homeland security coordination (Department of State Police), 69
Homelessness (Housing and Community Services Department), 55
Home Loan Program for veterans, 80
Homeownership Division (Housing and Community Services Department), 55
Home rule
    Charter (Metro), 227
    Constitution of Oregon, 342
Homicide, aggravated murder penalty (Oregon Bill of Rights), 328
Hood River County History Museum, 151
Hop Commission (Department of Agriculture), 29
Hops (agriculture), 3
Horse racing (Oregon Racing Commission), 73
Hospital, State (Health Authority), 51
Hospitals and seismic rehabilitation, 367–368
Hours of work (Wage and Hour Division), 17
House of Representatives, State. *See* Legislative Assembly
House of Representatives, U.S. *See* Congress, U.S.
Housing
    disabled and elderly, 365
    equal opportunity in, 17
    Housing and Community Services Department (OHCSD), 54–55
    Residential and Manufactured Structures Board (Department of Consumer and Business Services), 33
    veterans. *See* Veterans
Housing and Community Services Department (OHCSD), 54–55

Housing Stability Council (Housing and Community Services Department), 54

Housing Stabilization Division (Housing and Community Services Department), 55

Hoyle, Val (Commissioner of Bureau of Labor and Industries), 16–17

Hudson's Bay Company, 267, 292, 293

Human Resources Division (Secretary of State), 14

Human Services, Department of (DHS), 55–58

Hunting regulation, Department of Fish and Wildlife, 44–45

Husband and wife. *See also* Marriage
    divorce statistics, 2
    separate property, 373

Hydropower. *See* Electricity

I

Immigration to state (Oregon Bill of Rights), 327

Inclusion. *See* Discrimination

Income, per capita, 160

Income tax, 339–340
    corporate, 137, 160
    Kicker Provision, 135–136
    Measure 66 (2010), 137
    personal, 137, 160

Indian tribes, 173–178
    activism and restoration of tribal sovereignty, 306
    boarding and day schools for children of, 295, 302
    first Native peoples of state, 289–291
    gaming centers and casinos, 173, 308
    governments, 173
    Indian Gaming Regulatory Act (1988), 308
    Indian Reorganization Act (1934), 303
    Legislative Commission on Indian Services, 115, 173
    missionaries and, 293
    Museum at Warm Springs, 152
    preservation of culture of, 302, 308–309
    reservations, 173, 295, 302, 304, 306
    Tamástslikt Cultural Institute, 149
    treaties with, 295
    tribal courts, 173–178
    Tribal Gaming Section (Department of State Police), 70
    tribal termination, 304–305
    wars, 295

Indictment (Constitution of Oregon), 343

Indigent defendants, defense of, 107

Industry. *See* Economy

Information, criminal, 343

Information and Education Division (Department of Fish and Wildlife), 45

Information Management and Technology, Joint Committee on (Legislative Assembly), 115

Information Systems Division (Secretary of State), 14

Information Technology (IT) Governance framework, 25

Inheritance rights (Oregon Bill of Rights), 327

Initiative, referendum and recall, 14
    Constitution of Oregon, 333, 335
    history of, 242
    list of (with ballot title), 242–267

Injuries, occupational, 34–35

Inmates. *See* Prisons and prisoners

Insanity defense (Psychiatric Security Review Board), 71

Insect, state, 4

Inspections
    agricultural commodity commissions, 28–30
    aviation safety, 30

Inspector General Office (Department of Corrections), 36

Installations Division (Military Department), 64

Intellectual and Developmental Disabilities (I/DD) Services (Department of Human Services), 57–58

Internal Services and Consumer Protection Programs (Department of Agriculture), 28

Internal Support (Secretary of State), 14

International trade
    agricultural commodity commissions, 28–30
    consuls, 178–179
    economic impact, 158

Interstate agencies and compacts
    Klamath River Basin Compact, 82
    Western Interstate Commission for Higher Education, 144

Intestate succession when no known heirs (Department of State Lands), 75

Investment advisors, Financial Regulation Division (Department of Consumer and Business Services), 33

Investment Council (State Treasury), 16

Investment Division (State Treasury), 16

Investment of state funds, 15

Irrigation (Constitution of Oregon), 364–365

Iwetemlaykin State Heritage Site, 313

J

Jackson County Genealogical Library, 152

Japanese-Americans, 298, 300, 302, 304

Jessie M. Honeyman Memorial State Park (student essay by Aidan Lin), 230

Jewish Museum and Center for Holocaust Education, Oregon, 152

Joint Committee on Ways and Means (Legislative Assembly), 115

Josephine County Historical Society, 151

Judges. *See also* Courts
    Circuit Judges Association, 104
    Commission on Judicial Fitness and Disability, 106

Index

Index

Local government employees
    Employment Relations Board, 42
    Public Employees Retirement System
    (PERS), 71
    retirement benefits and plans, tax status, 348
Local Officials Advisory Committee (Department
    of Land Conservation and Development), 59
Logging industry. *See* Lumber industry
Long-term care
    Long Term Care Administrators Board (Health
    Licensing Office), 50
    Long-Term Care Ombudsman Office, 61
    Medicaid Long-Term Care Quality and
    Reimbursement Advisory Council
    (Department of Human Services), 56
Lottery, Oregon State, 61–62, 308
    Constitution of Oregon, 349, 370–372
    education support from, 134, 136, 140, 141
    Gaming Division (Department of State
    Police), 70
    Lottery Fund, 134, 140, 141
    state parks support from, 372
    veterans' services support from, 373
    watershed support from, 82
Low-income households, stabilization (Housing
    and Community Services Department), 55
LUBA (Land Use Board of Appeals), 59–60
Lumber industry, 346. *See also* Forests

M

Magazines, 167–168
Magistrate Division, Oregon Tax Court, 84
Malheur Country Historical Society, 151
Malheur Field Station, 153
Mandamus, 343
Manifest Destiny, 294
Manufacturing, 159. *See also* Economy
Maps
    Congressional Districts for U.S. House of
    Representatives, 172
    Oregon, cities and counties, 10
    State Representative Districts, 117–118
    State Senate Districts, 116, 118
Marijuana, recreational use, 61
Marine Board, State, 62
Marionberry (state pie), 6
Maritime Pilots, Oregon Board of, 73
Markers, historic (Travel Information Council), 79
Market Access and Certification Programs
    (Department of Agriculture), 28
Marriage
    divorce statistics, 2
    interracial, 296
    between man and woman, 309, 373
    separate property of husband and spouse, 373
    statistics, 4
Massage Therapists, Board of, 62

Mass transit
    Public Transportation Division (Department of
    Transportation), 77
    Special Service Districts, 229
McCall, Thomas Lawson, 312, 316
McLoughlin, John, 292, 316
McNary, Charles, 302
Measure 5 (1990), 133–134, 138, 140, 160, 307
Measure 50 (1997), 138, 140, 160
Measure 66 (2010), 137
Measure 67 (2010), 137
Measure 85 (2012), 135–136
Measurement standards, Weights and Measures
    Program (Department of Agriculture), 28
Mechanical Board (Department of Consumer and
    Business Services), 33
Media
    directories, 161–168
    freedom of press (Oregon Bill of Rights), 326
Mediation
    in appeals, 84
    in workers' compensation, 35
Medicaid. *See* Oregon Health Plan
Medicaid Advisory Committee (Health
    Authority), 51
Medicaid Fraud Unit (Justice Department), 19
Medicaid Long-Term Care Quality and
    Reimbursement Advisory Council
    (Department of Human Services), 56
Medical and paid family leave, 41–42
Medical assistance. *See also* Oregon Health Plan
    Medicaid Advisory Committee, 51
    Medicaid Fraud Unit (Justice Department), 19
    Medicaid Long-Term Care Quality and
    Reimbursement Advisory Council, 56
Medical Board, 62
Medical Examiner Division (Department of State
    Police), 70
Medical Imaging, Board of, 62–63
Memorials and monuments
    Fallen Firefighters Memorial, 72
    Fallen Law Enforcement Officers
    Memorial, 72
    national, 6
Mental health. *See also* Developmental disabilities
    Behavior Analysis Regulatory Board (Health
    Licensing Office), 49–50
    counselors (Oregon Board of Licensed
    Professional Counselors and Therapists), 63
    Psychiatric Security Review Board, 71
    Psychology, State Board of, 63–64
Mental Health Regulatory Agency, 63–64
Merkley, Jeff (U.S. Senator), 169
Metasequoia (state fossil), 3
Metro, 227
Metropolitan service districts, 358
Microbe, state, 4
Mid-Willamette Valley Council of
    Governments, 226

Index

N

Nail technology regulation, Board of Cosmetology, 50
Name of Oregon, 5
National cemeteries, 5
National fish hatcheries, 5
National forests. *See* Forests
National grassland, 5
National Guard, 64–65, 373
National Guard Youth Challenge Program, 64–65
National historic landmarks, 5–6
National Historic Oregon Trail Interpretive Center, 148
National Indian Gaming Regulatory Act (NIGRA), 173
National memorials and monuments, 6
National parks, 6, 301
National recreation areas, 6
National scenic areas, 6
    Columbia River Gorge Commission, 31
National University of Natural Medicine, 145
National wildlife refuges, 6
Native Americans. *See* Indian tribes
Natural and Cultural History, University of Oregon Museum of, 155
Natural disasters. *See* Disasters
Natural gas taxation, 347
Natural resources. *See also* Environment
    Department of Fish and Wildlife, 44–45
    fish. *See Fish and fishing; headings starting with "Fish and Wildlife"*
    forests. *See* Forests
    Land Conservation and Development, Department of, 58–59
    museums, aquariums, etc., 152–155
    Natural Resources Programs (Department of Agriculture), 28
    Plant Protection and Conservation Programs (Department of Agriculture), 28
    scenic areas. *See* National scenic areas
    wildlife. *See* Wildlife
Naturopathic Medicine, Board of, 65
New Deal, 303
Newspaper Publishers Association, Oregon, 166
Newspapers, 161–166
    freedom of press (Oregon Bill of Rights), 326
Nez Perce. *See* Indian tribes
Nike Corporation, 308
Nikkei Legacy Center and Endowment, Oregon, 152
Nobel prize winners from Oregon, 1
North Lincoln County Historical Museum, 151
Northwest Christian University, 145
Northwest Commission on Colleges and Universities, 144
North West Company, 267, 292
Northwest Power and Conservation Council, 65
Northwest Senior and Disability Services, 226
Northwest University, 145

Nuclear energy/waste
    Department of Energy, 42
    Hanford Cleanup Board (Department of Energy), 42
Nuclear medicine (Board of Medical Imaging), 62–63
Nurseries, plant. *See* Plants
Nursing, Oregon State Board of, 65–66
Nursing homes
    Long Term Care Administrators Board (Health Licensing Office), 50
    Medicaid Long-Term Care Quality and Reimbursement Advisory Council (Department of Human Services), 56
    Office of the Long-Term Care Ombudsman, 61
Nuts
    Hazelnut Commission (Department of Agriculture), 29
    state nut, 6

O

Oaths
    Bill of Rights of Oregon, 326
    Constitution of Oregon, 339, 370
    Supreme Court justices, 344
OBCE (State Board of Chiropractic Examiners), 31
Occupational Safety and Health Division (Department of Consumer and Business Services), 34
Occupational Therapy Licensing Board, 66
Ocean and Coastal Services Division (Department of Land Conservation and Development), 59
ODFW (Department of Fish and Wildlife), 44–45
ODOT (Department of Transportation), 76–79
Office of Academic Policy and Authorization (Higher Education Coordinating Commission), 52
Office of Community Colleges and Workforce Development, 52
Office of Degree Authorization, 52
Office of Economic Analysis (Department of Administrative Services), 25
Office of Legislative Counsel, 114
Office of Postsecondary Finance and Capital (Higher Education Coordinating Commission), 53
Office of Research and Data (Higher Education Coordinating Commission), 53
Office of Small Business Assistance (Corporation Division, Secretary of State), 14
Office of Student Access and Completion (OSAC), 53
Office of the Director. *See* Director's Office
Office of the Inspector General (Department of Corrections), 36
Office of the Long-Term Care Ombudsman, 61
Office of Workforce Investments (OWI), 53–54
OHCSD (Housing and Community Services Department), 54–55

Outdoor Recreation Office (State Parks and Recreation Department), 67
Overtime regulation, 17

P

Pacific daylight time, 7
Pacific Fur Company, 267, 292
Pacific Northwest College of Art, 145
Pacific Ocean. *See* Coastline
Pacific standard time, 7
Pacific University, 145
Paid Family and Medical Leave Insurance Division (Employment Department), 41–42
Pandemic. *See* COVID-19 pandemic
Pardons (Constitution of Oregon), 341
Pari-mutuel racing (Oregon Racing Commission), 73
Parks. *See also specific parks*
    lottery proceeds used for, 372
    national, 6
    state, 6, 66–67, 302, 312–317
    student essays, 108, 146, 156, 180, 230
Parks and Recreation Department, State, 66–67, 312
Parole and Post-Prison Supervision, State Board of, 68
Parole of criminal offenders
    Department of Corrections, 35, 36
    juvenile offenders (Youth Authority), 82
    parole and probation personnel (Department of Public Safety Standards and Training), 71
    State Board of Parole and Post-Prison Supervision, 68
Paternity order enforcement, 19
Patient Safety Commission, 68
Patrol Services Division (Department of State Police), 70
Pawnbrokers, Financial Regulation Division (Department of Consumer and Business Services), 33
Pears (state fruit), 3
PEBB (Public Employees' Benefit Board), 51
Penitentiary, State, 37
People's Party, 300
Per capita income, 160
Periodicals, 167–168
PERS (Public Employees Retirement System), 71
Personal income tax, 137, 160
Pesticides Program (Department of Agriculture), 28
Pete French Round Barn State Heritage Site, 314
Pharmacy, State Board of, 68–69
Physical dimensions of Oregon, 6
Physical Therapist Licensing Board, 69
Physician assistants (Medical Board), 62
Physicians
    Board of Naturopathic Medicine, 65
    Medical Board, 62
    Oregon Health & Science University (OHSU), 143–144, 366

Pie, state, 6
Planning Services Division (Department of Land Conservation and Development), 59
Plant Protection and Conservation Programs (Department of Agriculture), 28
Plants. *See also* Natural resources
    endangered, 28
    Plant Protection and Conservation Programs (Department of Agriculture), 28
Plumbing Board (Department of Consumer and Business Services), 33
Podiatrists (Medical Board), 62
Poet Laureate, 6
Police
    Department of Public Safety Standards and Training, 71–72
    Department of State Police, 69–71
    Fallen Law Enforcement Officers Memorial, 72
    seismic rehabilitation of emergency services buildings, 367–368
Policy, Data and Analysis Division (Department of Transportation), 77
Policy advisors (Governor's Office), 12
Political parties, 172
Polk County Historical Society, 152
Pollution. *See* Environment; Water
Polygraph examiners (Department of Public Safety Standards and Training), 71–72
Polysomnographic Technologist Licensing Board (Health Licensing Office), 50
Population, 6
    cities (1980–2020), 202–207
    counties (1980–2020), 207
    Economic Analysis Office (Department of Administrative Services), 25
    growth of, 304
    Native American, 173
Populist movement, 300–301
Port Districts, 227–229
Portland
    development of, 300
    ethnic communities in, 302
    gentrification in, 309
    income level in, 308
    Metro, 227
Portland Art Museum, 148
Portland Community College, 142
Portland Opera, 148
Portland State University, 143
Post-mortem examinations (Medical Examiner Division), 70
Postsecondary Finance and Capital Office (Higher Education Coordinating Commission), 53
Potato Commission (Department of Agriculture), 29
Poverty, 160
    Residential Service Protection Fund (Public Utility Commission), 72–73

Index

Rainfall, 6
Rainy Day Fund, 136
Ranches. *See* Agriculture; Livestock
Raspberry and Blackberry Commission (Department of Agriculture), 29
Read, Tobias (State Treasurer), 14–15
Real Estate Agency, 73
Real estate appraisers (Appraiser Certification and Licensure Board), 30
Real Estate Board, 73
Reclamation (Mineral Land Regulation and Reclamation program), 48
Records, public. *See* Public records
Records Center, State (Secretary of State), 13
Recreation. *See also* Parks; Tourism
    national recreation areas, 6
    state parks, 6, 66–67, 302, 312–317
Recreational marijuana industry, 61
Reed College, 145
Reforestation, 361
Refugees
    Refugee Child Welfare Advisory (Department of Human Services), 57
    Refugee Program (Self-Sufficiency Programs), 58
Regional Forest Practice Committees (State Forestry Department), 47
Regional governments, 226
Regional historical societies and heritage organizations, 150–152
Registration of business entities and secured transactions, 13
Registration of corporate names, 13
Regular Division, Oregon Tax Court, 84
Rehabilitation Program, Vocational (Department of Human Services), 41
Religion not to be supported by public funds (Oregon Bill of Rights), 326
Religious discrimination, 302
Religious freedom (Oregon Bill of Rights), 326
Rental housing (Housing and Community Services Department), 54–55
Representatives, State. *See* Legislative Assembly
Representatives, U.S., 1, 170–171, 285–287
Republican Party, 172
Research and Data Office (Higher Education Coordinating Commission), 53
Reservoirs, 7
Residential and Manufactured Structures Board (Department of Consumer and Business Services), 33
Residential Service Protection Fund (Public Utility Commission), 72–73
Respiratory Therapist and Polysomnographic Technologist Licensing Board (Health Licensing Office), 50
Restoration and Enhancement Board (Department of Fish and Wildlife), 44–45
Retirement Savings Plan, Oregon. *See now* OregonSaves

Revenue, Department of, 73–74
Revenue, Finance and Compliance Department (Department of Transportation), 78
Revenue, state and local governments. *See* Taxation
Right to bear arms (Oregon Bill of Rights), 327
Rivers. *See also* Dams
    Klamath River Basin Compact, 82
    statistics on, 7
    Water Resources Commission, 81
Roads. *See* Highways and roads
Rock, state, 7
Rogers, Major Robert, 5
Rogue Community College, 142
Rogue Valley Council of Governments, 226
Rogue Valley Genealogical Society and Jackson County Genealogical Library, 152
Rosenblum, Ellen F. (Attorney General), 18
Rough and Ready Botanical Wayside, 317
Rules of administrative agencies, 13
    Office of Legislative Counsel's role, 114
Ryegrass Growers Seed Commission (Department of Agriculture), 29

S

Saccharomyces cerevisiae (state microbe), 4
Safety
    Department of Public Safety Standards and Training, 71–72
    Occupational Safety and Health Division (Department of Consumer and Business Services), 34
    Operations Division (Department of Corrections), 36
    police. *See* Police
    State Fire Marshal, 70–71
    Transportation Safety Committee (Department of Transportation), 79
    Transportation Safety Division (Department of Transportation), 77
Salaries. *See* Wages
Salem (capital of state), 181, 369
Salmon
    Chinook salmon (state fish), 2
    dam construction's effect on, 303, 305
    history of commercial fishing, 299
    lottery proceeds for restoration and protection, 372–373
    Native peoples' harvesting of, 290–291
    threatened or endangered, 307, 309
Salmon Commission (Department of Agriculture), 29
Santiam Correctional Institution, 37
Santiam Historical Society, 152
Sarah Helmick State Park, 312
Savings and loan associations, Financial Regulation Division (Department of Consumer and Business Services), 33
Savings for college tuition. *See* Educational assistance

Index

Southern Oregon Historical Society, 152
Southern Oregon University (SOU), 143
South Fork Forest Camp, 37
South Slough National Estuarine Research Reserve, 75
Southwestern Oregon Community College, 142
Spanish expeditions, 291
Speaker of the House of Representatives, 109, 282–283
Special Districts Association of Oregon, 229
Special laws prohibited, 339
Special Litigation Section, Trial Division (Justice Department), 20
Special Service Districts, 229
Special Weapons and Tactics (SWAT; Department of State Police), 69
Speech-Language Pathology and Audiology, State Board of Examiners for, 74
Speedy trial (Oregon Bill of Rights), 326
Spills and clean up of waste and hazardous substances, 42
Sportswear sector development, 308
Spruce production, 301
Square dance (state dance), 2
Standard time, 7
Starting a business, 13–14
State Accident Insurance Fund (SAIF), 15
State Advisory Committee on Historic Preservation (State Parks and Recreation Department), 67
State Apprenticeship and Training Council (OSATC), 17
State Bar, 105
State Board of ... *See headings starting with "Board of"*
State Board of Psychology, 63–64
State buildings and lands
    address list, 20
    Department of Land Conservation and Development (LCDC), 58–59
    Department of State Lands, 75
    Enterprise Asset Management (Department of Administrative Services), 25
    Forest Trust Land Advisory Committee, 47
    Land Use Board of Appeals, 59–60
    parks. *See* Parks
    prisons. *See* Prisons and prisoners; specific correctional institution by name
    Salem (state capital), 181
    school lands. *See* Schools
    state authority for indebtedness incurred, 369
    State Land Board, 346
State Chief Information Officer (State CIO), 25
State Correctional Institution, 37
State Court Administrator, 88
State Debt Policy Advisory Commission, Debt Management Division (State Treasury), 15
State Department of ... *See headings starting with "Department of"*

State employees
    Chief Human Resources Office (Department of Administrative Services), 24
    Employment Relations Board, 42
    pension liabilities, state empowered to borrow to fund, 368
    Public Employees Retirement System (PERS), 71
    Public Officials Compensation Commission (Department of Administrative Services), 26
    retirement plan contributions, 348
State Fair Council, 74
State Fire Marshal (Department of State Police), 70–71
State Fish and Wildlife Commission (Department of Fish and Wildlife), 44
State Forestry Department, 45–47
State Forests Advisory Committee, 47
State General Fund, 133–134, 139, 140, 141, 160
State Historic Preservation Office (State Parks and Recreation Department), 66–67
Statehood, 295, 310–312, 319, 377–378
State Land Board, 11, 15, 75, 346
State lands. *See* State buildings and lands
State Lands, Department of, 75
State Landscape Architect Board, 60
State Landscape Contractors Board, 60
State Law Library, 104–105
State Library, 60–61
State Lottery. *See* Lottery, Oregon State
State Marine Board, 62
State Mortuary and Cemetery Board, 65
State parks. *See* Parks
State Parks and Recreation Department, 66–67
State Penitentiary, 37
State Police Department, 69–71
State printer (Constitution of Oregon), 369
State prisons, 37. *See also* Prisons and prisoners
State stationary, 348
Statewide Transportation Improvement Program, 77
Stationary, state, 348
Steamships, 298
Steens Mountain, 5
STEM Investment Council, 54
Stewardship Coordinating Committee (State Forestry Department), 46–47
Strawberry Commission (Department of Agriculture), 29
Streams. *See* Rivers
Student Access and Completion Office (Higher Education Coordinating Commission), 53
Student aid. *See* Educational assistance
Student essays
    Cove Palisades State Park by Jacob Hurd, 108
    Harris Beach State Park by Ivy Elseth, 156
    Jessie M. Honeyman Memorial State Park by Aidan Lin, 230
    Silver Falls State Park by Emma Arvin, 146
    Tumalo State Park by Luther Lawson, 180

Index

Department of Public Safety Standards and Training, 71–72

State Apprenticeship and Training Council (OSATC), 17

Youth Challenge Program (Oregon Military Department), 64–65

Transportation. *See also specific types (e.g., Railroads)*
climate impacts, 77–78
government and external relations, 78
history of, 297–299, 303, 304
public transit, 77, 358
roads. *See* Highways and roads
social equity in, 78
Statewide Transportation Improvement Program, 77

Transportation, Department of (ODOT), 76–79

Transportation Commission, 76

Transportation Safety Committee (Department of Transportation), 79

Transportation Safety Division (Department of Transportation), 77

Travel Information Council, 79

Travel Oregon, 76

Trawl Commission (Department of Agriculture), 29–30

Treason (Oregon Bill of Rights), 327

Treasurer, State, 14–16
Constitution of Oregon, 341
list of, by date, 270–271

Treasure Valley Community College, 142

Treasury, State, 14–16

Trees. *See also* Forests
Douglas Fir (state tree), 8
spruce production, 301

Trial Division (Justice Department), 20

Tribal Affairs Division (Health Authority), 51–52

Tribal courts, 173–178

Tribal gaming centers and casinos, 173, 308
Tribal Gaming Division (Department of State Police), 70

Tribal water rights, 81

Troutdale Historical Society, 152

Trucks, Commerce and Compliance Division (Department of Transportation), 78

Tsunamis (Department of Geology and Mineral Industries), 48

Tuition aid. *See* Educational assistance

Tumalo State Park (student essay by Luther Lawson), 180

Tuna (Albacore Commission), 29

Two Rivers Correctional Institution, 37

U

Umatilla County Historical Society and Heritage Station Museum, 152

Umatilla Indian Reservation
Confederated Tribes of, 173, 177, 223
Tamástslikt Cultural Institute, 149

Umpqua Community College, 142

Umpqua Lighthouse State Park, 316

Unclaimed property, 75

Unemployment, 40, 157

Unemployment Insurance Division (Employment Department), 40

Unfair labor practices (Employment Relations Board), 42

Unionization, 42, 300, 301, 307
Employment Relations Board, 42

Universities. *See* Colleges and universities

University of Oregon, 143
Museum of Natural and Cultural History, 155

University of Portland, 145

University of Western States, 145

Urban Indian Health Program, 52

Urbanization, 299–300, 304, 306

Urban renewal, 306, 347

Utilities
People's Utility Districts, 358
Public Utility Commission, 72–73

V

Vancouver, George, 292

Vegetables
Potato Commission (Department of Agriculture), 29
Processed Vegetable Commission (Department of Agriculture), 29

Vehicle registration, 77, 78

Verdicts, 343

Veterans
Aging Veterans' Services, 80
bonus, 362–363
farm and home loans, 359–360
lottery proceeds in veterans' services fund, 373
ORVET Home Loan Program, 80

Veterans' Affairs, Department of, 79–80

Veterans' Affairs Director, Advisory Committee to, 79–80

Veterans' Home and Farm Loan Program, 359–360

Veterans' Services Division (Department of Veterans' Affairs), 80

Veterinary Medical Examining Board, Oregon State, 80

Veto, governor's, 11, 111, 341

Victims of crime
Crime Victim and Survivor Services Division (Justice Department), 19
rights of (Oregon Bill of Rights), 329–330

Violence. *See also* Child abuse
Temporary Assistance for Domestic Violence Survivors, 58
victims' rights, 329–330

Vista House, Crown Point State Scenic Corridor, 313

Vocational Rehabilitation Program (Department of Human Services), 41

Index — Index

Women
Commission for Women, 27
equal rights, 331
Equity and Inclusion Office (Health Authority), 49
property rights of, 373
reform activism of, 300–301
rights movement, 306
Social Equity Office (Department of Transportation), 78
voting rights, 300–301
as World War II laborers, 304
Wood. *See* Lumber industry
Woodlands. *See* Forests
Workers' Compensation Board, 35
Workers' Compensation Division (Department of Consumer and Business Services), 34–35
Workers' Compensation Management-Labor Advisory Committee, 34–35
Workers' Compensation Ombudsman (Department of Consumer and Business Services), 34
Workforce and Economic Research Division (Employment Department), 40–41
Workforce and Talent Development Board, 53
Workforce Innovation and Opportunity Act (U.S.), 53
Workforce Investments Office (Higher Education Coordinating Commission), 53–54
Workforce Operations Division (Employment Department), 41
Working conditions, regulation
Bureau of Labor and Industries, 16–17

Occupational Safety and Health Division (Department of Consumer and Business Services), 34
WorkSource Oregon, 41
Works Projects Administration (WPA), 303
World Forestry Center, 155
World War I, 301
World War II, 303–304, 316
WOU (Western Oregon University), 143
Wyden, Ron (U.S. Senator), 169

X

X-ray technicians (Board of Medical Imaging), 63

Y

Yakima Indian War, 295
Yamhill County Museum and Library, 152
Yaquina Pacific Railroad Historical Society, 152
YDD (Youth Development Division), 40, 140
Young, Ewing, 294
Youth. *See* Children; Juvenile delinquency and corrections
Youth Authority, Oregon, 82
Youth Challenge Program (Oregon Military Department), 64–65
Youth Corps, 53
Youth Development Division (Department of Education), 40, 140

Z

Zoo, Oregon, 154–155